Praise for Ke[illegible]

THREE BL[illegible]

"Exhaustive . . . the network book to beat."
—*Time*

"This is an impressive work of thoughtful, thorough, on-the-record reporting. . . . Auletta has amassed a mountain of information and shaped it into a readable, sweeping saga of turmoil in corporate America."
—*Detroit Free Press*

"It's all here . . . Auletta has composed a valuable requiem for a dying industry."
—*Washington Post Book World*

"[A] captivating account of the three networks . . . the book's fascination and fun lie in the detail—Mr. Auletta's extraordinary access to the principal players, his eye for color, ear for anecdote and reporter's instinct for conflict."
—*Wall Street Journal*

"There is no better time to read *Three Blind Mice,* and no better explanation of the unsystematic system that is television."
—*Atlanta Journal-Constitution*

"[A] thorough, behind-the-scenes look . . . enlightening reading for anyone interested in television and how it became the way it is."
—*News-Observer* (Raleigh, North Carolina)

"A fascinating, disturbing, and admirably detailed volume which traces the gradual failure of the networks."
—*Christian Science Monitor*

"The best book ever written on network television."
—Frank Stanton, former president, CBS, Inc.

"A remarkable and extremely important book . . . careful, painstaking, understated journalism of the highest order."
—David Halberstam

ALSO BY KEN AULETTA

Greed and Glory on Wall Street
The Underclass
The Streets Were Paved with Gold
Hard Feelings
The Art of Corporate Success: The Story of Schlumberger

KEN AULETTA

THREE BLIND MICE

Ken Auletta is the author of the national bestseller *Greed and Glory on Wall Street* and also of *The Underclass, The Streets Were Paved with Gold, Hard Feelings,* and *The Art of Corporate Success: The Story of Schlumberger*. He is a columnist for the New York *Daily News,* and his work has appeared regularly in *The New Yorker* and *The New York Times Magazine.* His work has also appeared in such publications as *The New York Review of Books, Vanity Fair, The Village Voice, New Republic, Esquire,* and *Life.* Prior to writing this book, Auletta was the weekly political commentator on WCBS-TV in New York. He has also appeared regularly on WNBC-TV and hosted a weekly interview program on New York's public television station. He lives in New York City.

THREE BLIND MICE

How the TV Networks Lost Their Way

KEN AULETTA

Vintage Books
A Division of Random House, Inc.
New York

For Kate and Amanda

First Vintage Books Edition, September 1992

 Published in the United States by Vintage Books, a division of Random House, Inc., New York, and simultaneously in Canada by Random House of Canada Limited, Toronto. Originally published in hardcover by Random House, Inc., New York, in 1991.

A small portion of Chapter 3 of this work was originally published in *The New York Times Magazine* in June 1986.

Library of Congress Cataloging-in-Publication Data
Auletta, Ken.
Three blind mice: how the TV networks lost their way / Ken Auletta.—1st Vintage Books ed.
p. cm.
Includes bibliographical references and index.
ISBN 0-679-74135-6 (pbk.)
1. Television broadcasting—United States. 2. Television broadcasting—Economic aspects—United States. 3. Television programs—United States—Rating. 4. Television viewers—United States. 5. n-us. I. Title.
[PN1992.3.U5A96 1992]
384.55′4′0973–dc20 92-50105
CIP

Manufactured in the United States of America
10 9 8 7 6 5 4

CONTENTS

THREE BLIND MICE

—

Something or other lay in wait for him,
amid the twists and the turns
of the months and the years,
like a crouching beast in the jungle.

—Henry James,
The Beast in the Jungle

INTRODUCTION

Television has become a basic American utility, like water or electricity. The typical home uses a television more than it does a sink, stove, shower, washer, dryer, or automobile. On average, the TV screen is alive seven hours a day, which means that the typical household viewing week exceeds the typical work week.

While the amount of daily TV viewing has varied little in recent years, what is being viewed has changed dramatically. In the past decade an earthquake that would register a 10 on the Richter scale has struck the television industry. Four facts tell the story:

- The Big Three networks—ABC, CBS, and NBC—which fifteen years ago claimed more than nine out of ten viewers nightly, have lost a third of their audience—nearly thirty million viewers.
- The average home, which had seven channels to choose from in 1976, now has thirty-three.
- The VCR, which was not commercially available as recently as the late seventies, is now present in 70 percent of all homes.
- Cumulative profits of $800 million for the networks in 1984 shrank to $400 million by 1988, and will perhaps sink to zero in 1991.

For viewers, more choice has created something like a video democracy. But for once unassailable network empires the result has been shattering, even though the full impact of the transformation wasn't felt right away. We noticed the collapse of the Soviet empire in Eastern Europe because it came suddenly. In a flash, the Cold War was over, the Warsaw Pact terminated, the Berlin wall gone, the two Germanys reunited, and communist orthodoxy disgraced. The forces that struck the television industry did so less dramatically. Each year Americans received a few more channel options and cable increased its penetration by a small percentage. The upstart Fox network went from programming on only a single night, to two nights, then three, then four, then five. VCRs and video stores proliferated. Occasionally newspaper headlines blared about layoffs or major management changes, but viewers weren't much affected. They still watched *The Cosby Show,* the *Super Bowl,* and the nightly newscasts. This was an earthquake in slow motion.

It wasn't until the war in the Persian Gulf began in January 1991 that the cable revolution became dramatically apparent. Viewers realized that CNN, not the three networks, was a primary source of up-to-the-minute news. And they were getting the news the way they wanted it—instantly and without interruption from soap operas. For as long as the war held their interest, viewers could choose for themselves when to watch the news as easily as they could flick to an HBO movie, an ESPN basketball game, or a Disney cartoon. Suddenly, nearly everyone who thought about such things seemed to be asking whether network news had a future—indeed, whether the networks themselves had a future. Cable, which was now in 60 percent of all homes (only 15 percent had it as recently as 1976), seemed to have the upper hand.

The Gulf War exposed the frailty of the networks in other ways as well. Advertisers were pulling their ads, not wanting their friendly products juxtaposed with scenes of death. This provided a stark reminder that a network depends on a single source of revenue—advertising—while cable programmers such as CNN not only sell ads but charge a fee to cable subscribers for the use of their product. By 1990, cable had revenues of $17.8 billion, which dwarfed the $9 billion collected by the three networks. And while network ad revenues were relatively flat, cable advertising has more than doubled in the past five years to nearly $3 billion. Ten years ago, the three networks collected six out of every ten advertising dollars; today, less than five out of every ten.

The Gulf War was a vivid reminder of how dependent the networks are on others. A television network is not what many viewers assume. It is not a vast studio that manufactures programs. It is not a national grid of spaghetti wires linking 240 million Americans in more than 90 million households. A network owns few of the stations that distribute programs under the CBS, ABC, or NBC logo. A network is an office building, where executives package programs they do not own and sell them to advertisers and local stations they do not control.

To distribute their programs, the three networks rely on six hundred or so TV stations affiliated with them. Increasingly, these affiliated stations have been bumping their network's programming. Stations calculate that even after paying for the programs they can earn more money by airing syndicated shows like *Wheel of Fortune* or Billy Graham specials. Even if the audience is smaller, the affiliated station pockets more money since it gets to sell most of the commercials, whereas when a station runs a network program most of the advertising is sold by the network. In the world of the bottom line, traditions—like the "partnership" between the network and its affiliates—count for less. Not surprisingly, during the Gulf War, many stations—including KHOU, the Houston station at which Dan Rather got his start—bumped the news offered by the networks and substituted CNN coverage.

To most of us, television has always meant three institutions—CBS, NBC, and ABC. They have been our common church. But by mid 1991, with stations defecting and advertisers and viewers turning elsewhere, with the federal government refusing to significantly relax regulations that might open fresh sources of revenue to the networks or perhaps spur a merger between a network and a Hollywood studio, it was difficult to see how the networks could recapture the good times. Like blind mice, the people running the networks seemed trapped in a maze from which there was no way out. No matter how shrewd or tough the CEO—and the networks are run by able businessmen—as long as the Big Three each offered only one channel choice while viewers had as many as 150 other choices, the future of the networks was problematic.

My interest in this subject was piqued by Arthur Gelb, then managing editor of *The New York Times,* who suggested that I write a profile of Larry Tisch for the inaugural issue of the *Times Business World* magazine. The date was October 1985, and that previous summer Tisch and his Loews Corporation had first acquired CBS stock. Just months before, in March of 1985, Capital Cities Communications had taken on ABC. And in December of 1985, GE would announce that it had swallowed NBC. So as I wrote about Tisch, I could feel the ground shift. For the first time in history, the ownership of all three networks had changed hands.

From the time I started the Tisch profile, this book has taken nearly six years to write. By way of explaining the changes that transformed the networks, and television in general, I have tried to tell several stories, with an emphasis on the business and the people behind the

TV box. I have not probed in depth the television shows themselves or the impact of TV on our lives, though neither subject is neglected. I have written about an industry wracked by change, and of how some of America's most powerful business leaders have dealt with organizations they often can't control, try as they will. It is a story of how the Human Factor—insecurity, low morale, high ambition, vanity, pride, and panic—can dominate dollars and cents business logic. Even a titan of industry can be, as Arthur Miller described Willy Loman, just "a little boat looking for a harbor." This is a story of how the new owners of three venerable institutions arrived armed with the belief that their mission was what Joseph A. Schumpeter, trying to define the essence of capitalism, once called "creative destruction," and of the resulting battle between their devotion to profits versus their responsibility to the public. The book attempts to tell how a network works, how it decides what shows to buy from Hollywood producers, how it distributes its product to local stations, how it sells ads.

While gathering information for this book, I sought to be a fly on the wall, watching as CBS, NBC, and ABC tried to run their businesses while coping with competitors who in many cases did not even exist a few years before. My aspiration in writing was the one Flaubert set for his narrator: to be "everywhere present and nowhere visible." To succeed, an author requires the trust of the reader. Writers lose that trust if they conform to Janet Malcolm's description of a journalist as "a confidence man" who engages in "treachery" and betrayal, without "remorse." Malcolm's provocative pieces in *The New Yorker* seized on half a point—that writers of nonfiction are surprisingly unreflective, and when they sit down to write their constituency becomes the reader, not the source—and transformed this into a cartoon. A journalist can bring Orwell's "cold eye" to a subject without having a cold heart.

I try to avoid a similar pitfall common to network books, that of romanticizing the past in order to sharpen the portrait of current villains. It is an appealing intellectual construct, save that it is too simple. There are villains in this book, but not always the obvious ones. Sometimes the culprit is the new owners and their value systems, and sometimes it is people who believe in a world that doesn't exist. A preoccupation with costs and ratings did not begin the day the new network owners arrived. Yet I am also aware that in the endless struggle between profit and the public interest, increasingly the public interest cedes ground. In some ways, I believe the networks have cheapened their product. In other ways, I feel that television is better, not worse, than it was in the "golden days" when the Big Three held a virtual monopoly. It has always been fashionable to sneer at television entertainment. I no longer do that, in part because I watch more television.

A few words about method. Much of the information in this book comes from personal interviews or meetings I attended. A handful of people refused to see me, but no one I really needed to see at any of the networks declined to be interviewed. Most people both inside and outside the networks saw me at regular intervals. I am grateful for this generous access to people who were not required to talk to me. I had nearly fifty interviews with CBS president Larry Tisch, about twenty with NBC president Bob Wright, and a total of nearly twenty with Tom Murphy and Dan Burke of Cap Cities/ABC. I was free to pop in unannounced at ABC's twice-weekly Sales staff meetings, at CBS's Affiliates Relations meetings, and at NBC's Entertainment staff meetings, to watch producers Aaron Spelling and Bruce Paltrow develop their series, and to sit with Brandon Tartikoff and his Hollywood programmers as they listened to pitches and decided which programs might reach thirty million viewers on a given night. Sometimes people who saw me pretended that they hadn't. At my final interview with Cap Cities/ABC CEO Dan Burke, in February 1991, he said that he hoped I would not be unkind to chairman Tom Murphy because he had refused to talk to me. Burke was stunned to learn that Murphy, who had been reluctant to talk, did let me interview him on seven occasions. Sometimes the cat-and-mouse game was comical. In 1987, for example, the CBS board met and agreed that only CEO Larry Tisch would be authorized to speak to me; by that time I had already interviewed more than half the board. In all, this book contains about 1,500 interviews with 350 people.

The sources for quotes and facts will be found in the chapter notes at the end of the book. Unless otherwise indicated, the quotes from the principals were given to me directly. I use italicized dialogue where the principals or participants do not remember their exact words or where I wish to telegraph to the reader that I have reported what was said but am uncertain of the exact wording. Where I attribute thoughts to someone, I rely upon what my informants told me they had been thinking; in a few instances I rely upon information from someone else with direct knowledge. Principals' ages, salaries, and job descriptions are as of the time they are mentioned.

* * *

While I have tried to tell this story impartially, readers should know that four people who appear in this book are friends. I have known Howard Stringer for more than twenty years, since he was a researcher for CBS News. Because of this friendship, I probably give Howard less attention than he deserves. I am a friend too of Tom Brokaw and Tim Russert of NBC, and Peter Jennings of ABC. I mention this by way of full disclosure, but also to assure the reader, as I trust will become obvious, that this book is not dependent on information gleaned from them.

I owe much to various people who at one point or another helped with the research on this book, especially Gordon McLeod, Catherine Teehan, Jill Davis, and Clair L. Duffy. Sonia Campos, Kirsten Olsen, and Gail Timmerman also lent a hand. The *Daily News,* once again, generously granted me an unpaid leave of absence from my weekly column starting in April 1990; I am grateful to James Hoge and Michael Packenham. I am also grateful to the Gannett Center for Media Studies, which granted me a fellowship for part of a year, to the other fellows, who were provocative companions, and especially to executive director Ev Dennis. Various friends, including Richard Reeves, Nick Pileggi, Nora Ephron, Delia Ephron, Jerry Kass, John Scanlon, and Tully Plesser, have shared their wisdom and sometimes their living space. My agent, Esther Newburg, has been a valued friend and advisor.

This is the fifth book of mine Jason Epstein has edited. During the editing process, there were times I wanted to strangle him. Good sense prevailed, as did Jason's deft pencil and brains. My agent has never shopped around for a better price because I don't think there is a better editor. Jason's assistant, Maryam Mohit, is as well organized as any general, and less gruff. Sharon DeLano lent her skill and helped me pare the manuscript. Margaret Wimberger copy-edited this book as if it were her child, and when nature intervened and she had a baby, her task was completed by John McGhee and Chris Stamey. Their efforts were diligently choreographed by Beth Pearson. This book has enjoyed three Random House publishers—Howard Kaminsky, Joni Evans, and now Harold Evans. I am grateful to each. Thanks as well to Peter Osnos, Rochelle Udell, Mary Beth Murphy, Dona Chernoff, Carol Schneider, Mitchell Ivers, Steve Mentz, Eve Adams, Dennis Ambrose, and Oksana Kushnir.

Finally, a special word of thanks to the two women who put up with and sustain me—my daughter, Kate, and my wife, Amanda, who is one of the smartest editors I have ever known.

1

A FATEFUL DINNER PARTY, OCTOBER 25, 1986

Tom Brokaw knew the evening was going to be a disaster long before anyone sat down to eat. He knew it during cocktails, when he and the other male guests ignored the elaborate hors d'oeuvres and, half-crazed, grimly cased the house in search of a television set. He knew it when he heard his boss, Bob Wright, instruct Bryant Gumbel, NBC's *Today* show host, "You look in the kitchen." He knew it when Gumbel returned empty-handed and huddled in a corner of the living room with Wright, Brokaw, and their ultimate boss, Jack Welch. The four men giggled like coconspirators, but they were plainly upset. "They don't even have a television set downstairs," Wright moaned.

Jack Welch, chairman and CEO of General Electric, the new owner of NBC, had dreaded this dinner. Now here he was, imprisoned in a big old colonial house in Westport, Connecticut, on a springlike Saturday in October, the twenty-fifth to be exact, thinking only of baseball. The Boston Red Sox and the New York Mets were poised to play the potentially pivotal sixth game of the 1986 World Series, and Welch knew he could have had a choice seat at Shea Stadium in Queens. Hell, he could have had any seat in the stadium, since John F. Welch, Jr.'s company, NBC, was televising the games exclusively. *Okay. At least we can watch the game!* he had said to his wife as they drove to Westport from their New Canaan home.

But there didn't seem to be a damn television set. This mattered a lot, because the host was Lawrence K. Grossman, president of NBC News, and the purpose of Grossman's dinner was to impress Welch and Robert C. Wright, the forty-three-year-old executive Welch had plucked from GE and installed as NBC president in September. It mattered because the Red Sox, who were up three games to two over the Mets in the best-of-seven series, were on the cusp of capturing their first championship in sixty-eight years. And it mattered because Welch and Wright were Red Sox fans.

Actually, Welch was a Red Sox fanatic. He had been a fan from the time he was an altar boy in Salem, Massachusetts. His mother, Grace, the wife of a Boston & Maine train conductor and union leader, would take her only son by the hand to Fenway Park, where they sat in the bleachers. The day before this Westport dinner, the GE helicopter had whisked him to game five at Fenway Park, where he had season box seats. The Red Sox won, and Welch arrived at his office the next morning hoarse from cheering. The Red Sox were as much an obsession to Jack Welch as was getting rid of corporate waste. "Who played second base for the 1946 Red Sox?" was the first question he had asked Joyce Hergenhan, Con Edison's senior vice president for Public Affairs, over dinner when they met. The headhunter's report had told him Hergenhan was a sports trivia expert, and Welch was going to test her.

"Bobby Doerr," she answered.

"Yeah, but who held the ball?" asked Welch.

"Oh, you mean when Enos Slaughter scored from first base on a single?"

"What else would I mean?" growled Welch, his laser-blue eyes locked on her.

"Johnny Pesky!" shot back Hergenhan, who won a smile from the chairman and, eventually, the job as GE's vice president of Corporate Public Relations.

Larry Grossman didn't know his dinner was a disaster. "It was a perfectly decent social night," he revealed later, although he did notice a "locker room" quality to it. Anchorman Tom Brokaw remembers asking Grossman the day before, "Do you really want to go forward with this?" Brokaw was aware that the News chief often displayed the distracted air of a college professor, habitually donning a white cardigan with two red stripes on its right sleeve as soon as he entered the office, silently pulling at his trim, mostly white beard, which traveled in a thin line along the bottom of his jaw and blossomed at his chin, leaning back in his swivel chair and belching huge clouds of cigar smoke. Behind the boyishly handsome mask, Brokaw was as attuned to office politics as he was to Washington politics. He had done his homework, and warned Grossman that Welch and Wright were Red Sox fans.

Grossman telephoned his wife. It was too late, he reported back to

Brokaw.* The food and flowers were ordered, the caterer retained. What Grossman didn't say was that Alberta "Boots" Grossman, a Ph.D. candidate in learning disabilities at New York University, thought it silly that grown-ups should go *ga-ga* over a sporting event. Besides, there was a television set upstairs. Grossman reassured Brokaw they could all check in on the game at some point after dinner. Moreover, Grossman was intent on luring Welch and Wright into News's orbit.

From Grossman's point of view, the evening was part of a campaign. GE, America's third most valued corporation after IBM and Exxon, had officially taken over the network only months before, and Grossman didn't want to see the budget of the News division cut. Now that NBC was in first place in the nightly entertainment ratings, and News was poised to knock Dan Rather from his number-one perch, and *Today* had roared ahead of ABC's *Good Morning America,* Grossman wanted to spend more, not the 5 percent less Wright was asking each NBC division to accept as "an exercise." Rich in resources, NBC should open second fronts, Grossman argued—new bureaus, new equipment—and should aggressively recruit "stars" like Diane Sawyer, expand its celebrated investigative team, and aim for a knockout strategy to achieve the kind of dominance in news once enjoyed by CBS.

Grossman had so far failed to persuade Wright, but he was determined. His mission, as he saw it, was to teach his new corporate masters that News could not be judged solely on whether it made money. News had a public responsibility—to cover events everywhere in the world, to interrupt entertainment programs with momentous announcements, to take over the network after the polls closed on Election Day, to provide documentaries and gavel-to-gavel coverage of political conventions, to provide a place where Americans could repair in times of crisis. Larry Grossman—not unlike executives at the other two networks, which had also acquired new owners in 1986—worried that the goal of the new owners was not to educate, not to make television better, but to better control costs and maximize profits.

More than once Tom Brokaw warned Grossman, "Hey, Larry, they're not tenants. They own the place!" Like a man possessed, Grossman was undeterred. He had a mission, and on the night of October 25, 1986, it was to convert Welch and Wright to his religion. To help, thought Grossman, he would sprinkle a little stardust on

* Grossman doesn't remember Brokaw's words, but confirms it was too late to cancel dinner.

Carolyn and Jack Welch and Suzanne and Bob Wright by inviting Tom Brokaw and his wife, Meredith, Bryant Gumbel and his wife, June, and *Today* show cohost Jane Pauley and her husband, "Doonesbury" creator Garry Trudeau.

The Red Sox game was well under way by the time the two waiters finally began serving the four-course dinner to the guests seated in heavy French chairs around a rectangular walnut table. All the men save Grossman, who had an uncomfortable look plastered on his face, were deep in conversation about batting averages and ERA's. Only two women were faintly interested in The Game—Meredith Brokaw and Jane Pauley. Only one woman seemed passionate about it—Boots Grossman, who hated the idea of talking about baseball at her dinner table. "She had absolutely zero interest in the game," said Welch, who was seated beside her. "Boots was so upset," remembers Wright. "Her dinner party is literally being interrupted by people who are talking in Yugoslavian. She invited people and wound up with these Yugoslavs at her table. And they're all giving sign language and talking baseball and she was just fit to be tied."

During dinner a quiet struggle ensued, as five of the six men inquired about the whereabouts of a TV, about the score, while Boots Grossman tried to steer the conversation to weightier topics. For a while, they did discuss the differences between TV and print journalism. Bryant Gumbel, who had been singed by critics, argued that there was no reason for the network to cooperate by offering screenings to magazine and newspaper writers; Welch and Wright insisted that any press was good press. Briefly, Garry Trudeau, who sat across from Welch, poked fun at GE's "Star Wars" anti-missile defense-system contracts, dismissing it as science fiction; Welch shot back good-natured put-downs. And at one point the chairman, who was seated beside Boots Grossman at one end of the table, brought up a recent *New York Times* story which said that Grossman resisted Bob Wright's request that all departments pare their budgets by 5 percent. The *Times* quoted Grossman as saying, "I anticipate that we'll get what we need." Wright was quoted as saying he expected everyone, including News, to undergo this "exercise."

"Hey, Tom," yelled Welch, looking directly across the table at Brokaw. "I read this account in the *Times* that the budget differences between Larry and Bob is just jockeying. And then I read your view that it will all work out. Who's right here?"

Brokaw smoothly fielded the question, saying that when he talked to reporters he told them the dispute was not a serious one. Welch knew better, as did Grossman. But in this exchange, as in the others, Grossman did not join in. Grossman wanted to duck the issue, wanted to allow the passage of time and the exposure to his NBC guests to wear down Welch and Wright. To them, however, NBC's News president seemed paralyzed, his awkward smile suspended like a pose. "This was a loud, bang-around crowd and Larry's not a loud, bang-around guy," recalled Wright. Brokaw remembers Welch rolling his eyes, surprised that Grossman seemed "frozen in place." Gumbel, Pauley, and the others exchanged nervous glances.

Okay, Grossman. Where you hiding the TV? Gumbel jokingly inquired.

Boots Grossman scowled. After a moment of pained silence, she turned to Welch, who complained later to friends that she talked to him about how important Larry's job was, how awed her N.Y.U. classmates were by Larry's position, of how Grossman had engendered esteem on the many overseas and domestic trips he had made on behalf of NBC. "I was probably trying to sell Larry," she conceded later. "Part of the dinner was to introduce Welch and Wright to the News organization so they wouldn't think it was some alien organization. If I was tense it was because I was aware Larry was in trouble with the organization."

The GE chairman might have accepted a wife's tribute from Jane Pauley or Meredith Brokaw, for he was susceptible to the warmth of these children of the Midwest, with their wholesome peach-pink skin. But Alberta Grossman was the kind of woman Welch found annoying. Like his, her roots were working class. She was from Swampscott, Massachusetts, not far from Welch's hometown of Salem. But she had gone on to Radcliffe, and now at dinner her dark eyes moved about like sentries. She had short, fuzzy dark hair and looked to Welch like a middle-aged hippie. Despite her nickname, Boots Grossman was a serious person. She enjoyed entertaining, and was devoted to her husband. So devoted that when he had headed the Public Broadcasting System she spent eight dreary years by his side in Washington. To want to talk only baseball was, to her, as bad as the Washington custom of exiling women after dinner while the men sipped brandy and smoked cigars.

The dinner crawled—the hors d'oeuvres of mushroom philo tied with leeks were followed by salmon quenelles, which were followed by veal chops served with confit of onion, sautéed mushrooms, herb-broiled tomatoes, baby carrots with lemon butter, and herbed Basmati rice, which was followed by a salad of endive, watercress, and limestone lettuce bathed in lemon-walnut dressing, which was followed by black-currant, apricot, and strawberry sorbet in tulip-almond cups, which was followed by coffee. All the while, Jack Welch was going stir-crazy. Roger Clemens of the Sox and Bob Ojeda of the Mets were pitching against each other and here he was stuck at a table hearing how great Larry Grossman was! Throughout the first and second courses, Welch and Bryant Gumbel, a former sportscaster and also a rabid fan, kept interrupting the two catering-company waiters with pleas for the score of the game.

Boston is up one to nothing in the first, one reported.

Two to nothing in the second.

Clemens is pitching a no-hitter through the fourth!

Tied 2–2 in the fifth.

Gumbel sneaked off to Grossman's tiny upstairs den, where the TV was located, at least twice. Once he ran into Welch, and they stayed for an inning, though Grossman later said, "I didn't notice." By the sixth inning, Welch and Gumbel had abandoned everyone at the table and repaired upstairs. With Welch gone, Brokaw whispered to Grossman, "How do you think it's going?"

"I don't know," said Grossman.

By the seventh—the inning the Sox went ahead 3–2—Jane Pauley and Meredith Brokaw and all the men but Grossman were packed into the upstairs den. Although it meant an extra $5 to $7 million in profits to NBC if the Series went to a seventh game, Welch rooted for the Sox to win it in six. The game was an emotional roller coaster for Welch. He frowned as the Mets tied the game in the ninth; he was giddy with joy as his Sox pulled ahead by two in the tenth; he slumped as the Mets staged a two-out rally in the tenth to triumph, as Boston first baseman Bill Buckner let Mookie Wilson's squibble roll under his glove and Ray Knight scored all the way from second.

It was a significant victory. The Mets tied the Series and entered the decisive seventh game with a psychological edge. The dinner, said one guest, was also "significant because Welch and Wright made up their minds about Larry that night. They decided he was not one of their guys. He was not . . . in the traffic pattern of the evening." Welch was "turned off" by the "serious" Boots and Larry Grossman, admits Wright. Welch told friends he found the Grossmans too swollen with importance, too "haughty."

Larry Grossman was a serious man. While he was growing up in Brooklyn, his mother the teacher and his father the lawyer drummed into their son the notion of social responsibility, a belief nurtured later by his liberal arts education at Columbia University. Grossman's first job in television, at age twenty-four, was as a copywriter in the advertising/promotion department of CBS in 1956. Edward R. Murrow, the spiritual father of TV network news, was, he would recall, "a godlike figure to me," a tall, lithe presence passing by in his British cut trousers, wide ties, and crisp white shirts. Grossman's dream was to escape advertising and join Murrow's news division, but he was told he was more important writing promotion copy for CBS News. Soon he drifted to the advertising department at NBC, where he met Grant Tinker, vice president for Programming. Four years later, Grossman launched his own advertising and public relations firm. Always, however, he thought of how close he had come to becoming part of News, one of Murrow's boys. He came closer in the eight years between 1976 and 1984, when he served as president of PBS, where neither ratings numbers nor profits were central concerns. What was central, certainly in dealing with a Congress that helped fund PBS, was communicating a sense that public television was doing something special, as indeed it was. With an assist from Grossman, PBS launched the massive *Vietnam: A Television History* and such series as *Frontline* and *Inside Story,* and expanded the MacNeil/Lehrer news program to an hour. When Grant Tinker, by then chairman of NBC, offered him the News presidency in 1984, Grossman felt he had been entrusted with both power and privilege.

Yet now, two years later, Jack Welch sensed that Larry Grossman lacked support from his own people, who had also seemed uncomfortable at dinner. Welch arrived at dinner already suspicious of Grossman. Welch thought Grossman was being "underhanded" when he didn't confront the issue raised in the *Times* story. He suspected that Grossman or someone in News had leaked the story to the press to embarrass GE, to warn them not to desecrate the news priesthood. Larry Grossman, he sensed, didn't understand the new order.

Welch hadn't wanted to go to dinner, but how could he have refused? He knew that folks in the news division were concerned about their new corporate owners, as were employees at ABC and CBS. For the first time in history, each of the three networks was officially taken over in the blink of an eye in 1986—starting in January when Capital Cities Communications officially acquired ABC, followed in June by government approval of GE's acquisition of RCA and NBC, and ending in September 1986, when Laurence Tisch and the Loews Corporation ousted Thomas Wyman, assuming effective control of CBS.

Welch knew that people in News—indeed, employees throughout

the network—were nervous about Bob Wright, the protégé he had chosen to succeed Grant Tinker. He knew they were anxious about the departure of Tinker, who in five years as chairman had led NBC from third to first place among the networks, and had instilled employees with pride. Their programs—*Hill Street Blues, Cheers, St. Elsewhere, The Cosby Show*—had brought them Emmys and applause as "the quality network," as well as ever-expanding profits. And Tinker had done this with a soothing managerial style, without talk of "profit centers" and "downsizing" or "delayering," without arousing insecurity or insisting, as Welch did, that NBC "grow its profits" each and every year, even though under Tinker profits climbed annually. People in NBC News were particularly anxious, so Welch felt compelled to accept Grossman's dinner invitation. "We were new to the business," he explained later. "And the last thing you want to be is arrogant." Nor was he one to shun a confrontation.

Jack Welch was a lithe, five-foot eight-inch former hockey brawler with a love of conflict undeterred by a slight stutter. He was an only child, and his mother always praised "my Jack," to the point, recalls Welch, that "I never thought I stammered." His father, the union leader, was always working and "probably had no room to get between the two of us." They could afford a summer house and a new car because the railroad allowed his father to "featherbed," a practice the boy grew to detest. The spiritual force in the boy's life, however, was Grace Welch, who bore "my Jack" when she was forty. To hear the son speak of her is to hear a description of himself: "If you came to her house and said you liked her glasses, she gave them to you. She did taxes for people in the neighborhood. She was very quick with numbers. If somebody crossed her, I remember her remembering that. She was loyal to friends, and strong against those she felt wronged her."

At age fifty-one, Jack Welch had a stomach that was still firm, a chin that was still taut, and eyes like pale blue moons in a clear sky. Jack Welch believed the GE culture thrived on friction, on challenges. To him corporate competition was just another form of combat, like hockey or golf. As he played to win in sports, so now he competed to make GE the most valued company in the world. Since becoming chairman and CEO of GE in 1981, this Ph.D. in chemical engineering had shaken the foundations of the staid, 109-year-old industrial giant, shedding businesses and one out of four—one hundred thousand—GE workers. Welch questioned everything. A pet peeve of his was the belief, embraced by Grossman and others at the networks, that those engaged in national television had a unique public trust. Welch saw no difference between the public trust of his aircraft engines division and that of News. In fact, the public trust required in the consumer business was often greater, he thought. What if his refrigerators blew up? "Every GE engine attached to a plane," he said, "people bet their lives with. That's a public trust that's greater in many ways than a network."

The combative Welch saw Larry Grossman's dinner party as an opportunity to press home another point. He would demonstrate to the people in News that he knew their game, knew the positions of the political players, watched all the Sunday morning interview shows and the *MacNeil/Lehrer Newshour,* often preferring these to the "clipped," abbreviated reports he got on Brokaw's *Nightly News* or *Today.* Jack Welch saw himself as "a news junkie"—"It's why I watch television," he said. "That and sports." The chairman of GE and NBC ceded no moral high ground to those in News.

In contrast to the emotive, confrontational Welch, Bob Wright approached the dinner and the issues that provoked it in a more buttoned-down manner. He believed—as did Welch and the new owners of ABC and CBS—that the networks had become like the Big Three automobile companies in the seventies: fat and lethargic after years of enjoying a near monopoly. Wright had interrupted his GE career to spend a few years running Cox Cable Communications, and had been made aware of a world no longer dominated by three networks. He knew that cable TV, which began as an effort to deliver a better picture, had blossomed into a Goliath. A decade before, cable television reached a paltry 15 percent of American households. By 1985, almost forty million Americans were cable subscribers and 46.2 percent of all American homes could have a cable hookup if they wished. A viewer at home could choose from as many as fifty-five cable channels, ten pay-cable services, or a variety of independent television stations which offered movies and syndicated reruns of such popular network shows as *Cheers.* In the fall of 1986 Rupert Murdoch would launch the Fox network, which he vowed would become the fourth network. VCR movie-rental outlets or pay-per-view events like championship prizefights offered customers the movie or event they wanted when they wanted it. That the networks would lose viewers was, no doubt, inevitable. What wasn't inevitable, thought Wright and Welch, was the sloth, the complacency with which the networks faced this challenge. They believed the networks, like much of corporate America, had grown flabby.

In some ways, Bob Wright was like Jack Welch. Both were relatively short, lean, balding men. Both attended non–Ivy League colleges. Both had spent most of their adult lives working for GE. But Wright lacked Welch's electricity. He didn't figuratively grab you by the lapels; often he didn't look you in the eye but instead cast his hazel eyes elsewhere. He was a laid-back man, whose large, square eyeglasses and subdued paisley ties were the uniform of the corporate lawyer or credit manager. Wright had performed as both for GE, where he had held eleven jobs in twelve years.

When Larry Grossman or Grant Tinker heard the word *network,* they thought of NBC, CBS, or ABC; Bob Wright thought of a twelve-network universe, composed of HBO, CNN, ESPN, and other cable-programming services, many of which made more money in 1986 than the CBS or ABC networks. When Grossman or Tinker thought of the word *network* they thought also of the half-dozen or so network-owned TV stations in large metropolitan centers, stations which benefited from free network programming and were always awash in cash; Wright's calculus did not include the hundreds of millions in profits these stations delivered to NBC, CBS, and ABC. Looking only at the networks, Bob Wright knew that the Big Three, which only ten years before had monopolized 92 percent of all evening viewers, now claimed just 75 percent, and their share of the TV audience was heading south. As happened on the world stage, where powerful nation-states such as Japan, Germany, and South Korea had become economic forces the two superpowers were compelled to contend with, so Wright believed the cable sun was rising.

Wright was equally skeptical about network news. He believed people no longer automatically waited to watch the evening news at 6:30 or 7:00 P.M.They got their fix earlier from expanded local news, with free footage supplied by the networks or other pay services, from Ted Turner's Cable News Network, from all-news radio, from their computer terminals. Like a lawyer presenting his brief, Wright could recite the numbers: Just five years before, 72 percent of the audience watched one of three evening network newscasts; by 1986, only 63 percent did. Where Welch instinctively rejected the argument that News had a unique public trust, Wright relied on numbers. With less and less of the public watching, Wright wasn't certain that News qualified as a "public trust." It vexed him that NBC News had not earned a direct profit since 1979, when its costs were only $100 million. Now it was spending $275 million. It troubled him that CNN, which was on twenty-four hours a day, had a budget only one-third that size.

CNN was earning a profit, and Wright thought he knew why. CNN wasn't unionized, wasn't encrusted with strict work rules, wasn't burdened with an extra layer of field producers, wasn't bashful about using pictures provided by non-CNN sources. While the networks paid star salaries to its anchors and reporters—Brokaw was earning $1.8 million and most correspondents received six-figure salaries—at CNN no correspondent then earned more than $90,000 and no anchor topped $500,000. Wright was pained to note that the NBC News budget had ballooned at a compound annual growth rate of 14 percent between 1980 and 1984, and that in 1986 News would spend $64 million more than it collected in revenues. The new president of NBC thought all this, but like Welch he was wary of a public squabble with News.

Larry Grossman operated on a different set of assumptions. He believed the networks themselves were a public trust. The average American household watched television seven hours daily, and six out of ten owned at least two TV sets. On Sundays, the most watched night of the week, 100 million viewers gathered in front of their TV sets as if before a shrine, and the networks used this night to launch their miniseries; the early evenings, when the kids were still awake, were devoted to half-hour comedies; from 9:00 to 11:00, when adults were the dominant audience, the networks programmed more serious fare, including news specials and one-hour dramas. Not since the automobile had a new technology altered behavior as television had, thought Grossman. Television shrunk the world, made possible the "global village" Marshall McLuhan had prophesied. The Berlin wall could keep out people but not ideas. Grossman could remember the piece that ran on *NBC Nightly News* from tiny Belize, near Guatemala, in which correspondent Garrick Utley wandered about a Third World village which had no plumbing or electricity or metal television wires, but had plenty of battery-operated TV sets and backyard dishes receiving American TV shows from satellites whirling in space.

To Jack Welch or Bob Wright, Belize was a business opportunity; to Larry Grossman, it was an opportunity to advance a sense of community, the exchange of information that Third World nations might denounce as cultural imperialism but Grossman believed would one day infect nations with the spirit of freedom. Grossman rejected Jack Welch's notion that the same public trust applied to making an airplane engine. Relatively few people flew airplanes, and anyone could build them. Besides, the very reason television had more government-imposed regulations was that frequencies were relatively scarce and had to be rationed.

The public owned the airwaves, Grossman believed, and it was to them that a network owed responsibility to provide news, as well as to offer occasional evenings of dramas or symphonies. If political leaders shied from issues, he believed the press had a responsibility to highlight them. This was Larry Grossman's religion, one shared by many others at the network, even those who jumped aboard when an action-adventure series, *The A-Team,* helped pull NBC out of third place. To them the thought of requiring News to earn a profit or even to break even was a sacrilege. Before GE bought the network from RCA in 1986, Grant Tinker kept hands off News, respecting an invisible wall between it and business.

In the GE culture, on the other hand, nothing was sacred; the thought of accepting losses as normal was sacrilege. The primary responsibility was to GE shareholders, not to some romanticized notion of a public that was abandoning the networks anyway. To Larry Grossman, this was alien. For each of the two years Grossman had run the news division, he had spent up to $275 million, and each year lost money. Grossman was, of course, asked to justify expenses, but he did not feel the hot breath of accountants. Nor were news specials expected to match the ratings of entertainment programs. When he put *Today* on the road—sending it to Rome to interview the pope or to Moscow to interview Mikhail Gorbachev—the extra money spent on what he called "event television" translated into enhanced stature for Bryant Gumbel and a return to first place in the morning ratings. Larry Grossman believed in the virtue and power of liberal government—"The problems of poverty and inner city decay," he would say, "of education and pollution, of crime and drugs, of racism and discrimination, are well within our capacity to resolve." And Grant Tinker had supported Grossman's calling, which was to educate the public, to do good.

Grossman had known Tinker since the early sixties, and when Tinker retired as chairman and CEO of NBC during the summer of 1986, Grossman was deeply distressed. This was not just because Tinker treated News as sacrosanct. Larry Grossman carried a secret: Before departing, Tinker had recommended to Welch that Grossman be anointed his successor as head of NBC. Although he had not campaigned for the job, as others did, Grossman lived with the knowledge that he had been passed over in favor of Bob Wright. This might have been less of a burden had Bob Wright shared Larry Grossman's assumptions—his religion. He did not.

Being a man of reason and genuine sweetness, Larry Grossman did not let his wound fester, and early on he did what any former public relations executive might: He launched an offensive aimed at winning over the new corporate parent. The dinner at his Westport home was part of that offensive. He thought it would work, although Tom Brokaw was dubious. "I think they'll see it as a conspiracy," he remembers saying four days before the event.*

The event backfired. "You certainly didn't leave that dinner feeling close to Larry," said Welch. "You left feeling closer to Brokaw and Bryant." Because Welch feels that judging people and placing them in the right slots is his number-one task as chairman of GE, and because he liked Brokaw and was a news junkie, he soon developed an easy rapport with the anchor, calling him, seeking him out at the annual NBC Christmas party, inviting him to lunch or breakfast.

Grossman was another story. A month after the dinner, at an annual budget review at GE's campus headquarters in Fairfield, Connecticut, NBC, like the other thirteen divisions of the corporation, was expected "to make a case for the resources they require from us," said Welch. Grossman came proposing not the 5 percent cut Bob Wright requested but an increase for News.

"How dare you come in at 4 percent above 1986 when the word is out that you have to keep below the current budget?" Welch bellowed.

"That's what we need," said Grossman, who stammered as he tried to explain why. Welch sat across from Grossman and the other NBC executives at a large oval table in the GE boardroom on the third floor.

"You guys spend more money! My kids could do better!" Welch exclaimed to Grossman. He then followed with a barrage of questions: *How much does it cost NBC News per story covered? How many stories that are covered actually get on the air? How often is each correspondent on? Why can't we save money by allowing some of the two hundred or so NBC affiliated stations to cover stories?*

Grossman was stunned, and "hemmed and hawed," remembers Wright. What Jack Welch saw when he looked across the table was

* Grossman does not recall the warning.

Larry Grossman pouting. "He was sullen. I had a sense he was not buying in."

Grossman did not know the answers to many of Welch's questions about the news budget. But this was usually the case with network News presidents. With rare exceptions, they did not view themselves as "cost-control experts." The tradition at all three networks had been that the news division president protected News from the corporation, kept the efficiency experts with their flow charts and operating statements at a distance. Not having come from the world of journalism, Grossman was also anxious to demonstrate his news credentials. Like his colleagues, Grossman thought News was home for independent-minded, creative people, who operated best when they felt free. He was like a union leader representing News, struggling to keep the GE bosses at bay.

Welch glowered and recalls: "I was shocked. Shocked!" Welch didn't actually order Grossman to cut the budget, but he expected him to toe the line. He was appalled by what he took to be Grossman's stubborn, almost mulish resistance. Privately he railed, *Grossman is a damn socialist! He doesn't believe in profits!*

The next day, Wright telephoned Welch and said Grossman wanted to revisit the subject. The GE helicopter was in midair, ferrying former RCA chairman and new GE board member Thornton Bradshaw and his wife, Pat, to Martha's Vineyard, when Welch, without explanation, ordered the chopper to return to NBC to pick up Wright and Grossman and drop them off in Fairfield first. The former RCA chairman had no idea of the confrontation awaiting Grossman. The Fairfield encounter with Grossman, Welch and Wright turned into a two-hour summit. "The first words out of Jack Welch's mouth when I walked in," recalls Grossman, were, "This is the greatest day of my life!"

Grossman wondered whether one of Welch's children had just done something wonderful, whether he had become a grandfather or acquired a masterpiece.

"Our stock just hit a new high," explained Welch.

Grossman was stunned. "I couldn't comprehend his values," he recalls.

The three men sat on a sofa in Welch's giant modern office, facing the pictures of Welch's four children which flanked his glass-topped desk.

"I don't like the way the meeting went yesterday," Grossman began.

"What didn't you like?" asked the GE chairman.

"Look, I don't like this whole cost detail," said Grossman.

They went over and around the subject of the budget, and after a while, Welch remembers, Grossman looked at his watch and said, "I've got to get this over with. I have to get back to New York because I have dinner with Chief Justice Burger."

Welch was livid. "I was ready to fire him right there. That afternoon," recalls Welch. Not only had Grossman been remarkably self-important, he thought, he was also obstinate. "If you don't get your costs in line you won't be having dinners with Justice Burger!" Welch roared, pointing a finger at Grossman's chest.*

Welch did not let up: "You're going to do this stuff. You're going to follow our procedures. And if you like seeing Justice Burger you get this thing right. I want it clear that you cannot refuse to cut five percent. You work for Bob Wright! You work for GE!"

To Larry Grossman this encounter was like a nightmare, a scene right out of Paddy Chayefsky's prophetic 1976 movie, *Network,* in which the new network owner bellows to his anchorman: *"You will atone! Am I getting through to you, Mr. Beale?"*

Jack Welch got through to Larry Grossman. The News budget was pared 5 percent, although Grossman chose not to acknowledge the cut. Even so, Larry Grossman, like his counterparts at ABC and CBS, was compelled to recognize that a new order had replaced the old.

* Grossman does not remember that Welch had said this but adds, "If I mentioned Burger it was only to show off that I was having dinner with him."

2

A "LITTLE SHIRTTAIL COMPANY" TAKES OVER ABC, 1984-1985

A decade earlier, in the midseventies, the old order at the Big Three networks had been a comfortable cocoon, shielding those who worked there from bad news. Job security was a given. Hostile take-overs were unheard of. Like the Big Three American auto companies, the networks crushed all would-be competitors. The networks had paid little notice when Home Box Office, in 1975, requested permission to bounce its signal off a satellite. When the Federal Communications Commission held public hearings and invited public dissent, none of the three networks lodged a protest. No one cared. The networks felt impregnable. NBC's parent company, RCA, even leased one of its Satcom I satellites to the infant pay-cable channel.

Why should the networks feel threatened? Of the 85 million Americans who owned TVs in 1976, nine out of ten watched evening shows on one of the three networks. On a typical night, the average household received just seven stations, and *TV Guide* listed only fourteen viewing options. Neither Showtime, ESPN, CNN, the Disney Channel, nor MTV was included among the fourteen, since aside from services like the struggling HBO, cable programming barely existed. Only the Big Three could afford to exhibit recent Hollywood movies. There were fewer syndicated shows, and none bulldozed a time period as *Wheel of Fortune*, *Jeopardy!*, or *Oprah Winfrey* does today. There were, in early 1976, few commercially available VCRs, few cordless remote-control clickers, no satellite distribution of programs, no back-yard dishes, no superstations, no Fox Network, and about a hundred non-network independent TV stations in the entire United States. Advertisers wishing to reach mass audiences were held hostage by the networks. The revenues of CBS, ABC, and NBC racked up double-digit growth every year, swelling by an astonishing 324 percent between 1976 and 1984. The network was king.

Almost everything about the networks suggested comfort, from the silver limousines on demand to the chartered airplanes to the first-class air travel provided even technicians, to the mountains of caviar dispensed at network-sponsored conventions, to the party and conference planner on staff at ABC who did nothing but book hotels, reserve golf courses, and order custom-made ice sculptures for network parties. There was the luxury of knowing that the three networks were still controlled by the same founders or institutions—William Paley (CBS), General David Sarnoff and RCA (NBC), and Leonard Goldenson (ABC). In addition to job security, there was also the serenity that came from knowing that even the third-place network made money. Looking back, Paley conceded, "There was a sort of comfortable attitude on the part of the networks."

Competition came not from other methods of TV distribution but from the networks themselves, which were located within five blocks of each other along Manhattan's Sixth Avenue. It was a competitive but clubby world. There were enough advertising dollars to go around. Profits were assured. You lunched at the same restaurants, attended the same confabs of the National Association of Broadcasters, the National Association of Television Programming Executives, and the Association of National Advertisers, sat on the same industry boards, lobbied the same federal government. Mostly, you thought about each other. "In the old days it was *us* versus *them,*" recalls Brandon Tartikoff, president of NBC Entertainment, who had been an ABC programmer in the seventies. "We used to ask: Did we win Friday?" No one had to ask: What is the network share of the television market on a given night? The pie was sliced just three ways, with the nibblers vying for the crumbs.

Although the networks alternately fought cable or vied to invest in it, or battled the Hollywood studios, in general the Big Three were filled with their own power. When David J. Londoner, a respected media analyst with Wertheim & Company, issued a report in 1978 predicting that "new methods of entertainment distribution" would significantly erode network audiences, the Big Three were irate. Even under the worst circumstances, in the long run, proclaimed an internal ABC retort to Londoner, "the maximum negative effect on network audiences would be 6 percent or less." More than likely, the networks argued, their audience would grow because the population would. Nor were the networks worried about costs. As costs spiraled, they simply passed them along to advertisers by hiking prices. "The networks were gougers," admits Jake Keever, ABC's head of Sales. The networks would inflate the price of their ads, he recalls, and be stunned when advertisers agreed to pay them.

Meanwhile, they failed to focus on such emerging competitors as cable, independent stations, and the VCR. The pattern was not an unfamiliar one. As the networks paid too little attention when HBO requested access to a satellite, so a decade earlier the American auto companies missed the rising threat from cheaper, smaller, more fuel-efficient Japanese imports. Something similar happened earlier to the railroads, which were displaced first by the automobile, then by the airlines, and would happen to RCA and the American consumer-electronics industry as a whole, which lost its bet on video disc technology—or didn't bet at all—to the VCR revolution that would sweep America in the eighties.

Down the yellow brick road the networks skipped, blithely unaware of the bad news awaiting them.

For ABC, the first forecast of bad news concerned the price of its stock. The news was delivered on a radiantly sunny day in June 1984 by Michael P. Mallardi, the network's unpretentious chief financial officer. The setting was the vast, lavish green rolling lawn of the Crescent H Ranch in Jackson Hole, Wyoming. The occasion was a four-day ABC executive retreat, and the twenty-five executives present paid heed because Mallardi, fifty, was respected for his financial acumen and because he was without bombast, a down-to-earth man who preferred cutting the grass at his Rockland County home to attending cocktail parties or network junkets.

"Our company is worth more dead than alive," Mallardi warned his audience. "The breakup value of ABC is greater than the price of our stock." ABC stock, he cautioned, was trading at forty-two dollars a share, which suggested that the company was worth only $1.2 billion. Yet the book value was sixty dollars a share, suggesting a worth of about $2 billion. But Wall Street said that if the company were broken up and sold it would be worth about $4 billion. "So, fellas, people out there are saying ABC is worth more than twice its current market value. We are vulnerable." A raider, he was suggesting, could pay a steep premium for ABC, knowing he could dismember and sell off the parts—five TV stations, five AM and seven FM radio stations, seven satellite-delivered radio networks, ABC Motion Pictures, more than one hundred magazines and a book publishing arm, three cable-programming services, and various other assets, including extensive real estate holdings. ABC also made an inviting target, Mallardi said, since it was swimming in cash. Fueled by its robust TV stations, ABC would have a strong year in 1984, with $3.7 billion in revenues and $195 million in earnings.

Mallardi in his Jackson Hole speech was, of course, telling only part of the story. By the mid-1980s the television industry was wobbling from changes that shook the very foundation of the networks. *TV Guide,* which a decade before had listed fourteen viewing options each evening, now listed thirty-three. On a typical night, viewers could with their remote-control clickers flick from the networks to three times as many independent stations as existed in 1976, and to a veritable alphabet soup of choices, including A&E, ESPN, USA, SHO, HBO, FNN, NICK, LIFE, MAX, CNN, MTV, DIS, BET, C-SPAN. Movies and syndicated fare like *Wheel of Fortune* helped independent stations snare one out of five viewers. By the end of the decade, 60 percent of all homes would have cable. And if neither cable nor the broadcast stations appealed to viewers who increasingly grazed from channel to channel, technology offered still another choice not available in 1976. Viewers could now pop a rental movie into their VCRs. By 1985, VCRs would be in 20 percent of all American homes; six years later seven out of ten homes would have one.

With this variety of viewing choices, network TV viewership had plunged. By 1984, 75 percent of all homes were tuned on a typical evening to one of three networks, down from 92 percent in 1976; over the next seven years this number would slip to 62 percent, and dip below 50 percent on some nights. The networks would lose one of every three viewers.

By 1984, the world had changed in still other ways. Wall Street had turned predatory. Stocks were now traded mostly by money managers, who were graded on their short-term performance. Investment banks no longer acted as cautious counselors. Instead they vied to become financial supermarkets, and doing deals was their ticket. With Ronald Reagan in the White House, with the public less shamed by greed and eager to shrink government regulation, unshackled corporations engaged in what would once have been considered rapacious behavior. Speculation and hostile takeovers became normal. Leverage and asset-based valuations became the rage. With interest rates declining, investors could tap huge reservoirs of borrowed money to leverage their transactions. Investors believed that entrenched management was bureaucratic, resistant to change. New management, they insisted, could fatten cash flows by slashing costs, particularly labor costs. With an array of creative financial tools concocted by Wall Street, including junk bonds and other devices requiring minimal cash, relatively small companies could now ingest giants.

While Mallardi's depressing analysis shook many fellow ABC executives, it came as no surprise to ABC's patriarch, chairman Leonard H. Goldenson. To protect his beloved network, Goldenson had quietly retained the First Boston Company and its star employee, Bruce Wasserstein, to devise defense strategies. But while Goldenson knew that ABC was vulnerable, his people were still pretty insulated. What was new about the meeting in Jackson Hole was not the substance of Mallardi's warning but the fact that he was, for the first time, letting the possibility of a takeover out of the closet.

ABC's stock price was depressed, Mallardi continued, because network profit margins were shrinking. And he saw worse to come. ABC's ratings were down. After years of languishing in third place and being known as "Hard Rock," as distinguished from CBS's "Black Rock"—as its slate black New York headquarters was called—or NBC's "30 Rock"—named for its 30 Rockefeller Plaza address—in 1976 ABC had taken the ratings lead, and was now to be treated as seriously as CBS and NBC. But by mid-1984, ABC had stumbled from its number-one rating back to number three. Its daytime schedule, which once produced 50 percent of its profits, was slipping as women abandoned the home for work. Since a network earned about 70 percent of its income from entertainment programming—two-thirds of it from the prime-time evening hours between 8:00 and 11:00 when most sets are on and, consequently, advertisers could be charged the steepest prices—ratings translated into profits. And neither Sports nor News was providing alternative sources of cash. Roone Arledge had made ABC the place to watch *Monday Night Football, Wide World of Sports,* the Olympics. But ABC was now paying such a hefty price to televise these events—a then record $220 million for the 1984 Los Angeles Olympics—that profits had shriveled. The other piece of Arledge's domain—News—was at best a marginal money-maker, and still ranked third in the ratings, though the quality of the ABC newscast was now competitive with that of CBS and NBC.

Those gathered on the lawn under the bright sun at Jackson Hole were also acutely aware of another vulnerability. Everyone at ABC knew the network would soon need to fill Leonard Goldenson's shoes. Like the founders of the other two networks, he would be hard to replace.

* * *

Leonard Goldenson had taken a circuitous path to ABC. After graduating from Harvard Law School, he worked as a lawyer for Paramount Pictures, rising to chief executive of United Paramount Theaters before entering the network business. In 1951 the fledgling ABC, with its five fully owned and eighteen affiliated stations, which covered a mere 35 percent of the nation, was for sale. With only a single New York City station to call his own, William Paley of CBS sought to buy the potential rival. Lacking the stature of Paley and General Sarnoff, the somewhat bland Goldenson was expected to lose the test of wills. He didn't. With a plan to lure Hollywood movies to the small screen, Goldenson captured the prize for $25 million.

At this time, network TV was like radio. Most shows were live talking heads from New York. Unlike the owners of CBS and NBC, who had been in radio, Goldenson had come of age in the movie business and thought in terms of pictures. Eventually he convinced the Hollywood studios, which viewed the networks as a threat, to produce for ABC what Goldenson called "little motion pictures," and would soon become known as series.

Thirty-three years after he started out in television, ABC's eminence and largest shareholder was seventy-eight and surrounded by managers who were largely unknown on Wall Street. Between them, Leonard Goldenson and his team owned a scant 2 percent of ABC's stock. Three-quarters of the stock was entrusted to institutional investors, whose principal obligation was to maximize shareholder value. Goldenson's chosen heir was fifty-one-year-old Frederick S. Pierce, the company's square-jawed president, who had joined ABC in 1956 and whom Goldenson sometimes treated as the son he never had. Pierce looked the part of a chief executive, from his manicured fingernails to his thinning, neatly parted dark hair to the black-rimmed reading glasses he clenched in his fist as he gestured to make a point. But although he shared responsibility for many of the network's programming successes, Fred Pierce was not revered by the investment community. He probably didn't have the standing to confront the investor Laurence Tisch, as Goldenson did in 1981, and insist that the Loews chairman sell the 5 percent of ABC stock he had accumulated since November of 1980 (Loews sold). It was widely assumed that Pierce could not have outwitted a takeover attempt from the mysterious Howard Hughes, as the wily Goldenson had. "I was too preoccupied running the company and didn't spend enough time on Wall Street," Pierce would later admit. Had Pierce spent time on the

Street, it's doubtful his congenital optimism would have meshed with a financial audience increasingly worried that the networks might be dinosaurs.

The climate of the times, Mallardi warned the ABC executives in his Jackson Hole talk, was not good for the networks. "Most of us have relied on the FCC [Federal Communications Commission] to provide a veil," continued Mallardi. "We felt protected. No more." Traditionally, the FCC saw its mission as a regulator of a scarce public resource—the airwaves. Because television was such a powerful communications tool, because more than half of all Americans said television was their only source of news, because the radio frequencies over which electromagnetic radiations travel at the speed of light are finite, and because television was "free," the government felt justified in invoking "the public interest." Starting with the Federal Radio Commission in the twenties and extending to television with the Communications Act of 1934, the federal government treated first radio and then television, when it became commercially available in the late forties, as public utilities. The government doled out licenses, imposed minimum requirements for news or community programming, encouraged stations not to drench viewers with too many ads per hour. In 1941, when RCA owned two baby networks, the Blue and the Red, and threatened to strangle television competition when it began in earnest after the war, the FCC ruled that RCA should get rid of one of its networks, and in 1943 it sold the Blue Network to Edward J. Noble. Eventually, the Blue became ABC. Decades later, when ABC agreed to merge with ITT in 1968, the FCC stepped in and blocked the merger as not in the public interest.

The airwaves were considered a public trust; when David Sarnoff of RCA first broached the idea of a radio network in 1922, he saw it as a nonprofit "public service," with no advertising allowed, a public "library" of sorts. What Sarnoff really wanted was to sell radios, which RCA manufactured. Even Herbert Hoover, a champion of free enterprise, was repelled by what he called "ether advertising" on the sacred public airwaves. Because the airwaves were deemed public property, the government imposed the Fairness Doctrine in 1949, directing station licensees to provide "a reasonable opportunity for contrasting viewpoints," a doctrine that if imposed on a newspaper or magazine would be considered a violation of free speech.

At one time the Big Three produced many of their own shows and sold the reruns. To loosen the monopolistic grip of the networks, starting under Richard Nixon in the early seventies and extending through the administrations of Gerald Ford and Jimmy Carter, the government began simultaneously to reregulate and deregulate television. Under the financial interest and syndication rules (called the fin-syn rules), the networks were not allowed to produce or have a financial stake in most of the entertainment series that they ran, or later to participate in the profits from syndicating reruns of these shows to domestic or overseas outlets. The networks were compelled to rely on the studios to produce the shows that the networks broadcast.

The networks might have turned to the studios in any case, since Hollywood is proficient at manufacturing "product" for both the small and the large screen. But the networks had no choice. The system worked this way: Under the financial interest rule, the networks were allowed to produce made-for-TV movies, miniseries, and news shows. But they were not permitted to produce more than three hours of weekly entertainment programs out of the twenty-two hours of prime time.* Once a TV series idea was approved, produced, and scheduled, the network paid a weekly license fee to the studio that produced it. This fee covered about 80 to 90 percent of the cost to produce the show; in return, the network could, over the course of the required four-year contract, air each episode twice. If the series lasted the four years, the studio could renegotiate the license fee—or threaten to yank the hit series and sell it to a competitor. And after four years there would be enough episodes in the bank for the studio to sell reruns to local stations. But under the syndication rule, the networks could not participate in this two-billion-dollar (now three-billion-dollar) domestic secondary market, even though they helped conceive the series, financed it, and promoted it into a hit. The aim of the regulation was to make the airwaves available to more players.

And more players there would be. Under the prime-time access rule, the networks were allowed to air just three hours of prime-time programming each night (8 to 11 P.M. in most parts of the country), and four hours on Sunday night. Not only were the networks not to program in the 7 P.M. hour before the start of prime time, but local stations affiliated with the three networks were not permitted to air network reruns during this hour. Since there was too much product available, and too few outlets, these rules spurred the growth of both the syndication business and independent stations. One result was

* In 1988, this limit was raised to five hours per network.

that within a few years the number of independent TV stations tripled to over three hundred.

Meanwhile, the Copyright Act of 1976 granted the fledgling cable industry the right to distribute network shows to its cable subscribers without compensating the networks. Viewers were signing up for cable largely in the expectation of receiving better reception of network shows, and cable was using the proceeds to finance its own programming growth. By 1985, nearly half of all network viewers received their programs through a cable system. While the government opened the way for cable, it harnessed the broadcast networks, prohibiting them from owning cable systems (the hookup); a network was permitted only to own a cable-programming service, like ESPN or CNN.

All of these regulations were meant to protect the public interest, since they inspired competition and challenged network monopolies. Not surprisingly, the networks argued that the FCC was no longer a neutral referee. Yet even after all the regulatory changes of the Nixon, Ford, and Carter administrations, few challenged the bedrock assumption that the FCC had a right to monitor the airwaves in the "public interest." Then, under Ronald Reagan's first FCC chairman, Mark S. Fowler, that assumption was challenged. The year Mallardi delivered his Jackson Hole wake-up call, the FCC was in the process of amending the "seven-station rule," raising the ceiling on the number of TV and/or radio stations that could be owned by a single company from seven to twelve (provided the stations reached no more than 25 percent of the nation's households). Deliberately or not, the FCC was reversing itself, inviting more concentration of station ownership and therefore more mergers. Still another relaxed rule—repeal of the so-called "anti-trafficking" provision—made stations financially more attractive to investors. And invited turmoil. Since station owners had been seen as trustees for the public, they had been discouraged from flipping stations for a profit. The anti-trafficking rule required owners to hold on to a station for at least three years before selling it. By eliminating this rule in 1982, the FCC invited financial speculators to call themselves "broadcasters." Their path was eased further when the FCC also agreed to speed the processing of requests for transferring licenses. Inevitably, those who owned media licenses were no longer immunized from corporate raiders by the government.

Meanwhile, the Reagan administration and Congress were liberating cable companies from state and local price ceilings. This permitted cable subscription rates—and profits—to soar. These measures were, of course, accompanied by populist rhetoric: There was less need for regulation since viewers had options and could now vote with their remote control devices; let the public interest be determined by what the audience—from viewers to investors—desired. This was what Mark Fowler liked to call "marketplace magic." Because consumer choices were now so plentiful—with about 1,500 TV stations, 8,000 cable systems, and about 11,000 AM and FM radio outlets—Fowler claimed TV was just another business, another appliance, "a toaster with pictures." To Fowler, freedom was the only issue—freedom to speak, freedom to watch, freedom to buy and sell. The FCC was to become a bystander, not a referee. He wanted government to get out of the way, to let the marketplace decide winners and losers.

Once, as Mike Mallardi said, the FCC had been a guardian of "the public airwaves." But no longer. For those in Mallardi's audience at Jackson Hole, as for all those who had worked for the networks, the practices of a lifetime were about to end, even though the habits that accompanied them would persist. The security provided by a protective government that nurtured network monopolies became not so much a challenge to be met as an invitation to cling to familiar ways. As late as 1984, CBS issued a report predicting future network growth.

It is true that network officials often railed against cable, and each network strove to enter the cable-programming business. But for the most part, the networks focused on the competition among themselves. They had nothing comparable to the Japanese threat that rocked the car companies or the consumer-electronics industry. What "threats" there were came in the form of a mustached sailor from Atlanta by the name of Turner, with schemes for a twenty-four-hour Cable News Network and for beaming his Atlanta station to a satellite, which in turn would transform WTBS into a national superstation that sold and distributed its programs to cable operators. Ted Turner was "disparaged as a lunatic," remembers M. S. "Bud" Rukeyser, who for twenty-five years was the chief spokesman for NBC.

The networks failed to see the baby cable-TV industry as a potential outlet for their programs. According to John C. Malone, president of Tele-Communications, Inc., the nation's largest cable operator, "They failed to view themselves as programmers and instead saw themselves as broadcasters. It was a classic error. They fought a new technology rather than try to own it." The networks could have been more aggressive in launching cable services, or more patient in sticking with those they did launch, then selling their programs to cable operators like Malone.

Technology moves with blinding, ruthless speed, transforming innovations almost overnight into relics—as happened first to the gramophone, then the phonograph, then the hi-fi, then stereos, then cassette players, perhaps now compact disc players, which may be replaced at any minute by digital audio tape machines. It happened to typewriters, shoved aside by word processors. As in any industry under siege, the prevailing attitude at the networks toward rapid change was that of the Wicked Witch of the West in the Broadway musical *The Wiz: "Don't nobody bring me no bad news."*

In the months after Mike Mallardi's Jackson Hole talk, rumors about takeovers were rampant—there were stories of threatened raids by the Bass brothers, by Saul Steinberg and his Reliance Corporation, by Donald Trump and the Fisher brothers and Warren Buffett of Berkshire Hathaway. There was a buzz that the Tisch brothers were again acquiring ABC stock. From the beginning to the end of 1984, Leonard Goldenson's "tone began to change," remembers Roone Arledge. "He started out saying the stock should be higher than it was. It started out as a pep talk. Somewhere along the line it dawned on him that the more he talked about it [the stock price] the more it became not a source of pride but a source of fear."

This fear, coupled with what Arledge referred to as ABC's "inferiority complex" from having spent most of its life in third place, induced near panic. Frantically, Fred Pierce assigned task forces to review network expenditures. ABC wanted to prove to Wall Street that it was not vulnerable to a takeover, that it knew how to run its business, how to maximize its shareholder values.

But blood was in the water when Thomas S. Murphy, fifty-nine, the lanky, backslapping son of a former Brooklyn Democratic politician and state judge, paid a visit to Goldenson in December 1984. Some of his father's charm had rubbed off on Tom Murphy. He had a relaxed, easy way with people. And never for a day had he regretted following his father's advice to spurn an appointment at age thirty as postmaster of New York. Instead he would use his Harvard M.B.A. to embark on a career in business and ultimately become chairman and CEO of Capital Cities Communications.

In many ways, the careers of Murphy and Goldenson were similar. Each had started small. In 1954, after a few years in advertising, Murphy became WROW-TV's first employee when Cap Cities opened for business with this small UHF television station in Albany, New York. By 1984, Murphy had been CEO of Cap Cities for twenty years. Goldenson had run ABC for thirty-one years. Each felt that he had bucked the odds. Each had made a bundle of money. They were both active in charities, Murphy with the Madison Square Boys and Girls Club and the New York University Medical Center, Goldenson with United Cerebral Palsy, which he cofounded soon after learning a daughter was afflicted with the disease. And each was intensely devoted to his family. Throughout his business career, Murphy, like Goldenson, would often leave the office early to spend time with his wife and four children.

Ties between Murphy and Goldenson stretched back many years. Four of Cap Cities' seven stations were ABC affiliates. In all, these stations delivered 7 percent of ABC's total audience. In fact, Fred Pierce remembers planting the idea for a merger the year before when he spoke at Cap Cities' annual gathering of TV station managers in Phoenix. "You know, our companies would make a good combination. Our stations don't overlap much. ABC's revenues are 85 percent from broadcasting, and yours are split 50/50 with publishing. If the ground rules ever change, our two companies would make a pretty good fit." There was no question in Pierce's mind that ABC, the larger company, would be the senior partner.

But in December 1984 Tom Murphy had another idea. He had created a media company that nearly matched ABC's earnings even though its revenues ($950 million) were about one-quarter less. And he wanted his company to grow. He kept on his desk a list of properties he might like to acquire, provided he could do so in a "friendly" deal. From a single, weak Albany UHF television station, Cap Cities had become the owner of not only seven TV stations but twelve AM and FM radio stations, ten daily newspapers, thirty-six specialty magazines and newspapers, thirty-six weeklies and shopping guides, a variety of other magazines and specialized publications, and fifty-four cable-television systems in four different regions of the country. A single share of Cap Cities stock purchased for eighteen dollars in 1974 was worth two hundred dollars in 1984. And none of Murphy's many takeovers had been unwelcome. When it came to fellow businessmen, Tom Murphy was a gentleman.

Which is not to say that Tom Murphy wasn't tough. Cap Cities stations ran shoot-em-up, sensationalist local newscasts that did for crime and the seven-second soundbite what *Charlie's Angels* did for wet T-shirts. "We are giving the American people what they want," explained Murphy. "If you want to give people what you think they need, go into public broadcasting. More people read the *Daily News* than read *The New York Times.*" Behind Murphy's perfect row of white teeth and cheery salutations—his "Hi, pal," and his "Okay, pal"—lurked steel. "Tom is often underestimated because he's such a nice, open, friendly guy. You might miss his toughness," said his Harvard Business School classmate James Burke, then CEO of Johnson & Johnson and the older brother of Daniel B. Burke, Cap Cities fifty-five-year-old president and chief operating officer. One reason Cap Cities had the most profitable TV stations—earning an industry high of approximately fifty-five dollars on each one hundred taken in—was that Murphy and Burke managed costs ruthlessly. Cap Cities was known as a "lean and mean" company. When employees at the *Times Leader* in Wilkes-Barre, Pennsylvania, went on strike to protest work-force reductions in 1978, Cap Cities locked them out and continued publishing without them.* Murphy and Burke's philosophy was passed down from the founder of the company, Frank M. Smith, and is printed in its annual report each year: "Decentralization is the cornerstone of our management philosophy." And operating managers are expected "to be forever cost-conscious."

Murphy's visit to Goldenson in December 1984 was prompted by the soon-to-be-relaxed federal strictures on station ownership. Since the FCC would now allow Cap Cities to operate twelve rather than seven stations, and since TV stations were great sources of cash, the five stations owned by ABC were near the top of Tom Murphy's acquisition list, a list that also included the Chicago Tribune Company and McGraw-Hill. In four markets Murphy would wind up with both a TV and radio stations, which the FCC rules did not allow for new owners. But Murphy knew he could seek a waiver allowing him to keep each. And by imposing various economies on ABC, Murphy knew he could squeeze out additional profits, essential now that the networks could no longer expect double-digit advertising rate increases. And though he rarely watched or had much interest in the network's primary money-making product—entertainment programming—he knew how to read a bottom line. All in all, he expected network profits to remain relatively strong. Tom Murphy felt something else: For anyone in the broadcasting business, owning a net-

* To this day, the union bitterly continues to publish a rival newspaper, the Wilkes-Barre *Citizens' Voice.*

work was like conquering Mount Everest. Or, as Murphy would say when asked to describe himself, "I've loved the action."

Murphy and Goldenson met alone in the ABC offices. "Leonard, I don't want you to throw me out of the thirty-ninth floor here, but I have an idea I think we ought to consider," Murphy said affably, modestly.

"What's that, Tom?" said Goldenson.

"Capital Cities' four biggest affiliated stations are all at ABC—Philadelphia, Houston, Buffalo, Hartford/New Haven. Now that the FCC is going to allow us to go to twelve, and have one company own up to 25-percent coverage of the United States, I think it would be natural to put these two companies together."

"Tom, I'm not going to throw you out the window. It's an interesting idea," Goldenson responded. "I can understand what you're talking about, but I'd like to think it over."

The ABC chairman was ready for a merger, and had been quietly seeking a partner. He had already had discussions with IBM, and wanted to stall Murphy until he received its response. While IBM's huge cash reserves placed it at the head of the line, Goldenson felt warmly toward Murphy and Cap Cities. The two men sometimes played golf in Rye, New York, where they both lived. Goldenson admired Murphy's personal qualities, including his self-assurance. Experience also taught Goldenson that Cap Cities was a loyal station group, one that rarely preempted the network to run syndicated programs, as stations now did with alarming frequency. He knew that Murphy's stations emphasized local news, knew that years before Cap Cities had worked out a deal with the Israeli government to use its coverage of the Adolf Eichmann trial and to distribute the footage daily to stations around the globe while giving any profits from the deal to Israeli charity. In addition to his good feelings about Murphy, Goldenson respected Dan Burke, who had been Murphy's partner and number two for twenty-five years. He knew Burke was the builder, Murphy the architect.

"I must have had ten to fifteen people approach us over time," Goldenson recalls. "But I wanted to make a deal with broadcasters, and Cap Cities was the best." By "broadcasters" Goldenson meant people who had been in the business and understood its peculiarities and its unique public trust, people who were willing to sacrifice profits to air a documentary or broadcast election returns. By "broadcasters" Goldenson also meant people who knew what a strange business network television was. For a network was really a tenant pretending to be a landlord. Since government regulations did not permit the networks to own more than a handful of the stations that distributed their programs, the networks were at the mercy of the six hundred or so TV stations that agreed to call themselves affiliates. Having stitched together a national network of local stations that wanted to show the programs produced for the networks by Hollywood or the independent producers, the networks then went to advertisers and sold them mass audiences that were, in effect, rented from local stations. A network was, in fact, nothing more than a broker. It was an odd business.

But it could not fail, Goldenson thought, provided the people running the network cared about the product. "The people who run the company have got to have a feeling for programming. They've got to follow their instincts," Goldenson advised Murphy.

Murphy said that he lacked programming instincts. But he believed in finding the best programmers and delegating authority to them. This was the Cap Cities way.

The ABC chairman demurred, insisting that the CEO had to immerse himself in programming. But this was just a piece of brotherly advice. In the short run, more important matters had to be addressed. The main problem, Goldenson said, was that "the FCC has so deregulated the industry that broadcasters are no longer insulated from unfriendly takeovers." With financial pirates pillaging corporations, Goldenson wondered aloud whether the combined companies would have the resources to hold them at bay. There was much to think about: *What should be the price? Who would be the senior partner? Who the chairman and CEO? What would become of Fred Pierce?*

Goldenson didn't say it, but he wanted to delay because IBM was his first choice for a new owner. What he did say was that they should await FCC approval of the twelve-station limit, expected in January 1985. They agreed to ponder the matter over the holidays.

Early in January, Goldenson and Fred Pierce discussed the options. Pierce said he agreed that Cap Cities would "protect the integrity of the company," would treat network television as more than just a business that sold advertising, would recognize there was a public trust to uphold. But Pierce asked Goldenson to consider another possibility, one involving less of a shock to the network. "I wouldn't have sold the company," Pierce said. "I thought it would be equally productive to have a management-leveraged buyout." *Why not take the company private?*

This appealed to Goldenson's desire to protect his company, but

Goldenson was conservative. The idea of assuming a massive debt in order to take ABC private was abhorrent. So was the idea of selling off pieces of his beloved company in order to reduce the debt.

While Goldenson and Pierce were considering their options, CBS, just a block south, was already under attack from Republican senator Jesse A. Helms of North Carolina, who in January 1985 announced a bid to acquire it. Goldenson, who had spurned a bid in 1983 from MCA, the Hollywood entertainment conglomerate, now heard from his contacts on the West Coast that RCA was thinking of merging NBC with MCA. With speculative fever rising, with trading in ABC stock jumping, with rumors that pirates were about to plunder, even Fred Pierce was coming around to the view that ABC's last best hope was an arranged marriage.

Murphy telephoned again in mid-January, but Goldenson asked for more time to think. By early February, a new president of IBM had said no to ABC, and the FCC seven-station limit had formally been raised to twelve. Now Goldenson was ready to talk, so he telephoned Murphy over Presidents' Day weekend. When they met a few days later, Murphy said he was prepared to pay ninety dollars a share, a 35-percent premium over the stock price. Goldenson said that this was not nearly enough, and added that there were other considerations to be ironed out, which Murphy anticipated.

"Leonard, I've been trying to figure out how to make a deal work," Murphy said. Financing was the critical question. There was simply no way ABC could afford to pay for Cap Cities because "our multiple"—Cap Cities' earnings per share in proportion to the price of its stock—"was so high," said Murphy. Responding to a return on equity of nearly 20 percent, investors had driven up the price of Cap Cities stock. Goldenson knew that, but also knew Murphy needed what he called a partner with "deep pockets" to shoulder some of the financial burden of a merger and, above all, to ward off sharks. If Murphy could get help, Goldenson said he was ready to sell.

No problem, thought Murphy, who had in mind the investor Warren E. Buffett, the fifty-four-year-old chairman of Berkshire Hathaway and a Cap Cities director. Buffett and Murphy had been good friends since the day fifteen years before when Murphy flew to Omaha to ask Buffett to join his board. It had been an unforgettable experience. Buffett is one of the world's richest men. He operates out of a modern office building at Kiewit Plaza in downtown Omaha, and when the elevator opens on the fourteenth floor a visitor walks along beige industrial carpeting to a plain brown door that looks like the door to a dentist's office. Behind the door is just 2,500 square feet of space for four executives, two secretaries, and Gladys Kaiser, Buffett's assistant. This comprises the entire overhead for a $3 billion company whose stock multiplied in worth from $24.10 per share in 1965 to $1,643.71 per share in 1985.

To Murphy, Warren Buffett, with his bushy eyebrows, scuffed shoes, and a can of Diet Cherry Coke always by his side, was a soul mate, a kindred spirit. Neither man believed in hostile takeovers, or buying and selling stocks like commodities, or inherited wealth, or getting involved in businesses unless they liked the people. Each shopped carefully before supporting a political candidate: Buffett spurned requests from presidential contenders to fly to Omaha to visit, telling them to stay home because he would learn all he needed to know by watching them on *The Brinkley Show;* Murphy rarely got involved in politics, but when he did—backing Republican governor Nelson Rockefeller and Democratic senator Hubert Humphrey—he did so fervently. Both believed in decentralizing decisions. Murphy ran Cap Cities from the Villard House in New York, a brownstone on East Fifty-first Street off Madison Avenue that housed just thirty-three executives. Murphy, like Buffett, retained no public relations advisors.

Something else prompted Murphy to think of Buffett as a partner. Buffett shared his enthusiasm for the media. In addition to serving on the board of the Washington Post Company and tucking into his portfolio 13 percent of its stock, Buffett owned other newspapers. More, he cared about them. The most prominent spot on the wall of his modest office, the one facing his desk, was reserved for the Pulitzer Prize plaque won by his North Omaha *Sun,* for an exposé of how Boys Town, a prominent local organization whose board glittered with members of the Omaha establishment, was collecting $25 million a year and spending only a quarter of its budget to provide for the boys. Buffett swells with pride when discussing this exposé, noting that he suggested the idea because he wondered why Boys Town was raising more money when the number of those it provided for was declining. Seeking to unravel the mystery, he studied Boys Town's public tax returns and helped educate a team of four local reporters on the nuances of finance. A measure of the bond between Buffett, Murphy, and Dan Burke was that the financier was on record calling Cap Cities the best-managed public company in America. "It's like having Ruth and Gehrig batting in the same lineup," he said of Murphy and Burke.

On the afternoon of February 26, 1985, Murphy reached Buffett in

Washington, D.C., where he was visiting. "Pal, you're not going to believe this," said Murphy, who explained that he had just met with Goldenson. "I've just bought ABC. You've got to come and tell me how I'm going to pay for it."

Buffett had an answer by the time they met two days later in Murphy's brownstone office down the block from St. Patrick's Cathedral. They were joined by Dan Burke and Cap Cities senior vice president and chief financial officer Ronald J. Doerfler. Murphy was eager to go; Buffett was skeptical.

"I have two reactions," said Buffett, addressing both Murphy and Burke. "One is that at your ages you should think about whether you want dramatic changes in your life-style. You make a deal and your life will change. You will be a lot more visible."

Tom Murphy was not big on introspection. His mother, who was five feet tall, would touch his chest and say, "Tommy, you're the best!" He came, he said, to believe in himself. "I always tell him," said his pal Jim Burke, "his problem is that he doesn't know he has problems." Murphy asked, "What's number two?"

"In the present climate," answered Buffett, "soon after this deal closes the merged company would become vulnerable." The danger—the same one sensed by Leonard Goldenson—was that once a merger was announced it would trigger a bidding war, leading to an attack on Cap Cities.

After a pause, Murphy asked: "What do we do about that, pal?"

"You need a partner," responded Buffett, "a nine-hundred-pound gorilla" who owns a large stake. Someone who would treat Cap Cities/ABC the way the Sulzberger family treats *The New York Times* or the Graham family treats *The Washington Post.* Someone "who will not sell regardless of price." Someone with enough money "to help the company fight off an unwanted approach."

As he listened to Buffett, Dan Burke marveled at how Buffett had already "thought the whole thing through."

Murphy turned over his hole card: "Would you be our partner?" Once again Buffett had anticipated the question, and cited two obstacles. First, he had made a pledge to the Buffalo *Evening News* that he would not sell the paper, and he had to honor that. Since Cap Cities owned a TV station in Buffalo, and federal anti-monopoly regulations prohibited an owner from controlling both a newspaper and a television station in the same market, he couldn't participate unless Cap Cities agreed to sell the station.

No problem.

The second impediment, said Buffett, was The Washington Post Company. He owned 13 percent of the *Post.* Stock ownership was not the problem. Being a director was. It wouldn't be right to serve on both boards. Yet his friendship with the Graham family stretched back many years. In a decade, he had never missed a board meeting. Pictures of the Graham children pervaded his office. Buffett said he wanted to chew on this bone some more.

He flew home to Omaha, weighed the dilemma, and decided that *The Washington Post* was a settled success. ABC was a fresh challenge, one that allowed him to work intimately with men he admired. So that night he telephoned Murphy and said, "I'm in." He said he would say nothing to his friend Katharine Graham, who chaired The Washington Post Company, while the negotiations were secret. Before they could proceed as partners, however, Buffett and Murphy had first to agree on the percentage of Cap Cities Buffett would own, and the price. The telephone negotiations with Murphy took all of thirty seconds, Buffett recalls.

"Murph, how much would you like me to buy?"

"What do you think?" said Murphy.

"How's three million shares?"

"That's fine," said Murphy.

"What should I pay?" Buffett asked.

"What do you think?" said Murphy.

"$172.50," answered Buffett.

"Fine."

The total cost to Buffett was $517 million, which translated into about 18 percent ownership of Cap Cities. Buffett would resign from the *Washington Post* board and serve as a director of the new Cap Cities/ABC. With Buffett in the mix, Cap Cities could easily borrow three to four billion dollars to help finance the rest of the deal. Murphy wanted to do this merger with cash, not an exchange of stock. With Buffett's heft, Murphy had access to the cash as well as the protection he needed to fend off unwanted suitors. Murphy and Buffett agreed they would offer one hundred dollars a share to Goldenson for ABC's stock.

The offer was rejected by ABC on March 1, the day Murphy paid Goldenson another visit. ABC's patriarch wanted to exchange stock, not just cash, hoping to retain partial ownership of the network as well as to acquire the more valuable Cap Cities stock. Another meeting with Goldenson three days later revived the moribund negotiations, with Murphy upping his offer to $110 a share and Goldenson saying he would accept cash if the price were $120 a share.

They were getting close. Murphy and Burke had reason to feel good about the negotiations, particularly because Warren Buffett had volunteered to do something highly unusual, something he said he had talked over with his partner and vice chairman, Charles T. Munger. To insulate the merged company from the vagaries of a frenzied marketplace, Buffett proposed that as long as Murphy or Dan Burke ran the company, or until 1997, he would cede to them his "irrevocable proxy," in other words, his voting rights over the stock. Berkshire Hathaway couldn't sell its stock unless it first offered it to Cap Cities.* Buffett believed he was promoting long-term stability.

By March, while rumors were rampant that Ted Turner was soon to make a bid for CBS, word of the ABC negotiations had not leaked. The First Boston team, led by Bruce Wasserstein, labored quietly, prodding its ABC client to extract warrants from Cap Cities, allowing ABC executives (and shareholders) to purchase Cap Cities shares on advantageous terms. They wanted it spelled out that Fred Pierce would run the network, the owned stations, the cable-programming, and the video enterprises. First Boston was joined by Joseph Flom, the attorney who was also helping CBS fend off unwanted takeovers, and by a network team led by Pierce. The Cap Cities team included no investment bankers but did include Flom's friend and great rival in the mergers and acquisitions wars, attorney Martin Lipton. Lipton insisted that Cap Cities be allowed an exit if in twelve months ABC's profits were off by more than 25 percent from the prior year.

With all the demands and counterdemands from the bankers and lawyers, Murphy worried that they would never get to the altar. He did not want to go above $110 a share or to award to ABC executives warrants that would permit them to acquire Cap Cities stock cheaply.

On March 12, Murphy, Buffett, and Munger met through the morning with Dan Burke, Martin Lipton, and Lipton's partner, James H. Fogelson. In the afternoon they gathered with Goldenson and the entire ABC team. ABC seemed locked in concrete on its demand for $120 per share plus warrants. Wasserstein and Lipton grabbed calculators to compute the numbers. An awed Lipton recalls that Buffett did it in his head and got there just as fast. The meeting ended glumly at

* This was the same unusual arrangement Buffett had with the Graham family at *The Washington Post,* and with GEICO, the insurance company in which he was the principal investor.

6:30 P.M., with both sides further apart than when they started. Nevertheless, they agreed to meet once more the next morning.

Murphy and Buffett talked it over and concluded the negotiations were now "hopeless." It would be fruitless to negotiate in the morning. Instead Murphy was to call Goldenson that night at home and tell him, *No hard feelings but the gulf between us is too wide, pal.*

The deal was resuscitated by accident. Tom Murphy didn't have Leonard Goldenson's home telephone number, and was unable to reach him that night, so the next morning he trudged over to ABC's West Fifty-fourth Street offices to say the deal was dead. Goldenson was not in, and Murphy talked instead with attorney Joe Flom, who said that the ABC team did not have the same sense of deadlock. Flom insisted that Cap Cities was overreacting. ABC, he said, was flexible. Another negotiating session was set for noon at Flom's office.

Within two hours a deal was struck. Cap Cities agreed to pay $118 a share in cash plus warrants entitling ABC shareholders to purchase common shares of Cap Cities at $250 a share for a period of two and a half years. Those who received warrants were granted a choice of buying the stock at a potential bargain price or selling their warrants back to Cap Cities within ninety days for thirty dollars per warrant. Including the warrant, the estimated cost to Cap Cities increased to $121 for each of ABC's 29.1 million shares. Warren Buffett's company would be the largest shareholder, owning 18 percent. Not publicized at the time were the golden parachutes awarded one hundred or so ABC executives who, in exchange for their restricted ABC stock acquired through a longtime ABC incentive plan, would be given 268,725 shares of stock, worth $32.5 million, in the new company.

Next came meetings with the bankers to finance the merger. Cap Cities was seeking $2.5 billion in credit. The Chemical Bank, recalls Burke, was dumbstruck. No network had ever been taken over. And Cap Cities was just a station group. "They thought we were a little shirttail company. And we were!" said Burke.

Chemical granted the credit.

A company so frugal that it had not air-conditioned its original Albany headquarters and had once painted only the two front sides of the building facing the road, not the sides facing the Hudson River, was acquiring one of America's Big Three networks! Walking back from the Chemical Bank offices, Burke and Murphy practically skipped along Park Avenue with attorney Martin Lipton. Burke, who is Cap Cities' official worrier, punctured the cheerful mood by coming to a halt and declaring: "Tom, you have no idea how interesting this story will be when it comes out. We have no ability to handle it from a public relations point of view." Their only press liaison up to this point was Murphy's secretary, Ruth Fitzgerald.

"It will be a ten-minute wonder!" insisted Murphy, who had not taken to heart Buffett's warning that ownership of a network would alter his life.

"You're wrong!" snapped Burke.

"Marty, I'm not wrong, am I?" asked Murphy.

"Yes, you are," their lawyer replied. "It will be one of the big business stories of the decade." Lipton advised that they retain the public relations firm of Kekst and Company, which specializes in mergers.

Tom Murphy was very wrong indeed. The story of the $3.5 billion sale of ABC to a "little-known media company," as a *New York Times* headline referred to Cap Cities, generated enormous press coverage. It was the lead story in the next day's *Times* and splashed Murphy and Burke onto magazine covers as well as the network news.

Murphy ignored the stack of press clippings placed on his desk, shoving most of them into a wastebasket at the end of the week. "He's the only man I ever knew whose picture was on the cover of *Business Week* and he never read the article," said Dan Burke. He also paid little attention to ABC's prime-time schedule, which is where a network makes much of its money. That week ABC came in third, with only two of its shows ranked among the top ten, both prime-time soap operas produced by Aaron Spelling—*Dynasty* and *Hotel.* ABC was on its way to its worst ratings season in years. Murphy, Burke, and Buffett had acquired a network, and they could tell the difference between Peter Jennings and Tom Brokaw, but probably not the difference between *Dynasty*'s male lead, John Forsythe, and Brian Keith, star of *Hardcastle and McCormick,* one of ABC's ratings clinkers.

"To paraphrase Pogo: We have seen the news and it is us," is how Peter Jennings opened ABC's *World News Tonight* on the day of the merger announcement. That same day, CBS's stock jumped six points; the stock of NBC's parent, RCA, rose almost three points. People kept coming up to Mike Mallardi to say, "You were right!"

Which is not to say most ABC employees were pleased. If anything, they were numb; fearful that the new order, with its emphasis on costs, meant that not only was ABC's way of life endangered, so were its employees' jobs. "Everyone was worried," recalls Barbara Walters, who was accustomed to receiving congratulatory calls from the company founder after she did one of her high-rated specials (the phone was silent, she said, when ratings were low). "Leonard Goldenson was a warm grandfather. Suddenly we had these cold businessmen. At least that's what we heard."

Few were reassured by what they heard from analysts or even from Goldenson's own public statements, which predicted that Cap Cities would improve profitability by cutting costs. Nor could they have been comforted by Fred Pierce's standoffishness. Instead of celebrating the marriage, Pierce groaned about how "the laissez-faire attitude of the Reagan administration foisted this." Privately, Pierce worried that the network's two traditional goals—"profits and public responsibility"—would become uncoupled, and the new owners would think only of profits.

Nevertheless, Fred Pierce would stay as CEO of ABC, Inc., which included the network, the owned stations, and the cable-programming and video investments. He would also become vice chairman of the new company. Executives who had been reporting to Pierce would continue to do so. Goldenson would remain as chairman of the executive committee. Seven members of ABC's board of directors would join the board of the new hyphenated company. And employees were assured that Cap Cities' executives were *broadcasters.* As longtime affiliates, they were well known to many ABC executives. And then there was the issue of money and stability. ABC's stock, which traded at about $60 a share at the time of the merger, had been sold for $121 a share. Since he like most ABC executives owned stock, Jake Keever, head of ABC Sales, recalls, "I was happy because all of a sudden I was worth more money. I had the sense that the way we were heading at ABC meant trouble."

Besides, everyone at ABC knew there would be a breathing period of eight or nine months pending the approval of federal regulatory bodies such as the FCC. In the interval, Cap Cities was not very visible. "The FCC takes a dim view of anyone who anticipates what they will do," explained Dan Burke. From the March announcement until FCC approval in late November, the main point of contact between the two companies was Mike Mallardi. Through him Cap Cities came to know ABC's financial structure.

Over the summer ABC began to shed personnel, and the press office began portraying Fred Pierce as a champion of cost containment. The news division, which a year earlier had appointed a task force to explore phased reductions in personnel, decided after the merger to speed up its plan. "Everyone was trying to behave on the assumption of what Cap Cities would want," News vice president

David Burke recalls. "It was, 'Be lean and mean.' Everyone was just singing for their supper."

But despite the trims, ABC contained too many management layers for Cap Cities' taste. And unfortunately Cap Cities learned of the layoffs by reading about them in the newspapers. Fred Pierce hadn't told them. He explained that he wanted "no formal contact until the approvals of the FCC were in place." Others saw in this aloofness what Barbara Walters called Pierce's "emotional inaccessibility"; they sensed the resentments of a man who had been passed over. Pierce was a sometimes obdurate man. For years executives had referred to him, behind his back, as "The Jaw" or "The Great Stone Face." Now he seemed even more rigid. Pierce cut himself off from Murphy and Burke, who were getting all their information from Mike Mallardi.

Fred Pierce would not see the danger until it was too late.

3

TISCH FINDS AN EXCUSE TO INVEST IN CBS, 1985

On the morning of July 3, 1985, the telephone rang in the New York office of Laurence A. Tisch. As usual, the sixty-three-year-old chairman and chief executive officer of the Loews Corporation was working alone with his two-line telephone and his Quotron machine, which provides a steady parade of up-to-the-minute Wall Street news.

On the phone was one of Tisch's four sons—Dan, thirty-five, then managing director of the risk arbitrage department of Salomon Brothers. Dan Tisch told his father he had just spotted a Dow Jones wire service story flashing important news about CBS.

Larry Tisch reflexively reached for the Quotron keyboard and punched up CBS. Instantly, there appeared in green letters on the screen CBS's trades for the day, its stock price fluctuations for the year, its dividend and earnings summaries. The screen did not contain CBS's prime-time ratings, nor did it reveal that CBS was sliding in that department. Or that the previous night its lead-off comedy, *The Jeffersons,* was clobbered by NBC's *The A-Team.* Tisch pushed down the half-framed reading glasses parked on his bald head and peered at the financial numbers, which is what he knew best. While scrutinizing these, he talked to Dan for some time about CBS, and at the end of their conversation the elder Tisch made a move that would make him one of the most influential men in America.

Although Larry Tisch was already one of America's wealthiest men, few clues to that could be found in his corner office at Loews on the seventeenth floor of 666 Fifth Avenue. The spare furnishings and beige industrial carpeting were reminiscent of a Howard Johnson's Motor Inn, or of Warren Buffett's offices. The ten photographs bunched around his desk were a temple to his family, not to the powerful people he knows. Loews, the company he headed, with

$17.5 billion in assets, was among the nation's ten largest diversified financial corporations. Yet Tisch had no aides, wrote no memos, and usually left the office by 4:00 or 4:30 P.M., except on Fridays, when he left by 1 P.M. in order to play expert-level bridge. While his brother, Preston Robert, then fifty-nine, whom everyone calls Bob, focused on day-to-day management at Loews, Larry Tisch concentrated on trading stocks and bonds, on investments and long-range strategy. Only one part of the family business reported directly to his office—the management of the $13.5 billion Loews investment portfolio. Larry Tisch was one of a handful of investors who could shift billions of dollars—from stocks to bonds, from Treasury notes to blue-chip companies—all as part of a day's work.

Dan Tisch had the Loews portfolio in mind when he called his father. Thomas H. Wyman, the president and chief executive officer of CBS, a conglomerate with varied holdings, had just announced that his company was borrowing $954 million in order to buy back one-fifth of its stock for $150 a share, $32 over the current selling price. This was CBS's most aggressive defense yet against a hostile takeover by Ted Turner.

When he joined CBS in 1980, after a career as vice president of Polaroid, president of the Green Giant Company, and number-two man at Pillsbury, Tom Wyman had acknowledged, "I haven't had any broadcast experience, or publishing or toy business experience, and I don't know much about music." Over the five years of his reign, there were many who believed he had amply demonstrated his ignorance of CBS's main business—publishing, music, and broadcasting. Wyman's leading critic was the network's founder, William Paley, whom Wyman and the board had booted as chairman in 1983.

By mid-1985, CBS was clearly in trouble. Its entertainment programming was slipping in the ratings, barely clinging to its number-one ranking as upstart NBC threatened to pass CBS's lineup of worn-out hits such as *Falcon Crest.* Even *Dallas,* the second most watched series on TV, had been on for six seasons and was fading. Shows like *Dallas, Murder, She Wrote, Newhart,* and *Simon & Simon* attracted good ratings generally, but not the younger audiences advertisers were willing to pay premiums to reach. CBS's schedule featured neither such youth-oriented 8:00 comedies as NBC's *The Cosby Show* or ABC's *Who's the Boss?,* nor dramas to attract the upscale audiences who flocked to such serious fare as NBC's *Hill Street Blues.*

Nor were CBS's five owned TV stations performing as expected. Their profit margins—about 40 percent—trailed ABC's 50 percent,

NBC's 45 percent, and Cap Cities 55 percent. And surely Wyman had paid too much—$362.5 million—to the Ziff-Davis Publishing Company for its twelve consumer magazines. Surely, as Wyman would later concede, his diversification policy had failed. Events had not been kind to Tom Wyman. He was the victim of several inherited messes, including a mismanaged toy business acquired in 1966. He was the victim of a network advertising falloff that would slim CBS's 1985 profits. The CBS Broadcast Group, the core of the company, was said by analysts to be a "mature" business, meaning a business that was, as Ted Turner gleefully observed, suffering from a thousand razor nicks from competitors who ten years earlier had not existed. Even if he had known broadcasting, there seemed little Wyman could do to halt network audience erosion. CBS was bleeding to death from all the nicks, and urgently needed a transfusion. Anticipating a takeover, speculators had run its stock up as much as fifty dollars a share.

Tisch looked at the Quotron and noted that CBS stock this July day was trading at $118. Father and son discussed how Loews might purchase several million shares at a market price that would fluctuate, they guessed, between $110 and $120 per share. They could sell back one-fifth of the stock to CBS at Wyman's price of $150, and thus reduce Loews's average cost per share to about $105 for a stock trading considerably higher. They calculated that Loews would also gain a tax advantage because, according to the terms of the offer, the profit on the shares sold back to CBS would be taxed at the 7 percent dividend rate rather than at the much steeper capital gains rate.

Dan Tisch factored in something else. He knew Loews had once acquired ABC stock, and had once discussed a possible Loews/RCA merger. He knew his father had been interested in CBS for months. Perhaps, thought Dan Tisch, this was a way for Loews to be invited into the tent. Tisch could acquire a hefty slice of CBS under the protective umbrella of the exchange offer, and would thus be perceived as responding to an invitation.

Dan Tisch remembers saying to his father that either as a long-term investment or as a short-term arbitrage position, CBS was a no-lose proposition: "As an investment, it looks attractive at a low price. If people persist in a takeover attempt you will be in a position to sell for a profit or to increase your stake. And as an arbitrage position it's heads you win, tails you break even."

Larry Tisch was certain that CBS was a takeover target. As was true at ABC, the value of the component parts of the network were worth more—perhaps $150 or slightly more a share. And Tisch liked the tax benefits. He liked the network business because he believed it was a near monopoly, immune to foreign competition. He didn't know much about its domestic competition, about cable and independent stations and the VCR and how they were siphoning network customers just as surely as Japanese auto makers did the Big Three auto makers. Tisch saw something else, something outside his financial calculus. He saw CBS as an essential "public utility," as he called it, one whose independence must be preserved. The CBS network reached seventy-five million viewers every day, and was a five-billion-dollar communications colossus which for five straight years had the number-one-rated evening news program and had been number-one in the prime-time ratings race for twenty-five of the past thirty years. The CBS logo evoked legends—Edward R. Murrow, Jack Benny, Lucille Ball, Walter Cronkite, Mary Tyler Moore, Norman Lear, and of course William Paley, who had put it all together. And CBS had reach —in addition to the network, CBS owned two radio networks, five local television stations, seven AM and eleven FM radio stations, a cable sports-programming service, a research technology center; produced video-cassette rentals in a joint venture with Twentieth Century Fox; planned to launch in partnership with IBM and Sears a commercial videotex service for owners of personal computers; published books and magazines; and was the world's leading record producer and manufacturer.

CBS might provide the most significant investment the Tisch family had ever made. More significant than the Loews hotels and theaters, Lorillard tobacco, Bulova watches, or the CNA insurance companies. The presence of cash-rich Loews, he allowed, might stabilize CBS by chasing the vultures. Larry Tisch would be more than a shrewd investor; he would be a savior.

"Danny, you're right," said Larry Tisch. "Let's start buying stock."

The senior Tisch said he made the decision on impulse, without consulting the Loews board or anyone outside his family. "I trust my instincts," he explained.

In truth, Tisch had been looking for an excuse to invest in CBS.

Tisch's involvement with CBS had begun on an indoor tennis court the previous January. On weekends, Tisch and his wife, Wilma (whom everyone calls Billie), leave their Fifth Avenue coop for the splendid isolation of a thirty-seven-home enclave surrounded by a wildlife sanctuary on Rye's Manursing Island, in Westchester County. The wide windows of their split-level, contemporary stone house frame a giant lawn sculpture by Joan Miró and, beyond that, the panorama of Long Island Sound. On Saturday Billie Tisch puttered around the house, preparing a variety of salads for lunch, enough to feed any of their four sons, wives, and grandchildren should they pop in, as they often did. A cook fixed an early dinner for the family on Saturday night, and at 8:30 P.M. Larry's brother Bob, his wife, Joan, and a group of about twenty friends and their children—the same friends who have been getting together for twenty-five years—arrived to view a movie in their basement screening room, where hard brown plastic chairs are arrayed in theaterlike rows.

Most weekend mornings Larry Tisch plays tennis, jumping into his green Pontiac station wagon to drive to the nearby Century Country Club or the Rye Racquet Club, where Bob and a group of friends who have been playing together for years join in mixed doubles. After two hours of cleverly slicing or awkwardly pushing the ball over the net, Tisch and the group gulp soft drinks and swap information.

In January 1985, the hot after-tennis business topic was William Paley's company. Senator Jesse Helms of North Carolina had launched a letter-writing "crusade" urging his right-wing friends to "become Dan Rather's boss." Coming off the tennis court, Tisch turned to investment banker James D. Wolfensohn, a CBS director, and quizzed him about Helms. Tisch said he was agitated by the thought that anyone, of the political right or left, would try to harness a powerful instrument like CBS.

The passion Tisch displayed this day was unusual, for he is not a man to take up causes, the single exception being the survival of the state of Israel. He is a man most comfortable in the political center, and has contributed to the campaigns of an assortment of Democrats and Republicans, from liberal Democratic presidential candidate Walter F. Mondale to conservative Republican New York senator Alfonse D'Amato. His ideal candidate for president at the time was not Mario Cuomo, whom he dismissed as "a big spender," but rather, he said, "someone like Sam Nunn of Georgia."

After tennis, Wolfensohn recalls, "Larry told me that if we ever needed help on this public policy issue, he would offer it." Tisch said he was speaking at the time not as an investor but as a civic leader—a former president of the Greater New York United Jewish Appeal, the chairman of New York University's board of trustees, a trustee of the Metropolitan Museum of Art. Wolfensohn passed the offer of help on to Tom Wyman. "I told Tom he might get a call from Larry." Wyman never in fact got a call, but he remembers that "we knew here in January that among those concerned, Larry Tisch felt quite strongly."

January 1985 was the beginning of a siege that lasted almost a year. The Helms onslaught was followed, in February, by reports that arbitrageur Ivan Boesky and a group of investors had quietly purchased 8.7 percent of CBS stock.* CBS initiated a legal attack, and outmaneuvered Boesky as it had outwitted Helms. But around the time of the March announcement of the merger between ABC and Cap Cities, CBS was forced back on the defensive by a Ted Turner blitzkrieg, which began in April when Turner offered to buy the company for $5.4 billion in stock and debt securities, but no cash.

CBS was under assault from within as well. Tribal conflicts were erupting inside CBS News, between the Edward R. Murrow hard-news traditionalists versus the producers who were accused of wanting to soften the news, make it more entertaining. A not-so-silent war also raged within the CBS board, between Paley, eighty-four, whose title was founder chairman, and his anointed successor, the fifty-five-year-old Wyman. Paley had been ousted as chairman by Wyman two years earlier, and now he could count on the loyalty of only two board members, former anchorman Walter Cronkite and Marietta Tree, a family friend who first met Paley in London in 1940 and who had been the first woman assigned the rank of ambassador to the U.S. mission to the United Nations. Wyman could count on most of the other votes. "There have been five presidents of CBS since I've been on the board," observed Roswell L. Gilpatric, seventy-nine, who joined the board at Paley's invitation in 1970. "It kept you on the alert because it was always Paley versus the president."

Beleaguered throughout the first half of 1985, CBS came more and more to rely on Wolfensohn, the sole investment banker on the board.** Because of his experience as a former partner at Salomon Brothers, as principal executive officer of Schroders Limited in London, and now as president of the advisory and investment firm that bore his name, Wolfensohn knew the takeover game. And he inspired confidence. There is something about the silver-haired, Australian-born financier that puts people at ease, from the way he whispers into the phone to such clients as the CEOs of American Express, Du Pont, or Ford, to the framed letters on his office wall from such friends as

* Boesky in 1987 would plead guilty to one count of securities law violations for insider trading, pay a fine of $100 million, and be sentenced to up to five years in prison.

** That year, CBS paid advisory and investment banking fees of $700,000 to Wolfensohn.

Isaac Stern, to the Havana cigars he proffers to visitors, to his nimbleness with words or with a cello, to his luster as a former Olympic fencer or his chairmanship of Carnegie Hall, to the father/son or father/daughter Alaskan salmon-fishing trips with friends like Senator Ted Kennedy and *Times* publisher Punch Sulzberger he would organize each August. In addition to Wolfensohn, CBS relied on its own investment banking adviser, Morgan Stanley Group, and on Joseph Flom, the attorney who had represented ABC in its negotiations with Cap Cities.

Wolfensohn and Flom saw Ted Turner as a real threat, as did their friend Larry Tisch. People had sneered when Turner said he would use satellites to transform his Atlanta TV station into the first superstation, and when he promised an all-news cable channel. Yet by 1985, the reach of the station extended beyond the South and CNN was profitable. Tisch, Wolfensohn, and Flom had several conversations about Turner, and it was apparently around this time that Tisch began to contemplate one day owning CBS. Bob Tisch recalls that his brother first talked to him in March 1985 about investing in the network. Some time later Larry Tisch said he spoke separately to Wolfensohn and Flom, as a friend, not a predator. "What I said," he recalls, "was, 'Look fellas, if you're looking for a white knight, consider us a potential.' "

The message was transmitted to Wyman and the CBS board, who said thanks, but no thanks. CBS believed it could retain its independence without Tisch. Nevertheless, Wyman began cautiously to probe potential candidates who might save CBS from an unwanted takeover. One night in March he drove alone to Fairfield, Connecticut, to dine with Jack Welch, chairman and CEO of General Electric. "We had a very real meeting," recalls Welch, who then asked a team of GE people to study "this thing sideways, upside down." Leading the analysis was a Welch protégé, Robert Wright, the chief executive of the GE Credit Corporation (GECC). GE flashed the go sign, but CBS, recalls Wright, "never came back to us." Wyman also met with Al Neuharth, chairman of the Gannett Company. (Neuharth would write a book four years later —*Confessions of an S.O.B.*—in which he said they came within inches of merging the two companies, with Wyman agreeing to become chief operating officer. Until, that is, vanity got the better of both men; Neuharth, because he pushed too hard, Wyman, because he could not bear the humiliation of being pushed.) Wyman also began making discreet inquiries about Loews and Tisch, whom he had never met. "I talked to people in the motion picture business," recalls

Wyman. "Everyone thought Loews were pretty shrewd theater operators. When you ask ten people you get a good composite view."

Throughout that spring, as Wyman and the board struggled to retain their independence, there hovered the names of Tisch and Welch. Wolfensohn and Flom implored Wyman to meet Tisch. In late April, the Loews chairman was in the back seat of Wolfensohn's dark blue Mercedes when Wolfensohn telephoned Wyman to "arrange a meeting."

On May 2, Wyman phoned Larry Tisch and asked if he could come over that afternoon to Tisch's office to discuss CBS's anti-Turner strategy. At that meeting they did not talk television, about how poorly CBS's made-for-TV movie, *The Heart of a Champion: The Ray Mancini Story,* had fared the night before, ranking fifty-second for the week. Neither man had much appetite for the principal product of a network. Wyman got right to the point, asking Tisch to help line up Jewish and other civic organizations to urge the federal regulatory agencies to oppose Turner. Tisch readily agreed. Both men say they never discussed the possibility of Loews investing in CBS. But the lyrics, suggested Wolfensohn, were less important than the music: "The purpose of the meeting was to get them comfortable with each other."

Wyman felt comfortable: "It was very clear—there was a flavor—'that if you're ever talking about outside involvement of a defensive character, I'd be delighted and we can talk some more' . . . I had the impression, to be candid, that if I had said, 'Larry, look, I don't have a lot of time to discuss this but we need some money to do whatever,' I think he would have responded."

But Wyman didn't ask. The timing was not propitious for a union. Wyman was convinced there were other ways to slay Turner. One way was a leveraged buyout (LBO), by which CBS would buy a controlling amount of its own stock. The king of LBOs, Henry Kravis, told Wyman, "we're here," but Wyman spurned the offer. Instead, Wyman flirted with Jim Wolfensohn's idea of a leveraged buyout by CBS management, which would include a few trusted outside investors, including Wolfensohn's neighbor and Rye tennis partner, Larry Tisch. Like Fred Pierce's idea at ABC, the management-led LBO had the virtue of keeping the company from the grip of hostile outsiders. But as far as Wyman was concerned, an LBO would put him at the mercy of William Paley, since Paley owned the largest slice of CBS stock (9 percent) and his approval was essential.

Wyman rejected the LBO for other reasons as well. "I didn't think it was necessary" to preserve the company's independence, he said, and because to finance it CBS would be compelled to sell off its publishing, magazine, or records division. There were two other fears, observed then Publishing president, Peter A. Derow, who talked with Wyman about it: "No one could be sure where an LBO might end, and Tom was uncomfortable with uncertainty. If we couldn't get financing, the company might be put into play. CBS is a corporation using the nation's airwaves to serve the public and, as such, Tom believed that it should remain public. Tom is an eagle scout that way. He did not believe CBS should be owned by a private club."

The battle with Turner, and the search for alternatives, consumed Tom Wyman and much of CBS's management throughout the spring of 1985. The alternative Wyman chose to maintain the independence of CBS was a $954.8 million refinancing plan proposed by Morgan Stanley, a plan that made investment banker Jim Wolfensohn nervous. "The refinance plan weakened the company's ability to withstand a takeover since it reduced the company's capital and reduced the number of outstanding shares," observed Wolfensohn. He warned that Wyman might be making it easier for an unwanted suitor to succeed.

Wyman was confident he could fend off Turner; Tisch, like Wolfensohn, was not. "In the arbitrage world there's always a price on any package," Tisch explained. "Turner's was a serious offer. CBS should have been prepared to take Turner out by restructuring the company." The longer Turner's offer sat on the table, he thought, the greater the danger the Atlanta broadcaster would up the cash ante to CBS shareholders by vowing to sell off parts of CBS. Or, even more likely, another bidder would come after CBS. Tisch did not know it at the time, but on this point he had an ally in Bill Paley. "I never worried about Helms or Turner," said Paley. "I worried about people sitting in wait behind Helms and Turner. So we had to stop it."

The Tisch family wrestled that spring over CBS. Brother Bob and much of the family were enthusiastic; Larry's thirty-three-year-old son Jimmy was not. "We were really a house divided on that," said Jimmy Tisch, whose office was two doors from his father's and who worked closely with his father in setting overall investment policy. "I didn't see the same values he did . . . but Larry looked at it beyond just an investment."

CBS's assets are worth considerably more than its stock price, Larry Tisch said to his son. Media stocks, he said, were a great hedge against inflation—just as the cigarette business was—because advertising rates, like cigarette prices, were relatively easy to raise. And, the elder Tisch added, a broadcasting network was not like a widget company; it was a long-term national asset that must be preserved.

"Does it have to be preserved with our money?" asked Jimmy Tisch. CBS, he cautioned, would not be a characteristic Tisch purchase. "We're bargain hunters and bottom pickers," he said. Typically, in 1984 the Tisches had invested $5 million each in five super oil tankers constructed in the late seventies for $80 million apiece. The investment had no downside, because if the oil industry failed to revive, the scrap value of each tanker was $5 million.

The polite family disagreement was almost academic, for the family were united in the conviction that they should make no move without CBS's approval. Were Loews welcome, despite Jimmy's dissent, Larry Tisch was prepared to become either a white squire, investing to stabilize the network, or a white knight, investing to own the company. For this to occur, CBS had to feel sufficiently menaced, or had to grant Tisch an opening, an excuse.

That excuse came in July of 1985, when Dan Tisch called his father to say that CBS had just announced a recapitalization plan, to fend off Ted Turner.

Soon after he had called his father on July 3, Dan Tisch, acting as a broker for Loews, acquired 25,000 shares of CBS, the first of many daily purchases. Larry Tisch's next move was an act of courtesy. Within days he telephoned Tom Wyman to inform him that Loews owned nearly 5 percent of his company, and to reassure Wyman of his pacific intent.

Wyman and other members of the board were nervous about Tisch, as Leonard Goldenson had been about the Tisch or Bass brothers' stake in ABC. They wondered whether to fear him as the wolf who engaged in a hostile takeover of the CNA insurance companies in 1974, or to trust him as the statesman who had since declined to mount corporate raids.

William Paley was perplexed. Though their offices were only a block apart, and though Tisch said they had met a few times and had been in the same room at several dinner parties, Paley insisted he didn't know Tisch. In fact, Paley thought Tisch was someone else. "I got mixed up in my mind with him and Tishman," said Paley, referring to John Tishman, head of the Tishman Realty and Construction Company.

By the end of July, Loews owned 7 percent of the network. Before the summer was over, it owned 11 percent. It was a typical Tisch move, thought some. "Larry is a brilliant financial analyst who doesn't let himself get misled by current fads or, indeed, the crisis of the moment," said lawyer Martin Lipton, who, in addition to representing Cap Cities in its negotiations with ABC, had long represented Loews. "Instead, he focuses on long-term outlooks and long-term values. Larry is what you would call the typical contrarian. He doesn't ride with whatever the current learning is. He sees through smoke." Tom Tisch, thirty-one, who managed the joint investment portfolio of the four Tisch sons, cogently sums up the Tisches' investment strategy: "The sense here is that you want to make an investment that protects or preserves capital, and if you worry about the downside, the upside tends to take care of itself."

Other Tisch watchers thought the CBS stock purchase peculiar. The steep purchase price of CBS "was so out of character" for Tisch, explained one Tisch associate, that his only explanation was that Larry was "on an ego trip." It was true, this associate conceded, that Tisch was still modest, still did not engage in temper tantrums or vie to get his name in the gossip columns. But he had been seduced, suggested this associate, by pride, vanity, the stuff of novels. The Tisch brothers had never before permitted sentiment to play a big part in their business dealings. They sold Loews's Americana hotel chain to American Airlines, including the Americana in Bal Harbour, Florida, where Larry Tisch's children had been raised. They had built the Loews theaters, yet when the price was right twenty-five years later, they sold.

And yet no Tisch watcher would dispute that the brothers were cautious, long-term investors, not short-term speculators. In fact, in this regard Larry Tisch was a soul mate of Warren Buffett and Tom Murphy, both close friends. Twenty years before he had introduced himself to Buffett, whom he hails as "the greatest investor of this generation," through the U.S. mail. Tisch simply made out a check for $300,000 and invested it, unsolicited, in Buffett's company. Like Buffett and Murphy, Tisch was disturbed that Wall Street was no longer a place honoring prudence, no longer fearful of debt.

Tisch said he saw CBS as special, more than just an investment. CBS was his shining city on a hill. CBS had power, including the power to do good. And Larry Tisch, nearing the finish line of a distinguished career as an investor, wanted to do good, wanted a certain kind of respectability, a place in the history books. He had come to think of himself as a corporate statesman. He spoke reverently of the company Bill Paley had founded, in 1928, when he tapped his family's cigar smoking fortune to acquire sixteen radio stations that would grow into the Columbia Broadcasting System. CBS had broadcast its first black-and-white television programs to a single New York station in 1941 and the first coast-to-coast live TV transmission in 1951. Together with Edward R. Murrow, CBS invented network news. "My only desire," Tisch said soon after acquiring its stock, "is to keep CBS as a first-class, independent network. It's very important for the country. . . . It's a serious obligation. It's not a toy. I think Bill Paley took his obligation to report the news impartially very seriously."

Still, Larry Tisch acknowledged that the CBS purchase was, for him, unusual. Feet up on his desk in November of 1985, his eyes fixed on the Quotron machine, a wan smile parting his lips, Tisch exclaimed, "It surprises me too!"

Laurence Tisch and his younger brother, Preston Robert, were born three years apart in a middle-income section of Bensonhurst, Brooklyn, where they lived on the first floor of a two-family home owned by their grandfather. The Tisch family ate together, manufactured boys clothing together, and frowned upon any hint of rivalry between the two boys. Then, as now, the brothers were best friends. Always, however, Larry Tisch was accepted as the natural leader, the brilliant senior brother. In 1935 their father, Al, a former captain and star of the City College basketball team, acquired a summer sleepaway camp, Lincoln & Laurel, in Blairstown, New Jersey. The brothers worked at the camp and ran the canteen, selling candy. After school and on weekends, Larry worked as a salesman for his father's clothing business on Orchard Street. The family applauded when he received a diploma from DeWitt Clinton High School and entered New York University at fifteen, graduating with a major in banking and finance at age eighteen, and when he received a master's degree in business administration from the Wharton School at age twenty. Bob Tisch went off to the University of Michigan, receiving a B.A. there.

The business breakthrough that would one day make the Tisches billionaires came from Larry. In 1946, after serving in the army, where the math whiz deciphered enemy codes for the Office of Strategic Services (OSS) in Washington, Larry enrolled at the Harvard Law School. By the end of the first semester he was restless. Leafing through *New York Times* ads, he spied a successful Lakewood, New Jersey, resort for sale. In those days it was not uncommon to notice "for sale" signs on thriving businesses, for right after the war many entrepreneurs were deeply pessimistic. They had known only depression or war, and with the war over many assumed that America would again fall into a depression. So real estate came cheap. Larry Tisch sniffed a bargain. At his instigation, the family sold its summer camp and scraped together $400,000—$200,000 of it in cash—to acquire the three-hundred-room Laurel-in-the-Pines Hotel. It was Larry Tisch's idea to make this an even more successful winter hotel, one they could keep open from November through April. After completing almost a year of law school, he dropped out in late 1946 to enter the hotel business.

Laurel-in-the-Pines became a family enterprise. Al Tisch ran the overall business; Sayde Tisch purchased the food and furniture; Bob, while still a student at the University of Michigan, worked there during holidays; and Larry, in addition to manning the front desk, assigning rooms, and booking the acts, supervised all financial planning. On weekends, all were expected to gather for meals at the family table.

By 1948 Larry Tisch had fallen in love. He had taken the summer off to supervise the construction of an indoor pool and health club at Laurel-in-the-Pines and to scout for fresh business opportunities. Larry, who even then was nearly bald, was all work. A friend from Deal, New Jersey, where the Tisches were living, suggested he telephone a local girl, Wilma "Billie" Stein, who had graduated four days before from Skidmore College and had just been hired as a *Time* magazine researcher.

A whirlwind romance ensued. Larry would pick up Billie in his 1948 black Buick convertible with red leather seats. Their idea of a big date was to go to the Lavender Bull, a drive-in hamburger place on Route 35, often with Bob and his wife, Joan, who had met at the University of Michigan. Ten weeks after they met, Billie and Larry were engaged. After a year of marriage the first of their four sons was born, and the next three came twenty-one months apart. The second year together they rented a house with Joan and Bob Tisch. "Our only disagreement," remembers Billie Tisch, "was that we liked our leg of lamb rare. So we never made lamb." To this day, Billie considers Joan "my best friend."

Over the next several years, there was little time for leisurely family dinners. With Laurel-in-the-Pines thriving, after a time the combination of Larry Tisch's financial skills and brother Bob's managerial abilities would make each a billionaire. After Laurel-in-the-Pines, the Tisch brothers purchased for $300,000 a successful summer resort, the Grand Hotel in Highmount, New Jersey, followed by other bargains, including three hotels in Atlantic City and the McAlpin and Belmont Plaza in New York. The Tisches acquired these hotels, invested modestly in amenities, installed professional, cost-conscious managers, raised the rates, and were earning, Larry Tisch estimates, about five to six million dollars annually. The family had joint bank accounts, joint investments, and dipped into the common pool for whatever they needed, without accounting for every penny. "It was really a communist society," recalls Billie Tisch. "It was wonderful."

In the hotel business, the Tisches were pathbreakers. Before there were Sheraton or Hyatt or Howard Johnson hotels, the Tisches and the Hiltons forged the first large hotel chains in America. The Tisch brothers lured conventions and transformed seasonal into year-round hotels, with indoor and outdoor amenities. They were rolling in money, which started the brothers thinking about other investments.

By 1959, the brothers began accumulating stock in the Loews Corporation, which owned real estate, MGM, and a one-hundred-theater movie chain. Not wanting to be taken over, the Loews management at first resisted, confident that if they held out for a higher price the Tisches would run out of money. "They didn't want to recognize our stock ownership," said Larry Tisch, echoing a thought he would come to have about CBS management. "They were naive." Within the year, the Tisches owned 28 percent of the company. With the federal government insisting that movie studios could not also own movie theaters, Loews was compelled to sell MGM. Within three years, the Tisch hotels were merged into Loews and Larry became chairman and CEO. Bob was the chief operating officer. The Loews stock, which the Tisch brothers acquired for fourteen dollars a share, was by 1986 worth an estimated four thousand dollars per share, adjusted for stock splits.

There followed a variety of real estate investments, including hotels in New York, Monte Carlo, London, Puerto Rico, Chicago, and San Francisco. The Tisch brothers were also, in the early days of Loews, involved in a few stormy business deals. In a friendly 1968 transaction, Loews acquired for $600 million the Lorillard Corporation, a 208-year-old tobacco company. The investment banker representing Tisch was Felix Rohatyn, and this deal was the first to break the one-million-dollar investment banking fee barrier. Although it was a friendly transaction, the CEO and directors of Lorillard were ousted shortly thereafter, a detail that could not have failed to attract Tom Wyman's notice. Loews was rebuffed in its later attempts to take over the Gimbels department store chain, the Commercial Credit Company, and B. F. Goodrich. In 1971, Loews acquired a 25 percent controlling interest in the Franklin New York Corporation, which owned the Franklin National Bank. The next year the Tisches sold their stock to Michele Sindona, the Italian financier who was later convicted, to the embarrassment of the Tisch brothers, as a swindler.

Another Loews transaction also attracted attention. Beginning in early 1974, the Tisches commenced a nine-month-long hostile takeover of the Chicago-based CNA insurance company, which put up a fierce struggle, even trying (unsuccessfully) to induce the City Council to pass a bill blocking anyone who did not live in Chicago from acquiring a business there. But by November 1974 the Tisches had snatched CNA. The insurance industry was in a slump at the time, and within weeks they had brought in Edward J. Noha, an experienced insurance executive, to be CEO, and had dismissed eight hundred employees. Larry concentrated on devising a new financial strategy; Bob concentrated on management issues. Neither brother, however, tried to insert himself as a hands-on-manager; that was Ed Noha's domain. Nor did the brothers seek to replace once hostile directors, or to pack the board, a detail that may have comforted some CBS board members. Only Larry and Bob Tisch, and Lester Pollack, a top Loews executive, initially joined the CNA board.

CNA was the Tisches' most prominent hostile takeover. Chastened by a squall of criticism, they also made it their last. Around 1980, the Tisches developed an appetite for media stocks. Their interest was probably aroused by one of Larry and Bob's weekend tennis partners, ABC chairman Leonard Goldenson, and by Larry's friendships with Warren Buffett and Tom Murphy, who sits with Tisch on the N.Y.U. board. Every two years Tisch and Murphy and a group of business leaders and investors take a trip organized by Buffett—to such places as Aspen, Colorado, or to England on the *Queen Elizabeth II.* The group consists of people like Katharine Graham of The Washington Post Company and William Ruane, head of a fund that invests in the media. These one-week trips, said Tisch, broaden his horizons. "Half the time we discuss the media and media stocks and investments," he explained. "Certain things in the investor world when you don't have a working knowledge, you sort of shy away. When you get a familiarity with the subject, it makes it easier to take a position."

Tisch's initial media investment came in November of 1980. By January of 1981, Loews owned 6.5 percent of ABC's stock. "The size of his holdings made me nervous," Leonard Goldenson said of his former Rye tennis partner, and he prodded Tisch to sell the stock. "I have no reason to impugn Larry's motives," Goldenson dryly writes in his memoirs. "He's a good friend, and he has a well-deserved reputation as one of the country's smartest investors. But a few years later, in 1985, he . . . accumulated more [CBS] stock than Paley either owned or controlled."

In 1982, Tisch made an offer to purchase the New York *Daily News* from the Tribune Company, but refused to get in a bidding war and retreated when his offer was topped by Joseph Allbritton (who later lost out). Former CBS president Frank Stanton remembers having lunch with the Tisch brothers and Paley sometime earlier. "I think at that time they were looking for an opportunity to get in the business," said Stanton.

Larry Tisch was a self-effacing man. On the rare occasions when he yelled at a secretary, he quickly apologized. In all his years at Loews, he said he never fired anyone. He rarely brooded, and was not a man of hidden sides. He had few known enemies and even competitors thought of him as a nice man. "He's told me things about the New York real estate market for no other reason than to be helpful," observed real estate developer and publisher Mortimer B. Zuckerman.

Like Tom Murphy at Cap Cities, Tisch at Loews delegated management to professionals. He did not sit hunched over their shoulders second-guessing, and thus he could leave his office most days by 4 P.M. Asked to describe his talent, Larry Tisch said, "I think it's just being far enough removed from daily operations to have an overall view that comes in handy in the decision process." Larry Tisch kept on top of things at Loews through the financial reports that flowed through his office, through the questions he incessantly asked, and through his brother, Bob, who met regularly with the managers and averaged 120 days a year on the road and could hail doormen at their various hotels by their first names. Perhaps Larry rarely yelled because he had Bob to handle things. Bob was the early warning system for his brother on employee morale, the one who resolved jurisdictional and ego conflicts, the one who worried about raises and bonuses, who didn't forget the birthdays. Larry was less comfortable with management, as was Bob with financial matters. This led to a natural division of responsibility between two brothers who shared the same car, the same two secretaries, the same conference room and suite of offices, the same checkbook.

They also shared the desire for a new adventure. That Larry Tisch kept purchasing CBS stock through the summer and into the fall of

1985 suggests the emotion he felt. His modest initial investment in July was predicated—wrongly, it turned out—on the expectation that the price of CBS stock would plunge while he slowly acquired more of it. Nevertheless, he continued buying.

The Tisch brothers soon replaced Ted Turner as a subject of curiosity among the 26,000 employees who worked for CBS's many enterprises, particularly the 8,000 who worked for the network. Interest peaked in October of 1985, when Larry Tisch was invited to join the CBS board. Before the invitation was issued, however, the board debated how to handle him: as a man of peace or as a conquerer?

"There were long, extended discussions about what strategy made the most sense, and how to welcome him," recalled Franklin A. Thomas, president of the Ford Foundation, a CBS director and a close friend of Wyman's. Although he was a stranger, Thomas said: "Those who knew Tisch spoke highly of him." Besides, he added, "You want to have that person on the inside, not the outside." Hoping to stabilize the company, the board designated Wyman to present the invitation personally and to seek some assurances of Loews's peaceful intent. They were unanimous that only Larry, not Bob, was to be invited to join the board. "There was," recalls Wyman, "a very specific discussion not to invite his brother to be on the board."

Wyman walked a block to Tisch's office to extend the invitation, and he was greeted with a quick acceptance. Tisch hoped Wyman would extend an offer to Bob, but on this point Wyman was silent, and Tisch was too proud to ask. Wyman then asked, gingerly, "There's been a lot of discussion in and outside of CBS about what Larry Tisch's intentions are. The board would like some level of assurance as to your intentions."

Wyman never mentioned the words "standstill agreement," but Tisch understood that what the chairman was really asking for was a signed agreement that he would not purchase more than 25 percent of CBS's stock unless invited to do so. "I made it clear that I wasn't interested in a standstill agreement," said Tisch, who thought the request implied a lack of trust, like a prenuptial agreement. He felt he had already expressed his friendly intentions. The two men shook hands and Wyman departed, not totally reassured but convinced that with Tisch on his side he could now chase away any predator.

Tisch's refusal to sign a standstill made Wolfensohn and some members of the board uneasy about his true intentions, but they remained silent. On October 16, CBS announced that Loews would, in due course, increase its stake in CBS to 25 percent; Tisch's "confidence in the management of CBS" was proclaimed.

William Paley, who in July had thought Tisch was Tishman, now seemed comfortable with the situation. He had a new attorney, Arthur L. Liman, a partner at the firm of Paul Weiss Rifkind Wharton & Garrison, who also represented Paley's former son-in-law and friend, Steve Ross, who ran Warner Communications. Liman was also, along with Larry Tisch, one of thirty-seven homeowners on Manursing Island; and he was a protégé of his senior partner, Simon Rifkind, a former Loews attorney and a Tisch family intimate. Paley was encouraged by Liman to meet Tisch, who might be a future ally against Wyman. So, within days of Tisch's acceptance of the board post, Liman arranged for Tisch to visit Paley's Fifth Avenue apartment. Surrounded by princely Picassos and Rouaults, the three men nibbled on plain sponge cake and sipped tea. Paley did much of the talking, recalling the days when he founded the network. "I think he was very happy that I joined the board," said Tisch.

But CBS was still a company on edge. The network had ranked number one for six straight years, and now a resurgent NBC was shooting past it with such hits as *The Cosby Show* and *Cheers* on Thursday evenings and *Golden Girls* on Saturday. "The Tiffany network," as CBS liked to refer to itself, had had its "quality" mantle snatched as well by NBC, which offered viewers such highly praised series as *St. Elsewhere.* CBS had developed a reputation as the stodgy network, and no longer attracted innovative talent as it once had with the young Larry Gelbart of *M*A*S*H* or Norman Lear of *All in the Family.*

There was enormous unhappiness throughout the company. In the wake of management mistakes and shriveling profits, CBS employees knew that Wyman would have no choice but to start cutting costs. The $1 billion stock buy-back plan to fend off Ted Turner had boosted CBS's interest burden, forcing Wyman and the board to shed certain assets. In November, Wyman announced that CBS was selling the toy business that had lost $67 million in 1984. "We should have made today's decision a year earlier," Wyman admitted at a press conference. Many employees said good riddance to toys, as they had earlier to a string of failed CBS attempts to become a conglomerate, including Bill Paley's brief fling as owner of the New York Yankees in the sixties. There was fear, however, that other assets sold around this time were cutting into bone, not fat. CBS weakened its distribution system when it sold one of its five owned stations, KMOX-TV in St. Louis, to Viacom. Then, in rapid order, CBS sold its productions division, including its theatrical film production outfit; its one-third stake in Tri-Star, a movie production company; and the general books division of Holt, Rinehart & Winston.

The sale of assets brought fresh cash to CBS, but also great consternation. Strategically, CBS was going against the tide. The direction of the business, whether for networks or Hollywood studios or cable operators, was to integrate vertically: to do more of their own programming; to control the distribution of their product through their own local TV stations, or cable systems, or movie theaters; to own the book ideas and package them for sale to television or the movies. That was the game being played by CBS competitors like Rupert Murdoch and other communication giants, who were seeking to control the entire communication process, from idea to production to distribution of the product. It was the game the networks, including CBS, said they were anxious to play when they tried, unsuccessfully, to press the federal government to lift the fin-syn regulations to permit the networks to produce series and sell reruns to local stations. This was the way the business was drifting. Yet, in what looked like panic, CBS was going the other way; and at a time when its core broadcasting business looked grim. In November CBS announced it would write off $143.2 million in the third quarter, resulting in the network's first quarterly loss since its infancy. With a weakened advertising market, the Broadcast Group's profits alone fell 28 percent. By the end of the year, it was reported that CBS's earnings for all of 1985 had plunged from $212.4 million to $27.4 million.

Larry Tisch's first board meeting was on November 13, 1985, and for those who gathered around the twenty-foot walnut table in the thirty-fifth-floor room that was designed like a room in a French chateau where William Paley and his late wife, Babe, had once stayed, it was immediately clear that Tisch was not just another board member. He did not act like a freshman. "He's not shy about asking questions," Paley later observed: After getting through the formal agenda, which Wyman had called Tisch to review beforehand, the board retired to Paley's elegant green-and-white-wallpapered dining room, one of nine at CBS, where white-coated stewards serve a bountiful lunch and the real business of the board is usually conducted. On this day, Walter Cronkite aired his frustrations with the news division, which he complained had gone soft, preferring features to hard news, feelings to facts. Although Cronkite did not utter his name, it was clear to many in the room that he blamed Van Gordon Sauter, the executive vice president of the Broadcast Group, to whom the news division reported.

Tisch jumped in. Avoiding personalities, he wondered aloud whether the well-ventilated frustrations within News weren't at least partly explained by what he called the "layers" of managers. In the news division, for instance, the president of CBS News reported to an executive vice president, who in turn reported to the president of the CBS Broadcast Group, who then reported to Wyman. Tisch knew that people in News felt diminished, felt this extra corporate layer symbolized a lower status for News. But for Larry Tisch the core issue was not morale, but waste. Within News, folks worried about the desecration of traditions established by Edward R. Murrow; Larry Tisch worried about the desecration of his religion, which was maximizing shareholder value. Looking at his fellow board members, Tisch said he had scanned the organization chart of CBS and its subsidiaries in the annual report and was stunned to discover a total of forty-two presidents and vice presidents. *This is wrong! This is bureaucratic! This is a waste of shareholders' money!*

Other things bothered Tisch, which he chose not to discuss at his maiden board meeting. Don Hewitt, the executive producer of CBS's most enduring hit, *60 Minutes,* a show generating fifty to sixty million dollars in profits, and its outstanding correspondent, Mike Wallace, had recently signed similar contracts starting at two million dollars per year but averaging three million annually for Hewitt over the life of the agreement, and slightly less for Wallace. Tisch was "shocked," recalls Roswell Gilpatric, to learn that this contract, like anchorman Dan Rather's ten-year 1984 contract which started at $2.5 million dollars and quickly climbed to $3.5 million, had never gone before the board. The directors merely approved the news division's budget, not its components.

These contracts led to something else that agitated Tisch from day one, and that was costs. When he inspected CBS's budget he saw that while profits were going down in 1985, general corporate expenses were rising from $58 million in 1984 to $70 million. And there were —he couldn't believe it!—eight thousand employees in the Broadcast Group alone.

For the time being, Tisch contented himself with the questions he had raised. He would keep his own counsel, be a gentle prod, build relationships. Within weeks of his first board meeting, Larry and Billie Tisch joined Tom and Betsy Wyman for dinner at the Arcadia restaurant in Manhattan.

Tisch and Wyman are very different, not least in physical appearance. Wyman towers over the shorter Loews chairman, has a full head of hair and an unlined, handsome face; where the completely bald Tisch gets by on the tennis court with clumsy cunning, Wyman is all grace, overpowering his opponents. Their business backgrounds are also unalike. While Tisch is an entrepreneur and investor who does not immerse himself in organizational charts and chains of command, Wyman was trained as a corporate manager. In contrast to Wyman's obvious enjoyment of executive perks like CBS's private executive dining rooms and the exquisite wine from CBS's own cellar, at Loews Tisch ate in a tiny conference room he shared with his brother. Lunch began when a handyman placed a few eight-ounce bottles of soda on the blond wood table, followed by the single entree of the day, followed by a small bowl of fruit or a scoop of ice cream for dessert, and accompanied by green and white paper napkins stamped *Maude's,* one of the restaurants in the somewhat seedy Summit Hotel owned by the Tisches.

Another difference between the two men is religion. According to Walter Yetnikoff, president of CBS Records, Wyman once quizzed him about a strange object on his wall that turned out to be a mezuzah, a familiar symbol of the Jewish faith. Wyman had no idea what it was. In contrast, Tisch and two of his sons met one morning a week with Rabbi Nesson Scherman, a Talmudic scholar from Brooklyn's Borough Park, who came to Tisch's office to discuss the Bible and Jewish law and philosophy.

Despite these obvious differences, the dinner at Arcadia went smoothly. Over the meal the two couples rhapsodized about their children, about the elegant, inventive nouvelle-American menu at Arcadia, about the Tisches' early years in the hotel business and Wyman's experiences as a top corporate manager: they hoisted their glasses to celebrate the Wymans' wedding anniversary, which was the next day. "There was a sense of four people sitting down and getting to know each other better," said Billie Tisch. At least one piece of CBS business was slipped in: Wyman informed Tisch that he had decided to remove a management layer by shifting CBS News president Edward M. Joyce to another post, allowing Van Gordon Sauter, the executive vice president whom Cronkite had complained about at the board meeting a week earlier, to assume sole responsibility for the news division. Tisch complimented Wyman on his wise verdict.

Tisch's footprints could also be discerned in a decision CBS made regarding its $500 million employee pension fund. Knowing of his interest in investment matters, Wyman invited Tisch to attend a meeting of the board's retirement plans committee. Three months earlier, the committee had tied the buying and selling decisions affecting $300 million of its pension funds directly to the Dow Jones average of blue-chip stocks, which was then at 1,250. On the day Tisch met with the committee, the Dow average had climbed to 1,500. Committee members were ecstatic.

A dour Tisch was not, and inquired, "What do you do now?"

"We'll ride with the Dow index," replied Louis J. Rauchenberger, Jr., the corporate treasurer.

"Can I ask," said Tisch, "what chance is there that the Dow will go to sixteen hundred? Seventeen hundred?"

"Maybe 1,600. Not 1,700," said the treasurer.

"In the next few years, might it drop below 1,200 or 1,300?" asked Tisch.

The treasurer and the board members looked at one another as if a light bulb had popped on. "Everyone agreed it could drop," said a CBS director. Tisch had, once again, focused on the downside of an investment. That day, CBS sold $200 million of its pension fund's stock investments. "Everyone's genuine reaction was, 'Isn't that smart,' " recalled the CBS director. "Here we are euphoric about having made money and he threw cold water on it. What a terrific addition he is to the party."

The same director, just months later, would be embarrassed by his earlier enthusiasm, as Tisch was embarrassed by his advice. At least in the short run, the decision was a costly one for pensioners, since the Dow average by May had risen above 1,700 and passed 2,000 before it crashed in October of 1987 and then climbed right back up again.

In fact, this was not Tisch's first misreading of the market. Because Tisch had for years been bearish on the market, shifting Loews investments from stocks to bonds, in the eighties he missed the biggest bull market ever. Truth be told, Larry Tisch, child of the Depression, believed another depression was imminent. "The question on the table," he said at the end of 1985, "is whether it is 1926, 1927, 1928, or 1929. At the rate we're going—at the pace leveraging is accelerating—I would say it's certainly 1928."

This pessimism would color Tisch's view of Wyman's management at CBS. Why, he would come to ask himself, was CBS's return on assets over the past half decade a miserly 6 percent? Tisch tended to attribute this to poor cost management, not to too few hit programs, since he scarcely watched television. Costs, not revenues, were Tisch's preoccupation, though at first Tisch only raised such questions gently.

Tisch's presence seemed to have a sedative effect on CBS as 1985 drew to a close. Wyman boasted in his annual message to shareholders that although it had been a "turbulent and difficult" year, CBS could be proud because it had fought and won the battle "to retain its long tradition of corporate independence." Gene F. Jankowski, the former salesman who was president of the CBS Broadcast Group and who still radiated his salesman's sunny optimism, put it this way in a speech early in 1986: "Happy New Year! As I've said to my CBS colleagues, that's more than a greeting—it signals relief from the stresses and surprises of 1985 and welcomes optimism for the future." The broadcasting business had changed, said Jankowski, noting that there were $30 billion of media transactions in 1985 alone, including Rupert Murdoch's acquisition of six of Metromedia's seven TV stations, which he planned to link with his Twentieth Century Fox studios to create a fourth network. Jankowski resisted the increasingly fashionable idea that the networks were a "mature" or a declining business. He believed CBS's chief competition was what it had always been—NBC and ABC. He thought of cable and syndicators as minor nuisances. No matter the turbulence of change, Jankowski reassured his audience: "As good as our business is today, the best is yet to come."

As 1986 began, the wild gyrations of CBS's stock price ceased, the fast-buck artists were reportedly chased away, and Larry Tisch was hailed as a savior, without having to pay the usual raider's premium for the privilege and the power.

Where was Tisch's investment going? "I don't think he knows where his investment in CBS is going," observed Dan Tisch in late 1985. "Tisch has three options," said board member Gilpatric. "He could sell, buy, or insist on some overall changes in the management of CBS."

Whatever he was going to do, as 1986 dawned Larry Tisch was in an enviable position. If a rival bid for CBS, Tisch had three advantages: a head start on the necessary government approvals; a CBS board and management more comfortable with the devil they knew than the one they didn't; and a lower average cost per share, since Tisch had acquired 12 percent of the stock at an average share price of about $110. He could also opt to sell to a rival, at a handsome profit.

Or, observed his increasingly wary friend, director James Wolfensohn, "If the stock drops and he can't influence the company, he can make a bid for all the stock, or he can just continue to accumulate stock until he feels he has all the influence he needs. Either road leads to Rome."

4

GE SWALLOWS NBC, 1985 TO AUGUST 1986

If all roads led to Rome for Larry Tisch in 1985, there seemed to be nothing ahead but dead ends for Thornton F. Bradshaw, chairman of RCA, the company that owned NBC. In his five years at the helm of this unwieldy conglomerate, the sleepy-eyed, easygoing, pipe-smoking former Atlantic/Richfield oil company president and Harvard Business School professor, who sailed every chance he could with his buddy Walter Cronkite and encouraged people to call him "Brad," had steadied RCA. Led for most of its sixty-six years by "General" David Sarnoff, RCA had failed to find a suitable successor, and under Sarnoff's son and two subsequent CEOs had collected a variety of incompatible businesses. Soon after he became CEO in 1981, Bradshaw shed Hertz Rent-a-Car, the Random House publishing company, the real estate firm of Cushman & Wakefield, Banquet Foods, Gibson Greeting Cards, and C.I.T., a consumer finance and leasing company.

Bradshaw had reason to exult when he looked back on his tenure. Now, in the twilight of his business career at age sixty-seven, he believed he had returned RCA to "its roots," given it a sense of direction. He captained a $10 billion company, whose core businesses were electronics, communications, and NBC. The year before, planning for his succession, Bradshaw had appointed Robert R. Frederick, whom he had recruited in 1982 from General Electric, as CEO. Bradshaw remained as chairman.

Bradshaw was both proud and concerned. "Brad worried about the vulnerability of RCA not just to a takeover but to an economic downturn," recalls his investment banker, Felix Rohatyn of Lazard Freres & Company. Bradshaw knew, said Rohatyn, that the network business was cyclical, knew that even though NBC was streaking past its competitors, "hit" shows fizzled like meteors; you didn't know when they would appear but you did know four out of five shows would crash. CBS had been the ratings leader for nineteen consecutive years—until ABC captured the lead in 1975–76. Ten years later, ABC was back in third place. And with networks no longer able to monopolize audiences, hits were harder to come by. Bradshaw also knew that new technology conspired against the networks.

Television sends its signals over a narrow range of broadcast frequencies. Because this spectrum is such "a narrow highway," explained Julius Barnathan, ABC's president of Broadcast Operations and Engineering, "To get more cars through, we made the cars narrower." Broadcasters were allotted a spectrum width of just six megahertz, and this highway was crammed with traffic from VHF and UHF TV stations, from AM and FM radio frequencies. Competing for what was left of the slender spectrum were cellular telephones, private microwave links, and frequencies set aside for the military. Because the megahertz highway was so congested, the number of broadcast signals received and the quality of the picture was limited. Such technological advances as high-definition television, which produces movie-screen-quality pictures, require more spectrum space than was available. But if these narrow lanes were replaced by fiber-optic cables, which could one day bring thousands of laser signals into homes, or by individual dishes that retrieve direct signals from satellites, then the narrow broadcast lanes might—absent a technological breakthrough—become as obsolete as a country road.

Sometime in the nineties, according to Casimir S. Skrzpczak, vice president of Science and Technology at the NYNEX Corporation, homes will be equipped with large, flat screens with movie-quality high-definition pictures. Voice-activated television sets will rely on robotic technology. These "user-friendly" TVs will provide viewers with the equivalent of a "personal robot." A viewer will be able to plop in a chair and verbally order up on the screen a preview of the hundreds of sports or comedies or movie options available either from his small satellite dish or over his fiber-optic telephone wire. Viewers will become programmers, able to summon movies, news documentaries, newspaper stories, or tap into several hundred broadcast or cable channels. Or viewers will turn to interactive TV; by pressing buttons, they will choose camera angles, select their own instant replays, take part in games of chess with someone on the screen, customize spelling tutorials for the children, order theater tickets, or shop.

What most worried Thornton Bradshaw about the immediate future was NBC chairman Grant Tinker. He knew that Tinker planned to depart soon, and dreaded the impact on the network's delicate chemistry. Of all Thornton Bradshaw's achievements, perhaps the one that made him feel best was his recruitment of Tinker in 1981. Then fifty-five, Tinker was the cofounder of MTM Enterprises, a small company that produced such enduring series as *The Mary Tyler Moore Show, Hill Street Blues,* and *Lou Grant.* Tinker was a soft-spoken man with movie-star good looks, an aura of confidence, and that rarest of Hollywood qualities: humility. When you walked into Tinker's antique-filled office you were accosted by a large poster imprinted with the definition of the word "tink-er": ". . . an unskillful or clumsy worker; a bungler . . ."

Bradshaw looked back and contentedly remembered how Tinker led NBC's Long March from third place. The self-confident Tinker refused to cast aside the management team he inherited. He gave Brandon Tartikoff, a long-haired, thirty-three-year-old programmer, a new contract in December 1982, despite Tartikoff's third-place showing as president of the entertainment division for the previous two years. Tinker insisted he was committed to "quality" television, backing up his words by patiently waiting for shows such as *Hill Street Blues, Cheers, St. Elsewhere,* and *Family Ties* to find their audience and improve NBC's ratings. Though the conventional wisdom said TV sitcoms were dead, Tinker backed Tartikoff's push for a half-hour comedy with Bill Cosby in 1984. Tinker made only two major executive changes. He brought in a former colleague, Larry Grossman, to be NBC News president in 1984, the same year he discharged Robert Mulholland as network president. By offering stability and security, Tinker gave NBC back its self-assurance, its sense of pride. Profits followed, climbing from $48 million in Tinker's first year to $333 million in 1985.

Thornton Bradshaw feared Tinker might be irreplaceable. But the source of Bradshaw's enduring pessimism was RCA, not NBC. In the post-Reagan era, Bradshaw knew RCA's defense business was unlikely to enjoy the same governmental largesse. In addition, huge, technologically advanced competitors were on the move. "We didn't have the cash to compete with the Pacific rim countries or the giants like AT&T in the future," said Bradshaw. "We didn't have the resources."

What resources RCA had were, disproportionately, being generated by a single component—NBC—which in 1984 produced 43 percent of the parent company's $570 million in earnings. This troubled Bradshaw, because traditionally there was friction between the two parts of the company. The freewheeling culture of the network collided with the precise engineering culture of RCA. There was no way, Bradshaw believed, that RCA could thrive if the NBC engine drove the entire company.

It was only a matter of time, he guessed, before RCA would be sold and dismembered. Its breakup value was pegged at up to ninety dollars a share, and yet its stock market price had hovered all that year between thirty-four and forty-nine dollars a share, the same problem afflicting ABC and CBS. Warily, Bradshaw watched developer Donald Trump gobble up RCA shares, then sell them. He watched Irwin L. Jacobs, a Minneapolis corporate raider, buy about 4 percent of the stock, a bit more than T. Boone Pickens acquired around the same time. Then Henry Kravis approached Bradshaw, as he had Tom Wyman, suggesting a leveraged buyout. Bradshaw also remembered a talk with Larry Tisch "off the cuff, that he was interested in the networks."

To protect RCA, Bradshaw retained attorney Martin Lipton, the father of the so-called "poison pill" and a lawyer who would be involved in the transfer of power at all three networks. Lipton helped install a series of defenses—staggering the terms of directors, granting to RCA stockholders the right in the event of a raid to purchase three hundred dollars' worth of stock for half the price. "I saw all these attacks on the networks," said Bradshaw. "Maybe NBC would be protected by being in the bosom of a large company." It was the same thought that had visited Leonard Goldenson earlier at ABC.

There was at least one other parallel between Bradshaw and Goldenson: Each had doubts about his chosen successor. Robert Frederick, sixty, a former senior vice president at GE, had lost out in a 1981 power struggle to the man who became GE's chairman and CEO, Jack Welch. By 1985, Bradshaw and Frederick were estranged. Frederick did not share Bradshaw's fears about RCA remaining independent. And Bradshaw came to fret, as did a quiet chorus of RCA executives, that Frederick lacked the stature to lead the company. "He didn't think Frederick was good enough," said a Bradshaw intimate, "and felt he had no ability to deal with the people at NBC." However, since Bradshaw was then just three years shy of seventy and had chosen his successor at the prodding of the RCA board, he felt trapped. "I think he felt he could not revisit that matter with the board," said Grant Tinker. Selling RCA became a way for Bradshaw not just to secure the company's future, but to get rid of Frederick. The natural alliance, thought the RCA chairman, was with a "Big Eight" Hollywood studio.

The major studios had been as resistant to the birth and spread of television in the forties and early fifties as the networks had been to cable in the seventies and eighties. In its early days, network television relied on live studio shows and plays, many shot in New York, where the TV entertainment divisions were then located. So resistant to the networks were the Hollywood studios that Jack Warner even banned the appearance of a TV set in any Warner Brothers movie! That was easier to do in, say, 1950, when only 3.8 million homes had a television. But by 1957, 78.6 percent of all American homes had a TV set. And studios discovered that television production could offer a fresh source of profits for old movies, made-for-TV dramas, and sitcoms. By the eighties, many of Hollywood's eight giant studios wanted a network because it would allow them not only to produce movies and TV programs but also to control the distribution of their product. Already, studios owned movie theaters, television stations, cable systems and programming services, and produced video cassettes. A critical missing link to becoming a vertically integrated powerhouse was a network.

Owning a network would reduce their considerable risks. For each half-hour comedy or one-hour drama the studio financed, the fee paid by the network usually covered only 80 to 90 percent of the studio's weekly cost, leaving the studio to gamble that they could make up the deficit later by selling reruns of series that had been on the networks at least four years. But as the cost of series grew, deficits mounted. And studios grew restless with the long odds of getting a show on the network schedule, with their lack of control over the promotion of the show or whether it remained on the air long enough to enter syndication, which is where the real pot of gold lay.

The networks also felt hamstrung by a critical missing link. They were continually frustrated by the financial interest and syndication rules that prevented them from owning more than three hours a week of their own prime-time non-news programming and barred them from reselling entertainment shows to domestic or foreign TV stations or to cable. The Hollywood studios and the independent television stations were terrified that if a network owned the product and controlled its syndication it would inevitably choose to schedule its own product, or favor its own affiliated stations in the competition for reruns. Nonsense, replied the networks. It was ridiculous to think that they would favor their own product or stations, since to put weak shows on the network would sabotage their business. Nor would they miss a chance to maximize profits by evading a bidding process for their own syndicated programs.

Thornton Bradshaw, like his colleagues at CBS and ABC, hoped that if the fin-syn rules were lifted the networks could tap a new stream of revenue. Bradshaw knew the uncertainties of the broadcast business; he knew that today's adversaries—the networks, the studios, the cable companies, the telephone companies—might be tomorrow's allies. But of one thing he was sure: In the future those who controlled programming would control the entertainment industry. For however TV signals entered the future home—whether from backyard dishes collecting signals from satellites or from fiber-optic cable—the technology would work only if it had programs to deliver. In addition, Bradshaw believed that in tandem with a studio, a network could better control program costs, which now extracted about $1 billion annually from each network. The politics of a merger were also seductive. If the studios and the networks were partners, no longer would their friends in Washington have to choose between them. A studio and a network were a natural fit.

That is exactly the idea Lew Wasserman, chairman of MCA, had in mind in 1982 when he talked to investment banker and MCA board member Felix Rohatyn. The banker arranged a meeting between Wasserman and Thornton Bradshaw, who was also a client. MCA was then the major supplier of shows to NBC. After prolonged negotiations, RCA and MCA tentatively agreed to swap stock; Wasserman would run the combined MCA/NBC; and Bradshaw would oversee RCA. After almost two years of on-and-off talks, however, it all came to naught. "MCA pulled the plug on it," recalled Bradshaw. On the brink of signing a merger agreement in 1984, Wasserman put his pen down and exclaimed, "I just can't face putting my creative talent in the hands of engineers." Wasserman didn't believe the two cultures would mesh.

Enter Michael D. Eisner, chairman and CEO of the Walt Disney Company. Ever since joining the then sleepy studio in 1984, Eisner had dreamed of building a worldwide communications and leisure-time powerhouse. He would buy TV stations, get into cable programming, use internationally known Disney characters like Mickey Mouse to open doors overseas, including Euro Disneyland in France and Tokyo Disneyland. But what the forty-two-year-old Eisner really wanted was a network. For nine glorious years, starting in 1966, Eisner had been an ABC programming executive, helping propel ABC from number three to number one in both prime-time and daytime ratings. Owning a network would be fun.

In early 1985, soon after Bradshaw's MCA negotiations collapsed and around the time Tom Murphy was negotiating with Leonard Goldenson to acquire ABC, Eisner and his chief stockholder, Sid Bass, met with Bradshaw and NBC chairman Grant Tinker. Disney wanted to avoid entirely the problem that had stumped MCA, and proposed to exclude RCA from the merger. Disney "didn't want to be in the defense business," Eisner explained. Instead Disney proposed that in return for a substantial premium, RCA would spin off NBC and become a major shareholder in the new entertainment superpower.

Comfortable with Eisner, and tired of the weekly commute from his Los Angeles home to New York, Tinker was receptive. But Bradshaw, as he reflected upon the offer, was not. "We worked on the numbers and thought it was a great deal," said Bradshaw. "But then we looked at the other side and saw that RCA stripped of NBC couldn't make it." Bradshaw believed that without cash from NBC, the electronics and consumer-appliance parts of RCA could not compete with the Japanese. The MCA and Disney negotiations sharpened the cleavage between Bradshaw and his designated successor. "Frederick . . . felt enough things could be done at RCA so that eventually it could stand on its own," recalled Bradshaw. And Frederick was not averse to ridding RCA of those strange folks at NBC.

After months of talks, the Disney deal died in the fall of 1985. "We were moving towards a deal," recalls Eisner, but then the phone stopped ringing.

Phone communications were established instead with the General Electric Company. The contact was initiated by Rohatyn, who breakfasted regularly with Jack Welch to scout possible deals. In his almost five years as chairman and chief executive officer of GE, Welch had acquired approximately three hundred companies or product lines and sold about two hundred. Unlike frightened or cautious corporate chieftains who skimped on research in order to sweeten quarterly returns, over the preceding five years he had invested $20 billion in R&D, new plants and equipment, and improved productivity. Rohatyn knew that Welch was now sitting on a bundle of cash, not having made a major acquisition in years, and with 1984 earnings of $2.3 billion.

Rohatyn was a professional matchmaker, one of the best, and his job was to know his customers. He knew that Welch envisioned a highly competitive global marketplace. Losers and laggards were ruthlessly discarded, as were "excess" employees. If a GE company wasn't number one or two in market share, Welch usually got rid of it. Welch used words like "downsizing" and "restructuring" to describe what he was doing; critics called him "Neutron Jack," meaning that under him the buildings remained but the people disappeared. Welch pursued what he believed was his first obligation, to maximize shareholder values. To fulfill this obligation, he would say, quoting Richard Nixon, "Sometimes a good leader has to be a good butcher."

Jack Welch played at the game of business the way he had once played hockey, with elbows flying, crunching opponents against the boards, always driving toward the goal. *Growth* was his passion, and the way to achieve growth was through *deals,* through *alliances* and *synergies,* by using GE's massive resources to guarantee dominance and to escape the vagaries of national business cycles.

Fueled by his drive, GE in five years had grown from a company with $13 billion in revenues to a nearly $50 billion giant. Welch had streamlined GE into three basic components: five technology businesses (aircraft engines, aerospace, medical systems, factory automation, and plastics); a service sector led by the GE Credit Corporation, with $20 billion of assets; and a core manufacturing group (appliances, lighting, transportation, motors, construction equipment, power systems). Manufacturing had slipped within GE, generating just 30 percent of its business in 1985, down from 50 percent in 1980. Welch had targeted technology and services as GE's future, and by the end of 1985 the company proudly boasted that it was "the nation's largest exporter five of the last six years." Jack Welch was determined that GE become bigger than IBM or Exxon or anyone else, the world's number-one corporate superpower.

Rohatyn knew that Welch had made a bid for CBS, and knew that he had also made a friendly bid to purchase Cox Broadcasting in the early eighties. He knew Welch's aversion to hostile takeovers, his belief that the bitterness they engendered not only poisoned the partnership but, more important, prevented potential partners from turning to GE as a white knight. Rohatyn also knew Welch might like the synergies to be found between RCA and GE in defense, electronics, and consumer goods.

Rohatyn arranged a leisurely get-together between Welch and Bradshaw on November 6, 1985, at Rohatyn's apartment. Bradshaw arrived in the tuxedo he would wear to a Navy League dinner afterward. Because Bradshaw had to leave, the session lasted only forty-five minutes. The three men talked generally about the consumer electronics business and its future, about how difficult it was for American consumer businesses to vie with cheaper Korean and Japanese competition, and about the perils of being a defense contractor. No one talked about a merger, for these were all pros, who thought it bad form to kiss on the first date.

Welch left feeling unsure about whether Rohatyn had told Bradshaw before the meeting of GE's interest in RCA, but certain that he liked Bradshaw. Welch believed "there was some chance to do some business." Bradshaw said later that he was puzzled: "I asked Felix, 'Does Welch have any idea what we might do together, or was that just a meeting?' " But one of Bradshaw's friends insists that was just a pose. "Bradshaw went through a minuet for his own people," observed the friend. "He knew exactly what Welch was interested in." Bradshaw was maneuvering to sell RCA.

The next day Welch put together a team to discern whether RCA and GE made a good business fit. The secret effort was code-named "Island." There was a certain irony involved, because back in 1919 GE had been the sole owner of the Radio Corporation of America, and was a part owner of the NBC radio network when it was formed in 1926. With a boost from GE, NBC developed the first crystal set radios. The original partnership ended only because a federal court in 1933 compelled GE to divest.

Among those analyzing RCA for Welch was Robert Wright, CEO of the GE Credit Corporation.* With 1985 profits of $500 million, Wright managed the fastest growing component of the parent company and was thought to be Welch's protégé. Having left GE between 1980 and 1983 to run Cox Communications' cable business, and having earlier that year looked at CBS, Wright also had some familiarity with broadcasting. "One of the things I was doing at GE Credit was gearing up to finance media properties," recalls Wright.

Just before Thanksgiving, a sixty-page report on "Island" was circulated internally. The report concluded that RCA and GE's defense and aerospace businesses meshed well, as did their technology efforts. In the $57 billion defense electronics industry, GE combined with RCA would move from sixth to second among contractors. RCA had real strength in advanced radar and satellites, as well as an edge in the bidding to work on Reagan's "Star Wars" defense system. There were also savings to be realized from trimming overlapping overheads.

* Soon to change its name to GE Financial Services.

On the downside, the Island report expressed real concern about consumer electronics. True, there was a fit between the two, but low-cost competition from the Far East lurked ahead. GE, in fact, was planning to sell its consumer-electronics division. In addition, the Island report proposed to sell other components of RCA.

But about NBC there was unanimity. NBC that year was passing CBS to become the number-one network. "NBC looked good even though the network business looked bad," said Wright. Even as a so-called "mature industry," even with the onslaught from cable, VCRs, and independent TV stations, GE's analysts found that the revenues of the three networks had expanded by an average of 11.4 percent each year between 1980 and 1984. A network seemed inflation-proof, it produced mounds of cash, and there was no foreign competition. In addition, after years as a TV station owner, including a station it still owned in Denver, GE knew the five TV stations owned by NBC were an even better business than the network, with profit margins of nearly forty-five cents on each dollar of revenue. The stations alone accounted for four dollars of every ten dollars of NBC's profits, and fully half of NBC's market value. The future, the report said, was if anything even brighter for NBC, for its hit shows were youthful and appealed to the young, urban viewers advertisers craved. No question, NBC was the vital core of RCA.

During the Thanksgiving holidays, Welch jetted with his family to West Palm Beach and the other executives scattered. On Monday morning they all arrived at work eager to make a deal. Meanwhile, Thornton Bradshaw said not a word about GE to Robert Frederick, RCA's president; in fact, he spoke to no one but Rohatyn.

Welch next called Rohatyn, mentioned his continued interest in RCA, and suggested a second meeting with Bradshaw. The two principals met alone on Thursday, December 5, in Bradshaw's duplex at the Dorset Hotel on West Fifty-fourth Street, where he was staying while his apartment was being renovated. The day had not gone all that well for Bradshaw; at lunch, Grant Tinker announced that after four and a half years of commuting to New York during the week and back home to California on weekends, he wanted to call it quits. "Brad, I think we've done the job, and if you have no problem I'd like to leave at the end of five years," Tinker recalls saying. His timetable was to leave in July, his fifth anniversary.

Bradshaw said nothing of the meeting he was to have that afternoon with Welch.

When Welch arrived at Bradshaw's suite later that day, no sooner were the two men seated than Welch announced: "I'd like to buy your company!"

Bradshaw's eyes bulged. Welch explained his rationale, how the companies fit like a glove, how it would make both more internationally competitive, how it might strengthen the weaker parts of RCA and, if not, how they would be sold, but only after a testing period. Above all, said Welch, a merger would maximize shareholder value. Of the network, recalled Bradshaw, "He said they would treat NBC the same way RCA treated it, as an independent company with independent management."

"We'd like to pay in the sixty-one-dollar-a-share range," said Welch, or slightly more than thirteen dollars per share above RCA's stock trading price. "I hope you'll consider it and get back to me."

"You've given me an offer," Bradshaw responded. "It's too low. But I will have to go to my board." They would talk again soon.

That night *The Cosby Show* reached an astonishing 53 percent of all viewers who were watching television, powering NBC's Thursday schedule to another smashing ratings victory. But Bradshaw's mind was elsewhere. He phoned Robert Frederick and Grant Tinker, both on the West Coast, and asked each to fly east immediately. Tinker was not offended to have been kept in the dark about the November meeting with Welch, but Frederick was. Meanwhile Bradshaw phoned his directors to schedule a Sunday board meeting.

Frederick was not happy. Nor were some other board members. The chairman of the Marine Midland Bank, John R. Petty, according to a *New York Times Magazine* account, "had some strong doubts about the GE bid—specifically about Bradshaw's failure to inform the board about the November meeting with Welch, about the impact of a takeover on RCA's executives and other employees, and about the very notion of selling the company without some form of auction to get the best price."

But Petty was scheduled to be in Moscow on Sunday, December 8, the day of the board meeting, and Frederick, inadvertently confirming Bradshaw's doubts about his ability to assert leadership, chose not to marshal the board against the GE offer. Months later, Bradshaw took pains to protest that Petty never said he would oppose the merger. "He did say if we were pressed into selling the company we ought to open it to other bidders." Bradshaw said he reported this to the board. Respectful of the job Bradshaw had done and of his concerns for the future, directors decided not to seek other bidders, fearing it would put the company in play and invite what Bradshaw called "unsavory characters" to enter the bidding. In other words, Thornton Bradshaw alone had made a decision to sell, giving his board little choice but to follow his lead.

On Sunday, in the boardroom of Martin Lipton's law firm, by a vote of nine *yeas* to Frederick's solitary *no* and one abstention (Robert Cizik, CEO of Cooper Industries), the RCA board agreed to pursue discussions with GE. Frederick and Bradshaw were authorized to represent RCA.

First thing Monday morning, Frederick telephoned Welch to say that RCA wished to negotiate. But before proceeding he needed two things. First, GE had to sign a standstill agreement, vowing not to mount a hostile takeover if negotiations broke off. Second, he wanted to know the management philosophy GE would impose on RCA. Would GE retain, or sell, parts of RCA? Since GE under Welch had never mounted a hostile takeover, Welch—unlike Larry Tisch—that very day agreed to sign a standstill. In the afternoon he helicoptered to New York to meet at Bradshaw's apartment with the two men. Satisfied with Welch's pledge to keep an open mind on the sale of various RCA parts—a pledge at odds with the recommendations of GE's own internal analysis—Bradshaw and Frederick authorized Rohatyn to talk to John Weinberg, chairman of Goldman, Sachs & Company, who represented GE, and to commence serious negotiations.

By Wednesday evening—three days later—an agreement was ready and approved by both boards. GE would pay $66.50 per share, for a total of $6.28 billion in cash, the largest non-oil industry transaction to date. To break the news to their managers, Bradshaw and Frederick summoned their management team to the RCA boardroom on the fifty-third floor of 30 Rockefeller Plaza.

As Bradshaw readied for the meeting, Tom Brokaw prepared for his nightly newscast, where he planned to break the news. Brokaw paused to scribble a note to Bradshaw as an act of courtesy. But a few minutes later when Brokaw introduced correspondent Mike Jensen's story on the air, he felt vulnerable. "A great change was coming, and I felt unsettled," recalled Brokaw. "I worked for this company for my whole adult life, and it was always RCA and NBC. GE was this giant. I guess I felt for the first time like a cog in a machine. RCA had a human dimension. I knew the people."

The RCA and NBC executives who filed into the boardroom also felt uneasy. The drapes had been drawn and the room was dark. They sat at an immense walnut table, which overwhelmed them. At one end of the room, there hovered an oversized portrait of General Sarnoff, frowning. And the suspense heightened because as Bradshaw was about to speak he was handed Brokaw's note, which he paused to read.

Without betraying either the content of the note or a hint of emotion, Bradshaw coolly refolded it and filed it in his pocket. Then he announced to his apprehensive audience that what they were about to hear was privileged because they were "insiders."

Frederick took over and announced that RCA would be sold to GE, prompting pained outrage from Richard W. Miller, RCA's senior vice president of Consumer Electronics. "We didn't have to sell this company. And if we did, you should have gotten twenty dollars more per share," Miller exclaimed. Frederick, playing the good soldier, joined Bradshaw in defending the merger, arguing that without GE's resources RCA would not be able to invest in worldwide satellites and other new technologies.

The joint December 12 press release wrapped the merger in the flag. It would be good for America, they claimed, the same claim that would later be made when Time, Inc. and Warner Communications merged. The alliance, said the GE announcement, was "an excellent opportunity for both companies to create a combined company that will improve America's competitiveness in world markets." The merger was, of course, also good financially for RCA executives. GE gave employment contracts to nine RCA executives, including Frederick, guaranteeing their base pay through 1990 and bonuses no smaller than the ones they received in 1985. In addition, Frederick received \$5 million for his stock options; Bradshaw got a three-year consultancy paying \$500,000 annually and a \$7 million lump-sum payment for his stock options. NBC executives did not receive golden parachutes, though the nine members of Tinker's chairman's council did receive GE stock or stock options. Bradshaw and Tinker were invited to join the GE board. Bradshaw agreed, but Tinker, not much interested in jet engines or plastics, declined.

Reaction to the merger was mixed. Potential suitors were displeased. Martin Davis, chief executive officer of Gulf & Western Industries, which owned Paramount Pictures and the publishing firm of Simon and Schuster, immediately telephoned Felix Rohatyn. "I told him we would consider paying more," recalls Davis. "He said Bradshaw wouldn't listen to any counteroffers."

Among NBC's eight thousand employees, there was both pleasure and apprehension. For those employees who worked in the entertainment division headquartered in Burbank, California, RCA had been a distant or nettlesome parent, a fat bureaucracy leeching off the networks. In California, RCA was commonly thought to treat NBC Entertainment as a bunch of "kids." The head "kid"—Brandon Tartikoff —was thrilled. "NBC was always held back a little by RCA," said Tartikoff. "All we were out here were regional managers. GE is much more savvy and aggressive in maintaining a competitive sense of the marketplace. RCA was always trying to justify why some twenty-five-year-old kid was making more money than their guy who manufactured television sets." Several New York executives, including executive vice president Bob Walsh, shared California's disdain for RCA.

But most of NBC's employees—the bulk of them working out of 30 Rock—were probably apprehensive. They knew of GE's cost-cutting proclivities, feared they might be expendable. They knew that Welch boasted of having eliminated an entire layer of GE managers in early 1985. But there was another concern, one that went to what they found special about the network business. Whatever frustrations RCA aroused, at least RCA under Bradshaw left them alone; Grant Tinker was allowed to create a secure, collegial environment, in which NBC worried more about revenues than costs. They had achieved almost magical success. The dread was that GE would be so preoccupied with the bottom line that it would not have the patience to nurture, as Tinker had, outstanding series. After all, GE was, as writer James Traub would observe, run "by men who feel the world is on fire."

Another fear haunted NBC, particularly News employees. They were worried about censorship from a powerful conglomerate with major interests in defense and nuclear power plants. The specter of corporate interference worried journalists at all three networks. Admittedly, few believed Jack Welch would behave the way Brazil's Roberto Marinho did. Marinho is the sole owner of Globo TV, Brazil's dominant network, which attracts fifty million viewers—70 to 80 percent of the available viewing audience—for its nightly thirty-minute newscast. "We give all necessary information," Marinho told *The New York Times,* "but our opinions are in one way or other dependent on my character, my convictions and my patriotism. I assume responsibility for everything I run."

What troubled people at NBC and elsewhere was the danger of self-censorship, of a news department that would, for instance, avoid stories about nuclear power-plant safety. Accusations of self-censorship would continue to surface at the conglomerates. After Time, Inc. and Warner merged in 1989, for example, their book publishing unit killed a book by two former *Time* magazine writers—*Connections: American Business and the Mob*—which reportedly contained information embarrassing to Warner executives. In 1990 NBC's *Today* show killed—then restored when the incident was publicized—a report critical of the bolts GE used in some jet engines. Few believed that top executives at Time Warner or GE ordered the stories squelched, but what was generally believed was that underlings were simply trying to protect the boss and their own jobs.

Two opposing trends were unfolding at the same time. On the one hand, television was becoming a more democratic instrument, as viewers enjoyed many more choices for news, including CNN, C-SPAN, and expanded local and regional cable newscasts. On the other hand, the ownership of media was becoming more concentrated. Worldwide, five global media giants—Germany's Bertelsmann, Murdoch's Australian-based News Corporation, France's Hachette, and America's Newhouse Communications and Capital Cities/ABC—already controlled a huge slice of the world's magazines, book publishers, newspapers, book clubs, and record companies, and were now gobbling up broadcasting outlets. Group owners now claimed hegemony over 80 percent of the TV stations in the one hundred largest U.S. markets; chains like Gannett, with its 81 dailies, now monopolized 60 percent of America's 1,700 daily newspapers; Murdoch owned two-thirds of the newspapers in Australia. The top five American cable companies dominated nearly a third of all cable sets, and within a few years a single corporation—John Malone's Tele-Communications, Inc.—would control nearly one-quarter of all cable hookups and own pieces of cable-programming services that entered fifty million homes. A handful of chains claimed ownership of both bookstores and videocasette rental outlets. A few giants dominated book publishing. The reach of Hollywood's studios extended to most movie theater screens on which their pictures were displayed. While these mergers brought economic efficiencies, they also meant that many voices were being replaced by a few. Or as media critic Ben H. Bagdikian observed: "The basis for all liberty—freedom of information—is . . . in danger of being polluted, not by chemicals but by a new mutation of that familiar scourge of the free spirit, centrally controlled information."

These were some of the thoughts bouncing around people's minds at NBC as 1985 drew to a close, but the overwhelming fear was of the unknown. Executives were slightly relieved that Welch, soon after the merger was announced, pleaded with Tinker to stay. "I felt wonderful with the guy. I was comfortable with him," Welch said. "I felt good about him. Trusted him." Welch hoped to extract from Tinker a couple of years to allow a transition.

Beyond Tinker, the biggest unknown question at NBC was this: Would GE be an essentially benevolent owner, or an assertive one? Executives who feared the latter were not reassured by an encounter they had with Jack Welch in early January 1986.

Welch is a brawler. In interviews, when the conversation coasts, he may bark to a journalist: "Come on, gimme your best shot!" At the annual GE management retreat in Florida, the annual corporate officers meeting in Arizona, the smaller corporate executive council which gathers each quarter, or even at the annual management retreat of each GE company—Welch tries to attend each of these—his management style is to provoke people. And so in January, when NBC's managers joined five hundred or so managers of each of GE's other companies in Boca Raton, Florida, for a few days to exchange strategic plans, they were assaulted by Welch. At this meeting, like others, the GE chairman proselytized. "The people who get in trouble in our company are those who carry around the anchor of the past," Welch would bellow. Or: "It's a canard to say, 'If it works, don't fix it.' " True wisdom, Welch insists, "may lie in changing the institution while it's still winning."

Since NBC was clearly "winning," Welch's words did not soothe. Nor was it comforting to NBC executives to hear how important it was for all GE managers to attend classes for up to a week at its fifty-acre campus in Crotonville, New York. The mission here, as stated in GE brochures, was "to seek solutions for GE today and develop leaders for GE tomorrow." Every new GE manager or professional employee was sent there for two and a half days; five thousand employees attended every year. At Crotonville they would all wear GE name tags and come to share Chairman Welch's vision, bathe in the GE culture, swap information, and allow the eighteen faculty members and supporting staff of twenty to evaluate them, to identify future leaders. They would hear talk of how this facility nurtured "common purposes, common values," of how GE "is more than just a business you work for." To those NBC executives who had as little to do with RCA as possible, Crotonville conjured images of reeducation camps, of brainwashing.

And then there was the scene at the bar. Larry Grossman remembers standing at the bar in Boca Raton, next to Welch, while the GE chairman was "mouthing off in know-it-all fashion" about waste at

NBC, about how NBC's TV stations did not achieve the same 55 percent profit margin achieved by Cap Cities and how the networks imposed too many restrictions on what their stations could carry.

One of the joys of working for a network was the sense that it was more than a way to make a living, it was a calling. You were to enlighten as well as entertain, as people like Grossman believed the networks had done with news, with David Susskind's *Kraft Television Theater* or Martin Ritt's *Starlight Theater.* After the meeting in Boca Raton, a terrible foreboding arose that NBC's calling was now to maximize its profits to the parent company.

Despite these personal insecurities, as long as Grant Tinker was there, oozing confidence and watching over his flock, NBC relaxed. "Grant Tinker was the best guy I ever worked for, and I've worked for a lot of people," said Bob Walsh, fifty-eight, who had spent his entire career at NBC and then ran the owned stations, Sports, and Radio. In addition to admiring Tinker's accessibility and how he delegated responsibility and how there "was never a fear of failure," Walsh said: "all of us understood what he was for—quality." He remembered when WNBC-AM radio featured a foulmouthed disc jockey named Howard Stern. "Howard Stern got to be the most popular radio personality in the New York market, and was the difference between profit and loss at that station." But Tinker couldn't square Stern's on-air performance with his efforts to make NBC the "quality" network. "Look, if that's the only way to make money we shouldn't be in business," Tinker told Walsh. Because Tinker believed access to the public airwaves was a privilege, Stern was terminated in September of 1985.

Tinker altered the culture at NBC. Employees came to feel the network was special, a place that defied the tyranny of Nielsen's ratings, a place with the swagger to trust its gut instincts. Sometimes, to be sure, Tartikoff would chase after Nielsen numbers with a show like *Misfits of Science,* which even members of his staff believed crossed the line of bad taste. It featured bizarre characters—a man who could freeze anything he touched, provided he could sleep in a refrigerator and eat frozen candy bars, and a seven-foot four-inch giant who had invented a serum that allowed him to shrink to six inches for fifteen minutes at a time. Each of these characters teamed with a research scientist who, according to the NBC press release, "aims to make a difference in the world." Every network, including Tinker's, schedules embarrassing shows like *Misfits.* After all, it was an action adventure show—*The A-Team*—which Tinker and Tartikoff put on the schedule in 1982—that heralded NBC's resurgence. But what earned NBC its reputation for quality was its willingness to air good shows even though the initial research and then the Nielsen numbers were dismal. Bolstered by Tinker, the talented Tartikoff began to err on the side of more quality series, to boast of challenging the audience rather than giving it what it wanted.

Even in 1983, after Tartikoff put nine new series on NBC's schedule and all nine flopped, Tinker stood by him. Tartikoff at the time described how he felt: "It's not like you've just been rejected by your wife, or your boss, or your friends. You've been rejected by an *entire country.*" Even when the NBC affiliates and others wanted Tartikoff fired, Tinker calmly told the press: "His job is in no jeopardy. If he were to come to me and say, 'I've bombed again, and I'm packing it up,' I'd talk him out of it." Tartikoff said, "Had I been in charge of me then, I probably would have fired me."

Tinker bet not just on Tartikoff, but on the talent who would write and produce NBC's shows. Steven Bochco, who worked for Tinker when he ran the MTM Enterprises studios, said that Tinker was probably the most secure person he had ever come across. "He wants you to do what you want to do. He doesn't want you to do what he wants. My first week at MTM I went up there and said, "I want to run an idea by you."

"I'll listen," Tinker replied. "But we hired you to do what you want to do." The result, said Bochco, is that Tinker created "the only company in television run by writers. There's not a writer in television who ever had the privilege of working for that guy who has a bad thing to say about him. If Grant Tinker delegates to Brandon Tartikoff, and Brandon Tartikoff doesn't have to be afraid of Grant, then he can afford to operate in an environment where fear is not a factor."

The way Tinker treated Bochco, or Tartikoff, was at odds with the bottom-line managers then coming to dominate corporate America, including those who would take over the three networks. "Get your eyes off the bottom line and on the programs and the services people look to you for," Tinker said. Concentrate on revenues, not costs. Get out of New York. He knew viewers had no loyalty to networks, they watched shows. The product was everything. Produce hit programs and everything else would take care of itself. Unlike many executives, Tinker did not boast of his financial acumen. Just the opposite. "I have no financial background whatsoever," he declared. "I can't read profit and loss statements. When I would go up to RCA, if I had to give them a presentation in terms of dollars, I was a basket case.

But what I did know something about, or was supposed to know something about and it turned out I did, was how a network should behave and how people and programs should be selected. . . . It's a terrible mistake to work back from your bottom-line expectations and run a company that way."

What NBC employees didn't know that spring was what Tinker had told Bradshaw in December, and what he would tell Welch over dinner at the exclusive Knickerbocker Club on March 26, 1986.

My five years are almost up, Tinker told Bradshaw and Welch. *By July, when my contract expires, I hope to leave and return to California.*

But Tinker had a second item on his agenda at the March dinner. "I was selling succession from within," he said. Tinker advanced no candidate, because he was pushing a concept. Since NBC was, for the first time in TV history, in first place in the ratings during the 1985–86 season, Tinker did not want to risk disruption. NBC was enjoying a glorious year; it had added to an already potent entertainment lineup such future hits as *Golden Girls, ALF, Matlock, L.A. Law* and *Amen.* Its 1984 megahit, *The Cosby Show,* sometimes soared above a 50 share, meaning half of all homes watching TV were tuned to Cosby. And their shows captured the loyalty of younger, particularly female viewers, who advertisers believed did the shopping and were not, like many older viewers, already wedded to Crest toothpaste or Campbell's soup. For all these reasons and more, Tinker felt stability was the key to success. But Welch's totem was change, not stability. Welch chose, however, not to confront Tinker on this point, telling him he would think more about succession and that they would talk again.

Before Welch could think about succession, he had first to think about the possibility of losing Brandon Tartikoff, the programmer whom Tinker credited with NBC's thrust into first place. Welch had not had a personal conversation with Tartikoff, and Tinker, who shied from such conversations, had not talked with Tartikoff about his future either. Beginning in late January, Hollywood began manufacturing rumors. Rona Barrett reported that Tartikoff was being wooed by Twentieth Century Fox. Columbia Pictures, owned by Coca-Cola, actually did pursue him, as did Michael Eisner of Disney and Ted Turner, and these stories got around. Each promised to make Tartikoff rich.

Brandon Tartikoff had always been well off; he had never been rich, but he had grown up comfortably in an upper middle-income neighborhood in Freeport, Long Island. His father manufactured boys' clothing, and his mother had gone back to work organizing author's luncheons for *Newsday* when Brandon and his sister were of school age. At age twelve, he was one of 17 Jews among 650 gentiles attending the exclusive Lawrenceville School in New Jersey, where he was the state fencing champion in 1966. Next came Yale, where he was officially an English major but liked to say he "majored in girls." After graduation he struggled in the advertising business, tried and failed to sell a novella to *Esquire* magazine, and bounced from the sales department at a New Haven TV station to a job as director of advertising and promotion at Chicago's WLS-TV, an ABC-owned station. There his zany promotion campaigns caught the eye of Fred Silverman, then ABC's chief programmer.

Tartikoff suffered a setback when it was discovered that he had Hodgkin's disease, a usually fatal form of cancer. After having his spleen removed, he was subjected to taxing chemotherapy treatments. Then, miraculously, the disease went into remission in 1974, allowing Tartikoff to join Silverman at ABC as a programmer. Little more than a decade later, Tartikoff was the most successful programmer on television. But he earned only about $400,000 a year in salary and bonuses at NBC, paltry by Hollywood standards.

But Tartikoff also loved his work, thrived on the daily competition, the game of counterprogramming shows with appeal to women on nights when competitors ran male-oriented action-adventure shows or *Monday Night Football,* loved devising promotional pitches to lure viewers, waking up to check the Nielsen overnight ratings, courting talent like Steven Bochco, doctoring a script, sitting in casting sessions, watching Bill Cosby's monologue on Johnny Carson one night and later buying a series that billowed into *The Cosby Show,* the biggest hit that year on his or any other network. Two qualities set Brandon Tartikoff apart from most other network programmers over the years. First, he loved television. When he was in first grade, Brandon and some friends went around imitating TV westerns. "We'd disrupt class to play out scenes, picking up chairs and hitting people over the head with them—except, unlike on TV, the chairs didn't break, the kids did." As punishment he was not permitted to watch television in the months between first and second grades, which he calls his "dark period." Tartikoff believed that to be a successful programmer you had to be a fan.

Personality was the second key to Tartikoff's success. To those above him, Tartikoff was always perceived as "the good son"—sincere, loyal, humble, talented. He could defuse criticism with a quip. Once at a Hollywood Radio and Television Society luncheon he was asked about the smothering ways of Tinker's predecessor, NBC president Fred Silverman: "Is it true that no one at NBC makes a decision without checking with Silverman?"

"Could I get back to you on that?" Tartikoff instantly replied.

Talent gravitated to Tartikoff not just because he was smart but because he was fun. "He's a great creative executive. He challenges people," said Jeffrey Katzenberg, chairman of the Walt Disney Studios. "He has a wonderful sense of humor. When I look at my schedule and see that I have a meal with Brandon Tartikoff, I look forward to it. I don't have to think of things to say."

There was reason for Tartikoff to stay at NBC: his gratitude to Grant Tinker. Tartikoff remembered how Tinker stood by him not just when NBC remained mired in third place but in another, more important way. The year Tartikoff introduced nine new shows and nine flopped —1983—was also the year Tartikoff's Hodgkin's disease flared again. He tried to keep it secret, telling no one outside his family, his secretary, Barbara Barry, and Tinker. He hoped no one in the office would notice his condition, even though his Friday chemotherapy treatments left sores on his face and destroyed his long, wavy brown hair so that he had to wear a strange wig. Tartikoff stopped coming to the office only when Tinker ordered him to, insisting that his job was safe and his only concern should be his health.

Yet as much as he loved his job and was grateful to Tinker, Tartikoff was "dispirited" in the spring of 1986, said his friend Jeffrey Sagansky, who was Tartikoff's deputy from 1983 to 1985, and was so close to him that just before Sagansky's wedding Tartikoff took two full days off to prepare a This-Is-Your-Life bachelor-party video. Sagansky, who was now a motion picture executive, knew Tartikoff was nervous about whether GE would wait for a show like *Hill Street Blues* to find an audience. More important, Tartikoff was hurt. He didn't understand why Jack Welch didn't call, or why Tinker didn't discuss either his own departure plans or Tartikoff's future. For all his ease and grace, there was something distant about Tinker. Though he bucked them up in 1983, Tinker could be like a withholding parent. He did not lather NBC West Coast executives with compliments. When his four children were between ages two and nine, Tinker left his Darien, Connecticut, home and went west, missing much of their youth. Before he joined NBC in 1981, Tinker tended to let talented people leave his employ, never asking them to stay. When he and his second wife, Mary Tyler Moore, owned MTM Enterprises, both James Brooks and Ed Weinberger exited after their brilliant work on *The Mary Tyler Moore Show* and *Rhoda;* so did Gary David Goldberg, who worked on *Lou Grant.*

The nonchalance that was so attractive in Tinker could also be maddening. Among the few complaints from those who worked with Tinker at NBC—aside from the fact that he was "anal," insisting on returning every call, every letter, plotting every hour of vacation time —was that in Burbank, as opposed to the New York office, he seldom fought to get raises for his people or to offer them secure contracts.

Tartikoff felt ignored by both Tinker and GE that spring. "I felt—he never articulated it—that Brandon was hurt," said his good friend Dick Ebersol, the former producer of *Saturday Night Live* who had been at Yale with Tartikoff and in 1977 lured him to NBC, where Ebersol was head of Comedy. "No one had talked to him." By late April, said Ebersol, who also talked regularly to Brandon's wife, Lilly, "He told me he couldn't wait any longer. I kept thinking: 'How could I get to Jack Welch?' I remembered that Don Ohlmeyer [former executive producer of NBC Sports and now head of his own production company] told me he once played golf with Jack Welch." Ebersol tracked Ohlmeyer down in California. "Look, Don," he said, "I think Brandon wants to stay in broadcasting, yet it's only days before he leaves. Anyway, can you reach Jack Welch and tell him?"

Ohlmeyer called Welch and asked, "Jack, what are you doing? You're ignoring Brandon. He's liable to be gone."

"What are you talking about? He's fine," Welch recalls saying.

"Look, he's my friend," said Ohlmeyer. "I know him. He doesn't understand why you're not talking to him. Why are you ignoring him? You better call him!"

Welch probably couldn't tell the difference between ALF and the Fonz, but he knew that the entertainment division drove NBC's profits. The network produced five thousand hours of programming every year. But the twenty-two hours a week that counted most were prime time, those three golden hours each night (four on Sunday) when the network charged up to $450,000 for a thirty-second commercial on a leading show. Prime time was where NBC made 50 percent of its profit, with another 25 percent coming from daytime television and the rest from Johnny Carson's *Tonight* show and its other successful late-night programming. NBC Sports, which also populated the network schedule, made no money because the license fees paid to televise events had burgeoned. And NBC News lost money, even though individual programs such as the *Today* show were profitable.

Jack Welch was in the habit of selling businesses that made little money or trailed their competitors. As in the movie or record or book publishing business, Welch could see that the network business had become a business of hits. As audiences fled to cable, independent stations, and VCRs, the marginal shows no longer commanded top advertising dollars. Only the hits did. The license fees the networks paid the studios averaged about $475,000 for each half hour and about $850,000 for each hour drama. The studios paid the difference, gambling that their deficits would be recouped if the series remained on the air for at least four years so they could sell syndication rights. That's how the studios made their television money. The networks made theirs through a similar gamble. Of the top seventy-five rated network shows, the networks lost money on the bottom third, broke even on shows ranked in the middle, and made a bundle on the top twenty-five rated shows—where advertising revenues were from three to six times the license fee they paid the studios. And by the spring of 1986, NBC under Tinker and Tartikoff had ten shows in the top twenty-five.

No wonder Welch ignored the chain of command and telephoned Tartikoff that day—that hour! He asked if they could have dinner one night soon in New York. When the fall schedule was set in a few weeks, said Tartikoff, he would come to New York.

"Ohlmeyer did me an incredible favor," Welch said later. In his discussions with Tinker, said Welch, "It was sort of implied that everything was fine with Brandon. It was sort of an unsaid sort of thing." Tinker's explanation is that he believed Tartikoff wanted to stay at NBC. Although Tartikoff told him his phone was ringing off the hook, Tinker said he knew "Brandon looked forward to being out there in the sun alone. It was only human that he wanted to get the credit he well deserved."

The dinner was set for May, and in the intervening few weeks Lilly Tartikoff was skeptical. A perky former New York City Ballet dancer, she had sacrificed her career for family and her husband. She felt Brandon was unappreciated, and wanted him to leave. She was tired, she told reporter Lynn Hirschberg, of the way Brandon had been ignored, sick of the NBC peacocks on her towels. She told Brandon: "If you don't fall in love with this guy at dinner, you should leave."

Welch and Tartikoff met for dinner on May 12 at Primavera on Manhattan's Upper East Side, the same night NBC was offering a three-hour special with Bob Hope and more than one hundred celebrities to commemorate its sixtieth anniversary. In Tartikoff, Welch met his match as a psychological gamesman. No sooner were they seated in the expensive brick-walled restaurant than Tartikoff said, "Can I ask you a question?"

"Sure."

"I deal with a lot of characters. Before I came over here I read your research file. How'd you get a name like 'Neutron Jack?' "

Tartikoff had pressed the right button. At first Welch had hated the label, but now it had taken on almost "mythic proportions." "I think by asking him that question right out it put him at ease," said Tartikoff.

Over dinner they discovered that each was a baseball fan, that Welch was a walking encyclopedia on Bobby Doerr, and that Tartikoff, if he could come back in another life, would want to be Kansas City Royals third baseman George Brett. As Welch had to be a brawler to compete with more graceful athletes in hockey, so Tartikoff, as a Jew educated at a private prep school, had learned that "humor became a pretty good defense mechanism." As Welch had once quit GE over an issue of principle, so Tartikoff had rebelled against the Yale fencing coach, sacrificing a promising NCAA future rather than compete for an "incompetent" coach.

Welch could almost feel as if Brandon were his enterprising son as he listened to how Brandon missed his graduation ceremony from Yale because he was making "a fortune" as a Greyhound Tour guide—cracking jokes, playing games on the bus—and how he stayed in New Haven with the four thousand dollars he had earned for the summer. Brandon's girlfriend was a junior and he lived with her and four female roommates in a dormitory suite, going to the library each morning to read a book a day, to the gym in the afternoon to play basketball and take a steam bath, and to the Yale Film Society each night, where he paid a dollar to watch a film classic. A year later, he said, "I was getting tired of people saying to me, 'What are you doing?' " So he took a job for sixty-three dollars a week at a New Haven ad agency. He got the job because the guy who hired him was enthralled that he was living with five girls and hoped to meet one of them. Tartikoff recounted his career up until 1978, when he joined NBC as director of Comedy Development.

Halfway through dinner Welch leaned forward in his intimate way and asked, "What's going through your head?"

"I'm still excited about my job," said Tartikoff, who explained that after NBC's dry years, after surviving RCA and his mentor Fred Silverman's tumultuous regime from 1978 to 1981, he liked being number one. But he also thought about his family, and the long hours he worked, and the millions that beckoned from the Hollywood studios. He thought about the burnout factor after doing a job for six years, as he had. He had survived Hodgkin's disease twice. Maybe it was time to relax a bit, enjoy the sunshine.

Welch was not distracted. He asked about Tartikoff's frustrations. "I don't want to be Peter Pan," responded Tartikoff.

"What does that mean?" said Welch.

"I don't want to start every season by having to find new kids. I'd like to set up a system where I can keep some people and get some continuity here. We're now number one. And I want to be able to hold on to some people who might eventually be my replacement."

"No problem," said Welch. "Identify five or six key players, and it's done." He would be able to offer contracts, stock options, incentives. And not just to them, said Welch. *Stay and you can have a fat three-year contract. You can have stock options and bonuses. You can have the kind of contract to match what the studios are offering.*

"Do you have any interest now or in the future in Tinker's job?" Welch asked.

"No, it would be the worst use of me," replied Tartikoff, who interpreted the question as a potential offer. His interest was in the creative side of the business, not in managing, not in flow charts or cost-control meetings.

What other frustrations do you have? asked Welch.

I'd love for NBC to produce more movies, produce more of its own series. There's not one entertainment show on the air that NBC produces. If NBC produced more, it would keep Tartikoff's adrenaline pumping. Equally vital, it would enhance NBC's leverage with the Hollywood community.

Welch was turned on. He loved the idea of gaining leverage over competitors. Constantly he admonished subordinates: *Control your destiny.* If there were a way to institutionalize NBC's success, to branch out and become a powerful studio as well, NBC could reign forever. Something else excited the GE chairman: He saw himself in the boyish Tartikoff. Like Tartikoff, Welch had built something from ground level—GE's plastics business. Plastics was a $28-million-a-year company when Jack Welch, a young engineer, was put in charge; it was a $1 billion company in 1977 when he left. In the beginning he felt much as Tartikoff and his Burbank team did toward RCA: that no one cared about them at corporate headquarters. So at the end of year one, when they gave him a standard $1,000 raise on a $10,500 salary, Welch quit. His wife was pregnant, but he was off to Chicago for a job as a chemical engineer. A few days before he was to start, GE induced him back with more responsibility, more money. And, said Welch, "Someone told me they loved me." Now Welch, figuratively, told Tartikoff that he loved him. "I think we became very fond of each other that night. We just got along," said Welch.

Tartikoff saw in Welch the same competitiveness, the same compulsion to win, that he himself felt. Although NBC had just moved into first place, already Tartikoff felt some pressure from Brandon Stoddard, his counterpart at ABC. Despite ABC's third-place showing in the 1985–86 season, by early 1986 Tartikoff worried that Stoddard had the authority from his Cap Cities bosses and the taste to chase NBC in pursuit of quality, urban-oriented shows. As NBC's schedule filled with successful series, Tartikoff worried that talent would flock to a network offering more on-air openings. CBS, he believed, was tired, saddled with aging shows. But he worried about Stoddard, who had been his boss at ABC in the seventies. Finally, though Tartikoff was genuinely saddened that Tinker would leave, he was also exhilarated by the challenge of succeeding on his own. After a lifetime of operating in the shadow of mentors—Michael Eisner at ABC, Fred Silverman at both ABC and NBC, and Tinker—he would now rise or fall on his own.

At the end of dinner, Welch was convinced he had Tartikoff on the hook. They agreed to talk some more, and get down to the specifics of a contract next time they met. "I have only one request," said Welch. "I don't want to deal with attorneys. I want to deal with you." No problem, said Tartikoff.

During their dinner, NBC's sixtieth anniversary celebration easily won the Nielsen ratings race for the night, just as Welch had won over Tartikoff. When he returned to their New York apartment, Lilly Tartikoff spotted the look in her husband's eyes. "You're in love. I can't believe it!" she remembers saying.

"He's like me," Tartikoff reported. "He loves to win." Tartikoff wanted to stay, and now had to decide what he wanted in a new contract. He consulted Tinker and then, without lawyers, got Welch to double his salary and bonus to about $800,000 a year for three years, to give him more GE stock, and to sweeten his stock options, which promised to earn him from $500,000 to $1.5 million annually. Tartikoff also retained a couple of series commitments so that if he left

NBC he would be guaranteed work as a producer. It was the most sumptuous contract a network programming chief had ever enjoyed.

The announcement of Tartikoff's agreement was made in Maui, at the annual affiliates meeting in June, and for the two-hundred-odd NBC affiliated stations it took some of the sting from the news that Tinker would leave by summer's end. The affiliates, delighted with the revenues that accompany first place and the programs that entice viewers to leave their dials on one channel, treated the convention as a celebration.

One of the few jarring notes at the conference had been the sight of News president Larry Grossman entering a meeting wearing a colorful dashiki and a pair of wing-tipped shoes. Around this time, Grossman became the topic of a breakfast discussion among Tinker, Welch, and Thornton Bradshaw. The purpose of breakfast was to discuss succession, and this time Tinker unveiled his own plan. There were four possible internal candidates, he said—Raymond J. Timothy, who oversaw Sales, Affiliate Relations, Business Affairs, and, on paper, Entertainment; Robert Butler, who was chief financial officer and supervised some staff functions; Robert S. Walsh, to whom the owned stations, Sports, and Radio reported; and Larry Grossman. Tinker surprised Welch and Bradshaw with his recommendation:

What makes the most sense is to have a chairman as Mr. Outside. This person should be articulate, someone who could speak to the various publics NBC has to reach—viewers, regulators in Washington, press overseers, affiliates, advertisers. The chairman should be the CEO, and should be supplemented by an effective manager who would operate as Mr. Inside. We have four good men to choose from, but my choices would be Grossman as CEO and Timothy as chief operating officer.

Tinker admired the abilities of both men, but he came down on the side of Grossman because, explained a close associate, he saw Timothy, fifty-four, as a more remote figure, someone who was not as good with people. Unlike Tinker, he did not much venture from his office. Timothy had been at NBC his entire career, from the day he started work there as a page in 1954, rising through the accounting, production coordination, sales, station management, and affiliate relations departments. Timothy was respected by the broadcasting community. And he was a believer in the networks, much the way Gene Jankowski of CBS was, thinking it was "a miracle we have as much audience as we have." But Ray Timothy was not a visionary.

Unlike Timothy, Grossman, fifty-five, had not spent his entire career at NBC. His only prior journalistic experience, in fact, had been on his Brooklyn high school newspaper and at Columbia University's *Spectator,* where his colleagues included such lifelong friends as ABC's Roone Arledge and Richard Wald and *New York Times* executive editor Max Frankel. But under Larry Grossman, NBC News was on a roll. Not since Huntley and Brinkley said their last goodnight in 1970, had NBC News taken the lead. By the summer of 1986, Tom Brokaw's *Nightly News* often captured first place; the *Today* show—with a boost from splashy week-long visits to various locales, including a trip to Rome where Grossman's deputy, Tim Russert, managed to snag the pope to play host during Easter Week—had edged ahead of ABC's *Good Morning America;* they had just launched a magazine show —*1986*—hosted by Roger Mudd and Connie Chung, which they hoped might generate if not the kind of profits enjoyed by *60 Minutes* (about $60 million) then maybe those of ABC's *20/20* ($20 million). It was Grossman who pushed the network to enter into negotiations (which collapsed) to acquire a 50-percent interest in CNN, Grossman who linked affiliated stations by investing in a Skycom satellite system permitting stations to exchange live signals from remote locations, Grossman who proposed to replace the thirty-minute nightly newscast with a ninety-minute "newswheel," with the network integrating packages of national and international news with local news.

"I'll see these guys," Welch said after Tinker had made his case. "But if you're not going to be here I may want someone whom I have worked with and whom I know."

Welch was being polite, for he had already made a decision. Soon after Tinker told him in March of his firm intention to leave, Welch began talking to his own candidate—Bob Wright, president of GE Financial Services, a lending and deal-making company whose assets Wright had doubled in three years. Wright was a rising star at GE. Like Welch, he came from a Catholic household (in Hempstead, Long Island), and his father, like Welch, was trained as an engineer. The similarities between the two men were striking. Like Welch, Wright was an only son born when his mother was about forty, he did not go to an Ivy League College (Holy Cross), had made GE his career, had just a wisp of hair on top of his head, and didn't watch much television. Wright had worked his way up at GE, starting as a corporate lawyer, moving to various staff positions, and then rising to become general manager of the Plastics Sales Organization and later vice president and general manager of the housewares and audio electronics divisions, part of which he sold to Black & Decker. Wright had been employed by GE all his adult life, with two brief exceptions: He left for thirteen months in 1971 to serve as a twelve-thousand-dollar-a-year chief clerk for chief federal judge Lawrence A. Whipple of the U.S. District Court in New Jersey; and for a brief period beginning in 1980 he joined Cox Communications as executive vice president of their cable operations at a time when GE hoped to acquire Cox.

In May, Welch had quietly asked Thornton Bradshaw to meet Wright. Wright was a deal-maker, which Welch thought was important. He was more alarmed than either Tom Murphy or Larry Tisch about the future of the networks. Despite record NBC profits, Jack Welch fretted. It was his nature.

Bradshaw and Wright lunched at the Century Club, and Bradshaw came away a believer. "I thought he was a hell of a smart fellow," recalled Bradshaw. "I thought if we couldn't keep Grant here, this guy would be quite terrific. Besides, Grant had been brought in for one type of franchise—to get NBC off the floor and to get it to second place—we didn't even think of being number one. He did that, plus 100 percent. But that is a limited franchise in today's world. By the time Grant was ready to leave, the agenda had changed to: How do we adapt NBC to the new world of television and position NBC for the future? I don't want to say Grant couldn't do that, because I believe he could. But that wasn't his franchise."

Larry Grossman lunched with Welch on June 19 at GE's New York offices at 570 Lexington Avenue. Grossman admits he would have accepted Tinker's job if offered but did not lobby for it. What he did lobby for was for Welch to follow Tinker's advice and select someone from within NBC. Welch said he was thinking of bringing in someone he knew, someone he could talk to in shorthand. Grossman left convinced Welch would do as he pleased.

The three other candidates whom Tinker had advanced visited Welch on June 26—Bob Walsh in the morning, Ray Timothy for lunch, and Bob Butler at 3 P.M. "He knew a lot about me," recalls Walsh, an affable, popular executive who like Timothy had spent his entire career at NBC.

But from the outset, Welch made it clear that he had someone else in mind. Walsh raised the question of security—his own. "Welch indicated he wanted me to stay." A piece of paper came across the desk and Bob Walsh reached for it. On it were the number of shares of GE stock that were to be his and the stock options he would be granted. "It was very generous," said Walsh, who was mollified.

Ray Timothy was the most aggressive in pitching himself for the job, even asking to come back and see Welch a second time, which he did at GE's Fairfield headquarters on July 10. Welch awarded Timothy a generous stock plan, insisted he was an important player at NBC, but confided that he wanted his own man.

Welch was rougher with Bob Butler, who like Grossman had worked in various places before coming to NBC. Welch from the first treated Butler with contempt. The NBC executive recalled Welch's opening haymaker: "We've evaluated all you guys. You've come in fourth out of four. As of this point, I'm 90 percent certain I'm going to go with one of my guys. I'll give you the book on you: You're very thorough, competent, with impeccable integrity. And I want you to stay. But I got a hundred guys like you." Butler left knowing his days might be numbered.

By the time of these meetings, Welch knew both what he wanted and didn't want. He liked the four candidates well enough, he said. But he gave them little credit for NBC's resurgence—that credit belonged to Tinker and Tartikoff and their team in Burbank. And Welch did not think that any of the four men shared his sense of alarm over the future of the networks. He saw the NBC four as too appreciative of the distance NBC had traveled and not aware enough of the distance yet to go. Bob Wright, like Welch, was obsessed with the thought that "the clock is running and time is your enemy," that the network was fragile. Wright, he thought, was more attuned to the new video marketplace, a place where advertisers had other options and customers could purchase TV sets capable of reaching 150 different broadcast or cable channels. Wright, Welch said, "was far more qualified . . . to look at tomorrow than those inside the company."

That summer Welch and Wright were busy digesting a company they had acquired for $600 million in April—the Wall Street investment banking and brokerage firm of Kidder, Peabody & Company. Nevertheless, Welch told Wright he wanted to proceed quickly at NBC. To prepare the way, he said he was lending to NBC one of his bright M.B.A. types—J. B. Holston III—thus placing a set of GE eyes and ears smack in the middle of executive row at 30 Rock. It was as if Holston were parachuted behind enemy lines, but with a pass. Few welcomed him. To NBC employees, Holston's corporate career fit a yuppie stereotype—first the M.B.A., followed by the Boston Consulting Group, mergers and acquisitions for Salomon Brothers, and GE's strategic planning department. And yet Holston's background and manner belied the stereotype. He was born twenty-six years earlier in Fort Wayne, Indiana, went to public schools, spoke in a flat, barely audible voice, wore old-fashioned rimless round eyeglasses, a beard, and had unruly, thinning hair. Holston's task was to scout ahead for Wright, and to prepare a confidential memorandum outlining the issues the new CEO would confront when he arrived.

Meanwhile, Welch reported to Tinker that he had found his candidates wanting. Would Tinker, he now asked, dine with Bob Wright?

In early August, the GE helicopter ferried Tinker to Fairfield, where Bob and Suzanne Wright lived in a colonial-style house. Tinker noticed that Wright was conservative, a man described by his wife as "a stand-back kind of guy." Suzanne Wright, on the other hand, was a vivacious forty-year-old mother of three, who flipped her glasses on top of short, blonde hair and still spoke with the accent of her native Queens. The visit began with a drink outdoors on a vast, rolling lawn which yielded a sweeping view of the Fairfield Country Club and, beyond that, of Long Island Sound. As night fell they retreated to the dining room, where they ate lobsters. The dinner was strictly social, heavy on talk about family. They talked about how Suzanne Wright was the daughter of a Queens detective, how she and Wright met after her family moved to West Hempstead, where they attended the same Catholic church, how she dropped out of junior college to marry when she was twenty, living at first with his parents while he attended the University of Virginia law school.

Afterward, when Wright drove Tinker back to the helicopter, the ever courtly Tinker looked at the man who might replace him and said, "You've probably heard from Jack you're not my candidate. The job can be done well from within. That's not a personal comment on you." Tinker's attitude, Wright remembers, was that the networks "were a very in-house business and the reaction to a person from GE would be difficult. There would be a lot of suspicion and distrust. 'Why do you need that?' "

Wright appreciated the candor, but had already told Welch he would accept the job, would go down to New York and imbue NBC with a willingness to accept change. Wright was a believer in what he calls GE's "get-on-with-it culture." He found Tinker's view of NBC as an "in-house business" insular. It clashed not only with Wright's business philosophy, but with his self-concept. "My ability to deal in a successful environment is what I bring," Wright said of himself. "I have an appreciation for risk taking and understand the role people play. I'm also a flexible person."

Tinker came back to New York and told several glum associates: *I think Jack Welch has chosen a fella named Wright. We had dinner and he and his wife seemed like terrific people.* An explanation for Tinker's gloss might be that he desperately wanted to escape NBC, the suit and the ties, and return to California, where he could slip on his loafers, drive to work in his blue Mercedes convertible, and dine with his friend, Melanie Burke, an attractive woman in her early thirties. Tinker wanted to think well of Wright, wanted to reassure himself he was leaving the company in good hands. He would later tell friends that Wright was bright but he feared he was totally a creature of Jack Welch.

Wright and Welch certainly thought alike. And what Wright thought that August would have been considered blasphemous by Tinker and his colleagues who had been together in the lean days before NBC reached first place. The first NBC briefing Wright would receive came not from Tinker or Timothy or Grossman or Walsh or Rukeyser or Butler but from the GE whiz kid, J. B. Holston. Lugging a thick memorandum and charts, Holston briefed Wright on August 7. "He was trying to understand what type of business this was," said Holston. "He was looking for analogies to other businesses." One analogy Wright made was to compare the network to a "department store model." As the television business became "more fragmented and segmented" the network would have to branch out and add to its "wholesale" network such "retail" functions as cable, he said. It was a way of guarding against the cyclical nature of the network business, a way of opening another front, tapping another revenue stream.

Wright's appointment as NBC president was announced by Jack Welch on August 26, in NBC Studio 8G. Beside the regal Tinker, his forty-three-year-old successor appeared boyish, the more so because of his bright blue polka-dot tie, the shine on his high forehead, and the way he fidgeted with his hands and kept his eyes glued to notecards. Tinker ad-libbed his opening lines: "We want to share some happy news with you," and then introduced Welch as "a friend . . . I'm delighted by the way he thinks." Tinker was not displeased when it was announced that Welch himself would serve as NBC chairman, as he served as chairman of two other GE subsidiaries, Major Appliances and Medical Systems. Since he privately believed Welch would dominate Wright, Tinker wanted the relationship out in the open.

Welch, in a dark gray suit and bright red tie, returned Tinker's compliment, saying "we would have loved him to stay" and thanked Tinker "for putting together the team that made NBC the number-one network." NBC's new chairman noted that GE had been in the broadcasting business for sixty years, starting with RCA and a station in Schenectady, New York, and in all that time there was never an instant of GE "meddling" in news. He repeated the word "independence" several times, soothing Tinker and the NBC contingent, who sifted his every word for clues to GE's true attitude. They were pleased to hear Welch say he selected Wright because he was "someone accustomed to independence," someone who understood "independence was important . . . and it's been a key issue raised regarding NBC and its operating relationship to GE." No reason to fear, for News would not be expected "to show a profit." Every important GE division, Welch said, was "fiercely independent and that independence is encouraged."

Many at NBC chose not to hear that Welch was saying NBC would be treated like any GE division, that it did not have a special place. The words "public trust" were never uttered. They heard that News was not expected to earn a profit, but they didn't hear whether the news division's losses of $50 million to $100 million (depending on how the accounting was done) were acceptable. Similarly, only in time did it become apparent that when he introduced Wright the GE chairman laid out two contradictory objectives. "What Bob did at GE Financial Services," Welch said, "is remarkably similar to what we are asking him to do at NBC. He took a dynamic, rapidly changing business in General Electric and increased its growth rate and broadened its base through acquisitions, partnerships, team building, and creative, futuristic thinking." In other words, he changed things. Wright's second mission, said Welch, was a more conservative one—"to work with the outstanding team now in place at NBC" in order to build for the nineties. That second message was the one heard by the NBC executives seeking reassurance. They beamed as Wright, following his script, heaped praise on Tinker, spoke humbly of the "intimidating aspects" of "assuming responsibility for one American institution—NBC—and I'm attempting to succeed another American institution—Grant Tinker." Of Tinker's organization, he said: "I will stay with a winning team."

The press conference which followed was bland, except for four statements which proved untrue. First, Tinker put his imprimatur on his successor. "I am absolutely comfortable with the selection of Bob Wright," he declared. (He wasn't.) Second, Tinker predicted that since NBC pared costs five years before when it had been in third place, cost cutting was "not something he'll have to deal with" (which proved to be wrong). Third, Jack Welch said, "We find the characterization of the management at NBC very similar to GE. They drink beer, we drink beer. . . . We feel very comfortable with that team." (Untrue; from day one Welch was uncomfortable with the extra layer of senior vice presidents and one vice chairman.) Finally, Wright declared, "My job as I see it is not to fix or rebuild NBC," but to maintain its momentum (which was only half true).

Out of camera range, Wright was less humble. Leaving the press conference, he accompanied Tinker to a meeting of the chairman's council, now to be called the president's council. A creation of Tinker in his desire for collegiality, the council, which consisted of NBC's nine top executives, met once a week in Tinker's sixth-floor conference room. For this meeting, roughly thirty-five additional executives were invited. Wright was introduced by Tinker, who quickly receded into the shadows.

The new NBC president had thought about what he would say. "I was trying very early on to address what I considered to be the concerns of people who wanted to know as much about me and my thought process as possible," Wright recalls. "So I tried to cover seventy-five to one hundred areas. I was trying to pre-answer and anticipate questions before they were asked." Wright's one-and-a-half-hour speech rivaled one of Fidel Castro's. The monologue, which Wright delivered while he was seated at the head of the large rosewood conference table, undermined much of the public reassurance he had offered at the press conference.

His audience of NBC executives was shaken. "Instead of coming in and saying, 'I'm thrilled to be here. The company is doing great. I don't know a lot about network television, but you're going to teach me,' he came in from day one telling us about the business," recalls Bud Rukeyser. Wright did not chant the traditional network mantra, which was the reason people like Rukeyser liked to think they came to work each day—"The networks are a special business and 'maximizing profits' is not why we're all here." Wright paid no homage to the past.

Although NBC would earn record profits, Wright emphasized that the network business was "fragile" and predicted flat advertising revenues for the next year or so. To maintain profit margins they would have to cut costs. Wright believed the networks had often been guilty of narrow thinking, of tolerating federal restrictions that limited their profitability, including the ban on the networks owning cable systems or sharing in syndication profits. They—*YOU—had failed to curb program costs. YOU failed to cut the compensation paid to affiliated stations.*

YOU failed to staunch audience erosion. YOU failed to diversify. YOU failed to block the rise of a rival cable business the networks might have owned. In short, the networks had sinned by resisting change.

Wright stressed one other point—his authority. "One thing I remember is a veiled threat," recalls another senior executive. " 'If I don't succeed, none of you will succeed. I never want to hear of any of you withholding information.' He was saying, 'I am in charge and don't you ever forget it. This is the way *I* operate. These are *my* feelings.' " To some, Wright sounded like the killer in NBC's prime-time movie that very night, *Arizona Ripper.* Bob Walsh also heard the veiled threat, the lack of humility. "He was quickly trying to establish he was boss. No one was unwilling to accept that. Though the style was so contrasting to Tinker's it probably shocked people."

It certainly shocked Tinker. In his understated way the outgoing chairman described the speech this way: "I remember that it was more complete than I thought it ought to be." Tinker, like others, left the conference disheartened, more concerned than ever that the new order viewed the network as just another business, merely a way to sell advertising, not a public calling.

5

ABC: THE CLASH OF CULTURES, 1985 TO SUMMER 1986

One day late in January 1986, at the first management retreat after Capital Cities officially took control of ABC, David Burke found himself on his feet, clapping. He looked down at his hands and willed them to stop. "Christ, what the hell am I doing?" the vice president and assistant to the president of ABC News remembers thinking. A formal man, one who describes himself as "serious" and looks the part in his starched white shirts with gold cufflinks, round tortoiseshell glasses, and neatly trimmed sandy hair, David Burke hated feeling like an Amway salesman. He glanced about and saw 160 or so people, including maybe 80 executives from the old ABC, hollering like cheerleaders.

Officials of the two companies were meeting in the desert, and when David Burke looked up at the stage of the Arizona Biltmore in Phoenix he saw Tom Murphy, the lanky, avuncular chairman of the merged companies, winking at familiar friends. "He was like a politician playing to his old constituency," remembers Burke, who thought that Murphy was trying to reassure the folks from Cap Cities.

"Stand up and give them a round of applause," Murphy urged everyone, especially, Burke felt, the folks from ABC.

So Burke, like everyone else, jumped up and, a moment later, felt miserable.

For those who knew him, it was no surprise that David Burke would feel uncomfortable. One of five children in a working-class Catholic family from Brookline, Massachusetts, Burke was much like his father, a Brookline cop who did not get along with the chief of police. Rather than bend, his father paid the price by pounding a night beat. His father's convictions were reinforced by his mother, a "tough as nails," very "unforgiving" housewife, recalls her son. After graduation from Tufts University, David Burke set out to change the world, to become another Walter Reuther. He went to work at a Lever Brothers factory where he hoped to organize employees. But the plant closed, and Burke wound up at the University of Chicago. Under the tutelage of professor (and later, secretary of state) George Shultz, he completed an M.B.A. degree in economics.

Like Tom Murphy, David Burke loved politics. But unlike the Cap Cities chairman, who had declined a postmaster appointment, Burke spent most of his adult years in public service. Moved by John F. Kennedy, he joined the Commerce Department, rising rapidly there and then at the Labor Department. He became a legislative assistant to freshman senator Edward Kennedy, and was his chief of staff from 1967 to 1970. In the early seventies, Burke made some money with the Dreyfus Corporation, but he still burned to change the world and when asked in 1974 to become secretary to incoming New York governor Hugh Carey, he accepted. The high-minded Burke found dealing with the deal-minded state legislature seamy, and came to be thought of as an unbending "Headmaster," a moniker that would stick.

Burke's eagerness to escape Albany coincided with Roone Arledge's longing for an administrator to manage the news division he had just been appointed to run. The match was made in 1977, and together Arledge and Burke shaped ABC News into the equal of CBS or NBC. Burke was known around News as tough, the exacting taskmaster that the mercurial Arledge required. As a manager, Burke shared many of Cap Cities' precepts, including a desire to confront the unions in order "to break the seniority system so we can get rid of incompetents." Yet, for all their similarities, David Burke did not identify with the new owners.

He was not alone. "Phoenix was the place the ABC guys began to realize what really happened," said Stephen A. Weiswasser, general counsel of Cap Cities/ABC. "They realized that Cap Cities was the senior partner, and the company would be run differently in the future." Indeed, the month of January had been one prolonged insult to many old ABC hands. They had endured dramatic management changes. They had been accused of suffering from "a limousine mentality." Their new corporate parent had threatened to unleash drug-sniffing dogs to nab miscreants. And Cap Cities kept pounding away at costs, costs, costs, as if revenues were secondary. So as David Burke looked up at Chairman Murphy and his mind raced over the first month of Cap Cities' rule, he remembers thinking: "It will never be the same again. The business is going to evermore be different, be managed, be cost-conscious. So the first thing that goes through your mind is: Would they listen to a creative idea? Or does it all have to be cost-perfect?"

The new order had arrived first at ABC, which had been acquired nine months before GE had announced it would take over NBC. In the two-thirds of a year since the merger had been announced in March, but before it was officially consummated on January 3, 1986, Cap Cities moved gingerly, following the advice of lawyers who cautioned Tom Murphy to lay back until the FCC formally approved the merger. Meanwhile Fred Pierce had a free hand in managing the company he had always aspired to run.

But by the fall, Tom Murphy and his chief operating officer, Dan Burke, were alarmed. ABC was in third place in both prime-time and evening news, and advertising revenues were collapsing. Murphy and Burke were astonished by the costs—by the license fees Roone Arledge's sports division had agreed to pay for baseball, football, and the 1988 Winter Olympics; by the mounting miniseries costs incurred by the entertainment division; by sprawling overhead costs that now topped $500 million annually. Although Fred Pierce had begun to cut corporate overhead, his passion was programming. He was not leading a frontal assault on what Murphy and Burke perceived to be the enemy, a complacent, even slothful corporate culture. "Tom was never enthusiastic about Fred," admitted Dan Burke, who nevertheless convinced Murphy that Pierce brought attributes they needed, including continuity and programming talents. A believer in his own motivational abilities, Burke persuaded Murphy he would make it work.

However, Burke remembers being shaken in November 1985 when Pierce—as he had done in August when announcing payroll reductions—took a major step without consulting, or even telling, Burke and Murphy. Unhappy with ABC Entertainment's performance, Pierce decided to remove his friend, Anthony D. Thomopoulos, as president of the Broadcast Group. Ever correct, Pierce said nothing to Cap Cities; it would be improper to consult them before the FCC blessed the merger, he said. To Murphy and Burke, his silence seemed stiff-necked, stubborn, a side of Pierce they had heard about. Pierce had never courted the ABC board, and played things close to the vest. "I think he felt it would be a diminution of his power if he opened up more," Thomopoulus had said. The Cap Cities culture encouraged openness, sharing information. And though Cap Cities believed in decentralized management, this worked, Murphy need not remind Dan Burke, only if Murphy and Burke had confidence in their managers.

Again without talking to Murphy or Burke, Pierce, with an assist from Leonard Goldenson, prevailed upon Brandon Stoddard, the well-regarded ABC programmer, to become ABC's Entertainment head. Although unhappy not to be consulted, Murphy and Burke had reasons to be pleased with the appointment. Stoddard was a star. Since joining ABC in 1970, he had enjoyed a string of successes—first in daytime, then children's programming, then drama, including motion pictures and novels for television. He had been president of ABC Motion Pictures since 1979, where he shone again. Stoddard was a man who brought stature to the network, who went home at night and read books, who was proudest of the serious shows he had launched—like the miniseries *Roots.* Despite his successes, Stoddard resisted taking the top job. This five-foot six-inch wisecracking man, with the voice of an announcer and an almost feline shyness that masked his intensity, hated being a salesman—selling the virtues of ABC programming at regular meetings with affiliates, selling to advertisers, selling to the TV press, selling to the Hollywood production community. Even after Stoddard had lured *Roots, The Thorn Birds,* and *The Winds of War,* the three most watched miniseries ever, to ABC, as well as quality movies such as *Silkwood,* he had turned down the job as late as 1983. When first Pierce then Goldenson approached him again in the fall of 1985, Stoddard was still reluctant. But he admired the two men, felt comfortable working in tandem with Pierce, felt that success in TV programming often resulted from pairs—Tartikoff teaming with Tinker at NBC, Fred Silverman bouncing ideas off Pierce at ABC, the earlier partnerships of Robert Daly and Bud Grant or Michael Dann and Jim Aubrey at CBS.

Stoddard could not refute Pierce's argument that they would make a good team. Nor could he deny that it would be a challenge. Before he would succumb, however, he insisted on meeting with ABC's new corporate owners. "I was nervous," said Stoddard. "I didn't know these guys. What happens to programming? What happens to ABC executives, particularly Fred?"

The setting for the early November summit was Tom Murphy's brownstone office at the Villard House, and it came during the same week ABC's blockbuster miniseries, *North and South,* would catapult ABC to a rare weekly ratings victory. As the fireplace roared and the maestro of that miniseries, Brandon Stoddard, cracked jokes, Murphy and Dan Burke were smitten by his self-deprecating wit, by the contrast between this leprechaun and the solemn Pierce, who said little. They liked Stoddard's irreverence toward Hollywood, which they took as a sign of his independence. They suspected that Stoddard also wanted to attack Hollywood's extravagance. The networks, they were convinced, were being taken to the cleaners by Hollywood and were victims of cost-plus contracts like those awarded defense contractors. Producers just passed along the extra bills to the networks, which obediently upped the studios' license fee.

The Cap Cities executives were careful not to air their Hollywood grievances this day. Except for one item on the agenda, this meeting was meant to reassure Stoddard. He was indeed reassured. Expecting to meet bean counters, he was impressed with Murphy and Burke's humility. Murphy made a point of noting, as he would many times in coming months, that he knew a lot about the station business but was "a freshman" when it came to programming, and he had no intention of getting involved in Entertainment decisions. Like Wright and Welch at NBC, or Tisch at CBS, Murphy said he watched news and sports on television. He hardly even watched entertainment—with at least one exception: "Anytime Clint Eastwood is on I watch him," he said.

Stoddard sought to measure the new owners' commitment to "quality" programming, and to do so he requested their approval for *War and Remembrance,* a miniseries he wanted to do. ABC had had great success with another Herman Wouk novel, *The Winds of War,* which was the third most-watched miniseries in history. The most watched—*Roots*—had attracted an astonishing 71 percent of the TV audience. Even with the steady erosion of network viewing and the recent failure of several miniseries, ABC's twelve-hour *North and South* would reach, over the course of this November week, an estimated 100 million viewers. With this success in mind, Stoddard and Pierce proposed to offer another epic, the kind of big-event programming only the networks could package and promote, the kind of program that transformed thousands of separate communities into one American community of viewers, each sharing the same experience. Cable couldn't do this, because it was in less than half of all homes and because on its best night a cable channel reached maybe 2 percent of all viewers. Independent TV stations couldn't do this, because they were local. Stoddard argued that because viewers had many more TV choices than when *Roots* aired a decade before, blockbuster miniseries became franchises that set the networks apart, platforms from which to promote other network shows, a way to bring viewers back to ABC.

The problem was the price tag. ABC had already agreed to pay $60 million for twenty hours, said Pierce. But the material was so rich that Stoddard was asking for thirty hours and an extra $30 million. Pierce pushed hard for a *go* decision, even though Goldenson had advised him the costs would escalate to $110 million and he should cut his losses. To scrap the project altogether would cost ABC $14 million. One other problem, said Pierce: Author Herman Wouk, an orthodox Jew, felt it would be in poor taste to juxtapose commercials for deodorant or feminine hygiene products opposite his gripping saga of the Holocaust and World War II. In all, Wouk's list of unacceptable advertisers ran five typewritten pages.

Whatever the complications or costs, Stoddard insisted the miniseries would be wonderful. A go-ahead would be a sign to Hollywood that ABC under its new owners would pay for quality, would be a player. If Murphy and Burke spurned a project he had poured two years of his life into, Stoddard hinted he would leave. "If we don't do *War and Remembrance,*" Murphy remembers Stoddard's words, "I have to think about whether I want to stay in the job."

Murphy's instinct was to say no. He was deeply offended that the network, in his words, too often "programmed for glory rather than profits." He believed people like Pierce and Stoddard were not running ABC like a business. But this isn't what he said; he was afraid to lose Stoddard. Nor did Murphy or Burke feel secure with their own programming expertise. So, violating every fiber of his lifelong commitment to cost containment, the Brooklyn pol surfaced and Murphy, in effect, said, "Okay, pal."

Fred Pierce announced the news of Stoddard's appointment on November 12, 1985. Two days later, another piece of news arrived when the FCC granted formal approval to the merger of ABC and Cap Cities. Less noticed was the FCC's approval of Rupert Murdoch's acquisition of six Metromedia TV stations, which meant Murdoch could now reach 22 percent of the country and, if linked as promised to his Twentieth Century Fox studios, could form the foundation for a fourth network. As insular as the new owners thought the old order was, they could be insular themselves, so caught up in getting ABC's costs under control that they too would overlook their new competitors.

It remained for ABC to set a date when the two companies would be formally merged. For various reasons, Cap Cities wanted to wait until the new year, and settled on January 3, 1986. But as the date approached, Cap Cities got a bad case of jitters, not without reason. The two companies had agreed to allow Cap Cities to walk away from the marriage if earnings at ABC fell by 25 percent or more from the prior year. Now, as the day neared, network ad revenues nosedived and ABC slipped deeper into third place. The monthly revenue projections supplied by ABC had remained rosy throughout much of 1985. Yet, suddenly, as 1985 was ending, these projections were downgraded weekly as revenues collapsed. "We kept changing the numbers as they went down," explained Pierce's deputy, Marc H. Cohen. "We just couldn't keep up. It was happening so fast." Another executive offered a more jaundiced explanation: "ABC was not totally candid in all the reports they gave Cap Cities, and held back some forecasts for fear they would back out of the deal." For the first time since tobacco advertising was banished from television in 1971, total network advertising dollars fell in 1985—by 10 percent at ABC alone. While revenues rose for the new ratings champion, NBC, they were in a free fall for CBS and ABC. Net income plunged 19 percent at ABC.

Cap Cities knew that the reasons for the falloff were complex. There was bound to be a drop, since 1984 had been a presidential election year, which meant abundant political advertising, and since ABC in 1984 had telecast the Winter Olympics in Sarajevo and the Summer Olympics in Los Angeles. As local broadcasters, they knew the television marketplace had changed. They knew that cable had more than tripled its audience in the past decade. They knew that in the same decade the number of independent TV stations had also tripled. They knew that daytime television had sputtered. And Cap Cities knew that with the average prime-time audience of the three networks down to 77 percent in 1985—a ten-point drop in just four years—they should not be surprised if advertiser dollars were chasing audiences elsewhere.

What did surprise and alarm Cap Cities was the way ABC handled adversity. First, it tried to duck the bad news. Then it seemed to panic—yanking Jackson Pollacks and Willem de Koonings from the walls and selling them to pad their bottom line. A crisis of confidence loomed. Pierce claimed he had saved $30 million in overhead, but Burke advised Murphy this was as much a fairy tale as ABC's inflated monthly revenue reports. As Cap Cities chief financial officer, Ronald Doerfler, burrowed deeply into ABC's books, he said he found the network had overvalued Sports and Entertainment revenues by $600 million. Thus even before the merger was consummated, Cap Cities would be required to write down the value of the two companies by $300 million after taxes. At the December meeting of the Cap Cities board, Doerfler advised, "We probably could get out of the deal if we wanted to." All they need do was delay the close until April 1. Do that and the earnings for the twelve preceding months would have dropped more than 25 percent.

But Murphy and Burke did not want to wait. As with Larry Tisch's decision to purchase CBS stock, more than dollars and cents were involved. These businessmen were being softened by emotion, by pride. Dan Burke concedes that the network now held "a fatal fascination." But what Burke and Murphy wanted was the security of knowing that their fragile investment was in the hands of a manager who recognized the crisis.

Fred Pierce acknowledged there were difficulties, but not a crisis. He pressed Cap Cities to look at the brighter side—at the rising profits from ABC's 80 percent ownership of ESPN, the all-sports cable channel which was inaugurated in 1979; at the steady cash flow from ABC's five owned TV stations. The drop in ad revenues was temporary, Pierce assured Murphy and Burke. He was grasping for good news. He had even secretly hired a Hollywood psychic. Beginning in 1978, Pierce placed Beverlee Dean on the payroll at $24,000 a year, consulting her in strictest confidence about what programs ABC should schedule, what scripts or actors might catch fire.

While Murphy and Burke did not know of the psychic until after the merger was announced, it didn't matter. By December, Pierce had exhausted their patience. "Fred was a hostage to his experience," said Dan Burke. So when Pierce suggested they enter an expensive bidding contest to acquire rights to the National Basketball Association games, Murphy and Burke flatly turned him down. Murphy recalls wanting to fire Pierce outright. If alarms were ringing at the network, he needed Dan Burke, his dimpled friend with the scowl, in charge. Burke did not disagree; but he also wanted to keep Pierce, whose vast experience he knew was valuable.

As often happened on managerial issues, Burke prevailed. In private, the two men agreed to retain Pierce—if Pierce accepted a lightened portfolio; they decided the owned stations division, Radio, and all cable and outside investments would report to Mike Mallardi, and that ABC's publishing ventures would report to John B. Sias who was president of Cap Cities' publishing division. Only the network itself would be left to Pierce. Should Pierce refuse, Murphy and Burke agreed their fall-back would be Sias, fifty-eight, who had run Publishing for them since 1974. John Sias, they thought, was a natural salesman. Before joining Cap Cities in 1971, he had been Television Group vice president at Metromedia from 1968 to 1970, and before that he ran Metromedia's television sales effort for six years. "We have tremendous confidence in him," said Burke. They also enjoyed him. They still laughed about the time this ramrod-straight former paratrooper hid a water pistol in his pocket and squirted employees at Fairchild Publications, which Cap Cities owned; or used a boat horn to call meetings to order. And John Sias was loyal. So loyal that when he was summoned by Burke in early December and told that Murphy might need him to run ABC, Sias didn't even tell his wife. In John Sias's professional life, Tom and Dan were family; Cap Cities was more than a job, it was a vocation. He told Burke he would be available if needed.

With a substitute in their pocket, Murphy and Burke invited Fred Pierce to their townhouse office during the third week of December. "You don't need a vice president in charge of welching, but that's my job now," Murphy began. The Cap Cities chairman explained that the network's headaches were so severe that he needed Pierce to give them his undivided attention.

"Well, that's not the understanding," Pierce responded stiffly. "It's a violation of the contractual obligation that runs through 1989, with responsibility clearly spelled out."

In his soothing Brooklyn pol manner, Murphy tried to explain why the network needed everyone in Pierce's chain of command to know he was there full time. Pierce took the suggestion as an affront. Cap Cities was proposing to renege on a commitment. "Fred gets very macho, and decides to stick out his jaw," explained Roone Arledge. Pierce wanted to say *no* on the spot. But another part of Pierce—the cautious, studied part that Cap Cities came to think of as bureaucratic and many at ABC thought of as canny—asserted itself. "It's your nickel," he told Murphy. "It's your ball game. You have the right to run it as you see fit. I'll give you my answer right after the holidays."

Pierce was going skiing in Snowmass, Colorado, but at this very moment he was ready to quit. "I sensed they would be more comfortable if I left," he recalls. "I was leaning toward leaving. But I didn't want to react viscerally."

For the next two weeks while Pierce skied, the attorneys discussed termination terms should he choose to leave. Meanwhile, John Sias recalls, "I was in limbo, and just put it out of my mind until Fred came back from his skiing vacation." He had not yet told his wife he might have a new job. Outwardly, Murphy was equally calm. Inwardly, for one of the few times in his business career, he remembers feeling insecure. "We were station operators," he explained. He remembered Goldenson's advice—"People who run the company have got to have a feeling for programming." Murphy was not sure he did, so he seesawed and now rooted for Pierce to stay. Without Pierce, Stoddard might leave. Stoddard was becoming Murphy's obsession—How to make him feel wanted? How to demonstrate that Cap Cities cared about programming? How to send the right signal to Hollywood? The question Murphy and Burke and others kept asking themselves during the holiday season, recalls Ron Doerfler, was: "What would we do if Stoddard left?"

January 3, 1986, arrived, and the merger was consummated. The night before, an ABC comedy, *Shadow Chasers,* attracted just 7 percent of the available viewers against *The Cosby Show*'s 50 percent, which would help cement ABC's hold on third place. Whatever Pierce's decision, Murphy and Burke were convinced they had to move fast to resuscitate ABC, to change the old culture. Likening the networks to the American auto companies, Murphy and Burke saw both as high-cost providers undercut by cheaper competition. Yet by getting their costs under control, Murphy said, the auto companies regained profitability even though their share of the market declined. Similarly, with network shares shrinking, the way for ABC to boost earnings was to reduce expenditures. From day one, Murphy and Burke believed they could hack $150 million from ABC's costs; John Sias guessed the true savings could be $200 million, about 40 percent of the network's overhead.

The cost-control point man was Dan Burke, and to signal his determination, he moved quickly. Within the first forty-eight hours of the merger's consummation, Burke ordered a halt to the exclusive express elevator once reserved for Goldenson and eighteen other executives; even though it was otherwise used to haul garbage, employees referred to it as "the royal elevator." From now on all six elevators to the upper floors would be democratically available. Burke closed the six private dining rooms on the fortieth floor, where forty-five or so top ABC executives feasted on three- or four-course lunches. He eliminated multiple private phone lines and first-class travel privileges once enjoyed by hundreds of vice presidents. He terminated the six daily mail deliveries and the permanent duplex penthouse ABC maintained at the Plaza Hotel, consisting of seventeen rooms—including seven bedrooms, a dining room, kitchen, living room, parlor, and a billiard room.

The excesses were so appalling that Cap Cities executives used to swap tales of profligacy.

Can you believe that ABC News's Paris bureau has a chef?

Can you believe ABC pays to fly forty-two daily copies of The New York Times *out to the West Coast even though the* Times *publishes a national edition available in Los Angeles?*

Can you believe ABC executives insisted on private hot lines to one another, which cost $180 per month per line?

Can you believe Good Morning America *spends $2,600 a week on breakfast snacks for its guests?*

The star system also galled them, particularly the salaries awarded in Roone Arledge's past bidding wars. For example, Arledge bid $500,000 for CBS's talented Charles Osgood, even though a ranking CBS News executive said Osgood was asking only $150,000 from CBS. Fearful of losing him, CBS matched the offer. To Tom Murphy this all became an illustration of the network's limousine mentality. He felt shareholders were being cheated.

Cap Cities "looked at anyone who was in the network with suspicion. I understand that," said Roone Arledge. "When I came to ABC News we were number three. I viewed people there with suspicion too." Cap Cities inspired paranoia. Suddenly ABC felt like a conquered nation. Whatever its internal disputes or rivalries, to its employees the network had always felt more like a family than a corporation. Everyone had worked together for years, shared a sense of mission. ABC News didn't tote up the costs when it pioneered Ted Koppel's *Nightline,* or flinch when, in 1980, it ran a four-and-a-half-minute investigative report on its own network's cozy relationship with producer Aaron Spelling. Executives at ABC believed a network made money on what it put on the screen, not by cutting costs. They believed hit programs were nurtured in a climate of freedom and security. One hit show, they believed, would generate more revenues than could be saved by any cost-cutting campaign. Together they shared a sense that ABC had been their creation, that they had toiled together in the wilderness and finally succeeded in achieving parity with CBS and NBC, in making ABC a genuine network. An outsider might interpret this as arrogance, but you had to have been there in the lean days to appreciate the distance they had traveled to win their first prime-time ratings race in 1976, or to make ABC News or Sports competitive. Now, after a professional lifetime in which profit growth was as certain as a sunrise, suddenly there were men with calculators, asking questions. And for ABC to be taken over by one of its affiliates, to be told its success was really failure, was disorienting.

The paranoia at ABC rose a notch when days after the takeover Cap Cities announced a corporate-wide drug crackdown, with drug-sniffing dogs and maybe even mandatory urine tests for new employees. And then Fred Pierce returned from his Colorado vacation. Privately he told Murphy and Burke he was quitting. "It was a matter of principle," Pierce explained. "I'm a believer in agreements. I had gotten a lot of lashes on my back for developing cable networks and just when they were going into profitability, they prepared to take it away. I didn't like the way it was handled."

Murphy and Burke expected this, and asked Pierce to continue as a director of the merged company, to serve as a consultant. Pierce agreed. Then Murphy and Burke moved quickly to forestall a rush of applicants for Pierce's job.

ABC executives learned of Pierce's fate on January 9, when the top managers gathered in the conference room on the thirty-ninth floor. To Pierce's right sat the patriarch, who stunned the group by announcing that Fred Pierce had decided to step aside. Goldenson paid tribute to Pierce, and at one point made a passing reference to John Sias, which baffled people since Sias was unknown. Then Murphy and Burke entered to introduce him. "We didn't want Fred to leave," Dan Burke said. "But we understand why he did. When it came time to pick a replacement we knew there were a lot of good people here, but we didn't know any of you intimately."

Pierce announced that Sias would be president of the ABC network alone, leaving unclear who would lead the owned stations, Radio, or the cable and other investments.

Sias sat there, stone silent. It would not go unnoticed by those in the room that this longtime Cap Cities executive had absolutely zero experience in programming, where ABC most needed help. Sias's TV experience was pretty much restricted to sales. His résumé unnerved ABC executives, as did Burke's refusal to pledge that there would be no layoffs. The greatest worry, however, was the departure of Pierce, their protector. "Fred was tough but fair," observed Richard J. Connelly, vice president of Public Relations. "He was the father of the family, and Leonard was the grandfather." Now they would be reporting to a stranger, one who ranked third in the hierarchy.

This morning the fearsome pressures of the unknown converged on vice president of Corporate Communications, Patricia J. Matson, who had joined ABC in 1977 after working in the White House press office under Nixon and Ford. As chief spokesperson for ABC, Matson was pummeled by rumors and calls from reporters and employees; she had a press release set to go out at 11 A.M. announcing Pierce's departure and Sias's appointment. Tom Murphy was scheduled to come to her office around noon for press interviews, and Richard Nixon was on the phone to remind her she was expected at Lutèce, New York's great French restaurant, at 1 P.M. to help celebrate Pat Nixon's birthday. "The feeling I had," recalls Matson, a cool professional, "was of the final week before Nixon's resignation. It was as quiet as a tomb. Except my office, where the phone was ringing off the hook."

She would be late for lunch because Tom Murphy wanted to talk at length about John Sias and the network. He began by talking to *The Wall Street Journal.* Whatever Sias lacked in experience, said Murphy, was more than compensated for by his assets, which included brains, executive skills, and familiarity with Murphy and Burke. Look at his record, said Murphy. Under Sias's leadership, the publishing division generated 63 percent of Cap Cities' revenues and 48 percent of its profits in 1984. Murphy added that one of Sias's outstanding talents was that he was great with people.

Sias's so-called people skills were what most worried ABC executives. In succeeding days they kept hearing accounts of the strange things Sias had done. They heard about the time he ran across the roofs of cars in a parking lot to get somewhere fast, or wore a Captain Marvel T-shirt under his business shirt as a prank. Or the time Sias stopped an employee on the street and asked, "Where are you going?"

"I'm late, John. I've got a lunch appointment," said the employee, who kept hurrying down the street.

The employee had gotten maybe ten feet away when Sias wheeled and shouted, "Stop that man! He stole my wallet!"

Sias knew people were nervous, knew he had to calm them. His first task, he said, was to make Stoddard comfortable. "Brandon had not sought the job. He was leery of it," said Sias. "And he was to be given very careful treatment. My job, in large part, was to create an environment in which Stoddard had the minimum amount of distractions."

Meanwhile, Murphy and Burke sought to fill vacant jobs and clarify roles within the organization. Over the next few days ABC executives made pilgrimages to the Villard House for audiences with Dan Burke. "I wanted people to think I had a lot more information, a lot more insight, than I did," said Burke, who would rely on instinct to fill the managerial boxes on his new organization chart. "Everybody who saw me was a cardinal and hoped to be a pope, and came away a bishop," said Burke.

The first and most unpleasant visit was from News and Sports president Roone Arledge, perhaps ABC's best-known executive. In many ways Arledge, fifty-four, who draped expensive imported suits over his wide shoulders, personified the old culture of extravagance for the Cap Cities owners. It bothered them that Arledge wheeled about town in a chauffeured black Jaguar, the only non-board member with such privileges. It troubled them that Roone always seemed to have his own magic carpet, arriving at ABC meetings on chartered jets. They knew he often slept late and sometimes indulged in four-hour lunches and fifty-dollar bottles of Gavi di Gavi at Nanni Il Valletto, around the corner from his Park Avenue coop. They had heard the scuttlebutt from the news division of how Arledge sightings were sometimes treated like planetary occurences, as colleagues moaned about when he was last seen or how long it took him to return a call or how he made decisions through inaction. Like the Wizard of Oz, Arledge was behind a curtain, a man whose presence was more often felt than seen.

But few questioned Arledge's wizardry. In the nine years that he had been president of News and the eighteen years he had run ABC Sports, Arledge had introduced journalism to TV sports, had spotted the talents of Howard Cosell, had invented *Wide World of Sports, Monday Night Football, Nightline,* and *This Week with David Brinkley.* Arledge had brought hand-held cameras and close-ups to the games, as well as shotgun mikes, slow-motion and instant replays, and miniature cameras strapped to race cars and skiers, all designed to convey excitement. He covered the Olympics as if they were drama, with suspense, heroes, and villains.

Not without reason, Arledge saw himself as a visionary, as a creative producer, not as a day-to-day manager of ABC's two divisions. To ask Arledge details about the News or Sports budget was to abandon him in a Sahara of unfamiliar numbers. He knew one figure—News made $55 million in 1985—and he was proud of it. Unlike NBC, he had a money-making magazine show—*20/20*—and a late-night profit-maker in *Nightline.* To dwell on numbers was, Arledge felt, to ignore the larger franchise he had created. "There are certain things the networks have to do that lose money," he said. "The way ABC grew from nothing and attracted advertisers and affiliates was first sports, then movies." Arledge was making the same case for Sports and News that Stoddard had made on behalf of *War and Remembrance.* Big-event television, both believed, separated the networks from the pack, no matter the cost. "The more you give away to competitors," Arledge said, "the more you lessen the distinction and undermine your reason for being."

Murphy, Burke, and Sias viewed Arledge's argument as an excuse, as an assertion of blind faith. What was provable to Cap Cities were the expenses, which had risen alarmingly at ABC. They applauded the prestige and whatever profits Arledge brought. But as he ladled out salaries and sports-rights fees, profit margins declined. Whatever his talents, to Cap Cities, Roone Arledge was the father of television free agency. When Arledge, eager for a big-name anchor to boost his number-three newscast, dangled big-buck contracts in front of Dan Rather and Tom Brokaw at the start of the decade, he spurred a news star system, one pioneered by ABC in 1976 when it lured Barbara Walters from NBC with the first million-dollar News contract. To jump start ABC News, Arledge raided producers and on-air correspondents. Inevitably, everyone's salary rose.

Cap Cities was determined to regain control of the budget, and with Arledge's own contract expiring, now was the time to do it. They wanted it understood that it was no longer acceptable for the networks to pay $2.1 billion to the NFL for four years' worth of football games, or $309 million for the right to televise the 1988 Winter Olympics; not at a time when ABC Sports was losing money for the second straight year. Dan Burke had been told Arledge was spending only about 15 percent of his time in Sports. "We had serious hemorrhaging and morale problems in Sports," Burke recalls. "I wanted someone full time in there." And if Arledge was to give up Sports, Burke wanted him to cede a small portion of his roughly $2 million annual income. This message was delivered by John Sias during a rough three-hour meeting.

The message came as a rude slap in the face to Arledge. What he might accept from a longtime colleague like Pierce he could not accept from the new owners, and certainly not from John Sias, whom Arledge, like Stoddard, would have difficulty acknowledging as his boss. Ironically, the initial concern Arledge had about Sias—that he was not a serious man—was similar to that many had about Arledge himself when he became News president in 1977.

Arledge sulked. He felt he had been insulted by Sias. And he felt condescended to by Murphy, who privately told him, "You're the only ABC person we considered for Pierce's job." Despite Sports losses, he believed the new owners were shortsighted. "It troubled me that when these people came in they had a good view of me as a programmer but I was viewed as 'a spender,' " said Arledge. "My feeling was, and still is, that to build things you have to spend. That's the way Bill Paley did it." Sports losses were temporary, Arledge believed. He compared himself to a kid who had always kept his room spotless—except for the one day that Cap Cities decided on a room inspection. This enraged him, as did the effort to cut his pay.

To add insult to injury, Cap Cities' choice to succeed Arledge at Sports—Dennis Swanson, former general manager of WLS-TV, ABC's Chicago station, and for the past ten months president of ABC's owned stations division—did not meet with Arledge's approval. He had talked with Fred Pierce about leaving Sports for a year. *But give the job to Dennis Swanson? Why? Because he has a job offer from CBS?* Arledge had thirty Emmys decorating his office at ABC Sports. Dennis Swanson's office featured a University of Illinois football helmet on the wall. Besides, Arledge had his reputation, his stature, to protect. He didn't want it to appear that he was fired. Through his lawyer, Ron Konecky, Arledge argued for the freedom to choose his own successor.

To no avail. Although negotiations dragged on for weeks, in the end Arledge was replaced at Sports by Dennis Swanson. Arledge did get to keep his full $2 million compensation package by consenting to produce the 1988 Olympics in Calgary; and for appearance's sake, he was given a somewhat misleading title as group president, ABC News and Sports.

Negotiations with other ABC executives moved more rapidly. Within days of Pierce's exit, Cap Cities elevated Mike Mallardi from chief financial officer to president of the broadcast Group, responsible for the owned stations, Radio, broadcast operations and engineering, and ABC Video Enterprises; Mark Mandala would lose his title as president of ABC Television and would now be network president, responsible for Sales and Affiliate Relations but no longer responsible for the owned stations; the vice president for Sales, Jake Keever, who reported to Mandala, would now be a senior vice president; and in what was interpreted as an olive branch to Pierce's ABC family, Marc Cohen, a Pierce intimate and a working partner of Stoddard's, was asked to stay as executive vice president of the Broadcast Group. The only executive imposed from the outside on ABC was to be John Sias. And while it was clear that Cap Cities planned to shed jobs, among the executive ranks this shock was softened by a generous $30 million severance package. "On average, people probably got twice the severance they would have gotten from ABC," said Ron Doerfler.

As part of their pacification effort, Murphy and Burke headed west to meet with Stoddard and his team on January 21. Before leaving, Sias urged them to induce Stoddard to cut the Entertainment budget in order "to ameliorate some pain" in New York. If Stoddard took the initiative, argued Sias, Cap Cities wouldn't look to Hollywood like "a bunch of gimlet-eyed bean counters." Tom Murphy demurred, telling Sias the relationship with Stoddard was delicate, and reminding him to walk on eggshells when dealing with him.

In Los Angeles, Stoddard made a strong pitch to Murphy and Burke on behalf of still another miniseries—*Amerika*—a twelve-hour, $41 million project about life in America a decade after a Soviet takeover. Honoring the commitment would send a reassuring message to Hollywood, argued Stoddard. Even though the expensive miniseries violated the rules they had laid down to, say, Roone Arledge, Murphy gave Stoddard the same answer he had to *War and Remembrance*—*Okay, pal.*

In the month-old offensive to change the old ABC culture, Dan Burke planned one other effort. Each January the managers of the various divisions of Cap Cities were invited to a management retreat in Phoenix. With the mountains and desert as a backdrop, for three days the executives gathered at the Arizona Biltmore, a one-story sandstone building nestled among cottages, each with its own garden. Here they alternated sessions in the conference center with tennis, golf, swimming, jogging, biking, and, late each night, a high-stakes poker game orchestrated by Tom Murphy and Dan Burke.

Burke approached this annual event with the precision of a military commander. Months before the gathering, he brooded on his corporate goals for the meeting, worked on and rehearsed the speech and slide presentation he would make and the stunts he would pull. Day one usually began with a review by Burke of the financial results of each division; on the second day, Burke would concentrate on particular social goals, such as female and minority hiring; on day three he would focus on the targets for each business in the coming year.

Preparation for the event usually began with a phone call from Burke to Phil Beuth, a longtime Cap Cities employee who was then the general manager of their Buffalo TV station. "We're going to get rich together, Philly," Burke had told him in 1962 when he urged Beuth to borrow money to buy Cap Cities stock. By 1986, Beuth's initial $10,400 investment was worth $5 million. Philly, who walked with a limp from a birth defect and who almost never fastened his tie, would do anything for Murphy or Burke. He had held fifteen jobs at Cap Cities, and never once did he negotiate an employment contract, always choosing to accept Burke and Murphy's generosity.

"We want to show them what we're really like," Burke told Beuth before the 1986 retreat. "And if we are a little hometown and friendly and corny, so what? Our system has to prevail. . . . I want you to devise some sort of a game or scheme, Philly, to make people feel comfortable." "The Cardinal," as people at Cap Cities sometimes called Burke, saw himself as a setter of standards. To Beuth he outlined three objectives for the meeting: First, they must have a little *fun,* make everyone feel part of the family; second, *shock therapy*—to imbue ABC with what he saw as an essential part of Cap Cities culture—total candor, a willingness to confront bad news; third, there was a *mission,* which was to infect ABC executives with a zeal for cost cutting.

As the meeting approached, the eighty or so invited ABC executives were nervous as hell. "They were worried about room assignments," recalls a Cap Cities executive. Would they have single or double rooms? What was the appropriate attire? Would it be like boot camp? Should they prepare material? Would they be put on the spot? To help unite the company, Cap Cities took care to invite both Leonard Goldenson and Fred Pierce.

When the 160 casually dressed executives from the merged companies arrived at the Arizona Biltmore, a receptionist was waiting with a cut-in-half ten-dollar bill for each of them. The receptionist explained that they were to look for the person who held the matching half of their bill.

What horseshit! thought Fred Pierce, who said he noticed the halved ten-dollar bill but walked on by because, "I wasn't into it." *This was definitely not the type of thing a classy network did!* He was not alone. Many ABC executives found it jarring. And they were taken aback by the group-therapy aspects of the meeting. Although they thought of themselves as a "family," ABC executives tended to compartmentalize things, not to share information deemed "confidential." That is why Mike Mallardi's presentation at Jackson Hole in 1984 was such a shocker. Each department was like a mafia family—*You don't speak ill of the family to an outsider.* And they definitely didn't go in for the *rah rah* stuff—unless they were trying to whip up enthusiasm among affiliates or advertisers or the media over how *great* ABC's fall schedule was.

But in these cases, they were controlling the message; in Phoenix, they were the recipients.

The first evening featured a twenty-minute film produced by Phil Beuth, opening with Peter Jennings at his anchor desk reporting: "This deal did not go unnoticed in Washington." Cut to Vice President George Bush, a friend and neighbor of Dan Burke's from Kennebunkport, Maine, who said he was sure the combined company would be "a great success." Just then two trains race toward each other on the screen and collide!

Peter Jennings, as if doing *World News Tonight,* continued: "Cap Cities is known for its positive employee relations programs. . . ." Just then striking Cap Cities newspaper employees with placards appear on screen. Jennings continued: "ABC over the years has attracted executives of talent and of uncommon modesty."

"I can certainly go along with that!" declared Roone Arledge.

The film made fun of Arledge's propensity not to return telephone calls, as an announcer's voice boomed: "The answer is: St. Thomas Aquinas, Abraham Lincoln, and Roone Arledge. The question is: Who are the three people who never return your phone call?" The humor was meant to be self-deprecating, like the segment that hinted at the controversial drug crackdown with John Sias looking into the camera and, suddenly, stricken with a look of alarm, shouting, "Get away, dogs!" Cap Cities executives laughed more than those from ABC. "It was," observed News vice president Richard C. Wald, "like a sales meeting for a small-town newspaper. Some thought it was fun, and some looked down their noses at it."

When the lights went up, Dan Burke appeared on stage. Using slides, he did his tour d'horizon, skipping across each business, reviewing who was ahead or behind in spending and profitability, affixing green stickers to divisions that surpassed projections and red to the laggards. The message was unmistakable. ABC had a monopoly on red stickers. Profits, Burke emphasized, swelled every time an organization cut spending. While the ABC network made money in 1985, Burke saw a bleak profit picture in 1986. What ABC executives heard loud and clear was that they were expected to cut their way to profitability.

To impart his lesson, Dan Burke recounted the time when Cap Cities had acquired Fairchild Publications, and Fairchild executives came to the same management retreat and were shocked at how open he was, how willing he was to disclose Fairchild's earnings. What he intended then was shock therapy, just as he did now. He said that network revenues were in a nosedive, and if they didn't level off the network would lose money in 1986. He gave them the bleak numbers, and said he was troubled by ABC's tendency to present only good news to Cap Cities. Burke whacked them about Ron Doerfler's inspection of ABC's books, which had revealed that network revenue projections were inflated by $200 million. He whacked them about *Monday Night Football,* which nearly everyone at ABC considered a great success. Not so, admonished Burke. Because of the steep rights fees, *Monday Night Football* actually lost money.

"You could hear a pin drop as I went through the numbers," recalls Burke. Patricia Matson, ABC's chief of Communications, was so shocked by the numbers and the candor that she dared not write anything down, as she usually did. She did not want to risk leaks, or be blamed for them. This was Dan Burke's attempt at glasnost. He was entrusting the audience with the company's secrets.

But among many ABC executives, the spirit seemed less like glasnost then like the Cultural Revolution in China, where the intellectuals were made to wear dunce caps. Despite Burke's best efforts to bring everyone together, ABC executives felt picked on, and tended to huddle together. While appreciative of Cap Cities' candor, News vice president David Burke bristled, feeling that Cap Cities was mocking Arledge, who had devoted his life to ABC. "There was a time at ABC when there was nothing but him," Burke observed. "Entertainment was a failure. News was not on the boards. Sports was the only thing that brought black ink. Of everyone, Roone has had the toughest transition between what was and what is. At the old ABC he was a key player—the Olympics, *Monday Night Football, Wide World of Sports.* Fifteen years ago the only reason to know ABC was Roone Arledge." Now Arledge was the butt of Cap Cities' bad jokes. He had lost his jurisdiction over Sports. And his new employers threatened to judge his performance not on the quality of the shows he produced but on the revenues he generated.

After lunch the next day, company policies were reviewed, including affirmative action and pro bono records. Burke exhorted the executives, as he often did, to improve their efforts to hire and promote women and minorities. Here was another reason Burke was sometimes referred to as "the Cardinal." Burke was a tough man with a moral mission and rigorous standards. Once, when Murphy was having difficulty reining in his fifteen-year-old son, Tom Jr., the fathers decided they would swap Stephen Burke for Tom Murphy for sixty days.

Great idea! said Stephen Burke.

Young Murphy, however, was appalled. "Go live at Burke's house?" he exclaimed. "No way!"

On the final day of the retreat, on the way into the main hall of the Biltmore, executives were confronted with large picnic baskets. Above them were signs saying, "Definitely No Picnic." Inside the baskets were jars of delicacies, bottles of champagne, imported chocolates, jam, mustard, relish, ketchup. The executives were instructed to select one item each from the baskets and take it to their seats. Not surprisingly, most reached for the expensive items, leaving the relishes and the mustards for stragglers. A morose David Burke went to his seat empty-handed, thinking the game was "sophomoric."

He reserved an empty seat for Arledge, who arrived late, holding a jar of relish.

"Roone, there's better stuff there," Burke whispered to Arledge when he spotted the relish.

"Here, you have it," said a dispirited Arledge, tossing the jar to Burke.

From the stage Dan Burke called out, "How many of you have a bottle of ketchup?" Jake Keever's hand went up, and at that moment Dan Burke announced that inside was a gold Krugerrand worth several hundred dollars.

"How many have a jar of relish?"

David Burke tentatively raised his hand. Inside was another gold Krugerrand. Those who chose the expensive goods went away empty-handed; those who reached for the cheap condiments did well. Cardinal Burke had two homilies to impart: Those who take the hard road will be rewarded; and things are not always what they seem.

Of course, Phoenix was not a model of what Cardinal Burke wanted, or preached. It was, observed one ABC executive, "white, male-oriented, despite everything Dan Burke said." Only 9 women out of 160 attended, and only one black. To many it seemed like an old-boy network.

Day three featured Tom Murphy introducing the slight, rumpled Warren Buffett, with his scuffed shoes. Buffett described himself as Murphy's "gorilla," the dumb partner who just puts up some money and guards the network against a takeover. Speaking off the cuff or answering questions, Buffett was a very reassuring figure to ABC executives. After the turmoil they had weathered, many liked hearing him say that dealing with most stock speculators was "like being partners with a manic depressive"—they want to sell when they are depressed, and are happy only when the stock rises. They liked hearing Buffett praise Cap Cities for having paid only one dividend in its history. Why? Because Cap Cities invested its money for the long term, he said. And they were reassured to hear Buffett praise broadcasting as a stable, relatively inflation-proof business. He said little about increasingly intense competition from cable or independent stations.

In a way, Burke and Murphy tried to impart similar reassurances on the last day of the retreat, when they sat on a stage and accepted questions from the floor, conveying paternal authority. This aura was comforting to longtime Cap Cities personnel, who were as used to cost cutting as they were to rising profits. But Murphy and Burke unsettled many ABC hands who longed to hear there would be no more layoffs, who longed for more benign bosses.

With all their bruises, however, more than a few ABC executives were pleased. "The thing that surprised me," said Stoddard, "was the extraordinary candor and directness of these guys. Second was the incredible relationship these two men—Dan and Tom—had with every member of Cap Cities. There was lots of laughter. There was a sense of fun that was very special." Dan Burke came away pleased. "Phoenix was a watershed," he said, where a congenial atmosphere eased the transition from a little company to a big company. "They came out of there frightened, and hopeful."

Back in New York, Dan Burke and John Sias embarked on a whirlwind series of meetings with ABC managers, reviewing their operations, their budgets, the mission of each department, whether it was a necessary mission, and whether it couldn't be accomplished with fewer employees. Even wary managers were impressed by the provocative questions.

To reassure News, Dan Burke and Sias extended a hand to anchor Peter Jennings, among others. "They went out of their way," recalled Jennings, "to say to me on a number of occasions two things: Come and talk to us any time. And come and help us understand how your operation works." At one point Jennings, who had urged Arledge and David Burke to schedule a regular series of meals with prominent public officials, suggested to his superiors that he would play host at his Central Park West apartment to the chairman of the joint chiefs of staff. "Why don't we invite Murphy and Burke?" he suggested. "It would be a great way to embrace them and get them into the tent."

Out of the question! Arledge and Burke responded. They were worried that the new owners might not respect the line between business and News, might use these sessions to urge News to push for changes in federal regulations affecting the networks, or might push certain stories or pressure News to create programs more like Cap Cities' own racy local newscasts. At the time, Arledge and Burke were still seething. Every suggestion became a slight. Arledge was deeply offended when Murphy suggested—"not meanly," he conceded—"that I might talk to and get advice from the News director at their Raleigh, North Carolina, station about news. It was their sense that local stations were a source of all wisdom, and networks were screwed up."

Another reason for News's unease was John Sias. Arledge sensed Sias would enjoy sending ABC executives to collective farms to feed the pigs. Sias was perceived as a kind of zealot, who found the waste at ABC morally repugnant. When they cut a receptionist position, Arledge remembers Sias whooping, "Way to go!" But it wasn't only Sias's fervor that bothered Arledge. He had heard that Sias walked through the West Sixty-sixth Street newsroom on Lincoln's birthday disguised as the former president. Another time Sias visited News at 8:30 A.M., an hour when few—certainly not the head of the news division—were at their desks, and shouted at the top of his lungs, "Where's Roone?" To Sias, this was just having fun, meant to loosen people up. To Arledge and Burke, Sias seemed to have a screw loose.

Meanwhile, the grueling one-on-one sessions with department heads stretched into February. Over the course of three weeks, Dan Burke and John Sias went through each department job by job, probing for soft spots, places to cut. Several shocking facts emerged. While ABC's headquarters was a forty-story office building on Fifty-fourth Street and Sixth Avenue, ABC employees were scattered about Manhattan in thirty other locations as well. In addition to the communications difficulties this presented, it also meant ABC was constantly harassed by rent increases and lease restrictions beyond its control. At the same time, Cap Cities learned that ABC owned property on the West Side of Manhattan near Lincoln Center, a fact unknown to them at the time of the merger.

Burke realized that if he sold the Sixth Avenue office tower and invested a total of $200 million in the West Side site, all of ABC could be consolidated under one roof. Within months, Cap Cities/ABC unloaded the office tower for $175 million. By 1989, ABC would have a new campuslike headquarters.

Cap Cities' scrutiny of ABC yielded one other find. In January, Ron Doerfler had discovered that sales projections for 1986 were inflated by approximately $200 million. Why? both Burke and Sias asked in their February discussions with the sales department. The answer stunned them, for they learned that revenue projections for the network were made not by Sales but by Financial Planning. The reason Fred Pierce chose to rely on another department, explained his former deputy, Marc Cohen, was to "set up goals for Sales to reach." Setting the goals high became a "goad" to Sales, a guarantee that Sales did not set its sights too low. On paper, the check and balance idea worked; in practice, it did not. "The basic problem," said Robert S. Wallen, a Sales vice president, "was that Planning was trying to make the revenues fit" the profit goals. "Rather than controlling costs, they raised projected revenues." To Dan Burke it was a typical Fred Pierce move, an impression confirmed by Mark Mandala, to whom Sales reported. "Anyone who brought him bad news got their head cut off," said Mandala. Pierce used to tell Mandala, "We've got to think positive. I'm tired of all this negativism."

The antidote, Burke and Sias quickly decided, was to change the system, to make the sales department responsible for projecting revenues and setting its own prices. At General Foods, where he worked before joining Cap Cities, Burke had been schooled in Sales. And John Sias probably spent more time on the thirty-sixth floor, visiting with Jake Keever's sales team, than he did anywhere else in the organization. He would flatter them with reminders that he knew they were the one department responsible for collecting all network revenues. But Sias may have been saying something else, that Sales was where he felt most comfortable, most knowledgeable, particularly since he was instructed to keep hands off Entertainment, and dealing with News was for him like dealing with a sensitive Latin American ally, with whom there always lurked the danger of an "incident."

The situation made Sias uncomfortable. "I don't think I'm so good at allaying fears," said Sias. "I was trying to bring everyone into the real world." Burke, who was better at diplomacy, nevertheless kept alluding to his lifeboat theory: *You don't wait until the lifeboat is full before you recognize that half the occupants have to be let off.* Burke left no doubt that he believed ABC's boats were too full.

With neither Burke nor Sias shy about their pessimism, layoffs soon rocked the building. Among the first hit was the communications department, which was reduced from 17 positions to 6. Financial Planning, which now reported to Ron Doerfler, lost 16 employees. The research department, which was trimmed by 11 employees in reductions ordered over the summer by Fred Pierce, lost another 20. The publicity department, which promoted ABC's shows, went from 120 to 90 employees. The staff of 60 that once managed the five owned stations was slimmed to 6, and now they oversaw eight stations; one-quarter of the 400 employees at ABC's New York flagship, WABC-TV, were let go, as were the first 50 of an expected 100 employees at Los Angeles's KABC-TV. ABC News, insisting they were not responding to a decree, reduced its staff of 1,100 by 7 percent. Although privately unhappy, particularly with the humiliations he felt Sias had visited upon him, publicly Roone Arledge sounded like a spokesman for the new order, telling *The New York Times,* "There's a lot of people at all three networks who have grown up expecting the golden ring to always be there, and that's not a fact in this economy."

Sias, for one, wasn't satisfied. "They think it's terrific," said Sias of News's 7 percent staff reduction. "I think it's a beginning. . . . I don't happen to think we need 110 correspondents. How many of them are on the air every night?" Sias had "substantial doubts" about gavel-to-gavel coverage of political conventions and wondered why, since the ratings revealed that viewers rarely tuned to politics, News deserved one to three hours of prime-time programming on Election Night. Why, he wondered aloud, as would the other new network owners, did CNN produce twenty-four hours of news daily for one-third what it cost the network?

Folks within ABC News were unhappy, and usually offered one of three explanations. First, they thought Sias in particular didn't understand how a news department functioned. CNN didn't produce most pieces the way a network did; more often than not CNN just trained a single camera on a subject, producing a talking head, which it put on the air every hour or so, like all-news radio. During a given half hour, CNN achieved about a 1 rating, meaning it reached just under a million viewers; ABC's *World News Tonight* corralled twelve times as many viewers. By just measuring poundage, Arledge and others in News believed, Sias ignored the quality of the product. Correspondents couldn't be on the air daily because the twenty-two minutes of nightly airtime didn't allow it, and because reporting a story takes time —time to wait for plane connections or sources to return calls, time to dislodge information. A second complaint against Cap Cities was made by Josh Mankiewicz, then a bright young reporter in ABC's Atlanta bureau. He remembers doing his expense report early in 1986 when a corporate accountant asked, "Why do you need to make so many phone calls?"

Mankiewicz explained that reporters often live with phones attached to their ears, seeking information, following up leads, checking facts. The accountant kept pressing. Finally, an exasperated Mankiewicz said, "Boy, you guys are really taking the fun out of this!"

"Fun? This isn't supposed to be fun!" said the accountant.

Soon after, Mankiewicz quit.

The third reason for unhappiness was that people in News had divided feelings about Roone Arledge. They respected his programming skills, but waiting for Arledge to make a decision was exasperating, and when the decision came down it was not always a clear one. David Burke, for example, was ready to leave in early 1986. While he was loyal to Arledge, he was frustrated. In many ways Burke managed the news division, yet his title remained vice president and assistant to the president. In the spring, when Arledge finally promoted him to executive vice president, he did not define Burke's new job. The terse announcement merely gave Burke's new title and made clear that another News vice president, Dick Wald, would continue to report to Arledge.

In the first sixteen months of Cap Cities' rule, a total of 1,600 ABC employees would be severed, saving $100 million. This did not distress everyone there. The 172-person sales department was generally thrilled with the attention lavished upon it. But Sales was an exception. Much of the blame was heaped on John Sias, and the bill of particulars was long. Some ABC executives who had eyed Sias's job themselves resented the fact that an outsider had become president. Some complained that Sias was a floater, without convictions. They were enraged when he wondered aloud whether there was enough of a mass audience to support three network newscasts, or mused that "God did not ordain" the networks to be.

The doubts about Sias's judgment burst into public view in March of 1986 with a front-page story in *The New York Times.* Sias, who like other Cap Cities executives then avoided on-the-record press interviews, had impulsively picked up the phone to take a call from the *Times*'s enterprising television reporter, Peter J. Boyer. The story began: "John B. Sias, the new President of ABC, is a television executive of a sort the industry has never before encountered. Mr. Sias has never read a single television script. What's more, he says he probably never will." Then Boyer recounted some other unusual occurrences, including Sias stomping the halls of ABC with a whoopie whistle, emitting shrill sounds at random.

The front-page story further upset the people at ABC. The *Times* recounted several Sias anecdotes, but missed a few. Such as the time when Sias, while walking the halls, fliply said of the host of *Good Morning America,* "David Hartman is comatose!" (Sias called Hartman to apologize.) Or the time he went up to a news desk assistant and asked, according to one News executive who felt undermined, "Do you think we ought to have done two minutes on Honduras last night?" The problem with Sias, said this News executive, was that "he is a Doberman pinscher. I have no faith in his judgment on things. I see no policy design or vision, except what he thinks will get him some meat. . . ."

To Sias, the folks in News took themselves too seriously. They were, he complained, arrogant and elitist. Many ABC executives thought Sias the perfect symbol of the dreaded financial managers who now ruled corporate America. Sure they were elitist, that was a reason the networks could achieve quality. "If I came to work every day without being a little bit arrogant," said David Burke, "we'd have a pretty mediocre news operation. A little bit of arrogance and elitism drives a news division. Just as a professor at Harvard or a surgeon goes to work feeling" good about his work. "It's what makes an institution good."

Sias's initial encounters with the entertainment division under Stoddard, while not as fractious as those with News, were hardly smooth. The stricture handed down by Murphy was for everyone, including Sias, to get out of Stoddard's way. "Brandon wants John to leave him alone, and John largely does," said ABC's spokesman, Richard Connelly. The Cap Cities chiefs had granted Stoddard his miniseries wishes against their better judgment. And in the spring, when network executives gathered for a week in California to review the half-hour comedy and one-hour drama pilots contending for a place on the 1986 fall schedule, Murphy, Burke, and Sias let Stoddard make these fateful decisions. Burke actually skipped a good many of the screenings, as did Murphy. Sias attended them all, but said he asked only "a few questions and listened, and offered an observation or two. I had a minimal role." Sias kept most of his programming opinions to himself. In News many viewed Sias as the enemy; in Entertainment, Stoddard and his staff were more puzzled by Sias, not knowing what he believed.

Sias had his own frustrations. He was asked to run the ABC network yet was prohibited from managing Stoddard, and Roone Arledge went around him and communicated directly with Murphy and Burke. He was experiencing something unique in his career at Cap Cities. Because ABC was in such trouble, Murphy and Burke delegated less, were involved more directly in the management of the network. By nature a take-charge executive, Sias found himself caught in the middle, not wanting to offend Stoddard, not wanting to usurp the role of the chairman and chief operating officer he admired, and yet wanting to make changes.

Other strains began to show during the first six months under Cap Cities, perhaps the touchiest being those between the new owners and the affiliate stations. The first relatively mild clash came at the annual ABC affiliate convention in May, where the owners and general managers of the stations come to the Century Plaza Hotel in Los Angeles for three days to preview the fall schedule, to be stroked and stimulated and entertained. When Cap Cities assumed command of ABC, most of the 213 ABC affiliates were pleased. They knew Burke and Murphy as station owners, knew they understood the business from the bottom up; knew they understood that the era of ma and pa station ownership was ending.

But now, as owners of a network, Murphy and Burke saw things somewhat differently. When Dan Burke looked at costs, his eye went to the $120 million ABC paid its affiliates to air its shows. This was a bounty, called compensation, for agreeing to display the network's product. But the network owner felt that he was providing free programming to the affiliates, plus giving at least two minutes of advertising to sell during each hour of prime-time programming and more in other parts of the day, plus feeding them pictures and reports from all around the world for their local newscasts, plus giving them free promotion, equipment, an identity, and prestige. Not to mention that the network tie at least doubled the value of the local station.

Now that ABC was in trouble, wondered Murphy, why wasn't it reasonable for affiliates to share the pain? Instead, the affiliates were increasing their preemptions of weak network shows, substituting syndicated series that drew higher ratings than the network programs and that let the station sell upward of sixteen minutes of advertising per hour. "The typical affiliate talks about 'partnership' but at bottom it's about 'gimme,' " complained Sias. They "want more comp," and they want "to bump us more, to skim the cream."

To the affiliates, these were business decisions. A number of group owners acquired their stations through highly leveraged transactions, often with junk bonds or leveraged buyouts. Which meant they were faced with huge interest expense. The pressure to meet these payments and increase profits encouraged local stations to substitute syndicated shows during daytime hours, to bounce a weak night of network programming for local baseball or basketball, to delay *Nightline* into the wee hours in order to squeeze in a syndicated show.

There were, however, no sharp clashes at the May convention in

Los Angeles. Tom Murphy used his welcoming address as a platform to explain that the ABC network would lose money in 1986 and that the short-term network outlook was grim. Everywhere he had gone those first six months at ABC, Murphy had talked about corporate waste and ABC's limousine culture. Now he added to his litany the need for "a true partnership" between networks and their affiliates in which swollen compensation payments would be addressed.

Murphy, in fact, had become so obsessive, even strident, about waste and cost cutting that by late in the spring of 1986 he felt a need to pull back. So he began to emphasize that, aside from Sias, the people running the network—in News, Entertainment, Sports, Sales, Affiliate Relations, Communications, Research—were all familiar ABC hands, and he began to reach out to them. Soon after the May affiliate meeting he was lunching with ABC Sports president Dennis Swanson. "How are things going?" asked Murphy.

"Great," said Swanson. "But I wish Cap Cities wouldn't dump on the old ABC so much."

Tom Murphy recounted this story to a senior Cap Cities/ABC management gathering early that summer, and then added: "You know who's to blame? Me. I'm going to stop. It's time to end the complaining. We're one company!"

6

THE CREEPING TAKEOVER OF CBS, WINTER TO SUMMER 1986

The Tisches began to walk with a bit of a swagger in the winter and spring of 1986, for celebrity and power accompanied their CBS stock purchases. At a party at the Tavern on the Green to honor a book written by Don Hewitt, the executive producer of CBS's *60 Minutes,* correspondent Morley Safer ambled up to Bob Tisch, who immediately recognized the famous face and stuck out a hand. "Hi, boss!" said the impish Safer.

Within CBS, Morley Safer's joke was no laughing matter. By January of 1986, Loews owned 12 percent of CBS. As the largest CBS shareholder, Bob's brother, Larry, was not just another director. Nevertheless, at first Larry Tisch mostly listened to CBS chairman Tom Wyman, becoming something of a confidant. "It's very lonely to be chief executive of a large corporation and not have anyone to talk to," said Tisch. "I think I have an input there now that is helpful to the company." Wyman cultivated Tisch, calling or walking the block to the Loews offices regularly.

Wyman said he was grateful: "It's wonderfully convenient being three hundred yards away. His secretary sort of blows you through. It gives you a nice feeling." When investor Marvin Davis met with Wyman in February and proposed to buy CBS for $160 a share, one of the few directors Wyman consulted before formally rejecting the offer was Larry Tisch. So cozy were Wyman and Tisch that the CBS chairman invited his largest shareholder to meet with his management team—Broadcast Group president Gene F. Jankowski, Records Group president Walter R. Yetnikoff, and Publishing Group president Peter A. Derow. Wyman volunteered to have each man visit Tisch, but Tisch said he would rather come to them. After the initial meetings, Tisch felt freer to meet again, and would invite each executive to lunch twice, joined by Bob Tisch. By that winter, Larry Tisch was also seeing a lot of senior vice president for finance Fred J. Meyer, perhaps Wyman's closest friend in the company.

The more Larry and Bob Tisch learned about CBS, the more troubled they became. From Fred Meyer they learned that CBS's real estate expenses for 1985 were $30.9 million. Why, they wondered, did CBS own the thirty-six-story Black Rock building if it was also renting space all over town? And why did it have these long-term, non-cancellable leases? The Tisches were becoming agitated. "I heard, or Bob heard, or somebody heard, that Wyman wanted to take the restaurant downstairs and turn it into an employee cafeteria," complained Larry Tisch. He quickly calculated a loss of rental revenues amounting to perhaps $500,000 annually, plus an additional $1 million to convert the space. Even crazier, he thought, was the $362.5 million CBS paid in 1984 to acquire the twelve Ziff-Davis magazines.

Tisch became convinced that he was seeing at CBS the same extravagance, the same cavalier disregard for shareholders, that his friend Tom Murphy told him about at ABC. There was a tradition of not thinking about costs because profits were taken for granted. Like the new owners at ABC and NBC, Tisch would be accused of caring for nothing but making money. Over the next year or two, the battles at CBS would attract more attention than those at the other two networks, partly because the press had greater access there, partly because Tisch handled the press so maladroitly, partly because "the Tiffany network" was a magnet for the media. Of the three takeovers, surely CBS's was the most peculiar. Instead of an arranged marriage between two consenting corporations whose stockholders sold their shares for a substantial premium, CBS slowly succumbed to a forced marriage without benefit of either ceremony or dowry.

Tom Wyman didn't want to believe the worst about Tisch. He found his financial advice helpful, and he welcomed and followed many of his ideas. Larry and Billie Tisch traveled that winter to Hollywood to pick the brains of studio heads Michael Eisner of Disney, Barry Diller of Twentieth Century Fox, Frank Mancuso of Paramount, Robert Daly of Warner, and Lew Wasserman of MCA/Universal Pictures. "I went out to learn more about the business," Tisch said.

On these visits Tisch was all questions. "He's totally unself-conscious about the fact that he doesn't know something," observed Jay Kriegel, a former chief of staff to former New York mayor John V. Lindsay, who has been close to the Tisch family since 1975. "And he won't give up until he understands it, or until he learns that his guys don't know the answers."

At all of his CBS-related meetings, Tisch gathered information, including information and impressions about Wyman. It was part of his style to share the information. When Tisch returned from his Hollywood visit he reported to Wyman: "I was on the West Coast last week and my impression was that the CBS people were not being competitive and effective." Wyman was receptive, because publicly, and even privately, Larry Tisch spoke kindly of Wyman all through the winter of 1986.

However, within the extraordinarily close Tisch clan, it was known that Larry was developing broad concerns about Wyman in two areas —his management and his leadership.

When he arrived at CBS from the Jolly Green Giant company in 1980, Tom Wyman said he was determined to purge the network of its profligate ways. Over dinner with a CBS executive that year, he announced: "I am going to change the culture of this company, and I am going to change it fast." In the clash between the culture and Wyman, the culture won, or so Tisch believed. He saw Wyman as a cautious bureaucrat. And the proof to Tisch could be found in their varied definitions of cost cutting. During a March 13, 1986, meeting with Wall Street analysts, the CBS chairman loomed over a lectern and crowed that the takeover threat had passed and that CBS was "the envy of the industry." By selling off assets, including its toy, cable, and movie-production subsidiaries, CBS had reduced its long-term debt by $200 million. Equally impressive, he reported that rigorous management had resulted in a $20 million reduction in overhead. The original goal, said Wyman, which was to achieve this cost saving in three years, or by 1987; instead, the goal would be met a year early. Because of these measures and a robust records business, Wyman said that CBS would not experience a loss for the first quarter of 1986, as originally forecast; he predicted a twenty-five- to fifty-cent-a-share profit.

Tom Wyman seemed to impress his audience of analysts, but not his audience of one. The next day, Larry Tisch sat behind his desk at Loews and offered the same critique of Wyman that would one day be leveled at Tisch's own reliance on interest from treasury notes rather than on profits from the operation of CBS's broadcast business. "It's not meaningful," said Tisch. "Half the quarterly gains are from non-operating transactions. And the other part is primarily from the record company." Tisch projected that broadcast revenues would remain relatively flat for the near term. "I'm always more cautious,"

Tisch said. "I would get my budget in line to a lower projection. If given a choice between projecting a revenue gain of 3 or 7 percent, I'd pick 3 percent. And I'd get my costs in line to 3 percent." At a time when his fellow New York University trustee Tom Murphy was hacking away at ABC's costs, Tisch believed a three-year, $20 million slice from CBS's costs was a "piddling" sum.

Was there a danger that his pessimism might result in harsh dislocations? No, Tisch said, although his actions in the future would contradict his prediction. "Attrition can take care of 99 percent of your problem. You shouldn't disrupt the business with wholesale firings." As for the news division, he said, "deliverance of the news comes ahead of considerations for profitability." He would justify this approach to shareholders by explaining to them that if News is healthy, the likelihood is that the evening schedule would be as well. "Besides," he added, "we have an obligation, that comes with the franchise, to deliver news in a first-class manner." This was the kind of sentiment he offered freely at the time, although it was not clear whether his remarks expressed caveats or convictions.

Tisch's concern about Wyman's leadership abilities—the same concern that would be voiced about Tisch a year later—focused on repeated complaints of low morale and lack of programming expertise at the network: "TV is a creative business," he said. "Can Wyman create that sense of freedom to produce interesting programming, new programming? I don't know. Bill Paley understood programming. This is an art, not a science." Tom Wyman's background was consumer products, not entertainment.

By mid-winter, Tisch came to believe that Wyman, whom he personally liked, was in the wrong job and that it was only a matter of time before he would be replaced. Perhaps a good year for the networks would save his job temporarily, but in the long run, whispered a member of the Tisch clan, "we will only exercise effective control when we have someone we appoint as CEO and chairman." Then this family member let slip the thought that perhaps Larry Tisch himself sought a more elevated role than passive investor: "Who is better as head of a business than Larry Tisch? He could be chairman and CEO."

What Tisch really thought of Wyman then he didn't say, and one reason for this was the extraordinary support Wyman enjoyed from his board. Most directors gave Wyman high marks as a manager. They applauded his willingness to surround himself with what they perceived as strong executives. They liked his adroitness at juggling so many balls in the air, beginning with Jesse Helms's onslaught in January 1985. "He had to keep the troops' spirits up, he had to keep the wolves at bay, he had a board to deal with, he had a founder to keep happy, he had to deal with wild swings in the stock market," said director Franklin Thomas. "I think Tom has done an extraordinarily good job."

In addition, Wyman had personal or business ties to more than half the board. At Green Giant in Minneapolis, he became a close friend of Edson W. Spencer, the chairman and CEO of Honeywell Inc. which is also based there. Wyman served on the American Telephone and Telegraph Company board and the Business Council with Henry B. Schacht, chairman and CEO of the Cummins Engine Company, who first suggested Wyman to William Paley as a candidate for CEO at CBS. Along with Frank Thomas, Wyman was on Schacht's board. Together Wyman, Schacht, and Spencer were on Thomas's board at the Ford Foundation. The law firm of a fifth director, Roswell L. Gilpatric, retired presiding partner of Cravath, Swaine & Moore, was CBS's principal legal representative. CBS's only other outside law firm was Sidley & Austin, whose partner, former FCC chairman Newton N. Minow, was a sixth CBS director. The investment banking firm of a seventh director, James D. Wolfensohn, not only earned fees from CBS in 1985, but also served as an investment advisor to Schacht's Cummins Engine Company. The interlocking relationships among this board were rounded out by an eighth director—former secretary of defense Harold Brown—who was on the Cummins board with Wyman, Thomas, and Schacht and a general partner of Wolfensohn's in various venture capital businesses.

Larry Tisch's true attitude toward CBS was often voiced by brother Bob. In contrast to his more reclusive brother, Bob Tisch was a public figure, a gregarious man active in the Association for a Better New York and other organizations promoting the city, a gentleman who rarely said no to a charity, a cocktail party fundraiser, or a press interview. Bob Tisch caused a stir at CBS when the March 24 issue of *USA Today* appeared. During an interview, Bob explained Loews's goal this way: "The eventual goal is to control CBS and operate it as a first-class broadcasting company the way it was and the way it can and should be." This article was perhaps the first public warning of what the next half year promised for CBS, and directors were horrified. Their reaction was summed up by one of them, who said: "Is it Bob or Larry talking? I choose to read it as Bob. But a hair went up on the back of my neck when I read it." Bob Tisch was contrite, but he did not deny that the words were his: "I talked when I should have been listening. I did say it. It was stupid."

Bob Tisch's words served as a reminder of broader philosophical differences between the board and Tisch. Wyman and most directors were troubled by the takeovers at ABC and NBC, believing it unhealthy for any one man or institution to own more than 50 percent of a network that is, in effect if not in fact, a government-licensed public utility. Perhaps they came to this position out of self-interest or even naïveté—after all, one institution, RCA, had always owned NBC—but what stayed with them after a year of jousting with raiders was a conviction given voice by Wyman, who said, "The broader the ownership, the more accountable the ownership, the better it is. The managers should feel a sense of accountability to the shareholders." Tisch also said he believed CBS was a public utility, but, significantly, differed with Wyman and the board: "I think there's a greater sense of responsibility when it's placed in one individual or small group than if it's diverse. There's always somebody responsible."

Bob Tisch became an issue between Larry Tisch and CBS. On the thirty-fifth floor of Black Rock, they often referred to Bob as "Preston," evidence that they did not take him seriously. There was no appreciation of how Larry Tisch relied on his brother to manage Loews's day-to-day business, to assuage and motivate employees, to serve as Mr. Outside. They did not comprehend the emotional ties between the two billionaires. In late March, when the *USA Today* interview with Bob Tisch appeared, CBS executives wanted Larry to issue a denial. Although he was upset by his brother's loose tongue, he said nothing. Torn between embarrassing his brother or CBS's management, Larry Tisch chose not to embarrass his brother.

This issue erupted at the annual CBS shareholders meeting in Philadelphia on April 16. Irate board members grumbled that Larry was too concerned about Bob's feelings. "Larry, I'd like an explanation for the interview your bigmouth brother gave *USA Today* about CBS." said Edson Spencer in the executive session before the board met with shareholders. The question was premeditated. "Wyman knew beforehand he'd ask the question," said senior vice president Fred J. Meyer. "There was a lot of phone traffic prior to the meeting," said another CBS executive. Larry Tisch said he did not take Spencer's question as a challenge, but he would not rebuke his brother.

One of the reasons that Larry would not rebuke Bob was that in the spring of 1986, Bob Tisch was unhappy not to be more involved with CBS. After all, he was an equal partner in Loews, and half the investment in CBS was his. The brothers had always done everything together. Now, after years of the hotel, insurance, and tobacco businesses, they were owners of a company that Bob Tisch spoke of reverentially. He was proud of how they had saved CBS. And what was his reward? Bob Tisch had to skulk around for fear of upsetting people or upstaging his brother, as happened in the *USA Today* interview. He didn't blame his brother, but he did complain to him. And Larry Tisch agreed. "I think Bob would be a good addition to the board," he said privately at the time. Tisch said he had never uttered this thought to Wyman or the other directors. He just seemed to expect that someone—surely Wyman—would understand that the Tisch brothers were a team.

Wyman and a majority of his board were as unaware of Tisch's true feelings as Larry Grossman had been of Jack Welch's passion for the sixth game of the 1986 World Series. "I don't think that Larry sees Bob in such a role," said Wyman at the time. On this issue, Wyman and Bill Paley were aligned. Bob Tisch, said Paley, "is represented by his brother. I'd rather have variety."

The board's anxiety about Loews was exacerbated by a tangle of network woes. The once impregnable *CBS Evening News* with Dan Rather, which had enjoyed a string of 199 unbroken weeks as the number-one newscast, was now threatened by a surging Tom Brokaw on NBC. More ominously, CBS Entertainment was being nudged into second place that spring by the new ratings champion, NBC. And with the April resignation of Harvey Shephard, one-half of CBS's Entertainment team, morale was in the basement. The president of CBS Entertainment, old-timer B. "Bud" Donald Grant, was a wisecracking cynic who openly disparaged Broadcast Group president Gene Jankowski. Paley ridiculed the programming talents of Grant and Wyman, and longed for Robert A. Daly of Warner to return to CBS. Daly had resigned in 1980, one of the few men to leave Paley's employ voluntarily and a rarity among Entertainment executives in that he left while still considered a success. Paley was preoccupied with the Tiffany image; he had been since he hired his first public relations advisor when he acquired a few radio stations in 1928. This preoccupation with appearances—showing off to the federal government the symphonies and other quality programs the CBS radio network aired in the thirties, investing money in "Murrow's boys" and a premier news division in the forties, paying top dollar to lure talent away from network leader NBC in the fifties, sparing no expense in designing everything from a building to a logo—seeped into the CBS culture, became part of its self-image. For a quarter century, CBS was accustomed to being number one in entertainment and news. To slip, even momentarily, was to fail.

Determined to restore CBS's faded glory, in the spring of 1986 the founder asked to see Daly, who had worked for him for twenty-six years, at his New York apartment. "William Paley offered me Tom Wyman's job," recalled Daly, seated in an oversized office on the Warner lot, almost an entire wall of which featured an oval window that peers into a 240-gallon stainless steel fish tank. "He implied to me that Larry Tisch knew about it," though Tisch said he did not. Some weeks later, saying he was happy where he was, Daly declined Paley's overture. Trade press reports of Paley's visits rocked Wyman and his team. "This isn't helpful," Wyman said. "It raises questions about my authority here."

The rumors and bad news, some real, some fanciful, struck CBS with machine-gun frequency. The *New York Post*'s Page Six reported that Larry Tisch wanted to "dump" the CBS Records Group and sell while its profits were flush. Tisch assured Wyman it was untrue—*Why would I want to sell a business making such profits? The Washington Post* reported that Bob Tisch—"Big Mouth," as director Edson Spencer had referred to him—declared that Loews planned to increase its CBS stake above the agreed 25 percent to 35 percent. Larry Tisch assured Wyman it was untrue. In the art-filled, cloth-covered corridors of Black Rock, speculation reached fever pitch about Loews's intentions. *Was Larry Tisch just a passive investor? Would he buy more? Would he sell? Did he want to replace Wyman? Did he wish to run the company himself?*

At the same time, advertising revenues were off. So CBS announced still another round of layoffs. The total number of CBS employees—which reached 26,041 at the end of 1984 and dipped to 25,049 in 1985—was expected to fall by 9 percent to 23,745 by July of 1986. The Broadcast Group, which employed 8,000 and lost 305 positions in 1985, would lose another 140.

Morale was low. CBS was succumbing to a creeping takeover by the Loews Corporation. And it wasn't until midspring that Tom Wyman seemed to awaken to this. A gentleman to a fault, Wyman felt his anger rising. After months of what he described as "Chinese water torture," he had finally come to a decision. There was no one incident or point at which Wyman and his team decided that Tisch was the enemy. By May of 1986, however, Wyman recalled later, he had a "sense of intrusion," of "a foreigner who has plans to alter the structure." On this point, he said, there was no dissent. Even Bill Paley, who often opposed Wyman, was against Tisch's taking over CBS. "He thought it was unthinkable," said Wyman, who started visiting with the founder more regularly beginning in April and May. Board members Spencer and Wolfensohn began quietly pushing Wyman to come up with a white knight alternative to Tisch.

But Wyman still hoped to preserve CBS's independence, still hoped to keep Tisch in line, and toward this end he scheduled a strategy meeting of his "war group" on the afternoon of May 28 in the west conference room on the thirty-fifth floor. This was the same team that successfully fended off onslaughts from Ivan Boesky, Ted Turner, Jesse Helms, and Marvin Davis. The team consisted of investment banker Joseph G. Fogg III of Morgan Stanley, outside counsel Alan Stephenson of Cravath, and three CBS executives—counsel George Vradenburg III, senior vice president Fred Meyer, and senior vice president for Corporate Affairs William Lilly III. The one missing member of the team was attorney Joseph H. Flom of Skadden Arps Slate, Meagher & Flom, who had been retained by Morgan Stanley. Flom was not invited because of his longstanding links to Tisch.

The purpose of the meeting was to decide what CBS might do if Tisch were to buy more than 25 percent of the stock. Their dilemma was that the team worked within a strategic straitjacket. On the one hand they wanted to be aggressive, to repel Tisch and other potential invaders, and on the other they wanted to advance the impression of a serene CBS, a company unconcerned with a takeover. In addition, it was a lot easier to go after Ted Turner than it was Larry Tisch, a bland businessman with deep pockets. What was left to CBS as options were short-term defensive maneuvers—such as issuing more stock to dilute the percentage Tisch owned. Frustrated with such a passive approach, investment banker Fogg, sounding like a football coach, advised that the best defense was a good offense. He urged Wyman to draw a line in the sand and tell Tisch that if he crossed it CBS would consider it a hostile act. Wyman, he said, had either to sell the company to a friendly buyer or resurrect the idea of taking CBS private through a leveraged buyout.

The idea of selling the company didn't appeal to Wyman. He was intent on exploring other, more cautious options, including getting Tisch to sign a standstill agreement pledging not to acquire more than 25 percent of CBS stock. Such an agreement, recalled Fred Meyer, "was sort of a litmus test" of Tisch's intentions. Wyman would pursue this option himself, and promised to convene the "war group" again soon.

The war group never again met. Within twenty-four hours Wyman heard that Tisch knew of the meeting. *Where the hell did the leak come from?* Did it come from Joe Flom, who might have learned of the meeting from Morgan Stanley? Did it come from Morgan Stanley itself, which had extensive business dealings with Loews? Or did the leak come from inside? Tom Wyman was certain of one thing: Tisch knew, and he was furious. Wyman decided to disband the war group, and became even more dependent on the advice of two board members, Jim Wolfensohn and Ros Gilpatric. Wolfensohn, who had first introduced Wyman to his Saturday tennis partner, now played the role of Wyman's private investment banker; and Gilpatric, a man who had served as Tisch's counsel during the takeover of the Lorillard tobacco company, became Wyman's legal confidant.

Wyman didn't know if he was surrounded by assassins. Yet he had to be realistic. After all, Tisch was his major shareholder, and it would be best to clear the air. So Wyman decided to visit Tisch.* The CBS chairman walked the three hundred yards or so to Loews's offices and, according to Tisch, used as a pretext for the meeting a profile of Tisch that had just appeared in *The New York Times Magazine.* The article explored Tisch's frustrations with Wyman. Why, Wyman wanted to know, did Tisch feel the budget reductions Wyman had ordered were a "piddling" sum? Wyman recalls the meeting this way: "I went over to see him and asked, 'What makes sense here? How do we take some heat out of this gathering awkwardness?' "

"I think you should resign," Tisch replied abruptly. "I think you're a nice man. I've always liked you. But you're not the man to run this company." Tisch was pessimistic about the business and believed Wyman should cut costs more aggressively. To this day Tisch insists the meeting was not antagonistic, though he does recall this exchange:

"I'm not a rich man," said Wyman.

"Tom, if ever you left CBS I'm sure the board would be generous," said Tisch. Wyman remembers Tisch's words differently, almost as a bribe: "Financially, I don't have to tell you, Tom, that you wouldn't have to work another day in your life."

Wyman returned to CBS shocked by Tisch's "clinical forthrightness," and told his friend Fred Meyer: "I had a tough meeting with

* The date of this visit is disputed, but not that it took place or that it was unpleasant. Since several accounts indicate that Wyman briefly mentioned the encounter at a June 10 board dinner, and since Tisch was specifically excluded from this dinner, the likely date is June rather than July, as some recalled.

Tisch." Since charm failed, Wyman fell back on a plan to ask Tisch to sign a standstill agreement, the same request he had made in October 1985 when he invited Tisch to join the board. His messenger would be Gilpatric, who visited Tisch after "informal" discussions with fellow directors.

When Gilpatric entered Tisch's office on June 9, 1986, and proposed a standstill, the Loews chairman went ballistic. He would never sign a standstill—ever. He had already rejected the idea once. For the subject to be raised again suggested a lack of confidence in his word. Tisch shouted: *Since I have said publicly that I have no intention of going above 25 percent, you are challenging my word. Insulting me!*

Gilpatric shouted back: *CBS is a great institution, and has to protect itself, has to guard against the whispers that would panic investors and unnerve employees. If you won't accept a standstill, then how about agreeing to give CBS thirty to sixty days' advance notice if you plan to go above 25 percent?*

Absolutely not! said Tisch, who was both insulted and convinced that Wyman and his advisors were naive. What Tisch really thought was: *How dare board members with few shares try to dictate to a major shareholder? Gilpatric owns only 1,492 shares of CBS. Tom Wyman owns 10,867 shares. They are clerks! Loews owns more than 3 million shares! Only Tisch and Paley can think like owners because only we own major blocks of stock.*

Surprisingly, Tisch had a powerful ally on this point—Bill Paley. "A lot of our board members wanted him to sign a standstill," recalled Paley. "I never was for that. He didn't have anything to gain by doing that." Wyman's strategy at the time was essentially one of containment, hoping to separate Tisch from the board. The strategy hinged on keeping Tisch away from Paley, who could sway the votes of at least a couple of directors. Wyman believed this strategy would work, even though Paley plainly detested the man who removed him as chairman. On a personal level, Bill Paley resented that Wyman had banished him, the man with a proven feel for programming, from the deliberations to determine the fall schedule; Wyman had humiliated him deliberately, Paley felt, by selling his CBS helicopter and corporate jet, by charging him $72,558 annually for the 2,041 square feet of space he occupied at Black Rock, and by no longer allowing Paley to host a cocktail hour after each board meeting. Wyman had even changed the seating arrangement at board luncheons in Paley's own dining room.

Despite Paley's Lear-like rage, his aborted attempt to recruit and persuade directors to oust Wyman in the early eighties, Wyman was confident that Paley would not join hands with Tisch. Therefore Tisch would have to own more than 25 percent of the stock in order to gain control. "It never occurred to me, I never gave any credence, to the fact he might find a way to draw Paley into an alliance to produce 35 percent," recalls Wyman. Wyman thought CBS's founder was a snob, a man who would surely be offended by Tisch's ownership of hotels that saved money by using paper napkins and skimping on quality, by his relatively primitive grasp of art, by the few books adorning his home library. Paley was born a Jew but ever since he came to New York in the 1930s, his social set was mostly Protestant, as were his two wives. He did not think of himself either as a Jew or as a champion of Israel, as did Tisch. Bill Paley would cringe at the thought of a rabbi coming to his office to offer Talmudic instruction, or at the thought of spending Saturday nights sitting on plastic chairs while watching movies. Tom Wyman believed he and Bill Paley were of the same class. And Wyman also felt comfortable with Paley's attorney, Arthur Liman, a prominent corporate and criminal defense attorney who would serve in 1987 as chief counsel to the senate committee investigating the Iran-contra affair and would later become chief defense counsel for Michael Milken. Wyman felt that Liman was a bridge builder.

But unbeknownst to Wyman, Liman had forged a bridge between Tisch and Paley, who were now talking more, sharing their frustrations. "We see eye to eye," said Tisch that summer. The years were beginning to sap Paley's physical and intellectual energy; when visitors came to his office in the morning, he usually sat with a typed card before him to remind him of his guest's name. At eight-four, Bill Paley had become dependent on Liman. At one time Paley would have consulted more widely, seeking counsel from such friends as Felix Rohatyn or John Gutfreund, chairman of Salomon Brothers. But as he grew more frail, Paley leaned more on Liman.

So, in a different way, did Tisch lean on Liman. As he moved onto the CBS stage, Tisch took the precaution of engaging in exhaustive conversations that summer with his neighbor on Manursing Island. Liman, Tisch would say, was the person outside his family whose counsel he would seek first in a crunch. Liman, in a sense, wore two hats, as Paley's lawyer and as Tisch's friend. From conversations with his friend Liman and with Paley, Tisch realized one rock-hard fact that would stay with him: "Bill hated Tom Wyman. Wyman humiliated him. Wyman wouldn't allow Bill to come to program meetings. From that point on Wyman was dead in the water with Bill."

But as long as the overwhelming majority of the board was in his corner, Wyman would retain control. And Wyman's interests happened to coincide with those of most of the directors, who were increasingly alarmed that Tisch was slowly acquiring CBS without paying a premium—as any other raider would have to do—for the privilege. This offended them. They thought it was wrong. And, as a practical matter, it exposed the directors to legal challenge from shareholders. If they allowed control of the company simply to slip to Tisch without extracting a reward for shareholders, they could be charged with failing to exercise their fiduciary responsibility. How could they justify turning down the premium offered shareholders by Ted Turner or Marvin Davis and then let Tisch walk right in and buy his controlling shares on the open market? "No one was feeling good about the creeping tender," admits Michel Bergerac, the former chairman and CEO of Revlon who would become a swing vote on the board. Nor were they feeling particularly good about Tisch. His nagging and complaints, said Bergerac, "left some scars."

How deep those scars were could be gauged at an unusual dinner at the River Club on June 10. Informal director dinners the evening before a board meeting had become customary after Wyman early that spring had summarily rejected a $160-per-share bid for the company from Marvin Davis without fully consulting his board. What was unusual about this dinner was that Tisch was specifically excluded. Wyman and the board wanted the freedom to vent their frustrations and to devise a strategy. Wyman opened the dinner with a complaint: *The rumors and press stories are undermining the management of CBS, weakening our stock price, making my task extremely awkward.* Wyman did not share with the board the unpleasant message he had taken away from his private encounter with Tisch, but merely reported that they had met and that Tisch was combative. Gilpatric briefed the board on his session with Tisch, in which he had refused even to consider a standstill agreement. As a counterweight to Tisch, Gilpatric proposed that CBS adopt a defensive poison pill to repel Loews or any other raider. The directors were unswayed. Such a move, they said, would be interpreted as a sign of panic, inviting more rumors, more instability, and perhaps a bidding war. Instead, they informally agreed that a three-member delegation composed of Gilpatric, Jim Wolfensohn, and Frank Thomas should visit Tisch to argue their case for a standstill agreement and that at the next day's board meeting Tisch would be asked to offer a public pledge of support to Wyman.

Tisch attended the next day's board meeting and was confronted by directors who complained about their fiduciary responsibilities, about damaging rumors, about instability, about the depressed morale at the network and the wildly gyrating price of CBS stock. The most vociferous director was Ros Gilpatric, who was at a stage in life where he needn't worry about offending Tisch. The session was contentious. Tisch exclaimed that there wasn't a scintilla of evidence that he planned to go above 25 percent. "My present intention is to go up to 25 percent," Tisch told his inquisitors.

"What about your future intention?" Bergerac remembers one director asking.

Suddenly Tisch switched tactics, became more supplicant than challenger. He said, recalls Frank Thomas, "I'm not trying to undermine CBS. What can I do to be helpful?"

A public statement of support, in writing, would be helpful, the directors replied. Tisch at first refused, claiming it would bring more attention to CBS, but the directors were suspicious. "It was a bit like the girl who says, 'I love you but I don't want to go to bed with you.' It wasn't terribly convincing," recalls Bergerac.

Sensing that he was nearly alone, Tisch relented. Consider it done, he said. Members of the board sighed with relief.

The next day a brief, two-paragraph letter was hand-delivered to Wyman:

> Dear Tom:
>
> I have been concerned, as I am sure you have been, by recent articles in the press regarding the Loews investment in CBS. I want to reiterate to you that I continue to have full confidence in you and your management.
>
> Last October when I accepted your invitation to join the CBS Board, I advised you that Loews intended to purchase up to 25% of the outstanding shares of CBS. There has been no change at all in our intentions.

Some directors were initially satisfied. "There was a sense of relief on our board that the status quo would be resumed," recalls Marietta Tree, a regal woman of great breeding and charm. Tree's preoccupation, like that of her mentor William Paley and others, was that CBS remain independent. Wyman, however, was not satisfied, noticing that the original letter came over on Bob Tisch's stationery and had to be sent back. Instead of offering comic relief, this was seen as an indication of how lightly the Loews chairman took this matter. Of the letter, Wyman said, "I would not have shown it to my mother as evidence that everything was fine." It was a measure of Wyman's disappointment that Tisch's letter was not released to the press, as intended.

Tisch himself confessed privately that he had sent the letter only because "I didn't want to hurt the company. There are degrees of unhappiness. I could live with Wyman. If Wyman had played it straight with me, I could have protected him." The letter was, Tisch thought, a harmless fib, one that was in the interests of CBS. However, that was not how many directors would come to view it. To them it was part of a pattern of lies.

The next step in the board's containment strategy was for the three-member delegation to visit Tisch and "revisit the question of a standstill agreement." "We were trying to see if we could get him to firm up his intentions," recalls Gilpatric, who would serve as spokesman.

The meeting was scheduled for 3 P.M. on June 18, 1986, which happened to be the day after Loews's CBS stake had climbed to 19.7 percent. Instead of asking the delegation into his office, Tisch placed them in the spartan conference/dining room he shared with his brother, where they were offered Coca-Colas and told to wait. Tisch, sensing the purpose of the session, was particularly incensed to see his old friend and tennis partner Jim Wolfensohn in attendance. Acting as spokesman, Gilpatric raised the question of a standstill agreement. Tisch tried to cut him off.

But Gilpatric insisted on making his point on behalf of the board: *Surely, Larry, you understand our fiduciary responsibility. We spurned offers from Ted Turner and Marvin Davis. Yet we may be allowing Loews in the back door, at a lower rate, and without protest. We cannot accept that. We have to protect shareholders.*

All pretense to politeness dissolved. Tisch was furious, and by all accounts, including memoranda on file at CBS, railed at the delegation, insisting that he had already said he would not go beyond 25 percent. By persisting in questioning him, they were really saying they mistrusted him. "You get advance notice if I want to go above 25 percent," Tisch said. "I have to file a new Hart/Scott filing" with the federal government. Why wasn't that sufficient? Tisch was suspicious. Not only didn't they take him at his word, but he sensed they had a secret plan to adopt a poison pill, and he complained about this to his friend Arthur Liman afterward.

At least four things bothered Tisch about a standstill, only one of which—the mistrust it implied—he recited to his guests. As a business proposition, such an agreement would inhibit Loews's options, which no businessman desires. There was an emotional reason. According to his attorney, Martin Lipton, "Larry's attitude during this whole period was that he had a big stake in the company and people who didn't have a big stake were acting like he was doing something wrong. It drove Larry up a wall that someone who owns one hundred shares is trying to tell Larry what was good for shareholders." There was a final, more calculated reason, for Tisch's resistance. "Larry certainly was not going to sign a standstill after he had reached a conclusion on Wyman," said Lipton. But were there any circumstances under which he would have signed? Yes, said Lipton. "We would have signed a standstill if it were presented as a condition of Wyman leaving." The reasoning was simple. "As a practical matter," said a Loews executive, "we knew we couldn't go above 25 percent without opening the issue of a 'change of control.' " That is to say, under a federal rule imposed in 1970, no company could own more than a single radio or TV station or newspaper in one market. The only exceptions would be those companies—like the three networks—that owned such properties prior to the new rule. If Loews went above 25 percent, it might be compelled by the FCC to sell either a CBS radio or TV station in such cities as New York or Philadelphia. Or CBS might be forced to petition the FCC for a waiver, as both Cap Cities and GE were then doing.

Aware of this rule, and deeply insulted, Tisch was in a foul mood. So when the delegation pressed for his views on the CBS management, for the first time he blurted out what he had said only to Wyman and to close associates. "Do you really want to know?" said Tisch.

They did.

You asked me, so I'll tell you. There are too many layers of vice presidents and staff, and not enough hands-on managers. When he looked at the group presidents—he specifically mentioned Walter Yetnikoff of CBS Records and Peter Derow of CBS Publishing—he declared: *Yetnikoff is good. But Derow could go tomorrow and no one would miss him. He's superfluous. Wyman should cut more deeply into waste, the way Tom Murphy is doing at ABC. The programming people in Hollywood are in over their heads, and CBS could slip to third this season. I like Gene Jankowski and Tom Leahy*—president, CBS Broadcast Group and executive vice president, CBS Broadcast Group respectively—*but they are administrators, who add nothing to the creative mix. The outside directors are in a fog about what goes on inside CBS. And Tom Wyman is not a businessman, not a strong leader. A tough CEO could clean up that place in no time.*

The three directors were stunned by Tisch's diatribe but also enlightened. They walked away convinced that Larry Tisch had flashed his hole card, revealed his true feelings and intentions. Seven days after professing his public support for Wyman in writing, Tisch was telling them his letter was a sham. He was intent on removing CBS's management. Wolfensohn knew his relationship with his old friend was ruptured, that Tisch felt betrayed, though he didn't quite understand why. He thought Tisch demanded a personal loyalty to him at the expense of Wolfensohn's public responsibilities to CBS shareholders. Wolfensohn did not buy Tisch's protestations of innocence and believed Tisch was scheming to take over CBS. As an independent director, he felt he had no choice but "to call attention to the facts of the situation." But Lipton said Tisch expected at least the courtesy of Wolfensohn's coming to him and saying, "Look, I'm on the other side." Instead, said Lipton, "he felt Wolfensohn tried to play both sides." What also stuck in Tisch's craw was the belief that Wolfensohn harbored secret hopes of taking over CBS himself, which is why he had pushed so hard to do a leveraged buyout in the spring of 1985. Each man thought the other guilty of a lack of candor.

Gilpatric was also trying to follow the trail of facts, and these prompted him to write a memorandum describing the meeting. Tisch's outburst, he wrote, left CBS directors with two courses of action. First, there was a need for "contingency planning for the eventuality of Loews at some point going beyond 25% ownership in CBS," planning that could be done by the three-man committee, assisted by inside (George Vradenburg) and outside (Alan Stephenson) counsel. Second, "the management questions raised by Tisch should be discussed with the other outside directors" when they next meet for dinner on July 8, and then "perhaps pursued by another subcommittee of the board . . ."

Wyman was distressed by the briefing he received from the three-member delegation. He wanted to get rid of Tisch, and he asked Wolfensohn to speed up work on "the Project," as he code-named Wolfensohn's quiet search for a white knight. But a fundamental ambivalence on the part of both men would slow the task. Wolfensohn worried that by letting word out that they were seeking a suitor CBS would be inviting an auction they could not control. And Wyman, though he wanted to be rescued from Tisch, really didn't want to sell

CBS or to relinquish his crown. Foolishly, he still hoped that a powerful foe—Bill Paley—would save him.

That hope was dissipated when Gilpatric, Wolfensohn, and Frank Thomas visited Paley. Briefed by Tisch's friend Arthur Liman beforehand about the purpose of the meeting, Paley told them, flat-out, that he, too, was dissatisfied with Wyman. Still, in mid-June neither the independent directors nor Wyman suspected that Paley and Tisch, their link cemented by Liman, would come together. But the rupture that many board members hoped had been healed by Tisch's June letter to Wyman was now out in the open. Once again, the full board would have to address the question of Larry Tisch's true intentions.

The subject was placed on the agenda of the board's July 8 dinner at the Links Club. In discussing their options, Ros Gilpatric again suggested they should adopt a poison pill to chase Tisch, a suggestion greeted warmly by a few of Wyman's core allies—Spencer, Schacht, and Houghton—but skeptically by most of the board. Once again, the what-to-do question just floated away, unresolved. Most directors thought the poison pill option was buried for now; Gilpatric, however, came away thinking he was expected to craft such a pill. Privately, the core of Wyman loyalists pulled Wyman aside and asked him what they dared not ask in front of Paley loyalists like Walter Cronkite and Marietta Tree, or even in front of those swing votes like Michel Bergerac and Newton Minow: *What alternatives to Loews are you and Wolfensohn coming up with?*

In order to permit what diplomats call "a frank exchange of views," Wyman left at 9:30 P.M. and Tisch arrived after the dinner dishes were cleared. It was awkward. "It was like being called in to the grand jury," said Bergerac.

The directors came at Tisch like prosecutors. "Come on, let's get it on the table," Frank Thomas said, as he sought to "tease" information from a reluctant witness.

"What I said to Frank and Ros and Jim was in response to their questions," Tisch told them. "I didn't force this on the table."

Okay, but now that it's on the table we'd like your candid response.

Tisch answered that he was dissatisfied with Wyman and the management of CBS. On this point he had an ally, as Paley chimed his support. Like Wyman, most board members still gave hardly a moment's thought to a possible coalition between Tisch and the CBS founder. They believed that Paley's resentment of a rival owner would eclipse his hatred for a mere employee like Wyman. Yet directors could not ignore that the company's two largest shareholders were unhappy, so they offered a proposal: Since the agenda was full for the next day's directors' meeting and since the board did not meet in August, they would reserve time in September for these management questions.

Both Tisch and Paley were placated, for a time.

The directors gathered the next morning in the boardroom on the thirty-fifth floor at Black Rock, and peace reigned during the usual resolutions and status reports. At any rate, it reigned until Wyman handed Tisch and Paley another loaded weapon, this time in the form of a jumbled economic presentation from him and Broadcast Group president Gene Jankowski.

Not without reason did colleagues refer to Jankowski as "the Salesman." He was always up, always ebullient, always reluctant to dwell on bad news. And as Wyman introduced him, Jankowski looked the part, with his neatly parted hair, crisp, button-down shirt, and Gucci loafers. Wyman told the board a press release on their second-quarter earnings, which showed CBS revenues were running slightly ahead of projections for the first half of the year, was going out that day.

Jankowski explained that they were making progress on expense reductions—the Broadcast Group would eliminate 705 positions by year-end, with the timetable calling for 587 to be laid off in the month of July alone. Ever the optimist, Jankowski quickly added that this represented the final stage of layoffs. On the revenue side of the ledger, he reported that they were in the throes of what the networks call upfront sales, that crucial period at the beginning of each summer when the networks sell between 70 and 90 percent of their advertising inventory for the year. *It's too early to tell how strong the upfront will be. But I am encouraged,* said Jankowski, explaining that he expected total Broadcast Group profits to reach $334 million.

Tisch "went bananas," recalls Peter Derow, complaining that because revenues were not broken down "I can't get my hands around what's going on in the business." Just the month before, he noted, the Broadcast Group said its profits would total $370 million for the year, not $334 million. *What's going on here?*

Wyman backtracked, and was forced to admit that the profit picture was inflated by a one-time gain of $112 million from the sale of KMOX, the CBS-owned station in St. Louis. Even with this, said Wyman, trying to be upbeat, the Broadcast Group—which included the network, four CBS-owned stations, and CBS Radio—would still show a second-quarter profit of $8.1 million, which of course was so puny as to undermine Jankowski's rosy projection. It was so much wishful thinking, thought Michel Bergerac. With Wyman's allies as witness, Tisch had punctured the balloon. Wyman and Jankowski, said Bergerac, "gave the board the impression they didn't know what they were talking about."

The executive session that followed at around noon, and which included only the directors, was no less contentious. At one point Edson Spencer and James R. Houghton, chairman and CEO of Corning Glass Works, again raised the question of a standstill, again pursued the point that Tisch was slowly acquiring CBS without paying a premium, thus cheating shareholders. With a bored, this-has-already-been-discussed tone, Tisch reminded them that the stock he purchased was acquired on the open market. Then, heatedly, Tisch reiterated his opposition to a standstill and repeated his intention not to acquire more than 25 percent of CBS stock. Subject closed.

The subject is not closed, declared Ros Gilpatric, who felt Tisch was being duplicitous. As deputy secretary of defense, Gilpatric had said no to President John F. Kennedy. He had said no to Bill Paley. He had run one of the town's premier law firms and shed several wives, had squired Jackie Kennedy around town, had served on such prestigious boards as those of the Metropolitan Museum of Art and the New York Public Library. Ros Gilpatric was determined to stand up for the notion of truly "independent directors." He was determined to stand up to Larry Tisch. With barely controlled fury, he declared: *Well, Larry, since you won't clarify Loews's intentions and since the board has a fiduciary responsibility to assure CBS's independence and guard against a creeping takeover, the board agrees we have to consider the possibility of voting a poison pill to repel any predator.*

Board members were aghast. Gilpatric was proposing what they thought they had tabled the previous night. Now, as directors heard the idea hurled at Tisch, they were stunned.

Tisch charged at Gilpatric: *You are accusing me of duplicity. This is a declaration of war! This is personally offensive to me!*

Most members of the board did not care if Tisch was personally offended, and said so. "Larry blew his stack. Other people blew their stacks," said Bergerac.

The stormy meeting ended with the board hopelessly polarized and Tisch effectively isolated.

Yet, within days, Wyman would unwittingly hand more live grenades to Tisch. The first came on July 18 when Wyman passed on to the board a cheerful memorandum from Jankowski on the status of the upfront market. "The press has been giving considerable attention to this matter [upfront sales]," Wyman wrote the directors in a two-page cover memo. "The softness continues, but as the attached summary indicates our performance in the 'upfront' market is now essentially complete and is rather reassuring in relation to some forecasts of our 'collapse.'" The attached memoranda predicted CBS would end up with a larger network market share—35 percent or $865 million—than in 1985. However, it was silent on the prices CBS was charging. And the board wasn't told that CBS, in order to take more orders, was selling time at a discount.

"Probably Tom should have called and said to Gene, 'Market share doesn't mean a thing,'" concedes Fred Meyer. Wyman admits he didn't press Jankowski because "I didn't even understand it." Eager to communicate any ray of sunshine, Wyman passed along the memo at the end of the week.

That weekend Jankowski called Wyman at home to deliver shattering news: CBS upfront sales would be almost $100 million below projections. Jankowski explained that in the negotiations between CBS and advertisers, CBS was forced to sell inventory at rates 4 to 5 percent below last year's prices. Jankowski threw a blizzard of explanations at Wyman—inflation was down, depressing the prices they could charge advertisers; corporate profits were faltering, and advertising budgets were first to feel the pinch; the rise of independent TV stations and barter syndication opportunities was temporarily siphoning ad revenues from the networks; CBS's ratings were falling; all the talk of "tough times for the networks" gave a psychological edge to advertisers in the negotiations over ad rates; in a period of relatively low advertiser demand, a glut of fifteen-second commercials that sold at half the cost of thirty-second spots also depressed network prices.

Baffled, Wyman asked for a memorandum he could review Monday morning and hung up. When the CBS chairman arrived at work Monday he called in Fred Meyer and other members of his team to plot their next moves. Wyman was "shellshocked," said his friend Meyer, and resigned to the fact that Tisch would use this new weapon against him. "This will be an issue on which Tisch will get the support of the board," Wyman told Meyer.

Wyman knew he was in trouble, yet he told the group: "We've got to be candid with the board and bite the bullet." They decided Wyman would pass along Jankowski's second, gloomier report, accompanied by a three-page cover memorandum from Wyman detailing the $50 million in corporate cuts and salary freezes he would now impose. Dated July 29, Wyman's memo said "the price collapse" in upfront sales at all three networks "requires an important profit forecast revision for the balance of 1986." Profits in the Broadcast Group would be off by $96.5 million. But, Wyman hastened to add, these losses would be partially offset by an increase of $20 million in the estimated profits of the Records Group, and from another $30 million in savings from reduced interest and employee benefit payments.

Coming on the heels of the earlier memo and the board presentation—not to mention the overpayment for the Ziff-Davis magazines—the impact was devastating. "It was ridiculous," Tisch said of the final Wyman memo. "By that time I realized these guys didn't know what they were doing. They were always optimistic." Inexorably, the board was moving toward Tisch's position. Even Gilpatric, who in some ways was perceived as the most hostile to Tisch, said of the upfront debacle: "Some directors felt he [Wyman] should have anticipated it."

Then the news division set off another explosion. News, the pride of CBS, was in turmoil. In July, for the first time since October 1981, *CBS Evening News* with Dan Rather fell to third place, joining its morning news counterpart in the ratings cellar. *CBS Morning News,* which had disastrously experimented, at Van Gordon Sauter's urging, with former Miss America Phyllis George as cohost, was losing clearances from affiliates, which increasingly substituted their own programs. Rumors circulated that the morning time period would be snatched from News and turned over to the entertainment division.*

The news division was a cauldron of competing tribes. There were Rather's "Red Guards," as they were sometimes called, led by *Evening News* executive producer and Rather confidant Tom Bettag, a fierce advocate for traditional hard news; there were the Cronkite traditionalists, who felt estranged from Rather and blamed Sauter for ceding too much power to the anchor and for softening the evening news; there were younger producers like Andrew Heyward and Andrew Lack, who fell into no camp but who wanted television to be different from print, wanted it to use the power of pictures to tell stories, which led some to charge that they too really wanted to "soften" the news; there were Don Hewitt and his team of stars on *60 Minutes,* operating almost as a separate entity; and there were News's managers, led by Sauter, whom some perceived as unprincipled because they were eager to give the public the fluff it wanted rather than the hard news it should have.

At the red-hot center, as always, was Dan Rather, easily the most

* In late July, *CBS Morning News* was taken from News and awarded to a special broadcast group under the wing of executive vice president Tom Leahy.

powerful figure in the division. Rather was extremely uncomfortable that summer, torn between his role as a working journalist and his duties as managing editor, between his news values and his friendships. He was a jumble of emotions—eager to be polite and to please, yet determined to be a leader. Rather saw himself as an upholder of the Murrow tradition, yet he was not against donning a sweater on camera to soften his image, as he did in the winter of 1986. He saw himself as a manager when he selected stories and correspondents for the *Evening News,* yet he also saw himself as a rugged individualist. Rather felt an obligation to be the voice of lesser-known colleagues, but he also felt an obligation to Van Gordon Sauter, who was his fishing buddy and Connecticut neighbor. He considered Gene Jankowski a friend, called him "a mentor," yet he resented Black Rock, resented how, with the connivance of Sauter, they stole the morning show from the jurisdiction of News.

The one thing each tribe within News had in common was that nearly everyone blabbed to the media. All squabbles were public. For the Cronkite traditionalists, who felt most beleaguered, the ghost of Edward R. Murrow and the pioneering spirit of CBS News were invoked. They were angry that Sauter, who had taken over as News president for the second time early in 1986, was responsible for making network news more like local news, with more features, more pretty pictures and smiles. The brilliant and brash producer of *60 Minutes,* Don Hewitt, popped off freely about how the *Morning News* was an embarrassment and the public only wanted a half hour of news in the morning anyway, about how the news division should somehow do a leveraged buyout on its own, severing its ties to the network, and how the real curse of CBS News was that Sauter as head of News should be reporting directly to Wyman and not be caught in the squabbles of the Broadcast Group. For reporters who covered TV, CBS offered a daily public immolation and headline. In July 1986, after ninety more News layoffs were decreed, Andy Rooney wrote in his syndicated column: "CBS, which used to stand for the Columbia Broadcasting System, no longer stands for anything. They're just corporate initials now."

Sauter had little patience for this zoo. He was running a business, one he said would lose $31 million in 1986 if not for Hewitt's *60 Minutes.* Not to be concerned with ratings or whether affiliates would distribute your product, he felt, was like living on another planet. He hated the old Cronkite newscast, feeling it was nothing more than a wire-service review of the top twenty stories of the day. Television,

Sauter believed, should use pictures, tell stories, evoke feelings, and be different from print. His model was local news and tabloids. "Local news is the most democratic form of communications in this country," he told *Channels* magazine in an August interview. People wanted cozy entertainment in the morning, not unsettling news, and that's what they should have. Like Larry Tisch, Sauter also believed that CBS should be run in a more businesslike way. A newspaper that didn't make money, he said, would be bankrupt. Why was a network news operation different? "CBS is an organization protected from reality," he said. "Over the years money just came in over the transom. They say, 'We have to cover the summit.' I say, 'The money's not in the budget. It will cost two to three million dollars.' No one blinks an eye in saying, 'Do it.' "

Two truths were colliding. The news traditionalists advanced one truth, which was that theirs was a proud tradition threatened by those with too little reverence for hard news and too much devotion to the bottom line. Sauter and Wyman advanced another truth, which was that News had to stop bemoaning its lost virtue and hiding from the realities of network decline.

Sauter became a lightning rod, a symbol of unhappiness. Meanwhile, the signals sent by Tisch comforted many in News, for he spoke openly of preferring "hard" to "soft" news, of how he missed Charles Kuralt and Diane Sawyer on the *Morning News.* In casual encounters at dinners and elsewhere, remembers Mike Wallace, Tisch conveyed a sense "that he was on our side." But it was unclear what "our side" meant, and surely no one asked whether Tisch favored budget cuts or a fresh look at how departments, including News, spent money. This was an emotional battle, and many in the news division felt simply that Sauter and his benefactor, Tom Wyman, were on the other side of the barricades. Tisch, they innocently believed, *would make things like they once were.*

By now, Tisch was convinced Wyman was harming CBS, and harming his investment, which had climbed to about $700 million. So Tisch explored his options. Brother Bob, frustrated by his lack of involvement and perhaps wanting to strut his own stuff, had left Loews to become U.S. Postmaster General. But the brothers agreed that Wyman should go. Larry Tisch held a series of strategy meetings. "Larry didn't want to get into a public battle," recalls attorney Lipton. "He didn't want to appear like a raider. That was paramount in his thinking, and in all of our thinking. If they wanted him to make an offer for the company, he was prepared to do that. . . . One of the problems was that there was no clarity about what they wanted or if they wanted it."

If Tisch was sometimes as confused about the board's intentions as they were about his, one reason was that he was isolated. The board was his adversary. Through July, the only outside director with whom Tisch had a private conversation was Newton Minow, whom Wyman suspected was in Tisch's corner. But Tisch did have a crucial series of ongoing discussions with Paley through his proxy, Arthur Liman. Tisch knew that Paley was excited, and wanted to mount a comeback.

"I couldn't stand the idea that CBS was not being out front in terms of reputation," said Paley. Nevertheless, Wyman—and most of the board—were still convinced Paley would never join with Tisch. This was partly because they believed Paley was not always able to concentrate his energies and efforts, and partly because Wyman remembered tiny clues—like the board meetings when Paley asked for something to be repeated and "Tisch was a little rude."

Wyman began meeting more often with Wolfensohn on "the Project." "We were asked by a special committee of the board to provide whatever information we could on candidates," recalls Wolfensohn. "We did a hell of a lot of statistical work. We got together a list of possible white knights." This special committee of the board, he conceded, was not the product of a formal board resolution. Instead, it was an expression of the concern directors shared, of a desire to fulfill their fiduciary responsibility. On the list of potential white knights were General Electric, Gannett, Westinghouse, Gulf + Western. Wyman added Coca-Cola, for he had had a conversation earlier that summer with Francis "Fay" T. Vincent, an old friend who ran Coca-Cola's Entertainment Group, who expressed an interest. Director Harold Brown, who is on the Philip Morris board, added that company to the list. And in late July, Brown spoke with Hamish Maxwell, Philip Morris's chairman and CEO.*

Simultaneously, Wyman sought to strengthen his hand internally by cementing an alliance with Gene Jankowski. The president of the Broadcast Group was popular with people such as Dan Rather, Don Hewitt, and Mike Wallace, whose lucrative contracts he had approved. Jankowski got along with almost everyone at CBS. He was someone who always, in his words, "backed into things" after coming

* According to documents CBS filed with the Securities and Exchange Commission, Brown undertook this inquiry on his own. In any case, he had three conversations with Maxwell, who concluded he was not interested in CBS.

to New York from his native Buffalo—from Sales to Finance to the stations division to corporate comptroller to president of the Broadcast Group. One reason Jankowski was so popular was that he was such an adept mediator of disputes. Among the various divisions reporting to him—News, Sports, Entertainment, Sales, Affiliate Relations, Owned Stations, Radio—Jankowski would always insist there had to be "no winners or losers." When there were differences, he expected them to work it out, to compromise.

One of the few executives with whom Jankowski did not get along was William Lilly III, who as senior vice president for Corporate Affairs had been Wyman's chief image maker. The feeling was mutual. As Wyman sought advice in the spring and summer of 1986 about how to go on the offensive, he was urged by colleagues to purge CBS of Lilly. When Wyman fired Lilly in August, he chose as his new Communications chief David Fuchs, Jankowski's alter ego, a man who had been with the Broadcast Group for thirty-three years, starting in Sales with Jankowski. The appointment contributed to Wyman's difficulties, though this was not immediately apparent. Within CBS, Fuchs was much respected. He was a fountain of information about television. He wrote Jankowski's better speeches, adding a literate, learned quality. By television standards, Fuchs was an intellectual. He read books, he was relentlessly logical. Colleagues went to David Fuchs when they needed to analyze a problem rigorously, or to get a reading on Gene Jankowski. And they trusted him, thought he was a good man who kept confidences, thought he was a true Catholic, and not just because, like Jankowski, he went to church every day. But for all his virtues, Fuchs brought with him to his new job a major vice: He didn't believe in talking to the press. "Why should I talk to you?" he would say to reporters, not meaning to be hostile. He believed what went on within the halls of CBS was "sacred," and often blamed the press for CBS's predicament. His beloved CBS was a private corporation, he argued, and had no responsibility to talk to the media. So instead of concentrating on improving Wyman's image to the outside world, David Fuchs concentrated on plugging leaks, on smothering bad news. It was a futile mission.

In a way, however, it was in keeping with other Wyman moves, each carried out almost dutifully, without passion, without a sense of galvanizing leadership. Wyman began to shut out more people, to hunker down in his thirty-fifth-floor bunker. After the terrible upfront sales mess, observed his friend Fred Meyer, "Tom . . . told me that this was such a major piece of bad news in the war with Tisch. This was the final blow." Peter Derow remembers being shocked that Wyman explained the upfront mistake in a memo to the board, rather than visiting each director personally. When the memo was greeted by silence, Wyman told his managers, "Surprisingly, no one's called." After hearing this Peter Derow went home and told his wife: "This guy's not going to survive!" Without a strategy, Wyman was creating a vacuum.

This was a vacuum Tisch eagerly filled. The Loews chairman became bolder, more assertive. During dinner at Katharine Graham's home on Martha's Vineyard in July, Billie and Larry Tisch listened raptly as Warren Buffett and Graham discussed the media. Tisch asked informed political questions of historian Arthur Schlesinger, Jr., and queried *60 Minutes* correspondent Mike Wallace on the turmoil within CBS News. He was the attentive student. Wallace tried to draw Tisch out and used as bait an old friend. "Gene Jankowski's a very savvy man," Wallace said.

"Nice man, yes," answered Tisch. "Savvy man, no."

In August Tisch visited outgoing NBC chairman Grant Tinker at his home in Los Angeles and, according to Tinker, tried to recruit him to join CBS. "Can you help?" Tisch asked.

"No, if I wanted to do that I'd have stayed where I was," responded Tinker.

With Tisch becoming more aggressive and Wyman retreating into a shell, power was shifting to the board. Despite the crisis atmosphere, Wyman decided to maintain his, and the board's, regular vacation schedule. As was customary, there would be no board meeting in August. In prior years, this was a blessing. In the summer of 1986, it contributed to the leadership void. Even Wyman's hard-core supporters were losing their ardor. Disappointed in Wyman, and distrusting Tisch, eight of the outside directors began to talk to one another on the telephone more often, spurred by a shared sense of alarm.* "There was no evidence that Tisch and Paley were allied then," recalls director Frank Thomas, unaware of Liman's role as a go-between. "But Tom should have asked: 'Do I have Bill and Larry coming together in a lack of confidence in me?' If that's coming on, you got to get at the core of it. Tom should have led. . . . The directors looked to the chairman for a plan, a strategy. I don't understand what Tom

* The six directors not included in these conversations were Wyman, Paley, Tisch, Newton Minow (a presumed Tisch supporter), and two close Paley associates, Marietta Tree and Walter Cronkite.

was thinking that summer, from the disastrous meeting in July to September."

There was a sense that Tisch had a plan but Wyman did not. Describing how the directors felt in late July and August, Wolfensohn recalls: "You had this feeling that the chairman was not in control, and was not leading the board." Even Wyman began to feel heat from the board, though he misdiagnosed it. "The absence of an alternative to Tisch was a more serious problem than the upfront mistake," Wyman said. "That was the impatience the board expressed to me, to the extent they expressed any." They wanted a white knight, a savior, someone who would save CBS from Tisch and, not incidentally, save the board from a lawsuit for neglecting their fiduciary responsibilities.

The fragmentation spurred the board to become more assertive. To further probe Tisch's intentions, Wolfensohn suggested and the eight directors who were secretly talking agreed that they would ask a noncombatant, director Harold Brown, to meet privately with Tisch and convey their concern for the shareholders. Surely Brown's experience in negotiating with the Soviet Union while secretary of defense in the Carter administration couldn't hurt.

Unfortunately, it didn't help. The two men lunched together on August 14, 1986, at the Loews-owned Regency Hotel, and by all accounts it was a disaster. Brown, recalls Wyman, who was told about it later, called Tisch "a stone wall." Tisch was no more enthusiastic about Brown. Again he was offended that a director who owned hardly any stock would dare tell him what was best for the shareholders. And he was offended by Brown's manner. "With Harold," said Tisch, "no one is smart." For months thereafter he disparaged Brown as condescending and pompous.

Within Black Rock the sense of dread deepened, a feeling that the noose was tightening and that something had to be done. Wyman, in turn, felt defeated. Something had snapped in him; sometime in August he had come to the private judgment that his days as CEO were numbered. He was no longer fighting for his job. Instead, he convinced himself, he was fighting to preserve the independence of a great institution and to protect its shareholders. To these ends he recruited fellow warriors, including his associates in the Broadcast Group.

One such warrior was Van Gordon Sauter. Fed up with the uncertainty and turmoil within management ranks at the network, and believing that too many of his colleagues had run for cover and that it was manly to exhibit loyalty, Sauter stuck his neck out. Although he "barely knew the man," Sauter decided to transform a speech he was to give to News executives in Park City, Utah, into a defense of Wyman and a plea for stability. The "nagging questions of who will own this company and who will run it," he said, had "reached a point of distraction," sapping the strength of CBS. While Sauter said he conceived the speech himself, he first circulated drafts to Jankowski, Fuchs, and CBS's vice president of Communications and Information, George Schweitzer.

Utah was to be the opening of Wyman's second front, and the CBS chairman went there prepared to do battle. "I went out with Jankowski with the specific purpose being to settle who was in command of the news division—Van Sauter," said Wyman. On the morning after Sauter's speech, Tom Bettag, executive producer of the *Evening News,* shared a car ride with Wyman and two News bureau chiefs. "I can't understand why you won't support me" against Tisch, he remembers Wyman saying. "You don't understand the mentality of this guy. He's going to cut, and cut, and cut. I'm not sure he believes in the independence of News, the way I always have."

"What do you mean?" asked Bettag.

"Things like Israel," said Wyman cryptically.* The chairman did not elaborate on his statement at the time, but with others he did. "On at least two occasions I heard Wyman in social settings making comments expressing concern about the news division's independence in expressing views about Israel because of Tisch's strong support for Israel," said a Wyman confidant. *Newsweek* reported that while in Utah "Wyman offhandedly said at a cocktail party that Tisch's enthusiasm for 'pro-Israel' causes and charities might compromise the independent reporting of CBS News." Word filtered back to Tisch, who telephoned Wyman. "Wyman denied it cold," recalls Tisch.

"I don't believe it," said Wyman. "I never believed it. And if I had believed it, I'm too smart to say it."

Rumors were as plentiful as the fig trees beside Marietta Tree's villa outside Siena, Italy. On her annual visit to the Tuscan countryside for the month of August, Tree was visited daily by rumors, some in the form of transatlantic phone calls, some in the form of visitors. "I saw Felix Rohatyn in Italy and he said, 'Larry Tisch is angry.' My heart sank," she recalls.

Being away, Tree was unaware of how agitated her friend Bill Paley had also become. The board had not met since July 9. The outside

* "I don't remember saying it," said Wyman.

directors had been out of touch, scattering in different directions on business or to escape the August heat—Wolfensohn to Alaska, Frank Thomas to Martha's Vineyard. Wyman wrote no memos to the board, made no phone calls. "I had had no conversation with Tom since July," Thomas recalls. When the phone finally rang at his home on Martha's Vineyard, it was Bill Paley, who had placed Thomas on the board in 1970. "How can you guys just sit there?" Thomas remembers the founder barking. "The place is going to ruin! What are you going to do about it?"

Thomas respected CBS's founder, but he also knew that keeping Paley and Tisch apart was pivotal to denying Tisch a victory. The Ford Foundation president assured Paley he would make some phone calls, check in with fellow directors. One of the first calls Thomas made was to Jim Wolfensohn. *How's "the Project" going?* he asked.

As far as I know it's on hold, said Wolfensohn, who was just back from salmon fishing in Alaska. A quick survey revealed that the directors had not spoken to Wyman in weeks, and each shared at least two concerns: Why didn't Tom Wyman seem to have a plan? And what should the board do if Tisch wanted to go above 25 percent?

Thomas decided to assert himself and scheduled a luncheon at the Ford Foundation on August 26 for a select group of directors—Wolfensohn, Brown, Schacht, Gilpatric, Bergerac. The six men wrestled with many things. There was some support for the proposition that to protect shareholders they might have to sell the company, though everyone wished to avoid a bidding war. A list of hypothetical white knights was discussed, though there was no consensus as to who that white knight might be. No one was certain any longer that Wyman could survive. Michel Bergerac, who had been ousted as CEO of Revlon in a hostile takeover, wasn't sure a bidding war could be avoided. Once word spread that CBS was available, the board would be forced to accept the best price. And the best price was not necessarily what was best for CBS, or for the public. "If this company gets in the wrong hands," he remembers saying, "how are we to exercise our public trust?" On this point there was general agreement.

There was also general agreement that if they did not assert themselves, control of CBS would continue slipping to Larry Tisch; and if it did, it was their responsibility to shareholders to see that if Tisch gained control he paid a premium. On one other point they concurred: It was their responsibility to CBS and its employees to try to keep the company intact, to see that it was not dismembered. Implicit if unspoken were two other assumptions: Though uneasy about

Wyman's leadership, they were not ready to ask him to depart. And beneath the entire discussion was a certain wariness. They had endured much together, but the experience left scars of suspicion. "There were several people who played strange roles in all this," said a director. "I fear there were a lot of hidden agendas. I never knew whether in the back of Wolfensohn's mind was: 'If we can sell this I can get a fee of many millions.' Since Harold Brown was a partner of Wolfensohn's, was he a free agent? Since Henry Schacht brought Wyman into the company and had recommended pushing Paley out of the way, was he more concerned with his friend Wyman and with the threat of Paley coming back?" With all the interlocking relationships, the board was a conspirator's dream.

At the end of lunch, it was agreed they would meet again, clandestinely, on September 3. Neither Paley nor Tisch, nor their presumed allies, would be told of these secret meetings. Wyman, however, knew about them beforehand. "He regarded them as sessions the board ought to have to think through the strategy without him," recalls counsel George Vradenburg. "He did not think of these meetings as unfriendly." Wyman simply assumed that the board was on his side, aligned against both Paley and Tisch, in agreement that if they couldn't keep Tisch at 25 percent, their common task was to find an outside investor to save CBS from this awful little man.

Wolfensohn was off to his native Australia, and Wyman was hearing the tick of the clock. If he was to block Tisch's creeping takeover, he desperately needed outside help.

Enter Coca-Cola. Years before, Coke had branched into the entertainment business, which now accounted for 15 percent of its profits. With ownership of Columbia Pictures, Embassy, Tri-Star Pictures, and the Walter Reade Organization, Coca-Cola was an entertainment powerhouse. In television production alone it was then the largest, most successful programmer in the world, with more hours on television than Warner, MCA, Paramount, or Lorimar, its nearest competitors. Nor were CBS and Coke strangers, being partners until recently in Tri-Star. Coca-Cola was Tom Wyman's kind of company, led by corporate gentlemen who belonged to the Business Roundtable and spurned hostile takeovers.

Better, from Wyman's perspective, was that Fay Vincent, an old friend, with whom he lunched every couple of months, was chairman of Coca-Cola's entertainment business sector. Fay Vincent had the right kind of credentials. Wyman had attended Phillips Academy, Vincent attended Hotchkiss; and each had served as trustee of his school. Wyman graduated from Amherst College, on whose board he sat, and Vincent from Williams College, on whose board *he* sat. Wyman came to CBS to clean up the mess left by a succession of CEOs fired by Bill Paley; Vincent became president of Columbia Pictures to clean up after the scandal left by his predecessor, David Begelman. Wyman felt comfortable with Vincent and Coke, so comfortable that when Ted Turner made his pass at CBS in 1985, Wyman talked to Vincent. "At some point," he said, "I may want to come to you and see if you would buy CBS." Vincent agreed to consider it.

What prompted a call from Vincent to Wyman in August of 1986 was the avalanche of press stories and rumors. "How are you?" asked Vincent.

"Let's have lunch," answered Wyman.

They had a sandwich in Vincent's Fifth Avenue office on September 2. After the social pleasantries, recalls Vincent, Wyman began: "Look, Fay, I've come to some major conclusions. Number one, control of CBS is going to change. Either Tisch is going to take control or the company will be sold. I'm resigned to it. Number two, if there is a change of control of the company, a premium should be paid for that change. Number three, a perfect company for CBS would be Coca-Cola. I'm now making a specific proposal to you. The price should be $170 a share."

"That seems to me to be a respectable proposition. We've got to study it," said Vincent.

"In terms of me, personally," continued Wyman, "I'm not essential to the transaction. If Coke is not interested, I have a couple of other thoughts as to companies." He named Westinghouse and Philip Morris. But Coca-Cola, he made clear, was his first choice.

"Look, you're a four-star general," responded Vincent. "I'm a colonel. I need to report to the guys I work for." He asked for a week. If top executives at Coke's headquarters in Atlanta wanted to proceed, he would have a quick response. In the meantime, said Vincent, he and Coke's investment bankers, Allen & Company, would need to study CBS's financial situation.

Wyman left and remembers thinking: "There is a God, and he likes us."

Tom Wyman returned to CBS and summoned Fred Meyer and other members of his finance team, plus Tracy Schach of Jim Wolfensohn's office. Without telling them of his lunch with Vincent, he asked them to prepare and update CBS financial information and to add Coca-Cola to the list of companies they were profiling.

Meanwhile, the six outside directors, minus Wolfensohn, who was away, dined at Christ Cella on September 3, this time to discuss Wyman and the management of CBS. No resolution was reached, but it was clear Wyman had lost support, that his allies on the board were dispirited about his leadership.

Ironically, their somber mood was at odds with Wyman's. The CBS chairman's adrenaline was pumping again. He was a goner, he knew that. But at last he saw a way to outfox Tisch. There was a bounce to his step when he got back to the office and barked commands to Fred Meyer and the financial team. Three days later, with Wolfensohn not due to return from another trip to Australia for twenty-four hours, Wyman called Wolfensohn's associate, Elliott Slade, and asked him to deliver their analysis of Coca-Cola that weekend. In the days following their meeting, Wyman talked regularly to Vincent, who reported back that Atlanta was definitely interested in exploring a friendly merger. What Wyman didn't know was that Herbert Allen, Jr., the head of Allen & Company, a member of Coke's board, and the man who recommended Vincent for his job, was more dubious. The price, Allen thought, was too rich; revenues at CBS and ABC were heading south; and should the two companies merge, government fin-syn restrictions might force Coke out of selling reruns, its most lucrative entertainment business. "It was not promising," recalls Allen. "The conversations were social more than they were business."

Unaware of Allen's qualms, Wyman now thought he was ready to deliver something concrete to the board. By September 9, according to a document CBS later filed with the SEC, Wyman met with or telephoned the eight outside directors he presumed were his allies, telling them of his discussions with Vincent and of Coca-Cola's interest. Only Paley, Tisch, Tree, Cronkite, and Minow were not told. Wyman came away convinced that the directors were pleased. The plan, recalls Wyman, was twofold: He would send CBS's financial information over to Allen & Company so they could independently assess the company's health; and Wyman would make a presentation to the board at their regular meeting on Wednesday, September 10, and then, he hoped, commence negotiations with Coke the next day. "I'm not worried about this board meeting," Vincent remembers Wyman saying. "I've talked to a number of directors. I have their support."

While Wyman and the board schemed, unbeknownst to them, so

did Tisch and Paley and their intermediary, Arthur Liman. By the first week of September, the two largest CBS shareholders had forged a compact that could block Coca-Cola or any other white knight. Former CBS president Frank Stanton remembers that the compact was sealed in late August, and the adhesive was attorney Arthur Liman, who "was carrying messages back and forth" between his client, the CBS founder, and his friend Tisch. Larry Tisch insists that he and Paley never had a formal pact, but admits that by the end of August they were speaking "all the time" and "we would commiserate with each other."

So fiercely did Bill Paley want to remove Wyman that he was blind to other considerations, including his and Tisch's divergent interests. Liman might shuttle between the two men, but if his friend Tisch took control of CBS without paying a premium, his client Paley might not maximize the value of his shares. And while Tisch did not want his CBS investment to be managed by his aging ally, Paley wished to return and actively run CBS as chairman. Without Tisch's approval, Paley consulted with Frank Stanton, his colleague through four decades at CBS, about taking the company private. But the stock price was rising, making it prohibitively expensive. He even asked Stanton if he would return as CBS president under Chairman Paley. Although Stanton said he would, "I begged him not to do it," recalls Stanton, convinced the physical strain would be too great for either man.

While Paley and Wyman and most directors were under great strain, by early September Larry Tisch was at peace, like a man who knew events were tilting his way. His conscience was clear that he was doing the right thing in going after Wyman. "I lived up to everything I said," he recalled. "Did I know Wyman was the idiot of the century when I bought CBS stock? No. I found out later." Tisch wasn't counting heads on the board, wasn't making phone calls. His son Tommy wanted him to speak out, to denounce those who weakened the company by raging at "external forces." No, said the father: "Things have to stew in their own juices. No one can block me. They can't buy it, and I won't sell." Under New York State law no bidder could successfully claim CBS if one-third of its shareholders refused. Between them, Paley and Tisch owned 34 percent of the stock. And, said Tisch on September 2, "We see eye to eye."

There was another reason to let things "stew": Tisch and Paley didn't think they had the votes yet. While the board couldn't sell CBS without Tisch and Paley, Tisch and Paley couldn't oust Wyman without a majority of the board. As Tisch saw it, in a showdown Wyman would probably triumph by eight votes to six, with Tisch and Paley joined by Cronkite, Tree, Minow, and perhaps Bergerac.

Events, however, broke Tisch's way. In early September, CBS News's respected commentator, Bill Moyers, fed up with competing for airtime "with stories about three-legged sheep," announced that he was leaving the network. Andy Rooney rapped the network, again, in his syndicated column. So self-preoccupied had the folks at CBS become that beginning the week of September 2, and running for five straight days, Dan Rather signed off his national broadcast with a single word for the troops: "Courage." When asked why, Rather explained that "courage" was one of his two favorite words, the other being "meadow." The rival networks were, of course, ecstatic. ABC anchor Peter Jennings actually debated whether to sign off his broadcast that week with "meadow." Said Jennings, smiling, "I didn't have the *courage.*"

Bill Paley was distressed by the public travails of his creation, his baby. True, the public feuding undermined Tom Wyman, which pleased Paley. But more than Tisch, Paley bled with each nick. He couldn't stand what was happening to *my* company, as he referred to CBS. And then came the gaping wound delivered by *Newsweek* in the form of a cover story by Jonathan Alter and Bill Powell—"Civil War at CBS"—which reported on the "ceaseless turmoil" at the network. The article noted the "nerve-wracking tactical battle" being waged between Wyman and Tisch for control of the company and explored how the "soul" of this great company was being lost due to the short-term oriented cost cutters who now ruled CBS and much of corporate America. Perhaps the deepest cut came from a full-page interview that Bill Moyers granted the magazine. In the civil war between CBS news and entertainment values over the past two and a half years, Moyers claimed that entertainment values had won. "The line between entertainment and news was steadily blurred," said Moyers. "Our center of gravity shifted from the standards and practices of the news business to show business. In meeting after meeting, *Entertainment Tonight* was touted as the model—breezy, entertaining, undemanding. In meeting after meeting, the discussion was about 'moments'—visual images containing a high emotional quotient that are passed on to the viewer unfiltered and unexamined. Instead of . . . gathering, weighing, sorting and explaining the flux of events and issues, we began to be influenced by the desire first to please the audience. The object was to 'hook' them by pretending this was not news at all."

The day before *Newsweek* appeared—Sunday, September 7—Bill Paley and Tom Wyman separately attended the finals of the National Tennis Open in Forest Hills, Queens. Producer Don Hewitt had in his possession an early copy of the nine-page article. "What do you hear about the *Newsweek* piece?" Wyman asked Hewitt, who was seated in his box with Mike Wallace, Dan Rather, and others. Hewitt handed him his copy and watched as Wyman slumped in his seat. Wyman tried to appear nonchalant, first putting the article in his jacket pocket, as if to say it could wait.

But it couldn't, and Wyman pulled it out and began to read, then put it away, then pulled it back out. Each time he placed the article in his lap, Rather, Jankowski, and Wallace hunched to read it over his shoulder. "Jesus, Don, why did you do that here and now?" Wallace asked Hewitt, but Hewitt was silent, as if he were directing a segment for *60 Minutes.* Wyman was also silent, uttering not a word about the piece but thinking, "It was devastating." Wyman wandered over to Paley's box.

If there was a silver lining, it was that Wyman assumed Paley and he could link arms against the institutional harm the *Newsweek* article would cause. He still saw Paley's interests as separate from Tisch's, and so on Monday, the day *Newsweek* hit the newstands, Tom Wyman telephoned Bill Paley to ask if he could pay a visit. "If I had thought he had made a deal with Tisch I would not have visited him," recalls Wyman. Although he did not tell Paley of the Coke discussions, Wyman somehow assumed that Paley would go along with the sale of his company, particularly since shareholders would receive a generous price.

He was wrong on both counts. The two men sat alone, calmly discussing the company. To Wyman the conversation was relaxed, almost pleasant, and he felt comfortable enough near the end of his visit to solicit Paley's advice. "What would you do if you were in my position?" Wyman asked, according to the account Paley would share with Arthur Liman.

Paley's eyes turned cold. "I would resign because it is in the best interests of the company," he said. He added, *Larry agrees with me!*

It was now finally clear to Wyman that not only was Paley his implacable foe but Paley and Tisch were acting as one. Suddenly he knew the two men were talking regularly. A light bulb went on, and he intuited, in Fred Meyer's words, that "the glue binding Tisch and Paley was Liman."

Paley was all icy calm with Wyman. But with his friend Marietta

Tree, just back from Italy, he could not contain his emotion. Determined to catch up after being in Tuscany for a month, and responsibly wanting to determine how she should vote, Tree upon her arrival in New York made a series of telephone calls. Over the weekend she visited Wolfensohn. "About eight people telephoned him while I was there," she recalls. "He was quite critical of Tom." But Wolfensohn's criticism was targeted at Wyman's lack of hands-on leadership. Paley's criticism was much broader. "I never thought my company would be reduced to this!" he told her over dinner, pointing to the *Newsweek* cover. He was crying, she recalls, and spoke haltingly. She wanted information; Paley wanted to lambaste Wyman.

"I feel sorry for Wyman," his friend of almost fifty years told Paley. "Everything is breaking over his head."

"How dare you? You should feel sorry for the company!" declared Paley. "I've been saying this about Wyman for years. Why would no one believe me? I asked Arthur Liman why no one believed me and Liman said to me, 'No one would believe you, Bill, because you were like this with all the other presidents.' " Tree tried to comfort her dear friend, but he was inconsolable.

For Wyman, there was no solace back at the office. The aftershock from *Newsweek,* recalls Wolfensohn, was "dramatic. It was all out there. There was now a visible crisis." Wyman decided it would be best to cancel the board dinner scheduled for the next night at the Links Club. Within hours, Paley had phoned Wolfensohn to object and Wolfensohn phoned other outside directors, who agreed they must meet to search for a unified position. Led by Wyman's ally Henry Schacht, who made the calls to invite the directors, the dinner was rescheduled for the Ritz-Carlton Hotel, where Schacht was staying.

Pressures were escalating. On behalf of the directors, Wolfensohn telephoned Wyman to tell him the dinner was on. The directors, he said, wished to convene without Tisch or Wyman present. Wyman had no choice but to accede. No sooner did he get off the phone with Wolfensohn than Wyman took a call from Disney chairman Michael Eisner, who said Disney would be interested in talking about a merger if CBS so desired. Thanks, but no thanks, said the beleaguered Wyman. Then Larry Tisch called, lodging a complaint that he had heard rumors Wyman was shopping the company. Wyman assured him he was not, recalls Tisch.

Torn, as ever, between their fiduciary responsibility to shareholders, their ties to and affection for Wyman, and a sense that CBS was not just another company but a public trust, a somber board convened, without Wyman or Tisch, at 7 P.M. in a private room on the second floor of the Ritz-Carlton. The eleven men and one woman were tense, as were the two outside counsel invited, Samuel C. Butler, managing partner of Cravath, Swaine & Moore, who was representing the outside directors, and Arthur Liman, who was representing William Paley and, some directors now believed, Larry Tisch. A cold buffet was arrayed before them, but for a long while the food went untouched. Chilled wine was available, but no one drank. All anyone wanted to do was talk.

William Paley kicked off the formal discussion: "CBS is a public trust and should remain independent. I don't believe it can carry out its mission if it were part of another company. Many years ago I was asked to sell CBS and I considered it. The next day I called off the discussions because I thought of what might happen if the head of the parent company were disturbed with something on the network and called to say, 'Can't we tone this down?' These views, which I formed in the early days of CBS, have endured."

After making his case for the continued independence of CBS, Paley proceeded to offer a bill of particulars against Wyman, who he said was a "crippled leader." Tree remembers that Paley accepted responsibility for picking him and pleaded for a vote the next day on whether Wyman should go or stay.

Schacht and Wolfensohn, while never mentioning Coca-Cola, pressed Paley: *Suppose it were a first-rate company that wanted to merge with CBS?*

Paley deflected the question by repeating that CBS should remain an independent company, the only one of the three networks without a corporate parent. Directors moved to his second point—Tom Wyman. *What is the alternative if Wyman left?* they asked. Paley did not suggest his own return or Frank Stanton's, since, according to a Tisch confidant, the Loews chairman had told Paley this was unacceptable. Instead, Paley proposed a power-sharing arrangement: He would return as chairman and Tisch would become chairman of an executive committee consisting of the founder and board members.

The directors were unmoved. Most of them did not want Paley to return in an active capacity, though they were too polite to say this in his presence. Nor did they want Tisch "bullying his way in," said one board member. Paley countered that a committee could run CBS for an interim period, but directors insisted that in these troubled times CBS needed decisive leadership.

Tom Wyman has to go! insisted Paley. "I am very clear about this," he said, according to Marietta Tree's notes on the dinner. "And Larry is very clear, too." Now that he had Tisch's backing, he hoped he'd have the board's.

The directors glanced at one another nervously. "It was like neon signs when Paley said he and Tisch were together," said Thomas. "Then we knew the gauntlet was down." With Tisch and Paley bonded, Wyman might not survive.

Paley graciously exited, telling colleagues they should be free to discuss the subject in full candor. Like zombies, the directors rose to take plates and food. Thomas and Schacht invited Samuel Butler and select directors into a corner, where they whispered. Tree, Walter Cronkite, and Liman ate alone, feeling excluded from the conversation. After a twenty-minute huddle, the directors rejoined the table, where a long discussion ensued, much of it covering their now familiar dilemma. "Once this board reaches a state of mind that it can no longer remain independent and wants to sell the company," Bergerac remembers saying, "then the only responsibility of the board becomes to get the most money for shareholders. Therefore, the ability of the board to pick a white knight is illusory. I'm an expert on that." The board at that point turned to Liman and Butler, and both lawyers concurred: Bergerac was correct.

Walter Cronkite then made the case for changing the company's top leadership. Newton Minow echoed Paley's and Bergerac's conviction that CBS should remain independent. They talked, and talked, right through CBS's premier of *The Wizard,* an hour-long drama that racked up good ratings at 8 P.M., right through the Robin Williams movie *Moscow on the Hudson,* right through a rare Tuesday night CBS ratings triumph. Five hours after convening, the meeting ended inconclusively, with no agreement on resolutions to be introduced the next day.

Most directors left uncertain of what would happen next. Bill Paley, however, left confident that there was, he said, "a very good chance" they would oust Wyman. Meanwhile, off having dinner with a reporter at a steak house in lower Manhattan, News president Van Gordon Sauter was confident, even cocky, that Wyman, in his words, "has the cards" and that Tisch wouldn't dare make a lunge for the company. If he did, said Sauter, he would tarnish his cultivated image as a statesman. Sauter said he was certain of victory. As was Gene Jankowski.

Two other men who were not at the marathon board dinner—Tisch and Wyman—waited up for phone calls. Tisch's came from Arthur Liman, who reported on what was said, on how the directors now worried whether Wyman wasn't too wounded to rebound. A majority of the board, Liman guessed, was probably opposed to the sale of the company. Wyman waited for a call from Henry Schacht. The call came around midnight, and was witnessed by Frank Thomas, who was with Schacht.

Hank Schacht, Wyman's close friend and frequent tennis partner, came on the phone and was all business. *Tom, the board would like a presentation from you in the morning, and will then excuse you so we can deliberate privately. If you have something to present, my suggestion is that you get ready to present it sooner rather than later because Bill and Larry are now of like mind on the need to change the leadership.*

Schacht was aloof, almost officious. "Hank, this is Tom, your buddy, talking to you. What happened?"

Schacht remained distant.

Wyman said he would be pleased to make a presentation at the board meeting, then hung up. He was left with two conflicting emotions. On the one hand, he believed he retained the loyalty of a majority of the outside directors. On the other hand, as he played back the Schacht conversation in his mind he was distressed. Hank Schacht had sounded almost like a stranger.

"It doesn't look good," Wyman whispered to Fred Meyer first thing the next morning, recounting the frosty phone call. Wyman and Meyer turned to the business at hand, which was to review the slide presentation Meyer had prepared of the five years of Wyman's stewardship—"warts and all," said Meyer. In total, there were about eighty slides to run through. "Do you really have to give this many slides?" asked Meyer.

Sensitive to the charge that he had withheld information from the board about upfront sales in July, Wyman was determined to leave nothing out. He was also determined to proceed with the Coca-Cola discussions. As he entered the boardroom diagonally across from his suite, Wyman pumped himself up.

Silently, Wyman's core managers and directors filed around the twenty-foot-long walnut table that seemed to rise from a forest green carpet. They slipped into low-backed leather chairs with brass studs and casters. When they looked up from the papers laid before each setting, they saw round, lacquered columns painted pale yellow and paintings by Rouault and Ben Shahn. Light filtered through green silk drapes. "The tension was like a bomb ready to go off," recalls Patrick Callahan, the cheerful Irish steward who served coffee. "You could see the board members were tense. There wasn't that cheerful 'Good morning, Patrick.' "

Tom Wyman called the meeting to order from his customary seat at the far end of the table, like a distant CEO. Paley and Tisch sat directly across from each other at the middle of the long table. Following the usual practice, Wyman introduced the reports from the group presidents of Records, Publishing, and Broadcasting, and from Fred Meyer, who offered a financial projection, all from Wyman's end of the sleek table. These presentations were different—longer, with slides to buttress the points Wyman wanted stressed displayed on a wall panel screen.

The presentations backfired, reinforcing the gloom many directors felt. Peter Derow began his extensive report on the Publishing Group with the warning that "we are now projecting a $10.1 million profit shortfall" from budget. Fred Meyer's financial report was worse. While the Records Group was going strong, the Broadcast Group in particular was troubled, he said, with pretax 1986 profits now projected to plunge to $250 million, down $84 million in two months. And in 1987 the network alone was expected to lose $20 million. Wyman tried to put the best face on it, noting that profits had occasionally fallen in other years as well, as they did in the recession year of 1982. And while network profits might decline, earnings from their four TV stations were expected to climb to $154 million in 1987.

Juxtaposed against the board's growing sense of financial emergency, Wyman's optimistic charts seemed surreal. There were charts showing that the Broadcast Group had pared, over the past nine months, 140 out of 8,234 employees, a puny number to most directors. The charts and the two-hour presentation, by most accounts, were disjointed, misleading, exhausting. "It wasn't crisp," said Bergerac. And it was, said Wolfensohn, falsely optimistic: "The budget presentation did not hold together. There was a feeling that while not attempting to mislead us, Tom was not giving hard-edged information to the board." Several directors found Wyman distracted, as if he were going through the motions, which in a sense he was. "There was not a single question," Wyman remembers. "I didn't read that any particular way since most directors knew I had something else on my mind."

The something else was Coca-Cola. Soon after 11:00, the nonboard members were excused; lawyers Butler and Liman, who waited outside, were beckoned into the board's executive session. Wyman still held the floor and, according to Gilpatric, started off by claiming CBS "had really lost independence, that de facto control had passed. He didn't mention Tisch by name. He said the board had to consider whether they would do better by shareholders if they sold the company." According to the minutes of the meeting:

> Mr. Wyman stated that he had received an overture from the Coca-Cola Company that could lead to discussions for the purchase of the Corporation by Coca-Cola. His contact indicated that, if certain confidential information were to be furnished by CBS, Coca-Cola would be in a position to decide within 10 days if it was interested in entering into discussions with the Corporation. He stated that another major company had also contacted him. Mr. Wyman then recommended that the Board approve his furnishing the requested information to Coca-Cola and appoint a committee of outside directors (excluding himself, Mr. Tisch and Mr. Paley) to review and analyze any offer that might be forthcoming.

The CBS chairman was vague about price, about whether Coca-Cola was committed to entering negotiations, and about what other company (Disney) had contacted him. What he sought was approval to proceed. "When I made the presentation on Coca-Cola," recalls Wyman, "I expected it to be accepted."

Wyman misread his board. "It's all wrong. I'm 100 percent against it!" Tisch shouted, his bald head beet-red, his right hand pounding the delicate table. "My stock's not for sale at any price. What right do you have to offer this company for sale on your own?" Tisch continued: *This board fought off Ted Turner and Jesse Helms and Ivan Boesky. All so CBS could remain independent. Now you, without board knowledge, would contravene everything accomplished in the name of an independent CBS! Not only is the strategy wrong, so are the tactics. If CBS were to be sold, now is not the time. The time to sell is when the company is healthy, thus allowing shareholders to extract a maximum price. The Coke initiative is stupid as well as wrong!*

Equally angry, Paley seconded what Tisch said. With one-third of the stock not for sale, Coca-Cola was now a dead issue. But what was very much alive was the sense of betrayal felt by Paley, Tisch, and the three other board members who were unaware of the Coke discussions. Since none of the eight directors who had been briefed on the Coke discussions had said anything the night before, or spoke up now in defense of Wyman, these five directors assumed Wyman had acted on his own, was guilty of outrageous insubordination. He was, they thought, conniving to sell a company the board had specifically said was not for sale.

Directors who were aware of the Coke discussions would later say they were silent for one of three reasons. Wolfensohn said it was because he had been away and was not totally briefed on Coke and because he thought the subject had been "discussed the night before" at dinner and therefore was no surprise. Others said they were shocked that Wyman brought up Coke since he had given no warning. "We knew by September ninth he had an overture from Coke," said Gilpatric. "But we did not realize he would try and put the thing in motion on the tenth." Like most directors, Gilpatric thought the discussions were in their infancy, hardly ready for board deliberation. Finally, since Wyman had spoken to the eight directors individually, they said they were silent because they didn't know who else knew. "He should have said, 'I have approached Coke and here's the price they will pay. Do you want me to do it?' " said Bergerac. "Instead, he said, 'I have had conversations at Coke with this guy and that guy and they seemed interested, but I'm not sure; and they would be willing to pay a good price, but I'm not sure of the price; and, in any case, in ten days they'll let us know if they're interested.' It put the board in the position of putting the company up for sale without knowing if it would lead anywhere."

Wyman was vague, but he too had reason to feel betrayed. He had been under pressure from a majority of the board to come up with a white knight. He thought the board had discussed Coca-Cola at their dinner. He had even been told the night before on the telephone by Henry Schacht, who he presumed was speaking for the board, that he should lay his cards down and make "a presentation" at this meeting. Now that he had, he was being pilloried by Tisch, Paley, Tree, Cronkite, and Minow, and not one director, not one of his friends, rose to his defense, rose to say he was doing what they wished. In fact, in the press accounts that would appear in succeeding days, directors said they were "flabbergasted" that Wyman would want to sell when they were so intent on keeping CBS independent. Ironically, both Tisch and Paley, when they later learned that eight silent directors knew of the discussions with Coke, would come to share Wyman's sense of treachery.

Greeted by a ferocious onslaught of opposition, Wyman sensed his gambit had failed. He withdrew from the meeting to permit the board to deliberate, the theory being that Wyman was an interested party and they were not. Depressed, the chairman returned to his office, called in Fred Meyer, and asked him to retrieve the financial reports from Allen & Company. He then telephoned Fay Vincent, sketched what transpired in the board meeting, and told his friend the CBS directors were now meeting alone. "If I don't get support, I'm out. And so are you," Wyman said.

When he hung up, Wyman was alone. He ruminated on the past year, thinking with a clarity denied him in prior months. *It was brilliant!* he remembers thinking. *Larry Tisch had a plan all along to take over this company without paying a premium.*

For the rest of the afternoon, Wyman's office became a refuge for his management team—Jankowski, Meyer, Derow, Yetnikoff, Fuchs—who grimly wandered in and out, each baffled by the turn of events. Unaware of all this, at Alfredo's restaurant on Central Park South, Van Gordon Sauter was lunching with Robert Wussler, executive vice president of the Turner Broadcasting Company. "I had authority from Gene Jankowski to talk about acquiring partial ownership of CNN," recalls Sauter. CBS would be satisfied with a minority stake in the all-news cable network, with a first option to buy the service if it were put up for sale. "I was encouraged," said Sauter. Wussler and he agreed to talk again in a few days. Excited, Sauter called the office from his car and was stunned to learn the board was still meeting and that Wyman was in his own office.

Meanwhile, after deciding not to break for lunch and to have food brought in, the board deliberated through the afternoon, united by a sense, recalls Wolfensohn, that "we needed to resolve an intolerable situation." By midafternoon, the board did not yet know how they would resolve this crisis, but they quickly defined the four big questions to be addressed. The overarching question was: How to bring stability to CBS? Within that larger question there were three others: Should the company be sold? What to do with Tom Wyman? And if Wyman left, who should run CBS? They quickly reached a consensus not to sell CBS, to remain "independent." The board, led by Frank Thomas and Harold Brown, sought assurance that Tisch and Paley agreed with their definition of "independence":

Do you agree CBS should continue to be managed under the direction of an independent board? Do you agree that neither Loews nor Mr. Tisch should seek to make CBS a subsidiary or to dictate policy to the board?

Paley said he agreed.

All eyes turned to Larry Tisch, who said: *Loews has consistently stated that its present intention was to acquire only up to 25 percent of CBS common stock and not to seek control over CBS. That intention has not changed. Nor has Loews ever acted inconsistent with those stated aims. I never initiated any suggestion that Tom Wyman should resign. I only gave a candid response after being pressed to do so by a delegation of the board. Loews has not sought additional seats on the board, and has no plan to launch a proxy fight to gain control.*

The directors pursued Tisch, wanting to be sure that his "present" was also his future intention, wanting to be sure he agreed that CBS and its board should remain "independent." Tisch said he agreed.

What if the board, in its best judgment, concluded that Tom Wyman should remain as chief executive officer? asked James R. Houghton.

Tisch responded: *I would support whatever the board decided, and not say another word. I'm surprised you even ask, since I am not challenging the board's authority or seeking control of CBS. The management issue is not one of control. The issue is the responsibility of directors to see that CBS is well run.*

Paley, as he had the previous night, described his proposal to run the company, with himself as acting chairman and Tisch as acting chairman of an executive committee that would include Paley and several outside directors. Together, they would exercise the authority of the chief executive officer and immediately start a search for a new CEO. Paley, joined by Tisch, recited a litany of Wyman's alleged failures.

At some point it dawned on the directors that the fight was over. "When Paley and I spoke up representing 34 percent of the stock, they couldn't sell the company," said Tisch. Nor could they any longer protect Wyman.

Paley framed his management proposal as a formal resolution, asking that Wyman resign and be succeeded by an executive committee of the board with Paley as acting chairman of the corporation and Tisch as acting chairman of the executive committee. As they had when Wyman made a proposal on Coke, the board excused Paley, Tisch, and Liman, who retreated to an office where they would spend much of the next three hours together.

The first to speak was Marietta Tree, who had been silent. Tree was counted in the Paley camp. But unlike Paley, who Gilpatric would say "has no mercy in his soul," Tree was generous, giving Tom Wyman his due as a man, though speaking of him as if she were delivering his obituary. "Tom Wyman is a man of sensitivity and courage," she remembers opening. "I admire him as a man. He is a classic textbook CEO. The only problem is that a classic CEO deals through his managers. . . . But CBS is a different business, and he doesn't know that. Bill understood this business out of long experience, and his understanding of this business was to procure the best talent for CBS. I remember Lord Beaverbrook saying to me one time, 'A publisher has to eat, drink, and sleep his newspapers.' That's what Bill Paley did. That's what Tom Wyman doesn't do. . . . Larry Tisch doesn't have a lot of experience with Hollywood. But he ran the Loews theaters and he's a New Yorker, which makes him much more sensitive to this type of business. He has a reputation as a fine manager, a hands-on manager. As a director of CBS he has talked to more CBS employees in one year than Tom has in six years. You can't be born with taste or an eye. This takes work. Wyman has been here six years and he's never shown that ability. Again, he's a fine man. But I think the company should remain independent and that Bill and Larry should take over the company."

Bergerac spoke next. Unlike Tree, he was not perceived as aligned with the anti-Wyman camp. Wyman had, after all, met with Bergerac to tell him of the Coca-Cola discussions, a step he dared not take with Tree. Because Bergerac had been removed as CEO of Revlon in a hostile takeover, Wyman hoped his sympathies would lie with existing management. Yet he said he opposed the sale of CBS, a position shared now by every director in the room. So, Bergerac said: "With a very heavy heart we are confronted with a situation where the chief executive has made a recommendation that has just been unanimously rejected. And in view of the fact that one-third of the shares disagree with him and in view of the fact that we need to stabilize the company, Wyman must go."

Minow spoke next, then Cronkite, each concurring that it was time for Wyman to go. The final nail in the chairman's coffin was driven by Edson Spencer, the first person Wyman had appointed a director. Spencer said he had to catch a plane to Paris that afternoon on business. "I hate to say this because Tom is one of my best friends, and his wife is one of my wife's best friends, but it's inevitable," Spencer said. "He's got to go. Larry owns 25 percent, and Bill has 9 percent. And they can buy more."

No one disagreed with the logic. As Spencer left, the directors began mulling over the severance terms they would offer Wyman, the method they would follow to conduct a search for his replacement, and the temporary arrangements they might make to manage CBS until the search was complete. Bill Paley's motion to have a committee run CBS was offensive to their conviction that authority and responsibility ought be fixed on one chief executive. That's the way they liked to think they ran things. Better to locate one person to do the job for a few months.

They talked for a moment about asking former CBS president Frank Stanton to return, but since he was nearing eighty they decided to look elsewhere to rejuvenate the company. Of the available choices, one they could make this day, only Larry Tisch had the time, the energy, the experience to do the job starting tomorrow. Wary of Paley, they were at first prepared to allow him only a title, founder chairman, the title he now held. The question of the chairman's position was open, since the board was still suspicious of Tisch and did not want to give him the title of chairman as well, even temporarily. "We wanted to leave that open, to signal as much as possible that this was a temporary situation," recalls Bergerac. To further guard against Tisch, the board agreed that a management committee should be formed to share power with Tisch, and a search committee appointed to recruit a new chief executive immediately. As a precaution, the balance of power on both committees would rest with independent directors. The board approved, and asked Tisch alone to rejoin the meeting.

Surprised and pleased by the judgment the board had rendered, Tisch readily accepted the position of acting CEO. The appointment would be temporary, everyone agreed. Seeking reassurance, directors peppered him with questions, and were gratified by responses they had refused to believe on other days. When asked, recalls James Wolfensohn, "He made a commitment to keep the company intact." And Tisch reiterated that Loews had no intention to seek control. The board then directed Tisch to accompany Frank Thomas and Sam Butler, their attorney, to inform Bill Paley and Arthur Liman, who was with him, of their tentative conclusion. "They didn't want Paley to have a role," Tisch recalls.

Paley, joined by Liman, objected, insisting that it was important for CBS and its prestige that he have a role.

Tisch concurred, and went back to the board to urge that Paley be made acting chairman. Reluctantly, the directors consented.

The board, absent Paley and Tisch, then resumed deliberations about Wyman's severance. Their guilt was palpable. "Everyone felt sorry for Wyman," said Tree. The consensus, said Bergerac, was that "Wyman got sandbagged." Sandbagged by his own actions, but also by his board. They agreed to pay what Gilpatric said represented a "costing-out of his contract"—a lump sum of $4.3 million; and as compensation for the stock options he was reportedly sacrificing, they would pay him an annuity of $400,000 a year for the rest of his natural life. The current and the former chairmen of the board's compensation committee, Frank Thomas and Henry Schacht respectively, were asked to deliver the news to Wyman. Informed by his two good friends, Wyman chose to resign, effective immediately.

Thomas and Schacht returned to the boardroom just before 6 P.M., while Wyman summoned his management team to his corner office and simply announced he was leaving. "It was very businesslike," recalls Jankowski. No hugs, no kisses, no tears.

The board invited Tisch and Paley to return and informed them of Wyman's severance package. "I wasn't happy," recalls the tightfisted Tisch, who instantly calculated that they were awarding Wyman an eight-million-dollar package. He persuaded the board to stretch the lump-sum payments over Wyman's lifetime as well. "I couldn't say don't do it, but I thought it was outrageous," said Tisch.

Wyman's package resolved, the board unanimously approved five resolutions: First, they accepted Wyman's resignation; second, they approved the terms of his severance; third, "during the transition period" while they searched for permanent replacements, they agreed that Tisch would be acting president and chief executive officer, Paley acting chairman, and a management committee—consisting of Tisch, Paley, Wolfensohn, Brown, and Bergerac—would be formed "to review the corporation's operations during such transition period"; fourth, a search committee composed of the members of the management committee plus Frank Thomas, Walter Cronkite, and James Houghton would interview candidates and select a permanent chairman and chief executive "in the next few months"*; finally, the board approved a press release announcing the changes.

Over at the CBS Broadcast Center, Van Gordon Sauter was aware that something "momentous" was going on. The meeting had stretched through the afternoon; reports and rumors bounced off walls—that Wyman was packing to leave, that Thomas and Schacht had just delivered the bad news, that everyone in the boardroom looked ashen. By 5:45 P.M., Sauter recalls, he thought he had to put something on the evening newscast. The first feed to the affiliates went out at 6:30 New York time. Rather then did a second feed at 7 P.M., updating the news. By the time the board was passing its resolutions, Sauter knew the broad outline of what had transpired,

* CBS president emeritus Frank Stanton was listed as a consultant.

and felt CBS had to report Wyman's ouster. Wyman, not surprisingly, wanted to delay the announcement to allow time to tell his family and friends.

No way CBS was going to get beaten on this story, thought Sauter, who called down to the newsroom as the first feed was nearing its end. "As I dictated it downstairs," recalls Sauter, "I knew I was dictating my own adios." Gene Jankowski made a different assumption. There was no reason to think he would be ousted. "I never assumed that with anybody," said Jankowski. "With different styles you've got to be sort of adjustable."

CBS broke the news first, as Jennings and Brokaw had when their networks were sold. Dan Rather simply stared into the camera and adlibbed a single paragraph that Wyman was out and Tisch and Paley were in. How did Rather feel as he spoke? "I felt limited relief," recalls Rather. "Relief that it wasn't Ted Turner or Jesse Helms. And I had heard good things about Larry."

"CBS is a great company," Tisch told a throng of reporters waiting in the lobby of Black Rock shortly after 7 P.M., a beaming Paley at his side. "I am delighted to be a member of the CBS family and to help carry on its proud traditions." The pale Tisch stood beside the bronzed Paley and repeated the words of the press release: "I will hold office only during the brief transition period until we select a new chief executive. I intend to maintain the traditions and spirit of this company as established and nurtured by William S. Paley. I am fortunate to have Bill as my partner and mentor in this task. . . ." Paley also stuck to the script, saying he was "delighted" to welcome Tisch. "Larry has not only proven his extraordinary ability as a businessman and leader in the success of his own company, Loews, but most important, he shares the values and principles which have guided CBS throughout the period of its growth."

A mile away, guests had gathered at Mollie Parnis's Park Avenue apartment for a belated wedding reception for Mike Wallace and Mary Yates. Don Hewitt was there, as were Diane Sawyer, Morley Safer, Andy Rooney, and about seventy-five others, including the three network anchors, who came late. The buzz at the party was about CBS and the report Rather had just aired. At 7:15, Don Hewitt received a call from Paley, who confirmed the news. "Don looked twenty years younger, he was so happy," recalled author Kati Marton, wife of Peter Jennings. When Walter Cronkite arrived he was surrounded by guests, who wanted to know everything. At around 8 P.M. Tisch appeared and, said Marton, "It was as if the pope had just walked in the room. Everyone wanted to go and touch his robe."

"It was the most exciting party I've ever given," exclaimed Mollie Parnis. Don Hewitt told the *Times,* "I can't see any way that CBS will not recapture all that it once had." Mike Wallace left the party and told *USA Today:* "This sends the right signal to the troops—a signal that the old guard will take over once again."

Within CBS News, Wyman's departure was treated as a shootout at OK Corral, a showdown between heroes and villains, between the white-hatted Tisch and Paley and the dark-hatted Wyman. Forgotten were the faltering shows on CBS's schedule and the impact of cable and independent stations, which undermined the network's ability to tolerate News losses. Forgotten were the many forces that now preyed on News, including CNN and independent TV stations that now threw popular sitcoms up against network newscasts, or network affiliates that ran footage supplied by CBS in their own local newscasts, which sometimes made the network newscast seem stale.

Journalists are usually wonderfully skeptical, except when they are involved in a story themselves. And so the journalists at CBS hailed William Paley, just two weeks shy of his eighty-fifth birthday, as Cincinnatus, the statesman-general who restored glory to ancient Rome, rather than as El Cid, the dead Spanish warrior who was propped up by his troops for one final battle. Overlooked by many at CBS was Larry Tisch's record of cost cutting and how he had gained effective control of CBS without paying a premium for the privilege. Somehow, Paley and Tisch were going to make things what they once were at CBS.

7

ABC: MORE SANCHO PANZA THAN MACHIAVELLI, SEPTEMBER TO DECEMBER 1986

By the time Larry Tisch and Bob Wright became CEOs of CBS and NBC in September of 1986, Tom Murphy of Cap Cities/ABC had a head start of eight months; eight months to inject a sense of alarm into what all three new owners saw as an indolent network culture. But after steering ABC for two thirds of a year—after firing Fred Pierce and eliminating jobs and stripping Roone Arledge of his Sports fiefdom and closing the executive dining room—Tom Murphy and Dan Burke still weren't sure their message was getting through. They wanted very much to avoid an *us* versus *them* atmosphere, and had consciously pulled back from publicly complaining about the network's "limousine mentality." Nevertheless, they were determined to insist that the good times had stopped. The contract negotiations late that summer with David Hartman of *Good Morning America* provided the opportunity.

The ex-actor had hosted ABC's two-hour morning program for a decade, a period in which ABC surpassed the *Today* show in the ratings race, only to slip back into second place early in 1986. While Hartman brought the network success, he also was expensive, and powerful. He was earning two million dollars annually, and his contract gave him a veto over everything from which segments to air to the naming of substitute hosts. He was widely perceived as both a talented TV performer and a sometimes difficult "star," one who barely spoke to his cohost, Joan Lunden. Now, with Hartman's contract due to expire on November 30, 1986, Cap Cities insisted on reducing his power and regaining editorial and spending control. The person to accomplish this task would be Phil Beuth.

One of the first calls Tom Murphy made after the merger with ABC was to Beuth, who had been with Cap Cities almost from day one. He asked Beuth to take a look at Hartman's contract and to oversee *Good Morning America,* among his other responsibilities. Murphy had reasons to make this match. Philly Beuth had always enjoyed producing a show, from the programs he cobbled together for the original Cap Cities Albany station to the pranks he orchestrated at the annual management retreat in Phoenix. But above all, Beuth's code was their code. "My interest is really business," said Beuth. "I like to know what effect what I'm doing has on the audience, but I like to influence the bottom line."

When Beuth arrived he encountered not just Hartman's enormous clout, but waste, waste that subtracted from the bottom line. Almost immediately he sliced $95,000 a week from *Good Morning America*'s budget—nearly 10 percent of the $40 million it spent annually.

Then Beuth turned to Hartman's two-million-dollar salary, sliding ratings, and immense clout. Hartman was playing hardball, demanding a new contract which would give him more leverage, more money. Beuth felt his demands were too steep, a view shared by his colleagues at Cap Cities. So they decided to risk losing Hartman by insisting that he cede power to management. At the core of Hartman's contract negotiations, explained Murphy, "was not money. It was control of the show. He wanted it, and we didn't want him to have it." A split second after uttering this sentence, Murphy the pol softened what he had said with a tribute to Hartman: "Nice man." Hartman departed, replaced by a competent ABC News correspondent, Charles Gibson, whose salary was approximately one-third Hartman's, and who was not a temperamental star.

A message had been sent. The way to pound that message home to every ABC manager was at the August/September 1986 budget review meetings. The year 1986 would turn out to be a horrible one for both the ABC and CBS networks, since ABC would lose money and CBS's profits would dwindle. Only number-one-ranked NBC would enjoy robust profits this year, triggering speculation that instead of a business with no losers, network television had become a business with one winner and perhaps two losers. Murphy and Burke were patient men; they knew that to become number one took time. What they could accomplish immediately was to control spending. The budget process would become their vehicle. Under the old ABC, said Cap Cities' chief financial officer, Ronald Doerfler, the operating heads of each division "had a tendency to budget like government, on a worst-case basis. And if they didn't spend it, they worried." Not surprisingly, the first round of budget drafts submitted by most divisions early in the summer of 1986 were returned with instructions: Redo them the Cap Cities way.

By August of 1986, each department was ready for its budget review. Few were prepared for what awaited them. "In Cap Cities the budget process is the essence of management," observed counsel Stephen Weiswasser. "It is the exemplification of how Cap Cities runs the company. People at Cap Cities pride themselves on being able to look at hard realities. Tom Murphy often says, 'We did wrong with that decision because we wished our way into it.' The ABC guys were far less prone to that rigorous way of thinking—obviously, there were exceptions. At Cap Cities you don't get into trouble for giving bad news to your superior. You don't get into trouble for being wrong. You get into trouble for not admitting mistakes. That is the ethic of the place."

With Dan Burke, John Sias, Ron Doerfler, and sometimes Murphy as the audience, each department was subjected to rigorous cross-examination, sometimes extending over a period of days. The sessions at Cap Cities' Villard House headquarters could be rough. None were rougher than those experienced by Roone Arledge and his news division. By September 1986, Arledge and David Burke had trimmed one hundred jobs from their budget, without fanfare. And News, under their management, was earning a profit—$37 million in 1986. While News profits were falling, ABC, unlike NBC, was not losing money. Arledge had a money-making magazine show—*20/20*—in prime time. Unlike CBS or NBC, ABC News had a late-night entry—*Nightline*—that was the envy of the industry. ABC dominated Sunday morning with David Brinkley, and in Peter Jennings had an extraordinarily skilled anchor. Arledge and his team felt they deserved a pat on the back.

But Arledge came to this budget review unprepared, at least by Sias's and Burke's lights. Like his friend and former Columbia University classmate, Larry Grossman—like most network News presidents—Arledge didn't have budget facts and figures at his fingertips. He couldn't tell them off the top of his head how many subscriptions to *The New York Times* his news division ordered; couldn't explain why Hilary Brown, who had left ABC five years before, still had five newspapers delivered to her at ABC; couldn't describe the cost savings he'd like from a new NABET (National Association of Broadcast Engineers and Technicians) contract. Dan Burke would ask questions in his firm but polite way; John Sias would play the bad cop, always hollering, "Cut them in half!" But Sias played second fiddle to Burke, who ran these meetings, chewing his sugarless gum and fastening his intense blue eyes on those in the dock. Burke would ask, "Why do you need this computer graphics software? How many machines do you use? How many people does it take to operate? Do you really need one next year?"

On the second day the subject was News salaries, and the session was even rougher. Cap Cities executives asked, *How can a producer make so much more than on-air talent? How come you pay this guy $200,000?* The responses failed to impress. Sias felt that Arledge and his people were "kings of obfuscation." His displeasure was matched by Arledge's, who felt demeaned. Arledge and his people felt Cap Cities was missing the point. News succeeded, they fervently believed, not because of management controls but because of what it put on the air. The chasm between Arledge and Cap Cities widened because each side was making a different point. Cap Cities wanted to talk about *management,* Arledge about *quality.* Between them there was a tendency in these early days to treat the two—management and quality programming—as adversaries. If you favored cutting costs, you were deemed anti-quality programming by those who ran News. If you emphasized quality programming, you were dismissed by Cap Cities as an opponent of cost controls and profits.

The news division's budget review extended over three full days and led to the elimination of another fifty positions. News was not the only division to feel the heat. When the Affiliate Relations people came in they were asked: *Why, at a time when the network is losing money, did ABC continue to pay its stations $120 million in compensation?* William Grimes, who ran ESPN, ABC's sports cable service, recalls how Murphy and Burke were startled to learn that ESPN's thirteen thousand cable affiliates paid so much to the cable-programming channel. Instead of one stream of revenues (from advertising), ESPN had two, explained Grimes. From the first—advertising revenues—ESPN expected to collect $120 million in 1987; from the second—compensation paid by the cable operators to ESPN as a program supplier—they budgeted another $120 million. With both a healthy ESPN and a frail network in mind, Tom Murphy said it was "vitally important" that ABC receive relief from its affiliates.

In the end, the budget review served several purposes. On one level, since the network would lose $70 million in 1986—the first network loss since 1971—the review became a way to narrow the losses, to plant the idea that cost containment or profitability for each division was a requirement, not a luxury. More, the budget review was a tutorial, serving to educate Burke and Sias in depth about the business they had acquired. By asking *Why do you spend money on this? Why do you need ten rather than eight people working on this? Why can't it wait till next year?* Cap Cities gained mastery over ABC's budget. And ABC was compelled to think about priorities.

The message got through. ABC learned, said News vice president Dick Wald: "We can't continue as we did before if the whole company loses money. The company has to make money. So it is not unreasonable to ask the news division to cut."

Dan Burke walked away pleased after three weeks of budget reviews. Just as he had done in preparing the first Cap Cities/ABC management retreat in January, Burke thought long and hard about these budget sessions. He saw them as a way to get on top of the business and to judge his executives. These were the obvious hard business reasons. But Dan Burke also saw these sessions as a bonding experience. During one long, particularly contentious budget review, he leaned over to a stunned ABC executive and whispered, "You have to let people know someone is watching."

Even as a youngster in Slingerlands, New York, a small bedroom community seven miles southwest of Albany, Dan Burke had a fierce sense of right and wrong. His father was a decorated World War I major who became an executive with the New York Life insurance company; his mother was a Wellesley graduate and an early feminist who briefly taught English but gave it up to travel where her husband's job took them and to raise four children. James Burke, who is four years older than his brother Dan, said of his father: "His gift to us was that he had a deep conviction of right and wrong, an almost simplistic view of the world." The four children were reared as strict Catholics, attending parochial schools in part because their father disdained "the lax standards" of the public schools. Only after his father was appointed to run the Northeast region for New York Life and the family moved to Wellesley, Massachusetts, was Dan permitted to attend a public high school. "My father was very rigid," recalls Dan Burke. "My mother was intellectually curious and well read. But my dad was tough. My brother was interviewed after he became president of Johnson & Johnson and he said, 'Thanks to my mother and father I never had any difficulty deciding right and wrong.' My father could not stand an edited recital of facts, where you left something out. That was worse to him than a bald-faced lie."

If the senior Burke intimidated his children, so Dan Burke sometimes intimidated his talented older brother and two sisters. "Dan has some hot buttons," said Jim Burke of his brother's temper. "We were all in the family a little afraid of him. I think he was the smartest." And the most verbal. And the funniest. And the cheapest. "We used to think of him as a real tightwad," Jim Burke said. "He was always careful with his money." Many of these traits persisted. At Cap Cities he declined a company limousine. When their four children were growing up, Dan and Harriet "Bunny" Burke conducted an at-home study hall for them. They read and discussed books. The children were subjected to strict discipline and lessons in manners.

Dan Burke met Tom Murphy through his brother Jim, who with Murphy was in the Harvard Business School's legendary class of '49, which also included future SEC chairman John Shad, Xerox president Peter McColough, Bloomingdales president Marvin Traub, and General Housewares founder John Muller. After graduation, Jim Burke and Murphy shared an apartment in Manhattan, where each set out to conquer the world of business. Meanwhile, Dan attended the University of Vermont, fought in Korea, and received a Harvard M.B.A. in 1955. Then he joined General Foods, where he quickly rose within the executive ranks. By 1961, when Dan Burke was in charge of new product development, Tom Murphy mentioned to Jim Burke that he desperately needed someone to run WTEN, his Albany television station. "I need somebody like your brother," Murphy said.

"Why don't you ask him?" said Burke.

"I can't do that. I don't want to risk our friendship," said Murphy.

Jim Burke convinced Murphy that their friendship was too secure for that, and Dan became the station's general manager. "I had concluded I would be more comfortable in something smaller," said Burke. "I had begun to sense it would be impossible to get involved in pro bono activities. General Foods' headquarters was in White Plains, and I didn't live in White Plains. I sensed that to go to a small city and be head of a TV station would be more of a pro bono act." And it would mean a return to his Albany roots.

The same demanding standards Dan Burke imposed on his children he imposed on Cap Cities employees. To Burke, waste not only denied shareholders their full value, it was almost sinful. He carried, said Steve Weiswasser, "a sense of obligation, one that parallels fundamental Catholic notions about one's obligations to people around you and the world." Like an evangelist, Burke sometimes painted an apocalyptic vision; he fretted about everything. He spoke often to employees of obligations—to tell the full truth, to stay humble, to get home early and spend time with their families. He lashed them to improve budget performance, to place all their cards on the table, to avoid gossiping about colleagues, to hire more minorities and women. A visitor to Burke's office could not fail to notice the only plaque exhibited—the Ida Wells Award for encouraging minority journalists.

Burke is a stickler for detail as well. "People tell me I'm sort of forbidding-looking," said Burke, with his chiseled nose and neatly parted silver hair that is rarely out of place. "Maybe I am a son-of-a-bitch. I don't think of myself that way. I do know I can turn a group on and excite them, because I've done it. Most often I can get a deep reaction with bad medicine."

For all his sternness, Burke is generous with compliments. He sends thank-you notes to ABC people who show him around the newsroom or the sales department. He appears unexpectedly on weekends to cheer at ABC employee softball games. He designs the annual Phoenix management retreat, in part, to recognize achievement and spotlight good performance. "My tendency is to lead the cheers," explained Burke. "It's an important ingredient in a business of creativity, intuition, artistry. I've never met anyone who tires of getting complimented." It is partly because Tom Murphy paid Dan Burke the compliment of allowing him to feel as if he actually managed most parts of Cap Cities' business (which he did) that Dan Burke was content to remain as Murphy's number two. It explains why Burke, a sports enthusiast like his friend and neighbor in Kennebunkport, Maine—George Bush—spurned a chance to be commissioner of baseball in 1984, and why he said no to headhunters and others who dangled job offers before him, including Katharine Graham, chair of The Washington Post Company.

The talents of "Murphy & Burke"—they're referred to almost as a trade name—blended. Like Burke, Tom Murphy set a moral tone. They liked to tell executives: "Are you the kind of a person who stops at a traffic light way out in the country when no one else is around? If so, you're one of our guys!" Yet Murphy and Burke had different management interests. Murphy was more instinctual, the optimist who concentrated on strategy and doing deals and Washington and Hollywood relationships and being the place the buck stops on big decisions. Burke was more analytical, the skeptic who concentrated on day-to-day management issues and fixing things. Most personnel questions come to rest on his desk. "One of the reasons my relationship with Tom works is because he is not out front all the time," explained

Burke. "I would be appalled if he were out front and being misquoted all the time, or if he were quoted and I had to clean up after him."

Still, there were lots of messes left behind, particularly in the wake of the merger. A year afterward, Burke spoke of the "enthusiasm we've encountered every step of the way at ABC. I don't know whether it's because they realize we were headed for worse troubles, or because of John Sias's skills." But Burke also acknowledged the cultural conflict between the old ABC and the new Cap Cities: "There have been hurt feelings."

Burke underestimated the extent of these hurt feelings. By the fall of 1986, the emphasis on cost cutting and changing established ways of doing business had rattled ABC. There was a widespread impression that Cap Cities sometimes wanted to humiliate old ABC hands. And, of course, everyone was insecure about his or her own job.

Like a lot of talented people in the news division, producer Christopher Isham was dispirited in the summer and fall of 1986. At thirty-three, Isham was one of ABC News's star investigative producers. He had uncovered secret nuclear arms sales to Pakistan and Israel and torture in South Africa. Yet Isham saw his world changing in ways he did not like, and thought of quitting. "I don't like the way the business has become bureaucratized," he said. "When I first got to ABC, if you had a story, you were told to do it. Now for an investigative story you have to go through enormous hoops with the accountants. I don't mind working hard. What I mind is being nickeled and dimed. The accountants have more influence on how we cover the news. They ask whether it's cost-effective. There are whole parts of the world we don't cover because it's not cost-effective. We have not covered Haiti in the last four months. That was a financial decision." The producer did not blame Cap Cities for ordering a blackout of Haiti; he blamed the managers at ABC whose eagerness to accommodate their new bosses provoked blind cost cutting. When White House chief of staff Donald Regan was sworn in and Ted Koppel tried to order up file footage of then treasury secretary Regan and other chiefs of staff, the librarian told him, "We can't find it now, and tomorrow we're going to erase half the library for savings reasons." Koppel phoned Dick Wald, who ordered a halt to the file purging. Koppel found there was no directive to gut the library. Rather, he said, "It was a general cost-cutting mood and someone said, 'We can really save a lot of dollars if we had fewer tapes.' "

On the other hand, Koppel and others agreed there was extravagance at the old ABC. Chris Isham, who would eventually come to admire Cap Cities, acknowledged, "No question, there had been lots of waste at ABC. During the hostage crisis in Iran we had maybe twenty crews sitting on their ass waiting for orders." Nevertheless, what bothered people like Isham in the fall of 1986 was a feeling that Cap Cities seemed to pay more attention to what went on in headquarters than to what appeared on the TV screen. Which brought to mind Leonard Goldenson's warning to Tom Murphy: "The people who run the company have got to have a feeling for programming. They've got to follow their instincts." Someone who manufactures cars ought to drive one.

John Sias became the lightning rod for much of the unhappiness within ABC. Stoddard's entertainment division was incensed at some of Sias's public utterances, including the statement he made to the May 1986 affiliate convention. Asked to grade ABC's programs, Sias responded: "I might say a D plus. Of course, I've always been an easy grader." Sias, for his part, found Stoddard too much of an elitist for television. Although Sias could appreciate fine things—he is a committed environmentalist and serves on the national board of the Nature Conservancy—he cared more about profits than about what appeared on a television set he rarely watched.

The conviction grew that Sias looked only at numbers, not at people. Few were as despondent that fall as Roone Arledge. He had spent three decades at ABC. But Arledge was so miserable the first year of Cap Cities' reign that he became even more reclusive than usual. His office door stayed shut. He returned fewer calls. Visits to the newsroom became rarer. He disappeared for interminable lunches and sometimes did not return to the office, preferring the TV consoles at his Park Avenue apartment. There was a feeling that the Visigoths had arrived. David Burke, his deputy, said they felt a jumble of emotions, including: "Who are these people to judge me? It must be the same thing children suffer when their father remarries."

With Arledge the feelings fused with a broader concern. During the course of one four-hour lunch at his favorite restaurant, Nanni Al Valletto, Arledge said, "My biggest worry, even though there are highly intelligent individuals involved, is that at this point in time I don't see anyone with a dream or vision or concept of what television ought to be. There's a general awareness of how costs must be cut, styles changed. All three networks undoubtedly had to cut back. A rational person would say it was necessary. What troubles me is that once that's done, the people at all three networks don't have a vision of what the networks should be."

The problem with the new owners, Arledge believed, was that they were businessmen, not showmen. "Everyone wants to be appreciated by their peers," he continued, picking at a plate of angel hair pasta twirled in tomatoes and basil. "And the people running the networks have as their peers all businessmen. The blend doesn't seem to be there. . . . What worries me is that I don't get a sense this is temporary and that after the cost cutting we'll resume the 'vision' and do creative things. If you have access to the airwaves, there is some responsibility beyond just to stockholders."

Arledge acknowledged that the issue of public trust was not easy to define, certainly not easy to codify. He was aware that other businesses—such as banks—had a public trust, which is why the federal government insured deposits. But to Arledge, owning a piece of the public airwaves was a special privilege. Under Cap Cities, he said, "No one sits around talking programs. It's all CPMs [cost per thousands] and multiples." Would Murphy and Burke—or Sias—insist on news documentaries because they were important? Even if they lost viewers?

A final fault line between old and new concerned the future. While only a fool could fail to recognize that the networks were no longer as dominant as they once were, executives like Arledge had more faith in their future. Like others who had grown up at the networks, he believed "the networks are always going to be a major player." Only the networks, Arledge believed, had unrivaled access to the mass audiences advertisers needed to peddle their products efficiently. Although the three networks no longer reached 92 percent of all viewers each evening, they still reached 75 percent. And even if that number dwindled to 65 percent—or 55 percent—Arledge knew no competitor even came close to such numbers. The new owners, on the other hand, focused more on the downside. They weren't sure that the roughly $3 billion the three networks spent on entertainment programming gave them insuperable advantages over smaller competitors. They were suspicious of those, like Arledge, who preached the old-time religion that "this is a business of hits." These were prudent businessmen, managers of risks, and in the fall of 1986 they saw more risks than opportunities.

The biggest risk they saw was from cable, which by 1986 was in nearly half (48.7 percent) the roughly ninety million TV homes. Between pay-cable channels like HBO and basic cable viewing, each day about 19 percent of the TV audience watched cable. By 1986, subscriptions brought in $10.2 billion and advertising revenues totaled $932 million. Cable companies were in the narrowcasting business, satisfied with small, targeted audiences. They didn't have huge overheads to feed. Since cable was still in its infancy, it rarely dealt with unions or established management layers. ESPN, for instance, put on twenty-four hours a day of programming with a staff of just 450, compared to the ABC network's roughly 8,000 employees. People like John Sias openly fretted that ABC might follow the pattern of mass picture magazines like *Look, Life,* and the *Saturday Evening Post,* which were rendered obsolete by the instant pictures of television, or of AM radio, which had been decimated by FM radio and by smaller stations that specialized in soft or hard rock music, or country and western, or all-news radio. Listeners, readers—or viewers—were being given more options, and they were responding accordingly. Television was being cannibalized—and democratized.

The new owners were much more likely to listen to Wall Street analysts than to Roone Arledge. And what analysts like Rich McDonald of First Boston were saying in the fall of 1986 was this: "The reason the networks are a big dinosaur is the fact that their one channel analogizes to the dinosaur's small brain. The networks have no flexibility. Cable has fifty to seventy-five channels." Now that cable operators were talking publicly of pooling their resources into a single programming consortium—and TCI's John Malone went so far as to talk to producer Norman Lear about running it—the assumption was rampant that the future belonged to cable.

The future also belonged, some feared, to Rupert Murdoch's scheme to make Fox a fourth network by acquiring stations in six of the top ten markets, lining up affiliated stations, and setting up a programming department, just as the three networks did. Attempts to start a fourth network had been launched before—by DuMont in the fifties, by the United Network in the sixties, by Paramount in the seventies, and by Metromedia earlier in the eighties. Murdoch, however, was credited with a better shot at success, now that the three networks no longer dominated. By acquiring Metromedia's six TV stations and linking them to one other station, plus his ownership of the Twentieth Century Fox studios, Murdoch could now become what he called "a fourth programming force in American network television. . . ." There were network executives who disparaged Fox at the time, saying it relied on weaker stations whose signals did not radiate far enough, had affiliates in only 75 percent of the country, and lacked a great advantage enjoyed by the networks: the ability to promote shows by platforming them with promotional ads during peak viewing hours.

But Nielsen's numbers told a different story. Already, independent stations not affiliated with any of the three networks attracted 13.5 percent of the national audience. And now Fox was offering these stations free programming, and as it added nights to its schedule it promised to siphon more network viewers. Fox was set to premiere in November of 1986 with a new late-night entry, *The Late Show Starring Joan Rivers,* and to begin regular programming on Sunday nights starting in the spring of 1987. Since Rivers had often substituted for Johnny Carson, she was not an unknown. Nor was the chief executive officer of Fox, Barry Diller, who had been a successful programmer at ABC in the seventies and was a money-maker when he next ran Paramount Pictures. Diller's programming talents, teamed with Murdoch's deep pockets and business acumen—plus the Murdoch Fleet Street formula of gossip and hype—was still another menace to the networks. Already Fox had introduced at its owned stations a new show—*A Current Affair*—which would be widely syndicated and would pioneer the sensationalism and hyperkinetic writing that would come to be called "tabloid television." Another Fox advantage was low overhead. "The main thing Fox has going for it," observed ABC president John Sias, echoing the cost-conscious outlook of both Bob Wright and Larry Tisch, "is that they don't have the $300 to $500 million overhead each network has. They have only fifty people—the size of the ABC research department!"

Fox and cable were already beginning to poach on another network monopoly—televised National Football League games. The networks' five-year contract with the NFL, which had always been exclusive, was to expire after the 1987 Super Bowl. To keep cable from getting a foothold, the networks in 1981 agreed to pay the NFL $2.1 billion over five years for the right to televise games. However, as football salaries soared and the cost of tickets no longer covered expenses, as the league expanded and some club owners found themselves heavily in debt, football came to place greater emphasis on broadcast rights. By 1986, observed Val Pinchbeck, the NFL's director of broadcasting, two truths dangerously collided. On the one hand, football teams were becoming more dependent on TV revenues, which in 1986 accounted for two-thirds of the average club's income. On the other hand, the networks that were the sole source of those revenues claimed—and Pinchbeck did not challenge—that they were losing money on the games. ABC was paying $7 million a game for *Monday*

Night Football—$150 million a season—and yet its ratings were tailing off, depressing the price it could charge advertisers. Further confusing this picture was politics. The political system might deregulate, but would it go so far as to permit a popular American pastime to be removed from the free airwaves? "If we put the Super Bowl on anything else but a network," said Pinchbeck, "the Congress would pass a bill the next day." Since just under 50 percent of American homes had cable, to air the games on cable would black out half the population.

But the new owners of the three networks refused to sweeten their NFL contract. In the preliminary rounds of negotiations, Pinchbeck was informed that the networks planned to reduce the cost of their contract. They were less concerned with the long-term threat of cable or Fox than they were with the immediate cost of the games. That was the emergency they focused on. Ironically, the short-term needs of the new owners blended perfectly with the long-term strategy of the NFL. For the NFL, the ideal solution was a compromise. With cable willing to pay more to get a foot in the door, and able to pay because it could pass along the costs to subscribers, the NFL wished to hedge its bets. "This is a good time to get our end wet with someone else, like cable," Pinchbeck said in late 1986. If it were just a few games on cable, he didn't believe Congress would interfere. With the new network owners demanding to pay less, and with ESPN, HBO, Turner Broadcasting, Fox, and others vying to broadcast NFL games, here too leverage was shifting from the networks. Once again, it could be argued the consumer would benefit. Without commercials, said HBO president Michael Fuchs that fall, "We think we can do a football game that is forty minutes shorter than a network NFL game." Of course, if cable gained access to the games, the networks would lose more audience share.

With audiences shrinking, what Tom Murphy and his counterparts at the three networks desperately wanted was another source of revenue, and they felt that their best hope was to alter their business relationship with another competitor, the Hollywood studios. Fearful of a network monopoly, Hollywood remembered how once, prior to 1970, the Big Three had produced many of their own programs, and sold the reruns. Often, the studios were denied a spot on the network schedule. Flexing political muscle, the Hollywood studios helped persuade the Justice Department to enact the so-called financial interest and syndication rules in the 1970s. The rules would be relaxed to allow each network to produce up to three hours of prime time in the 1986–87 season, rising to five hours in 1988–89. Perhaps, the networks hoped, the deregulation-minded Reagan administration would soon eliminate these strictures altogether. Not so. When his own FCC tried to relax the rules in 1983, President Reagan—with a last-minute nudge from his former agent and friend, MCA chairman Lew Wasserman—sided with the studios for whom he once worked as an actor. There would be no modification of the rules.

But the rules were scheduled to lapse at the end of the decade. Tom Murphy and his fellow new network owners were convinced that if they could speed the process, could own a piece of the product whose value they helped create by placing it on their schedules in the first place, they would have a gold mine. They also believed that if they could be partners with the studios in producing shows, the financial incentives would be altered. Perhaps if the option rule were eliminated, the studios would no longer be able to hold them up at the end of a required four-year contract, demanding that the network pay a lot more weekly for a successful series—or else risk losing the series to another network just as it became a hit. Perhaps, together, they could better control costs. There was one other incentive: If an agreement could be struck between the networks and Hollywood, no one would be happier than Washington. No politician eager to be reelected longs to choose sides between two generous campaign benefactors.

By the fall of 1986, Murphy and his compatriots believed the merits of the case were on their side. Only one network—NBC—earned healthy profits. Then there was the fairness issue. The networks were hamstrung by regulations that didn't apply to their competition. In addition to being prohibited from owning and syndicating programs, the networks were not permitted to own cable systems, though they could own cable-programming services like ESPN. Nor could they own TV stations reaching more than 25 percent of the nation. Nor could they acquire both a TV and a radio station in the same market. By contrast, the giant Hollywood studios were, theoretically at least, free to integrate vertically as well as horizontally, as were the big cable companies.

It bothered Tom Murphy & Company that ten Hollywood studios, which supplied six out of ten prime-time network programs in the fall of 1986, at times enjoyed the kind of dominance they claimed the networks had. For instance, Lew Wasserman's studio—MCA/Universal—not only produced TV shows and movies, it also distributed movies to its own theater chains, created an aftermarket for its movies by producing them for its own home-video production business, made programs for cable through its partial ownership of the USA cable network, and would soon produce programs for a TV station it was acquiring in New York—WOR-TV. WOR was a superstation, and as such it would compete not only with the network-owned stations in New York but with the networks directly, since a pact with cable operators allowed WOR's signal to reach a national audience. Warner Communications then claimed partial ownership of six TV stations and produced and distributed TV programs and movies, owned major pieces of both MTV and Nickelodeon, and as the nation's third largest cable system owner was in a position to showcase its own programs. Paramount was the number-one distributor of its movies to its own 470 movie theaters, as well as a major syndicator of shows to independent TV stations, a partial owner of cable's USA Network, and sole owner of the New York Knickerbockers and Rangers, as well as the Madison Square Garden cable-programming service that displayed their games. Besides making TV shows and movies, Disney owned KHJ-TV in Los Angeles, the nation's second largest market, and held a dominant position in the cable industry through the Disney pay-cable channel. Columbia's various production arms made TV programs and movies and generated substantial profits in the syndication marketplace. Twentieth Century Fox made TV shows and movies, distributed them to the networks or to cable, and was also becoming a direct rival as a fourth network. Some studios also owned publishing houses, and made and distributed movies in a VCR format. To new network owners like Tom Murphy, real power resided with the Hollywood studios. The studios were becoming less dependent on the networks for distribution, while the networks were coming to rely more on the studios as suppliers.

The game had changed, but not the rules. The same was true in cable, where cable-system owners like Tele-Communications Inc., Time, Inc., and Warner Communications, three of the nation's biggest cable companies, owned the cable systems that carried signals from their own programming services; and TCI had a controlling interest in United Artists Theaters, the nation's largest theater chain. In short, these cable giants had the means to distribute the product they produced and the potential power to lock out competitors. Though they enjoyed nearly monopolistic power, there were few government-imposed restrictions on the studios or cable companies.

The networks under both old management and new negotiated with the studios in search of common ground, a way of sharing both costs and profits. The government encouraged these talks, hoping to avoid choosing sides. During the spring and summer of 1986 a half dozen meetings were held, bringing the participants to the brink of a compromise agreement. The network negotiators were representatives of the old order—Gene Jankowski of CBS, Robert Butler of NBC, and Mike Mallardi of ABC. On October 8, 1986, they received a compromise proposal from Robert Daly, chairman of Warner Brothers and head of the studio negotiating team, the same Robert Daly whom founder Bill Paley had tried to lure back to CBS to replace Tom Wyman. What Daly offered was to let the networks co-own up to 50 percent of four prime-time series or to produce up to five hours weekly of prime-time programs, while at the same time extending the financial interest and syndication restrictions through 1995. Knowing the distance they had traveled, the negotiators on both sides thought they had a deal. "Had we gotten this proposal last February or March, I'm convinced it would have passed," said NBC's Bob Butler. "But when we went to the three new owners they said, 'Why do we have to do this?' " The new owners, who now talked regularly, decided the compromise would become a straitjacket. They still believed they could change the world, and preferred no loaf at all to the quarter loaf offered by Daly.

The gulf between the networks and Hollywood was too wide to bridge, and involved emotion as well as substance. Few were as passionate as Daly, who once sat on the network side of the table as the head of Business Affairs for CBS. Behind the gold and silver doors that open to his huge sunken office, with its wall of tropical fish on the Warner Brothers lot, Daly conveyed the emotion he and others in Hollywood felt: "Even Larry Tisch and Tom Murphy and Bob Wright don't understand what takes place with Business Affairs at the networks and studios. The networks take 50 percent of your profits and don't pay you for it. The power of the networks is awesome. When you go into negotiations over an idea all you're dealing with is an idea. When you write a script you have to lock in a deal over how much the networks will pay you for a pilot and for the first four years of the series. You have no leverage when you make the deal—unless you're dealing with superstar Tom Selleck. You have to make whatever they suggest. Their power is no different today than it was twenty years ago. Who do we sell to? Nobody but the networks, because nobody has the circulation they have." Daly was saying that, whatever its audience erosion, only a network reached enough viewers to pay the license fees of $400,000 to $850,000 per week for a series. Daly was frightened to allow them to get in the syndication door. "If they have the back end of the deal they'll take the little guys and try and squeeze us," he said. "That's what I used to do. I picked the weakest guy in town and made that deal first, and then used that as the basis to bring everyone else in line."

In many ways, the emotion—and the system—made no sense. Both sides were shouting past each other, the networks complaining that the studios were inflating their deficits, the studios screaming that the networks were out to murder them. But by the fall of 1986, several of the studios were ready to ease the rules. Because of the expense of making one-hour dramas—about $1 million per week, and more for an action-adventure series like *Miami Vice*—and because the licensing fee the network paid the studio to produce each episode usually fell between $100,000 to $300,000 short of the studio's actual weekly costs, a partnership that would share both costs and gains might make sense. Otherwise the studios might have to give up hour-long dramas altogether. Everyone at the networks, both old and new owners, said this publicly. Privately, it was acknowledged by those on the other side of the table as well, including Fay Vincent of Coca-Cola's Entertainment Group, which owned Columbia, Embassy, and Tri-Star Pictures. "Isn't the way we do business now ridiculous?" declared the man who thought briefly of acquiring the CBS network and later went on to become commissioner of baseball. "The networks put up all the costs for *Who's the Boss?* It runs. They get all the money from advertisers. We take the risk that after four years we'll make money from syndication. That's the legal form. I'd rather the law said: 'Take *Who's the Boss?* and share the up-front costs and share the back-end profits.' "

But a compromise with Hollywood was not possible in the fall of 1986. Despite Fay Vincent's private comments, both sides were locked into firm positions. Though Tom Murphy and Dan Burke had failed with the studios, by late fall they were clearly succeeding with ABC. People at the network more readily accepted that the world had changed. "It's more a business now," said ABC Sales and Affiliate Relations head Mark Mandala. "Places like ABC thought they were bulletproof."

Cap Cities mercilessly hacked away at costs. Not only had more than one thousand ABC employees been dismissed, but by November, Dan Burke claimed that one-third of ABC's paperwork had been eliminated. An impatient John Sias, who believed News was "insular" and rooted in "habit and traditionalism," in November 1986 persuaded Arledge's division to reduce spending, on an annualized basis, by another $25 million. Arledge agreed to slim the London, Paris,

Warsaw, and Chicago bureaus, and eliminate twelve correspondent slots, among other measures.

Because the change in corporate culture was so sudden, the mood at the end of 1986 was sometimes funereal. "I can't smile when I walk into work for fear of making somebody feel bad," Dan Burke told the *Buffalo Evening News.* There was considerable anxiety that this somber mood would depress morale and creativity. "They run their business like the Harvard Business School," observed Fred Pierce from his office-in-exile at Cap Cities' townhouse. Pierce thought Cap Cities engaged in too much "bravado," too much boasting to the business community of how "lean and mean" they were. Like Arledge and others, he was concerned that in their rush to cut costs and transform the old culture, Cap Cities was forgetting what was special about a network. Pierce said, "The last major thing I committed to before I left was the Statue of Liberty coverage [for the bicentennial]. I don't think any of these regimes would do that. It's risky. It takes a certain amount of vision, not just in terms of what the audience is attuned to but what advertisers are willing to pay for. . . . The new guys want predictability in costs and sales and the bottom line. Extraordinary things, which make network TV stand out, are what will suffer."

Few ABC hands were as depressed that fall as David Burke. Although he was the hands-on manager of the news division—and seemed to be someone who would agree with Cap Cities' tough approach to management—he had, in a sense, checked out. When News executives met to decide on cuts, Burke was often not there, unlike Arledge, who tried to be a good soldier. One would have thought that Burke, coming from politics and Wall Street, would have been comfortable with fellow Irish Catholics Murphy and Burke, who shared his interest in politics and efficient management. But David Burke couldn't hide his contempt for Sias. And behind Tom Murphy's backslapping charm he sensed coldness, the same glazed calculation he knew so well from politics. Of the three Cap Cities officials, the one he most admired was Dan Burke, but he saw too little of him. So David Burke, with his white starched collars and his carefully manicured nails, became a fierce guardian and protector of News.

In a series of interviews beginning that fall and running through 1988, Burke always spoke on the record, always freely expressed his doubts and fears. Although some colleagues would say he acted the role of news purist to compensate for his "impure" political background, David Burke was in earnest. He praised Cap Cities for eliminating many of ABC's "inefficiencies." In years past, he said, "95 percent of our time was spent" trying to get ABC News to be competitive with CBS and NBC, trying to be creative and work on new programs; only 5 percent was spent on budgets. "Now that has changed drastically. Now at least 50 percent of our time is spent on the budget. 'Why are we sending this guy to the Sudan? Can we send him from Rome?' " The questions were healthy, said Burke. But they aroused two concerns: "Do I become a good German? First you give your finger. Then your wrist. And then you say to yourself, 'Sometime I'm going to draw the line.' Then there's no line, and your arm is gone. My second concern is that we may be under the control of people who don't know where the line is. If Frank Stanton said, 'We have to adjust,' I'd roll up my sleeves and I'd do what has to be done because I'd know I'm under leadership that knows. Leadership that understands this is a public trust as well as a business. . . . With me it always comes down to the last day in the hospital room when you've got to make an accounting to yourself. Larry Tisch may be in that hospital room and be very pleased with the stock market price of his company. But those are not my values."

David Burke's fears were heightened in November when Cap Cities permitted the owned stations division to move *World News Tonight* from 7:00 to 6:30 P.M. on its flagship station, WABC-TV in New York. It would be replaced at 7 P.M. by *Jeopardy!,* a syndicated game show that boosted station profits. The eight owned stations were ABC's major source of profits. Coupled with Cap Cities' faith in decentralization, the leverage of the stations over the network had grown. It had always been the stations' belief that they could fatten profits by moving *World News* to an earlier time slot and replacing it with a show that drew a wider and a younger audience. In what old hands would describe as a self-fulfilling prophecy, John Sias explained the move simply: "The networks are no longer the center of the universe." To those who claimed the move was a sacrilege, Sias could point out that earlier network newscasts were now commonplace. For instance, by 1986 three ABC-owned stations and about half the six hundred-plus three-network affiliates already aired network news at 6:30, and sometimes earlier in the West. Nor was this the first time a News program had lost an intramural tug of war. Just this fall, for example, Sias and Cap Cities management decreed that News could not preempt the entertainment schedule for a midterm Election Night special. And even in the so-called good old days when News was supposedly sacrosanct, Edward R. Murrow's sparkling *See It Now* had been dumped for a quiz show.

WABC-TV calculated that if *Jeopardy!* were up against Tom Brokaw and Dan Rather in New York, *Jeopardy!* would win. And if Jennings were the only network newscast in New York at 6:30, WABC might win that time period too. The logic was unassailable—as long as WABC moved first.

The decision was left to the owned stations group. "My goal is to get to the point where I can go back and put my head on my desk and take a nap," said Dan Burke, explaining Cap Cities' philosophy of decentralization. "We mentioned it to Burke and Sias," recalled Mike Mallardi, to whom the owned stations reported. There were "no prolonged discussions, no summit meeting. They understood it. The big difference was a change of philosophy: Each operating division should be permitted to make its own calls. In the old days, the network would have said no."

Something fundamental had changed. As it lost viewers, News lost some of its sanctity. In the old days one reason the network would have said no was that News was not expected to be a profit-maker, nor to compete against game shows. News was the division that conferred status on the network, that fulfilled its obligation as a privileged franchise. "I don't like the idea of being another commodity, which the move to 6:30 suggests," complained Peter Jennings. "They just move News around. There's no thought, 'Let's put Jennings in at 6:30 to make News stronger.' The move was made to get *Jeopardy!* in at 7:00. Even the Romans believed in bread and circuses! *Jeopardy!* is cutting into Tom and Dan. I'm not pleased by that. It's not fair that network news shows go up against a game show."

Measured by ratings, the move turned out to be a success for WABC and for Jennings. *Jeopardy!*, as expected, dominated the 7 P.M. time period. And Jennings, who had been trailing both Rather and Brokaw in New York, now had a higher rating at 6:30 than either had at 7 P.M. Most surprising, more viewers in the New York metropolitan area were watching the three network newscasts after the move than before, which seemed to confirm Sias's suspicion that vanity, not principle, drove News's resistance. "The ego of, say, Peter Jennings, who says 7:00 gets more viewers, is crazy," Sias said at the time. "Hell, they get more viewers now. It's the dumbest thing I ever heard."

Actually, Jennings wasn't dumb at all. He and others in News rightly perceived another long-term menace. By ceding the 7 P.M. half hour, the network was subtracting a half hour from traditional network time, allowing syndicators who had previously been able to sell only the 7:30 half hour to now sell the full 7 to 8 P.M. hour. ABC was strengthening the very syndicators who attacked network dominance. Soon after WABC-TV slotted *Jeopardy!* at 7 P.M., Stuart Hersch, then the president of King World, which owned the top three shows in syndication—*Wheel of Fortune, The Oprah Winfrey Show,* and *Jeopardy!* —exclaimed triumphantly: "The networks have just lost a half hour to the syndicated marketplace. . . . ABC is backing out, cutting back time the network delivers programming."

One other decision reminded News that the old rules were out the window. Over the years, when contracts of performers or correspondents came due, a bidding war for their services was common. Bill Paley built up CBS by stealing the radio and recording services of Jack Benny, Amos 'n' Andy, Al Jolson, Edgar Bergen and Charlie McCarthy, Groucho Marx, and others from his friend David Sarnoff. In the early eighties, Roone Arledge tried to steal first Dan Rather and then Tom Brokaw, and even before that he had successfully raided and plucked some of the best correspondents and producers from CBS and NBC. To attract talent from another network required an open purse, one Arledge enjoyed under Leonard Goldenson and Fred Pierce.

With Diane Sawyer's CBS contract expiring at the end of 1986, Arledge began talking to Sawyer and her agent, Richard Leibner, hoping to bring her to ABC. Leibner made it clear that Sawyer would leave only for a coanchor spot. To push Sawyer as coanchor at CBS was ticklish for Leibner, who also represented Dan Rather, his most important client. So he shopped her at ABC and NBC. Word of these discussions soon leaked, and did not please Peter Jennings. "I used to work in a three-anchor system," Jennings said in December of 1986. "Now I'm solo. I didn't take this job and go through all the crap I did for three years in order to divide up twenty-two minutes."

Jennings's attitude did not please Arledge, who at the time was concerned that the other anchors were encroaching on management prerogatives, had become temperamental stars. It bothered him that Jennings was feuding with—indeed, barely spoke to—his executive producer, Bill Lord. Jennings was making noises that when his contract expired in the summer of 1987 he wanted economic parity at least with Tom Brokaw, who was earning $1.8 million a year versus Jennings's $850,000. In addition, Jennings wanted the same managing editor title that Rather and Brokaw enjoyed. Arledge and David Burke were angry enough to want to put Jennings in his place. But with Jennings climbing in the ratings, they dared not risk losing him or his making life so miserable for Sawyer that their on-air chemistry would suffer, as happened when ABC paired Barbara Walters and Harry Reasoner in the mid-seventies. With Jennings effectively vetoing Sawyer as coanchor of *World News,* and with Sawyer refusing to leave *60 Minutes* except for an anchor opportunity, Arledge was stumped. Nevertheless, he was determined to add Sawyer to his galaxy of stars.

Then Arledge ran into a bigger obstacle—Cap Cities. Tom Murphy told Arledge he didn't believe the networks should compete for stars. It was ungentlemanly. And "wars" got to be expensive. "We didn't want to get into a bidding contest and up the ante," recalls Sias. Arledge countered that NBC was hot in pursuit, which was true. Seeking to avoid a blind bidding contest, Sias thought to telephone a Westport neighbor—NBC News president Larry Grossman. "I'm going to ask a question which you don't have to answer," Sias said. "Are you interested in Diane Sawyer? The news division says you are."

"That's an inappropriate question and I'm not going to answer," an offended Grossman replied. (Sias confirms the conversation.)

The telephone call—and the unwillingness of Cap Cities to bid for talent—aroused concern about collusion among the three networks. When Sawyer re-signed with CBS before Christmas for $1.2 million—$400,000 less than Larry Grossman was willing to pay—whispers were rampant that Tom Murphy had spoken with his friend Larry Tisch and, in effect, engaged in restraint of trade. After all, Tom and Larry usually breakfasted twice a week to raise funds for New York University, and they were social friends. Murphy and Tisch deny they ever spoke about Diane Sawyer, and in a way it didn't matter whether they had. In many respects, the three new owners were triplets. They shared investments—Loews, GE, and Berkshire Hathaway's Warren Buffett were major investors in Macy's. They shared a preoccupation with costs, a determination to transform the network cultures they inherited and to put "stars" in their place. They shared a value system. "They're all alike," remarked Billie Tisch admiringly.

In one sense, this was nothing new. The networks used to rotate coverage of the annual Emmy Awards, with a tacit agreement to showcase the industry awards show by throwing feeble programs up against it. And despite savage ratings competition, the Big Three have always had a stake in one another's success. The more ratings leader NBC charged for its ads in 1986, for example, the steeper the prices ABC and CBS could extract from advertisers. Or as CBS's Gene Jankowski observed, "The best and the healthiest thing for the industry is three strong networks." But something was different about the competition starting in 1986. The new owners, observed one prominent, longtime network executive, "have a common goal to get the industry under control. That's different, and that's where I see the danger. David Sarnoff didn't look upon Bill Paley's costs as a common problem." All through that fall and winter, Tisch and Murphy in particular swapped tales of the latest cost outrage they had stumbled upon. In conversation, each was intimate with the budget travails of the other two, and used this information as leverage. Though they competed, they were helping each other.

Perhaps their biggest shared lament was the money each ladled out to affiliates as compensation for airing network programs. Tisch boasted, recalls Murphy, that he would cut $50 million out of CBS's $168 million in compensation. Murphy was determined to curb the $120 million ABC paid. Murphy also wanted to stop affiliates from preempting poorly rated network programs in favor of syndicated shows or movies. Murphy would put the affiliates in their place, as he had David Hartman.

Tom Murphy had been in the business long enough to know preemptions were nothing new—in the seventies, forty-one ABC affiliates refused to air the network's weaker evening newscast. But Murphy also knew two things were different. First, preemptions had become much more common, since stations had a broader menu of syndicated product to choose from, and since the networks, particularly on weekends, were losing their mass audiences. A second major difference was that the networks' very lives were now at stake. The ABC network would lose $70 million in 1986, and Murphy believed the affiliates were being greedy and should accept compensation adjustments.

There was one catch: Murphy and Tisch believed Bob Wright and NBC should take the lead in paring compensation. NBC was now the number-one network, and the ratings leader always had more clout with its affiliates since it lifts their ratings as well. After NBC reached first place in the prime-time ratings in 1986, 136 of its affiliates ranked first in their markets, 28 were second, and only 18 were third. Although Bob Wright shared Murphy's and Tisch's view that compensation should be pared, and believed that the $141 million NBC paid its stations was excessive, Wright thought CBS and ABC had to take the lead. "It would be difficult for me to explain cuts to our affiliates because we're doing so well," Wright said.

By the annual ABC Affiliate board of governors meeting in Hawaii in December 1986, Tom Murphy had decided to be the first to make the plunge. Standing before his "partners" and delineating the networks' travails, Murphy proposed to cut affiliate compensation by a modest $3.7 million in 1987 and $10.5 million the following year, for a total of 9 percent. Despite his extensive experience as an affiliate station owner, Murphy was unprepared for the reaction. Affiliates threatened to increase preemptions if the network followed through. They produced charts showing that smaller stations were much more dependent on network compensation for their economic health, and that reductions would send them to the trauma unit. "We perceived the affiliate cuts as minor," recalls counsel Steve Weiswasser. "We were really shocked by the reaction."

Despite fierce opposition, Murphy believed his position would be vindicated because the other networks would form a solid front, robbing stations of their ultimate weapon—to shift their affiliation to another network. Instead, ABC twisted alone for a month. Then, in January, while Tisch remained publicly silent, NBC announced that it would boost the compensation it paid affiliates by an average of 3 percent, though this was somewhat misleading since NBC would also gain revenues by reclaiming certain spots once given to local stations to sell. By offering more cash, NBC devastated ABC's hopes of granting less. Like the three networks' decision to allow cable to get a foot in the NFL door, or ABC's decision to shift *World News Tonight,* short-term considerations were in conflict with long-term network needs. Two years later NBC Network president Pier Mapes would concede that it was "the wrong psychology" to appear to boost compensation in 1987.

In the wake of NBC's announced compensation hike, Tom Murphy felt he had to surrender. Fearing what Sias called a wave of "one-time-only preemptions at a time when we could not afford them," Murphy rescinded the proposed cuts. The only change ABC would insist on was that it would no longer pay the affiliates compensation for airing either NFL games or the World Series, events the affiliates would never think to preempt. Looking back three years later on his decision to back off, Murphy conceded, "We were wimps!"

But Murphy and Burke were also skilled managers of people. The imbroglio with its affiliates was a rare instance in which ABC's difficulties spilled into the press. Unlike NBC, where executives would leak damaging memos from Bob Wright, or CBS, where Dan Rather or Andy Rooney would publicly challenge Larry Tisch, Cap Cities was spared similar turmoil by its ability to keep its recriminations out of the media despite deep budget cuts. By the end of its first year, said

Ron Doerfler, ABC had reduced its overhead by $50 million. ABC News, which according to Dick Wald employed 1,450 people at the close of 1984, by the end of 1986 had reduced its News staff by 300, without fanfare. At least part of the credit for the public tranquility is owed to skillful Cap Cities management.

The process Cap Cities followed to make the cuts also made their cuts somewhat more palatable than those that would be made at CBS and NBC. Murphy and Burke patted people on the back, walked the halls, had human contact with employees. They exchanged jokes. They did not look over the shoulders of managers, specifying where cuts should be made. Said an appreciative Robert Murphy, vice president of News Coverage: "They came up with the environment that allowed us to take a look at things that should have been obvious in the beginning." Murphy and Burke, from their first official day at ABC, borrowed a technique used by Grant Tinker at NBC. They conducted regular closed-circuit dialogues with employees, in which anyone who worked for ABC could telephone to ask questions or make statements. They openly shared budget numbers. They made quick decisions. They better understood the broadcasting business. Unable to control their outrage at the excesses they encountered, at first Sias, Murphy, and Burke were rough on ABC and its "limousine culture," but by the end of 1986 they seemed more appreciative of the executives they inherited. "They have changed more than we did," observed one top holdover. "They used to think we were all dummies." Much sooner than would happen at NBC or CBS, the new owners of ABC strove to convey a sense of pleasure, openness, and humility.

At the end of their first full year at ABC, Murphy and Burke had reason to be pleased with their stock price, which climbed from a low of $208 and closed 1986 at $268. But after a full year at ABC, Murphy and Burke were learning a lesson, one that would be painfully learned by the new owners of CBS and NBC. They were learning that their power was limited. No matter how smart they were, how skilled at management, the fate of their business was partly beyond their control. More than most businesses, the networks depended on others—affiliates, advertisers, Hollywood producers, the press, government regulators—whom they did not command. Ready to impose their will, the new owners learned that their powers were circumscribed not just by the sputtering economics of a "mature" business. A network, wrote former NBC vice chairman David Adams in 1980, was like "a flywheel that helps maintain a system consisting of many parts it does not control. . . . It is a business that requires the reactions and sensitivities that grow from long experience in the field, and an outsider can be effective only after a period of high-level apprenticeship learning the nuances of a very singular business."

The three networks could refuse to meet the NFL's demands—but at the cost of opening the door to their cable competitors. ABC could boost *World News Tonight*'s ratings by shifting it to 6:30 P.M. in New York, but by doing so ABC strengthened the very syndicators who were nibbling away at network dominance.

Looking back on the way ABC bungled the compensation issue and the other mistakes made at the three networks, ABC executive Mark Mandala astutely remarked, "The longer I've been in this business the more I believe less in the cunning of a Machiavelli than the bumbling of Sancho Panza."

8

NBC: A NEW QUEEN BEE, SEPTEMBER TO DECEMBER 1986

By the time a queen bee is five she is old and no longer reproduces, leaving her army of honeybees torn between loyalty and survival. Since the hive cannot survive without a productive queen, the beekeeper reaches into the hive with a long-gloved hand and squashes the enfeebled queen. With the entire hive as witness, all know the queen is dead. Absent the scent of their leader, the honeybees panic.

But the beekeeper is prepared, having ordered a new queen from a bee breeder. Arriving in a two-inch-long wooden box with a screen at the top and bottom, the queen is accompanied by a court of six to eight escort bees who care for her every whim, cleaning and feeding her, removing her waste. At one end of the box a tiny piece of hard candy blocks access to the queen. When the box is inserted into the hive, the first instinct of the worker bees, who immediately know she has the wrong scent, is to kill the new queen. The workers struggle to reach her, but are blocked by the candy. Soon they become diverted by the sweet, and over the two or three days it takes to eat through it they succumb to the enticement. Their fealty is won. All hail the new queen bee.

Something akin to that happened when Bob Wright was inserted in place of Grant Tinker in September 1986. NBC's workers did not want to lose Tinker, and were wary of the substitute supplied by GE. But Welch and Wright were determined to substitute not just a new queen but a new type of leadership. Toward this end, Wright offered something sweet—an invitation welcoming all NBC employees to Studio 8H on September 16, between 4 and 6 P.M., to bid farewell to Grant Tinker. Studio 8H, where Toscanini once played for NBC and where *Saturday Night Live* was now produced, filled with tearful employees, each waiting to shake hands with the departing chairman.

"People stood in line to touch him," remembers Melissa Ludlum, an executive assistant. "He was like a religious figure."

NBC employees were proud. Proud of the way Tinker helped stabilize the network after the buzzsaw presidency of Fred Silverman; proud of the quality programs NBC aired and the thirty-four Emmys they had won in September, the most ever captured by NBC; proud of the way Tinker stood by Brandon Tartikoff and of the good times they enjoyed; and proud, after being third for nine straight years, to be number one and to tote up record profits. But NBC employees also knew they were bidding farewell to more than Tinker. They were saying goodbye to yesterday.

The man who represented tomorrow, Bob Wright, circled Studio 8H and tried not to show his contempt for the self-congratulatory mood. Repeatedly, NBC employees came up to him and exclaimed, "Gee, aren't things great! Isn't everything just terrific!" Wright politely smiled, even made a speech praising Tinker's accomplishments. But Wright didn't feel terrific. "Who are they kidding?" he remembers thinking to himself. NBC might be number one, might produce astonishing profits, but he knew there was trouble ahead. Wright was a GE man, and the GE way was not to stop and applaud but to keep the pressure on, to concentrate on tomorrow, not yesterday. Even though NBC was in first place, Wright viewed the broadcast future with alarm. What he saw were twelve national programming services —including cable's HBO, Showtime and MTV, and Ted Turner's WTBS superstation—ten of which would make more money than the ABC network. Wright's job, as he and Jack Welch saw it, was to prepare for a future when networks might no longer dominate. Part of Wright's task was to kill the culture left by his predecessor.

Bob Wright's impatience was reflected in the way he spent his first weeks on the job. Tinker had graciously agreed to stay on the first three weeks of September for consultations. But in this period, Tinker would later marvel to friends, Wright never once consulted him. Instead, Wright spent September in meetings, learning what he could about NBC.

Meanwhile, Grant Tinker was considering no less than seventeen serious offers. One of these was the possibility of running CBS (he said no). Tinker instead accepted an offer from the Gannett Company to finance the start-up of a new studio. In Gannett chairman and CEO Al Neuharth Tinker saw a risk-taker, a man who would bestow on him the freedom Tinker liked to give subordinates. Within days of announcing the birth of GTG Entertainment, as it was christened,

Tinker received a ten-series commitment from CBS, which would have first right of refusal of his work for a period of five years. With NBC's schedule stocked with young hit shows, Tinker felt he had to take his business to one of its competitors.

Bob Wright did not come to NBC surrounded by loyalists. The only other GE person joining him at the network was J. B. Holston, the young GE corporate planner Wright had met only a month before. At Jack Welch's instigation, he also interviewed another bright young man, Thomas S. Rogers, senior counsel to the House Telecommunications Committee, but Rogers would not join the team until January 1987. Meanwhile, Wright was dependent on the staff he inherited from Tinker, a team that did not share his skepticism toward network television.

By contrast to Tinker, who had devoted himself to resuscitating an ailing network and took a traditional view that the network should not compete with itself by investing heavily in cable, Wright saw himself as a deal-maker. Among his happiest professional moments, his wife Suzanne said, was when he ran GE Credit. "The deal-making was fantastic. You walked in every day and everyone was on fire with: 'What deal are we going to do next?' " When he came to NBC, Wright viewed his task as "70 percent future oriented and 30 percent today." As a result, he was often out of the office. "We already have a group of people in here capable of dealing day to day," he explained. "What I'm good at is positioning a company for the future."

When Wright concentrated on current network business, he plunged like his ABC counterparts into a careful review of the budget. Over the summer Tinker had asked each division to prepare no-growth budgets. The idea was to pare some of the 8,465 NBC jobs through attrition, not layoffs. Now Wright asked each department: *Why do we spend $141.5 million on affiliate compensation? With such miserable ratings, do we really need the news magazine show* 1986? *Why does the news division spend $275 million annually, almost three times what CNN spends? Can the 45 percent profit margins at the owned stations match the 55 percent margins at Cap Cities/ABC? With sports rights escalating and with NBC Sports losing $50 million annually, does network sports have a future? Since our nonnetwork competitors don't have one, why does NBC need a forty-eight-person broadcast standards department to prescreen shows?*

Skepticism greeted Wright at nearly every turn. By constantly invoking the "future," Wright seemed to be implicitly degrading the network's value. Those who worked at "the quality network," as Tinker licensed them to think of themselves, were appalled when Wright said in October it "would be exciting" to do a home shopping show, though the logistics of taking frying pan orders from 18 million viewers might not be so "exciting." At the time home shopping was something of a fad—in four years cable's Home Shopping Network had rocketed from $900,000 in sales to $150 million. NBC officials worried that Wright would cheapen NBC.

The greatest anxiety was felt at NBC News. Larry Grossman was shaken when Wright, noticing the relatively small audiences news documentaries attracted, wondered aloud why News didn't ask NBC stars like Don Johnson of *Miami Vice* to host a documentary on AIDS, or have Bill Cosby host one on teachers. "They would attract a 40 share!" Wright exclaimed. Grossman did not think to counter that maybe Don Johnson could host a special for Entertainment as opposed to News, but instead he stiffly dismissed the idea out of hand, adding to Wright's frustration with what he saw as the self-ordained News "priesthood." Wright was puzzled. While Grossman upheld the purity of News, he also ordered a new score from composer John Williams to accompany *Nightly News.* Didn't he spur the *Today* show to go on the road more, as if it were a circus? Was it news or promotion values that prompted Tom Brokaw to do live news updates from the World Series or the Fiesta Bowl? *Who is Grossman kidding?*

Grossman believed these gimmicks did not cross the line into hucksterism. But to let an actor host a news special would, he believed, cross the line. Nevertheless, Wright had half a point. Those in the news division were hardly virgins. Tom Brokaw did the David Letterman show because, he conceded, it exposed him to a younger audience and "shows me as a person," a normal human reaction from an intelligent man often reduced to reading an anchor's script. Brokaw, like others in News, including Grossman, worried about both the declining and aging audience for news. Brokaw was amenable to NBC News consultant Gordon Manning's suggestion that three hours of Election Night 1986 could pivot around Johnny Carson and Bill Cosby. "They could go for forty minutes," said Brokaw, "and Cosby could say, 'We now go to Tom Brokaw. We'll be right back with Billy Joel and Christie Brinkley." Asked if he thought this blurred the line between news and entertainment, Brokaw demurred, "You're not blurring the line at all. Cosby would not be standing in the studio with me! I'm looking for a way to get a larger presence for us in News."

That larger presence for News was what Wright, in his own peculiar way, was after. But Grossman and others in News saw Wright as a threat. A pattern was forming in Grossman's mind, connecting Wright's Don Johnson idea with others, including the time Wright asked why NBC had to provide gavel-to-gavel coverage of the national party conventions when both CNN and C-SPAN were doing it already? Wright argued that network news should be unique. "It is no longer attractive for us to do a C-SPAN. C-SPAN does C-SPAN," said Wright. "CNN can have microphones there in front of people all night. When there wasn't any CNN . . . it wasn't so bad for networks to do that."

Not that Larry Grossman didn't try at times to accommodate the new order. Since 1986 was not a presidential election year and no major electoral surprises were expected, he recommended that NBC for the first time should not take over the entire three hours of prime time for a special, as CBS would. Grossman instead proposed a 10 to 11 P.M. election results special featuring Tom Brokaw. While Wright quickly agreed, the decision dispirited Brokaw, among others. "We should have gone on at 9:00, not 10:00," Brokaw said, and he blamed Grossman for losing the extra hour.

Grossman was feeling heat from below, as well as from above. Like every News president before him, he had the unenviable task of convincing the corporate hierarchy that he was a no-nonsense manager while at the same time convincing his underlings that he put news first and money second. Of these twin pressures, Grossman was most troubled by the heat from above. He just wasn't comfortable with Wright and GE. He was troubled that Wright seemed not to watch much news; the only opinions Wright offered about NBC News concerned costs, not content. His fears were confirmed when Wright visited the newscast set in early October and quipped as Tom Brokaw read the news: "Here it is: the summary for the hearing impaired!" What might have been taken as a joke from Tinker or Frank Stanton, who had proven their devotion to News, became an insult. And so Grossman, whose own thin credentials as a newsman were questioned within NBC News, saw himself as the guardian of News, much as David Burke did at ABC.

Rather than cut costs, as the new owners wanted to do, Grossman wanted a profitable NBC to spend more. So he submitted a News budget calling for a 4 percent rate of growth (8 percent after factoring in an estimated 4 percent for inflation). "We have an opportunity to dominate this industry for a decade, as CBS did," Grossman said in mid-October. "The momentum is going our way." It was Grossman's request for a budget increase, just two months after Wright became

CEO, that set in motion the events that would lead to the climactic summit confrontation later in Jack Welch's office, the confrontation that interrupted the Bradshaws' helicopter trip to Martha's Vineyard and that would cement bad feelings between Grossman and his new employers.

Wright was stupefied when he saw Grossman's new budget proposal. He could not comprehend Grossman's logic. Looking at the numbers, he saw that NBC News brought in 10 percent of NBC's revenues, yet its $275 million budget accounted for 16 percent of network expenses. And on top of this, NBC News would lose $64 million in 1986, exclusive of overhead costs. Looking at the entire network, Wright believed revenue growth had stalled; yet its payroll costs, which accounted for 20 percent of the budget, had climbed from $368 million in 1980 to just over $500 million; program costs, which accounted for just under two-thirds of all spending, had nearly doubled in that period, reaching $1.3 billion. Bob Wright rejected the notion that NBC News could spend its way to more success. "The history of business is marked by people who have gone down with that unique strategy," he said. "All you have to do is guess wrong once or twice." The argument assumed, he continued, that if a network like ABC had poor ratings it was because it did not spend enough. No, Wright believed the networks had to "downsize" because they were more "fragile," surrounded by low-cost competitors.

Like his new counterparts at ABC and CBS, Wright was pessimistic about the short-term future, projecting "relatively flat advertising" revenues for at least another couple of years. At the time he envisioned no dramatic employee cutbacks at NBC, just some pruning, though he would have liked to do more. But Wright said, "I'm going to keep the heat on. I don't think there's any alternative."

Wright applied more heat in early October when his executives gathered in his sixth-floor conference room for the weekly president's council. To this meeting of his top dozen executives Wright invited another two dozen department heads, for after a month on the job he felt he had something important to say. Seated at the head of the rosewood table, Wright was dead serious. Revenues were expected to remain relatively flat in the next year, he said, and the divisions had already been asked by Tinker to prepare no-growth budgets for 1987. Now he was asking for more. "What I'd like to ask you to do—as an exercise—is to rework those figures and let me see what a 5 percent cut would look like rather than a no-growth budget." Assuming an inflation rate of 3 to 5 percent, Wright was really asking for cuts of up to 10 percent.

Wright's exercise was common within GE, but foreign to NBC. Executives were pained by what they took to be Wright's brusque manner—his "exercise" was obviously an order! The process would not be easy to sell to employees who were being asked to treat good times as if they were bad. Entertainment and News were especially unhappy. But only Grossman challenged Wright in front of the others, insisting he didn't know how he could cut $15 million, and complaining that because Wright did not include the cost of inflation he was actually asking for an almost $30 million reduction. If he put it down on paper, even as an "exercise," Grossman warned, word would get out; News morale would plummet. Further, since he was sure Wright didn't truly favor such cuts, why risk riling the troops over an "exercise"? When the meeting ended Wright was not sure if Grossman, who struck him as sullen, had said "no" or "maybe." He was certainly not happy about how Grossman, as Jack Welch recounted it later, "challenged him in front of others."

Brandon Tartikoff and his business affairs deputy, John Agoglia, also demurred, but they did so privately, explaining that contractual commitments—the heart of the Entertainment budget—made it impossible to pare 5 percent, at least in 1987. Because he handled the matter privately, and because Tartikoff, like Brandon Stoddard at ABC, was treated as a prince—Wright backed off, excusing Entertainment from the exercise.

"It became a big issue in News," recalls Wright. "In the rest of the areas of our business it was a nonevent, or only a modest issue." Over the next few weeks Wright and Grossman waltzed around the subject, with Grossman promising to "do the best we can," believing he could cut $15 to $30 million if he could spread the pain over a twelve-month period. In the meantime, Grossman launched a campaign to "educate" Wright. To accomplish this, Grossman would use his "stars," arranging a series of lunches and dinners with NBC's president.

One of these was Grossman's ill-fated dinner for Welch and Wright during the sixth game of the 1986 World Series. Four days earlier, Peter Boyer of *The New York Times* had broken the story of Wright's 5 percent budget exercise and told how Grossman "refused to participate." This "leak"—which Welch had questioned Brokaw about at the Grossmans' dinner—was the first of three Wright would angrily endure that fall. "Leaks" were unheard of at GE, seen as a violation of the privacy a corporation requires to function efficiently. It was—there was no other word for it in GE's vocabulary—insubordination. The *Times* story aroused suspicions that the "leak" came from Grossman or someone close to him, which did not help Grossman's relations with Wright.

Neither did the dinner four days later at Grossman's Westport home; nor did it help Grossman that some of his supposed allies in News agreed with Wright, at least in part. Tom Brokaw, for one, said at the time of Wright's 5 percent exercise: "I think it's a useful exercise he's putting everyone through." Steve Friedman, then the executive producer of the *Today* show, who openly mocked Grossman by calling him "Ted" (for *The Ted Mack Amateur Hour*), agreed with Wright. News, he said, had to be operated more like a business, had to eliminate needless duplication. Of the Reagan/Gorbachev summit, Friedman asked, "Why shouldn't the local stations and the networks pool their cameras?"

But on one question Grossman and most everyone else in News were united. "What was best about Grant Tinker," Tom Brokaw said in October, "was that he encouraged people to raise their sights to what TV could do. He encouraged you to believe that people want more, not less, from television. And I hope that doesn't get squandered."

Wright's communications chief, Bud Rukeyser, was determined to educate his boss as to the difference between a network and most businesses, and wrote a memo to him:

> We do not have a tangible product, yet it is "used" in nearly every home in America every day; we buy programs and sell audiences; we have regulatory constraints that many of our competitors do not; our distribution system is dependent on two hundred affiliates who often have a different business agenda from our own; we are required by statute to serve the public interest, yet every home we serve has a different idea of what that interest is; our main business is entertainment, yet we are the primary source of news for most Americans; and we are the most widely-covered business by the press. . . .

With growing impatience, Wright ignored such counsel as an excuse to do nothing. By mid-October, Wright said he was displeased both with the speed and the content of the responses he received from most divisions to his 5 percent exercise. "I was very concerned that the message was not getting through. A lot of people were saying, 'We don't do it that way.'" Like hell we don't, thought Wright, who exclaimed, "We need to change the culture!" The NBC president poured his frustration into a blistering three-page memorandum sent on October 24 to every senior NBC officer. The memo, he announced in paragraph one, was intended to "set out some guidelines which may help you in understanding my operating philosophy and the objectives I am trying to achieve." He was seeking, he wrote, to move away from a "cumbersome, layered organization . . ."

Then came the kerosene:

> Many of you appear to be uncomfortable dealing with numerical or financial explanations of your business plan. I, in turn, have been uncomfortable when you arrive at meetings with no hard data to back up your positions. This is a big business, and we must have executives who are capable of dealing with the creative, business and financial aspects of their responsibility. . . . This business is in a mature cycle, a cycle often characterized by inflexibility, reverence for the past, isolation from other realities. You must be intolerant of waste, bureaucracy, and those who do not carry their fair share of the load. *We will not operate this business with both belt and suspenders.*

Without warning the "belt and suspenders" memo appeared on the desks of forty-four senior executives, and was widely interpreted as a sign of Wright's insecurity within GE. "I think it's Jack Welch," said chief financial officer Bob Butler. "I can see Jack talking to Bob Wright and saying, 'When you walk in the school yard you punch the first guy in the nose and let them know who's boss.'"

Wright's memo was also taken as a sign of his insecurity within NBC. "I think he's very smart," said one NBC official who saw a lot of Wright. "He sucks up enormous amounts of information. But he reminds me of a kid who skipped a couple of grades and has to show you he knows the answer to your question before the question is asked." There was a prevalent sense that, although Wright was accusing them of being isolated and unresponsive, it was he who was out of touch—his whereabouts a mystery to the executives who reported to him, his schedule a closely guarded secret. "Even in the wackiest days of Fred Silverman," observed Bud Rukeyser, who briefly left the network in the late seventies rather than caddy for the volatile former NBC president, "I always knew where he was. With Wright I honestly don't know." What did Wright's Communications chief communicate when he had an audience with his boss? "When I'm in there," answered Rukeyser, "I feel like a crazed bell-ringer in with the king. I've got all these ideas to get out, but I don't have much time with the king."

People were confused. And angry. Which may be why Wright's memo was leaked to the press. Within the halls of NBC, the reaction was a whispered salutation, "Have your suspenders on?" Outwardly, executives joked; inwardly, they were afraid of Wright.

On the West Coast, the reaction to Wright was different. Wright and Welch felt an affinity for Tartikoff's entertainment group in Burbank. From New York, they got dour faces and newspaper leaks; from Burbank, they got laughs and the largest slice of the 100 million viewers who turned on their TV sets each night. With News and Sports losing between them about $150 million, NBC's 1986 profits of $407 million came primarily from the success of the group working out of a squat, three-story Burbank building that looks like a motel. To get closer to Tartikoff and his team, Wright and Welch flew to Los Angeles and dined with them at Morton's restaurant on October 29, 1986, then spent the entire next day at NBC's Burbank offices, reviewing the ideas in development for comedy and drama shows to be selected in May for the 1987–88 season.

Wright and Welch were turned on by the free flow of information and creativity in Burbank. With Wright, however, there was a certain initial awkwardness in the relationship with Tartikoff. After Silverman and Tinker, Tartikoff was wary of another courtship. For Wright it was even more unsettling. In New York he understood what Bob Butler or Bud Rukeyser did. He was less sure that he understood what Tartikoff did. And like John Sias at ABC, Wright had instructions to keep his head programmer happy. So the buttoned-down Wright strove to keep out of the way of his entertainment division.

Welch seemed more relaxed around Tartikoff. At one point in the afternoon review of projects under development, Welch asked Perry Simon, the head of Drama Development: "How come you don't do an *L.A. Law* type show about Wall Street?"

"I'm not sure how accessible and related to the public it is," Simon answered.

Warren Littlefield, Simon's immediate boss, put it more simply. "Nobody gives a shit about people on Wall Street," he said. "You can't root for them. All they do is make money."

"I'm just going back to Connecticut where people listen to me!" Welch said, smiling.

Welch loved the exchange, and the people. "We vibrate with that company," he said of the Burbank group. New York he saw as full of "administrative," not creative, people. "I happen to like Brandon a lot. If he were unhappy I'd feel terrible."

Tartikoff was happy. The message communicated by Welch and Wright, he recalls, was: "You're the ones making this thing go. You're doing great!" Welch and Wright brought other tidings, which also pleased Tartikoff. They were troubled that their chief suppliers of programming—the studios—were also their competitors. John Agoglia, the head of Business Affairs, had spoken of "the weird relationship between the network and its suppliers. We're a major purchaser, and yet our suppliers hate us. They think we have the power of life or death over their programs and whether they make or don't make a profit." Altogether, the network was paying about one billion dollars a year in license fees to studios. Yet since the production costs were controlled by the studios, the network had little leverage over projects they funded, despite Bob Daly's claim that the networks held life-and-death power over the studios. Welch and Wright now wanted to strengthen NBC Productions so the network could produce the three hours—soon to go to five—of prime-time shows permitted under the financial interest rules. They remembered the $40 million NBC made by selling Columbia Pictures the rights to *Punky Brewster,* a children's show NBC produced itself; although the show got mediocre ratings on NBC, Columbia was able to sell it to stations all over the world.

Welch and Wright had one final mission on this trip, and it was to buck up Tartikoff's team. Welch had promised Tartikoff he would offer contracts to key members, and on this visit Wright came to terms with eight members of his team, including Agoglia, Littlefield, Simon, and Comedy head Michele Brusten. Unlike the unhappy New York executives, people here were generally content. "None of us liked RCA," observed Michele Brusten. "We were like children to them." But Welch and Wright conveyed respect. With "Brandon and his team," as they referred to the group, Welch and Wright felt they were dealing with entrepreneurs, experts.

Back in New York, change came more slowly than Wright liked. That fall the network pared about three hundred jobs, mostly through attrition and the elimination of unfilled positions, including fifty jobs in News. A member of Tinker's chairman's council—Vice Chairman Irwin B. Segelstein, sixty-two—also announced his departure. But the pace was too slow for Wright. He agreed with Jack Welch, who complained that NBC believed it would "always get taken care of" because revenues invariably rose.

Wanting to position NBC for an uncertain future, Wright also sought an antidote to the effective Washington lobbying effort mounted by Jack Valenti, head of the Motion Picture Association of America. NBC's lobbyists complained that the networks were failing to compete with the well-oiled lobbying machines created by the Hollywood studios and the cable operators. In recent years Washington had deregulated cable television and the telephone companies, had privatized satellites launched into space, had relaxed limitations on TV station ownership. Yet the networks were still strictly regulated. Wright felt he had to convince Washington to loosen these strictures, and was determined to overcome internal inertia or opposition. It irked him that network executives had always given money to members of Congress sympathetic to their point of view or to members of key committees, but that this giving was usually unorganized. The networks trailed both the cable industry and Hollywood in political contributions. Bob Wright wanted to steer NBC's contributions into a more organized assault on Congress.

Wright dashed off a seven-paragraph memorandum to general counsel Corydon B. Dunham on November 6, with copies to each member of the president's council, asking for the formation of an NBC political action committee (PAC). "It is time for us to get off the dime on our political action plans," the memo began. "I would like to take charge of our coordination efforts to ensure the creation of an NBC PAC." Dunham was instructed to link his efforts with GE's PAC. It did not go unnoticed at NBC that Wright adopted the same combative stance Jack Welch had taken earlier that year when he drafted a statement of company values and declared that those GE employees who were uncomfortable with these values should work elsewhere. Wright wrote:

> The key point that must be emphasized is that we are in a business that continues to require significant political interface. Employees who earn their living and support their families from the profits of our business must recognize a need to invest some portion of their earnings to ensure that the Company is well-represented in Washington, and that its important issues are clearly placed before congress. Employees who elect not to par-

ticipate in a giving program of this type should question their own dedication to the Company and their expectations.

Once again, Wright was startled by the reaction. Larry Grossman told him that because News couldn't take political sides it should not participate in a PAC. Wright quickly acceded to Grossman's request, suggesting he had not thought through the implications of his memo. But Grossman was not alone in raising a complaint. "I didn't really know what a PAC was," Brandon Tartikoff joked. "I thought it was like an athletic conference when I first heard it!" While defending Wright's "healthy exploration" of new ideas, he added, "I wouldn't want somebody in Iowa or Montana or Michigan or someplace to think that the programming arm of a network had any sort of political debt. . . ."

The story exploded on page one of *The New York Times*. Wright was livid, and at a breakfast with Bud Rukeyser he tried to fathom why company memos became public property. Rukeyser was blunt: "We haven't even decided to have a PAC, and here you are saying what happens to people if they don't comply." Rukeyser wanted Wright to think of himself as part of NBC, not as Jack Welch's agent. But what Rukeyser and others at NBC did not understand was that Wright really did believe that Jack Welch was his NBC boss. "I'm the COO [chief operating officer] if Jack Welch is NBC's chairman," explained Wright. In any case, to separate the two would be all but impossible, the more so since Welch shared Wright's views and publicly defended his PAC memo, though privately, Welch said it was "naive" of Wright to have sent a memo with copies before first "having a chat" with his counsel.

Welch pointedly said of NBC: "Those who dwell in the past do nothing but create a tired organization, an inward-looking organization. We've been through that at GE. People like yesterday." Welch cited his consumer appliance plant in Louisville, Kentucky, as a model for change: "We now make 15 percent more appliances with 60 percent fewer people." The way to judge Bob Wright, Welch said, was by how "he deals with his changing business environment." If anything, Welch added, "We haven't been bold enough" in attacking NBC's costs.

Welch was more confrontational than Wright, more radical, and privately worried that as Wright immersed himself in the network he might be co-opted by it. In fact, Wright had to juggle pressures from both Welch and NBC. He had to answer Welch's insistent questions—

Why does NBC need a fifty-person program practices department?—and at the same time deal with the fact that government and advertisers and viewer organizations expected a program practices department to screen for good taste. "Bob is in a position," observed J. B. Holston, "where he has to manage Jack as well as NBC. Jack tends to be hands-on until a company is going the way he wants it to. Physically, that means Bob has to spend a lot of time with Jack."

Within NBC a conscious effort—no, a conspiracy—arose to separate Wright from Welch, to make Wright more responsive to the network. NBC executives hatched a plot for the November affiliate board meeting in Laguna Niguel, California. The scheme was to transform Wright's maiden meeting with the thirteen-member executive committee into a consciousness-raising session. Usually, such three-day meetings are an opportunity for the network to present its new Entertainment, Sports, and News programming plans, and also to exhort its affiliates to promote and clear more network shows. But weeks before the meeting, the affiliates and the News division planned a secret agenda. Grossman was popular with NBC's affiliates. He had successfully turned around the *Today* show, had provided them with trucks and equipment and network news feeds, and he was always available to speak at their functions. Unlike other News presidents, he opposed an hour of network news, which pleased affiliates who wanted an extra half hour of their own money-making local newscast. Instead, Grossman came up with the idea of an hour newswheel, where the network and its affiliates might share an hour, alternating packages of local, national, and international news.

Larry Grossman may have had his difficulties within the news division, but the affiliates and the press were his base of support, and with Brokaw's *Nightly News* coming in first during half the weeks of 1986 and by a full rating point the week prior to the board meeting—its largest lead in eleven years—Grossman was feeling almost cocky. So when an affiliate board member called before the meeting to express concern about Wright's memos and his attitude toward News, Grossman responded, "He's a good guy but he's made mistakes."

"Would you be embarrassed if we asked him questions about News?" the affiliate asked.

"No," said Grossman.

Grossman stage-managed the agenda. The affiliate board "asked us what we wanted on the agenda," admitted one executive. "We said we wanted an opportunity to talk about the future of network news." There was a natural affinity between network news and the affiliates.

Yes, it was true that local and network news competed—local stations regularly sent their own reporters to cover national or even international stories, displayed pictures on the local news that were supplied free by the network, even though these feeds upstaged the network newscast, and signed up with CNN or other news services who were network competitors. But it was also true that network news remained a centerpiece of the relationship. A station made most of its income from local news, helped by the network, which supplied two to three daily feeds of breaking national and international news packages free of charge. In addition, network news was a source of prestige. Whether in Omaha or Phoenix, billboards featured the local anchor alongside the network anchor.

When the thirty-five network and thirteen affiliate representatives gathered to hear Bob Wright speak, they heard Wright refer to news as "a very, very expensive product for us." They heard him say that network news was considered "a dinosaur." The fixed costs of the worldwide NBC News operation were $200 million, Wright said, and "we shouldn't be out there as your partners spending $200 million on something that you think is nice, but not something that we really think is a high priority."

The word "dinosaur" would live in the memory of Grossman and others long after this meeting ended: *Wright thinks News is a dinosaur.*

After Wright spoke, Eric Bremner, chairman of the affiliates news committee, rose and urged Wright "not to take too seriously the publicity that says network news is a dinosaur." News is what differentiates NBC from cable or Fox. It's "what makes us what we are," and "if you feel we don't recognize that, then I think you need to know how we feel." Affiliate board chairman James Lynagh chimed in that news is what makes "us different and special compared with our many video competitors." A chorus of affiliates agreed.

The conspiracy worked. Afterward, J. B. Holston said of Wright, "He got the message."

And Grossman would begin to get Wright's message after having his first run-in with Jack Welch at the meeting at GE headquarters before Thanksgiving. Grossman and his executive team had traveled to the GE campus, off the Merritt Parkway in Fairfield, Connecticut, to review the proposed 1987 budget, and Grossman was struggling to explain why he couldn't comply with a 5 percent cut in expenses, and in fact needed a 4 percent increase. Grossman outlined for Welch his plans for an early morning show, a business show, a weekend *Today,* and a late-night news show; he was pouring extra dollars into a prime-time magazine show—*1986*—which Grant Tinker had vowed to keep on the air "forever," or until it made money, like CBS's *60 Minutes* or ABC's *20/20.* He spoke of plans to introduce three robotic cameras. And since Tom Brokaw was gaining on Dan Rather and the network was pulling ahead in prime time, Grossman said now was the time to put more, not fewer, resources into News.

"S-s-s-hit!" shouted Welch, whose slight stammer was more pronounced when he was upset, as he pounded the table. "Ted Turner puts on C-C-N-N-N-N for twenty-four hours a day for only $100 million! Ted Turner makes $50 to $60 million. We do three hours of news. We spend $275 million and lose $100 million." To Welch, Grossman was behaving like a typical bureaucrat. "I have yet to find," Welch said, "a functional organization in twenty-seven years of running a business that ever had enough money." He said he expected Grossman to comply.

Grossman resisted. To cut 5 percent, even as an exercise, he replied, would demoralize the news division. Grossman said no one had ever before asked News to be "a profit center."

Welch felt that Grossman's attitude toward the budget was mulish. He had fired executives for less.

Wright tried to mediate, but was confused. Neither he nor Welch had ever said News should be "a profit center." In fact, Wright had said that News "is a cost center, not a profit center. You want to pay attention to how much it is costing you and whether it is reasonable." Nor did he want to sacrifice News. Entertainment programs and Sports, he explained, the network rents; News is one of the few products the network manufactures itself. "In my mind that is the last thing you want to give up—uniqueness," Wright had said, but if he heard these words, Larry Grossman didn't believe them.

Personal and stylistic differences widened the split between them. It bothered the GE-trained men that Larry Grossman was not familiar with his own budget. "He was hemming and hawing," recalls Wright. "It occurred to me that he did not know how to do this, that there was no management system in the news division." Neither Wright nor Welch had felt comfortable with Grossman since the fateful World Series dinner when Welch thought he sounded almost like "a socialist," like someone who thought of NBC as a giant public utility whose costs should be paid by a benevolent, unquestioning GE. Welch complained that Grossman acted like the head of a "priesthood" who lived in a monastery, spoke in code, and believed no one could question him. What crap!

But Welch and Grossman did not collide on this November day. Welch did not order Grossman to trim his budget. And Grossman did not offer to do so. Grossman left depressed, and told his deputy, Tim Russert, that he was thinking of quitting.

Back in New York, Wright huddled with Grossman. "This process is not working," he said. "You have to come to grips with your costs." Wright said he wanted to know whether Grossman disagreed with him about the cuts, or didn't know how to achieve them.

"I'm not sure where Welch is coming from," Grossman replied. "I'm not sure he likes News."

Wright insisted that costs were the issue. Period. "You either have to become comfortable or this is not going to work here." Wright suggested another meeting with Welch.

The next morning Grossman telephoned Wright. "Obviously, this is not doing you or the news division any good," he said. "I'm not going to hang around if I get under Welch's skin and he gets under mine." He asked if they could meet with Welch together. At 4 P.M. that same day—November 16, 1986—the call from Welch's office came, prompting Wright to interrupt his weekly president's council meeting. The GE helicopter was on its way to take them to Fairfield. "We have to go," Wright told Grossman as the two men hurried out the door, leaving their colleagues wondering what was going on.

For this two-hour-long summit the three executives sat on the sofa in Welch's office, as Wright mediated. Wright tried to isolate the issues, including the issue of his own role at NBC. Welch wanted to get right to the point, wanted to force Grossman to comply with Wright's original directive. But not wanting to provoke a furor by firing the president of NBC News, he struggled to arrest his temper. Politely, he said that though he was kept informed, Bob Wright was the day-to-day boss. They circled the issues, until Welch could no longer contain himself. Jabbing his finger at Grossman's chest, Welch reminded him: "You work for GE!"

In the end, Grossman agreed to keep his 1987 expenses at the same level as those of 1986—$273.5 million, actually a cut of roughly 5 percent after inflation was factored in. Wright brought up one other matter. He believed Grossman needed help. "Larry's not a newsman," he explained. "He's not a businessman. He operates on a consensus approach. And he's in a situation where there is no consensus." So Wright suggested they should hire a consultant to analyze the cost structure of News, to help Grossman sort through the options.

"That's a terrific idea," said Grossman. "We're doing three hours of full-time programming every day. It's hard when you're going full speed to look at the engine and see if it needs an overhaul." He added, "A consultant will help us because they'll help convince you we need the money." Wright and Welch, however, thought a consultant would find ways to save money. Welch suggested that John Stewart of McKinsey & Company was "the ideal candidate," and since his company had worked for both GE and for Grossman when he ran PBS, Stewart was chosen. Provided, said Grossman, that Stewart and McKinsey reported to the president of News. The three men shook hands.

"It kind of cleared the air like a spring storm," Grossman said happily. Over the next several weeks, Grossman took the public posture that News would be spared any cuts. "We got the budget we asked for," he told Edwin Diamond of *New York* magazine. But as Grossman went through the budget with his staff, he learned of the hard choices to be made. If he wanted a new business or Sunday *Today* show, then he would have to close bureaus or terminate correspondents. Or kill *1986*. He soon realized that the simplest way to shed 5 percent of the News budget without harming NBC News's three hours of daily programming was to cancel the magazine show whose ten appearances on the schedule tied it for last among all 112 weekly shows on the three networks. By cutting the thirty staffers from *1986*, plus a total of sixty-two more actual or budgeted positions that would be eliminated by the end of the year, News could meet Wright and Welch's target. And Grossman could sugarcoat the losses by announcing that in place of *1986* NBC News would substitute a total of fifteen documentaries—"the kind of programming that made network news great," Grossman told the *Times*.

Bob Wright was pleasantly surprised by the decision. The twenty-million-dollar cut "was very useful to Larry in meeting his budget objective," he said. Besides, added Wright, "He wasn't very happy with the show." Roger Mudd, the coanchor of *1986*, blasted the change as another example of "pressure for profits," and left NBC a month later. Mudd had an ally in Grant Tinker, who said that NBC had too hastily "abandoned" the show. Tinker believed a network had obligations that sometimes transcended business or budgetary considerations, that it was wrong for NBC not to have a news and information show in prime time.

But Grossman was hopeful. He now believed that it was possible to improve his relationship with Wright and Welch. He welcomed John Stewart, the McKinsey partner who would direct a team of four consultants and four NBC News executives in analyzing how News spent its money. In some ways, Grossman and Stewart were alike—good listeners, soft-spoken, gentle, skilled at conciliation. Stewart, a thin man with graying blond hair was, like Grossman, in his mid-fifties, and had nursed more than a few sick companies back to fiscal health. Stewart was able to explain to Grossman how his clients in the American automobile, steel, and electronics industry had also undergone wrenching changes in the face of new competitors.

"Managers get paid to avoid trauma," Stewart said, citing Frank Lorenzo's effort to lay off Continental Airlines employees by declaring bankruptcy as an approach to avoid. Stewart sounded to Grossman like a fellow incrementalist.

Stewart began by interviewing News people to see what they actually did. To serve as a liaison, Grossman assigned Tom Ross, a News vice president with an ease of manner that matched Stewart's. Ross had been a print journalist for twenty-two years before becoming Washington bureau chief of the Chicago *Sun-Times,* followed by a stint as chief spokesman for the Pentagon in the Carter administration. When GE acquired RCA, Ross was senior vice president for Corporate Affairs at RCA, and worked closely with Thornton Bradshaw and Welch on the transition. Because Ross knew Welch and other executives in Fairfield, Grossman had another task for him, a secret task. In addition to working with Stewart, he wanted Ross to be his liaison to Wright and Welch, to help decode them. Grossman confided that he felt that his Fairfield meeting had been "terrible," and he asked Ross to "find out what the feeling was."

Ross liked the assignment, but was dubious. He was aware of the chasm between GE and NBC. While NBC congratulated itself on how far it had come from the dark days of Fred Silverman, Wright and Welch believed that what separated NBC from ABC and CBS was mostly *The Cosby Show* and a few hits on Thursday night. On the other side, Ross understood "the subconscious sense of annoyance" at NBC toward the intruders from GE who were "asking Larry to change what he perceived to be a success." Like Grossman, Ross saw the McKinsey effort as a way to educate Wright and Welch.

Bob Wright was pleased to have Ross serve as a liaison to McKinsey and in December invited him to lunch in his private dining room. Wright saw in Ross a man of experience in a world—journalism—he did not fathom. And he saw him as another source of information. Their December lunch would become the first of a series of clandestine meetings, several kept secret from Grossman, that Wright and Ross would have over the next year and a half.

Grossman was confident he had found the key to managing his relationship with the men from GE. Ross would be his personal emissary to Wright and Fairfield. His deputy, Tim Russert, would be his ambassador to the news division as well as his political advisor. And in John Stewart he had someone who could shore up his management weaknesses by helping set up a system to better manage news. Now he would concentrate on improving his relationship with Tom Brokaw.

Like the presidents of the other two network news divisions, Grossman flattered his anchor. He had given Brokaw the title of managing editor of the evening newscast, and publicly called Brokaw "the team leader of NBC News." Privately the two men were hardly a team, too different to be close. Larry and Boots Grossman were fairly private people, who maintained a small apartment in Greenwich Village and who spent as much time as they could in their suburban Westport home. In contrast to the Jewish-intellectual upbringing and Ivy League schooling enjoyed by the Grossmans, Meredith and Tom Brokaw were from Yankton, South Dakota, where they were high school sweethearts, where Meredith was Miss South Dakota of 1959, and where both graduated from the University of South Dakota. Despite their rural roots, the Brokaws treated New York as if they owned it. He jogged with Robert Redford in Central Park, she opened Pennywhistle, a store that sold inventive games and toys for children. The Grossmans often arranged their vacations around his overseas speeches, going off to tour museums and landmarks; the Brokaws safaried with their three daughters in Africa, went mountain climbing in Pakistan, shot the white rapids of Idaho and Wyoming. Brokaw glided gracefully through a cocktail party or a room full of GE executives, and not just because he was a "star." He was quicker on his feet than Larry Grossman, seemed never to forget a joke, told them well. By contrast with the more reclusive Grossmans, the Brokaws enjoyed entertaining, skimming the cream of New York's journalistic and literary world and inviting its members to dine at their Park Avenue duplex.

The relationship between Grossman and Brokaw was as clumsy in some ways as Grossman's was with Welch or Wright. Unlike Grossman, Brokaw had spent his life in News. He began at KMTV in Omaha in 1962, moved three years later to WSB-TV in Atlanta, where he covered civil rights; he then shifted to reporter and anchor with KNBC in Los Angeles in 1966. Seven years later he was hurling questions at Richard Nixon as NBC's White House correspondent; he began anchoring *Today* in 1976 and *NBC Nightly News* in 1982. The elevation brought him satisfaction and power, but also a feeling of constant siege. A network anchor is always on the go, racing from subject to subject, traveling from place to place, more so in recent years as the networks try to retrieve lost viewers by making news more immediate. But the great weight the anchor carries is that he is public property. Brokaw, not Wright or even Tinker, was the public face of NBC. The affiliates wanted to grab a piece of his time for a local promotion. Community groups wanted him to serve as MC. The media sniped or demanded an interview. Advertisers wanted him to speak. The public wanted his autograph. Whatever their fame or salary, TV anchors feel vulnerable. What an anchor expects from his News president is protection, assurance that his boss can shield him from turbulence, can manage the corporate owners and bring a sense of calm, of solid news judgment. With Tinker there, Brokaw felt a measure of security. But he never felt secure with Grossman, never felt his boss brought enough news experience or judgment—or decisiveness—to the table. Looking younger than his forty-six years, Brokaw hated being thought of as a pretty boy, as just a news reader, especially since he didn't need a script to ask intelligent questions. But he would have liked to be able to turn to someone he considered a wise news partner.

Grossman had his own problems with Brokaw, whom he found too defensive, too sensitive to criticism. "I was very concerned about his image as a lightweight," said Grossman. "He appeared in the gossip columns too often." Grossman worried that Brokaw's boyishness and celebrity, the fame he had achieved on the frothier *Today* show, plus the relatively small amount of foreign travel he had done compared to his two competitors, made him seem less experienced. Grossman pointed to a confidential 1984 NBC Research report on the three network newscasts that found that while Rather then had the highest personal appeal and Jennings's was steadily rising, Brokaw's appeal had actually declined. Moreover, the report concluded that while Brokaw bested his two rivals in not a single authority or personality measurement, "He is perceived as having strong disadvantages on experience, knowledgeability, and clarity of speech." While the report also found that NBC News ranked third in the quality of its correspondents and "team of experts," Grossman tended to think the weaknesses of the newscast would fade if the anchor appeared stronger.

To put more heft in his image, Grossman urged Brokaw earlier in 1986 to travel more, to become active in the Foreign Policy Association, to avoid the gossip columns, and, above all, to practice his delivery. Brokaw, like Barbara Walters, has a slight lall—he forms the letter *l* in the back of the throat instead of with the tongue against the roof of the mouth. Even Walter Cronkite had difficulties—he mispronounced the word "million." But Cronkite had a white mane and oozed experience. Since anchors were readers as well as journalists, and since Brokaw sometimes garbled words when he was tired, Grossman felt more practice would help. Grossman also pushed for Connie Chung as "a regular nightly presence" on the newscast, which Brokaw took as a mild rebuke since Chung, while popular with viewers, was not generally perceived within News as a heavyweight.

A more direct affront came when Grossman sought—as had Roone Arledge at ABC—to lure Diane Sawyer to NBC. Unlike CBS, which had luminaries like Sawyer or Charles Kuralt to back up Dan Rather, or ABC, which had Ted Koppel to substitute for Peter Jennings, NBC didn't have a backup with marquee value. Knowing Sawyer's CBS contract would expire at the end of December, and of her eagerness to be an anchor, Grossman, like Arledge, spoke to Sawyer and her agent, Richard Leibner. Grossman proposed a dual anchor, with one anchor always on the road. This was a way, Grossman thought, to get around the problems coanchors Brokaw and Roger Mudd had when both were competing for nightly anchor airtime. It would be a way to get Brokaw out from behind the anchor desk, a way for both anchors to show depth by reporting more and reading less. It would also be a way to strengthen ties in weaker NBC markets—Washington, D.C., Dallas, Chicago, Philadelphia, Houston—because the traveling anchors could often go there.

Since Arledge's Cap Cities bosses had refused to enter a bidding war for stars, Sawyer and her agent were enticed by Grossman's discussion of a coanchor spot, and by the $1.6 million NBC would pay her, double her CBS salary. Grossman, according to Leibner, went out of his way to stress that Brokaw was numero uno. "NBC never promised she would sit next to Tom, but said that given time they would try to create an atmosphere where that would happen." But if Brokaw should slip in the ratings, added Leibner, he was convinced "it would have happened."

Grossman got a green light from Bob Wright, who felt a network had to be willing to pay for those "few people who are extremely attractive." Grossman then approached Brokaw.

Roone Arledge had talked to Peter Jennings about Sawyer as a coanchor, but was spared a confrontation because his network was uninterested in paying the price. Not so at NBC, where Grossman confronted an obdurate Brokaw. According to Grossman, Brokaw exclaimed, "No way. If that happens, I leave."

"I didn't erupt or threaten to leave," said Brokaw. "I said I didn't think it will work. But I think we should get her here." He had compelling reasons to oppose a dual anchor. Back in 1981, when Brokaw and Roger Mudd were teamed as coanchors, they began with high hopes. Even though Brokaw's father had died the day before, Brokaw flew back to New York to keep a previously scheduled dinner he was hosting in Mudd's honor before turning around the next morning to return to Yankton for the funeral. Nevertheless, the Mudd/Brokaw alliance dissolved in acrimony. Dual anchors, Brokaw now felt, led only to competitive cannibalism. After subtracting time for commercials and station breaks, the newscast was only twenty-two minutes long—the script of the entire newscast if laid out would cover only two-thirds of *The New York Times*'s front page. Subtract another minute or so for music and credits, then add the correspondents' reports, and the anchor was left with about five minutes to read the news and do bridges between stories, which Brokaw thought was too little time to divide in two. "To drive these programs with a single anchor is hard," Brokaw said. "It takes a single authority figure, male or female. . . . If you add another body you couldn't do the same stories because you would be worrying about finding a role for the coanchor. It worked with Huntley and Brinkley, but that's because Huntley did most of the anchoring and there was a specific role for Brinkley with his Washington bon mots and his wonderful way of putting news into perspective." It didn't work with John Chancellor and David Brinkley.

Brokaw exercised his veto, but it was awkward. After all, they were friends. Tom and Meredith and Diane and her then beau, investment banker Richard Holbrooke, played tennis together every Thursday night. The job of a News president was to take the heat. Grossman went back to Sawyer and Leibner and told them the coanchor idea wouldn't fly. Instead, he proposed that Sawyer become the "primary substitute" anchor for Brokaw, the "prime" correspondent for *Nightly News,* the anchor of some NBC specials, and the host for both *Meet the Press* and a new Sunday *Today* show. Abandoning the top-rated *60 Minutes* for a regular anchor slot on Sunday mornings held little allure for Sawyer. Nor did the uncertainty of changing networks. "Ninety percent of this business is atmospherics," said Grossman. And for Sawyer, the atmosphere was right to stay at CBS, at least for the time being.

The Diane Sawyer incident stoked the smoldering Grossman/Brokaw fire. Brokaw was feeling more and more contempt for his boss. He credited Grossman with standing up to Welch and Wright on behalf of News, but he asked: "Did he do it skillfully? He didn't. We knew this was coming. There were principles involved, but he hurt News in the process. GE thought we thought we were the high church." Brokaw saw himself as a pragmatist and Grossman as a naif. Grossman, he felt, was in over his head. "Welch is tougher than he is," he said. "Welch and Wright are the World Series of poker."

Brokaw's contempt was fed by mistrust. Grossman's approach to Sawyer gave Brokaw reason to feel insecure. And what Grossman took to be Brokaw's intimacy with Wright and Welch made Grossman insecure. Soon after the World Series dinner at his Westport home, Grossman said, "I got a sense that Tom was seeing Welch and seeing Wright." Grossman accepted that "Tom was a political animal, and had to protect himself." But Grossman felt that it was "not done in a forthright way." Feeling undermined, he spoke with Wright at one point in December and said, "I have to get clued in when you're seeing Tom." Wright agreed.

By the end of 1986, Grossman was feeling vulnerable again. He had done battle with his anchor and his boss. He was operating without a contract, and was beset by recurrent rumors that he was about to resign. "You have a contract for life, but it's renewable each day!" Tim Russert used to joke. The past few months, Grossman admitted at the time, had been "rough." But on good days, he said hopefully, "it is clear they want me to stay."

While it was obvious to many NBC executives that Grossman sometimes felt orphaned, no one realized that Bob Wright did, too. "It has been difficult," admitted Wright, referring to his first four months as president. Not only was he expected to walk in Tinker's large shadow, he was alone, with executives he inherited, without allies who shared his vision. His memos were leaked to the newspapers. He complained to Bud Rukeyser that he was "surrounded by assassins." These first months at NBC, explained Suzanne Wright, her husband felt ostracized. "How would you like to walk into a place and not have anyone that you know?" she asked. "I mean, as uncomfortable as they felt with Bob because he was the new leader, there were many more of them than there were of Bob. . . . Bob was here by himself. And he was surprised by people's reactions." As a boy from the working class and the daughter of a Queens cop, perhaps Bob and Suzanne Wright felt they were victims of a kind of elitism. Throughout much of their first year at NBC, observed Al Barber, a former classmate of Wright's at Holy Cross and a GE colleague, "Bob and his wife were lonely. The people at NBC didn't extend themselves to Bob, or to Suzanne."

Many NBC colleagues, on the other hand, thought Wright was succumbing to a classic syndrome, one explained in a book then popular among GE's executives—*The Dynamics of Taking Charge,* by John J. Gabarro of the Harvard Business School. New business leaders most often failed, he wrote, because instead of involving others they operate "in a more solitary fashion, leading to what I describe as the 'Lone Ranger Syndrome.'" At NBC, Wright was dealing with new people and a strange culture, with an infrastructure that had grown over the years like a sturdy oak tree. To his friend Al Barber, to whom he began talking in late 1986 about joining NBC, Wright sounded like the Lone Ranger: "I don't have enough people who think beyond the broadcasting business."

What Wright didn't understand, what particularly irked him, was what he called "the extreme concern" about General Electric from the media and from NBC executives. He didn't understand why people thought he was Welch's puppet, since he talked to Welch as little as three times a week. And although Welch was listed as NBC's chairman, he also served as chairman of two other GE businesses. NBC was a small fish, representing only 7 percent of GE's earnings. Hadn't NBC been part of RCA, another giant company? So why should there be paranoia about GE? It was as if, he said, "We are going to do something dramatic, like go back to black and white or something, or do something that only the criminally insane might do. Like decide to only do sports programs during prime time! It was as if we had some sort of agenda to harm network television, something that God should not allow." Wright did not grasp the paranoia partly because he was a GE man through and through. He thought first of his responsibility to public shareholders; many NBC employees, particularly in News, thought first of the network's responsibilities to the public.

Wright's self-perception was also at odds with how he was generally perceived at NBC. He had been a twelve-thousand-dollar-a-year law clerk for a federal judge in New Jersey, had written sentencing reports in the trials of mobsters and sorted through mountains of data without being captured by either side—"the single most exciting thing I've ever done," remembers Wright. He felt that dealing with life-and-death decisions taught him to be sensitive to people. Had he been insensitive, Wright said he would have ordered wholesale personnel changes at NBC. While many at NBC saw him as strictly a dollars-and-cents businessman, Wright saw himself as a creative executive. He heard all the talk about "creativity" at the networks, but after his first two months he had concluded that the investment banking world he had just left was just as "creative," just as frenetic, just as exciting. Wright thought he was a regular guy, an attentive father who broke early from the office to attend the school or sporting events of his two sons and daughter, who always vacationed with the family in Nantucket in summer and Aspen in winter, who drove Triumph and Austin Healy convertibles, who enjoyed climbing under old cars, fixing and selling them. And although it was then largely a secret to NBC colleagues, Wright has a sharp sense of humor.

To his NBC colleagues, however, Wright conveyed an almost puritan sense that having fun was slothful, wicked. A mood of uncertainty gripped much of NBC. No matter that NBC revenues surged 15 percent in 1986, topping $3 billion for the first time, or that pretax earnings were $407 million, or that GE's stock had climbed from a low that year of $66 to $87 a share, or that NBC was firmly in first place in the Entertainment ratings, or first with the *Today* show, or, finally, with Tom Brokaw's *Nightly News.* Too few people at NBC headquarters in New York were in a celebratory mood. Wright frightened them.

Unlike Dan Burke or Tom Murphy of ABC, Wright was cheap with compliments. Everyone acknowledged that Wright was smart, but unlike Murphy and Burke he seemed short of human smarts. Because Wright "from day one conveyed the sense that all ideas in the company were wrong and were yesterday's ideas," said one NBC executive, "no one gives him the benefit of the doubt." Rukeyser thought the new network owners were making a classic mistake. "Firing people as a way of cutting expenses is wrong," he said. "If you fire three hundred people and it saves you $15 million, it's not worth it. The turmoil created in doing that, and the atmosphere it creates may not make it $15 million worth of anything. Let's say Diane Sawyer is on the fence about coming to NBC and two networks are in turmoil and NBC under Tinker is stable. Perhaps Diane Sawyer would make a different decision about coming here. We had an opportunity to solidify what we had under Tinker. Instead, we've behaved like losers."

In truth, Rukeyser and Wright were each half right. Nearing the end of the twentieth century, network television was reeling from the kinds of changes convulsing other industries. The networks were losing market share; they had grown fat and lethargic. Cost cutting was inevitable and necessary. At the same time, people like Rukeyser understood the price of cost cutting and the importance of a collegial atmosphere, and the sense that working at a network was special. "I don't mean to detract from what Grant Tinker accomplished in prime time, but he wasn't concerned with managing the cost side of the company," said Franklin J. Havlicek, then NBC's director of Labor Relations. "Wright has shifted the focus to the cost side. That's good. But on the other hand, maybe neither of them struck the right balance."

Network people were suspicious of Wright because they believed he did not view his current job as the capstone of his career but aspired higher, to the presidency of GE. Folks at NBC believed GE had no emotional tie to NBC, and only wanted to milk it for cash. It was difficult for Wright as an outsider to allay these fears, the more so because he and Welch tended to debunk the past in sweeping terms. They were like revolutionaries eager to stamp out history, to convert people to a new order. Comparisons between Wright and Tinker were inevitable, and diminished Wright. Tinker was associated with quality television shows, both when he produced programs like *The Mary Tyler Moore Show* or *Lou Grant* and when he helped dot NBC's schedule with *Cheers* and *St. Elsewhere.* But Wright, said his wife, watched very little television and told TV critics at an October luncheon that he preferred shows that weren't "overly complex" and didn't "require an emotional commitment" because "I don't have time."

The contrast with Tinker became Wright's heaviest cross. Wright's friends tended to be fellow businessmen—"country club types," said one NBC employee who remembers meeting a developer, an accountant, and a banker at NBC's World Series box at Shea Stadium; Tinker's friends tended to be from the entertainment world. Wright's speeches were usually monologues, Tinker's were brief; Wright conveyed certitude, Tinker humility. Wright was brusque, Tinker affable. As often as not, Wright looked at the floor—or at a chair—when talking to someone, while Tinker looked one in the eye. Wright was often inaccessible, and executives complained that phoning or sending him a memo was like dropping it down "a black hole"—nothing ever came back; Tinker was a fussbudget about answering mail, returning every call. Of Wright, senior vice president for Finance Donald Carswell, who joined NBC in 1956, said at the time, "I honestly don't know what he does."

Indeed, Wright perceived the business differently than did most people at NBC, and he probably had a more pessimistic view of the networks' future than the new owners of CBS and ABC. Instead of focusing on how well NBC was doing, he concentrated on how well the networks' competitors were doing, including most of the other eleven networks. Wright pounded home the point that the television world was no longer dominated by three superpowers.

To prove his point, Wright asked his corporate planning department to draw up a chart estimating the 1987 operating income of the twelve major national TV-programming services. The chart, which he shared with NBC executives in late 1986, projected NBC as the earnings leader, with 1987 profits of $300 million (exclusive of profits from its owned stations). By this measure, the number-two network would be HBO ($87.5 million in profits). Ten of these networks—including cable's Nickelodeon, Showtime, MTV, and the USA Network—would make more than ABC; four cable services—HBO, ESPN ($65 million), CNN ($57.6 million), and Ted Turner's superstation, WTBS ($53.6 million)—were expected to make more than CBS ($25 to 50 million). The lesson Wright drew from this chart was that, despite its current success, the future would look different from the past, and NBC had to branch out into cable. Wright knew the Hollywood studios had almost committed suicide by resisting the networks and VCRs, just as the auto companies had ignored smaller, fuel-efficient cars. He was determined not to make the same mistake.

And Bob Wright wasn't alone. Certainly there were those who, meaning no disrespect for Tinker, welcomed Wright and GE. One of those was Brandon Tartikoff. "Bob is changing," said Tartikoff in January of 1987. "Bob is inherently a good guy. . . . He's smart. It would be a mistake to write him off for a couple of foibles, or to make the mistake of thinking that if only Grant Tinker were signed up for another five years NBC would be far better off. These are different times. They require shrewd and creative businessmen. It is naive to think if I keep coming up with hit shows everything will be fine. . . . What GE is doing is forcing us, in good times, to confront issues." There was a school of thought, put down as "revisionism" by Tinker advocates like Bud Rukeyser, which claimed that Tinker's programming successes hid the management mess at NBC. Whispering this view into Jack Welch's ear was Edward L. Scanlon, RCA's senior vice president for Personnel and the executive who worked closely with Welch while integrating RCA into GE. "The networks are like the record business," Scanlon said. "Hire Bruce Springsteen and you can make mistakes and no one will notice. Grant Tinker was superb. But . . . between a superb program executive and a guy who can take you into the future, right now NBC needs someone who can take it into the future."

Meanwhile, Tinker sat in Hollywood and seethed. He was no wild-eyed idealist. He had put his share of garbage on the air. He could barely read a budget. But he believed budgets mattered less than product. While he supervised construction of a fourteen-acre Culver City lot that would house the forty-million-dollar production company he had formed with the Gannett Company, Tinker was distressed by what he saw as a "slavish devotion to the bottom line" on the part of the new network owners. Network television was a business, and should be run as one, he said. But a network also had what he called "a unique franchise obligation. . . . There is a civic duty there that relates to a public trust." There was a difference, Tinker believed, between a network and other businesses. Owning a network was a privilege.

Poppycock! said Jack Welch at the end of the year. On the morning he was interviewed, the GE turbines division had laid off hundreds of employees, with barely any notice. "You think they're happy?" Welch said combatively. Turbines and NBC both had obligations to shareholders. Each had a responsibility to customers—Turbines for their physical safety, NBC for their mental safety. Both had suppliers and distributors to contend with. And government regulators. The only difference between Turbines and NBC, Welch insisted, was simply this: "They have no press to write about them!"

9

CBS: MANAGING BY THE NUMBERS, SEPTEMBER TO DECEMBER 1986

Larry Tisch arrived early—7 A.M.—for his first day of work as acting CEO of CBS on September 11, 1986, and before he reached his desk he was asking questions. Entering Eero Saarinen's black granite slab between West Fifty-second and Fifty-third streets on Sixth Avenue, Tisch made a mental note—*Why does the lobby need six Wells Fargo guards?* Then he stepped into the elevator that one of those guards converted to an express by pressing a button at the reception desk. When the elevator glided to a halt on the thirty-fifth floor and Tisch walked onto the taupe carpet, the only CBS employee on hand to welcome his new boss was steward Patrick Callahan. "I was standing there with a big smile on my face because I knew his son Tom," recalls Callahan, fifty-one, who was born in Tipperary. "I took him on a tour to see every office."

They wandered down corridors covered with sound-smothering ivory fabric that was taken down and cleaned four times a year. They passed other walls covered with French walnut, and some of the nine private dining rooms, which Tisch paused to peek into. They passed CBS's collection of Chagalls, Calders, Rouaults, Hockneys, and Mirós, which Tisch did not pause to admire. He was quiet as he walked, but Callahan could tell he was drunk with anger. "Look at all this empty space!" Tisch cried out as he glanced at the empty suites.

Office space was not uppermost on Tisch's mind that first morning, though empty space was a reflection, he thought, of the "waste" at CBS. One of the first things Tisch said to chief financial officer Fred Meyer was that CBS was "50 percent overstaffed." Since Tisch felt there was little he could do in the short term to boost network revenues, he was determined to cut costs. And among the costs he would address first was debt. Larry Tisch was an old-fashioned businessman, who believed debt was a burden, not an opportunity for expansion. When the recession came, as he expected it surely would, a tide of bills would drown the company. With CBS earnings down and working capital below $300 million in 1985, and with long-term debt swelling from $400 million to about $1 billion, Tisch felt CBS was overly leveraged. The debt pushed Tisch toward a conservative position he was most comfortable with anyway, which was that CBS should not be "a so-called conglomerate," but instead, as he told *Broadcasting* magazine that fall, it "should be a media company with an emphasis on broadcasting. . . ." People assumed Tisch meant that CBS shouldn't be in the toy business, but should remain a communications company, involved in broadcasting, magazines, books, records, video cassettes and some cable programming. His goal, Tisch told *Fortune*, was a return on assets of 12 percent, or double the best return Tom Wyman had achieved during his six-year reign.

There were other questions on Tisch's mind. Could he share the throne with CBS founder William Paley, who was returning as acting chairman? What executive changes should he make? How would the pessimistic Tisch mesh with the ever-optimistic Gene Jankowski, president of the Broadcast Group? How would he relate to a board so intent on resisting him that they were prepared to sell CBS? In particular, how would he get on with his old friend, James Wolfensohn, a leader in the effort to keep CBS from Loews's clutches and a man whom Tisch's friends now delightedly disparaged as "the Inspector Clouseau of investment banking"?

Among the first calls Tisch would make this first day was to Roberto Goizueta, chairman and CEO of Coca-Cola, to inform him CBS was not for sale. That matter settled, he summoned Jankowski to his office.

As he climbed the flight of stairs from his thirty-fourth-floor office to Tisch's corner suite, Jankowski trembled. After twenty-five years at CBS, he was understandably nervous that he might lose a job that had paid him a total, including bonuses, of $847,885 in 1985. The natty Jankowski was Tisch's opposite. Tisch always seized on the bad news first; Jankowski latched onto a strong overnight rating, a "good word of mouth," a favorable press clip. Tisch's impatience was betrayed by the way he spoke, crisply, always getting right to the point; Jankowski was almost Oriental in his patience and the convolution of his answers.

But Gene Jankowski was safe, for the moment. No sooner did he enter Tisch's office than his new boss got right to the point. He wanted Jankowski to fire News president Van Gordon Sauter. Tisch felt that Sauter was now the focus of discontent within News, the person who was thought to have desecrated the Murrow temple by, among other transgressions, hiring Phyllis George to cohost the *Morning News.* And Tisch still bridled at the speech Sauter had made in August in Utah, defending Wyman and censuring the instability Tisch had brought to CBS. "It is something everybody is ready for," Tisch said. "It is obvious to everyone he has to go."

Done, said Jankowski. But, he reminded Tisch, Sauter had recently signed a five-year contract guaranteeing him at least $350,000 a year. Would the frugal Tisch eat this expense?

Do it anyway, Tisch said. *We need to make a fresh start in News. Let Sauter's deputy, Howard Stringer, serve as acting News president, and see if he can gain the confidence of the organization.*

Jankowski's secretary reached Sauter in his car, summoning him to Jankowski's office. When he arrived, Sauter was ready for the worst. He had heard that Walter Cronkite was in Washington that morning boasting of management changes before nightfall. Jankowski was all business. "I want you to resign," he said as soon as Sauter shambled into his office and closed the door. "It's entirely my decision."

Sauter didn't believe Jankowski had come to this decision on his own, but he simply said, "I don't want my contract abrogated."

No problem.

The meeting lasted only a few minutes. Sauter had been loyal to the side that lost, he felt, and now he paid the price. Sauter headed home and as soon as he got there he had his secretary book him on the first plane the next morning to Bozeman, Montana, where he would fish. He phoned and told his fishing buddy, Dan Rather, and his wife, lawyer Kathleen Rice Brown, daughter of former California governor Edmund G. "Pat" Brown and sister of former governor Jerry Brown. Within the hour Kathleen Brown met her husband at their Park Avenue apartment, and together they drove to Connecticut to collect his fishing gear.

It did not take long for word of Sauter's ouster to explode in the newsroom. *"The wicked witch is dead! The wicked witch is dead!"* sang out producer Richard Cohen as he skipped through the newsroom. "I really felt he was a very evil force," said Cohen. The breach between Sauter and those he led was vast. Sauter was a producer, an impresario, not a hard news journalist; he believed TV news had to grab people's emotions. Cohen and other News traditionalists, on the other hand, saw themselves as journalists whose medium happened to be television; they believed that if the criterion for a good news story was emotion then the evening news would be tarted up with conflict and human interest stories, much as local news was. There was, of course, more than a touch of hypocrisy involved, since "entertainment values" are not alien to a newscast concerned with such cosmetics as theme music or softening Dan Rather's image with a V-neck sweater; *60 Minutes* had thrived for nineteen extraordinary seasons, in part because the talented News traditionalist who created it, Don Hewitt, focused his cameras on personalities, on storytelling, on making viewers care about the adventures of Mike and Morley and other correspondents.

But Sauter was indeed guilty of trying to soften network news, to blur distinctions between local and network newscasts. Even he recognized that it was time to move on. "I had exhausted the good will of the organization, and my patience for it," recalls Sauter.

With Sauter gone, Tisch turned to another matter: reassuring the three group presidents—Jankowski, Peter Derow of the Publishing Group, and Walter Yetnikoff of the Records Group. Late this first morning, he summoned them to his office and declared that there would be no more executive beheadings. Nor would they have to attend twice-monthly management committee meetings with the company's top forty executives. He was abolishing the management committee. "It's all nonsense," said Tisch. "It doesn't do anything." As a signal to the organization that calm had returned, Tisch immediately dispatched a one-paragraph memorandum to all employees. He had met with the three group presidents, Tisch wrote:

> I assured them of my complete confidence in them and in the organizations they head. I would like to add that I have the same level of confidence in the men and women who serve this company so well.

To further reassure the news division, the next morning Tisch, accompanied by his son Tom, paid a surprise visit to the set of the troubled *Morning News* show, where he was greeted as a conquering hero. An hour later he hustled to a meeting with all of Jankowski's top managers, where Tisch asked questions. Like his counterparts at ABC and NBC, he was not satisfied with the answers. "The company was sort of being run as if it were IBM," he said. "It had the kind of overhead IBM had. The first thing I did was look at the body count. And the first thing I found was that the 500 people the board and the press had been told were laid off was incorrect. Only 150 had been laid off. It reflected the fact that no one wanted to let anyone go." Why? They were "lazy," Tisch said. The real culprit, he thought, was Tom Wyman. "It wasn't their fault," Tisch explained. "There was no leadership from the top."

Now, despite his reassuring memo, Tisch alone would supply that leadership, for he felt there was no one at CBS who instinctively acted like an owner, who shared his sense of outrage at the waste of shareholder money. As he told *Broadcasting* magazine, what he alone brought was "an objective point of view on the business, the industry, the company." In Tisch's view, CBS was overstaffed, arrogant, detached from reality. Almost immediately, Tisch got his arms around the 1,350-person corporate staff and dismissals were accelerated. One-third would be fired, and with other reductions this would save CBS $40 to $60 million annually.

David Fuchs, who had served as de facto chief of staff to Jankowski before being summoned to assist Tom Wyman, tried—as did Bud Rukeyser at NBC—to warn his boss that from now on he was in the fish bowl. "From this moment on people will be looking at you and measuring your words," he said. Tisch nodded, but like Bob Wright, he didn't grasp at first what his sudden visibility could mean. After all, he had made billion-dollar investment decisions before and the press yawned.

Tisch told reporters that cost cutting was merely a sideline and programming was the heart of his mission, but this was not the way he acted at CBS. He was determined to keep CBS on its toes, focused on expenditures. Aware that he often sold assets, reporters asked if he planned to sell any parts of CBS, as Ted Turner said he would have done had he bought CBS and as Fay Vincent said Coca-Cola would "seriously consider" doing. Tisch told the *Times,* "Nothing is going to be sold for the sake of selling. It is not my nature to make blanket statements about anything. But as far as I am concerned, it [a sale] is ridiculous!"

Programming commanded some of Tisch's thoughts this first week. He rarely watched entertainment programs on television, but he had enough friends in the business who warned him that CBS's schedule needed intensive care. Its hit shows, such as *Dallas* and perhaps *60 Minutes,* were aging. It had no 8:00 comedy hits, which meant it had no hook to attract viewers to the three hours of network prime time. Its shows appealed more to rural audiences, not the younger, urban/suburban viewers whom advertisers craved. And it had little luster—

no *St. Elsewhere,* no *L.A. Law,* no *Cheers*—the kind of gleaming series that made NBC the "quality" network and attracted the best writers and producers. Tisch wanted to do something about it. But what?

Tommy Tisch suggested he consult Robert Pittman, thirty-two, a friend who was the principal creator of the hip, fast-paced MTV. MTV went on the assumption that television viewers ingest information in quick bites, feeling it rather than analyzing it. With its music videos MTV had eliminated the barrier between the program and the ad; viewers enjoyed the commercial as if it were the program. Now Pittman was running Quantum Media, a programming supplier with 50 percent backing from Hollywood powerhouse MCA.

When they met at Tisch's Rye home that weekend, Pittman argued that unlike older people who grew up reading books, the younger generation "process information differently. Kids can do homework, watch TV, listen to the radio, talk on the phone, all at the same time. My parents can only do one thing at a time." Books require a reader to concentrate, to translate words, to follow characters, to make connections—to work. Television is passive, requiring less effort. Reared in households that averaged seven hours of TV daily, younger viewers were less riveted by plot or language or character than by impressions—likeability, warmth, excitement. Television had shortened attention spans, altered the way teachers taught, sometimes forcing them to use entertaining or freakish gimmicks to seize their students' attention, as Geraldo Rivera or Oprah Winfrey did on their syndicated talk shows. Pictures forever altered the perception of things. Calvin Klein didn't sell his jeans by advertising their sturdiness or comfort. He sold an image, a surface feel, just as *Miami Vice*—with its mix of pulsing music, stylish clothes, action, and quick cuts—sold an image, a contemporary feel. Like Sauter, whom Tisch had just fired, Pittman believed television had to hit viewers in the gut.

Tisch wasn't sure if Pittman was correct; in fact, he rarely pondered such matters, and wasn't much interested in doing so. But he was intrigued. What he liked about Pittman was that he wasn't attached to the past. Tisch offered Pittman a job—Tisch later said it wasn't Jankowski's job and Pittman said he wasn't sure if it was Jankowski's job or that of CBS's Entertainment head, Bud Grant. They never got around to defining the position because Pittman declined, telling Tisch he wanted to remain an entrepreneur.

Tisch's passion for change was tempered not just by the perceived limitations of the people reporting to him or by a culture resistant to his corporate values. There was also a nettlesome lawsuit, filed just days after he accepted the job. On September 17, the FCC invited CBS to respond within two weeks to a lawsuit brought by Fairness in Media, a politically conservative group. The group alleged that since power at CBS was now in Tisch's hands, a "change of control" had occurred at the network; therefore CBS should no longer be allowed to own a radio and a TV station in a single market, which they had previously been permitted to do because they had been in business prior to the passage of the legislation. If the FCC ruled against CBS, Tisch would have to sell either a radio or a TV station in four cities where CBS owned both. CBS resisted, filing a fifteen-page memorandum along with a three-page covering letter from Paley. There had been "no transfer of control," insisted Paley, because Tisch and the Loews Corporation owned just under 25 percent of the stock and because the company had been guided through the summer of 1986 by "an independent board of directors" composed of only two individuals employed by CBS (Paley and Cronkite). Recent events demonstrated, wrote Paley, that the eleven outside directors championed CBS's successful effort to ward off predators, that they had ousted Wyman and replaced him with Laurence Tisch only after first determining that Tisch was committed to an independent CBS. Independent directors, added Paley, now comprised a majority of a management committee to whom Tisch reported. And independent directors would help locate Tisch's permanent successor.

What Paley left unsaid was that he, the founder of the company, also served as an independent check on Tisch's power. Although Paley was old and often sick, he was once again chairman, in the office part of every day, traveling to the West Coast again for program meetings, asserting himself. He sat on the management committee, and he was a member of the search committee for a permanent CEO and chairman, which announced it would move promptly.

With one eye on the board and the other on the FCC suit, Tisch was constrained to demonstrate that he ran but did not rule CBS. Tisch began telling reporters he was uninterested in the job. "I don't want to be chief executive of CBS," he told *Newsday.* Perhaps a concern for appearances also prompted Tisch to write a letter to *Newsweek* denying that "I am irritated with my friend and fellow CBS director James Wolfensohn because he allegedly supported Thomas Wyman's efforts to sell the company. . . . Mr. Wolfensohn assured me repeatedly that he opposed the sale of CBS, and to the best of my knowledge he made no efforts to sell the company." Privately Tisch sang a different tune. Asked at the time about Wolfensohn's claim that his and CBS's staff had run some numbers on Coca-Cola and other companies while Wolfensohn was out of town, Tisch could barely contain himself and snapped, "That's his story!" But mindful of the FCC suit and of a board suspicious of his motives, publicly Tisch held his tongue.

To function in such a circumscribed way was unusual for Tisch, who ran Loews with a free hand and dominated its board meetings. At Loews he made instant decisions about investments, about executives, about deals. He was the absolute, unquestioned boss. At CBS he suddenly had to learn to operate in a different environment. Sometimes he bulled ahead anyway. For example, during Tisch's second week on the job he skipped a Museum of Broadcasting meeting, and at lunch the next day with Paley and former CBS president Frank Stanton, Paley said to him, "We missed you last night."

"Oh, I was having dinner with Mariette Hartley. We made a deal to put her on *The Morning Program.*" Paley's jaw dropped. Without telling Paley first, Tisch had met with actress Hartley and executive producer Bob Shanks, whose lighter, more entertainment-oriented *Morning Program* was scheduled to replace the *CBS Morning News* in January. "I was surprised," said Stanton. "I thought the understanding was that on matters of programming Bill was to be consulted, if not given the final word." Paley pouted but said nothing.

The news division, however, was generally grateful to Tisch for ridding the company of Wyman and Sauter, and Tisch basked in Dan Rather's florid praise. "I like the look in his eye, the warmth of his handshake, and I like what he says about News," said Rather at a Los Angeles press conference. "In a rough and tumble business, the first thing anyone says about Larry Tisch is that he's trustworthy."

News was prominent in Tisch's mind, and not just because he enjoyed Rather's praise. News was what he most watched on CBS. Like Murphy and Burke, or Jack Welch, he was a serious consumer of news. And he was a fan. A fan not just of stars such as Rather and Diane Sawyer and Charles Kuralt, but of such correspondents as Lesley Stahl and Bruce Morton. He believed News was the jewel of CBS. To reassert that belief, on September 19 Tisch boarded a Metroliner to Washington with acting News president Howard Stringer. Together, they would tour the D.C. bureau on M Street, sit in the control room and watch Rather do the evening newscast from Washington, and then with much of the bureau in tow, retire around the corner to Il Giardino restaurant. In the discussion over dinner, Tisch mentioned the travails confronting the networks, but what he stressed was his belief that CBS News had to remain the best and that he was prepared to do all in his power to advance the Murrow tradition. "I am cutting bureaucrats who don't contribute," he said. "I am not cutting News. I am a friend of News." Eager for reassurance, the journalists lobbed softballs. The subject of cutting the News budget, recalled Tisch, "never came up. No one ever said to me, 'Are you going to let anyone go?' " Perhaps only because he had to rush to catch the 9:00 shuttle to New York was Tisch saved from being kissed.

Still, Tisch was Tisch, a man with an almost religious fervor for cost cutting. He remembered talking to Barry Diller of Fox, who boasted of managing the Fox network with just fifty people. This piece of information stuck like a bone in Tisch's throat, as it had in Sias's. Tisch was committed to a frontal assault on CBS's overhead; what held him back was a lack of confidence that the people at CBS could make the necessary cuts. So as a substitute for his own staff, he recruited the management consulting arm of the Coopers & Lybrand (C&L) accounting firm, announcing on October 1, 1986, that they would "assist in a review of financial and operating systems and procedures within CBS." The C&L team was to be housed in unmarked offices on the twentieth floor of Black Rock, and would be led by Thomas C. Flanagan, a partner. With his preference for keeping things simple, Tisch instructed Flanagan that he wanted no written reports and wanted him to "tell me once a week where, and how many, people can be reduced."

Flanagan saw things simply as well. "Entertainment is just another business," he said. Nothing special. His task was no different from what it was at any other company. Within weeks, 70 employees were cut from the personnel department, 170 from Research and from Broadcast Standards, 8 of 28 from Public Relations, 8 of 8 from Corporate Stockholder Relations; all outside consultants were severed, limousines and messenger services were curtailed; two of the five CBS kitchens serving the nine private dining rooms were closed, as were two of the dining rooms. Eliminated as well was the CBS store, which sold CBS T-shirts, records, books, toys, and other products to employees at bargain prices, and the CBS medical center, an office with four nurses and two consulting doctors to treat sick or injured employees. Many CBS employees came to feel that Tisch didn't care about their welfare. To them proof that Tisch cared more about head counts than the future came when he cut all 26 CBS pages in New York. The blue-jacketed pages, who earned six dollars an hour and received no benefits, were a trivial cost item. What they represented were entry-level jobs for those wanting careers in broadcasting.

Another budget whack with future implications was Tisch's decision, taken alone, to close the CBS Technology Center in Stamford, Connecticut. This was the laboratory where a passionate and brilliant young scientist, Peter Goldmark, pioneered the LP record and color TV, where CBS engineers blazed the development of one-inch tape and electronic news gathering (ENG), where the network strove to develop new technologies, including high-definition television, which promised twice the picture clarity of current TV sets. In the short run, by shuttering the technology center Tisch was able to save upward of $20 million annually. In the long run, CBS was ceding its technological self-sufficiency.

Tisch saved much less—$300,000—by eliminating CBS's minority advancement program, an effort to rotate minority employees throughout the company and to advance them by having the personnel department subsidize their salaries. Tisch was so intent on ridding CBS of waste that he sometimes sounded as if nothing else mattered. In an interview with the AFTRA union's magazine that fall, Tisch was asked, "What do you think the future holds for women and minorities in television?"

"Is there a problem?" Tisch replied. To Flanagan, the issue posed by the minority advancement program was, simply, its $300,000 cost. Tisch quickly agreed to eliminate it.

Flanagan and Tisch were doing it by the numbers, said Records Group president Walter Yetnikoff, who had welcomed Tisch's victory in September because he thought Tisch would bring stability and because "I thought I would relate to him better—in an ethnic sense." By October the bearded, hot-tempered Records chief who wears gold chains and talks with the speed of a stand-up comic was no longer so sure. "They didn't look beyond the budget box," he said. Yetnikoff resisted cuts, which prompted a call from Larry Tisch.

"This bullshit record company has too many people," Tisch snapped.

"I don't like you making these statements," Yetnikoff replied. Tisch reminded him that he, not Yetnikoff, ran the company.

"I report to you, but I don't work for you," replied Yetnikoff, whose Records Group earned $87.2 million in 1985. Soon tempers cooled, and they made a lunch date, which turned out to be just as tempestuous. "We're getting rid of dining rooms!" Tisch insisted.

"You have to get rid of yours. We'll set one aside for you on the thirty-fifth floor."

No way! exploded Yetnikoff. "The dining room is an extension of my office." He used the rust-carpeted room with two simple leather couches, a phone, and small round table as a waiting room for visitors, and used a bigger conference room for more formal lunches. Yetnikoff was incensed. He ran the world's largest record company, one with eleven thousand employees, many of them concentrated in the manufacturing arm. And yet Larry Tisch was worrying not about a new contract for Bruce Springsteen but about his dining room! In the end, Yetnikoff won. He kept his dining room and agreed to cut only forty employees. More than any other CBS division head, Yetnikoff frustrated Tisch's body-count goals, his desire to triple the seven hundred or so people allegedly severed from the payroll by Tom Wyman earlier in 1986. Nevertheless, Yetnikoff was left uneasy by his encounter.

He was not alone. Executives brooded that despite Tisch's September 11 stability pledge, he would eliminate vice presidents at any moment. "I'll do it—if I'm here next week!" became a refrain among executives. In October, when Tisch was on the Sales floor, one executive bolted from a meeting to call his secretary and tell her to shut his door. "This way Tisch won't see the nice furniture and be shocked," he explained.

Peter Derow, the crew-cut president of the Publishing Group, was convinced Tisch was offended by the stylishness of his nineteenth-floor corner office, with its thick beige carpet, private bath and shower, and array of bright paintings. On October 16, 1986, the day he was fired, Derow wrote a memorandum to the file describing how Tisch performed the deed. They were to meet in Tisch's office to review publishing matters, including budgets. "After reviewing the progress on the two division budgets and the 1987 budget for the Publishing Group staff," Derow wrote:

> Mr. Tisch said that I wouldn't have to worry about "that anymore because we're eliminating the entire 19th floor operation." I asked him if he meant the entire Publishing Group staff and he answered that he did, including my position, but that he knew that I had a contract with two years remaining and that he'd "try to find something for you to do here."
>
> "I asked to review both the logic and the timing of the change, given the fact that we were two weeks away from completing the

> 1987 budgets and that the Coopers & Lybrand study of the entire company was not scheduled to focus on the Publishing Group until late in October or early in November. Mr. Tisch responded by saying that I shouldn't worry about the budgets and that I should "get the 19th floor thing done by tomorrow." . . . Given the nature and timing of the change, I asked Mr. Tisch if he planned any announcement to the employees and/or the press. He answered that none would be necessary, that it was Thursday and "the news will die over the weekend." I suggested that given the potential for anxiety both in the publishing divisions and in other parts of the Company it might be useful to issue a statement to the employees explaining the action. Mr. Tisch said "that's nonsense."
>
> Finally, I told Mr. Tisch that I was personally disappointed regarding the decision to eliminate the Publishing Group staff and that I was concerned about the timing and style of the change. Nonetheless, I said that I would do my best to assure that the change was executed as effectively as possible. Mr. Tisch stood, neither thanked me nor offered me any personal words, and I left his office. . . .

Asked to explain the firing of Derow, particularly after he had granted him a vote of confidence on September 11, Tisch responded: "What is a vote of confidence? I don't want to hurt the man, but did you ever listen to his line of taffy? We had a whole floor of people without a job."

Concerning Derow, Tisch was not without supporters. Some found Derow too turf-conscious, complained he had overpaid badly for the Ziff-Davis magazines, and were aware that CBS Publishing Group profits had declined in 1985 to $41 million. It was now the smallest group contributor to the company. Nevertheless, Derow was a decent guy. Few thought he deserved such an undignified exit. As one CBS executive observed, "We began to worry: Are we dealing with a man who says one thing and does another? What it did was signal to a number of us that we have to question everything Tisch says."

The angst within CBS was compounded by another incident, this one involving Dan Rather and another set of damaging headlines. While the CBS anchor was walking alone along Park Avenue one Saturday night early in October, two men in dark suits reportedly approached him and asked, "Kenneth, what's the frequency?"

"I beg your pardon?" said the courtly Rather.

Without another word, a fist crashed into Rather's face, propelling him backward and toward a building. The two men chased him inside and pummeled him to the floor, ignoring shouts from the doorman. A moment later they casually walked away. They were never found, the case never solved. In the meantime, this incident ticked away within CBS, for colleagues feared that some horrible disclosure would surface, shredding Rather's credibility. Coupled with the cuts, the insecurity—and the resignation of commentator Bill Moyers—drove the network once again to the brink of a nervous breakdown.

In some ways, the angst did not really reach Larry Tisch. He was a trader, who kept his distance, focusing on hard numbers, not personalities, never dwelling on mistakes. In his business career, Tisch had never fired anyone personally until Peter Derow. He always left this to others. At CBS, Tisch was making his decisions by looking at the numbers produced by Flanagan, not by encountering the real people involved. In fact, he didn't want to encounter them, believing it would lessen his resolve to do what had to be done. Tisch believed he was sending a crucial signal to his employees. He said of the CBS store: "The store was costing CBS one million dollars a year, and it did no business. The more important signal is that people understand this has to be a vital company. People don't like working for a company that is not doing well, that is not well managed." And Larry Tisch's definition of a well-managed company was something quantifiable in dollars and cents, not ephemeral things like *morale* or *trust* or *quality* or *investing in the future.* Besides, Tisch believed his actions were compassionate. "We take good care of the people let go," he said. "The job market is very good. And if we have to let people go, now is a good time. There is no recession." This attitude, expressed publicly, enraged people, none more so than Grant Tinker, who had recently signed a production deal with CBS but nevertheless declared: "One of the least attractive things Tisch did was to say that people were almost lucky to be fired because there was a good job market. Never once did I hear him say, 'Gosh, this is agonizing.' "

While the cuts didn't play well with his CBS audience, Larry Tisch was a hit on Wall Street. "He is doing everything every analyst and investor would love to do if they had the power: Run CBS more like a business, find out what all these people do, and make more money in what is inherently a good business," a media analyst told *The Wall Street Journal.*

CBS News was harder to please. In October, a full-fledged campaign was mounted for the presidency of CBS News. Much of the old guard that had worked for Cronkite pushed Burton R. Benjamin, a beloved figure within News, to replace Sauter as president. After many years as a producer for CBS, including service as Cronkite's executive producer, "Bud" Benjamin had left the network to write a book and become a senior fellow at the Gannett Center at Columbia University. Like his friend Cronkite and other traditionalists, Benjamin was deeply disenchanted with the "softening" of news, thought the evening newscast was different, not necessarily better, worried that graphics and technology were becoming the "dog, not the tail," as he put it.

Another group, led by *60 Minutes* executive producer Don Hewitt, was pushing David Burke, Roone Arledge's deputy at ABC News. After nine years as number two, Burke wanted to run his own operation. And Burke had another incentive. When he was preparing to leave state government in early 1977, Felix Rohatyn phoned Bill Paley and arranged an interview for Burke, who hoped to join CBS News. Instead of getting a job, he got a form letter of rejection from Paley. Now, nine years later, Hewitt hosted a mid-October lunch for Burke at his apartment on Central Park South, to which he invited Mike Wallace. In effect, they were interviewing their prospective boss. "I have a guy for you," Hewitt recalls saying to Tisch after lunch. Burke was a manager, which appealed to Tisch, and a believer in CBS's traditions, which appealed to Hewitt. Ever up-front, Burke had informed Arledge of this lunch, and as part of a chess game Arledge telephoned acting CBS News president Howard Stringer, knowing that Stringer might depart if he were passed over. Arledge said that he and Stringer, whose work as a producer he respected, agreed Stringer would come to ABC if Burke got the job.

Meanwhile, Stringer had been active on his own behalf, orchestrating a series of breakfasts and lunches that fall with the various CBS News tribal chiefs, including Cronkite, Benjamin, Hewitt, and ex-News presidents William Leonard and Richard Salant. Stringer had the fervent support of the most important chieftain—Dan Rather—who looked upon the president of News as a kind of campaign manager for the anchor and wanted someone in that job he both respected and trusted. Like the other two anchors, Rather felt vulnerable to attack. Just how vulnerable was explained by Walter Cronkite in a remarkably candid moment while offering a eulogy to a former producer:

> Those who are closest to us gorillas are cast in something of the role of keeper. . . . They feel that they have to listen to our complaints—mostly unreasonable, sometimes irrationally directed at the keeper himself. They feel that they have to humor the beast in his most ridiculous suggestions. They frequently are put in the demeaning role of valet, seeing that the gorilla's personal needs of transportation, lodging, board, are magnificently catered.

Rather naturally wanted a hand in choosing his own "keeper," and his choice would not be someone linked to his predecessor, like Benjamin. Nor could it be a stranger to CBS, like Burke. Stringer had been Rather's executive producer, had replaced a Cronkite producer at a time when Rather was tense and slipping in the ratings, and in three years he pumped up both Rather and the ratings. Rather told Larry Tisch he thought Stringer deserved the post. This suited Tisch, though not William Paley, who invited Benjamin to lunch in October, a lunch that Tisch was invited to join in Paley's dining room. "Paley offered me the job as interim president," recalled Benjamin. "I wasn't certain that Tisch was on board on that, but I passed." At sixty-nine, Benjamin told Paley he would be a "lame duck the minute I sat down." *No, you need a young, forceful personality,* he said. His recommendation: forty-four-year-old Howard Stringer.

Tisch, who had been silent, relaxed. He had been dazzled by the Welsh-born, Oxford-educated son of a Royal Air Force officer. The curly-haired, six-foot three-inch Stringer could wow an audience by quoting the classics. His shelves were crammed with books, including many valued first editions; the gaps on Tisch's shelves were filled by family photos. Stringer, a genuinely funny man, made the dour Tisch laugh. And he had impressed Tisch earlier that month at a meeting when he proposed that CBS be the only network to allow News to take over three hours of airtime on Election Night in November. (Tisch agreed.) Stringer then argued for a one-hour nightly newscast, something that had long been a dream of the three network news divisions. As part of his presentation, Stringer expounded on how television, unlike print, "was all eyes and ears" and how "less can be more in television. You must have all the right information," he would say, "but if you clutter the story much of it gets lost. People need intervals to absorb the information. You have to recognize the limitations of the medium. People are at home. They are not alone more often than not. Their powers of concentration are not focused. You want people to walk away with facts, a sense of shared experience, and sometimes an emotion that will stay with them. The trouble with the evening news programs is that too often they try to condense too much information into too little time."

That was a compelling argument for an hour newscast, but could also be an argument for Sauter's emotional "moments," for softening the news. Would Stringer continue moving away from what Cronkite and others who started in print journalism felt was the Murrow tradition? It bothered members of the old guard that Stringer did not have a linear approach to the medium, that he had, they would whisper, *little hard news experience.* They would note that in the eighteen years Stringer had been with CBS most of his experience was with the documentary unit, not on breaking news stories. Stringer's defenders would reply that he had been executive producer of the network newscast for three years, that as executive producer of CBS Reports between 1976 and 1981 he had crafted outstanding hard news documentaries, including the five-hour *The Defense of the United States,* that he had won thirty-one Emmys and three Peabodys. Because passion and emotion were involved, these points mattered less than which side Stringer had been on in the various internecine wars. There were misgivings about Stringer because he had been a loyal deputy to two unpopular News presidents, Sauter and Ed Joyce. Some wondered whether he had the backbone to resist Rather. Would he stand up to Tisch? Was he, in short, *strong*? But after a successful CBS career, and after years of shared laughs and meals, Stringer had the broadest support internally. "I'm proud of Howard," said his former mentor at CBS, Bud Benjamin. "The question is: Is he tough enough? I think he is."

On the morning of October 29, Tisch's secretary called to invite Stringer to lunch. A moment later the man to whom Stringer reported, Gene Jankowski, called to ask if he had talked to Tisch yet. *No, what's going on?* asked Stringer.

Never mind, said Jankowski, leaving the impression he knew a secret while not usurping Tisch's right to tell it. "Come see me after lunch."

When Stringer arrived for lunch, Tisch was walking out of the office with Jim Babb, a member of the CBS affiliate board. Spotting Stringer, Tisch announced: "This is the new president of CBS News!"

A less popular figure at CBS was Bud Grant. Not only had CBS Entertainment slipped from number one during his regime, but Bud Grant was widely considered to be lazy and sour, a man who arrived at work late and often left after lunch. "Bud didn't seem to like anyone he reported to," said a CBS executive. Gene Jankowski wanted Grant fired, but he didn't press his case on Tisch the way Paley did. "Gene didn't take stands like that," recalled Tisch two years later. But Tisch liked Bud Grant, felt he was bright and was owed a season under the new management to succeed or fail. There was one other factor: Larry Tisch was grateful to Bud Grant for openly feeding him information all through the tense year Tisch spent on the board with Wyman as chairman. Tisch decided to fly to California in October to light a fire under Grant. "The word in Hollywood was that Bud was capable but had no enthusiasm," said Tisch. After meeting with Grant, Tisch returned to New York reassured.

Larry Tisch was having fun. "I've been bitten by CBS," he told *Broadcasting* magazine in October, admitting that he had rethought the matter of becoming permanent CEO and would now "consider it" if the search committee asked him. Among the reasons Tisch was having fun was that he was beginning to do what he knew best—cutting costs and exploring the sale of CBS's parts.

Although the Tisches began as hoteliers, Loews had become a giant holding company, with Larry Tisch sitting at his Quotron terminal, buying and selling. He always sold a business when he thought the price offered would never be repeated. Sentiment was not a factor. That is why when investors stampeded to enter the hotel business he sold the Americana (where he and Billie were married), or sold his New York flagship hotels. It is why, more recently, he had sold the Loews movie theaters. And it was why many suspected he would one day sell CBS. But Tisch had another idea: to dismember and sell off parts of CBS, as Ted Turner or Coca-Cola would have done. In October 1986, he would sell the CBS songs division and CBS's interest in a record catalogue business for approximately $68 million. Tisch was also visited early that month by William Jovanovich, chairman of Harcourt Brace Jovanovich, a leading publisher of textbooks, professional and general books, and periodicals.

"I'll give you one offer for your publishing company," Jovanovich told Tisch, who was all ears. "He mentioned a price I thought was much higher than we could get for it if we went out to sell," recalls Tisch. "Plus publishing had zero to do with broadcasting, which to me is CBS." By October 24 the CBS board of directors granted telephone approval, and it was announced that CBS sold most of its Educational and Professional Publishing Division to Jovanovich for $500 million. Over the next three months Tisch shed the remainder of CBS's book publishing empire.

Tisch was in his trading element, publicly denying—as professional traders usually do—that he was selling anything while privately slipping potential bidders into his office. Before the month of October ended, Tisch began receiving feelers to sell the magazines division, and calculated he could get about $600 million for CBS's twenty-three magazines, including *Woman's Day* and *Modern Bride.*

But the magazines sale would take time. Meanwhile, uppermost in Tisch's mind was the sale of CBS Records, a business he feared was haunted by drugs and payola, a fear Frank Stanton shared when he ran CBS. Tisch was aware that Leonard Goldenson had sold ABC Records to MCA in 1979, and that GE sold RCA Records to the German media giant, Bertelsmann, earlier in 1986. Besides, Tisch was never comfortable with a business whose profitability gyrated wildly, depending on whether Bruce Springsteen or Michael Jackson or some other superstar that Tisch never heard of had a hit album that year. So Tisch was pleased to be visited by Nelson Peltz, who, with the backing of Drexel Burnham's junk bonds, had transformed a small vending-machine company that was losing money into Triangle Industries, the world's largest packaging products company. The flamboyant Peltz wanted to get into the entertainment business and had his eye on CBS Records. Tisch told Peltz he hadn't thought about selling Records, but if he were inclined to sell, Records should fetch $1.25 billion. The record business was hot, Tisch explained, with profits from the Records Group zooming to $160 million. Peltz thought the price steep and asked to see some numbers, which Tisch told Fred Meyer to gather.

Walter Yetnikoff learned of Peltz's visit when a friend at Drexel Burnham called to ask if he could escort Peltz to a meeting to review the numbers. Enraged that Tisch had neglected to inform him, Yetnikoff stalled the investment banker. Pressing another line, he got Tisch on the phone and screamed: *You lied when you pledged never to discuss selling Records without first talking to me!*

Tisch had grown decidedly impatient with Yetnikoff and his tantrums, but he could not squeeze a word in.

"You don't own this record company!" Yetnikoff exclaimed to Tisch, shouting so loud that his voice barrelled down the corridors. "You can't sell this record company without me. And I can't sell without you. We are co-owners." Since Yetnikoff owned little stock, Tisch didn't like hearing that. If Gene Jankowski ever pulled that on Tisch, he would be gone. Finished! Tisch, however, had learned enough about the records business to know that performers like Michael Jackson or Bruce Springsteen were loyal to Yetnikoff, not to CBS. If Yetnikoff walked out the door, as he threatened to, so might Springsteen. *Calm down, calm down,* Tisch pleaded. *I didn't tell you about Peltz because I thought it was a hundred-to-one shot he would come up with the money.* Tisch pledged not to sell Records except through Yetnikoff.

Yetnikoff was pacified, yet guarded. CBS directors were also upset when they learned of the Peltz discussions. "Larry did what he accused Tom of doing," complained a former Wyman ally on the board, recalling how Tisch erupted when he learned of Wyman's secret talks with Coca-Cola. Within weeks, Yetnikoff had three bids for the company—from Peltz, from Disney, and from Sony.

Sony had the most money and a compelling dream: to mate the software of CBS Records with the hardware customers use to play the music. For Yetnikoff Sony had something else: its leaders were farthest away and left their managers alone. After several huddles with Sony officials, Yetnikoff was enthusiastic. He pestered Tisch in what reporter Peter Boyer would call "a sort of a divestiture-by-annoyance approach," until Tisch, too, was enthusiastic about both Sony and getting rid of Yetnikoff. "The guy's a nut!" Tisch would come to say of him.

But Paley and the CBS board did not like the idea of selling Records. "My logic tells me to sell it," Paley told Tisch. "My instincts tell me not to. Records were part and parcel of CBS, and had a bright future." Paley had nursed Records to life, and he told Tisch he could not part with it. Besides, Paley said, directors had told him that after hand-to-hand combat with those who threatened to dismember CBS, they were resistant to the idea of selling. Tisch feared that he had climbed too far out on a limb, and telephoned Yetnikoff at home.

"I don't know where the board sits on this," Tisch said. "Stop all discussion." This was difficult, since Sony executives were at that very moment in his living room. He put Sony's investment banker, Peter G. Peterson, chairman of the Blackstone Group, on the phone with Tisch, but Tisch excused himself and hung up. Sorry, Yetnikoff said, they had to await the board meeting scheduled for November 13.

On Tisch's agenda for the meeting was a discussion of the sale of Records to Sony and board approval to pursue the sale of the magazines division as well. Directors entered the boardroom briefed, there having been considerable telephone traffic prior to the meeting. "Everybody on the board was talking to everybody," said director Michel Bergerac. "And one reason was that Tisch was not making an effort to get close to the board."

Directors felt that Tisch had not been straight with them. They resented that he had refused to sign a standstill and felt it was because all along he schemed to own CBS. They said he had fired Peter Derow less than a month after pledging there would be no bloodletting. They thought he had been devious for not consulting the board on the sale of parts of the company. They thought he was engaged in a charade with the CEO search committee because the committee rarely met and because they suspected Tisch secretly wanted the CEO job himself. The search committee was a "joke," observed Frank Stanton, who along with Walter Cronkite was a consultant to a committee that never once consulted them. "I had a list I was prepared to talk about, but no one ever called me up." Even among some of Tisch's supporters on the board there was a sense that he had betrayed what they remembered as his September 10 vow not to liquidate CBS. And a clear majority of directors were unsettled by Tisch's attempt to accumulate cash by selling off parts of CBS. At a time when companies vied to become global communications giants, it made no strategic sense to them to narrow CBS's scope. A principal proponent of this viewpoint was Jim Wolfensohn, who reminded board members that Tisch was doing what they had denied Ted Turner and Marvin Davis the opportunity to do.

The November board meeting was tense and interminable. Tisch was livid that directors had conspired behind his back. He shouted that they had formed "a cabal" to undermine his leadership, which prompted Wolfensohn and Harold Brown to complain that it was he who had conspired to circumvent the board. Tisch was especially angry with Wolfensohn and Brown, who he believed secretly shopped CBS over the summer and who, several board members attested, were ringleaders in polling the board by phone before this meeting. In Wolfensohn, Tisch saw Brutus, someone who pretended to be a friend and then stabbed him. In Brown, Tisch saw a man he thought had the highest IQ of almost anyone he had ever met, yet who was a dumbbell when it came to business, a flaw compounded by Brown's condescending air. He also blamed Henry Schacht, who kept quiet at board meetings but who was in the thick of the telephone traffic. According to a board member, Tisch threatened at one point to "buy shares" in Schacht's Cummins Engine Company "and put it in play." The meeting became personal, ugly. Tisch concedes he was "disappointed," but said he threatened no one.

Tisch was also disappointed when the board unanimously rejected the sale of CBS Records, and directors flat-out said they were uninterested in selling CBS Magazines. Tisch was not appeased that they agreed to sell CBS's one-third share in Trintex, an electronic service meant to provide home banking, shopping, and information services. The board bought Tisch's argument that since its initial 1984 investment, Trintex—which didn't promise to be workable for another two years—had drained CBS of about $40 million; but they didn't agree that Records and Magazines were bad businesses to be in.

The board's refusal to sell CBS Records troubled Tisch. He believed nostalgia was clouding their judgment. In fact, Tisch and the board prized different things. Tisch wanted cash; the board wanted to keep intact a diversified communications company. For Tisch, who was used to getting his way at Loews, the pain of rejection was acute.

Ties between Tisch and the CBS board were further strained by the November release of directors' SEC depositions. It dismayed Tisch to learn that despite their silence at the September 10 board meeting, eight directors had been alerted by Wyman of his discussions with Coca-Cola. "I was shocked," admits Tisch. Added to his sense of treachery was a conviction that the board was preventing him from taking effective business action. Here he was the CEO, the major shareholder, and yet he couldn't do what was necessary to run the company. On top of all this, the search committee resisted anointing him the permanent CEO, a position he now coveted.

Did he have to beg for the job? These sons of bitches still don't understand Loews owns 25 percent! Just as they don't understand Bob Tisch belongs on the board! Tisch raged, and among the options he explored with counsel George Vradenburg and others was a proxy fight to rid the board of at least three members—Wolfensohn, Brown, and Schacht.

Tisch's relationship with the acting chairman was more complicated. The board's refusal to sell Records or consider unloading the magazines demonstrated Paley's sudden sway over the board—and over the public, since he was Mr. CBS. While Tisch was obsessed with Wolfensohn, Brown, and Schacht, it was Bill Paley who most impeded his freedom, including his freedom to speak his mind. A board that by the early eighties had tired of Paley's sniping now invited him to hover, protecting them from Tisch. Paley's presence also impeded Tisch's introduction to the programming side of the business. So while Tisch concentrated on streamlining, he left Paley to foray out to the West Coast. "Tisch always addresses Paley with the greatest respect and defers to him on programming in all meetings," observed Michel Bergerac. "And after he does that, he relies on his own counsel." Publicly, these two allies had rid CBS of Tom Wyman. Publicly, they professed mutual admiration. Within the walls of CBS, however, they treated each other in "ceremonial fashion," said a top CBS executive, like two senators, ever polite, ever wary.

Nevertheless, Tisch was not deterred from his drive to cut costs. Starting on November 11, he commenced a series of budget reviews with the twelve CBS divisions that were preparing their 1987 budgets. Each division came to the boardroom for two to three hours. Of all the numbers that he reviewed, Tisch was especially annoyed by the $168 million CBS was budgeted to pay its 206 affiliated stations in 1987. This figure—which was more than double the network's 1986 profits—was the compensation CBS would pay to its stations for carrying the 115 hours a week of programming the network supplied them. Tisch didn't comprehend the logic. *CBS was paying stations to air programs the network supplied them free of charge? And on top of this the network gave them forty or so minutes of ad time to sell locally each week?* At a time when CBS network profits would fall to about $80 million and only because NBC had record profits would the three networks together earn $300 million—down from $800 million in 1984—why, Tisch asked, couldn't the affiliates make some adjustment in compensation? And why did CBS pay $30 to $50 million more than either NBC or ABC paid?

At a meeting with the Broadcast Group, Tisch was told how the system worked: *The only distribution system CBS owned was its four stations, reaching just 19 percent of the country. Otherwise it depended, as the other networks did, on its local affiliated stations to show network programs on local screens. In effect, the network was renting viewers by paying stations to carry its shows. Then the network went to advertisers and assured them that if they purchased ads at a certain hour they would reach a nationwide audience.*

How many hours of network programming don't the affiliates run? asked Tisch.

They clear about 98.5 percent of prime time, answered Tony Malara, president of the CBS Network, to whom the affiliate relations department reported. *They clear about 96 percent of our daytime schedule and just under 90 percent of CBS's late-night offerings.*

Tisch was offended by the entire concept. *Why shouldn't there be changes—immediately?*

The room fell silent. Gene Jankowski, to whom all of the Broadcast Group reported, said nothing. Nor did other executives speak up. It fell to Tony Malara to respond. In contrast to the smooth-faced, somber-suited types in the room, Malara stood out. He was a college dropout who favored bright polka-dot ties and sported a neatly trimmed beard shaved around the cheeks, which gave him a cherubic look even though he is built like a retired offensive guard. In the twenty-one years before he joined CBS in 1978, Malara had worked first as a radio disc jockey and then as general manager of WWNY-TV in Watertown, New York, a CBS affiliate. Malara brought to the task of cajoling affiliates one other qualification: He was the former Republican chairman of rural Jefferson County in upstate New York. In contrast to the "cool" types in this room with Larry Tisch, Malara was unafraid to show emotion. He was grateful for the exalted office he had achieved and displayed his devotion to CBS by logging up to 200,000 miles on the road each year and by always wearing to work a set of cuff links embossed with the CBS eye.

But the verbosity that charmed Republican party functionaries or CBS's affiliates did not help Malara with Tisch. To Tisch's rat-tat-tat questions Malara offered no quick responses. Instead he countered with a long-winded explanation of how the concept of affiliated stations began with General Sarnoff in 1926 as a way to get radio stations to play music and thus entice listeners to purchase RCA radios. The bounty paid to the stations went up in 1928 when William Paley decided the only way CBS radio could compete with the two NBC radio networks was by hiking compensation in return for exclusive access to the affiliate. Tisch invoked dollars and cents logic, Malara network tradition: *Compensation has existed for nearly sixty years. It's tradition, a partnership, a sacred bond. This is not a good time to cut compensation since CBS is no longer number one. If we anger our partners they could switch to NBC or ABC. Or replace more of our shows with syndicated product. Besides, we couldn't cut all at once since we sign two-year contracts with each station.*

Tisch erupted: *Partners! A true partner would offer relief. Why won't they help us? Why won't they share the bad times as well as the good?*

It's the way the business works, and has worked for sixty years, said Malara. *If we go back and ask for relief, the affiliates will say, "Why should we help you? My business is no different than yours. I have to pay for programming and sell ads.*

Their profit margins are larger! Tisch shot back.

True, said Malara. *But compensation is a small piece of our cost of sales. Every business pays for distribution, from Pepsi-Cola to CBS. And everyone knows that CBS has the best stations in the business.*

If they don't cooperate, we should cut or drop the affiliation! declared Tisch, who by now was beet-red.

The only weapon the network has in its arsenal is to drop the affiliate, said Malara. *That is like the atom bomb, the ultimate weapon. You want to save it and use it only if you have to.*

By this point Tisch was no longer listening. *Everyone knows a network affiliation at least doubles the value of a station. Why? Because the network is providing programming—free. If we add to the value of a station, shouldn't we get some consideration in return? This is all bullshit!* To Tisch, Tony Malara was full of windy excuses. One of Tisch's strengths as a businessman is that once his mind is made up he does not look back. What Malara was trying to tell him, without success, was that the network was a different business. He did not control the affiliates the way he did bellhops at Loews hotels. Malara was being candid, but to Tisch he came across as another network slave to the past. "Tony alienated Tisch because he didn't know how to sell it to Larry," observed one of Jankowski's associates. "Gene knows how to sell."

Tisch ordered Malara to prepare a study exploring where they could cut compensation, a study to be ready before they met with the affiliate board in January. He asked Malara to come back with $50 million in savings.

Another saving Tisch had in mind was to cut CBS's stock option plan, which in 1985 conferred stock on 17,044 eligible employees, many from the ranks of management. The stock was held in trust for them, and upon leaving CBS the extra value belonged to the employee. With still another round of layoffs and falling network profits, Tisch thought it inequitable and in bad taste to reward executives. "I wanted a period to evaluate who was valuable and who wasn't," he said. The current plan, he thought, was more in the interest of managers than shareholders, some of whom would pocket fifty thousand dollars or so if the plan remained intact. With the board's concurrence, Tisch announced the plan would be suspended at least until the spring.

Having been on the job nearly three months and having gone through the budget reviews, Tisch was ready to alter the management structure as well. He still thought the structure cumbersome, with too many layers of managers. So Tisch asked Jankowski to prepare a new, streamlined structure—*delayered* was the preferred word—for the Broadcast Group. Jankowski offered a draft, which Tisch altered, and in December it was announced that an entire layer of upper management would be reduced. Gone would be the three executive vice president titles. Instead, there would be five operating division presidents—Entertainment; News; Sports and Broadcast Operations; the Television Stations; and the CBS Television Network—reporting to Jankowski. Tisch's assumption was that as he shed organization boxes he would be better able to identify duplication.

At first blush, the executives could claim this was a lateral move since they were losing only a title, not functions. All, that is, save Tony Malara, who lost the network sales department, lost direct access to Jankowski, and was returned to his old job as head of Affiliate Relations. Malara also lost his title, president of the CBS Television Network, which was awarded to Tom Leahy, to whom he now reported. Malara would be called senior vice president, Distribution. "It was the first time it ever happened to me," said Malara, depressed by the demotion. Malara was seated in his well-appointed office, thinking of leaving the network, accepting condolence calls from general managers and other friends in the industry. "Yes, we're in a new environment, and we can change," he said in December of 1986. "But . . . affiliates are the only way we have to reach people, except through direct broadcast satellites and backyard dishes, which viewers can't afford."

Malara was not the only morose CBS employee. The delayering of executives, the drumbeat of layoffs, the elimination of the medical center, the CBS store, the affirmative action program, the management seminars, the employee newsletter, and such perks as the stock option plan all saved money, but there was a cost as well. "There's no question CBS had to cut," said a dispirited executive at the time. "But what's missing is an incentive for those who stay behind. Tisch missed the point that this type of compensation gives us an incentive in tough times. We would only be rewarded if we turn the company around. At Chrysler Lee Iacocca gave stock rights to employees and said, 'If the company turns around you'll be rewarded.' " No one, this second-tier executive complained, was telling Tisch this, certainly not Gene Jankowski, who was trying to demonstrate that he was a champion of change.

CBS employees fretted that Tisch was not spending enough time thinking about employee morale and how to motivate an organization. The fear was that he had spent too many years in front of a Quotron machine staring at lifeless numbers. There was little contact with Tisch, little corporate interchange since Tisch had eliminated the employee newsletter, the management seminars they would attend at a Long Island retreat, and even the monthly breakfasts with employees from various departments Tom Wyman used to conduct. Reaching out, trying to make employees feel good, was not Larry Tisch's style.

In fact, Tisch's style of management became a subject of intense speculation at CBS. By December, employees felt that he was neglecting the human factor.

Tisch did not follow the practice that had worked so well for him at Loews—that is, hiring people he trusted and leaving them alone while he functioned as chairman of the board. At CBS, Tisch did not have people he knew and felt he could trust. So he was serving as a hands-on CEO, a job for which Larry Tisch had little experience.

"It's clear to me," said one executive, "that Larry thinks that anyone who works here is a fool. *'If you're so terrific, why aren't you out there making millions?'* He knows we have talent, but we're less than the people he really admires, who make big dollars in their own business. He's friendly to me, but there's never any sense of 'Who are you? Who are your kids?' " There was a coolness he detected in Tisch, a distrust also communicated by the way he brought in Coopers & Lybrand.

Unlike Wyman, Tisch was an owner, treating the company's money as if it were his own, as one-quarter of it was. In December Tisch and Yetnikoff were in California to visit Barry Diller at Twentieth Century Fox, and Tisch invited Yetnikoff to breakfast at his Beverly Hills Hotel suite. Yetnikoff was hungry. As Yetnikoff studied the menu, Tisch said, "You can have half a grapefruit or orange juice."

"I'm hungry," answered Yetnikoff. "I want a bagel!"

"You know how much a bagel costs in this hotel?" exclaimed Tisch.

Sulking, Yetnikoff decided not to eat. His attention shifted to transportation. "Let me call Diller and have him send a car for us," he said.

"No," snapped Tisch. "I'll drive."

They hurried downstairs where the doorman ushered them to a two-year-old Mercury from the CBS motor pool. Tisch had no cash and, whispering, asked Yetnikoff to leave a tip.

"How much?" asked Yetnikoff.

"Five dollars," Tisch said.

"What? It's too little!"

They fought over the tip. And they fought over who should drive. Yetnikoff lost both times. The only satisfaction for Yetnikoff was that Tisch got lost on the way to Fox. And, to make a point against a man he came to detest, at CBS's subsequent monthly board meetings Yetnikoff always brought along a bagel.

"Larry is terrible at articulating things," observed a member of the Tisch family. "He just went around the world and I asked him how it was. He said, 'Fine.' " Perhaps this would have mattered less if Tisch had had beside him his brother, Bob, who always served as the more human face of the two. When Loews decided to fire eight hundred insurance employees at CNA in Chicago, it was Bob who did the dirty work, handling it smoothly. Without brother Bob, Larry had no sounding board, no trusted advisor. He was performing executive functions that were new to him. He was surrounded by people he didn't know, and who more often than not were so eager to get to the point for fear he would snap off their heads that they volunteered little information.

Like Bob Wright, Tisch was flying solo. Typically, he would spend his day breakfasting and lunching in his private dining room with outside people, often asking them what they thought of various CBS executives, which also served to arouse insecurity at CBS. As did the regular appearances in the office of his sons. One day, it was feared, the Tisches would transform CBS into a family dynasty. With a son sometimes present, Tisch would conduct CBS meetings around his nearly empty desktop, one eye cocked to a single TV monitor which, with the sound off, was set to the Financial News Network. Tisch would usually rush through the agenda, and meetings were brief. During his first months at CBS, Tisch rarely visited Loews's offices a block away. Nor was it necessary, since his son Jimmy filled his father's financial role and they talked on the phone incessantly. But by December, Tisch was wandering over to Loews more often and had resumed his customary afternoon departures to attend his daily bridge game at the Regency Whist Club.

Tisch paid no attention to office furnishings; the only changes he made in the office he inherited from Wyman were the family pictures surrounding the plain oak table he used as a desk and the single TV set, which substituted for the now-unused wall unit containing three TV sets silently tuned to each network. Tisch could be equally unpretentious in his dealings with people, and far less remote than people at CBS thought. In December of 1986, for example, Jim Jensen, the anchor at New York's WCBS-TV, wrote Tisch protesting the decision to cut free newspapers delivered to the newsroom and the local anchors. "In order for the anchor correspondents to have the necessary background for the stories we report," Jensen wrote, "it is absolutely essential for them to daily read four and five newspapers. . . . I once in my lifetime worked in an auto plant assembling transmissions. I don't recall the company asking us to bring to work with us nuts and bolts from home. For journalists, having a daily supply of newspapers translates into our form of 'nuts and bolts.' I ask you to reconsider this decision. . . ." Within days, Tisch's secretary had called to announce Tisch had rescinded the order.

Tisch loved the challenge of CBS. At lunch that fall with Leonard Goldenson, his old friend asked, "What do you think of the business?"

"Leonard," Tisch responded, "the business is getting so bad it's getting interesting."

Tisch saw himself as the taskmaster, and his task, as he saw it, was to alter CBS's culture, to get employees to focus on problems in a different way. The way, Tisch thought, he had done at CNA when Loews took over the Chicago-based insurance conglomerate in the early seventies. CNA had been a go-go company, which had branched out into nursing homes, dental and medical supplies, cable TV, and real estate, among other businesses. *Get rid of them!* Tisch ordered. *Get rid of the huge overhead staffs! Get back to basics—to the insurance business.* That is what he planned to do at CBS: get back to the basics of broadcasting.

For this task Tisch would lean on Gene Jankowski. The amiable Jankowski, the son of a Buffalo truck driver, had some difficulty adjusting to Tisch's style. Jankowski had reported to three previous CBS presidents, each of whom had come to think of Jankowski as a friend —until each was fired. After he was booted from CBS, Tom Wyman had more time for leisurely lunches. One of these was with his predecessor, John Backe. One subject that intrigued them was Jankowski, who had been a stalwart loyalist to each. "Let me ask you something," said Backe. "Did you ever hear from Gene Jankowski after you left?"

"No," said Wyman. "Have you?"

"No," said Backe.

Jankowski was most comfortable working within a structure, with memos and a chain of command; Tisch was a manager who discouraged memos and flaunted chains of command, preferring to pick up the phone and call one of Jankowski's people directly or to get his information from a network of sources outside CBS. To watch Jankowski and Tisch together was to be struck by the awkwardness of their relationship. On more than one occasion, Jankowski stopped a reporter coming from a meeting with Tisch and asked, "How am I doing with my boss?" But whatever discomfort Jankowski felt was camouflaged from employees, and offset by the conviction, said a key aide, that "he was hanging on to the steering wheel in rough seas."

That is not always how Jankowski's role was perceived from the inside. He was viewed as compliant. "Gene has the bumper-car concession," observed Tony Malara. "He's the bumper. Tisch takes advantage of him being there. Gene is the soul of morality, probably the straightest arrow in our business. By keeping him around when he makes all these moves, Larry gains from the comfort Gene's presence provides."

He also gained from Jankowski's flexibility. Never a champion of cost cutting, after Coopers & Lybrand appeared on the scene Jankowski plugged their virtues. "They have effectively worked with all of us and helped us get some things done that in the past we couldn't get done," he said, sounding as if he had long been a frustrated reformer. In fact, Gene Jankowski frustrated many of the executives who worked for him because they found him maddening slow to make decisions and utterly averse to risk. Often Jankowski would tell his people, "I want no winners or losers." Everything had to be compromised. "Gene never wanted to come to his own conclusion out of a meeting," said News vice president Eric Ober. "He wanted consensus. The problem is if you want strong people in your broadcast division, it's very hard to get a consensus." The real loser, some CBS managers felt, was initiative.

But Tisch appreciated Jankowski's loyalty, as well as his ties to the broadcast community. In fact, as 1986 was drawing to a close Tisch was feeling pretty content with the job he had done. His biggest impact, he said, was in "making people realize we're in a changed business." He didn't think he had made any "major mistakes." His one great frustration was his recalcitrant board of directors. He had done a superb job, he thought, and yet they resisted him, resisted selling Records or Magazines, resisted offering him the permanent CEO job they should have known he was prepared to take. Instead, he had to listen to professorial lectures from the likes of Harold Brown, had to make nice to directors who had sat like stones while Tom Wyman was ruining the business. Informally he suggested to the board late that fall that they add some new blood. Specifically, he recommended two friends—attorney Arthur Liman, who had been such an important bridge to Bill Paley during the effort to oust Wyman, and New York University president John Brademas, whom Tisch as chairman of the board of trustees had recruited to N.Y.U. and later added to his own Loews board.

The directors turned Tisch down. As the board once worried that Tisch had a clandestine plan to take over the company, now they worried that he planned, in the words of one director, "to dismember the company, and one of the ways to prevent it was to keep the same board."

While Tisch felt undermined, so did some directors when they gathered on December 10, 1986, for their monthly meeting. Their unhappiness was part personal, part policy. James Wolfensohn, his full head of dark hair flopping like an orchestra conductor's, entered the board meeting smarting from what he perceived as a series of insults from Tisch. He resented, he said, Tisch's "constant reiteration that I tried to sell the company, that I acted improperly, that I wasn't giving him support on the sale of Records." There was more. Wolfensohn resented Tisch for conveying the impression to mutual friends that he had been disloyal. And he was still angry at Tisch for accusing him and Harold Brown of "a cabal" at the November board meeting. Wolfensohn said nothing, simmering quietly through the open session of the December board meeting. But when the staff was excused and the board entered executive session, Wolfensohn erupted. Turning to Tisch he declared, "I object to being brutalized at board meetings."

You object! I object to having my leadership undermined by you and Harold Brown! retorted Tisch. "The assertions of pain and suffering came fast and furious," said one longtime board member.

After this brief outburst, the combatants retreated, seemingly embarrassed by their display of raw emotion. However, the ceasefire did not bring peace. Real policy differences between Tisch and most of the directors were now apparent. Directors were alarmed that Tisch the trader lacked a strategic plan. Why was he breaking up the company? Three months earlier a search committee had been appointed to find a permanent CEO, yet directors noted that Tisch had not interviewed a single possible candidate. Tisch was sixty-three years old, and directors were concerned that while he concentrated on getting rid of employees he failed to plan for his own succession. The directors liked Jankowski, but they did not see him as a number one.

At this executive session, directors pressed Tisch to explain his plan of succession. Tisch answered their queries, but he wasn't happy with what he took to be their preoccupation with planning. It was all so bureaucratic! But he curbed his temper and responded that he had identified just three executives at CBS who might one day become president and CEO: Sports president Neal Pilson, Stations president Peter Lund, and a choice that surprised board members because they barely knew him, News president Howard Stringer.

Stringer had caught Tisch's eye. With Pilson and Lund he talked about sports rights fees or profit margins at the stations. With Stringer he could talk about the Middle East, invite him to his apartment to meet Sam Nunn when the Georgia senator was in town and came to dinner, or get the inside poop on Ronald Reagan. Tisch was a fan of News, and a fan of Stringer's, with whom he probably spent as much time as he did with Jankowski.

Another reason Tisch and Stringer talked a lot was Diane Sawyer's contract, which expired at the end of the month. Tisch was distressed to hear that NBC had dangled before her a $1.6 million offer. Like his friend Tom Murphy, Tisch disapproved of the kind of raiding practiced by the "old culture," a mindless competition that raised costs for everyone. Tisch felt strongly about Sawyer. She popped over regularly to lunch at Black Rock with Tisch and was sometimes escorted to functions by Paley. Sawyer and her friend, investment banker Richard Holbrooke, had dined at the Tisches' Fifth Avenue apartment, where she fastened her porcelain face and baby blue eyes on Billie as well as Larry Tisch. At public dinners, while crowds gathered about Larry Tisch, Sawyer could be seen chatting alone with Billie Tisch. "Diane would be a loss for any network," Tisch said at the time. The matter is in Stringer's lap, he said, adding, "If I can help Stringer I will."

Stringer would need help. Sawyer's agent, Richard Leibner, was seeking a lot more than the $800,000 she now earned annually at CBS, and had already spoken with Larry Grossman at NBC and Roone Arledge at ABC. "Diane," Leibner complained, "would like to do more than *60 Minutes,"* where she appeared only three out of every five weeks. Leibner wanted a coanchor slot for her at one of the three networks, preferably not at CBS where his main client, Dan Rather, presided.

For Stringer, the negotiations with Sawyer posed ticklish problems. He had to contend with *60 Minutes* executive producer, Don Hewitt, who didn't want to lose Sawyer yet was "mightily upset" that she seemed to be disparaging the value of *60 Minutes.* Like the other network News presidents, he also did not want to risk offending his anchor. No matter what syrup Rather poured on Sawyer publicly, Stringer knew how Rather really felt. Like Jennings and Brokaw, Rather didn't want Sawyer or anyone else sitting beside him when ten million viewers tuned to the *CBS Evening News.* Stringer felt a coanchor team was too cumbersome. Moreover, survey research showed that viewers sought "authority" and strong journalism from their network anchors; and fair or not, these qualities were usually associated with male correspondents. Unless the anchor was perceived as callow—like the twenty-six-year-old Peter Jennings when he failed as an ABC anchor in the sixties—there was a fault line in most research separating male and female correspondents; a line between "authority" and "likability." Reporters like Sawyer and NBC's Connie Chung ranked relatively low in "authority," but considerably higher than males such as Rather in "likability." The concern news executives had was that viewers might treasure likability in Oprah Winfrey or a local anchor, but that they expected authority from their network anchor.

There was one other factor in Stringer's mind, a more personal one: Diane Sawyer made him uneasy. While she charmed the people above him like Tisch and Paley, she was less popular with colleagues, some of whom found her habit of cupping her face in her hands and asking solicitous questions contrived. "Diane is a beautiful, bright lady, in whose arsenal charm is a major weapon," observed Eric Ober, one of Stringer's two deputies. Ober recalled that Stringer was not pleased when Sawyer telephoned him that fall from Billie and Larry Tisch's apartment and said, "I want you to know I'm here with Larry and Richard and I told him very good things about you."*

Tisch did not promote Sawyer as an anchor, but neither he nor Stringer wanted to lose her. So with a nod from Tisch, Stringer offered her a four-year contract at $1.2 million annually and promised to expand her duties, including substitute anchor when Rather was away. Between the thirty or so million viewers Sawyer reached three weeks out of five on *60 Minutes* versus hosting low-rated Sunday morning shows or filling in occasionally for Brokaw, Sawyer chose to remain at CBS. In addition to more money, Leibner negotiated a window in her new contract which would allow Sawyer to leave if she was offered an anchor position elsewhere.

Satisfied that he and Stringer had retained a budding star, Tisch was now looking forward to another encounter with Stringer in the form of a combined holiday/work tour. Billie and Larry Tisch would be accompanied on visits to CBS News's European bureaus by Stringer and his wife, Jennifer Patterson, a dermatologist. Tisch, who planned to be in Venice over Christmas, said he would like to visit some of the bureaus to get a better understanding of how News functioned, a curiosity that Stringer welcomed. Tisch had been asking questions about News's budget, complaining about excessive spending, as he had about other areas of the network. The trip, Stringer thought, would expose Tisch not just to the numbers but to the real people behind those numbers, which he was confident would work to News's advantage.

Stringer decided on a loosely structured visit, a decision many col-

* Diane Sawyer did not return phone calls seeking confirmation of this call.

leagues would later come to regret. "In preparation for the trip," said Mark Harrington, a Stringer deputy, "the bureau chiefs were all told they would be meeting the head of the company and he was concerned how they spent money and would ask a lot of questions and they should be prepared for it." No one was warned, said Stringer, to be careful, to watch what he said to the boss, to clean things up. The people in the bureaus were all invited to come and meet and talk with Tisch, with no thought that Tisch might wonder why such busy bureaus could, in effect, suspend operations for his sake.

The trip did not go as planned. On December 28 the party arrived in Rome to visit the bureau, dine with bureau chief Peter Schweitzer, do some sightseeing, and meet with the pope the next day. Within moments of his arrival, Tisch kept asking why twenty-two people were necessary when they often sat around like firefighters waiting for an alarm to go off. Schweitzer explained how journalists often had to wait for sources to return their calls, often had to do stakeouts, which took time, often had just returned from weeks on the road and were unwinding. Unlike print reporters, Schweitzer said, they needed time to set up cameras and assemble the team of producer/correspondent/cameraman/soundman for travel. Television was a collaborative business. It was also dependent on pictures; most times a telephone interview wouldn't do. Tisch was hearing an argument that sprang from an ancient journalistic battle between "headquarters" and the "field." Reporters always complained that the "boss" in New York didn't understand. Bud Benjamin recalled the time Bill Stout of CBS was in Saigon and was urgently dispatched to Sydney, Australia, where the executive producer in New York wanted him immediately. "Jesus, you know how far Sydney is from Saigon?" said Stout.

"It's an inch and a half on my map!" shot back the producer.

The Tisches and Stringers arrived in London on the thirtieth, in time for dinner with the bureau staff, which would be followed by a visit the next day to bureau headquarters, New Year's Eve at Covent Garden, and a party at Claridge's. The London visit convinced Tisch that CBS News was even more wasteful than he imagined. At dinner with the bureau staff at the Hotel Connaught, he met a producer who was staying at this expensive landmark and who announced he was off to Scotland for a story.

"What will you do for a room when you get back?" Tisch remembers a colleague asking.

"Oh, I'm going to keep the room at the Connaught while I'm away," answered the producer.

It went downhill from there. One old hand marveled at how in earlier days they produced at least as much news with only nineteen rather than the approximately eighty people CBS now had there, which naturally made Tisch wonder why CBS needed such a big bureau. Later Tisch sat in a control room and watched feeds from Eurovision, a news consortium that supplies pictures from all over the world and adds narration in its own studio. He wondered why CBS couldn't replace some of its overseas staff by substituting this inexpensive, easy-to-use service. Stringer and his people explained that Eurovision was not always available or reliable, and the only way CBS News could authenticate stories was to remain a worldwide news service. Besides, they explained that part of the mission of the London bureau was as a satellite production point for much of CBS's overseas news gathering. London was where pieces were edited and film converted to tape and signals were bounced up to a satellite and back down to New York.

Tisch didn't press the point, but he was still skeptical about the size of the staff, the more so when the London bureau chief wasted everyone's time by arranging for him to meet with the chief rabbi of London.

On January 1, the party arrived in Paris, dined with bureau chief Joel Bernstein and two correspondents, followed the next day by a visit to the new bureau headquarters and dinner with the staff. Tisch was struck by how plush the rented office space was, and was troubled that *60 Minutes* had its own separately rented space.

They arrived in Moscow on January 3, in time for dinner with bureau chief Wyatt Andrews and his three-person staff. Over the next two days they would tour, attend the ballet, and meet with government officials. Tisch was startled that the bureau consisted of just four people, one of whom boasted that they got more pieces on the air than any other European bureau. "Tisch thought Moscow was the perfect bureau," said a News executive who did not make the trip but got an earful. "It consists of four people—a cameraman, a correspondent, a sound man, and a local assistant. What he didn't understand is that Moscow limits reporters to a thirty-mile radius. And you only cover Russia. In Rome you must also cover Africa. From London and France you go all over Europe and the Middle East."

Tisch returned to the U.S. convinced he had to change News, fast. Before the trip, he confided that he knew there was waste but planned no News budget cuts until 1988. After the trip, he would not delay. "I think their budget could be reduced by $100 million," he complained to Fred Meyer. To friends he wondered aloud whether he couldn't cut the roughly $300 million News budget in half, bringing it closer to CNN's $110 million 1986 expenses. And with a third of CBS's costs, CNN was making a profit of almost $40 million. It bugged Tisch that the "culture of News," as he called it, was so self-satisfied, so closed to rethinking how they might deliver quality news more cheaply. CNN, which had almost as many bureaus (eighteen, as opposed to CBS's twenty-three), nevertheless put on six times as much news in a given day for one-third the cost. And CNN was much more aggressive about selling its news overseas, offering services in fifty-three countries, including CNN news packages in fifteen thousand European hotel rooms. With technologically more versatile cameras, editing machines, and video equipment, News staffs had nevertheless swelled rather than shrunk. And Tisch wondered why CBS News had a dozen people earning more than $500,000 annually.

The "trip," as it came to be called, bonded Tisch and Stringer on a personal level. Tisch enjoyed his company and was more convinced than ever that he had chosen wisely. The trip also provided Tisch with what many in News came to feel was the wrong kind of education. "The questions he asked were remarkably narrowly focused—'Why couldn't you save a little money here?' " remembers Tom Bettag, Dan Rather's executive producer. "He didn't ask: 'Help me understand the mission and process.' " The absence of planning before the trip became a common lament. Dan Rather remembers telling Stringer, "Howard, you've got to tell those European bureaus to get everyone out on assignment. Larry ought to walk into a ghost town everywhere he goes." It was, concluded Rather, "a mistake not to carefully plan that trip. It was a mistake on all our parts." Stringer disagreed. Some things, he suggested, couldn't be anticipated: "I never thought people would run around saying, 'We don't have enough work.' "

Tisch was incensed. "I saw waste and inefficiency and redundancy. . . . CBS News had an $89 million budget in 1978. And it skyrocketed to $300 million in 1986! If you took the normal inflation increase, it would have been just $145 million in 1986." Tisch told Stringer he thought CBS was overstaffed and could probably find $50 million in savings. "Don't get to know these people," he advised Stringer. "You may have to lay them off."

Stringer agreed with Tisch that people in News too often equated "quality" with money spent. Like Tisch, Stringer saw waste and overpaid, self-satisfied "stars." On the other hand, he was the captain of a crew that had been through three News presidents in little more than a year and some awful storms. They desperately needed calm. He wanted to slow Tisch down, and to prepare Rather for the leaner times ahead. Rather told Stringer that if Tisch tried to slash News it would be the third set of News cuts in little more than a year. *The news division can't handle that, Howard. Cut the budget and I'm off the reservation.* Rather, like Grossman at NBC, believed News should be spending more money, not less. He wanted, he said, to "put more reporters both overseas and at home," believing that CBS could win by investing resources its competitors wouldn't.

Stringer was struggling with two gorillas at once. Seeking to co-opt Rather, Stringer invited him to meet with Tisch to discuss the trip. Over lunch, recalled Rather, Tisch kept asking: "Don't you think waste and redundancy are important?" Rather said they were, but emphasized that "quality" required a worldwide news apparatus, which cost money. It also required a team united in its pride, secure that a pink slip was not in the next interoffice mail.

"There was a lot of posturing at lunch," remembers Rather. "Larry was coming on strong—'I see what I see.' He was not in a listening mode. Howard, who usually is very good in these situations, was very nervous. I tried to finesse the lunch."

The pressures on Stringer grew. Gene Jankowski, who anticipated Tisch's moods and sometimes overreacted to them, was pushing Stringer to *get tough.* Flanagan of Coopers & Lybrand, from whom News had been roped off, was asking questions. Somehow Stringer had to reconcile an alarmed Tisch and a defensive news division.

Stringer felt his team should hear from Tisch directly and, perhaps, challenge the boss. He arranged for Tisch to come over to the West Fifty-seventh Street Broadcast Center on the morning of January 12, 1987, to meet the senior News staff of managers and producers. Avuncular in manner at this meeting, Tisch nevertheless was direct. He announced that News spent too much money, was overstaffed, and could save $50 million over the next twelve to eighteen months.

News executives replied: *If we cut too much, CBS will no longer have a twenty-four-hour news service. We could package news pictures, as Eurovision does, but cut too deeply and we will no longer be able to report what goes in the package. Or mine sources. Or provide the contextual reporting that distinguishes a network from a local newscast. We might have to rely on unproven twenty-four-year-old stringers or free-lancers, as CNN does. We might have to forego the "body watch" on the pope, the cameras that trail the pontiff just as they trail the president's every public appearance, always ready should an assassination attempt occur.*

"We have to take acceptable risks," Tisch responded. To make choices was not censorship. And one choice News should make, he said, was to figure out, as Ted Turner's CNN had, how to generate fresh revenues by selling film from its archives or distributing its newscasts in Europe. *The world is changing. News must change,* he declared.

"The people who came out of that meeting were really shaken," said Tom Bettag. "I heard people saying, 'Boy, we really misjudged that guy.' " There was a feeling of betrayal, which perhaps said as much about their illusions as it did about Tisch. And there was a future concern—as there was at NBC and ABC—that their new owner was about to redefine the mission of network news. Would they remain a twenty-four-hour news-gathering operation with a large group of correspondents? Or would they become a packaging operation with a few stars parachuting into distant lands they did not know intimately?

Jankowski defended his boss: "Larry has a way of using numbers to get people's attention." Certainly Tisch succeeded in getting the attention of the news division, and just to make sure, a few days later someone—Tisch says it was not him—set Flanagan loose. Flanagan and his auditors appeared at the broadcast center to meet with Operations and Engineering and induced near panic when they talked to Stringer and requested a meeting with his executive producers. The last thing in the world Howard Stringer wanted was for the accountants to meet with the staff. To do so, he felt, would be inflammatory. Nimbly, he asked Tisch to keep Flanagan out of News operations, and in return News would devise its own expenditure reductions. Tisch agreed, and Stringer knew he could now use Flanagan to scare his own team.

Tisch sensed things were going his way at News, as indeed they were at the company as a whole. Embarrassed by their open spat at the December board meeting, Tisch and Wolfensohn managed to patch their differences, aided by a call from Tisch to tell his fellow director he accepted his good faith. The search committee, which had collected a file full of names but had conducted no formal interviews, realized it could hardly deny Tisch the job. As always, Tisch had the power of an owner. Bergerac remembers telling fellow directors, "Either we tell Tisch he can't have it, and if we do how long before he packs the board with people we don't want? And then in a year they will do worse things. So why not give him a crack when he has the desire to do it?" Despite a lingering mistrust and budding strategic differences, the board was in many ways pleased with what Tisch had done. He had excised waste, streamlined management, shed certain businesses, reinvolved Paley. Even Gilpatric, who had been a leader in the anti-Tisch coalition, said he was pleased: "He and Paley are still on a parallel course. I don't think there has been any loss of confidence on the part of the board in Tisch. . . . He got a good price for the publishing division. The board feels he lets everyone have their say. There's been only one flare-up between Jim Wolfensohn and Larry. . . . And we all sense that if we brought someone in to be CEO, Larry would want to be chairman and Bill wouldn't want to give it up."

Paley, as Wyman had learned months earlier, was a linchpin. To insure tranquility and, not incidentally, his own permanent chairmanship, the founder, along with Frank Thomas, helped broker a peace. They would convene the directors for a special dinner, where it was unanimously agreed that the entire board would be renominated for another term. "I have no problems with the board," Tisch recalls saying. "I have no intention to change it." In return, directors would make Tisch the permanent CEO and Paley the permanent chairman. With Tisch away at a brother-in-law's funeral, the board voted unanimously on January 14, 1987 to make him the CEO, Paley the chairman, and to renew the directors' lease.

Tisch was happy, even though the CBS network ended 1986 with a meager pretax profit of about $80 million. Still, that was a good deal better than ABC, which lost $70 million. Tisch was not content that CBS's stock price closed the year at a relatively low $128 a share, but he had many reasons to be pleased. The uncertainty over the leadership of the company was over. He had gotten the body count down—there were one thousand fewer positions at CBS at the end of the year than at the beginning. He still had hopes of reducing affiliate compensation, though he had lost leverage when his friend Tom Murphy announced in January that he was dropping plans to cut compensation and NBC announced it would boost parts of its compensation package. He had hopes of buying at least three stations in the top twenty markets, though he would stay with the four stations CBS already owned rather than be stampeded into paying what he considered exorbitant prices, as he thought GE did when it bid $270 million in early 1987 to acquire WTVJ-TV in Miami. Tisch could note with satisfaction that CBS expected $154 million in profits from its four stations in 1987. Tisch also felt that he had begun to dent the CBS culture, had goaded it to be more alert, more cost-conscious. And he was pleased with the applause from Wall Street, which was beginning to proclaim that CBS shares were undervalued.

But during his first months as CEO Tisch paid less attention to traditional measures of network success. He did not improve CBS's distribution system. There was growing consternation among network executives that Tisch was too much a prisoner of his cost-conscious past to recognize the importance of acquiring a station on the rare occasions when one became available in a major urban market. In refusing to match GE's bid for Miami's WTVJ-TV, Tisch was doing what he had done in hotels or with oil tankers—looking for a bargain. There were none, so he and CBS were left with their four owned stations covering 19 percent of the nation, compared to NBC's 22 percent or ABC's nearly 25 percent coverage. Nevertheless, Tisch assured CBS shareholders that he was earning more annually (7 percent) on two-year treasury bills than the return CBS could achieve from another TV station, which did not reassure the board since a station was an asset that usually appreciated in value each year.

Perhaps the greatest source of unease at CBS was over programming. A network spends between 70 and 80 percent of its budget on what goes on the air, including license fees and rights and production costs for entertainment, news, and sports programming. And programming was where networks, if their ratings were strong, made most of their money, particularly from prime-time shows. Unfortunately, CBS's entertainment schedule had not only slipped into second place, but in 1986 CBS actually lost 5 percent of its prime-time audience. While Tisch concentrated on quantifiable things—costs, profit margins, return on treasury bills—CBS's product faltered.

Finally, there was the morale problem. No one disputed CBS's poor morale—not even Tisch, who said it was to be expected while the network was getting its house in order. Others were less stoic. "If you look at him in terms of morale, he's wrecked it," complained Frank Stanton. The former CBS president worried that Tisch couldn't motivate people, and this was a business where people—not a bond issue, not an assembly line, not technology, not a patent or a formula—produced a successful product. Tisch, the worry went, was trying to quantify too much. A producer who lunched with him that fall in Paley's private dining room paused to marvel at the Ben Shahn and Jasper Johns paintings.

Impatiently, Tisch cut him off, gesturing at the paintings. "They belong in a museum!" he declared, eager to get back to concrete business.

10

ABC: MARRYING TWO COMPANIES, JANUARY TO SEPTEMBER 1987

By January 1987, the start of Cap Cities' second year at ABC, the Cold War within the network had thawed. At the annual January Phoenix management retreat, the ABC contingent laughed more easily at the jokes, seemed more relaxed. There was a sense that "we're a single company," John Sias felt. By then, Sias had toned down his own act and was playing fewer practical jokes. He even had some praise for Roone Arledge and the news division.

But there would be fresh reminders starting that winter not of enemies within, but of those without. The new network owners at Cap Cities—and at GE and Loews—brought with them the confidence, even hubris, that comes with success. They were determined to be masters of their fate, believed they could quickly impose changes, believed they could continue to be the lions they had always been. Yet now, for the first time in their careers, these eminent businessmen sometimes felt more like dazed mice, lost in a maze. Tom Murphy thought he could dominate the affiliates when he roared his intention to trim network compensation, but the stations fought back, and by January Murphy had scampered for cover. "Maybe one day we'll take more overt steps," said a subdued John Sias. Despite Murphy's pacific gesture, affiliates continued to snipe at their network—that winter fourteen affiliates preempted part of ABC's weekend schedule and substituted *Star Trek,* a syndicated show.

Viewers were just as uncooperative as affiliates. In the three-network competition, ABC Entertainment was still stuck in third place with such clinkers as the *The Charmings* and *Sledge Hammer!,* both purported comedies. Even though Entertainment chief Brandon Stoddard continued to elicit praise from Hollywood for patiently lining up what Brandon Tartikoff at NBC called "interesting ideas" for future shows, the ABC network still lost money in 1986. And when Cap Cities loosened the purse strings—as it did for Stoddard's $35 million, fourteen-and-one-half-hour *Amerika* miniseries, which they had reluctantly approved only because Stoddard insisted—ABC couldn't escape hostile reviews and low Nielsen ratings.

Stoddard said that he knew the way out of the maze. He insisted network television was a business of "hits." To win big, networks had to gamble big. One hit could rocket ABC to profitability, just as the movie *Dirty Dancing* had done for Vestron, a marginal video distributor, at around this time. The new owners of ABC heard these arguments, but they had no desire to gamble on revenues. They focused on controlling costs. Since eighty percent of a network's budget is committed to what goes on the air, however, there was no way Tom Murphy and Dan Burke could escape by concentrating on the twenty cents of each dollar spent on overhead and engineering.

Then there were the NFL negotiations, another trap from which the new network owners could find no escape. Altogether, the networks expected to lose $125 million on National Football League games. Determined to reduce costs and avoid a bidding war, the three network owners adopted a common posture. They would not pony up the fees demanded by pro football. The football owners countered by saying the NFL would find other customers. The network's were faced with a Hobson's choice: lose money and keep football away from cable, or turn down the NFL and open the door to competition from cable. The networks short- and long-term interests warred, as they did when the networks over the years saved money by airing reruns in summer, which chased away more viewers.

The network owners decided not to pay. There would be, explained Dan Burke, "a natural migration to cable" of sporting events. It was inevitable, the new owners believed, because cable could cover escalating costs by tapping their two sources of revenue (subscription fees and advertising) to subsidize the games, and because cable had many more hours of airtime to devote to sports.

In February 1987, the twenty-eight NFL team owners signed a $1.4 billion five-year agreement which, for the first time, included cable. Thirteen games would be aired on ESPN, the all-sports cable channel. In the short run, Cap Cities, which owns 80 percent of ESPN, would benefit. But in the long run, ABC, CBS, and NBC's decision to save money would hurt the networks, giving audiences an excuse to shop elsewhere.

Cap Cities handed viewers still another excuse to flee the networks.

Because of its devotion to decentralization, Cap Cities decided to allow its owned stations to preempt the ABC network for ESPN games on Sunday night, which is the most watched television night of the week, a night when more than 100 million Americans sit before their TV screens. The irony was delicious. The same network owners who wailed about affiliate greed when the local stations refused to clear network programs were now declaring—as they did when they allowed WABC-TV in New York to advance the network news to 6:30 P.M. for a game show—that the stations' interests came before the networks'. Potentially more worrisome for the network was that the NFL games were just the sort of big event that cable craved. It would hook viewers on the cable habit and become a great advertisement for cable, just as the America's Cup in January of 1987 was for ESPN.

The NFL rights, said Ted Turner, were "a milestone," the beginning of a "continuing migration of the most important programming to cable." At a Cable Television Advertising Bureau convention soon after the negotiations concluded, Turner clucked, "I consider the networks kind of like the Germans were in late 1942: They held a lot of territory very thinly. Two out of three of them are unprofitable now. . . . There has been a basic financial power shift." Cable was coming on strong, nourished by improved programming and by its physical expansion into half of all homes, doubling its reach of the previous four years. While cable thrived, only one network—NBC—made big money in 1986.

What was happening to network television paralleled a shift in the way businesses serviced consumers everywhere. Moviegoers now enjoyed ten choices at their local multiplex theaters. Consumers browsed in a video store with twenty thousand rental options. The convenience of takeout food siphoned customers from restaurants. In retailing, specialty shops and mail-order catalogues helped to empty many department stores. Specialized publications displaced mass circulation magazines. Huge independent booksellers offered thousands of titles instead of the handful of bestsellers featured in the shopping mall chain outlets. In advertising, increasingly the mass market gave way to hundreds of demographically distinct markets, which advertisers now reached by shifting their spending from national advertising to targeted promotion budgets.

A greater democracy of choice was altering the face of television. Network television was reeling from a blow nearly as powerful as the one the industrial revolution delivered to traditional craftsmen. By standardizing production, the industrial revolution made mass-produced goods cheaply available to all consumers. In turn, a mass market heralded the rise of mass advertising. But today new technologies have created markets for a variety of specialized products, targeted to particular groups of consumers. "Our whole system of consumption and marketing and distribution is still based on a mass-production model," said Lester Wunderman, chairman of Wunderman Worldwide, the direct marketing innovator. "Network broadcasting is still in the mass-production business at a time when computer chips allow manufacturers to customize cars or suits." While the public was learning to expect variety, a network offered only a single choice.

"Cap Cities and Larry Tisch are perfect to keep the dinosaur," Wunderman observed. "They will teach it to eat a little less each day. That's what they know. They are not innovators. Not that they're stupid. It's not what they learned to do. They learned cost efficiency. I'm not sure about the GE guys, because the GE culture is innovative. What I am sure about is that the networks have been taken over by the efficient rather than the creative. To generate more value, they've got to be more creative. And that's not their talent. . . . America is dying of efficiency."

John Sias was perhaps proving Wunderman's point about cost cutting at the expense of innovation when he said that "I can see stripping in prime time by the networks." What Sias meant was that instead of producing fresh programs, ABC could reduce costs by purchasing cheaper syndicated game shows or series produced by others and stripping them into the prime-time schedule each day at the same time.

"I don't know how thrilled I'd be to announce to the world that we're going to strip *The Dating Game* at 8:00," said Brandon Stoddard. Ideas like stripping reignited fears among programmers and others that the new owners were not interested in what appeared on the screen. Tom Murphy, for instance, before hosting a press conference for TV reporters and critics in October of 1986, confessed to a small group at lunch that while he liked *Moonlighting* and *Hill Street Blues,* "I'm not a big fan of programming in prime time." The point he was making was not that he had sampled and rejected what prime time had to offer viewers each night, but that he preferred news and sports.

Statements like that alarmed people in the business. The new owners "are not broadcasters," declared Fox chairman Barry Diller. "They are not interested in what the network founders"—Sarnoff, Paley, Goldenson—"were interested in, which is how the product looked and felt." Diller had a point. When William Paley took his family to

Nassau for its annual two-week holiday in the fifties, he spent much of his vacation viewing prints of future and current CBS shows, to his family's chagrin. Good or bad, his shows were his children. Lorimar's hit TV series of the 1970s, *The Waltons,* began as a two-hour movie called *The Homecoming.* The CBS executives who screened it loved it, recalls Merv Adelson, who ran Lorimar. "But we didn't get the order for the show until Bill Paley saw it. The CBS executives began to worry that it was 'soft.' Paley listened to his gut. That's showmanship." Lorne Michaels, executive producer of *Saturday Night Live,* summed up the difference between the old and new owners: "Network television was organized by people who . . . knew television was a business of hits. They have now been replaced by businessmen. The process of making hits is a disruptive one. And it goes against the grain of smooth-running, structurally sound operations."

Of course, the "good old days" had not always been so good. In the early days of the networks, advertisers largely controlled the schedule, producing their own shows. Seeking mass audiences and friendly settings for their commercials, the networks usually played it safe. Back in 1953, ABC couldn't find a sponsor for a show it was enthusiastic about because it featured a "colored" star named Sammy Davis, Jr. Homogenization was the rule when mass audiences had no choice, a point pounded home by the astute Les Brown in his still relevant 1974 book, *Television: The Business Behind the Box.* "Television is a cheerleader for the team that has already won," wrote Robert MacNeil in his coruscating 1968 memoir, *The People Machine.* Perhaps the most telling critique of network programming was delivered not in the "terrible" eighties but in the "good old days" of 1961, when former FCC chairman Newton N. Minow delivered his now famous "vast wasteland" speech to the National Association of Broadcasters:

> I invite you to sit down in front of your television set when your station goes on the air and stay there without a book, magazine, newspaper, profit and loss sheet or rating book to distract you—and keep your eyes glued to that set until the station signs off. I can assure you that you will observe a vast wasteland. You will see a procession of game shows, violence, audience participation shows, formula comedies about totally unbelievable families, blood and thunder, mayhem, violence, sadism, murder, western badmen, western good men, private eyes, gangsters. . . . And endlessly, commercials . . .

But it is nonetheless true that the networks under the old owners would more often choose their programs for reasons divorced from the bottom line. None of the three networks would air commercials or entertainment programs during the four days when President John F. Kennedy's body lay in state, for instance. Each set aside public service and cultural hours in prime time. NBC in 1963 turned over its entire three hours of prime time for a civil rights special. The owners did not expect network news to earn a profit, and led by Edward R. Murrow, the news divisions saw themselves primarily as educators. Said Richard Salant, who had been president of CBS News for sixteen years, "the news was considered something that CBS owed to the public and to its conscience. . . . More often than not, I spent more money than was budgeted each year. . . . Senior management hardly raised an eyebrow." Network documentaries usually zeroed in on serious subjects. If the airwaves were a scarce resource owned by the public, it followed that those who held a television frequency were borrowing public property. Which raised a question that Congress began to ask, again, of the networks in early 1987: Did the network owners recognize their public trust? Did their preoccupation with profits come at the expense of their public obligations? Did they feel a responsibility to inform as well as to entertain? Would they set aside some portion of their schedule not for the masses but for programs for those with special tastes—a symphony, a ballet, a news documentary—and thus expand the tastes of the masses? Was it an accident that the three networks aired seventy-nine prime-time news documentaries in 1970, and just fifteen in 1986? Was the obligation of a network owner, as Jack Welch said, no different from or no more special than the obligation of a helicopter manufacturer? Did Tom Murphy, Larry Tisch, and Jack Welch feel a sense of obligation to viewers as well as shareholders?

To explore these issues, and to discuss reimposing some of the rules that had been lifted during the early Reagan years, the House Telecommunications and Finance Subcommittee invited the three new network CEOs to testify in late March of 1987. The new owners appeared and assured the Congress of their fervent commitment to news and to the public trust. Congress was quickly sedated, and the threat of network reregulation seemed to pass.

The news divisions at the networks would prove more difficult to appease than Congress. The aftershocks of the "financial power shift" cited by Ted Turner hit News especially hard. No longer assured of profits, the networks looked even more intensely at ratings, and here news came up short. Unless it was Barbara Walters doing a special at home with Nancy and Ron or an international crisis, news could not compete with entertainment or sports.

A real fear at all three networks was that a ratings test would be applied to the evening newscast. The challenge uppermost in the minds of ABC News executives in the first half of 1987 was how to attract new viewers to *World News Tonight,* which was then third in the ratings race. Would a new format, they wondered, tempt new viewers?

To most viewers, the three network newscasts seemed like the same program. Each had a single studio anchor, who smoothly served as the bridge to and from stories that were often so alike on all three networks that they seemed to share the same assignment editor; each story was of roughly similar length, each professionally produced, each newscast more often than not opening with the same lead story and ending with a soft feature that allowed the anchor to smile as he bade the viewers good night. And each network's audience was treated to pictures they had already seen on a local newscast or on CNN, which may explain why the network news audience was dwindling. "We have to do something to differentiate ourselves from the bulk of news," said ABC News president Roone Arledge, who offered no specifics.

John Sias agreed that something should be done, though he took care not to push Arledge, fearing that "it would tend to be threatening" if the recommendation came from him. Where Sias and Arledge did agree was that any changes in the newscast had to be introduced gradually. "The changes can't be so monumental that viewers notice them overnight," said News vice president David Burke. "*World News* produces half our revenue."

Arledge and David Burke decided to ventilate the subject at an all-day session on January 13, 1987, at Manhattan's elegant Lowell Hotel. A dozen or so people from News, including anchor Peter Jennings, attended. The questions they grappled with were these: In the roughly twenty-two minutes allotted the newscast after subtracting the ads and local station breaks, should ABC increase the number of stories by making them shorter? Or should there be fewer and longer stories? Should they emphasize headlines or analysis? Should they rely on many correspondents or a few stars? Hard news or features?

For the first two hours, ideas were tossed around inconclusively. Then Paul Friedman, ABC's director of news coverage for Europe, Africa, and the Middle East, rose and, between drags on his cigarette, sketched what might be a new twenty-two-minute format, one that would "differentiate itself from local news and other newscasts, and do something valuable at the same time." A new format might begin, said Friedman, with a five-minute opener that would include a report and an analysis of the most important story of the day. "Essentially," said Friedman, "we'd be saying to the audience: 'You may have heard on local news that the hostage deadline passed. We're going to tell you *why*.' " The second segment might consist of "all the rest of the news in four and one-half minutes"—headlines, really, that the anchor would read to graphics or tape, or that correspondents would knock out in thirty-second pieces. The third segment could last perhaps seven minutes, and would feature Jennings. It could consist of an interview conducted by Jennings or a longer piece on a single subject, with the correspondent later talking live with the anchor. Like the first segment, this would be a place for one of a dozen star correspondents to report a piece in depth. Segment four would extend for up to three minutes and consist of what local news used to call "news you can use"—consumer and medical news, for instance. Finally, there would be the closer by one of the star correspondents. "A really good closing piece," said Friedman, "has either got to be funny or have some poignancy or emotion, or get the viewer to say, 'I never knew that.' "

The meeting lasted five hours. Dazzled by Friedman's self-assurance, Arledge assigned him the task of devising a new format. "I picked Friedman because he was not a threat to anybody," said Arledge. "He seemed like a good, neutral choice." The assignment, however, sparked rumors that Arledge would ask Friedman, forty-one, a former executive producer of NBC's *Today,* to replace Bill Lord, executive producer of *World News Tonight.* Implicit in Arledge's search for a "neutral choice," and unspoken at the Lowell Hotel meeting, was the fact that Bill Lord and Peter Jennings detested each other. Tensions between the two would help slow the search for a new format to end News's ratings slide. Once again, day-to-day considerations —including personalities—diverted attention from the core problem, which was network erosion.

It was hard not to be diverted by the personality clash between the star anchor and his producer, for it hung over the entire news division, putting everyone on edge. From Jennings's point of view, Bill Lord—who was Ted Koppel's original executive producer when *Nightline* started in 1979—was an irascible, miserably moody man, who offered no support. Like the other anchormen, Jennings was a genuine celebrity, a face that entered ten million homes nightly, more homes and with more frequency than that of any Hollywood star. And unlike actors, the anchor was involved in a business—news—about which everyone had opinions. Jennings wanted the comfort of knowing that the executive producer was a shield. "I carry the public can for this broadcast," he said. "People don't get angry at Bill Lord." It bothered the anchor that he, unlike Dan Rather at CBS or Tom Brokaw at NBC, had no say in the choice of an executive producer. It bothered Jennings that his set for the previous year and a half had been a glass bubble that required him to use more makeup but still made him look, Jennings felt, "washed out," pasty. And yet Bill Lord did nothing. It bothered Jennings that though he and Lord hardly spoke, Arledge and the management of the news division allowed the situation to fester, unresolved.

Then there was the ambivalence that Jennings felt about being an anchor. After spending years based in Europe and roaming the world as a correspondent, he had been stuck for the past four years at a desk in New York, loving the clout and the money and the power to educate, yet hating feeling like he was a "pitchman." Jennings's mood that January was fouled by a winter diet he had put himself on and by his struggle to quit smoking. His sense of vulnerability was heightened because he had just fired his agent.

The compromise that every anchor makes between the responsibilities of a journalist and the obligations of an entertainer had been on Jennings's mind frequently. An anchor, Lynn Darling once wrote, is "part journalist, part master of ceremonies," and no matter how good a reporter you are—and Jennings, Brokaw, and Rather are good reporters—you live with the knowledge that any "announcer can be an anchor," can read news. Constant telephone calls from Arledge insisting on dark suits and straight collars because they conveyed *authority,* complaining that *tough guys don't wear polka dots,* became so oppressive to Jennings's predecessor, Frank Reynolds, that at his funeral his wife, Henrietta, decided to make a silent statement. From his coffin Reynolds would have the last word, albeit privately. As Arledge and others filed by the closed coffin, what they did not see was that Reynolds wore a cream-colored suit, blue button-down shirt, and polka-dot tie.*

Jennings was perhaps particularly sensitive on this issue because of his background. He has always been self-conscious that as a boy in

* Reynolds's son Dean, who works for ABC, admits the family considered this outfit but says that at the last moment they decided against it. A close family friend insists that Frank Reynolds wore polka dots to his funeral.

Canada he dropped out of high school without graduating. Then when he tried to get a job with the Canadian Broadcasting Corporation, where his father, Charles, was known as "the Edward R. Murrow of Canada," a nepotism rule blocked his path. If he was unfairly held back in Canada, however, Jennings was rewarded too early in the U.S. After serving for several years as an ABC correspondent, covering civil rights in the South among other stories, suddenly at age twenty-six, in 1965, Peter Jennings was made a network anchorman. He was, he thought, totally unqualified, and viewers agreed with him. The anchor experiment was short-lived. It wasn't until Jennings went overseas as a foreign correspondent that he finally achieved acclaim.

Jennings was especially sensitive to assertions that he was just another pretty face. He felt Lord treated him like a bimbo. Jennings couldn't get out of his head something Lord said three years before: *The anchor performs a role much like Ed McMahon's on the* Tonight *show. He is the pitchman, the person who sells the show.*

To which Jennings cried, "I'm a journalist!"

"I'm not saying you're not a journalist," said Lord. "But your job is to get people into the tent." To Lord, this was self-evident. "When I would say that to Ted [Koppel], he agreed," Lord remembered. "Ted isn't pretentious about that."

From Lord's viewpoint, Jennings was often impossible to work with. "Peter has been a bitch, awful, since he quit smoking," explained Lord, who had held an impressive string of jobs since joining the network in 1961. "He has been abusive to the staff. He went off and came back from vacation and his first day back he destroyed a producer by being real nasty." Even before he quit smoking, Lord said, Jennings would be chary with praise, would nitpick. Lord's disagreements with Jennings were one part personal, one part philosophical. Lord believed—and was supported by management in this belief—that the executive producer, not the anchor, was the final arbiter. After all, management fought that battle in 1986—and won—over David Hartman. "The anchorman is terrifically important," Lord said. "But there is a boss, and the boss is the executive producer. In a live show there are things an anchorman can't know." The show was—and had to be—run from the control room. Let Jennings alone decide what gets on the air, Lord worried, and ABC News would be freighted with foreign stories, with lugubrious news. "It is far more difficult to manage the relationship with your anchor than it is with your wife," mused Lord. "Sometimes I do badly. Sometimes Peter does badly."

If this had been a voluntary marriage, both mates would have sued for divorce. Because it was a marriage imposed by management, they could not. And management was not prepared to move. "Peter is a difficult person. So is Lord," said David Burke at the time. But Burke found Jennings so "extreme" in his resistance to management that in the winter of 1987 an entire meeting among News executives was consumed with stories about how sensitive Jennings could be. *Jennings is threatening to abandon the anchor chair and go back to being a reporter!* warned Dick Wald.

"Let him leave!" Burke finally snapped. There was always the multitalented Ted Koppel to take his place. Although Burke liked Jennings, he was fatigued by what Jennings himself concedes is a reflexive aversion to management. "Ingrained in Peter is *us* versus *them,*" said Burke. "Peter feels toward us the way we feel toward the new management."

Caught in the middle was the staff. It was an article of faith at ABC that Jennings was perhaps the best of the three anchors. Even the competition praised him. "Peter is very good," said Tom Brokaw. "He has a kind of anchorman's élan. He always exudes a sort of confidence." Dan Rather's executive producer, Tom Bettag, put it this way: "Jennings is such a sophisticated, savvy anchor that he masks a lot of ABC's weaknesses." Everyone admired how hard Jennings worked, how diligently he prepared for big stories. And there were colleagues, such as correspondent Barry Dunsmore, who said of him: "Peter is a man who has succeeded without leaving any dead bodies behind." Those who knew admired him for quietly spending most Monday nights as a volunteer for the Coalition for the Homeless. Despite the encomiums, in 1987 Jennings admitted, "I have been very prickly," adding, "I am enormously frustrated."

The "Jennings problem" played out against a backdrop of frustrations within the news division, including doubts about Cap Cities' intentions and the insecurities inflamed by budget cuts. It vexed many in News when, in 1986, Cap Cities encouraged News to launch *Our World,* a retrospective look at yesterday's headlines and people. Using free-lancers and relatively inexperienced producers and relying on ABC's film library, the show was cheap to produce—about a third the cost of a typical network hour. *Our World* was thrown into the 8 P.M. Thursday graveyard opposite *The Cosby Show.* The show had its fans but not much of an audience. And because it skimped on costs, many in News believed *Our World* revealed something awful about Cap Cities. "Quality is not their priority. Cost cutting is," said a senior network producer. Cap Cities' preoccupation with costs induced the same depression felt at NBC or CBS. "There is a feeling among people my age," said a young producer, "that we ought to think of another line of work. The message from Cap Cities is that this is a business. Period. But we didn't get into this business to make money."

By the winter of 1987, ABC News was unhappily struggling to sweat $20 million from its budget. In pushing these cuts, Cap Cities had some allies, including *20/20* executive producer Av Westin, who in February wrote an extraordinary eighteen-page memorandum—"Days of Penury, Days of Affluence"—criticizing the waste within News. Westin meant to publish the article in *Channels* magazine, a lively publication covering the broadcast and cable industry, but yanked it at the last minute. As if to undermine Arledge, he sent copies to Tom Murphy, Dan Burke, and John Sias. Somehow Westin's memo leaked, prompting a rare public furor at ABC. Westin was alone in his methods, but not in his opinion. There was fat at ABC News, said one bureau chief. "We have ninety-six correspondents, and only forty or so are on the air a lot." It was wasteful, said a senior producer, for a studio show like *Nightline* to have an editorial staff of thirty-five or so, or for a program like David Brinkley's to operate as a separate duchy, without a central desk coordinating the staff working on all network news programs.

News made the cuts. And they did it quietly, without the leaks that bedeviled Bob Wright at NBC, without the public bleats common at CBS News. In all, ABC News pared its staff from 1,450 to 1,150—a bigger cut than CBS News's tumultuous layoffs in March of 1987. But little adverse publicity accompanied these reductions or ABC's third-place finish. Marveled NBC Communications chief Bud Rukeyser, "Rarely is a network in third place given the luxury of avoiding the glare of publicity. Aside from the Av Westin memo, they have gotten little bad press. When Fred Silverman ran NBC and we were number three there was a daily drumfire of negative comments. A picture of chaos, no matter what you did."

The appearance of tranquility was a source of enormous pride to Arledge and his team, who took it as a sign that they were managing their shop in a more humane way, offering counseling help and generous severance pay. This cost-cutting success, in turn, warmed Cap Cities managers. John Sias, who had said the previous June that Arledge "endures me," now said, "He's been very cordial. People who work with him have volunteered how amazed they are to see him take the lead now in restructuring. In the past it had not been his *schtick.* He liked to spend money."

Despite appearances, Arledge had still not fully softened, certainly not toward Sias. He was still "unhappy," said David Burke. Arledge and Burke viewed Cap Cities as experienced local, as opposed to network, broadcasters. They didn't know, he thought, about how or when a network had to take precedence over local broadcasters during a crisis. They didn't share a sense of calling. Arledge and Burke remained ever vigilant against intrusions from the new owners. So on guard, said one middle-level News executive, that instead of feeling protected by the wall Arledge and Burke erected against Cap Cities, there was concern they were being too belligerent and therefore not serving the broad interests of the news division: "They don't ingratiate themselves to Cap Cities," observed a middle manager in News. "What Howard Stringer is doing at CBS is very smart. Why haven't they tried to ingratiate themselves?"

Even after Cap Cities refused to support what David Burke called Av Westin's "Bay of Pigs" memo, even after it stood behind the decision to suspend Westin, Arledge and Burke kept Cap Cities at arm's length. But Sias thought Cap Cities' support for Arledge "probably had a positive effect." Arledge came over to discuss the Westin matter with him, Sias remembered. They had a good chat, agreed that short of firing the talented producer, which Arledge and Cap Cities did not want to do but David Burke did, Arledge was a free agent. As Cap Cities delegated authority to WABC-TV to switch *Jeopardy!* and *World News Tonight,* so it delegated authority to managers like Arledge.

But tougher decisions lay ahead. May is the month when each network establishes the prime-time schedule for the fall season. In Los Angeles Brandon Stoddard and his team watched the thirty-one pilots submitted, compared these with shows already on ABC, and then readied a draft schedule to present to the Cap Cities/ABC hierarchy in New York on May 15, 1987. The approximately forty executives who entered the thirty-eighth-floor conference room had received tapes of the pilots. They knew ABC had lots of holes to plug. Because of ratings duds such as *Starman* and *Life with Lucy,* ABC would end the 1986–87 season in third place. Few in the room knew what Stoddard would recommend, though John Sias had a clue. Before the meeting he had phoned Arledge and told him "to get his research together." Since Arledge had only two shows in prime time—*20/20* and *Our World*—Arledge understood he had to be prepared to defend them against Stoddard.

But Arledge was not prepared for what happened next. Standing beside a magnetized board containing the seven-night schedule of shows that probably would run on ABC, NBC, and CBS (but not the Fox network), the short, perky, self-confident Stoddard enumerated at machine-gun speed the three key props that would sustain his proposed schedule: First, he had a hot new variety hour—*Dolly*—starring Dolly Parton—which he wanted to air Sunday at 9 P.M., the single most-watched hour of the entire week. CBS, owing to a strong lead-in from *60 Minutes* at 7 P.M., followed by Angela Lansbury in *Murder, She Wrote,* easily won the ratings competition on Sunday evenings. *Dolly* could dent CBS's lead, Stoddard insisted, partly because it would appeal to many of the older viewers now tuned to CBS and partly because it would be up against movies on both CBS and NBC. Dolly Parton was *hot,* a proven winner, Stoddard assured the executives. Her *Smokey Mountain Christmas* on ABC was the fifth-best-rated made-for-TV movie of the 1986–87 season. When she teamed with Kenny Rogers for a Christmas special on CBS, the ratings went through the roof. Just to be sure, Stoddard proudly announced that they had tied her up with a three-year personal and production contract which, it later was revealed, would cost the network $34 million.

The rub was that in order to schedule Parton on Sundays, Stoddard said he had to find another night for ABC's Sunday movie, which was his second major prop. He couldn't shift the movie to Monday, since ABC had a proven winner in *Monday Night Football.* Tuesday was out of the question, since it was already a triumphant night with comedies like *Who's the Boss?* and *Growing Pains,* and viewers loved the witty, sexually charged verbal fisticuffs between Cybill Shepherd and Bruce Willis on *Moonlighting.* Wednesday was also out of the question since it was already a strong night, with an "audience flow" of younger viewers from the two comedies that began the night—*Perfect Strangers* and *Head of the Class*—viewers that wouldn't necessarily stay tuned to a movie. And Friday or Saturday nights were out, since the advent of the VCR deflated these as movie nights. So the natural home for the ABC movie would be Thursday evenings. Which brought Stoddard to his third prop: In order to wedge a two-hour movie in at 9:00 he would have to move News's magazine show, *20/20,* from Thursday at 10:00 to "right here"—and he slapped a magnetized *20/20* plate next to Thursday at 8 P.M. Each move, he said, is "interconnected."

People gasped. Everyone in the room understood that to move *20/20* meant it would be up against NBC's blockbuster Thursday schedule in general and *The Cosby Show,* the number-one-rated show in the universe, in particular. And not only would *20/20* star Barbara Walters and News suffer this hopeless time slot, News would lose *Our World,* which had already been sacrificed to Cosby at 8 P.M. In the way intramural score was kept at the networks, Arledge's division was "losing" an hour of programming to Entertainment, and the one prime-time hour News had left was being offered as another bone tossed to Cosby.

Because everyone understood this, all eyes turned to Roone Arledge, who was silent for what seemed an eternity. "I deliberately didn't speak for four or five minutes," said Arledge. Edward W. "Ted" Harbert, Stoddard's deputy, filled the void, telling the assembled executives: *Research reports that the audience at 8* P.M. Thursday is potentially larger. 20/20 *could kick off ABC's entire night. And if the movie was terrific, and if it ran more than two hours, it would be possible to shorten* 20/20 *and start the movie earlier.*

"Stop!" Arledge remembers shouting. "This is out of the question!" Not only did the move enrage him, equally outrageous was the contempt it reflected, he felt, toward News.

"Why don't you run Dolly Parton at 8 P.M. on Thursday?" David Burke asked.

"What are you, crazy? You tell Dolly!" said Stoddard.

"You tell Barbara!" shot back Burke.

"This is the way it's gonna be," Stoddard announced, recalls Sales head Jake Keever. Stoddard, after all, had reason to feel emboldened. Murphy and Burke backed every decision he made. They approved his miniseries. They kept Sias out of his hair. They treated him as if he were an "expert," as if he, and he alone, knew the secrets to the kingdom.

The room fell silent. Glancing about, Stoddard knew Arledge had some allies beyond David Burke, the one other executive from News in attendance. Sales, for instance, played a bigger role in programming since Cap Cities had taken over, and Sales was a big fan of the magazine show. They were partial to the prestige prices it commanded. The affiliates liked it because among ABC's lowly rated prime-time programs, *20/20* ranked relatively high and was a natural lead-in to their own nightly newscast. And from a corporate viewpoint, the roughly $20 million *20/20* generated helped put News in the black. Seeing they were at an impasse, Stoddard was prepared to offer a compromise, and wandered over to the schedule board. He reached up and moved *20/20* from Thursday to Friday at 10 P.M.

Try Tuesday at 10, countered Arledge, picking ABC's strongest night and a position right after *Moonlighting.*

Impossible! said Stoddard, noting that he had a terrific new series—*thirtysomething*—slotted there. *The audience flow from a hip, younger-appealing* Moonlighting *to a series about yuppie angst fit. To stick* 20/20 *there would suddenly skew to older viewers.*

Arledge lost Tuesday. He didn't much care about losing *Our World*—its executive producer was Av Westin, and the show ranked last in the ratings among the ninety-seven prime-time shows. It lacked "production values," the Arledge flair—and so he made no impassioned plea for it. But Arledge did feel passionate about Barbara Walters and *20/20.* More than once, Arledge had said that if he were stranded or in a jam the one person he would call was Walters. To move *20/20* from Thursday to Friday at 10:00 meant a smaller available audience, he said, since Fridays and Saturdays were the least watched nights of the week. This in turn meant a revenue loss, because advertisers paid less for smaller audiences. Even if *20/20*'s audience ratings dropped on Thursday nights, Arledge reasoned, the show was still likely to make more money since the audience pool to draw from was greater. Arledge was genuinely irate, for *20/20* was a workhorse for the third-rated ABC. In its eight years on the air, the share of audience it attracted always eclipsed its lead-in show.

There was another issue for Roone Arledge as well. He worried that News might lose its internal clout if it no longer produced a profit. And he cared about something else. Arledge, more than anyone else in the room, had put ABC on the map. He respected Stoddard's talents, but he didn't understand why he was treated with such reverence. After all, as a scheduler Stoddard was surely no genius. Recently he had made the mistake of scheduling *The Betty Ford Story* against the second installment of CBS's smash miniseries, *I'll Take Manhattan,* which appealed to the same female audience. Lose this fight, and Stoddard would be king, free to move News wherever he pleased. This was, in part, a power struggle. Roone Arledge would not meekly accept Thursday night at 8:00.

Tom Murphy sat nearby, taking this all in, brooding. Murphy and Burke freely admitted they didn't understand Hollywood or entertainment programming, which is one reason they delegated such matters to Stoddard. They had not imposed their own judgment on Brandon Stoddard because they had no judgment of their own. Now, because

Entertainment and News could not agree, they were being forced to intervene. What ran through Tom Murphy's mind at that moment, he recalls, was how vexing this decision was, how "the program people were too rough." As he thought this, Murphy heard Arledge throw down the gauntlet: "If *20/20* goes to 8:00 Thursday, we won't produce the show!"

With that, the stalemate was complete, the meeting ready to adjourn so tempers could cool. The limits of Tom Murphy's belief in decentralization had been reached. He would have to choose between News and Entertainment, and even were he an experienced network hand, the decision would have been daunting. Rising, Murphy looked squarely at Stoddard and said, "You are one tough son-of-a-bitch." They would sleep on it, announced Murphy, and gather in a smaller group tomorrow.

The next day, Murphy, Burke, and Sias met separately with both Arledge's News team and Stoddard's Entertainment group. In the meeting with News in the thirty-eighth-floor conference room, Arledge made a pitch to move *20/20* to Wednesday at 10:00. To bury it on Thursday at 8 P.M., he argued, was to weaken a show that not only cost less to produce than a normal hour of programming but also had a track record 40 percent better than the ABC show preceding it. Murphy was persuaded, and told Arledge that Wednesday made sense.

Now he had to talk to Stoddard. "It's the most difficult decision we ever had to make," sighed Murphy, who stretched out on a couch in the conference room, research reports strewn on the floor and on his chest. The research told Murphy that *20/20* would do better in its original slot, Thursday at 10 P.M., but Stoddard had been given free rein to set the schedule. Dan Burke invited Stoddard to come in alone to discuss it privately. Murphy, the *20/20* magnetic card in his hand, said he didn't want to move *20/20* to Thursday at 8 P.M. "What do you think of moving it to Wednesday at 10:00?"

Stoddard took the magnetic card from Murphy and went to the board. *Put* 20/20 *on Wednesday and we have to move* Dynasty. *The half-hour comedies and dramedies preceding* 20/20—Perfect Strangers, Head of the Class, Hooperman, *and* The Slap Maxwell Story—*would appeal to a younger audience than the one that tunes in to a newsmagazine show. Therefore we lose our audience flow. And where do we put* Dynasty? We would have to rip up our entire schedule.

By this time Stoddard's team had entered the room, and Stuart Bloomberg, vice president of Comedy and Variety Series Development, erupted: "How can you hold the entire schedule ransom to one program, *20/20*?" Stoddard was fuming quietly. Every time he had gone to the mat, he had won. Stoddard was not used to losing. The prime-time schedule was his job, not Arledge's. And the last time Arledge complained of a scheduling shift—when WABC-TV moved News up to 6:30 P.M. in November—the ratings for *World News Tonight* jumped from a 6 to a 9 in New York, which translated into a national ratings rise of three-tenths of a point! So choked with anger was Stoddard that Sias leaned over and whispered to Tom Murphy, "Brandon is close to quitting."

Feeling trapped, again Murphy pulled back, scuttling Wednesday at 10 P.M. They would meet again tomorrow, he announced.

When Murphy conferred with Arledge, the News president did not resist Stoddard's logic concerning Wednesday. He would be quite content, he said, to go back to square one, to remain on Thursday at 10 P.M., opposite *L.A. Law.* It made sense to Murphy.

Let's keep it on Thursday at 10 P.M., said Murphy the next morning to Stoddard and his team. This was the third position Murphy had taken and, by this time, recalls Stoddard, "I'm tired. I'm thinking, 'It's time to be a good trooper. Be a good boy.'" So he moved the card to Thursday at 10:00 and tried rearranging the other pieces. But they ran into the same dead ends on Monday, Tuesday, Wednesday, Friday, and Saturday, prompting Stuart Bloomberg to ask, "Tom, could you tell me again why you think it should go there?" Murphy started to explain but wasn't satisfied with his logic so he put the meeting on hold while he left the room to caucus with Dan Burke and Sias. A moment later they returned and Murphy announced his fourth and final position: "We'll go with Friday at 10 P.M."

Stoddard's staff broke into applause.

"How dare you applaud!" exclaimed Murphy angrily, disturbed that Stoddard's people viewed this decision as if it were a victory for themselves rather than a decision that would benefit the entire network. Murphy adjourned the meeting, saying he would talk to Arledge. Until he had, Murphy said he expected silence from the group.

After a bumpy start, Murphy, Burke, and Sias had come to appreciate the job Arledge & Company were doing. They still weren't entirely pleased with News's cost cutting, but they believed Arledge had built a first-class News operation, had adjusted to the new ownership without any of the public whining emanating from CBS and even NBC. Arledge had launched *Nightline,* which now brought in up to $20 million in annual profits and cost an average of only $500,000 weekly. And now, as he dialed Arledge from his office, Tom Murphy knew he was about to kick him in the groin.

The decision is Friday at 10 P.M., Murphy announced. Arledge remembered that Friday had been Stoddard's original compromise offer, so he knew Stoddard had gotten his way. He blew up. Murphy asked if he could come over to Arledge's ABC News headquarters at 7 West Sixty-sixth Street that afternoon.

We've made a decision, he announced as soon as he, Burke, and Sias were seated in the fourth-floor conference room, where they were joined by Arledge, News vice presidents David Burke and Richard Wald, and Irwin W. Weiner, News's senior vice president for Finance. *We're going to move* 20/20 *to Fridays at 10 P.M. We know that doesn't make you happy, and we welcome your candor.*

Welcome my candor! David Burke was ready to shout, but before he could speak Arledge did. The News president was hardly mollified, but Arledge tends to circle things. "We have had eight years of success with *20/20,*" began Arledge. "And we are being badly treated. The decision is wrong. The research department said it is wrong. The affiliates said it was wrong. Sales said it was wrong." The jab stung, for the Cap Cities people felt uneasy with the decision they had made.

Before they could respond, however, David Burke squared off against Tom Murphy, one Irish pol to another. Burke said: "It's been hard on everyone going through the merger, hard on you, Tom, and hard on us. We've tried to anticipate your management style. The people involved on both sides don't share the same jargon or history. And we in News are arrogant, for good reason. We feel the weight of public responsibility." At this point Burke paused, then threw a wild punch: *"That little twit on the West Coast has no right to push aside News!"*

"He isn't a twit!" shot back Murphy.

"Yes, he is!" countered Burke, releasing some of the frustrations that had been pent up in him since the merger. He continued: "But as time went on, Tom, I got comfortable. This News management and I were on the team. And you were my leader. And yet, as my leader, you come in and say, 'Brandon Stoddard, not Tom Murphy, is my leader!' Well, I don't want to have Brandon as my leader!"

Dan Burke was stunned and upset, but before he could utter a word in his leader's defense, an unruffled Tom Murphy said, "I understand how hurt you are. This is the toughest decision I've ever made."

"Why are you listening to Entertainment when Roone has been here longer and has a record of success?" shouted Irwin Weiner.

"Only one network has a successful prime-time magazine show," added Dick Wald. (CBS's *60 Minutes* aired at 7 P.M. Sundays, a time reserved for public affairs or children's programming.) "What you're doing is taking our successful time period and giving it to someone else. Then you're telling us, 'You get one of the two least favored nights of the week while the better time periods—Tuesday and Wednesday—are being given to Entertainment.' " And on Friday they would follow a one-hour show—*Max Headroom,* featuring a robot—that the mature adults who tuned to news shows wouldn't watch.

"It may help the network," Dan Burke replied hopefully.

David Burke was unmoved. He had gone to confession his entire life, and he could spot insincere contrition. He felt that Tom Murphy was being sympathetic only because he wanted to escape the meeting without any resignations. Murphy, in fact, remembers thinking to himself, "I don't blame David Burke for saying what he said."

David Burke was not easy to soothe. "The network is in the shithouse!" he cried out. "News is strong. Peter Jennings is only one point behind the evening news leader. Last week Ted Koppel beat Johnny Carson. You're saying to News what was said in Vietnam: 'You have to destroy my village in order to save it.' "

"If *20/20* looks like it will fail, we'll move it to Tuesday or Wednesday at 10 P.M.," Murphy promised, trying to reassure them. Dan Burke and John Sias wanted to deflect the punches thrown at Murphy, to whom they felt great loyalty. They respected his serenity and decency. The tale was told more than once of the time in November of 1986 when "Murph," as they called him, was coming back from Chicago on the company airplane with Corporate Communications chief Patricia Matson. They encountered a heavy rainstorm as they tried to land at Westchester County Airport. The jet burst through low cloud cover too fast and skidded on the wet runway, spinning out of control, its nose and one wing breaking off as the plane cascaded from runway to field, finally tumbling to a stop in the mud. All through the ordeal, Matson remembered that Murphy was calm, and as soon as the plane came to a halt he had the presence of mind to unbuckle his seat belt and race to open the exit door. Seeing that Matson was shaken, Murphy invited her to his Rye home for coffee. "Honey, I'm home," he called out to his wife as he entered the house, as if nothing had happened.

The conversation with Arledge's people may have been rough, but Tom Murphy was serene because he saw it as another step toward encouraging candor, unbottling feelings. That attitude had become part of the Cap Cities culture, and was why Sias could say: "It didn't leave any scars on me. Letting their people talk was constructive." This belief was reaffirmed when in the weeks and months afterward they never picked up a newspaper and read—as they did with squabbles at CBS or NBC—about the sulfurous things David Burke had said to Tom Murphy.

What drove David Burke to take such an uncompromising stand? In part, he was playing the bad cop for his boss, Roone Arledge. In part, he may have been expressing the frustrations of someone too long in the job of number two. In part, he was sticking his neck out for News. David Burke had fought to harden the news, fought to keep News independent from the bottom-line businessmen at Cap Cities, fought to transplant the Murrow tradition to ABC. And perhaps there was one other factor with David Burke. "He's like a convert," explained Dick Wald. "When Mrs. Luce converted to Catholicism she became more Catholic than the pope. When David converted from spin control and politics, he became purer. And the Cap Cities people weren't pure in his sense."

Arledge, like Burke, felt there had been a breach of faith. The next day—Saturday—copies of a memorandum from Arledge explaining the *20/20* shift from Thursday to Friday littered the ABC newsroom:

> As you may know, the management of ABC News feels very strongly about this matter. We argued strongly in opposition to the change for over three days. In the end we did not succeed primarily because of the enormous pressure placed on the decision makers by the extraordinarily poor performance of ABC's prime-time programming, and the resultant economic loss facing the network.

Arledge's blast was greeted unhappily by other ABC divisions. Entertainment was incensed, and wondered why Murphy & Company didn't silence News as they had Entertainment when they stood and cheered. Jake Keever said, "I thought he made a mistake putting out a memo." There were snickers about how Arledge's memo was silent about the departure of *Our World,* and smirks about how he was playing his own favorites. But Murphy, Burke, and Sias were almost nonchalant. "Oh, he has to do that," Murphy said, calming a fellow executive. "He has to show the troops he's fighting for them." Besides, he knew Arledge was also saying that though he disliked the decision, News would live with it. Even Stoddard later conceded, "If I were Roone Arledge I would have done exactly the same and made the same points he did."

But there were larger lessons to be drawn from the battle. This was the first big institutional fight within ABC in the seventeen months since the takeover, and the perils were too stark to miss. A network was not like one of Cap Cities' stations or its publishing division. Institutional rivalries and conflicts came with the turf. The number-three network could not afford to siphon its energies in fratricide. As the day-to-day manager of this enterprise, Dan Burke wouldn't allow it. In order to manage the inevitable "fractiousness" between Stoddard and Arledge and the other divisions, Cap Cities had to modify its traditional decentralized approach. It had to be more involved in decision making.

A second lesson was that Brandon Stoddard had to operate on a somewhat shorter leash. Although Entertainment had won the battle, maybe it had lost the war. Soon after this meeting, recalls Sias, "Tom and Dan told me they wanted me to be a little more heavy-handed. Tom was frustrated and concerned that we were not making progress in prime time. By insisting that *Dolly* be on Sunday at 9 P.M., it caused us to lose the Sunday movie. And we had invested $350 million in movie product. . . . After May, I was a little less reluctant to come in there and have a say." This was Brandon Stoddard's first full schedule, the first to bear his complete, personal stamp. And Stoddard and his team would leave these meetings with less luster than when they arrived.

Maybe, Murphy & Company began to believe, picking programs and deciding on a prime-time schedule was not the arcane science they had thought. Maybe they had to be more engaged, as Leonard Goldenson first suggested to Tom Murphy back in December of 1984. After the May 1987 scheduling battle, Murphy said, "The area we're least comfortable with is the most important—entertainment. But we're no longer virgins."

The network's fall schedule decided, ABC then turned to the task of bringing in potential advertisers. When the public turns on their TV sets, they think program. But a network thinks advertiser. *Buy* Monday Night Football *and Miller Lite will reach adult males. Buy* Dynasty *and Charmin will reach women. Buy* Who's the Boss? *and Disney's latest movie will be introduced to teens. Buy* World News Tonight *and sell more Polident to mature adults. Buy a half hour on Saturday morning for G.I. Joe toys, and get your own* G.I. Joe *show.* "The network is paying affiliates to carry network commercials, not programs," explained Mark Mandala, the ABC executive to whom Sales and Affiliate Relations reported. "What we are is a distribution system for Procter & Gamble and other advertisers."

The stakes associated with success are enormous. Advertisers would spend just under $9 billion on the networks in 1987. When they had a new national product to introduce, the three networks were the preferred vehicle, for only they could reach mass audiences. But advertisers were fussy. "I wouldn't buy *Tour of Duty* [a Vietnam War series on CBS]. I sell nice, friendly products," said George F. "Pete" Tyrrell, vice president for Advertising of Johnson & Johnson. For the networks the stakes are also high. Since there were then 87.4 million TV homes, a single Nielsen rating point equaled 874,000 households. A one-year jump of just one rating point for the entire daytime schedule, for instance, netted an extra $60 million a year for the network; a point jump for the evening news equalled about $9 million; and one point in prime time could add $100 million.

Advertisers seek different customers, and the networks break audiences down into demographic categories. The seven "demos," as they call them, are: women eighteen to forty-nine; men eighteen to forty-nine; adults eighteen to forty-nine; women twenty-five to fifty-four; men twenty-five to fifty-four; adults twenty-five to fifty-four; and total number of households. Generally, the most desirable "demo" is thought to be younger adults, particularly women eighteen to forty-nine, since it's assumed younger viewers have not yet developed brand loyalties and can be seduced to buy a new product, and since women generally watch more television and do more of the shopping. Typically, adult women account for about 48 percent of the prime-time audience, men 34 percent, and teens and children 18 percent. Older adults tend to watch more news, men more sports, women more series. With advertisers willing to pay a premium to reach younger demos, particularly women, it is not uncommon that a program with a smaller audience but better demos can charge more than a program with a broader but older audience. For example, although CBS ranked number one in daytime ratings in 1987, number-two ABC actually hauled in more money because it reached more women aged eighteen to forty-nine.

Television is a preferred medium for advertisers since Americans are addicted to it. In addition to the nearly 90 million households owning at least one TV set in 1987, six out of ten of these owned at least two sets and the average household watched seven hours and ten minutes daily and fifty hours per week. But the composition of the television audience has changed as the demographics of American viewers have changed. For instance, while television viewing has increased, daytime shows have a shrinking audience because the number of women who stay at home has declined, since 65 percent of all mothers work. With women having shed their assigned roles as homemakers, decisions about what products to buy have inevitably changed as well. More men now share these choices. And with both parents working and with shopping malls nearby, more teenagers are shopping for the family. Even so, some analysts questioned whether the networks and the advertising community weren't too infatuated with younger demos, since the average age of the population continues to inch up. The fastest growing segment of the population is those thirty-four to forty-four. With advances in medical science, the second fastest-growing group of Americans is those over seventy-five.

The network's task is to negotiate a price for advertising space in a show, the key determinant being the cost per thousand (CPM)—the cost for reaching each one thousand viewers. For instance, a popular series like *Moonlighting* was charging fourteen dollars per thousand, while the low-rated *Heart of the City* could charge only six dollars. In the early days of television, the basic units the network sold were usually entire half-hour or hour blocks of time. The network sales force then dealt with relatively few clients, who often made season-long commitments. But as television sets multiplied and the reach of the networks became national, the cost to the advertiser went up, as did program expenses. Only the larger advertisers could afford to subsidize an entire program, and as clients became more sophisticated they realized it wasn't in their interest to be locked into a single audience on a single night.

Thus were born sixty-, thirty-, and, finally, fifteen-second spots. Since a network is not permitted to own cable systems or sell reruns of entertainment shows, these spots become a network's sole source of revenues, except for the few dollars made from the sale, say, of a news documentary overseas. During the 8 to 11 P.M. prime-time hours when network shows command an average price of about $100,000 and up to $450,000 for a thirty-second spot on a hit show, the networks sell between seven and eight minutes an hour in prime time (twelve minutes in daytime and late-night programming).* Over the course of the 1986–87 season, ABC's national Sales force of thirty-

* Another two to three minutes of each prime-time hour are given to the local station to sell.

four account executives and fifteen managers sold a total of 75,958.5 spots. Most of these spots were sold in the so-called upfront market, where advertisers buy 60 to 90 percent of a network's entire inventory in the course of a few summer days; in exchange for network guarantees that the advertiser will reach a specified minimum audience, the advertiser agrees to commit to an annual spending schedule. Spots are also sold year-round in what is called the scatter market, in which the buyer is not given an audience guarantee and may end up paying higher prices if a show succeeds, while the network loses the certitude of a fixed price and guaranteed advertisers. Whether the advertiser chooses to buy ads upfront or in the scatter market, either way he gambles. By pouring most of his money into buying upfront, an advertiser gambles that the cost will be less than if he waits and buys each quarter in the scatter market.

The job of selling ABC's inventory fell to Jake Keever's department. Keever is not a stereotypical smooth salesman. He is a man of immense girth, who waddles down ABC's corridors in shirtsleeves and baggy pants, always ready to chat. After twenty-four years of selling ABC ads—of playing golf with his customers and taking them to *Monday Night Football* games—Jake Keever had developed a foundation of solid relationships.

Nevertheless, he was nervous each summer as the upfront market approached—"the Super Bowl for Sales," he called it. This is where decisions are made that determine winning or losing seasons. The network has to decide: How much to sell? At what price? At what guaranteed audience? The network and the advertiser are playing for huge stakes. Think of the network as a supermarket, its shelves stocked with inventory. Sell 90 percent of this inventory upfront, and the network is left with only 10 percent on its shelves to sell throughout the rest of the year. That's great—if the network receives good prices upfront and if the schedule proves a disappointment. For unlike a supermarket, which can replenish its inventory, or magazines, which can add pages, a network can't easily add spots. Viewers are already sated with ads. If a series blossoms into a hit when most of its inventory has already been sold, then the network loses an opportunity to boost prices in the scatter market. On the other hand, if the network is willing to bet that a new show will be a hit and refuses to sell inventory upfront, and the series actually becomes a hit, the network cleans up in the scatter market. In the 1985–86 season the total prime-time upfront market for the three networks was $2.6 billion.

ABC itself, according to Keever, sold $850 million worth of time, or just over 80 percent of its inventory.

The upfront is a mating dance which begins sometime in March, when the networks invite the ad agency representatives out to Los Angeles for their first taste of the programs being developed for the new season. In 1987 when ABC Sales returned from the Coast it had spent the better part of April gathering intelligence. Each ABC account executive was responsible for a cluster of four to six advertising agencies, and from these familiar contacts they were expected to gauge how much money each customer might spend upfront. By testing demand, they determine the price they can charge—but only after deciding on "the comp," or the audience composition. The more young adults, particularly women, the higher the comp, and therefore the steeper the price. For example, ABC's *Moonlighting* in the 1986–87 season enjoyed a .66 comp among the key target group of women eighteen to forty-nine, which meant that sixty-six of every one hundred homes watching included this group. Although the ratings on *Moonlighting* trailed, say, those of *Murder, She Wrote* (22.7 versus 25.5 percent), its comp was almost twice that of the .38 comp for the CBS hit. Since *Moonlighting*'s demographics were better, ABC could charge more. The urban appeal of ABC's stations also gave it an edge over CBS; ABC affiliates tended to be grouped in what are called the A and B counties, which are the urban/suburban markets with the most upscale audiences, while CBS led among the more rural C and D counties with their elderly, less affluent audiences.

All through the spring of 1987, as was true to a lesser extent throughout the calendar year, Sias would often drop in on ABC Sales' 9 A.M. meetings. Sometimes Tom Murphy or Dan Burke would stop by. Unlike News or Entertainment, Sales welcomed the involvement from above, welcomed being asked to play a more active role in grading current and prospective network shows.

This process of grading shows for upfront sales had begun in April, before the prime-time schedule was finalized, when the Sales staff gathered in the bare white-walled conference room on ABC's thirty-sixth floor, jamming their brown leather chairs around a huge conference table often sticky with the remains of late-night Chinese take-out dinners. Here Keever and his team devised an unscientific rating system to ascertain which of ABC's current prime-time shows to keep on the air. The "white" programs were the sure successes, the "black" the failures, and the "gray" those borderline shows that may not have done well in the ratings but had good demos. A poll of hands from each of the fifteen members of the New York Sales team in attendance indicated the weaknesses of the ABC schedule. Only seven shows were classed as white, including *20/20*; two were black; thirteen were gray.

A week later, Ray Warren, the vice president to whom the eastern account executives reported, reviewed the initial "gray" show choices with his ten account executives, asking them to make hard choices—"black" or "white"—so that Sales could make its recommendations. Seven of the thirteen were moved to the black category. The discussion revealed how subjective the process of selling ads is.

Everyone agreed that *Max Headroom,* which was then airing at 10 P.M., had to be moved to 9:00. The older audiences available at 10 P.M. didn't watch the show, and its only hope was to tap a younger audience. There was unanimity that *Hotel*—a one-hour drama—was stale, yet most of the eastern sales force agreed its ratings were adequate. The majority wanted to kill the two hours devoted to the Disney show on Sundays, but they were willing to recommend a one-hour Disney entry. To replace the two hours, said Ray Warren, would mean Sales was urging the network to come up with eight and one-half hours of new programming, which everyone agreed was too much. There was a consensus that Av Westin's *Our World* made sense because it was cheap to produce, but concern was expressed that by staying with such a low-rated program ABC was surrendering Thursday evenings, opening an opportunity for a show with a different kind of youth appeal—Fox's *21 Jump Street* was mentioned—to walk away with big numbers, as *The Simpsons* would do in the 1990–91 season. Ray Warren's boss, George Cain, liked *The Charmings,* a half-hour comedy.

"And she's got great tits!" joked account executive Peter McCarthy, referring to its female star, Caitlin O'Heaney.

They were uncertain whether weak-rated shows such as *Starman* and *Webster* were better or worse than their untried replacements. "You got to remember," said Mark Mandala, to whom Sales reported and who entered while the meeting was in progress, "that if *Webster* comes back they have to order twenty-two shows. If they pick a new show they only have to order six. Do we want to order twenty-two of those peckerwoods?"

The Sales team didn't always play to win. No one, for example, wanted to sacrifice ABC's stronger comedies—*Who's the Boss?* or *Head of the Class*—against Bill Cosby. They recommended retaining *Our World* on Thursdays, said Ray Warren, because "we have better chances of making inroads against other networks on other nights." It came down to simple triage: "Do you put your best stuff against Cosby, where it doesn't get watched?"

In early May the account executives—whose base salary is about $26,000, which with commissions and bonuses brings the compensation package to about $100,000 annually—performed what Peter McCarthy called their "tap dance" for regular agency clients, visiting the ad agencies with a list of thirty-one pilots in production and reviewing the bare information then available on each. The intention was to give advertisers a second taste of what might be *hot,* to get them thinking about which shows might help sell a Mars bar or a Ford Taurus.

Later in May, each of the three networks invites about a thousand of its customers to an auditorium or ballroom filled with loud, pulsing music. At ABC, this meeting was held on May 28, 1987, two weeks after the Stoddard/Arledge contretemps. It featured Brandon Stoddard standing before a lectern on the stage of the Minskoff Theatre, where he unveiled ABC's eight new shows and those returning. The lingo was about demos (the audience composition for each show). "ABC expects to strongly challenge CBS for second place in households and surpass CBS in young adults," read the glossy booklet handed out to advertisers. "Additionally, ABC should begin to close the gap with NBC in both categories." The prime-time presentation was followed by an open bar and lavish buffet, another in a long series of treats—free trips for clients and their spouses to the British Open, the U.S. Open, *Monday Night Football* games, each leg of the Triple Crown, the World Series, the Super Bowl. There seemed to be genuine enthusiasm among ABC's advertisers, but as Tom Murphy cautioned after circling the buffet room for more than an hour, "Advertisers are always floored after a presentation. You need time to decide what you like."

After the May sales pitch, ABC's account executives again visit individual ad agency clients, this time on an intelligence mission; they want to gather detailed information on the shows to which advertisers might be willing to make a season-long, upfront commitment beginning in September, and to figure out how much money they might spend. The information, which was due in Jake Keever's office by mid-June at the latest, included a sketch of clients' approximate annual budgets, an analysis of which of the shows they preferred and which they did not, and of which of the four quarters they wanted to spend their money in. Getting this information was relatively easy, and not just because it was in everyone's interest to share it. Selling TV spots is not like selling a car or a house. In TV sales the relationships are ongoing, not episodic. You deal with the same clients daily, year-round. You swap information. You learn whom to trust. You become friends. Customers become clients. Often, since the advertising agency is paid a commission based on the value of commercials purchased, the network and the agency share a common interest in maximizing the sale.

Once the intelligence was collected, Keever and his Sales team spent much of June shaping a final sales strategy for the upfront market. With help from ABC Research, Sales estimated the demographics of each series on the schedule and the minimum share of audience ABC would be willing to guarantee advertisers. The problem with these estimates, in fact the central confusion over the approaching 1987–88 upfront market, was something called the people meter. In September, the Nielsen rating service was switching to a new measurement system. In place of the thirty-year-old audimeter system in which 1,700 households were monitored as to *whether* their TV sets were turned on and *what* channels they were watching, and a diary system that encouraged viewers to fill out forms so Nielsen could determine *who* was watching, the new people-meter system promised to expand to 4,000 households, providing each with an electronic device for viewers to press in order to report what they were watching. In some ways, the people meter was a much more accurate system, one that did not rely on memory and thus might provide a more vivid portrait of the viewing audience; but based on the initial tests, the networks were convinced that the people meter would falsely conclude that network audiences had shrunk. People meters, they complained, were not user-friendly—too many viewers wouldn't know how to use them. "It appears that better educated, more technologically conscious persons may be more willing to accept and use people meters than perhaps blue-collar, high school–educated persons who frequently view more television," said Marvin S. Mord, then ABC vice president for Marketing & Research Services. "This may be one reason that Nielsen's people meter ratings appear lower with the new system."

Since there was quite a bit of uncertainty about the new meters, explained Jake Keever, "we have to gamble more on setting prices. Therefore one thing to do is not to sell as much upfront. . . . This year it may go down to 60 percent." Maybe, he said, the network guarantees had to be flexible. Maybe ABC should just guarantee demographics and not the size of the audience. Or maybe they should offer no guarantees at all.

The other great unknown as the upfront approached was a potentially weak advertising marketplace. There had been a wave of mergers among consumer-product companies and advertising agencies. Would the debt service resulting from these mergers siphon advertising dollars? Everyone knew that the prior year, 1986, saw one of the worst network advertising slumps in history. There was mounting concern that the slump was due to the clutter problem. Viewers were said to be grabbing their remote-control devices as a defense against the onslaught of commercials, and advertisers were frantically searching for other outlets. The typical consumer is bombarded by an estimated five thousand advertising messages daily—two million yearly. These messages cost domestic advertisers more than $100 billion annually for TV, radio, and newspaper ads alone. Billions more are spent on marketing campaigns. Brand names are now plastered on our cars, clothes, coffee mugs, church bulletins, parking meters, and restrooms. To stand out, increasingly advertisers produced ads intended to shock. Ads began to resemble the rock videos played on MTV—sexy, sultry, slinky. Advertisers were no longer selling the taste of a beer, or the sturdiness of a pair of jeans. They were selling an emotional association, a look, status. They were preaching: *Consume.*

With network TV flooded by ads, new devices—such as supermarket scanners—are enabling advertisers to identify who is buying their products, and thus better target their desired audience. Increasingly advertisers have turned to "more addressable" outlets—cable TV, direct mail or telephone, coupons, contests, billboards, cooperative advertising exchanges between, say, Disney theme parks and Mars candy bars, sales promotion campaigns such as posters in McDonald's windows, regional magazines, local newspapers, or TV and radio—to sell their products. By 1987 advertisers could reach 80 percent of the U.S. through syndicated shows on independent stations—at half the cost of network advertising. Money was tilting away from network advertising, and Jake Keever could recite the numbers by heart: *In 1980, $5.1 billion of the $81 billion spent on marketing products in the U.S. was spent on the three networks. By 1987, the total monies available for marketing doubled, but so did the promotional budgets. And though network advertising rose to just under $9 billion, its relative share of the total was declining.*

All of which lent a sense of urgency to the 1987 network upfront sales effort. By June 17, 1987, Jake Keever was able to distill his meetings and consultations into a three-page, single-spaced strategy memorandum containing the following assumptions:

> 1) Together the advertising revenues for the three networks would grow at about the 5 percent inflation rate. 2) The total upfront market would grow from $2.6 billion to $2.8 billion. 3) ABC would write 30 percent of the upfront business, a dip from the prior year "due basically to our poor program performance." 4) ABC expected to charge an average of $7.54 as its cost per thousand (CPM) in reaching television households, up from $7.03 over the prior year. ABC assumed NBC would charge the most ($7.82) and CBS the least ($7.02). 5) ABC would "attempt to limit our liabilities on guaranteed sales while remaining flexible on marketplace needs and conditions."

Central to ABC's strategy was its intention to follow the leader—NBC. Or as NBC's own internal strategy memorandum—which called for a 6 percent unit price increase—correctly anticipated:

> The competition is facing the same pattern of program cost increases. If they are smart, they will hang back to see what NBC does, let NBC take the heat for the price increases, then adopt the same strategy and tuck in behind us. . . . We believe this is a year to go for unit price increases rather than volume, although a minimum upfront sales volume of 50% is essential as a sales "base."

The last component of ABC's strategy was pricing and assigning a schedule to each advertiser, a task that fell on the slender shoulders of Elaine Chin, vice president for Prime Time Planning. Chin, an eighty-seven-pound Chinese-American whose lingo is sprinkled with phrases like "real gross dollars," wears Brooks Brothers jackets and oxford shirts and says of herself, "What man would listen to me if I wore dainty clothes? I've got to boss these guys around." On the eve of the upfront sales effort every year, Chin, along with her staff of four, collects the minimum ratings the sales department expects for each program on the ABC schedule. They then divide these into four categories. The A category consists of their best-watched series—that year, *Who's the Boss?*, *Moonlighting*, and other series that aired mostly on Tuesday and Wednesday evenings; the B group is those estimated to be solid but not spectacular performers, which then included *Dynasty, The Slap Maxwell Story,* and, surprisingly, *Dolly,* revealing that Sales did not share Stoddard's enthusiasm for this new variety show; the C group consists of returning shows—like *Hotel* and *Max Headroom* that year—that were expected not to have great allure for advertisers; the D group are the turkeys—*I Married Dora, The Charmings, Sledge Hammer!, Ohara*—shows that advertisers didn't want.

Chin's job was to come up with a rate card or "unit price" for each show in category A through D, using as a starting point ABC Sales' revenue goals for the year and then factoring in two other questions. First, which of the four quarters did the advertiser wish to buy? The second quarter (including April and May) and the fourth (October to December) drew the biggest audiences and thus cost more; the first and third quarters went for a lower price. The upfront sales conformed to the program season, starting with the fourth quarter, or with the fall launch of the network's series, and then carried through the first, second, and third quarters. The next and more important question for Elaine Chin was the comp expected for each show. If advertisers had their way, they would "cherry pick" only the most watched series. It is Chin's task to come up with a balanced schedule, one balanced in ABC's favor. To sell the weakest shows in group D and C, she would structure a rate card that offers "your best to sell your worst"—take two from column A *(Who's the Boss?* and *Monday Night Football)* and get one from column D *(Ohara.)*

Once Chin prepared her pricing recommendations and her bosses signed off in early June, the Sales force fanned out, giving their clients a recommended plan for how to spend their ad dollars. Then Sales waited for each agency to assign its own numbers for the shares and comp each show might command, numbers the advertiser and the network would battle over. They waited for the network leader, NBC, to make the first upfront sale so ABC and CBS could follow along. They waited because waiting was psychologically important for the three networks. To appear too eager to sell, even after the agencies had reworked and submitted the proposed plans, might give the advertiser the edge. There were no secrets in this business—the three network sales forces plied the same large ad agencies for the same nearly $9 billion worth of business—so that if ABC seemed too eager the suspicion would arise that its vast intelligence operation had yielded evidence of a weak market.

The ABC Sales team waited the way surgeons do before an operation. Nervously, they checked off—*Did you bring your overnight bag in case the upfront breaks? What hotel will you stay at?* Screw up, and cost ABC a bundle. Fibbing might be okay, like a candidate saying he expected to win an election he knew was already lost. But telling a blatant lie in this small world, where no one is a stranger and people jump from networks to ad agencies and back was verboten. As in any clubby world, members could be unforgiving.

Day after day went by in June of 1987, with Keever and members of his Sales force relaying rumors, meeting most mornings, passing on information about whether the ad agency or the advertiser insisted on guarantees, whether they would forego them for the right price, whether they wanted to be among the first to take the plunge, or to wait. Daily, Jake Keever's big waistline expanded as he and his deputies courted advertisers at expensive breakfasts, lunches, and dinners.

The advertisers' perspective was a little different. Some ad agencies looked at the networks and saw weakness. Irwin Gotlieb, senior vice president at D'Arcy Masius Benton & Bowles, saw the networks in decline. All of Gotlieb's data—about how much each network sells each quarter and to whom, about how much is sold upfront, the average cost per thousand, the number of fifteen-, thirty- and sixty-second spots sold—are computerized by network. From the vast data at his fingertips he concluded that the network upfront was no longer crucial to advertisers. "My office used to be called 'Network Programming.' It isn't anymore," he said. "It is now called 'National Broadcast.' So in some respects what we do with networks is tactical, not strategic. . . . For one large client in prime time we spend more in syndication and with Fox than we do with any network. The larger the client, the more strategic you can be. The smaller, the more you need the networks." Even though Gotlieb's agency spent about $550 million of its $700 million broadcasting dollars at the three networks, he said that ten years ago it spent 100 percent with the networks.

Despite the erosion of the network advertising dollar and audience share, the Big Three still retained enormous clout. Pete Tyrrell of Johnson & Johnson, who spent $160 million on network television, making J&J one of the top ten network advertisers, saw the Big Three differently than Gotlieb did. For the past seventeen years, Tyrrell had been overseeing the advertising side of the consumer health products company, and he knew all the network people. Although he was the buyer, by mid-June Pete Tyrrell felt as helpless as a seller. "One thing I know for sure, the networks always have more information than I have," he said on June 16, on the eve of the 1987 upfront. "That's their leverage—intelligence." The network sales team had access to one hundred ad agencies. Unlike Irwin Gotlieb, Pete Tyrrell saw only network power: "Everyone wants them. He who has the shows has the dough. That's Fox's problem"—by the summer of 1987 the new fourth network had shows only on Saturday and Sunday nights. Tyrrell remembered how arrogant the networks had been, how they used to threaten advertisers: *The upfront train is about to leave the station. Better get aboard.*

While network "arrogance" had abated, Tyrrell thought the networks still retained the balance of power. He was determined in June of 1987 to cut the best deal he could, and toward this end he conducted eight strategy meetings with J&J's five ad agencies, including their principal agency for the networks, Young & Rubicam. Over lunch at the Italian Pavillion, a restaurant then located along Network Row, Tyrrell outlined J&J's upfront strategy: "We'll go to NBC first with a big number"—$60 million. "We'll probably go to NBC early. We'll let them think they're getting J&J out of the way early. We're thinking that if we make an early deal we get the best inventory and we do it before they get too cocky." Tyrrell was prepared to throw them a bone. "NBC daytime sucks," he said. "Two years ago we closed them out of daytime. If we give them $10 million in daytime, that's a big favor. In return, they give us some benefits in prime time and in *Nightly News.*"

Once he had locked up a deal with NBC, Tyrrell said, "we go to the other two networks and offer them all of our remaining money, or part of it, and threaten them with a two-network buy. And it is a threat because we don't need them both once we buy NBC." That is precisely what Tyrrell did to number-one ABC in 1977—shut it out after ABC demanded prices he found unreasonable. With ABC this time, he hoped to complete an early daytime deal, which was important since J&J usually invested half its daytime monies with the network with the best daytime demographics, which was ABC. By getting ABC daytime out of the way early, said Tyrrell, "That helps us because if we have to take a walk we know we at least have daytime."

Because he believed that prices would rise later in the scatter sales market, Tyrrell decided that J&J would try to buy as much upfront as possible. As for audience guarantees, Tyrrell was of two minds, torn between wanting the safety net of a guaranteed audience, yet knowing he could get a better price if he waived it. Tyrrell's ad agencies urged him to get guarantees from the networks, and his instincts told him to see the heads of Sales at the networks and cut his deals without guarantees. What he didn't want to do, even with all J&J's advertising clout, was play a game of chicken with the networks. He needed them. J&J was a company with forty mass brands, a company that constantly introduced new products. For J&J's familiar products—such as Tylenol—he could steer some advertising monies to the Fox network, or CNN, or to syndicated shows. But when Tyrrell wanted to introduce a new product, the networks were the only place that offered him sure reach and frequency—the only place he could potentially capture 100 percent of all Americans who had televisions. The Fox network didn't have enough affiliated stations to reach 100 percent of viewers, and they programmed only two nights. Ted Turner's CNN reached an average of 1 percent of viewers at its most watched hour. Cable, which was in not quite 50 percent of all homes and consisted of dozens of channels, couldn't command a mass audience. Nor could syndicators who sold station to station. No newspaper or magazine or billboard or cooperative ad attracted a rival mass audience. So the networks had leverage. "The networks line us up like ducks in an amusement park and knock us off one at a time," Tyrrell sighed. "They create this turmoil and say, 'If you don't get in line we won't sell you anything.' "

The network had leverage as long as the sale was made by the end of July. By August, leverage would tilt to the advertiser because the fall season starts in September and it would by then be obvious that there was plenty of unsold time. So the question as the upfront approaches becomes: Who would blink first?

By June 27, ABC had done just one upfront deal—with MGM. The other movie companies, as they do each year, would also sign up early, for two reasons. First, their schedules changed constantly, and studios were willing to pay a premium for flexibility. And second, to attract weekend moviegoers studios preferred to advertise Tuesday through Thursday, and to get the best spots they needed to beat the crowd. But the other advertisers were not budging, not yet anyway. Everyone trafficked in rumors. "The street has it that NBC is about to make a deal with Y&R [Young & Rubicam], Leo Burnett, and BBDO," said Keever on June 30 of three of the five top-spending ad agencies. "Y&R told me they're working with NBC. CBS we haven't heard anything about." Only rumors.

By the last day in June, Keever's department had not made a sale but they had already prepared and submitted to advertisers eighty-two plans worth $599.8 million. One $12 million plan for a packaged-goods manufacturer offered seventy-five prime-time units (spots) on their stronger shows.* The cost per thousand women aged twenty-four to fifty-four, said Keever, would be $23.29—a jump of nearly 40 percent over what the same advertiser paid a year before. Why? Because, said Keever, "we're not giving them any weaker shows." The more important reason for the steep price rise was that this was only the opening gambit. Until Keever knew what NBC would charge, ABC didn't want to ask for less than the market might bear. The price would drop after NBC made its move; after advertisers offered to take weaker shows; after ABC shifted units from the stronger second and fourth quarters to the weaker first and third quarters; and, even more important for networks facing the uncertain implications of the new people meters, after the advertisers indicated they would accept lower viewer guarantees.

The upfront market broke for ABC early in the week of July 6, 1987, only hours after NBC cut its initial deals. By the time Keever lunched on Tuesday with top executives from J. Walter Thompson, which ranked fourth in broadcast spending among all ad agencies, he was determined to impress upon them that ABC had already sold $145 million in ads. "They were surprised," he said. "When the lunch started they only knew of the movie-company deals. But by the end of lunch we showed them that other people were finding ABC an attractive buy." The next morning Keever met with the fifth largest ad agency, BBDO, to spread the same message. They promised to get right back to ABC. "The more orders you write," observed Keever, "the more people feel comfortable with the marketplace."

All through that week on Keever's thirty-sixth floor, hollow-eyed account executives sat behind closed office doors, huddled with ad agency representatives or bent over phones negotiating deals or whispering of other deals already made, warning that the ABC rate card might rise. Bedlam ruled the corridors as nervous agency honchos waited outside the suite of offices shared by Keever and his deputy, John Tiedemann, and one by one were taken inside, like patients being wheeled into surgery.

Jake Keever was sixty, and most of his twenty-three previous upfronts had been like this. At a certain point the advertiser panics. By sundown advertisers had flooded Keever's office with $2 billion worth of requests, even though ABC planned to sell only about $850 mil-

* In return for being granted access to Sales meetings and deliberations, I was asked at times not to name the advertiser.

lion worth of ads, meaning Keever would have to say no to a lot of customers.

This thought was very much on Keever's mind when Dan Burke, doing his daily check on morale, ambled into his corner office carrying a large blue and white umbrella. "How'd the day go, kiddo?" he said to Keever, who looked like a tired elephant stuffed into a small swivel chair behind his modest desk.

Keever gave his COO a rundown of what they had sold so far and how the clamor had become so intense he had asked Elaine Chin to recompute some deals. It would be a late night, with take-out Chinese food for twenty-two.

"Happily," said Burke, standing in the doorway, "there is still a tendency to panic by the other side."

Helping to induce this panic was part of Ray Warren's job. The bearded Warren had played the game from both sides, having worked at Benton & Bowles. Although he was now the seller, he acted like a buyer. Late that night he telephoned one of his agency customers at home. The customer was willing to spend $12 million upfront, and since this client was a public utility it wanted its spots in a serious setting and chose *20/20*. But the price was high.

"The price is $9.68 per thousand," Warren said into the speaker phone. "We did everything we could to get the number down to $9.50, but couldn't. . . . Are you happy?"

"I'm getting happy," answered the account executive. "How can we move this a little bit more? The $9.68 is still a tad high."

"We'll split the difference—$9.59."

"How about $9.55?"

"I'm really not going to get below a 13 percent increase, which is $9.58," said Warren. "Maybe I can shave a nickel off by dropping ads from a better to a weaker show. What if we knock off a few *Hoopermans* and *Slap Maxwells* and move them to the Monday movie and *Ohara*?"

Deal.

After the account executive hung up, Warren said his real bottom line was $9.22 per thousand.

Between Wednesday at 4 P.M. and Friday morning, ABC wrote out orders worth $600 million. But success brought problems. With ten New York account executives selling on a first-come, first-served basis from the same inventory pool of twelve thousand prime-time spots, ABC worried that it might have oversold, particularly on Tuesdays and Wednesdays, their two best nights. With orders pouring in, the

ABC computer broke down. Doing a manual calculation, Elaine Chin's department reported to Keever that ABC had oversold the third quarter. Which meant forty advertisers had to wait while she figured out who had been first on line and renegotiated a schedule for those who bid later.

It turned out to be a much stronger upfront than anticipated. The three networks wrote over $3 billion for prime-time ads in three to four working days, not the usual two weeks, a record. ABC had planned to sell only $850 million and wound up selling $985 million upfront. In all, ABC sold 90 percent of its entire year's prime-time inventory in the upfront market, leaving just 10 percent for the scatter market.*

Prime-time upfront sales at the other two networks were equally robust in 1987. CBS sold about $900 million, and NBC $1.2 billion. And each network got price increases—5 percent per unit in ABC's case, even though its ratings for the 1986–87 year had dropped 12 percent in prime time. By contrast, NBC's ad rate jumped by about 10 percent and CBS's by less than 5 percent. "By not holding back inventory and by pricing aggressively, ABC did better than CBS, which waited too long to sell and priced themselves too low," observed Robert Blackmore, NBC's Sales chief.

But why should a network sell more ads even when its audience declines, as ABC's did? Supply and demand is one answer: The demand was greater for network time than the supply. But why would demand be up? One explanation is that advertisers still needed the networks' mass audiences for their new products, even if the audience had eroded. A second explanation is that the ad agencies were even more anxious than the networks about the new people meters and sought the security of the minimum audience guarantees offered upfront rather than risk higher prices in the scatter market. A third explanation is that since 1988 would be cluttered with ads for both the Olympic games and a presidential contest, advertisers chose to beat the clutter by pouring more resources into 1987. Another explanation is that since all three networks held out for price increases and none folded, advertisers could not play one off against the other, as Pete Tyrrell hoped to do for J&J. Finally, there was panic. As ABC's

* By the end of 1987, ABC would sell a total of $2.5 billion in advertising—43 percent of it in prime time, 19.3 percent in daytime, 14.2 percent in news, 17.9 percent in sports, 3.1 percent on *Good Morning America,* and 2.4 percent on children's programming. Entertainment accounted for nearly 70 percent of revenues.

Ray Warren explained: "It's when Benton & Bowles hears that Y&R is doing business and everybody says, 'What did they think of that we did not think of?' "

Jake Keever chose not to gloat, but Pete Tyrrell was willing to complain. "It happened just as we said it would," he said after the upfront was over. "They got all the lemmings lined up and convinced them it was a good thing to cross the river. And all of them drowned."

Tyrrell did not blame just the networks. Johnson & Johnson, like many corporations, had begun to build its own in-house ad agencies, in part to reduce agency commissions and in part because executives like Tyrrell were suspicious of the advertising agencies. "I often sit around here and ask, 'Are the agencies working for us or for the networks?' " he said, aware that the agencies usually made their money by charging the client a commission of 15 percent on each dollar of billed advertising. The more ads placed and the steeper the price charged by the networks, the more money the agency pocketed. Since a one-stop buy with a network was simpler, and cheaper, than patching together different cable outlets and stations and syndicators, Tyrrell suspected that the agency had a built-in bias to do business with the networks. This bias was abetted by what Tyrrell called the "strutting" rights that came to agency honchos—like the twenty couples Jake Keever took along as ABC's guests to the British Open right after the upfront, or those who got a hello from *Moonlighting* star Cybill Shepherd. Tyrrell believed that the interests of the ad agency and the client sometimes diverged, a point stressed in an internal NBC memorandum. The memo outlining NBC's upfront strategy stated that its inventory was "oversold" by June of 1987, and among NBC's options were "welshing on some obligations or renegotiating." The downside of such an option, NBC wrote, was this: "Neither networks nor agencies are particularly interested in giving money back to the clients."

In the end, the 1987 upfront was a boon to the networks. "It looks like it gives us another year to screw up," Dan Burke announced to Tom Murphy. Yet the strong upfront did not reduce Burke's pessimism about the networks or his commitment to cut costs. Neither he nor Murphy—nor the other two network owners—believed the economics of the business had changed. Between them, cable and independent stations now siphoned more than a quarter of the average nightly prime-time audience. The new owners could not overlook the fact that a syndicated show like *Wheel of Fortune* was on 199 stations with a 33 share, as big an audience as ABC's hit comedy *Who's the*

Boss? reached. One good upfront did not constitute a trend. "I think it's aberrational," said Burke. "I never pay attention to the revenue line. . . . Even if the upfront were 15 percent better, I'd still be struggling to get the organization to be as trim and as efficient as possible."

Dan Burke's preoccupation with costs led, late that summer, to tough negotiations with two News stars. The first was Kathleen Sullivan, the $500,000 anchor of ABC's weekend news and substitute cohost of *Good Morning America,* who eventually went to CBS for $1 million per year when ABC refused to match this offer.

Far more important were the negotiations with Peter Jennings, whose contract would expire in August. Jennings was making $850,000, considerably less than his two counterparts at the other networks. He wanted a raise, though he had no expectations of matching Rather's $3.5 million salary.

The summer of 1987 was an ordeal for Jennings. There had been no movement in his tug of war with producer Bill Lord. He was frustrated with Arledge, chafing, as did others, at Arledge's tendency to disappear for lengthy stretches of time, or not to focus. Jennings was upset—as was David Burke—that Arledge had not settled the Lord matter. And after Arledge had asked Paul Friedman to work with Jennings on a half-hour pilot for a newly formatted *World News Tonight,* Arledge had done nothing with it, treating it like a state secret, not even showing the pilot to David Burke. "I'm always fighting Arledge," Jennings admitted. "We go back a long way. If Arledge says yes, I say no." Added to these professional frustrations were personal ones. His great friend, ABC correspondent Charles Glass, was taken hostage that summer in Beirut. And Jennings and his author wife, Kati Marton, were having marital difficulties, much to the joy of the gossip columns. Jennings was hurting. He felt as if he were "public property," felt that the anchor job had cost him his privacy and maybe his family.

"I'm trying to figure out what fulfills me," Jennings said at the time. "What I have now is a job that is well paid, with enormous visibility. But it's five to seven days around-the-clock, having to be more of a politician than I ever thought I'd be. This job is a lot more than just journalism." He hated doing news breaks from the World Series. Or wrapping his arm around a local anchor to promote an affiliate. Or serving as ABC's spokesman. Or going to what he thought were small dinners and finding he was the bait to lure others. Ironically, among the few people Jennings felt he could talk to about this was Dan Rather. Each shared a sense—the same one shared by ex-presidents—that only a fellow anchor could truly understand his travails, his vulnerability. "Peter and I have talked about the general pressures, special and otherwise, that go with the job, comparing how we feel and how we deal with the corrosive and damaging aspects and its effect on family life," said Rather. "There are not many people you can talk to about it."

In his contract negotiations, Jennings wanted three things in addition to more money. He, of course, wanted the same managing editor title enjoyed by Rather and Brokaw; he wanted to get rid of Bill Lord as well as the power to name Lord's successor; and he wanted the right to veto any coanchor. The three, said Jennings, would represent "recognition from management." Jennings had some leverage. He was good at what he did, and everyone knew it. His ratings were rising. And Howard Stringer at CBS had made him an offer to become a kind of coanchor with Rather. He could do more reports from overseas or from other cities, could work on longer pieces, could enjoy coanchor billing and yet not be chained to an anchor desk. Rather had even added his support, urging Jennings to come on over to CBS.

Jennings wanted to stay at ABC. "Emotionally, I hope I can work out a deal here whereby this becomes a more sensible job," he said. But what he liked about CBS is that he could "do what I do but have more time to think about it, to plan for it." The top managers of Cap Cities and Arledge also wanted Jennings to stay, but they were prepared to replace him with Ted Koppel. "It's no reflection on Peter," said Dan Burke, "but ceding editorial control to anyone on the air is a no-no." They would not make him managing editor, not give him an explicit veto over his producer.

The protracted negotiations with Jennings increased insecurity within News, but nothing compared to the anxiety that ABC's fall schedule aroused. Everyone was worried about the new Dolly Parton show, worried that it might bomb when it debuted on Sunday night in the fall, as ABC's Lucille Ball show had done the previous year. If Dolly failed, so would ABC's entire Sunday night schedule. ABC was already in third place three nights in a row—Thursday, Friday, and Saturday; and management was distraught that Entertainment was not doing a better job of managing one of its few hits—*Moonlighting,* which was chronically over budget. And even though ABC produced this series itself, it had produced only fifteen original episodes in the past season, not the usual twenty-two to twenty-five.

However, even with these headaches there was a sense that in 1988 ABC could climb out of third place with the World Series, the Super Bowl, the 1988 Winter Olympics, and some promising new shows. *Variety* proclaimed: "NBC Has the Momentum; ABC May Be Hot."

Despite the anxieties, there were other signs of progress. By the autumn of 1987, nearly two years after officially taking over ABC, Cap Cities was further ahead of its two principal competitors in making its network a happier place to work. "In the last six months," David Burke said, Cap Cities had changed, particularly toward News. "We see less of Sias. There's a constant effort to praise. We keep hearing that the news division is highly regarded. If two years ago we heard that, we wouldn't have believed it."

Roone Arledge now acknowledged that he had also changed, that he had "more of a business perspective." Routinely now, departments vied to show the efficiencies they had made. "What pleases me," Dan Burke said, "is that there is now pleasure in the pursuit of efficiency."

People at ABC now felt that perhaps Burke and Murphy truly were different from the dreaded new owners at CBS and NBC. Unlike Bob Wright or Larry Tisch, longtime ABC employees assured themselves, they were broadcasters and publishers, who knew about the business. In fact, Murphy did, at least publicly, express greater concern for the public trust than either Wright or Tisch did. Murphy, unlike them, had been a broadcaster. He blamed the FCC for encouraging professional finance types to enter television, buying and selling "stations like they were buying and selling cows." He favored the rule that a company had to own a station for at least three years before it could sell it. "A network," Murphy said, "touches 100 percent of the people every day. . . . I consider being in broadcasting special, and with it comes a special responsibility."

More so than at either NBC or CBS, the new owners of ABC seemed to care for people's feelings, as an incident involving the executive dining room demonstrated. For cost reasons, within weeks of the actual merger Cap Cities had closed the six executive dining rooms and kitchen on the fortieth floor. About a year later, Tom Murphy presided over a big meeting in a conference room at lunchtime. Concerned with costs, no one dared order lunch. But Murphy was hungry, so he sent out for sandwiches, which took a while. "We have to send out for sandwiches because the dining room is closed," explained one ABC radio executive.

"You guys used it?" exclaimed Murphy. "I thought no one used it." He asked Dan Burke to look into establishing another dining room.

By the fall of 1987, ABC had opened a lunch buffet room. Unlike the old dining rooms, it was to be democratic—any one of 145 people at the vice presidential level or above could wander in without a reservation, choose from the cold buffet, and sit at large tables without placecards. Burke and Murphy made it a practice to dine in the communal mess two or three times a week. This was in sharp contrast to the situation at CBS, where Tisch had his own private room and a handful of executives had access to their own rooms, or at NBC, where Bob Wright had his own dining room and only sixteen top executives had access to a cramped sixth-floor dining room. Each time Burke and Murphy used the ABC buffet, they got to know a different executive and helped nudge ABC toward a greater sense of community.

11

NBC: MANAGING THROUGH INSECURITY, WINTER 1987

As 1987 opened and Cap Cities focused more on employee morale, Bob Wright and Jack Welch were preoccupied with advancing their cultural revolution. They were determined to alter both NBC and the television business. In January, they seized on an opportunity to pound home this message, and to best Larry Tisch. Wright announced that NBC would dump its longtime Miami station, WSVN-TV, and replace it with WTVJ-TV, previously a CBS affiliate. Not only was this the biggest switch of affiliates in history, it was the most expensive. For NBC didn't just switch affiliate contracts, but paid an astonishing $270 million to acquire WTVJ. It was the first acquisition by a network of a station aligned with another network.

Counting a Denver station that GE had owned before it acquired NBC in December of 1985, this acquisition gave NBC seven owned stations, reaching 22.4 percent of the nation's homes, nearly the maximum allowable limit of 25 percent. But unlike its two-hundred-plus affiliated stations which distribute network programs to 75 to 80 percent of viewers, an owned station lets the network pocket the profits; it also guarantees that the station will not preempt network shows without permission. The Miami move was a raw display of GE's power.

The message: NBC's affiliates might win a skirmish, as they had when the network sweetened parts of its compensation package in January, but the networks and their affiliated stations were not equal partners. Affiliates could preempt network shows or sign up with CNN, but if they thought this was real power, said Welch on the January day he personally closed the Miami deal, "they were living in yesterday." No, leverage lay with the networks, which could withdraw the affiliation, slashing overnight the station's market value by at least half. No longer would the station be supplied with free network programming. The NBC move "put the fear of God into station operators," admitted Martin Pompadur, whose company then owned eight stations. In any TV market with more than three strong VHF stations, the network affiliate had reason to fret that its network might take its business across the street, diminishing their asset. That's what happened to WSVN in Miami; not only did it lose its NBC affiliation, it was forced to become an independent station.

A second message sent by NBC's bold move was aimed at its network rivals: This is war. Larry Tisch, true to his reputation as "a bottom dweller," had refused to pay a penny more than $170 million for WTVJ-TV. Tisch said of NBC's bid, "They could have bought the station for much less." By buying the Miami station, however, NBC threw CBS off stride in the three-network competition. The appearance at least was that NBC had outmaneuvered Tisch. CBS had lost a valuable affiliate and would be forced to scramble to link up with the station NBC was dumping, to try to raid ABC's affiliate, or to affiliate with an independent station whose weaker signal reached fewer homes in Miami's burgeoning market. Tisch chose to save money and lose viewers, at least in the short run, when he spent $59 million to acquire WCIX, an independent Miami station whose signal reached 20 percent fewer potential viewers.

CBS, whose four owned stations covered just 19 percent of the U.S., was ceding an opportunity. Large urban stations are such cash cows that rarely do they become available, which is why Peter Lund, who ran the CBS stations, urged Tisch to make the deal. Stations generate forty to fifty-five cents of profit for every dollar of revenue, and in 1987 the seven NBC owned stations would yield more than $200 million in profits, half NBC's total. The compound annual profit growth of NBC's owned stations from 1979 through 1987 was 20 percent. "I don't think GE has another business as good as that," said Bob Walsh, who oversaw NBC's station group before it, like the networks, felt the profit squeeze.

The Miami move sent an internal message as well. "The GE bias is towards action," explained J. B. Holston. "The NBC bias was towards inaction." NBC set up committees; GE made quick decisions, and worried less about traditions.

In this spirit, Bob Wright in January 1987 reviewed NBC's negotiations with the National Association of Broadcast Employees and Technicians (NABET). Instead of improving the contract when it expired on March 31, as was normally the case, Wright told Gene

McGuire and his Personnel team he wanted changes, particularly work-rule concessions. Wright also intensified the review started under Grant Tinker to determine whether NBC should move from its home at 30 Rockefeller Plaza when its lease expired to larger, more modern space, and he retained the consulting firm of Booz, Allen & Hamilton to find out why NBC spent $470 million on operations and technical services, including its studios, crews, office space, and satellite time.

In early 1987 GE Capital freed more money for acquiring and financing media properties, including local stations, cable-program services, cable-system ownership, and movie studios. Meanwhile, Wright had Holston look overseas for additional opportunities. At Welch's instigation, in January Wright hired Thomas S. Rogers, senior counsel to the House Telecommunications Committee for five years, to search for new business in America. Although the network and its stations would make over $400 million for NBC in 1987, Rogers, like Welch and Wright, believed the networks were "out of step ultimately with where the business may be going."

Wright traveled frequently, still attended meetings that were kept secret from NBC executives, and often canceled weekly president council meetings, alienating its members. While Wright was aware of some unhappiness, he was determined to bring NBC around to his vision of the future. So he gathered eleven of NBC's top managers for a three-day seminar, led by a college professor, at GE's Fairfield conference center in February. Each executive was asked to prepare a brief paper about NBC ten years into the future, addressing these questions: *What impact would technology have? What is the future of cable? Sports? News? High-definition TV? The VCR? Would the three networks still exist? The Fox network? How will the global television marketplace change? What will happen to government regulations?*

When the executives had composed their thoughts, each of them—News president Larry Grossman and group vice presidents Ray Timothy, Bob Butler, and Bob Walsh, among others—stood up and read what they had written, then divided into teams to see if they could agree on a single draft. What Wright wanted—if not from this meeting then from subsequent ones—was a common statement expressing "the visions and values" of NBC. The executives failed to reach a consensus. Bob Wright wanted to focus on new business opportunities—in cable, overseas, in new alliances; many NBC executives wanted to concentrate on widening their ratings lead over CBS and ABC. But before the meeting broke a committee of ten was appointed to produce a "visions and values" statement. This committee would work for months and come up empty.

A larger group of about a hundred NBC executives gathered on March 22, 1987, at the Sheraton Bonaventure Hotel in Fort Lauderdale. After a Sunday evening welcome from Chairman Welch, they spent the better part of three days in a series of meetings. The objective of what was to become an annual spring management rite was still to seek a "consensus" concerning a strategy for NBC.

Wearing an open-necked shirt and sports jacket, his scalp pink from the Florida sun, Welch seemed relaxed. But then he began to tell the hushed executives how NBC was only one of fourteen large GE businesses, how "the goal in our company is to be the number-one or number-two player in every business we're in. In fact, our long-term goal is to be the most highly valued [American] corporation in the world." He asked whether NBC was better off under RCA or GE, and answered: "I'd say for the good people, it's a dynamite deal. For the *turkeys,* it's only marginal."

The advantage GE brought, he said, was "buckets of money," as well as the ability to act fast. But unlike RCA, it didn't tolerate "turkeys. . . . Those of you who aren't good, who aren't winners . . . don't get on the NBC boat."

Most NBC executives sat there absolutely stunned. Welch could have emphasized how successful the merger had been for GE. He could have said the merger with RCA "has exceeded our expectations," as he would tell GE shareholders a month later. He could have hailed NBC as the most profitable network in history, the prime-time leader for each week of the 1986–87 season, with a two ratings-point lead over CBS and four points over ABC. He could have mentioned NBC's triumphs in late-night programming with Johnny Carson and David Letterman, or its morning victories with *Today,* or its number-one ranking more weeks than not in 1986 with Tom Brokaw's *Nightly News.* But Welch wanted to send a stern, parental message. As he explained later, he wanted to instill "insecurity."

In the course of his lengthy presentation, Welch offered only four stray compliments to NBC. And each time he did he hastened, as if correcting a mistake, to compare NBC to the four GE companies with greater profits, or to warn that NBC was unprepared for tomorrow. He offered no congratulations. He did not speak of the privilege of running a network. Welch stood before them as a proponent of change—"quantum change," not "incrementalism."

"Layers are the bane of the corporation," he warned. "Layers not only cost, they screw up communications." He didn't say to them what he said privately, which was that he thought the top layer of NBC vice presidents were bureaucrats, "little bears," and with the possible exception of Ray Timothy, he expected them all to leave over time. He was eager for them to go, and had told Wright, "I think you've got to make some calls over the next twelve months." What Welch said to these NBC executives who sat frozen in their chairs was: "We're going to demand from you earnings growth every year. And don't give us any shrugs about that. Those are the rules of the road. . . . You take charge of your destiny. If you don't, we will."

Some NBC executives found Welch's speech inspirational. "I wasn't intimidated. I was inspired," said Tartikoff's deputy, Warren Littlefield. He believed Welch's message encouraged change, not fear. But most NBC executives believed Welch's speech was a put-down. The word *turkey* stuck. They were offended by the paucity of praise, by how Welch mocked the past, by his failure to say that NBC was special.

In Hollywood, Grant Tinker, who saw a tape of Welch's speech, was troubled. He felt "the people at NBC should have been allowed to celebrate, to savor their triumphs. I thought Jack could have paid more attention to that triumph." A leader should instill a sense of security among employees, he said. "My idea of a productive company is a happy company," not "an anxious company."

Tinker believed that morale mattered, that NBC or CBS would pay a penalty for its unhappy employees. Business consists of more than rigorous cost control and "downsizing" and brilliant strategic planning. So, too, the best ball teams are not necessarily those which, man for man, have the best athletes. Sparky Anderson's Detroit Tigers enjoyed tremendous success throughout the first half of the eighties—just as the Portland Trail Blazers did in the late seventies—not because they had the best ballplayers, but because of intangibles—team chemistry, constant communication, the manager's or coach's contribution to a clubhouse environment that made players feel wanted, feel good about themselves and the team.

The new network owners were conveying a debilitating signal, said Warner Brothers chairman Robert Daly. "I don't believe you can run the business and be so negative. They talk about losing their share and of rising costs. People have to come to work every day trying to figure out how to be successful. To walk in and say, 'This is a terrible business!' only demoralizes the staff. I feel I have to come to work every day and pump up my managers." Daly's boss, Warner Communications CEO Steve Ross, broadened the point: "I probably could have saved $5 to $10 million dollars. But by not 'saving' $5 to $10 million I didn't lose one good person I didn't want to lose. And I didn't affect the morale of the entire company."

Since a network made the bulk of its money from its entertainment product, and this product was created by free-agent suppliers who were at liberty to work elsewhere, a congenial atmosphere and a sense of freedom mattered. Told of Welch's speech, Ross sought to explain why morale mattered. He talked about Daly and Warner Brothers, which makes about twenty-five movies a year. "How many are successful? Seven or eight. Do I want him to think he's a 'turkey' when only seven or eight are a success? I want him thinking he's the best. I want him to take risks. If he releases a movie and it's not successful, I'm on the next plane out there and I'm saying, 'Guys, I would have made the same goddamn movie!' That's my opening statement. When a movie is a big hit, they don't see me. I want them to take the credit. . . . Jack is wrong. You can't operate a company by fear, because the way to eliminate fear is to avoid criticism. And the way to avoid criticism is to do nothing."

Of course, Welch spoke of better communications, insisting that employees should be free to advance their ideas, to take chances, to thrive in a less bureaucratic atmosphere. But that's not what many NBC executives heard. Nor was it what many Kidder, Peabody executives heard after GE acquired their Wall Street firm and behaved as if any smart GE executive could step in and make it function smoothly. Welch meant to say: *You can't relax.* Many at NBC heard: *You can't enjoy.*

There might have been less of a negative reaction to Welch's speech if Wright had regularly gone through a buffet line with NBC managers, as Tom Murphy and Dan Burke had begun to. Or had he spent more time talking about their product—the programs aired on NBC—rather than their cost. Or had Wright been more sensitive to his own echo, had he answered their memos or patted more backs.

After the Florida management retreat what remained with Welch were the private conversations he had over drinks with NBC executives. "They refused to acknowledge the word cable," Welch remembered. "It was as if it didn't exist. . . . People in the midst of change just get frightened to death by change." Wright shared Welch's sense of frustration.

The news division had another reason to be fearful, since earlier in the month Larry Tisch had cut CBS News's budget by 10 percent.

Now they heard Wright say on the last night of the conference that NBC News was losing $150 million annually, including some questionable corporate overhead costs charged to News. In the presidential-election year coming up, Wright estimated that the three network news divisions would together lose $450 million. "That isn't good management, that's not good anything. That is just dumb. . . . I wouldn't be doing my job if I don't help [find] a solution. . . . And you're not in the right company if we don't act on controlling some of that." He had read about the $4 to $8 million or more Rupert Murdoch lost each year on the *New York Post*. Yet he said tartly, "Cumulatively, forever, the *New York Post* hasn't lost half as much as we lost last year in News. I mean, sometimes I walk around and I just can't believe the numbers. And I come from a big numbers business. I'm just amazed."

Grossman and his colleagues in News were now resigned to some budget reductions, though until the McKinsey report was delivered no one would know how much "waste" there was in News. NBC News had not earned a profit since 1979, and in 1987 was spending $275 million. Tom Ross, working with McKinsey and helping Grossman decode Wright, noted, "No one manages the news division. Larry is the publisher, and there's no editor. Seventy percent of the people in the division earn more than seventy thousand dollars a year. How many reporters at *The New York Times* or *Washington Post* earn more than seventy thousand dollars?"

By the spring of 1987, talking about costs was no longer heresy and Grossman was no longer pleading for a larger News budget, as he had the previous November. He was now prepared to cut. But he was puzzled. Did Wright and Welch want News to earn a profit? Or simply to break even? Would GE be content if News simply reduced its losses? At the time Grossman believed that the best News could do was trim its losses.

Wright did not say how much he planned to cut the News budget. He had learned from his initial encounters with the media to avoid putting anything in writing, or even from making sharp demands that might get into the papers. He would use stealth, and the facts generated by the McKinsey study, to wear down News. Privately, however, Wright whispered that his "theoretical objective was to break even," though he wasn't sure he could achieve that. Privately, Jack Welch said it wouldn't be unusual if News continued to lose money. GE's medical business lost money, as did the GE business that manufactured panels for circuit breakers. It was part of servicing the customer.

"News is one element that makes a network a network," said Welch. "People identify with it. It provides lead-ins. It's why I watch television—that and sports."

Had Grossman and the journalists within NBC News heard this, they might have been less upset, or even relieved. They did not hear it because Welch and Wright wanted to force News to "examine the way it does business." They wanted revolutionary change. Only slowly would Jack Welch and Bob Wright learn that a network changed incrementally.

12

CBS: TISCH CUTS NEWS–AND HIMSELF, MARCH 1987

There were fresh flowers on Larry Tisch's private dining-room table at CBS, the bacon was crisp, the English muffins toasted just the way he liked them. His expensive navy blue pinstripe suit and red and white polka-dot tie reflected Tisch's elevated status and power. And yet, as he chatted with a visitor* the morning of March 10, 1987, he was feeling both powerless and hurt. It was seven days after he had backed down and told CBS affiliates he would not reduce their compensation; eight days after the Writers Guild had struck CBS and ABC News over proposals to give management more flexibility in hiring and firing; four days after CBS News announced that it was firing 215 people and slashing its budget by $36 million or 10 percent; one day after he narrowly averted the resignation of News president Howard Stringer by insisting that the *Times* got it wrong when they quoted him as saying that these cuts were Stringer's idea, not his. And *now this!*

Tisch was sullen as he glanced at the morning papers. Once again the man once hailed as CBS's savior was being reviled. Dan Rather, who was paid $68,000 of shareholders' money each week, was pictured on the picket line, proclaiming that to avoid layoffs he and others at CBS News had volunteered to reduce their pay. Andy Rooney, the outspoken *60 Minutes* commentator, was calling Tisch a heartless cost cutter. In *The Washington Post,* TV critic Tom Shales, who is read along Network Row like an ayatollah, said that the "Morale at CBS is, if possible, lower than rock bottom" and blamed Tisch. With impunity, CBS news correspondents—his employees!—told Shales that Tisch was a liar and an ogre. Then when Tisch turned to the editorial page of *The New York Times,* his bible, the one paper his family and friends all read, there at the top of the opposite page was

* The author was the visitor.

an op-ed piece by his most famous employee, Dan Rather. Entitled "From Murrow to Mediocrity?," under Rather's byline were these words:

> Our new chief executive officer, Laurence Tisch, told us when he arrived that he wanted us to be the best. We want nothing more than to fulfill that mandate. Ironically, he has now made the task seem something between difficult and impossible.
>
> I have said before that I have no intention of participating in the demise of CBS. But do the owners and officers of the new CBS see news as a trust . . . or only as a business venture?

If Rather or any of these other critics worked for Loews, Tisch would undoubtedly have fired them. And no one would have noticed. But at CBS nothing was private. Every single day the media reviewed the TV shows on his CBS network, displayed a daily Nielsen ratings scorecard of how miserably the shows were performing, published accounts of internal battles, including interviews with the losers. For the first time in a distinguished career as an investor, Tisch was being mocked by the media. He couldn't even control his own employees without inviting more bad publicity.

"I feel hurt because it's a lot of nonsense," Tisch exclaimed, leaving untouched his English muffin and bacon while he read and reread the morning's insults. Was it true that Rather and others had offered to cut their salaries? "These are the biggest bunch of liars I've ever seen in my life!" Tisch sputtered. He noticed that in *The Washington Post,* CBS's congressional correspondent, Phil Jones, accused him of betraying a September pledge made over dinner with the Washington bureau that "there wouldn't be any cuts, no cuts in people involved in news gathering."

"Who is Phil Jones?" Tisch asked, unaware that Jones was his chief congressional correspondent.

At one moment Tisch's bald head could not be seen as it sunk beneath the newspaper he held in front of his face, and then his nostrils flared as he released the paper onto the flowers and wailed about the awful things CBS employees said about him. He read aloud the words of CBS correspondent Lem Tucker, who said that at the September dinner in Washington Tisch "looked us all in the eye and obviously lied when he said this wasn't going to happen."

"He's a son of a bitch, Lem Tucker!" cried Tisch. "Wait till I tell him what I think of him."

Tisch was incensed, and became more so when he read that News president Stringer wanted to stretch the cuts out over a longer period but that Tisch had refused. "Unbelievable!" Tisch moaned, again tossing the newspaper against the flowers. In fact, said Tisch, he had left the reductions to Stringer. "If anything, I reduced the size of the cuts. I took six correspondents off the list to be fired!" One of them, he said, was Lem Tucker. Yet Larry Tisch was wounded that he got no credit for rescuing them and saving Tucker, who was a network rarity, a black correspondent. He dismissed Andy Rooney as "an old blowhard who makes $400,000 a year for two minutes a week!" It was true, as Shales reminded readers, that he had said employees were "lucky" to be fired now. "It's as good a time as any," he again explained, since U.S. unemployment was at its lowest level in years. "Would they rather get laid off when there were no jobs available?"

It enraged him that the conflicts between Black Rock and News, between entertainment and news values, were presented as if they started with Larry Tisch. After all, hadn't Edward R. Murrow thirty years before warned of the "clash between the public interest and the corporate interest"? When Murrow exposed Senator Joseph McCarthy in a 1954 *See It Now* broadcast, a timid CBS refused even to promote the show. Did Dan Rather not remember that Murrow and producer Fred W. Friendly reached into their own pockets to pay for an ad in *The New York Times*? Did Rather forget that Friendly resigned as president of CBS News in 1966 when the network chose to televise reruns of *I Love Lucy* rather than present live Vietnam War hearings before the Senate Foreign Relations Committee? And even the sainted Murrow, as great a journalist as he was, made compromises. Was his *Person to Person* broadcast, where he entered the homes of, say, Bogart and Bacall, so very different from *Lifestyles of the Rich and Famous*? And, more recently, was it Larry Tisch who had hired a former Miss America to host the *CBS Morning News*? *What hypocrites!*

Tisch was still boiling when Jimmy, the third of his four sons, entered the dining room and commiserated with him. Jimmy urged Tisch to write his own op-ed piece to attack those who called him a liar. Tisch liked the idea, and after pondering who could draft it decided to ask Jay L. Kriegel, the public relations consultant who had worked on and off with the Tisches for a dozen years. But before calling Kriegel, Tisch first wanted to talk to Howard Stringer about Dan Rather.

Trailed by his son, Tisch marched into his office, placed his feet on a nearly bare desk, and pressed the Stringer button on his phone.

Without bothering to say hello, Tisch asked Stringer: *Is it true Rather proposed to cut his salary?*

Not exactly, said Stringer.

"They never approached you on anything? They never approached me!" said Tisch.

Yes, but Rather's agent, Richard Leibner, and several well-paid members of the news division had raised the issue, vaguely, said Stringer.

"So even though they didn't give you a proposal, you shot it down," Tisch said into the phone. "So there is some truth to it. But they didn't present it to me!"

I thought they presented it to you! said Stringer. *Maybe they presented it to Gene Jankowski?*

Tisch's laugh sounded like a cry. "This is great! Sickening!" Then he asked another question: "Should I answer in an op-ed piece?"

Not yet, said Stringer. *Unless you can make a commitment that there will be no more layoffs!*

"I won't give them any promises on layoffs!" Tisch snapped.

"Calm down, Dad," said Jimmy.

"I just won't do that!" exclaimed Tisch. He felt passionately about making binding pledges, and not just because he privately hoped to cut more. He wouldn't sign a standstill agreement in 1986, and he wouldn't make promises about layoffs now. "You have to do what's right for the company." He made it clear that the issue for him was "waste." How else to explain, he said, why CBS News's budget had tripled to nearly $300 million since 1978 "with no additional news?"

The powerful Tisch was learning, as were the other new owners, that there were limits to his power over affiliates, or Hollywood, or cable. But now he was confronting limits to his power over his own people. If not for these News tantrums, Tisch thought he could "take half the people out of News." Instead, he was cutting a mere $36 million, 215 jobs, including a paltry 14 correspondents. CBS News would still be left, at the end of the year, with 1,105 full-time and 245 part-time employees. *What a bunch of babies!* Tisch thought. Half of America's steelworkers lost their jobs over the past decade without half the fuss.

When Tisch gave examples of fat and waste to people like Rather, he said, they privately did not challenge him. "They just don't want to say it publicly. Journalism is a fraternity." He had invited Rather to lunch three weeks earlier. "He understood everything," Tisch said. "I thought we had an understanding—he didn't agree with everything—but he understood." Now he was hurt that Rather wasn't "the team player" Gene Jankowski assured him he was, and flabbergasted that Rather went public with his opposition while over at ABC his friend Tom Murphy made cuts without a public peep from News. Tisch was chagrined that Rather "never talked to me" before writing the op-ed piece, the way, for instance, Tom Brokaw first sent to Bob Wright and Larry Grossman copies of a *Washington Post* op-ed piece he had written in which he conceded that NBC News had to be more cost-conscious. Rather simply announced to Stringer what he was doing. Tisch knew that Rather hadn't even written the piece himself, but that it had been drafted by senior political producer Richard Cohen, and this made him even angrier.

As angry as he was, Tisch was intimidated by Rather's power to portray him as a cost-cutting ogre. This might not matter to Tisch's Wall Street friends, who kept score by the numbers. But among his newer friends on the boards of the Metropolitan Museum or the New York Public Library it did matter. On Wall Street, money mattered. Uptown, respectability mattered. By "saving" CBS in September 1986, Tisch had achieved social respectability. Now his own employees were scandalizing him.

Tisch also knew that the controversy would undermine public confidence in CBS News, the jewel in the network's crown. He knew he was making the new owners of ABC and NBC look good. Tisch was so shaken as to concede that perhaps he had mishandled it. "Maybe I am [guilty]," he said.

But he was ambivalent. On this March day, Tisch drew strength from his conviction that he had done the right thing by his shareholders. Anyway, he said unconvincingly, "Time heals most of these things." In the end, Tisch would not write his own op-ed reply for fear it would prolong the controversy.

The same morning, over at the Broadcast Center a half mile away on West Fifty-seventh Street, Dan Rather, wearing yellow and blue suspenders, sat in his dimly lit, antique-filled office off the newsroom, and in a measured but steely voice said of his boss: "I'm finding it dangerous to deal with Larry Tisch. He takes things literally. And he takes things too far . . . he doesn't allow for light and shade. If you say, 'Yes, there is fat,' that gets turned around to, 'Dan agrees with me there is waste.' And the next thing is you have $30 million in budget cuts, and that's not the end of it." Was it true, as Tisch had claimed, that Rather had agreed to cooperate in exchange for minimal *Evening News* reductions? Yes, he was consulted, Rather said, without acknowledging a deal. But he never "signed off on firing 215 people!" Nor did he sign off on the way it was done—"all in one whack."

Why, if Rather agreed there was fat, were he and others resisting cuts? Why so much emotion? "Nobody here ever calls CBS a company," Rather explained. "Nobody ever thinks of it as a company. One speaks either of CBS News, or the Organization, or the Institution. No one calls it 'the Company.' They don't because there is a sense here of being in a religious order. It's more what might be called a calling than a craft. People here invented broadcast journalism." Some of the fourteen correspondents who were fired—like twenty-two-year veteran Ike Pappas—had risked their lives covering wars for CBS News. They were loyal, and yet Tisch discarded them.

"Nearly everybody believed Larry Tisch when he came in and said he would do nothing to diminish News's quality," Rather continued. And yet Rather felt conflicted. Time had changed him, and not just by softening the sharp dimple on his chin. To watch clips of a young Rather is to be struck by how much more relaxed and conversational he had been on the air then, before he carried the weight of the broadcast on his shoulders as managing editor. He didn't want to let people in the news division down. "In many ways the reputation of their work depends on me," he said. Coach Rather would defend his team against Tisch. Rather was responsible for an organization and not just for himself.

He took a certain joy in being Coach Rather—standing up to Tisch, or Richard Nixon, or Senator Jesse Helms—on behalf of his CBS team; and yet he liked being close to Tisch and the group in power at Black Rock. In many ways Rather was old-fashioned—he still wore button-down shirts and wide, big-knotted ties, and opened doors for others; yet he could be a tough-as-nails politician, as he was when he outclawed Roger Mudd to succeed Cronkite as anchor—"Roger Mudd didn't even see Dan go by him," said one News executive. Rather prided himself on loyalty, yet was torn between two sets of loyalties—to his own staff and to his friend and immediate boss Howard Stringer because, he said, "the next person in that job might be from Coopers and Lybrand."

Rather's forced TV smile, said some colleagues, reflected a tormented soul. "He does things to impress people," producer Richard Cohen said in 1987, before he had a falling-out with Rather. "Every time an outside reporter is here he goes into his aggressive managing editor routine. It's embarrassing. One of Tisch's sons visited the fish bowl [as the newsroom is called] a few months ago. I couldn't stand everyone kissing this guy's ass. Dan was in front of the room. After the broadcast, Dan came in and conducted the most thorough, ludicrous postmortem I ever saw. 'What did the opposition do?' 'Did they beat us?' It was like he was auditioning for *Lou Grant.* At a lunch with Senator Al Gore, Dan went around handing out cookies! I think Dan Rather is playing himself."

Rather was clearly upset with Tisch's cuts, but he coolly managed his feelings. Outside his corner office and within the news division, however, there was a riot of emotion. Andrew Heyward, a rising young producer on the *Evening News,* said, "We perceived Tisch as a white knight. Yet it is possible that when he takes off his helmet he is Darth Vader." Like the people at NBC, Rather's colleagues now feared that their new owner had only begun to hack away. They blamed Tisch, not themselves, forgetting their own innocent September tributes to him as someone who would restore past glories and lost viewers. They ignored their own failure to inspect Tisch's record of remorseless cost cutting. They only remembered the generalized promises Tisch had made to their Washington bureau in September 1986, how he pledged to be a friend of News. They had forgotten how he had reassured CBS's three group presidents that their jobs were secure—and a month later fired Peter Derow.

While it was true that Larry Tisch never ordered News to cut its budget, everyone in the division knew he didn't have to. The events leading to this very public fratricide began when Tisch returned from Europe in January and asked to meet with Rather, then with the management of the news division. He told them News could reduce its expenditures by 20 percent—by over $50 million. Howard Stringer and his managers knew that if they didn't make the cuts, Coopers & Lybrand would, and the carnage would be awful.

Starting on Saturday, February 28, the senior News staff met for six straight days in Stringer's conference room. They fought and cajoled and in the end got everyone from Rather to Tisch to sign off on their $36 million budget-reduction plan. When the cuts were announced on March 6, Stringer and his team sighed that despite the pain, they had managed to avoid Tisch's $50 million target. They were pleased to have sneaked past Tisch the fact that one-third of the cuts actually represented unfilled budget lines or people about to retire. And News had arrived at these cuts without turmoil. They had even, they assured each other, made improvements, particularly in ending the practice of having producers work exclusively for the *Evening News.* From now on producers would be in a pool, available to all the broadcasts.

"Howard was a lion tamer," observed Eric Ober, one of Stringer's deputies. "He had a chair in one hand and a gun with blanks in the other. And he had Dan Rather on a stool, and Mike Wallace on a stool, and Don Hewitt, and everyone else. The problem is that at any time the lions could eat the lion tamer, as they did Howard's two predecessors. But they thought this time the gun had real bullets." They knew that Tisch was "backing the lion tamer."

By March 6 Stringer thought he had accommodated everyone, including Tisch, and went to bed pleased, determined that this was the last purge he would have to endure. He was awakened Saturday morning by a call from the *Times*'s Peter Boyer, who told him he had just called Tisch and the CBS president told him the cuts were Stringer's idea. Boyer's piece appeared in Monday's paper and quoted Tisch as saying, "I never said to Howard, 'We have to cut the budget at the news division.' That's the truth. Howard called me a month ago and said, 'Larry, I've got some ideas on restructuring the news division. It'll take me about thirty days to put them together.' I said, 'Fine, Howard, I'll be happy to go over them with you.' "

When members of the news division read Boyer's story, they exploded: *Larry Tisch, that liar, is blaming Howard!* Tisch's disingenuous statement to Boyer made Stringer a hero within news, and Tisch a villain. Dozens of supportive phone messages from correspondents and others greeted the News president on the day Boyers's story ran in the *Times.* But this offered no solace to Stringer, for he was convinced that he looked to the outside world like Tisch's fall guy or ambitious errand boy. Either way, unless he extracted a clarification of some kind from Tisch today, Stringer told associates, he would have to resign.

Stringer left the Broadcast Center and went over to Black Rock to see Jankowski. Meanwhile, Mike Wallace and Don Hewitt called Tisch, whom they had publicly defended, and asked if they could talk. Tisch suggested lunch that day. In Tisch's private dining room, Wallace and Hewitt warned that Stringer was close to quitting.

What should I do? Tisch asked.

Acknowledge that the budget reductions were your idea, they told him.

A floor below, Stringer sat with Jankowski and said the same thing, that his future credibility in the news division required a public clarification from Tisch. A public statement was drafted, and clutching it, Jankowski bounded up the flight of stairs and joined Tisch, Hewitt, and Wallace. Jankowski explained that he thought there was a way out of this bind, a way to make everyone happy, and he handed Tisch the draft statement.

Ask Howard to join us! Tisch told Jankowski.

"The *Times* took my quotes out of context completely," Tisch told Stringer as soon as he entered. "The cuts were instigated by me." He explained that after the dismissal of Stringer's two predecessors within a single year, he was actually trying to build Stringer up, not undermine him. There were those at CBS who believed Tisch, who believed his problem was his carelessness with words and his impatience to move on to the next point. To friends, Tisch was imprecise; to many at CBS, Tisch shaved the truth. Both explanations might be true.

Stringer accepted Tisch's explanation. Shortly after lunch, CBS issued a public clarification from Tisch: "I suggested having Coopers and Lybrand do an in-depth study of the division," but instead accepted "Howard Stringer's suggestion that the news division examine itself . . ." Although Tisch didn't mention the 20 percent News budget reduction he had proposed in January, he added: "I accepted wholeheartedly their recommendations of an approximately 10 percent reduction."

The News budget would continue to polarize CBS. Unlike NBC, which was using McKinsey & Company to establish a common ground of facts, at CBS there was little common ground. As long as the facts were disputed, the argument could never be resolved. And as long as the debate was public, Larry Tisch, perceived by the outside world and by those within CBS as all-powerful, would privately feel victimized, powerless.

13

NBC NEWS GATHERS FACTS ON ITSELF, MARCH 1987

The same struggles between public versus shareholder responsibility, the same almost religious conflict between old and new values tore at each network. What was different was the way each battle was fought. CBS engaged in a full-fledged public war in which Larry Tisch was left bloodied and the casualties were chronicled in the press. ABC's was a quiet skirmish, attracting little notice, even though the new owners would slash their News budget as deeply as Tisch did. The battle at NBC was neither as loud as at CBS nor as quiet as at ABC.

What was odd about the news divisions at the three networks was that when it came to self-analysis they often practiced bad journalism. They lacked hard facts. Neither the journalists nor management knew the average pay of correspondents or camera crews, or the actual cost per story, or how many pieces a producer averaged per year, or how many assigned stories got on the air, or the savings to be realized if the networks sometimes pooled a camera at presidential press conferences or relied on an affiliate to report a breaking local story. There was not even an account of the true losses within the news division. The two sides substituted opinions for information. This is why Bob Wright felt he needed McKinsey & Company to do the reporting not only for him but for NBC News itself.

In the end, the most intelligent battle was waged at NBC because the combatants had access to the best reporting—McKinsey's. John Stewart started gathering facts in December of 1986. By March of 1987, he had quietly interviewed hundreds of News employees and had told Larry Grossman that News—like the auto companies—had "to find a new way to make cars with fewer workers who are higher paid and do more things with more technology." The central task for News managers, said Stewart, was "to avoid trauma."

NBC News would have to change, but not radically, for the changes could be parceled out over five years or so. Stewart felt that Larry Tisch's 10 percent reduction in CBS's News budget was not excessive, certainly not compared to the reductions in other American industries. What was excessive, he thought, was the brutality of the cuts, the sudden layoffs rather than phased attrition, and the resulting headlines. "All these guys come in and think 'cut, cut,' " said Communications chief Bud Rukeyser. "Then they learn when they cut 10 percent that they are in the papers portrayed as a bad guy. In any other business if you cut 10 percent you're a good guy."

Stewart wasn't sure it would be easy to find common ground between Wright and Welch on the one hand and News on the other. He knew that if Wright aspired to succeed Welch at GE, the peer group that mattered most was at GE, not NBC. "There are fourteen Bob Wrights in the company," said James P. Baughman, a key member of Welch's headquarters staff, and of Wright, GE didn't "really know the full story about [him] yet." John Stewart was aware as well of the gap between the GE culture and the network news culture. Stewart defined the GE culture as: "hard driving, numeric . . . competitive, analytic." They were a group that tended to challenge "each other up and down about how they're going to win or lose." In contrast, the NBC News culture asked: "Where's the story? How am I going to get it?" And they were "not highly analytic about themselves." Stewart knew the two sides were "searching for common values with uncommon languages."

Early on, Stewart agreed not to offer his recommendations in McKinsey's name but to let Grossman present them as if they were his own. By the end of March, Grossman would edit Stewart's memo and prepare for an April 3 summit meeting with Wright as if he were cramming for his oral exams.

But Grossman was still confused as to whether Wright wanted News to show a profit, break even, or produce a smaller loss. Grossman believed there was no way News could break even. "It's out of the question. But we can operate more efficiently," he said. Nor was there agreement on the size of NBC News's deficit. Wright claimed that News was losing either $150 million or $120 million (Wright now used both figures) and Grossman's staff estimated $50 million, excluding network overhead costs charged to News. Grossman was further confused because he had no relationship with Welch or Wright. Or as one NBC executive said, "He can't read them. Grossman can't whisper to Wright, 'Let's compromise at $50 million.' And Wright can't confide in him, 'How do we sell this to Welch?' "

On the eve of their April 3 meeting, Grossman handed to Wright his version of Stewart's draft. The memo revealed the distance Grossman had traveled. Instead of blocking budget cuts, as he did in November, Grossman now welcomed them. And he accepted that News losses were closer to Wright's figure than his own. "News represents 10% of NBC's net revenues," the memo stated, "and 16% of its expenses. . . . Including corporate overhead, the [News] Division's loss in 1987 will increase to $100 million, excluding $20–$40 million in indirect revenues from news product." Grossman spoke with enthusiasm of reducing management layers at the top of the news division, of decentralizing the correspondent assignment process so that bureau chiefs, the central news desk, and the assignment desk on each news program no longer "overlapped"; of how there had "not been a premium on management systems" to oversee union contracts or dampen overtime; of the need to cut out the dead wood among those correspondents who rarely got on the air, to save money by relying more on affiliates to cover local stories, by pooling the three network cameras at press conferences, or by using CNN footage.

By all accounts, the meeting attended on April 3 by Wright, Grossman, Stewart, Tom Ross, and a few staff members went well. In June, the full three-volume McKinsey report was submitted to Grossman and Wright. While NBC News ratings had improved steadily in both the evening and morning segments, McKinsey reported that News's average annual costs between 1981 and 1987 expanded faster (11.4 percent) than its revenues (9.2 percent). After 1979 the revenue and expense lines on the McKinsey charts moved in opposite directions, and were drifting further apart. Another chart revealed that News costs inched up slowly in 1981, 1982, 1983, 1985, and 1986, and rose sharply in only one year—1984, a presidential election year. What was unexpected was that after jumping from $207.3 million in 1983 to $282.5 million in 1984, instead of slipping back down in 1985, a nonelection year, costs actually continued to climb—a textbook example of Parkinson's Law.

Big losses resulted. The McKinsey report concluded that NBC News's true bottom-line loss in 1987 was going to be $91.1 million. Stewart arrived at this number by adding the cost of corporate overhead (which included the cost of preempting entertainment programs for presidential press conferences or crisis coverage, as well as News's $32 million share of corporate administration), and then subtracting the revenues News generated for other parts of the company (the $13.5 million of *Today* show ads sold by NBC's seven local stations and the sale of News product overseas, for instance). McKinsey gloomily projected that News, like network television in general, would continue to lose viewers. And the viewers News was left with tended to be older—62 percent of the audience were men or women over fifty years of age; only 21 percent were women eighteen to forty-nine. Thus News could not command the premium prices advertisers paid for younger demos.

Nor was there much hope for revenue growth. At the margins there might be some improvement—if *Today* ran the same number of commercials as ABC's *Good Morning America,* NBC's annual revenues would grow by $12 million; a full-point rise in *Nightly News*'s ratings would add another $11 million. But overall, McKinsey's revenue projections were grave. Even if NBC had a news magazine show like CBS's *60 Minutes* or ABC's *20-20,* McKinsey reported it was "unlikely to be successful economically." To reach this conclusion McKinsey introduced the new network math, one at odds with News traditions. Instead of calculating News's profits and losses by themselves, McKinsey measured News's performance against what NBC could make if it ran an entertainment show instead. On this basis, it was inevitable that, with the exception of *60 Minutes,* most newsmagazine shows or documentaries would be losers. Even if a newsmagazine show made money, the new network math would say it lost money because it would not make as much as an entertainment program.

Volume two of the McKinsey report criticized the way the news division was managed. News decisions were made with only "minor" consideration given to cost. No one in management tracked the costs of a story. In breaking down News's 1987 budget, McKinsey found that more than half ($131.4 million) was payroll costs; $36 million went for office space and telephones; $32 million for travel; $31 million was mostly satellite charges to transmit news; the rest was spread among a variety of areas, including $7.1 million for advertising. These costs were comparable at ABC and CBS.

One of the facts that stood out in the analysis of NBC was that between 1977 and 1987 the number of stories aired on *Nightly News* fell (from 2,496 to 1,564) even as the average cost per story multiplied (from $12,400 to $63,000). The same pattern held at the *Today* show. Another glaring fact: After subtracting six minutes for commercials and one minute and thirty seconds for theme music, credits, and teasers, the average nightly newscast actually offered less news (twenty minutes and fifty seconds) in 1986 than it did in 1977 (twenty-two minutes and forty-five seconds).

NBC News was paying more for less, yet McKinsey concluded hopefully that News's economics "can be improved without reducing editorial discretion, quality, or timeliness. . . ." The key was more rigorous management. There were four basic types of stories—breaking news, features, special segments, and major planned events. Analyzing each category, McKinsey found that breaking news assignments were generally made by producers who gave almost no thought to the average $63,000 cost for each story or to whether they really would use the story. The report singled out what is called "protective coverage," when a network dispatches a crew to cover a press conference which it is not certain will lead to a story. On January 22, 1987, for example, NBC's Washington bureau sent out thirteen crews and used film from only four of these. To McKinsey's accountants, this was wasteful; to many journalists, this illustrated how news is rarely predictable, and if it were it might not be news.

Half of the nightly newscast was made up of prechosen or feature stories. Here, too, McKinsey found waste. Over one two-month period, half of the fifty-six assigned *Nightly News* stories were not aired; of twenty-three feature stories ordered by the weekend *Nightly News,* seventeen were canceled. If more thought went into making the assignments, McKinsey said, real savings could be realized. There were also savings to be found if the three networks and CNN more often pooled coverage; or if NBC used the seven NBC-owned stations for more domestic stories; or if NBC used pictures from overseas news services. Of course, these recommendations carried risks: NBC might lose its claim to be a worldwide news-gathering organization and might find itself relying on organizations that did not share its standards.

The third McKinsey volume focused on personnel management, which was central to both the performance and economics of News. A better-managed division might generate another $20 million in revenues; staff cuts would probably be necessary. The news division employed 1,261 people, half of whom (653) were "involved in coverage activities." This number, the report found, was excessive. To make its case, McKinsey drew a chart of the on-air work of the ninety correspondents on all NBC News programs. The top twenty correspondents were on the air nearly half the time (46 percent); the bottom forty correspondents were on only 10 percent of the time. The traditional network argument for a large correspondent pool was that it was necessary for "crisis coverage." Yet McKinsey analyzed four crises —the *Challenger* shuttle explosion, the U.S. raid on Libya, the Pan Am and the *Achille-Lauro* hijackings—and found that ten correspondents monopolized from 85 to 97 percent of the airtime.

NBC News would air 5,900 stories in 1987, of which half would be breaking stories which appeared the same day they were assigned. These breaking stories relied on a small pool of regulars, like the White House or Pentagon correspondents. The remaining 2,925 stories had a longer lead time, and fewer made the air. Better management could reduce the number of correspondents and three-person camera crews used for nonbreaking stories. Then there were salary levels. The average NBC correspondent earned $84,000 in 1981 and $174,000 in 1986 (the average for the four "star correspondents" was listed at $540,000); the average pay of each camera-crew member rose from $63,000 to $96,000; field producers' pay rose from $51,000 to $75,000. What impressed Bob Wright was McKinsey's conclusion that there was "little correlation between salary levels and performance"; lower-paid correspondents such as the Pentagon's Fred Francis had the most airtime; the best paid—such as respected commentator John Chancellor—had the least. Wright believed the networks were paying too steep a premium for network correspondents, and to him proof of this came with a comparison of pay scales. Seeing little difference between the work load of those engaged in local and network news, Wright was bothered that the average affiliate paid its correspondents just $41,000 (versus $174,000 on the network); or that the average network producer earned $89,000, while the affiliates paid $31,500; local news crews received $38,100, about 40 percent of the network rate.

McKinsey made no cost-savings recommendations. The report did say that either attrition or early retirement would be the least "disruptive approach to reducing staff levels." The key to reform, it said, was to improve management of the news division. Executive producers and bureau chiefs had to assume "greater responsibilities for hiring, firing, promotion, and salary determinations." A personnel evaluation system was needed, as was a chief of correspondents to speak for the on-air reporters. Top managers needed guidelines to police poor performers. Managers needed training in the art of management.

The three-volume McKinsey report was not released. To control rumors, on June 9, 1987, Grossman released an eight-page internal telegram to News employees, signed "Reliable Sources," which sketched some of the results and changes he planned. Privately, Grossman credited McKinsey with teaching him a lot. The biggest surprise, he said, was the inefficient way News managed nonbreaking stories. These stories took the most time, cost more, got on the air less, and decisions to do them were "made as casually as deciding what to eat," he said. While saying he wanted to take care not to convey a sense within the division that management cared only about cost, Grossman said "it is not unreasonable to ask the producer: 'Is this a $150,000 story?' " Nor was it unreasonable, he continued, to ask why the average cost per story had multiplied five times in the past ten years, though he emphasized that this "problem was more difficult to solve" since the reasons were varied. While the number of NBC correspondents had shrunk from 110 to 90 in the three years Grossman had headed News, he said the number would shrink further, to about 70. In the future, Grossman predicted, there would be more specialized beat assignments—education, science, etc. And there would be just two categories of correspondents—those who get on the air regularly, and lesser-paid producer/reporters.

Since he was acknowledging waste on his watch, did this prove that News was mismanaged? Attired in his customary white cardigan and seated at the conference table he often used as a desk, Grossman pondered the question between puffs on a thick cigar. "When I came here we were number three," he said. "My first task was to improve. My second task was to fix the systems. My third task was to transform News from a loss leader to a profit center. We have achieved the first goal. Now the second priority has to be addressed, which is to make sense of the processes and management of News."

The argument that there was waste in News was greeted very differently by Tom Brokaw than by Dan Rather, at least publicly. "It is time for a reordering," said Brokaw of the McKinsey report. "We want to make a substantial investment in News, but that investment has to be efficient. Journalists ought to be able to look at themselves sometimes, as McKinsey helped us do." Still, Brokaw was concerned that McKinsey was trying "to quantify things that can't be quantified"—such as the output of chief investigative reporter Brian Ross, who wasn't on the air much, but only because he was a careful reporter who tackled the toughest subjects. One reason News produced fewer stories even as their costs rose was that the *Nightly News* allowed longer pieces, which took more time. Still, the pieces were not long enough. Garrick Utley, one of NBC's principal correspondents, was allotted a relatively large amount of airtime—four to four and one-half minutes—for his pieces from around the globe. Yet Utley admits, "In four to four and a half minutes you're very often going over something lightly." Real depth, he said, required about seven minutes for a piece. But the seven-minute pieces, which help distinguish network from local news and provide viewers with more context, take days, often weeks, to report. Therefore they are more expensive and reduce News "productivity."

The report suggested the need for a chief of correspondents to give voice to reporters, which became a point of contention. Wanting to improve the tense relationship he had with his anchor, Grossman offered the job to Brokaw, who reluctantly accepted. This aroused quiet controversy. The most common lament of correspondents is a lack of airtime, often because the anchor lobbied for another story, or insisted he would do the voiceover himself, or jumped on an airplane and did the story personally. Thus correspondents grumbled that the fox was now in charge of the chicken coop.

But Larry Grossman and his team were generally happy with McKinsey's work. Unlike CBS, Grossman and NBC were now dealing with a common set of facts. Grossman and Wright eventually agreed that News would try to break even over the next three years, by 1991. They agreed on a $91 million budget gap, and agreed to close it without fanfare or layoffs, relying on attrition and early retirement buyouts. Jack Welch joined the consensus. The process "is moving along nicely," he said, though he was careful to note, "We haven't done anything yet." They had done enough, however, to impress Larry Tisch at CBS. After word of the McKinsey study leaked to the press, Tisch said CBS should "do more by attrition. Like NBC."

Grossman had reason to be content. He had skillfully handled McKinsey, had steered clear of the bloody battles at CBS, had seemingly calmed the anxiety of his staff and met the demands of his superiors. He sensed the greening of Wright, and maybe even Welch. Grossman, too, had grown. He now acknowledged that better management of costs need not be the enemy of better news. If News operated more efficiently, it would free more money "to spend on breaking news," he said.

The news division remained uneasy with Grossman. One of his managers complained "that he was not a leader, didn't take charge." But the greater unease, the one shared by the news divisions at all three networks, was that the new owners cared more about budgets than about news, didn't feel an obligation to educate—didn't *love* News.

14

CBS: TISCH GOES HOLLYWOOD, MAY 1987

Although News often attracts more headlines and probably delivers more prestige, the financial heart of a network beats in Hollywood, at its entertainment division. From day one, each of the three new network owners chose to cede Entertainment decisions to their Hollywood programmers. But by May of 1987—nine months after he had taken charge of the network—Larry Tisch was growing restive. He could no longer contain his fury toward what he considered waste in Hollywood. And he was coming to share the sense within the Hollywood colony that his Entertainment president, Bud Grant, was lazy and was not attracting his share of talent to CBS. Now that he had asked basic cost questions of News, Tisch was ready to ask questions of the division that spent most of the network's money.

So when CBS executives gathered in Hollywood in May to make their fall programming decisions, Tisch went at them with questions: *Since movies attract smaller television audiences because viewers now rent them or watch them on HBO or independent stations, why does CBS still devote three nights a week to movies? If multinight miniseries are so expensive and fail to hold viewers, why is CBS still pouring resources into that rathole? Why aren't CBS programmers bold? Why can't you think of something else to put on the air but old—and expensive—movies?*

Cornered, Bud Grant and his Entertainment team decided to gamble. By the end of its May Decision Week, CBS would replace nearly 40 percent of its prime-time schedule, introducing eight new hours of series programs in the fall, the most new hours CBS had ever scheduled. The eight-hour hole came about partly because of another Tisch-inspired decision: CBS would abandon two of three movie nights, substituting regular series programming for the two-hour Tuesday and Saturday night movies. In a bold cost-saving move also provoked by

Tisch, CBS decided to curb miniseries and made-for-TV movie development, slashing about thirty-five people from the staff.

Though the conventional wisdom said comedies were crucial to reach the younger audiences CBS lacked, CBS included only two half-hour comedies among its eight new hours—*Frank's Place,* a series about a black professor who inherits a New Orleans restaurant, which CBS believed would be an instant hit, and *Everything's Relative,* about two brothers who room together, one a bookish workaholic who can't find love, the other a construction worker who can't avoid it. Instead of comedies, CBS kicked off four of seven nights with hour-long dramas, including *Tour of Duty,* about a platoon of soldiers in Vietnam, *Beauty and the Beast,* a variation on the classic story, set in New York, and *Wiseguy,* about an undercover cop in the mob.

Tisch didn't have strong feelings about *Tour of Duty,* the casting of Linda Hamilton as Beauty, comedy versus drama, or even about the quality of the other series selected. He felt strongly about movies and miniseries not because he watched them but because they cost a lot—just under $3 million for the average made-for-TV movie, and just above that sum for a feature film. In getting rid of two movie nights, however, Tisch was making some shaky assumptions. First, he assumed that CBS's new dramas and comedies would snare larger audiences. And second, he assumed that his preoccupation with saving money would go unnoticed in Hollywood.

Both assumptions were wrong. Why send TV ideas to CBS, asked Robert Daly whose Warner Brothers was a major supplier of network programs, when all they want to do is think about costs, not hits? The movie decision in particular irked Daly, because it suggested that Tisch didn't understand the business, didn't understand that revenues were what counted. Daly agreed with Tisch that three movie nights were excessive. But he thought Tisch should have cut back to two, not one. CBS just didn't have enough good series to fill in for two movie nights. So what CBS was doing was plugging holes on its schedule with filler, with mediocre shows like *The Law and Harry McGraw,* which would die expensive deaths after just a few weeks on the air. "The difference between Bill Paley and the managers today," said Daly, who once worked for Paley, "is that Paley never thought about costs. He thought about profits. Coming up with hits is the name of the game. In the entertainment business most things fail. Most albums, most books, most movies, most TV programs. You got to think *hit.*" To succeed, Daly believed, the new owners of the networks had to be more involved in programming.

In fact, CBS's May 1987 program meetings did herald Tisch's greater involvement in programming. The meetings, observed long-time Tisch associate Jay Kriegel, who after the March News uproar was now giving regular advice to Tisch, provoked Tisch to rein in Bud Grant. "When Larry sat in the program meetings in May he found the emperor had no clothes. He's not pretending to be a programming genius, but he is now more a part of the process. He is stripped of illusions," Kriegel said.

Like Murphy at ABC and Wright at NBC, Tisch still basically ceded programming decisions to his West Coast team, but the more attention he paid to Hollywood, people at CBS thought, the more Tisch would realize that Bud Grant and the team he assembled in Hollywood were not as good as Tartikoff or Stoddard.

A more assertive Larry Tisch might have reminded Bud Grant of a story Coca-Cola's Fay Vincent liked to tell. "I've left you three envelopes for your first three crises," said a network Entertainment chief upon meeting his successor. The fired Entertainment president explained where the envelopes were located, and left. The new honcho wouldn't touch them—until his first crisis.

"Blame your predecessor!" read the note in the first envelope.

After his second crisis, he opened the second envelope, and the note advised, "Reorganize."

After his third crisis, the CEO reached into the drawer and eagerly ripped open the final envelope, which read, "Start preparing three envelopes!"

Within five months of these meetings, Tisch fired Bud Grant. By the fall Larry Tisch was shuttling between New York and Los Angeles more often.

15

NBC: TARTIKOFF IN HIS SANDBOX, 1987

Brandon Tartikoff was like a boy in a sandbox. His job as NBC's chief programmer was fun, as visitors learned when entering his Burbank office. A "Be There" motorcycle jacket from *Saturday Night Live* was mounted on the wall, the same jacket Tartikoff wore when he hosted the show in 1983 after learning that the Hodgkin's disease which had threatened his life had gone into remission. It was fun for Tartikoff to have an idea, and then see it on his own network. Like the time in the early eighties when Tartikoff jotted down the phrase "MTV Cops," which blossomed into *Miami Vice.* Or the time he visited an aunt in Miami and came back with the germ for *Golden Girls.* Tartikoff likened his job to that of a football quarterback, because "you can call an audible at the line"—surprising opponents by shifting a series on the schedule, selecting a strong lead-in show to open holes, tinkering with scripts and promos, summoning a new star actor or writer or executive producer from the bench, keeping score of touchdowns by winning the time period.

After nearly a decade as NBC's Entertainment president, Brandon Tartikoff had, by the spring of 1987, led his team to one victory after another. For the second year in a row, NBC captured the September through April season ratings race, winning twenty-seven of thirty weeks, stretching its lead over second-place CBS from one to two ratings points (each rating point was worth about $100 million). NBC boasted a powerhouse lineup of such leading half-hour comedies as *The Cosby Show, ALF, Cheers, Family Ties,* and *Golden Girls,* as well as such one-hour successes as *L.A. Law, St. Elsewhere,* and *Miami Vice.* Unlike CBS, which had too few half-hour comedies, or ABC, which had too few one-hour dramas, Tartikoff's schedule balanced both. And not only were NBC's ratings climbing, the network was pulling further ahead among the younger, urban, female demographic categories advertisers wanted.

Bob Wright and Jack Welch treated Tartikoff, Bud Rukeyser said, like "some sort of Tibetan prince." "I love Brandon," Welch said. "I feel he loves me. I trust him." Unlike Tisch or Murphy, who were backing into programming, Wright after nine months as president of NBC trusted Tartikoff to act on his own. By May 1, 1987, Tartikoff said he had not spoken to Wright in a month, the last time being when the NBC president came to California for no other reason than to hear a speech given by Tartikoff. Their only regular communication was a terse biweekly status report Tartikoff dictated. Wright was "comfortable" with Brandon.

Nevertheless, the thirty-seven-year-old, always slightly disheveled Tartikoff developed a bad case of jitters as the May meetings to decide on the fall schedule approached. For the first time in his NBC career, he was out from under the shadow of a mentor. He would be drawing up a schedule without Grant Tinker or Fred Silverman. The "kids" were on their own, and this year Tartikoff's challenge would be different. The previous May, said Tartikoff, the question was: Would NBC come in first? In May of 1987, Tartikoff was confident that NBC would remain number one next season, but scores of smaller questions remained. Could NBC find another signature show like *Hill Street Blues* and thus remain "the quality network"? Would NBC still be perceived as the innovative network, the place that dared sign up *The Cosby Show* in 1984 when everyone said that comedy was dead, the place that launched *Golden Girls* when everyone insisted stars had to be young? Could NBC find replacements for two 10:00 shows—*St. Elsewhere* and *Hunter*—which Tartikoff suspected had only another year of life in them? Were there enough good series in the NBC pipeline to reduce the number of movie nights from two to one? Could the "kids" succeed without Tinker?

Tartikoff had also to think of his many constituencies. He wanted to take care of his newest toy—NBC Productions. Could Tartikoff find a place on NBC's schedule for any of the eighteen shows NBC Productions was developing? Tartikoff also thought of his core team of producers. By awarding so many series commitments to established writer/producers, even NBC staff members wondered whether Tartikoff was inadvertently signaling that NBC's door was shut to fresh talent. On the other hand, wasn't it crucial to retain the devotion of four of NBC's most important creative producers—Marcy Carsey and Tom Werner (*The Cosby Show*), Gary David Goldberg (*Family Ties*),

Michael Mann (*Miami Vice*), Stephen J. Cannell (*Hunter*)—each of whom was working on new shows? Would Tartikoff placate his late-night ratings champion, Johnny Carson, by renewing *Amen,* a lame comedy set in a Philadelphia church and created by Carson's own production company?

Tartikoff also had to think about *Hill Street Blues,* the most honored dramatic series in TV history. The Steven Bochco–created show was retiring after seven years, taking with it the gloss (and the demographics) that were key to NBC's resurgence. This unusual police drama collected a truckload of Emmys; it also diverted critics from labeling Tartikoff's first big hit—*The A-Team,* an undistinguished shoot-em-up action-adventure show—as NBC's emblem. Tartikoff knew that a network schedule required hits like *The A-Team* to galvanize mass audiences, and series like *Hill Street,* which radiated glamour and beckoned other talented writers and producers to work for the network that took chances. One part of Tartikoff, the one Grant Tinker nurtured, wanted more shows like *Hill Street;* the other part, the one Tinker helped temper, wanted more *A-Team*s.

By 1987, Tartikoff had reason to feel that, as good as he was, as good a team as he assembled, perhaps his impact was at the margins. Perhaps he exercised as little control over NBC's fate as Larry Tisch exercised over Dan Rather. Tartikoff knew that after a one-year hiatus Nielsen was once again reporting dramatic erosion in the audience for the three networks. On a typical evening in the 1986–87 season, only 75.8 percent of those watching TV were tuned to one of three networks, down 1.6 percent from the prior season, and down from the 92 percent recorded in 1976. And next fall the networks were expected to show a still sharper drop when Nielsen introduced the people meter. In just over a decade the networks already had lost an average of ten million viewers a night to cable, independent stations, VCRs. Which is a reason Tartikoff searched for hits that would expand the viewing audience, compel viewers to plan their nights around a network program, as they once did for *The A-Team* and were now doing for *The Cosby Show.* But Tartikoff was not sure he could keep network audiences from eroding further.

Nor could he control how long NBC would remain a favorite of the TV press. "You can sense the press is totally bored writing about NBC being number one in the ratings," Tartikoff observed, slumped behind his desk. "I feel sorry for the guy in the local press who has to write the ratings story each week. Reporters like to build up heroes and take them down. They're sitting out there dying to write that we've become crass and commercial." The most influential critic, he thought, was Tom Shales of *The Washington Post,* who actually enjoyed TV and snapped heads back with his vivid, sometimes wicked, jabs. Tartikoff was preoccupied with the media, and spent many hours each week seeking to put his spin on a story, to sell TV critics on a series, to debunk ABC or CBS programmers. Yet he knew the tribe was restless. Perhaps he could hush them with a few "quality" shows, but in the long run he knew they were beyond his control.

The economics of the business were also largely beyond his control. Increasingly the Hollywood studios resisted spending an average of $1.2 million to produce the one-hour dramas Tartikoff wanted. Would they continue to make these dramas when the network license fee, averaging $850,000, did not cover the studio's expenses? Or when the studio could rarely recoup its investment in the syndication marketplace, since local stations preferred half-hour comedies? Local stations already used a precious hour a day of their time for talk shows like *The Oprah Winfrey Show* and *Donahue.* And viewers now seemed to prefer reruns of half-hour comedies. Everyone in Hollywood noticed when local stations refused to buy the hour-long *Miami Vice* reruns, forcing Universal to make a bargain-basement syndication deal with cable.

Nor was Tartikoff sure that with the explosion of buyers—from cable, Fox, and first-run syndication, among others—there was sufficient talent to stock a twenty-two-hour prime-time schedule. Tartikoff knew that success in network television often came when a producer believed passionately in a project—be it Norman Lear with *All in the Family,* James Brooks with *The Mary Tyler Moore Show,* or Steven Bochco with *Hill Street Blues.* But Tartikoff also knew the network television production system was a sausage factory. "What fucks up television is compromise," Bochco said. "It homogenizes it. You're serving all kinds of masters. You've got to satisfy the studio. And the networks. So compromise is born of fear. There's a difference between a guy who manufactures a product for a buyer and a guy who wants to create something artistic. If I'm a volume supplier of a product, my agent's concern is to sell what the buyer wants. If the buyer doesn't want it, he changes the product. As opposed to someone who brings a vision to the network. . . . This is a failure-oriented business. People fear failure. Out here, every *putz* in the world is 'a writer' or 'a director.' It's such a high-profile business. And so glamorous. It's like heroin. People in the business are junkies. The guys at the networks and the studios have all the heroin. But you're so desperate for heroin you'll do anything. This desperate need robs you of your courage." And, Tartikoff knew, it robbed the networks of an adequate supply of good product.

The pressures on Tartikoff grew more intense in the months leading up to May's Decision Week. During March and April the networks bounce their marginal series around on the schedule and experiment with new shows to see if they have a pulse. By the last week of April 1987, Tartikoff was spending much of his time with his staff, watching pilots, sorting through contracts and license-fee arrangements and figuring out how to introduce more "likable" characters into a series or how to kill off dislikable ones—questions he wanted answered before Bob Wright and his executive team visited Burbank to preview the fall schedule.

This was to be Wright's first Decision Week, and Tartikoff naturally wondered what role he would play. As they watched the pilots together, Tartikoff was struck by at least two differences between Tinker and Wright: "Bob wore a tie and Grant wore a sweater. And Bob laughed more at the comedies. He was a good audience."

Although the May week of meetings featured lots of discussion, everyone knew that Tartikoff, not Wright, was the final arbiter. Unlike the jaded Bud Grant at CBS or the highbrow Brandon Stoddard at ABC, both of whom had fierce detractors, Tartikoff was a fan of television. He watched it with an almost childlike enthusiasm. And his memory for shows and time slots and their ratings when shifted around on the schedule was elephantine. Tartikoff could rattle off Nielsen statistics like an accountant. Everyone attending these annual soirees, watching him retrieve facts from memory, came to understand that to be a good programmer one had to be a good scheduler. And to be a good scheduler, one needed memory, experience, instinct. "He's got to be one of the best ever," observed his ABC rival, Brandon Stoddard, comparing Tartikoff to such past programmers as Michael Dann of CBS and Fred Silverman of ABC. "I think he's as good a scheduler as I was," said Michael Dann. It was clear that Wright would leave the decisions to his programmer when he arrived late, missing most of Monday's screenings, and then departed after Thursday's sessions, missing the final day of formal deliberations.

In the end, the already successful NBC schedule would have the fewest new series of any of the networks for 1987–88—just five. There was a new drama—*A Year in the Life,* starring Richard Kiley—which Tartikoff boosted as his "special" quality offering, NBC's heir to *Hill*

Street Blues. NBC had several other shows that "skewed older"—*Highway to Heaven* with Michael Landon, *Matlock* with Andy Griffith, and *J. J. Starbuck* with Dale Robertson—which displeased Sales but satisfied Tartikoff's desire to counterprogram against ABC's youth-oriented shows on Tuesday and Wednesday. Though Hollywood feared that NBC would favor shows from its own studio, Tartikoff didn't like any of NBC Productions' eighteen pilots and none made the schedule.

In making scheduling decisions, however, Tartikoff sometimes compromised for the sake of its producer. *Crime Story,* for example, was a well-written and well-acted drama that followed a federal anticrime unit as it battled mobsters in Las Vegas in the sixties. It was a "dark" show—dimly lit, with little humor, terrific but unknown actors like Dennis Farina, no female lead or love interest, and few characters to root for. But what helped *Crime Story,* in addition to research showing that it tested stronger with the new people meter, was that its executive producer was Michael Mann, who also produced *Miami Vice.* Other series that made the schedule but might not have save for their sponsors were *Amen* (produced by Johnny Carson), *A Different World* (produced by Bill Cosby and Carsey-Werner), *J. J. Starbuck* (produced by Stephen J. Cannell), and as a "pinch-hitter" in midseason, *The Bronx Zoo* (produced by Gary David Goldberg). All but *Amen* and *A Different World* failed.

This year at least, Tartikoff took internal pressures more seriously than he took the fledging Fox network. Since Fox was then open for business only on Sunday nights, when it attracted 8 percent of the audience, Tartikoff's scheduling board had no magnetic cards for Fox entrees on Sunday night, as there were for ABC and CBS. This would prove to be a mistake. After a safe and sluggish start, once Fox began to take programming risks, it became a magnet for viewers. Within three years, the Fox network would program four nights and offer series like *The Simpsons,* which elbowed its way onto the list of the top ten most watched shows.

In retrospect, Tartikoff's refusal to contend with Fox was consistent with a 1987–88 NBC schedule that critics and advertisers would say was too safe, a schedule that featured no breakaway or daring shows. In May 1987, Tartikoff seemed to be coasting. Certainly he did nothing to rival Robert D. Wood, who as president of CBS Television in 1970 boldly replaced three successful longtime hits—*Petticoat Junction* and the Red Skelton and Jackie Gleason shows—because they were now old and featured aging performers when Wood knew advertisers sought younger demos. Wood gambled—winning the allegiance of younger, more urban audiences, and the advertising dollars followed.

Bob Wright walked away from his first Decision Week struck, he recalled, by the general "mediocrity" of the pilots he viewed. He blamed not NBC's programming department but a surprisingly pedestrian Hollywood. He had expected "to see that our people were 'homogenizing everything' we put on TV," that NBC was somehow "interfering with the raw product. . . . I expected to be impressed and knocked over by things. Yet largely what I saw was material that required an awful lot of work from our people to get it into shape, to be better." Wright came away thinking less of the so-called "creative community" and more of how vast "Brandon's challenge was."

Tartikoff bristled that Wright was "a little bit quick to write the whole development season off." But the sting did not linger. Tartikoff felt bullish, perhaps complacent, particularly after ABC and CBS released their fall lineups. ABC, he said, scheduled its shows poorly, either by moving them around too much and confusing viewers, or by not shifting established comedies to shore up weak nights. While he respected Stoddard's eye for quality, he did not respect his scheduling skills. "My guess is that ABC will make a management change by November," he predicted. As for CBS, their successful series—like *Dallas, Newhart, 60 Minutes*—were getting old, he thought. And CBS's much ballyhooed new shows for the fall—*Frank's Place, Tour of Duty*—he dismissed as overrated. By November, Tartikoff guessed, CBS would return to two movie nights.

In two more seasons Tartikoff would have been on the job for ten years—longer than anyone else in network history. Already, speculation was rife that he might be suffering from "burn-out." The word was that this would be his last year, that he would soon run a major studio, that his deputy, Warren Littlefield, would replace him. Among the minority who disagreed was his good friend and former NBC deputy Jeff Sagansky, then president of Production at Tri-Star Pictures: "I wouldn't be surprised if he stayed beyond his contract. I never hear him say, 'Boy, I'm getting sick of this.' "

More so than Bud Grant or Stoddard, Tartikoff hatched his own series ideas. "Ten years ago," said Tartikoff, "90 percent of the ideas came from the creative community. Now it's only 20 percent." Which meant that NBC came up with most of the series ideas, and then pitched these to writers and producers. Warren Littlefield guessed that one third of their projects in development in 1987 derived from commitments made before a script was even written.

According to Tartikoff, this approach was driven by the limited supply of talented writer/producers. Besides, he insisted that while the original idea may have been NBC's, the execution was not. Tony Yerkovich, the writer, and Michael Mann, the executive producer of *Miami Vice,* took Tartikoff's skeletal idea—"MTV Cops"—in totally unexpected directions. The fast cuts, the Armani clothes, the Ferraris, the Miami setting, the characters of detectives Sonny Crockett and Ricardo Tubbs, and the story lines—came not from Tartikoff but from the producers and writers. Of course, often the final "idea" for a series —whether *Miami Vice* in 1984 or *Twin Peaks* in 1990—was not an idea at all but a look, a feel, a sense of novelty, a show in which mannerisms dominate substance.

By generating their own ideas and selecting the writer/producers, Tartikoff and his team had come to believe, as did GE, that they could control their fate, keep ahead not just of ABC and CBS but Fox and cable and all the forces assaulting the networks. Tartikoff believed he had a formula to defy the cycle.

He also believed the changing economics of the business dictated a top-down model. Series production was so expensive that the studios were taking fewer risks. And since the syndication marketplace wanted half-hour comedies rather than one-hour dramas, studios were loath to subsidize hour-long series to the tune of $200,000 to $300,000 a week unless they had an extended commitment from a network. Partly for these reasons, the three networks, led by NBC, increasingly offered "commitments" to producers—skipping the traditional pilot process in which a network signs up a writer/producer to prepare a half- or full-hour pilot, which is then judged against twenty-five to forty other pilots. Instead, Tartikoff was awarding writer/producers six- or thirteen-week commitments. The process had now become so expensive that everyone was looking for a *sure thing*—the studio for a sure shot on the network schedule, the network for an idea it knew would add balance to its schedule. What Tinker and Tartikoff figured out before their ABC and CBS counterparts did is that there were only a couple of dozen or so talented writer/producers likely to craft outstanding shows. Scoop up the top talent, tie them up with commitments, and NBC might remain number one.

It was network weakness, not strength, that drove Tartikoff to adopt more aggressive tactics. It was because the networks' monopoly had ended that Tartikoff believed this top-down approach would work. With the erosion of network audiences, networks were no longer the sole buyer. Tartikoff recognized that a network could no longer sit back, wait, and react. "When I started in television, being at the network was being the buyer," observed Jeff Sagansky. But no longer. "In the last five years—and not all the networks know this—the network became the seller," said Sagansky in 1987, "because there are so many places for talent to go—video cassettes, films, Fox, the syndication market. The network now had to chase them. . . . The reason CBS and ABC lag behind now is that NBC locked up the great producers."

Except for the few dozen or so writer/producers Tartikoff considered talented, NBC still acted like a buyer. Starting in the late spring, soon after Decision Week, and extending into the summer, hundreds of producers, writers, and studio heads pitch ideas to the networks, hoping to get an order for a series for the following year's schedule. Knowing that the networks are looking for sure things, no matter how unlikely they are to find them, producers tend to pitch formulas that worked before. And so it follows that soon after the Huxtables of *The Cosby Show* arrived on NBC in 1984, all three networks were flooded with proposals for family comedies, a familiar pattern seen more recently in the wake of ABC's success with *America's Funniest Home Videos.*

From the studios' vantage point, landing a spot on a network schedule is a crapshoot. Every year, for its twenty-two hours of prime time, each network is pitched about 2,000 ideas. Only about 150 of these ideas become actual scripts, of which perhaps 30 will be turned into pilots, and of these maybe 5 to 8 will make the schedule. And only 1 or 2 of these series will last a season. So, among the three networks, maybe 6 ideas out of 6,000 actually succeed. Few producers feel they are in a position to insist on their own ideas, as Bochco did when he fought for *Hill Street Blues* or *L.A. Law.* Few are powerful enough to resist the networks—as producer Gary David Goldberg did when NBC's Broadcast Standards wanted him to change the dialogue on *Family Ties* from a "crazy person" to "disturbed." When Bochco was doing *Hill Street,* he remembers spending "endless hours reinventing language so we could create a raw language cops might use"—instead of "shit," they came up with "dirt bag" and "wet brownie."

By the summer of 1987, Tartikoff's attention had shifted to the fall of 1988, more than a year away. He was determined to streamline the development process by looking for only five or six new dramas and three comedies, hoping for "a couple of shows that explode" into hits. He narrowed his sights to Wednesday and Friday nights, where he was in second place. On Friday he had *Miami Vice,* now limping in its fourth season, and he wanted a strong replacement. On Wednesday *Highway to Heaven* was in its fourth year and *St. Elsewhere* in its sixth; and *A Year in the Life* might not survive its rookie season. All were hour-long shows. Tartikoff saw the 1988–89 year as particularly "crucial" for NBC. "I could probably go on vacation and come back in February and we would still be number one next season," he said, noting that starting in January of 1988 NBC owned the Super Bowl, the Olympics, and the World Series, not to mention such stalwarts as *The Cosby Show*. "But at some point I have to face the reality that there will be no Cosby; *Family Ties* and *Cheers* will only be on this year and next probably. Johnny Carson will one day want out." The challenge this year, he said, was to plant the seeds in 1988 that would flower in the fall of 1989.

Near the top of Tartikoff's list of writer/producers was Bruce Paltrow, whom he considered among the best writers in television. Like Tartikoff, forty-four-year-old Paltrow was born on Long Island and was a child of television. As a boy, Paltrow attended a public school that had split sessions so his classes began at 12:45 P.M. Naturally, Paltrow blamed the school when he stayed up late to watch TV. He became addicted. While attending Tulane University, or directing off-Broadway plays in the late sixties, or waiting in line at the unemployment office in the early seventies, where he met and began courting his future wife, actress Blythe Danner, Paltrow preferred watching television to reading a book. He could not recite from the classics, but he could recite lines from *The Fugitive*.

Paltrow was a big, enthusiastic kid, his curly hair reaching to his shoulders, his standard uniform sneakers and jeans, his walk a bounce. Fifteen years previously, Paltrow had been writing and directing TV pilots in Los Angeles. Then he wrote *The White Shadow*, a series about a white former professional basketball player who becomes the coach of a black high school team, which ran on CBS for three years and established Paltrow in the business. Paltrow's breakthrough series was *St. Elsewhere* in 1982, which he supervised as executive producer. Its mix of black comedy, anger, searing dialogue, and the constant dance with death at St. Eligius Hospital glued viewers to their TVs; like *Hill Street*, it won Emmys, not smash ratings.

Now Paltrow was ready for another series, this one loosely based on his own life. Throughout the eighties, Paltrow had an idea for a one-hour series set in a New York restaurant. Paltrow himself is part owner of restaurants in L.A. and Aspen. The character Paltrow conceived, restaurant owner Nick Tattinger, would be good-looking, witty, passionate; he would have two teenagers in private school, like Paltrow, and a Main Line WASP ex-wife (Blythe Danner is a Main Line WASP). For various reasons, *Tattinger's,* as the show was to be called, remained in his drawer, even though as early as 1983 Tartikoff said he liked the idea. It was different, he thought, an odd mixture of action adventure and domestic drama. Nick Tattinger wasn't a cop, a lawyer, a teacher, or a doctor. Besides, as Grant Tinker observed, "Bruce is a leader people want to follow." But in the case of *Tattinger's,* people would follow him right off a cliff, for the series would bomb when it debuted a year later.

In 1983 Tartikoff offered a thirteen-week commitment for *Tattinger's,* but Paltrow was busy with *St. Elsewhere* and unable to find the right male lead, so did nothing. Then early in 1987, his wife had a flash: Why couldn't their friend, actor Stephen Collins, play Nick Tattinger?

Paltrow liked the idea. "The decision," recalls Paltrow, "was made the way one decides all important things: caprice." NBC, looking for a male lead with the kind of universal sex appeal Tom Selleck had, was interested. For Paltrow, a working-class kid from Great Neck, Long Island, the money was staggering. NBC would eventually pay a weekly license fee of $900,000 to MTM, the studio Paltrow worked for. Paltrow, in turn, received from MTM an annual salary of $2.5 million as executive producer. Plus, he would be paid the regular union scale for each episode he directed, about $18,000, and a bit more to direct the pilot. Plus, for those episodes he wrote or coauthored, Paltrow would be paid the Writers Guild minimum of about $16,000. Plus, if Paltrow managed to get several series on the air simultaneously, MTM promised him bonuses that would exceed his $2.5 million annual salary. Plus, should *Tattinger's* air for at least four years, and if it sold in syndication for, say, a modest $100 million, Paltrow would get about $20 million more.

The amounts of money to be made in television—typically the head writer on a series made from $7,500 to $15,000 per episode—suggests why so many writers are eager to please the networks. Money was not, however, Paltrow's sole concern. "No one, to the best of my knowledge, has shot a very sophisticated show," he said. "This one will be very urban. I want to use Gershwin music on the show. We're going to use theater actors. It's going to be a kind of contemporary rhythm piece. Like *The Thin Man.* It's not going to be a show about car races." In September 1987, Paltrow would shift his base of operations from California to New York, build a sound stage, and assemble a staff to produce the *Tattinger's* pilot so that it would be ready for Decision Week in May 1988.

Meanwhile Tartikoff was pursuing a second executive producer, Aaron Spelling, who would take an entirely different direction from Paltrow, though his series, like *Tattinger's,* would also bomb. Aaron Spelling was certainly among the wealthiest producers in the nearly half-century life of television, a man who lived the lavish life of the characters he created on series like *Dynasty.* The white-haired, rail-thin, sixty-three-year-old Spelling was probably the most prolific writer/producer in television history, a man who since 1956 had packaged 2,500 hours of television and netted a fortune estimated at $500 million or more, who created such smash hits as *Charlie's Angels, Fantasy Island,* and *The Love Boat.* In 1979 alone, Spelling produced an astonishing seven of ABC's twenty-two prime-time hours. But Spelling hadn't had a hit in years. Hollywood whispered that he was over the hill. Brandon Stoddard had just terminated his nearly two-decade-old exclusive contract, though three years earlier ABC had rented an entire train to transport him and his entourage to New York. Spelling was notoriously afraid to fly. Now his phone was cold, unlike Paltrow's.

Aaron Spelling had something to prove. He always did. Spelling never forgot growing up poor in Texas and being called "Jewbaby!" The memory lingered of casting directors and others who never said "thank you" when the skinny young actor read for a part. As a result, Spelling was unfailingly, obsessively, polite. He left cigarettes on silver trays in his office so that those who came for interviews knew they could smoke and relax. No matter his successes, Aaron Spelling continued to think of himself as an "insecure man." He wondered, "Will I be able to write a show again?" Spelling's insecurity had intensified by 1987. No longer was he a fixture at ABC. He felt estranged from the Yale-educated Brandon Stoddard, of whom he said, "Brandon does not like television."

Spelling is a worrier even when things are going well—he paid cash for his houses because he fretted that maybe one day he wouldn't be able to meet the mortgage. By early 1988, Spelling felt even more vulnerable. Not only had ABC terminated his exclusive arrangement the previous year, but he was no youngster, had recently taken his 1,340-employee company public, and had not had a new hit in years. The series Spelling had on the air, ABC's *Dynasty* and *Hotel,* were growing tired. People in the Hollywood colony made fun of Candy Spelling's shopping forays and the 40-carat diamond ring she purchased from the Shah of Iran's estate. Visitors to the Spelling home on Mapleton Drive sometimes mocked the two Warhol paintings of her (one with a pink backdrop, the other blue) that faced each other on opposite stucco walls of their living room. All of Hollywood seemed to be obsessed with the 65,000-square-foot, $45 million palace Candy and Aaron were building in Holmby Hills. They were moving from their 14,000-square-foot Mapleton Drive home, Candy Spelling said, because it had "become a crowded home for us." To make her point, Candy turned to the bulging library shelves groaning with red leatherbound volumes. The volumes contained not Homer or Dickens but thousands of five-to-a-volume Spelling scripts. Hollywood snickered, *Can you imagine, Candy and Aaron have to move because their home doesn't have three kitchens or a bowling alley?*

The Spellings were extreme, even for Hollywood. Hollywood, Spelling sighed, is a place of "envy," of seething "jealousy," a town where people proclaim "their sensitivity to racism, to women's issues, and yet this is a town of the greatest insensitivity to the feelings of others. They feel they are 'sensitive' because their feelings are hurt easily. They're sensitive to themselves." His new home, said Spelling, was designed as "a mental fortress. Leave me in my new house and I'm safe."

Spelling's series for NBC was born in the Twentieth Century Fox parking lot in January 1987. Tartikoff had attended a meeting at Fox because NBC Productions was making a movie produced by Spelling that Fox was going to distribute to theaters. The two men had worked together at ABC in the mid-seventies and liked each other. Before sliding into his silver Lincoln Continental, Spelling turned to Tartikoff and said: "I read somewhere that you're interested in doing summer series."

True, said Tartikoff. The networks had always used reruns in summer, which alienated viewers. To get them back, Tartikoff said NBC should do more original summertime programming, the kind that would appeal to mass audiences.

"There's an idea I've always had and it would be perfect as a summer series," said Spelling. It would be a modern-day *Charlie's Angels.* Brandon Stoddard had said that Spelling's idea was vulgar, one he thought viewers would dismiss as exploitative. But Spelling was eager to try it out on Tartikoff.

Unlike Stoddard, Tartikoff was not trying to escape Spelling's shadow; nor was he striving, as Stoddard was, to upgrade his network. NBC under Tartikoff already had a reputation for quality programs.

Tartikoff could afford to see if Spelling had another *Charlie's Angels* in him. "What's the idea?" said Tartikoff, aware that Spelling was no longer tied exclusively to ABC.

"I can pitch it to you in a sentence," said the Texas-born Spelling.

"Okay, what is it?"

"Student nurses in Dallas in the summer and the air conditioning doesn't work so they sweat a lot!" said Spelling.

"It's a 40 share!" exclaimed Tartikoff, describing a megahit. "Let's do it!" He didn't need a story meeting, a script, a pilot. All he needed was one sentence, one sentence from the producer who had already given the nation Farrah Fawcett in a wet T-shirt.

Spelling was delighted by this chance to regain some status in Hollywood. Despite his vast fortune, Spelling was hurt that people said he had lost his touch, that he had never won an Emmy, that even when he produced a quality series like ABC's *Family* in the late seventies or knocked down racial stereotypes by starring a black cop before it was common in *Mod Squad*, he rarely got credit for it. Aaron Spelling was thrilled to have another chance to prove to Hollywood that he still knew what grabbed mass audiences. And he was determined to prove Brandon Stoddard and ABC were wrong to let his exclusive contract lapse. ABC, which used to send him lavish gifts, hadn't even sent him a Christmas card in two years.

As he zipped back to Burbank in his Mustang, Tartikoff was enthused about Spelling's idea. Maybe it was time, he thought, to bring voluptuous women back to network television. Tartikoff thought that the 1980s were sexually repressed, and he blamed the conservative mood and the AIDS epidemic. But he thought that a show with "five extremely attractive women" could be "hot." He couldn't think of five drop-dead-looking women in the entire sixty-six hours of prime time on the three networks. He believed Spelling was a master storyteller who could produce acceptable "soft porn," and that a network owed its viewers variety. Tartikoff had given them the gritty realism of *Hill Street Blues* and *St. Elsewhere* and upscale comedies like *The Cosby Show* and *Cheers,* and now he was convinced the time was ripe for sex. Tartikoff and Spelling could fill "a vacuum."

Within days, a Tartikoff invitation beckoned Spelling to visit NBC's Burbank offices. Spelling was nervous because he had never been to NBC, so he asked Bill Haber, his agent, to accompany him. Nothing could have prepared Spelling for what awaited him when he got off the elevator on the second floor: A red carpet was rolled out, and hostesses handed him flowers. A marching band struck up "The Yellow Rose of Texas," and two hundred or so NBC employees applauded as he was steered toward the WELCOME AARON sign at the end of the hall, right above Brandon Tartikoff's head. Smiling, Tartikoff pumped his hand. "I felt ten feet tall," Spelling later said.

Like every great programmer before him, Brandon Tartikoff understood what F. Scott Fitzgerald meant when he said of intelligent people that they must be able to hold two contradictory ideas in their heads at once and still function. He wanted to do shows that he could be proud of. But he lived—and died—by the Nielsen ratings. Tartikoff was so excited by *Nightingales* that he told his team: "This is a guaranteed 40 share!"

"We'll be shot for this!" exclaimed Warren Littlefield. But a moment later Tartikoff's deputy began to rationalize: "Aaron is his own best critic. He knows what is trash. It will be an eighties show, with nurses with interesting lives. It won't look like tits and ass!"

The "kids" were on their own. Around the office *Nightingales* was known as "the silver nipple show."

Spelling, like Paltrow, signed a thirteen-week commitment. The pilot for *Nightingales,* like the pilot for *Tattinger's,* was to be ready by May of 1988. Both series were expected to compete for a spot on the fall 1988 schedule. Despite the proven record of the producers and Tartikoff's brilliant record as a programmer, both series—one upscale, the other down—would fail.

16

TWO SCORPIONS IN A BOTTLE: THE NETWORK/AFFILIATE "PARTNERSHIP"

Since a television network is neither a giant studio that manufactures programs nor a national grid of network-owned wires connecting 240 million Americans, once it buys an Aaron Spelling series, a network rents time on its 200-plus local affiliated stations to display the series. A recurrent fear haunting network executives is that its affiliates will refuse to feature its programs.

The nightmare came true on October 28, 1987. Out of nowhere, a syndication company called LBS Communications stitched together for one hour this night its own ad-hoc national grid of 141 stations—including 97 stations affiliated with each of the three networks. In contrast to the networks, which supplied free programming, LBS would extract a toll from each station. Nevertheless, the syndicator enticed the stations with promises of up to twenty minutes of advertising time to sell, as opposed to the two to three minutes the networks would have allotted to their affiliates. The bait to lure the 141 stations was a one-hour special—*Return to the Titanic . . . Live,* hosted by Telly Savalas. The prime-time special was accompanied by a barrage of publicity and a measure of suspense—for the first time, a team of experts would reveal the Titanic's secrets, long buried with the ship on the ocean floor.

The Big Three, like the once impregnable *Titanic* itself, were also under water that night. The Nielsen numbers told the story. The syndicated special was seen on 24.7 percent of all the TV sets in America—and more than a third of all sets in use that night. The runner-up was ABC's *Head of the Class,* with a 13.8 rating. The *Titanic* special was among the top five shows of the week, eclipsing *60 Minutes.* Only once before—in April of 1986, when Geraldo Rivera hosted *Al Capone's Vaults*—had a syndicated show beaten the networks, and they considered it a fluke. People are always intrigued by mobsters, the networks said. The promotion for the Capone special was brilliant. No need to worry.

This time the networks were worried. They had seen their affiliates preempt network shows for Billy Graham or *Star Trek* specials, or for local sports contests. But more than any other experience in a dozen years at NBC, the *Titanic* special "made me feel like a dinosaur," said Warren Littlefield. "The three-network power base was knocked on its ass for one hour by a piece-of-crap special!"

At the weekly staff meeting of the CBS affiliate relations department vice president Scott Michaels warned his twelve somber district managers and supervisors, "We're going to have more of these next year." CBS divided the country into six districts, each consisting of thirty to thirty-five stations. Each district manager helped negotiate the compensation paid to the station, lined up clearances, kept track of the preemptions, informed stations about changes in the CBS schedule, made sure stations had the technical information they needed to receive network programs off the satellite. The district manager expedited requests (Can Dan Rather pose with our local anchors for a billboard ad?), relayed complaints (Why are there so many sports overruns knocking out local news?), and served as the local station's contact with the network. Affiliate Relations used to be a snap—a decade before, most affiliate stations were ma and pa operations and felt like part of a network family. Rarely did they deny networks their airtime. When KXLY-TV, the CBS affiliate in Spokane, preempted the network in 1976, for instance, it was promptly terminated.

There were several reasons for the rise of preemptions. By mid-1987, only two of CBS's top fifty stations were privately owned; forty-eight were run by station groups like Group W, Gannett, Cox, Hearst, Scripps Howard, and the Gillett Group. These corporate owners lacked shared history and old loyalties. Run by bottom-line managers, and often burdened by the debt incurred to meet the steep purchase price, stations were constantly trying to better last year's numbers. "It's commodity trading to us," admitted Martin Pompadur, chairman of Television Station Partners, who managed eight stations from his New York headquarters. "We don't know the community. We're short-term players."

Squeezed by financial pressures, station managers now had a variety of products to choose from. Syndicators like LBS Communications offered bounties to bump network shows, just as food packagers offered cash or promotion dollars for supermarket shelf space. Movies were plentiful and relatively cheap. News was supplied free of charge several times a day through network news feeds. Inexpensive regional and world news services were also available at nominal charges, allowing stations to expand their local news hole. By preempting the network, the station manager could sell from twelve to twenty minutes per hour rather than the two to three minutes granted by the network. Like free-agent athletes, affiliates increasingly sold their loyalties to the highest bidder. And every time Tisch or Murphy suggested cutting their compensation, stations took it as an excuse to show less loyalty.

By 1986 CBS affiliates preempted 5,103 hours of network prime time; 60 percent of the affiliates delayed the start of the network's late-night programming for the sake of a more profitable syndicated show, and 20 percent delayed the 10 A.M. start of CBS's daytime schedule. No CBS affiliate was a worse offender than KMOV-TV in St. Louis, the station CBS sold to Viacom in late 1985. In all, KMOV preempted 103 network prime-time hours in 1987, almost 10 percent of CBS's evening schedule. These preemptions, in addition to tightened management, helped boost KMOV's profits from twenty-two to forty cents of each dollar taken in. But the preemptions reduced CBS's audience and threatened its ad revenues. In 1986 alone, prime-time preemptions from CBS stations forced the network to give back to advertisers a total of 128,000 thirty-second spots.

If a station fails to submit sufficient notarized forms agreeing to display CBS programs, the network has two options: to offer the preempted show to another station in the market, as the FCC permits it to do, or to bestow its affiliation on another station, as NBC did in Miami in January 1987 when it snatched CBS's affiliate and dumped its own station. But these options did not always exist. Since most markets had only three VHF stations, the networks were reluctant to affiliate with a UHF station carrying a weaker signal that reached fewer viewers. And to raid the station of another network was expensive.

With so many other programming alternatives, affiliates now sensed that the balance of power had shifted in their favor. And as CBS's ratings collapsed, its affiliates gained even more leverage. The networks were unable to strike back—unless the affiliate was flagrantly abusive. "There is nothing I can hold over their head," said Jeff McIntyre, who supervised thirty-two affiliates for CBS in the Midwest. McIntyre couldn't support the termination of an affiliation just because a station preempted a single show or if CBS offered a pathetic late-night schedule. He understood the pressures the local general managers were under from above. And he understood the program options available to local stations. "My typical day is heartburn," McIntyre said. "What I'm trying to do is force thirty-two different businesses to follow my lead without any real power to do it."

The story of the power shift away from the networks is found in the grassy backyard of KCTV-5 in Kansas City, one of the thirty-two affiliates McIntyre supervised. Behind KCTV's two-story brick building sit five large satellite dishes, only two of them devoted to CBS. A third satellite was set aside to receive syndicated shows like *Return to the Titanic . . . Live* or *Geraldo;* a fourth was set aside for another network competitor, CNN, since KCTV paid seven hundred dollars weekly for an hour of *CNN Headline News* at 5 A.M. daily and for the right to plug CNN stories into local newscasts; the fifth was for KCTV's two satellite news-gathering trucks, which also reduced KCTV's dependence on CBS because they helped expand local news. These $550,000 trucks, one third of whose cost was subsidized by CBS, permitted the station to go live, to roam far from home, to bypass the network by hooking up directly with other stations and regional and even worldwide news services. From one of the two CBS satellite dishes, KCTV received three daily network news feeds, permitting the station to run pictures before the network did. "In my day we wouldn't let them use the feed until after the 7:00 News," said former CBS News president Fred Friendly. "One of the reasons News ratings are down is that people say, 'I saw that already.' "

KCTV is one of seven stations owned by the Meredith Corporation, based in Des Moines. In 1987, this Kansas City station was ranked seventh from the bottom among all CBS affiliates in clearances of network programs. Five nights a week KCTV substituted two syndicated shows—*The Fall Guy* and *Hawaii Five-O*—for CBS's late-night fare, and daily it bumped a half hour of daytime programming. This was of more than passing interest to CBS since the general manager of KCTV was Phil Jones, chairman of the CBS Affiliate Advisory Board.

In 1987, KCTV employed 120 people, 37 fewer than when Phil Jones became general manager in 1980. "That's one of the reasons I respect Tisch," said Jones, forty-three, a former ad salesman. A real good ol' boy—gregarious, University of Missouri-educated, a weekend hunter, fervent opponent of gun control, and sports car enthusiast—"Herky" Jones cuts a dashing figure in Kansas City, where he has spent most of his life. This $250,000-a-year executive waves to half of Stroud's restaurant as he consumes his three chicken breasts, cinnamon buns, mashed potatoes, salad and soup—all for $7.95. He zips around town in a blue 500 SL Mercedes convertible and his station perennially ranks at or near the top in this five-station market. In Kansas City, Phil Jones, not Larry Tisch, is the face of CBS.

CBS provides Phil Jones's station, free, thirteen of its twenty-four hours of daily weekday programming, including all of its prime-time shows, which, since this is the Midwest, air between 7 and 10 P.M. CBS notifies its stations when its Telstar 302 satellite will be beaming shows, and the KCTV engineering staff aims a receiver on its twenty-three-foot-wide satellite dish that sits out back to capture the signal and then either tapes or transmits it live to the 1,044-foot KCTV tower and antennae. In addition CBS provides much of KCTV's sports programming, as well as the morning and evening network news and the three daily news feeds. CBS also provides its stations with free promos, as well as steep discounts on broadcast equipment. The network also offers about two minutes of advertising time—called adjacencies—for the local station to sell during each hour of network time. These network adjacencies alone provide KCTV with roughly 40 percent of its annual sales revenues. And on top of this, CBS in 1987 paid $1.1 million annually to KCTV—$164 million to all of its affiliates—in cash compensation.

A network does still more for an affiliate. "A network," said Phil Jones, "gives me national continuity, as McDonald's does for its stores. . . . Advertisers see my product, and it makes me a part of everyone's life. No matter where you go, you see my product." And you see CBS News, which takes KCTV places it cannot afford to go on its own. Then there is the identification, and prestige, of being able to associate KCTV with Mike Wallace or Angela Lansbury. And because the network provides free programming and assures vast audiences for advertisers, its network affiliation "at least" doubled the value of KCTV, admitted Jones.

But a station has two bottom lines, its long-term value and its short-term profits. Increasingly, economics worked against the network. KCTV made more money replacing weak network series with syndicated shows. About a third of KCTV's revenues are from selling local ads on syndicated shows, which the network does not share. When KCTV took back from CBS the 10:30 to 11:30 P.M. hour on weeknights to run syndicated shows, the difference was substantial. In

1986, KCTV paid the syndicator $7,000 a week for five episodes of *Hart to Hart,* which earned the station $35,000 per week in revenues. CBS's late-night action-adventure series would have brought only $12,000 a week to the station, a difference of almost $1 million a year. Another bonanza for local stations in the heartland of America are Billy Graham specials. As often as four times a year KCTV, like other stations, replaces CBS's prime-time programming for an hour on each of three consecutive nights. In 1987, 40 percent of CBS's affiliates bumped the network for Graham specials. The economics were simple: Graham paid KCTV $25,000 for each of the three nights, far more than the $10,000 in local spots and another $200 in network compensation that KCTV sacrificed.

By far the biggest money-maker for KCTV was local news, which generated roughly 50 percent of its annual revenue. When advertisers buy time, they usually want local news as part of the package. And they pay a premium for it. KCTV's late news at 10 P.M. costs as much as a prime-time spot. On the early news at 5 P.M., the station billed from $600 to $800 per thirty-second commercial, compared to the $150 to $250 for the syndicated show at 3 P.M. And the station shared none of its nine minutes of commercials and promos on a typical half hour of local news with the network. Because KCTV was rated number one in news, because local news offered KCTV its community identity, the station had an incentive to crowd out the network with a total of two hours daily of local news. It was no surprise, then, that KCTV and other affiliates opposed the expansion of network news to one hour, or that KCTV ran Dan Rather at 5:30, before most viewers were home.

With its successful local newscast and selective preemptions, and by keeping expenses under 2 percent growth each year, KCTV thrived. Its total revenues for 1986–87 had climbed to $26.5 million. Local ads accounted for $14 million of these revenues, the adjacency spots allotted by the network added $11.5 million, and the remainder came from the $1.1 million in network compensation. KCTV's expenses were $13.5 million, with local entertainment programming costing $5 million, a forty-two-person news operation $2.3 million, technical expenses $1.5 million, sales $2 million, and administrative expenses $1.9 million. The bottom line: $9.5 million in pretax profits. Because roughly 60 percent of KCTV's revenue came from local ads, because the economics of syndication were so alluring, and because of a faltering CBS schedule, the future looked even bleaker for the network.

KCTV's sales manager Patrick North predicted, "Clearances will continue to decline."

Despite KCTV's relatively poor network clearance record, CBS did not accuse Phil Jones of violating the "partnership," as it did other affiliates. One reason was Jones's position as chairman of the CBS Affiliate Advisory Board. At least equally important was Jones's agreeable personality. He was someone who always tried to understand the network's point of view, who extolled "the partnership" as if it were sacred. In this federal system, Jones was the leader of an independent state; but he always professed a belief in a healthy central government. When CBS ran the movie *Gandhi* on the Wednesday before Thanksgiving, which happened also to be the night of KCTV's annual telethon to raise money for the homeless, Jones volunteered to bump his own late-night schedule to air the movie. When CBS wanted to experiment with a new late-night show on Fridays, Jones agreed to try it for six months, giving CBS a chance to lift off the ground.

Tension between the network and its affiliates was, of course, not new. But by the end of 1987 these tensions had spiraled, threatening the partnership. The new network owners were determined to shift the balance of power. Station owners were just as determined to maintain the status quo. "They are like two scorpions in a bottle," observed former NBC vice chairman David Adams. "The network and its affiliates have always wanted to kill each other, but they feared killing themselves." With networks and stations alike beset by economic pressures, the chances were greater that they would kill each other without meaning to. The networks would cut compensation—and risk losing viewers to preemptions. Affiliates like KCTV would insert syndicated shows—and damage their network. As a station manager, Phil Jones's primary task was to maximize KCTV's short-term profits. "We don't pay attention to industry problems," he said apologetically. "We live in a vacuum."

With VCRs then in five out of ten homes and more than twenty choices on KCTV's cable box, Phil Jones had his own nightmare. He worried less about lost network viewers than he did about the cable companies assigning his station a higher and less desirable number on the cable box. He worried about spurting regional sports and news cable networks. He worried about CBS one day distributing its programs through cable or direct broadcast satellites, in both cases bypassing local stations. He worried about the telephone company one day linking up with a network or a studio and delivering shows to the home directly through fiber-optic telephone wire. But mostly Phil Jones worried about his short-term needs, which were not always the same as those of CBS. More than they cared to admit, the interests of the "partners" diverged.

17

ABC: A HAPPIER PLACE TO WORK –THE SECOND HALF OF 1987

The new A. C. Nielsen people meter would take a huge bite out of the three networks in the fall of 1987. The size of this bite was sketched by Lawrence S. Hyams, ABC's director of Audience Analysis, on the second Tuesday in November 1987. A competent man with a droning, matter-of-fact voice, Hyams sat with his back to the window at one side of a conference table as his dismal report on the first six weeks of the fall 1987–88 season was distributed to a dozen members of the ABC Sales staff.

Hyams's report was, of course, laced with the jargon of audience research. There were figures on the *HUT* level—Homes Using Television—which is the percentage of the ninety million television households with their sets on. There were figures on each show's *share,* which is the percentage of TV sets actually in use that are tuned to a particular show. Then there was the show's *rating,* which is a smaller number because it calculates the percentage of the total TV potential viewing audience watching a particular program, counting sets not in use as well. Finally, there were the *demos,* or the age and sex of the actual audience. By each of these measures, Hyams told the Sales team, the Nielsen people meter found that during the first six weeks of the fall season the three networks had lost 10 percent of their prime-time audience from the year before; the share of homes watching one of three networks in prime time sagged from 79 to 75 percent; the HUT level fell 2.5 percent, to 60.3 percent; and the younger demos were evaporating.

Hyams flipped through the dreary statistics, starting with CBS, which was the biggest ratings loser. CBS's ratings plunged 38 percent on Saturday and 22 percent on Tuesday evenings, for instance. But this offered little solace to ABC. Nor did the slight decline at seemingly invincible NBC. The weekends were becoming a graveyard for all three networks, as viewers fled to the local cinemaplex, or stayed home and popped a movie into their VCRs. The three-network ratings dropped an astonishing 14 percent on Friday nights, 17 percent on Saturday, and 9 percent on Sunday, usually the most watched night of the week. Brandon Stoddard had assured Tom Murphy that the new Dolly Parton variety hour would be a winner for ABC. Instead, when compared with the previous year, ABC's Sunday ratings fell 12 percent; the Parton show, which opened with a strong fifth-place finish in the September weekly ratings, had slumped to fortieth by November. Members of the ABC Sales force were not reassured by another chart. It revealed that ABC had lost less of its overall audience than CBS and even NBC. One hard, ineradicable fact remained: ABC still had fewer viewers this fall than last.

People in sales are conditioned to be optimistic, but Hyams's dire report served as a reminder that viewers had more choices. While the three networks lost viewers, the big gainers were independent stations, including those affiliated with the fledging Fox network, which now programmed on Saturday and Sunday nights. The audience on nonnetwork-affiliated independent TV stations rose 12 percent over 1986, and now averaged a 10.1 nightly rating, compared to ABC's 14.5 and CBS's 13.8. Which meant that of the TV sets actually on between 8 and 11 P.M., nearly one out of five viewers (17 percent) was now tuned to a nonnetwork-affiliated independent station. Fox had become more than a nuisance, with 113 affiliated stations and nearly $100 million in summer upfront sales, almost twice what was expected. Fox even beat one ABC show on Saturday, a lame comedy called *Sable,* and Fox shows appealed to younger viewers.

Hyams paused and looked about at a room filled with dejected Sales executives. The gloom deepened when Hyams reviewed the cable numbers. Cable viewing had jumped by nearly a third over 1986. Basic cable-programming services like CNN and pay-cable channels like HBO gave cable an average 8.4 rating, siphoning nearly 15 percent of nightly viewers. Cable did not command the mass audiences of the networks—with the exception of sporting events, a cable show rarely achieved a 1 percent rating. Nevertheless, with its dozens of choices, cable took a massive bite out of the networks. And cable, unlike network TV, was young. Already half the homes in America were wired for cable. Within a decade, it was expected that at least 70 percent of all homes would have cable. And with piles of cash, cable programming was improving. HBO offered such choices as *Not Neces-*

sarily the News and Robin Williams and Billy Crystal specials, while its rival, Showtime, had *It's Garry Shandling's Show* and *Uncle Tom's Cabin;* the Arts & Entertainment Network carried John Gielgud in *Time After Time;* ESPN featured NFL games; Ted Turner's superstation, WTBS, presented MGM movie classics. Already, cable networks were bidding against local stations to acquire reruns of network shows; by 1987 cable had captured the syndication rights to *Miami Vice, Remington Steele,* and *Cagney and Lacey.* Then there was CNN to worry about. As network news cut back, Ted Turner's twenty-four-hour cable news service expanded, and in addition to its nineteen bureaus now included the only full-time network correspondent based in Africa outside Cape Town. Already, 180 local U.S. stations were CNN subscribers. If there was a single moment that symbolized the official end of the three-network monopoly, it came in December 1987 when President Reagan sat with the network anchors for a year-end interview and the Big Three became the Big Four; for the first time CNN's Bernard Shaw was included.

In fact, Hyams's report showed that the Big Three had become the Big Five, as cable and independent TV stations assailed ABC, CBS, and NBC. The combined audience of cable and the independent TV stations now exceeded that of any of the networks on most nights. Then there was the VCR, which hadn't even existed a decade before. A year earlier, 30 percent of all American homes owned a VCR, Hyams reported. Now, in a single year, 46.1 percent had one, a jump of 54 percent. Even public television (PBS) viewing, which dipped 8 percent, stole viewers with an average 2.4 rating and would, in one fall week in 1990, triple its normal audience with the extraordinary miniseries, *The Civil War.*

The ABC Sales team arrayed around the conference table listened intently, rarely looking up from Hyams's charts. There was little to celebrate in the Nielsen numbers, even though Hyams guessed that half the network losses resulted from flaws in the people meter itself. Cable subscribers, who were already accustomed to punching up dozens of cable channels, were presumably more at ease pressing the people-meter button than less-sophisticated viewers. Still, at least half the audience loss was real, said Hyams. And his graphs revealed that the culprit was not just increased competition. There were no new "hits" on any of the three networks this fall—certainly none approached the 59 share once reached by Aaron Spelling's *Charlie's Angels* in its 1976 premiere season, nor the 40-plus share of *The Cosby Show.*

Everyone in ABC Sales knew the theories behind the network falloff. They knew the argument of people like Spelling, who claimed the networks offered too much realism and too little escape, too few shows like *Fantasy Island, The Love Boat,* and *Dynasty,* each of which Spelling produced. Within ABC Sales there was another explanation, which was that the networks offered too much of Spelling's escapism and too few shows of distinction. Surely there was evidence in Hyams's charts that the worst shows were weaker—eight series registered less than a 15 share, compared to only three in 1986. Perhaps the networks bore some blame, as Brandon Tartikoff had suggested in a speech earlier that month. The networks were guilty of slashing the number of weeks in which they offered original series episodes from thirty-five or so to between twenty-two and twenty-five, of accosting viewers with too many commercials, of relying too much on stale formulas, of scheduling clinkers against competing hit shows. The greatest audience erosion for the networks came from these mediocre shows, not from the hits, since as late as 1987 the top ten hits attracted nearly the same ratings as the hits of 1977 did.*

Larry Hyams's report on the fall 1987–88 season could be read as a devastating rebuke of network television in general, and of ABC in particular. ABC's schedule from Thursday through Sunday nights, the principal targets of Brandon Stoddard's May 1987 scheduling changes, fared poorly. *Dolly,* Hyams said, might not be able to reclaim the audience it had lost on Sunday. "It's doubtful," he said, especially "with ESPN on Sunday night." When the networks allowed cable to televise eight Sunday night NFL games, they did not calculate that many stations would preempt the networks' Sunday night schedule, as even WABC in New York had done the previous Sunday when the New England Patriots played the Detroit Lions. Cap Cities' decentralization philosophy tolerated such freedom, and since ABC owned 80 percent of ESPN, its cable investment benefited—at the expense, however, of its network investment. By the end of the season, in fact, ESPN's Sunday games claimed a combined rating on their broadcast and cable outlets of 12.4, in contrast to *Dolly*'s 10.3 Nielsen rating.

With a collective sigh, the Sales meeting ended, Hyams went back to his research desk, the Sales force returned to its telephones, and vice president Jake Keever lingered in the conference room. Normally buoyant, the white-haired Keever was morose as he looked out the window toward the black granite CBS building a block south. "For

* Within a few years, even the hits would no longer attract the same network ratings they once did.

CBS it's a lot worse," he said. "It's like the farmer down the road who lost six pigs. We only lost four!" But Keever wasn't kidding himself. He knew that for his department, Hyams's report offered nothing but headaches. If the ratings dropped below the guarantees Sales had made in the upfront market, ABC would have to come up with "make-goods," drawing on its reserves to give advertisers free commercials in shows with comparable audiences, thus depleting network revenues. The season was only six weeks old, and already ABC had diverted five hundred ad units worth $40 million from its inventory for make-goods.

While network spirits rise and fall depending on the overnight Nielsen ratings, in the autumn of 1987 the analogy hounding Cap Cities/ABC executives was the fate of AM radio, whose decline could also be traced to a proliferation of choices. They could remember that back in the early seventies, AM radio dominated 75 percent of all listening. Fifteen years later, seventy-five percent of listeners now tuned to FM stations, which usually spared them the blitzkrieg of commercials encountered on AM. While the network owners were often preoccupied with day-to-day crises—cutting costs, negotiating contracts, adjudicating among News, Sports, and Entertainment for a spot on the schedule—the larger foe remained. Viewers continued to abandon the networks. Dan Burke was pessimistic. "I think it is possible there will come a time, maybe in ten years, when the networks no longer have a critical mass," he said.

But ten years was far away, and in the meantime ABC had a prime-time schedule to fix. ABC's new owners admitted to some disappointments. By going along with Stoddard and scheduling *Dolly* on Sundays at 9 P.M. and bouncing its Sunday movie, the new owners had substituted Stoddard's judgment for their own. "*Dolly* wasn't ready to go on the air when it did," John Sias said. "And when the show aired Brandon stuck with its producer too long." Now, after ABC had sunk $44 million into it, the show was about to fall on its face. The *20/20* move to Friday was not turning out as badly as Arledge had predicted, but since many fewer viewers watch television on Friday nights, its audience was off. The Thursday movie was fizzling. *Moonlighting* was behind its production schedule and way over budget. After an overheated media buildup, *Max Headroom* collapsed, and by November that failure and others would, Tom Murphy calculated, cost ABC $16 million.

Despite these disappointments, ABC was number two in the ratings, ahead of CBS. And Stoddard had discovered a few new series with promise. "I'd say that ABC has planted a few seeds that could develop into something," observed Tartikoff that fall. Shows like *thirtysomething, Hooperman,* and *The Slap Maxwell Story* had their own distinct voices, trod the same path Tartikoff and NBC had taken. This fall the TV critics, who as Eugene McCarthy once said of journalists were like blackbirds—when one jumps off the wire the others tend to follow—latched onto one or two of these quality series as emblems of ABC's entire twenty-two-hour prime-time schedule. Although he had concerns about *Dolly* and Stoddard's skills as a scheduler and cost manager, Tom Murphy said he was content that Stoddard had delivered "the kind of quality programming he had promised." It was, Murphy said, only Stoddard's "sophomore year"; he knew it had taken Brandon Tartikoff five years to succeed at NBC.

By the fourth quarter of 1987, Murphy was moving toward Hollywood. He had come to have a greater appreciation of programming's impact, was now studying more closely the research reports on entertainment shows, was attending focus groups designed to spot the strengths or vulnerabilities of series already on the air. His confidence grew. "I have very common taste," Murphy explained that fall. "I have been surprised by the correlation between what I like and what the viewers like. I'm more confident of my own judgment now."

Murphy had come to appreciate that in Hollywood a network had to spend to make money. Talent was expensive, but it was even more expensive to watch NBC lock up the best writer/producers. So Murphy in November signed an extraordinary talent contract with Steven Bochco, creator of ABC's promising series, *Hooperman,* and NBC's breakthrough *Hill Street Blues* and *L.A. Law.* In return for the writer/producer's exclusive services for six years and for three nonexclusive years thereafter, Bochco, who had won eight Emmys, agreed to create, develop, and produce ten television series. ABC paid Bochco a $5 million signing bonus and agreed to both pay a generous license fee for each series and absorb any deficits. Additionally, ABC would pay Bochco a $1.5 million kill fee if it chose not to air a series. With Fox joining as the syndicator of any Bochco series, the twin package was said to be worth $50 million to Bochco.

ABC, said Bochco, was sending a message that it was "willing to make commitments to the production community. People assume, correctly, that if I'm willing to work at ABC it's because I've got freedom. That's a wonderful message to send to this community." Said fellow producer Bruce Paltrow, "The truth is, if he gets two hits, what does it cost ABC?" Too much, answered both NBC and CBS.

Larry Tisch in 1987 just didn't believe in spending that kind of money for talent or entertainment, for sports rights or TV stations. "I respect the deal he made," said Tisch. "But if you look at it in the cold light of day, it raises the cost of every program for the future. Every producer will say, 'If you pay this to Bochco, why not me?' When I was in the hotel business, all that was important to the performers was what we paid their peers!" Brandon Tartikoff made a similar point: "Would Cosby want twenty commitments if I gave Bochco ten?" Besides, he added, as the ratings leader NBC just didn't have the open slots on its schedule that ABC or CBS had.

In addition to making Bochco happy, by late 1987 Cap Cities continued to make ABC a genuinely happier place to work than the other two networks. But Dan Burke was dissatisfied. Burke had been particularly upset by the bickering he had encountered during May's Decision Week. News and Entertainment were still battling over the schedule. Sports and News vied over time on Sunday mornings. ABC executives still complained about Stoddard's scheduling decisions and Arledge's disappearances. Sports chief Dennis Swanson, shaken after a son's auto accident, ranted and abused an aide in front of thirty colleagues in September, and Burke felt compelled to order Swanson to take a six-week leave of absence. Entertainment and News regularly maneuvered around John Sias. Some old-timers at the network found nothing unusual about all this, insisting this was the price of having highly skilled, competitive individuals. Others blamed John Sias, who even friends acknowledged was not as assertive as he wanted to be because he was sandwiched between Burke and Murphy and didn't want to upstage either.

After two years as president of ABC, Sias conceded he was not entirely happy. "I've had enormous frustrations," Sias said. "I've been spoiled. From 1963 on I've been used to running my own business, and succeeding or failing at it. I had freedom in publishing, and only consulted Tom and Dan. Now Murphy and Burke are more involved, understandably." Murphy and Burke had separate offices over at Cap Cities' East Side townhouse, but they spent much of their day at ABC, where their thirty-ninth-floor offices surrounded Sias's. Below Sias was Brandon Stoddard, who, Sias mused, called him "Mr. Cutrate TV," suggesting that "I'm just interested in costs"; and Roone Arledge, Sias laughed, "would love to be in my job." Any time Arledge or Stoddard had something important to discuss, they maneuvered to have Murphy and Burke present at a meeting with Sias, who, not wanting to upstage Murphy or Burke, rarely spoke up. Sias was having difficulty adjusting his brash personality to a subdued management style.

Sias decided he had to be "less bashful" in asserting himself, and late in the fall of 1987 he talked to Murphy and Burke, who agreed that they had, inadvertently, impeded him. Burke began to pull back, no longer attending meetings with News or Sports, no longer telephoning Stoddard. "I felt my absence sent a message," Burke said.

Those less sympathetic to Sias said that he, not the management structure, was the problem. They said this former salesman got excited about the wrong things, that he was, in the words of a senior executive who liked him, someone who could "probably play a great trumpet. I'm not sure he's an orchestra leader." News vice president David Burke agreed that Sias wasn't a leader. "A leader," Burke said, "is supposed to be someone who can get you to moderate your zeal for the good of the company. That's a strength John doesn't have." Tom Murphy and Dan Burke, however, faulted ABC executives for being too fractious. Dan Burke likened ABC to a family where one kid blames the other or runs to a parent to "complain rather than try to fix things." It was the way former pitching star Johnny Sain operated as a pitching coach. "He creates a terrific feeling of cohesiveness among his pitchers," said Burke. "But he does it by blaming the shortstop. It's why he never stays as a pitching coach or gets to be a manager. A lot of people manage that way." Burke wanted to see more teamwork.

An obvious problem was the ongoing war between Peter Jennings and his producer, Bill Lord. All anyone who worked on *World News Tonight* could talk about was whether and when Lord would leave, and who would replace him. Or whether Lord would step out of character and smile. The venom, and Lord's dark mood, were sapping the newsroom's energy. Jennings often sulked. When Sam Donaldson sat in for Jennings as a substitute anchor, as he occasionally did, calm returned. People laughed and tension drained from the newsroom.

The battle between Jennings and Lord had been going on for more than a year, and News employees blamed Roone Arledge for procrastinating. Even his deputy, David Burke, blamed Arledge. "I would have moved a long time ago," Burke said of Lord in November. Those close to Jennings complained that Arledge delayed because "he loves the game, loves the exercise of power," loves to keep people guessing. It had been almost a year since he assigned producer Paul Friedman to work up a new news format, yet Arledge still had made no decision on that. "Roone, for whatever reason—pressures in a lot of areas, etcetera—drops in and out of people's lives," explained Paul Friedman, who admired Arledge. "You never know quite where you are."

That summer and into the fall, Jennings wrestled with the offer to move to CBS as a coanchor with Rather. His contract had expired on August 9, 1987, and by November he hadn't signed a new one. One day, as Jennings relaxed on an oversized couch in his airy office, surrounded by family photographs, the battered trenchcoat that was his trademark hanging on the door, he declared: "I want this company to trust me and give me freedom to say this is stuff we should have on this broadcast or not have on this broadcast." Jennings lacked confidence in Bill Lord. "I want them to understand that the key to making this job work is having a relationship between the executive producer and the anchor. My problem with Lord has always been the authority problem. A good anchor and executive producer shouldn't have that problem."

It was Jennings's impression that ABC felt Dan Rather had too much power and, by God, they weren't going to make the same mistake with him. The Bill Lord question became entangled in this larger issue, which helps explain part of Arledge's reluctance to make a change. There was also the question of whom to choose as Lord's successor. Jennings wanted Paul Friedman, who had gone back to his job in London as director of News Coverage for Europe, Africa, and the Middle East; Arledge was hard to pin down but hinted that his choice was Dorrance Smith, thirty-six, executive producer of *This Week with David Brinkley* as well as the weekend news and *The Health Show.* Jennings told Arledge he worried that Smith, who had served in the White House under President Ford and had become an Arledge protégé but had never worked overseas and had little experience with breaking news, lacked Friedman's seasoning. Arledge urged Jennings to meet with Smith, which he did.

By December, Jennings had signed a new $1.8 million contract, one which did not name him managing editor but did stipulate that he would be consulted on a new executive producer. Jennings joined Arledge for a leisurely lunch on December 14 at Café des Artistes on West Sixty-seventh Street, a block from News. "I've seen both," Jennings told him. "I think Friedman is the person we should have. He has the experience. At a time when overseas news is more important, we can use that experience. And I've worked with him." Jennings saw Dorrance Smith as a smart and able young man, much the way old ABC hands once viewed Jennings when he was a twenty-six-year-old anchor. But Friedman had covered wars, produced documentaries, served as executive producer of *Today* and *NBC News Magazine* during the fourteen years he spent at NBC before joining ABC in 1982. Jennings believed that Friedman, though only forty-two, was mature, worldly. He had asked Smith what he thought of the broadcast, the direction in which he would take it, and he received vague answers, the kind of answers those without experience or certitude would give. From Friedman he got crisp responses, a sense of authority, and confidence that he would have a protector, someone who would both give the newscast a new identity and exhibit some loyalty to the anchor.

Jennings left lunch confident that Arledge would pick Friedman. How could he not? Even if Arledge preferred Smith, unless he was prepared to replace Jennings he had no choice. Typically, the decision was made circuitously. Friedman was asked in late November to fly to New York, where he lunched with Arledge, and the two were later joined by David Burke. They talked about the newscast, but no job offer was rendered. The next day Friedman and Burke lunched. Again, no offer, and Friedman returned to London. Meanwhile, Irwin Weiner, who oversees finances for News, telephoned Friedman and began to negotiate a what-if-you-were-executive-producer contract. "I negotiated a contract before Roone offered me the job," laughs Friedman. On Christmas Eve Arledge called.

"I'm really pleased you're coming and that we've worked out a deal," Arledge said.

"Are you offering me the job?" asked an incredulous Friedman.

"Yes. Merry Christmas."

Friedman's appointment was greeted with enthusiasm within News. Friedman declared that one of his most important tasks was "to make Peter feel comfortable." Arledge was also happy. "We are what CBS used to be," he declared. Arledge thought he had the best team of anchors in Jennings and Ted Koppel. "We have the best bench. We have the most creative programming. No one else does *Capital to Capital.* No one else does *Viewpoint.* No one else does *Nightline.* Or a town hall meeting in Israel. Or a three-hour program on AIDS."

Something else pleased Arledge. By the end of 1987, he was feeling more comfortable with Tom Murphy, Dan Burke, and even John Sias, who seemed to him more subdued. Arledge had taken to calling the Cap Cities people "broadcasters," contrasting their background in television with that of Larry Tisch and Bob Wright. He was proud that when Murphy and Burke announced the formation of a corporate PAC that fall, they specifically excluded News from participation, unlike Bob Wright at NBC. Arledge, who counted such businessmen as investment banker Felix Rohatyn and RJR Nabisco CEO Ross Johnson among his friends, also took some pride in proving that he was a businessman too. This year Arledge smoothly answered Burke and Sias's pointed questions at his annual budget review and was accorded respect, like a fellow corporate chieftain. While ABC Sports, from which he had been unceremoniously removed in January of 1986, was only marginally profitable, Arledge delighted in reminding people that ABC News was a profit-maker. Even David Burke was feeling a bit mellower about Murphy and Burke, if not Sias. He said of Cap Cities, "The people who acquired ABC were broadcasters. They had been in the publishing business. The people who acquired CBS and NBC were different."

But unlike Arledge, David Burke didn't want to dine with the people from Cap Cities. He preferred to head for his Westchester home and dinner with his wife, Trixie, their daughter, and four sons. He would keep his distance. "I'm paid to be uncomfortable with these people," Burke said.

What also made David Burke uncomfortable as 1987 drew to a close was Ted Koppel's contract, which expired in December. Burke knew that his friend Koppel was unsure whether the new owners were really committed to network news. He knew Koppel saw an opportunity in the burgeoning syndication marketplace to ensure the integrity of his work by controlling his own company; there was also an opportunity, Koppel saw, to make real money. In conjunction with the Tribune Company, Geraldo Rivera had recently launched a syndicated talk show to compete with Oprah Winfrey's and Phil Donahue's. Grant Tinker had hired Steve Friedman away from *Today* and was paying him a bundle to create a syndicated *USA Today*. Surely Ted Koppel could command an audience. David Burke knew that Koppel fretted about something else. "He kept saying to me, 'The networks are dead, and the news divisions will soon follow.' " So Burke went to Arledge and Murphy with a plan. Murphy would lunch with Koppel and call him regularly. Warren Buffett would fly east and explain to the newsman why he invested in ABC and why he was in for the long haul. "I knew they would be soul mates," said David Burke.

Whatever the daily agonies, the larger point people outside began to notice was that ABC had become a congenial place to work, thanks in large part to the people skills of Cap Cities managers. Contented, less fearful employees, Dan Burke and Tom Murphy assumed, would be unafraid to take chances. This was one reason Murphy and Burke moved, after the wave of 1986–1987 layoffs, to say they would try to avoid layoffs in the future. It is a reason that Burke, when he searched for managers, said that besides the obvious qualities he always sought humor. "I have never met anyone with a well-developed sense of humor who is not capable of being a good manager," said Burke. It is a reason that Burke made a major effort, beginning in the fall of 1987, to identify the next generation of company leaders. Working from the bottom up, he compiled a list of 150 ABC middle managers, and invited the first group of 50 to attend a November 15–17 retreat at Arrowood, a conference center in Westchester County. Throughout the two days, Burke moved freely among them, full of questions. When he heard that Northeast News Bureau chief Mimi Gurbst's baby daughter had a fever, he asked her three times in two days about the child.

At the end of two days, Burke noticed that the words "family" and "loyalty" kept recurring. That was half Burke's message, for he wanted his managers pulling together. But Burke wanted to teach them another lesson too. So when he stood up at the end of the retreat to offer a few final words Burke put on his best scowl and declared: "This is not my 'family.' My family is ten miles away in Rye. You have to succeed on your own. I know you learned always to talk about family. I never subscribed to that. I have a lot of friends in this company, but they're not my family." The group was chastened, but Burke had made his point. He wanted them to act like a family, but he also wanted them not to lose their initiative, not to wait for *daddy* to do it.

Confidence grew that one day soon the good feeling would translate into higher ABC ratings, just as it seemed to do under Grant Tinker at NBC. Handicapping the three-network competition in late 1987, former CBS executive Peter Lund, who left Larry Tisch's employ in March of 1987 to become president of MultiMedia Entertainment (and would return as executive vice president of CBS in October of 1990), echoed a common refrain about Cap Cities when he said: "I keep thinking that ABC will be the winner of this crowd. Why? Because Murphy and Burke are broadcasters, and because I have never heard so many people say so many nice things about their boss. People at ABC think they're terrific managers, and that they don't take themselves overly seriously. They have created an atmosphere that can lead to success. At a time of insecurity in the business, that's important." Said Michael Fuchs of HBO, "Cap Cities seems to have the most respect in the industry. Murphy and Burke are good solid citizens. They have more people skills than Larry Tisch. Murphy and Burke are not on an ego trip."

As they neared the two-year anniversary of their merger with ABC, the new owners from Cap Cities were both pleased and disappointed. The ABC-owned stations made more money than Cap Cities anticipated, the network less. The eight ABC stations made close to 55¢ on each $1 of revenue collected and in 1987 earned $390 million pretax. ESPN, which they inherited, would earn $70 million in 1987, about equal to the $74 million profit from the network. They were satisfied that the network lost no money, as it had in 1986, but depressed that its profits stacked up so poorly against NBC's, which earned five times as much. Still, Murphy and Burke were pleased with the Cap Cities/ABC stock price, which despite the stock market collapse of October climbed 28.7 percent in 1987, to $345 a share, up from $268 the year before. A reason the stock price rose was that investors had confidence in Cap Cities' management. The company had succeeded in its cost-reduction efforts, cutting in two years a total of 1,800 jobs at both the network and the owned stations. And they had succeeded in settling the place down. ABC's demographics were good and improving, its news division profitable and on the move. They sensed that Brandon Stoddard had nurtured some programs that might be hits.

However bleak the Nielsen numbers, deep down Murphy and Burke did not believe the three networks were dinosaurs. Cable, they knew, had its own woes. Earnings at pay-cable channels like HBO were flat, with audiences static and costs rising. The entire cable industry had to keep an eye on the telephone companies, which were prohibited from entering the programming business but were advancing arguments that consumers would benefit if existing telephone wires could be used to bring programs into the home more cheaply. A more immediate concern for the cable companies was the government in Washington, D.C. Having freed cable from many of its regulatory strictures in 1984, Congress was now restive, concerned that network television had been restrained in order to prevent monopolies while cable itself had become a monopoly which raised prices at will. A single cable operator—John Malone of Tele-Communications Inc. (TCI)—had acquired 150 cable companies in the past three years and now owned nearly 25 percent of the country's cable systems. At the same time, Malone had a significant equity stake in nine of the top twenty basic cable networks, including the Turner Broadcasting System and CNN, the Discovery Channel, American Movie Classics, and Black Entertainment Television. The very thing the networks were restricted from doing—serving as both the exhibitor and the producer—Malone was free to do.

John Malone, said an envious Jack Welch of GE, was "getting as much as he can before the sheriff gets to him. And he's doing it very well. . . . I see a guy getting himself positioned to control distribution." If Welch did it, it would be an antitrust violation, but because the laws differed for cable it was legal for Malone to be vertically integrated. "My hat's off to a smart guy," said Welch.

Whatever the outcome of Congress's closer scrutiny of John Malone and the cable industry, Cap Cities/ABC at the end of 1987 enjoyed some advantages. Unlike NBC, which under Bob Wright would try to catch up, or CBS, which had shed most of its cable-programming investments and under Tisch would sell its nonbroadcasting holdings, ABC had a video enterprises division with numerous cable and entertainment investments, including 80 percent of ESPN, America's largest cable-television network, with 44 million subscribers. Tom Murphy had also inherited one-third ownership in two cable-programming services—the Arts & Entertainment Network (A&E), with 27 million subscribers, and Lifetime, with its female-oriented programming for 33 million subscribers—both of which became profitable for the first time in 1987. In addition to being the largest group owner of TV stations, Cap Cities/ABC claimed nine AM and eight FM radio stations, seven ABC Radio networks with ties to 1,900 affiliated stations, numerous newspapers and magazines, a video-cassette publishing venture, a high-speed information-delivery system called INDECSYs, was a manufacturer of movies and specials on video cassettes, and had a stake in an Australian venture to track video-cassette rentals electronically and to distribute cassettes in vending machines. In conjunction with the Shubert Organization, ABC was the third largest overall investor in Broadway theater, owning major stakes in such hits as *Cats, Phantom of the Opera, Amadeus,* and *Dreamgirls.* These theatrical investments were made with an eye on the future potential of pay-per-view. Said Herb Granath, who ran ABC's video enterprises division: "One night on pay-per-view there will be a thirty-million-dollar opening night. At that point, I don't care what Frank Rich writes in *The New York Times.* It will be the salvation of the theater."

Overseas, Cap Cities/ABC was in a position to become what Dan Burke described as one of "the six or so integrated companies" that would compete in global communications. Although Cap Cities moved more cautiously than, say, GE, by the end of 1987 it did more business overseas than either NBC or CBS. There were $75 million in overseas sales of ABC entertainment and news product. With European governments ending their broadcasting monopolies and welcoming private competition, and with satellite technology, the European market was a new frontier for well-financed adventurers. Between 1982 and 1986, the number of European TV channels nearly doubled from 38 to 62, and Young & Rubicam projected they would multiply to 110 by 1990; already, there were ten million European homes wired for cable, twice the number just two years before.

Tom Murphy and Dan Burke's pleasure at being better positioned than either NBC or CBS in the broad communications competition was tempered by a shared frustration. To get back into the business of producing their own programs and selling reruns in the syndication marketplace, and to remove the roadblocks set up by the federal government, the networks needed to reach a political settlement with the Hollywood studios. The network owners were prepared to accept some limits on the number of shows they produced or to divide more of the upfront cost of producing shows with the studios. But in return they wanted to share some of the syndication profits. The networks hoped to collect studio allies by meeting individually with each, and a few studios were even receptive to a peace pact which, presumably, the government would then ratify. Martin Davis, CEO of Gulf & Western, which owned Paramount Pictures, said, "If common sense would prevail a peace pact could make sense." But by "common sense" Davis meant that he expected the networks to guarantee his studio certain program hours, to share in both the deficits and profits, to engage in joint ventures and, perhaps, even agree to merge a studio and a network.

The effort came to naught. Hollywood's opposition to suspending the fin-syn rules remained implacable throughout 1987 and beyond. Ronald Reagan, their staunch defender, was in the White House. And Bob Daly of Warner Brothers, still the chief negotiator for all the studios, was still immovable. "I wake up every single morning and check with our people in Washington on the financial interest rule," said this former CBS executive. "They [the networks] could wipe us out. . . . The networks make their money upfront. We don't. When I hear them complain that Viacom is making so much money selling the Bill Cosby show, I laugh. Look at all the money they make from the sale of ads on the Bill Cosby show! If they want to share profits, fine. Let us share in their profits. Can I have a piece of their Thursday night revenues?"

As 1987 ended, Murphy and Burke had learned a few lessons about network reality. They were less optimistic about budging Bob Daly and the Hollywood studios. They had surrendered, for now, the idea of cutting the compensation ABC paid its affiliates. They reluctantly agreed that they had to pay star salaries to people like Bochco and Jennings. There were limits to what expenses Cap Cities could cut, because they ran a business whose principal cost—programming—they couldn't control. They worried about the erosion of network viewing, which Murphy and Burke now predicted would bottom out near 60 percent. Their silent partner, Warren Buffett, admitted that if he had known how ABC would perform by 1987, he would still "have been as aggressive as we were in pursuing ABC, but not a lot more."

The new owners didn't control their Hollywood program suppliers. Or the local stations that distributed their product. Or the advertisers on whose revenues they were solely dependent. Nor did they benefit from shows promoted on their network and which returned in syndication to bite them. The union contracts and work rules restricted how they scheduled their work force. Sometimes ABC couldn't even control its own managers, for executives like Roone Arledge and Brandon Stoddard—or anchors like Peter Jennings and Ted Koppel—couldn't be ordered about at will. In many respects, the networks were supplicants of the same federal government their news divisions covered. Murphy and Burke were now, personally, exposed to public scrutiny as they had never been before. "It's a tougher business than I thought," conceded a subdued Tom Murphy at the start of 1988.

Nevertheless, Tom Murphy had reason to be hopeful. The after-tax income of Cap Cities/ABC rose 53 percent in 1987. His company was solidly positioned for the future. As for Hollywood, Murphy could wait, knowing that the fin-syn rules were due to expire in 1990, when Reagan would be out of the White House. Perhaps one day the studios would come around. A strong network was in the interests of Hollywood, as well as advertisers who needed access to mass audiences. "It would be a disaster to the entertainment business if the networks went under," admitted Michael Eisner of Disney, who had sought to acquire first NBC, then CBS. "It is very difficult and expensive to produce quality programming" without the networks, for "no one entity can put up enough money. It could lead to what happened in Europe—a lot of junk. I believe in diversity. But I don't want so much diversity that there is not enough money. So I am very interested in the networks remaining strong."

Tom Murphy had turned his considerable political charm on Hollywood and it was working. He had become more involved in Stoddard's programming, had seen that Hollywood was where the success of his network rested. As he gained more confidence in his own programming taste, Murphy became more assertive. In December he prodded Stoddard to revamp the prime-time schedule, moving Dolly Parton's show to Saturday night, putting seven series into different time periods starting in January. Nevertheless, and very privately, because that was his style, Tom Murphy slowly began to worry that ABC Entertainment had not made sufficient progress. Which did not bode well for his pal Brandon Stoddard.

18

"CREATIVE DESTRUCTION": NBC IN THE SECOND HALF OF 1987

The lunch went well—terrific, in fact. Jack Welch and Bob Wright were eager to meet Richard Burt, then U.S. ambassador to West Germany and once a respected *New York Times* reporter. Over lunch the three men discussed East/West relations, the fate of journalism, and the possibility of Burt's joining NBC or GE—in some undefined News capacity, or to spearhead NBC's efforts to expand in Europe, or to serve as an international consultant to GE. Or perhaps, it went unsaid, Burt could be president of NBC News? Welch and Wright walked away from lunch impressed. So impressed that Welch telephoned Burt that afternoon and, with the same gusto he brings to Boston Red Sox games, Welch exclaimed into the phone: "We *love* you! I mean, we *really love* you!" He was determined to bring Burt aboard.

Then Welch and Wright began to make some calls—to Henry Kissinger, George Shultz, Tom Brokaw, and others who knew or worked with Burt. The reviews were mixed. Almost overnight, Welch's ardor cooled and he moved on, discarding Burt as if they had never met.

In some ways, this incident captures both Welch's and GE's restlessness. When Welch was not happy—with employees or with the performance of a GE company that was not number one or number two—he usually cut the cord and moved on. Unlike Cap Cities, which sought to reassure ABC employees, GE still aimed to instill insecurity in its NBC work force, to demonstrate that Schumpeter was right: Capitalism is indeed a form of "creative destruction."

In the summer of 1987, the combined RCA and GE consumer-electronics business, which in 1986 generated $3.5 billion in revenues and manufactured nearly one-quarter of all U.S. TV sets, was sold to Thompson S.A. of France, in a swap for a medical-imaging business with higher profit margins. This transaction left Zenith as the only U.S. manufacturer of television sets and video equipment, even though Thompson was allowed to retain the RCA brand name. Consumer electronics was the sixth RCA business that GE had sold or closed since the December 1985 merger was announced. In a year and a half, GE had cut the number of RCA employees from 87,577 to 35,900 through the sale of assets or layoffs.

To NBC employees, the most jarring disposal of assets was the sale that summer of the NBC Radio networks, which mostly distributed news and sports to AM stations around the country. Selling NBC radio was like selling a family heirloom. Founded sixty-one years before by the Radio Corporation of America, it had, over the years, been home for Amos 'n' Andy and Jack Benny, and had fathered the NBC television network.

"It caught my attention," Tom Brokaw said of the sale. "Does that mean Jack Welch won't sell NBC? I don't know." It also caught the media's attention, and reporters asked Bob Wright whether he also planned to sell the television network.

The sale of NBC Radio sent Larry Grossman into a deep funk. "These guys have no commitment to the businesses they're in," he said. "They buy and sell companies. GE is a venture capital company. That's what makes the light shine in Jack and Bob's eyes. . . . There's no commitment to people or product." Something else troubled Grossman. Under the terms of the sale, the company that bought NBC Radio could continue to use the network's name. "They sold the name NBC News to another company. There was no sensitivity that our name was put on a news product over which we had no authority," Grossman complained.

One other tradition seemed to be breached that summer, and that was the separation between News and the business side of the network. Late in July, at a Los Angeles press conference, Grossman was asked why ABC, and not NBC, reported that people in Ohio were suing GE for allegedly building leaky nuclear power plants. Grossman replied that NBC not only did not miss the story but was actually "doing a major investigation." Then Grossman seemed to contradict himself, stating that the original story had been uncovered by the Cleveland *Plain Dealer* some months before and therefore, Grossman said, "it was not a news event." Which begged this question: Why do a "major investigation" of a nonnews event? In any case, Grossman assured reporters, "you can bet that we go after major GE stories, positive and negative, as hard if not even somewhat harder than we would about anybody else's stories."

People in News were upset by Grossman's remarks. "I never talk about stories we're going to put on the air," said a senior producer. "What if the story doesn't get on the air? Then we'd have stories about how we caved to GE pressure." Jack Welch was also upset and telephoned Grossman. Welch said that he was not trying to influence News or its reporting and that he wanted NBC to follow the facts no matter where they led. But on the other hand, he didn't think it fair that NBC should go after GE "somewhat harder" than they would another company.

This was not the first time a network head called down to News about a story: Leonard Goldenson once telephoned Roone Arledge in 1980 to express concern about an ABC report on fraud allegations, investigated and later discarded by the D.A., against producer Aaron Spelling; and even the great Edward R. Murrow was successfully censored at times by William Paley. But the head of RCA had never called Larry Grossman. While Welch said later that he did not remember phoning Grossman on this or any other story, he was not shy at management retreats about denouncing "off-the-wall stories" or complaining about shoddy investigative reporting. Obviously Welch and Grossman had had some kind of encounter, for Grossman on July 29 told those at his daily News executive meeting of Welch's call. Grossman did this in order to insulate himself and News, but colleagues thought it was rash on his part to risk both a press leak and further polarization between News and its corporate parent. (Science correspondent Robert Bazell did an extraordinarily long four-minute-and-forty-six-second piece, "GE and Nuclear Safety," which aired on *NBC Nightly News* on August 7, 1987.)

Bob Wright tried to ignore such episodes and focus on NBC's future. Unlike Larry Tisch at CBS, who thought first of the downside or potential losses associated with any investment, Bob Wright adhered to the GE philosophy, which was to think of the upside. GE was a company steeped in technology, and under Jack Welch it had always been rewarded not for its caution but for its daring. Were each new owner running a football team, GE would field an offense-minded team, going for the long touchdown bomb; Tisch would stack the defense and play for turnovers; and Cap Cities would grind out a few yards each play.

In a speech to the Cable Television Administration & Marketing Society in San Francisco in mid-August, Wright spoke of a television future in which the networks and cable need not be foes, in which they pursued "cooperative ventures," including joint investments, in which the network programmed for cable. While insisting that NBC was committed to the network business and its two hundred-plus affiliates, Wright, typically, emphasized change. No longer would NBC be preoccupied with the three-network competition, he said, "because if I did that, I would be looking at a smaller and smaller world."

The cable industry, which felt it needed improved programming to reach mass audiences, welcomed Wright's speech; many at NBC did not. They worried that Wright was proposing to build up a competitor. Wright, however, saw that ABC was better positioned in the cable industry than NBC, whose sole cable investment was one-third ownership of the Arts & Entertainment cable network, which earned a few hundred thousand dollars that year. NBC's only other sources of income beside the network and its owned stations were the small sums it collected mostly from selling international rights to news shows and the $20 million it earned in a joint videotape venture with Columbia/Tri-Star, the same kind of venture CBS had with Fox.

Meanwhile, Welch was impatient to uproot the present NBC management team. It wasn't enough that under Wright NBC had already discarded an estimated 5 percent of its staff. Welch had his eye on a bigger management issue. After a year under Wright, only one member of the team Wright inherited from Grant Tinker—vice chairman Irwin Segelstein—had departed. To friends, Welch said he held "a gun to Bob Wright's head" to decide in the next year—he made it clear it was Wright's call, not his—whether to retain Larry Grossman. He was impatient with the senior layer of vice presidents at NBC. Although Welch had no direct role in firing the first of NBC's top managers—group executive vice president and chief financial officer Robert Butler—he applauded when Wright let him go.

"Do you have a minute?" Wright said to Butler on the morning of August 24, after a 9 A.M. meeting to discuss whether NBC should move its headquarters to the Upper West Side or New Jersey, or remain at 30 Rockefeller Plaza.

"Sure," said Butler, a low-key, pleasant man.

Bob Wright closed the door, Butler recalled, and got right to the point: "I'd like to buy your contract out." Although they had never discussed it, he said he assumed Butler, fifty-seven, planned to take his $1 million lump-sum retirement package at the end of 1988 anyway.

Bob Butler accepted the verdict with equanimity. Grant Tinker did not. He was unhappy to see the first of his former management team sacked. The move, he said, was "disgraceful" because Wright and Welch had made up their mind from the start about Butler. Bob Wright's explanation was that he wanted a more dynamic "leader," not a "low-key" person, and he had just such a man in mind.

Albert F. Barber, forty-one, first noticed Bob Wright when they were students at Holy Cross, and met him again when they were both at GE. Barber had admired Wright at Holy Cross and at GE, where they became, as Barber says, "close." In early June Wright offered Barber Bob Butler's job as chief financial officer (without finance in the title) at Barber's insistence. A strike by NABET workers delayed the move, but by late August, even with the strike on, Wright wanted his own man in the job.

Al Barber, a round-faced man with wavy dark hair and the backslapping personality of a politician, moved into a sixth-floor corner office on executive row. He saw himself as "a cajoler, not a hit-em-over-the-head-with-a-two-by-four type of manager. I don't try and embarrass people. I have a desire to be a long-term player here, and I don't plan to be a finance guy." Barber thought of himself as a kind of chief operating officer, plugging the management holes as Wright concentrated on strategy, on deal-making. He saw a natural fit. "Bob is much more intense than I am," he said. "I am a devotee to his intellect. He is a devotee to my style." Wright, he explained, "is not a good atta-boy kind of person," and better communications within NBC was "a big part of my portfolio."

Barber's appointment was the first management change Wright made. The second came in the fall, and this time Welch was the instigator. Edward L. Scanlon, formerly RCA's senior vice president for Personnel and the person who worked shoulder to shoulder with Welch in "downsizing" RCA after the merger, was being wooed by other companies. GE already had a chief of Personnel—Frank Doyle, one of Welch's close associates; and NBC itself had Eugene P. McGuire, a longtime employee. McGuire was "a good fellow," said Welch, but not as good as the wiry, red-haired Scanlon. "I think Scanlon is a 'ten' relations guy," declared Welch. "I mean, not an eight or nine. A ten!" Welch described Scanlon as "a good fingertip. Very trustworthy. Very open. Very fair." So Welch in May asked Wright "to spend some time with Scanlon." Like CBS and ABC, NBC had no systematic way of evaluating its executives or identifying successors. At GE, by contrast, Jack Welch evaluated each of his top executives twice a year. The GE system sought to identify backups for each, to groom successors, to foster better communication between managers.

Wright wanted an "agent for change" running Personnel, just as he did in finance, and Scanlon shared his and Welch's sense that NBC's culture was too insular. NBC, Scanlon would say, was staffed by people who were too "comfortable," convinced they possessed "unique skills." GE was comfortable only with discomfort. Although Scanlon had worked at one company for thirty years—RCA—he was an instant GE man. He perceived himself much as Al Barber did, as a chummy fellow who smoothed rough edges—which is not necessarily how he was seen by people he worked with at RCA. "Ed Scanlon never bowled me over," said Grant Tinker, as upset by this appointment as he was by Barber's. However, Scanlon did seem to bowl over Bob Wright, who took him into his confidence immediately, telling him in October he wanted him to launch what Scanlon called "a platonic search" to replace another NBC executive—Larry Grossman. The decision was not then made to oust the News president, recalls Scanlon, but only to explore NBC's options. The search would go slowly, extending over many months.

Scanlon's appointment was delayed until October because NBC was in the throes of the NABET strike. NBC, like ABC under Cap Cities in 1986 and CBS under Larry Tisch in 1987, was determined to achieve a more flexible contract from its 2,800 NABET employees. The network wanted a contract permitting the hiring of some part-time workers in order to reduce overtime costs, a contract that didn't insist that a $600-a-week technician in Denver be given the same $825 weekly wage as a technician in Cleveland, a contract that allowed robotic cameras to replace camera operators and that relaxed work rules in general. Not surprisingly, NABET employees were unhappy. Allow NBC its way, and scores of employees would be terminated. Even more ominous, the union would be busted, and with it whatever leverage it exercised over GE and its NBC subsidiary. It was a typical labor dispute: The union wanted job security, and management wanted efficiency.

The strike, which was called on June 29 and entered its fifth month in October, was bitter. It infuriated NABET that NBC was demanding worker concessions from a third of its work force when the network was in first place in the ratings and would, that year, earn twice as much as ABC and CBS combined. But Wright used different arithmetic. He lumped together all three networks and showed how they had all lost market share. Striking workers circled the entrances to 30

Rock, handing out leaflets and petitions, chanting demands and, as the strike wore on, insults. NABET picketed Bob Wright's Connecticut home and once paraded outside what they thought was the Connecticut home of Jack Welch. "I can't get rid of you no matter what I do!" exclaimed Carolyn Welch into the phone to the husband she was now legally and amicably separated from. "I've got your representatives out here!"

The strike exhausted nonunion NBC employees and taught Jack Welch a lesson that would damage NABET. It was a lesson he grasped immediately in October when he arrived at the Arizona Biltmore in Phoenix for the GE corporate officers meeting. This was a regular review at which the operating heads of all GE divisions arrive with their key managers and, before their peers, offer twenty-minute slide presentations sketching the current competition and what they might do over the next three years to better position their companies.

The most significant event of this management retreat came not from the podium but on the tennis courts, where Welch overheard congratulatory remarks about how NBC, despite a NABET strike, was managing with 2,800 fewer people, roughly one third its work force. Welch couldn't believe what he was hearing. To him, this was another example of NBC's complacency, of how "they hadn't thought through the implications." Would NBC hire the workers back when the strike ended? Should it? Welch worried that Wright, who had been traveling a lot the past few months—to Wimbledon and the French Open in July, to Nantucket for three weeks in August, to Rome, California, and on to Korea for two weeks to plan the 1988 Olympics coverage, and to China with Tom Brokaw and 130 News employees in September—was becoming co-opted by the NBC culture. Welch was visibly angry.

Coming off the tennis court, he cornered Wright and said, "I want to get up to my elbows in the muck and wallow in this NABET issue." Once again it was time to discard people. There would, Welch announced, be a full-scale meeting with Wright and his team at GE's Lexington Avenue headquarters. Welch was so noticeably impatient with Wright that executive vice president Bob Walsh, who witnessed the encounter, said, "I felt bad for Bob Wright."

The meeting in Welch's conference room at 570 Lexington Avenue lasted from 2:30 to 6:30 P.M. on October 14, 1987, and by all accounts it was lively. So lively that during the four hours not one of the eleven executives who attended left to visit the bathroom. Bob Wright would say little in this meeting, having selected Bob Walsh to present the overall NBC plan of attack once the strike was settled. Walsh explained how NBC would lay off 250 employees by the end of 1987, and another 250 by the end of 1988.

When Walsh finished, each executive then explained how his department would function with fewer employees. Al Jerome, who reported to Walsh, talked of his plans for the seven owned stations, declaring at one point, "The stations did a terrific job during the strike!"

"Who did the best job?" asked Welch. "Which of your general managers did the best job?"

"Cleveland and Chicago."

"Who's next?"

"Washington, D.C. But each station faced different problems," said Jerome.

Welch was undeterred. "In other words, your two highest paid general managers"—New York and Los Angeles—"did a shitty job!"

It was tougher in the larger markets, explained Jerome. *Everyone worked hard, filling in for striking people. Although we kept the shows on, the quality of our product suffered!*

It didn't hurt the ratings! Welch shot back.

"It got a little heated," recalls Bob Walsh. Larry Grossman again wondered whether Welch cared only about numbers and not about quality. When Grossman spoke he offered News's plans for its 551 NABET workers, mentioning how many worked on *Today.* Welch interrupted to ask: "Why don't we charge for those book interviews on the *Today* show?"

Stunned, the room fell silent.

"It wouldn't be journalism," Bud Rukeyser finally said. "It would be paid flackery!"

"Not if you selected the authors to interview!" Welch replied. Then, having dropped his impractical and ethically dubious suggestion, Welch moved on.

"Maria Shriver is too shrill!" Welch now declared.

Why? asked Grossman.

Welch said he found her voice grating, particularly on Sunday mornings. Her cohost on *Sunday Today,* Boyd Matson, he compared to *white bread*—"plastic," is the word Welch remembers using.

"I ended up the meeting very satisfied," said Welch, who felt he had performed as a chairman is supposed to. "I firmly believe my job is to walk around with a can of water in one hand and a can of fertilizer in the other and to make things flourish," he said. When the NABET strike ended in late October, new Personnel boss Ed Scanlon said he hoped to dismiss about 12 percent of all NABET employees, saving up to $25 million.

Jack Welch had been involved in the acquisition of the Miami station and the hiring of Ed Scanlon, but the NABET strike was the first operational issue in which he acted like a CEO. NBC executives groused that he was guilty of micromanagement. "Bob Wright was upset," observed a friend, who said Wright and his NBC team were on top of the situation, had a plan, and that Welch was second-guessing them needlessly.

Welch was, in fact, beginning to second-guess Wright. He was displeased by Wright's "tactical" presentation at the corporate retreat. Welch told an NBC official around this time "Bob's going to have to spend more time in that building managing the place." Wright had been on the job more than a year, and what Welch saw in his handling of NABET was a failure of good management and leadership. Welch was frustrated that Wright had continued to endure a News president he barely communicated with. People within NBC thought Wright was like a son to Welch, or the brother he never had. They believed Welch would back Wright no matter what. And, it was true, Welch did feel close to Wright. But not that close. If necessary, he would cast the same cold eye upon Wright that he did upon Richard Burt or NABET employees.

For Welch, the jury was still out in late 1987 on whether Bob Wright was a "transformational leader." The phrase was coined by GE consultant Noel M. Tichy of the University of Michigan's Graduate School of Business to describe a corporate leader who rises above the inertia of his organization, transforms its culture with a vision, and communicates it simply and emotionally enough to sway an entire company. Jack Welch, as Tichy described it, was such a leader, a man who had become chairman of GE in 1981 when he was forty-five, the same age as Bob Wright was in 1987.

Was Bob Wright too much the analytic lawyer to be such a leader? Wright was relatively untested as a manager. James P. Baughman, a member of Welch's executive management staff to whom GE's Crotonsville training center reported, observed that before Wright left GE to join Cox Cable in 1980, "he was basically an attorney." When he returned to manage the housewares division in 1983, said Baughman, he sold it to Black & Decker within a matter of months. "He was just beginning to hit his stride at GE Financial Services when he joined NBC. So in one sense, I don't think he maxed out at GE Financial Services. I don't think we got a full take. We got a very exciting take. But we don't have a full take on him at NBC." The take that will count, Baughman said, revolved around the question of leadership—"the follow-me dimensions. We have people in this company who can lead two hundred people, but not five thousand. People who can do deals, and people who can't. People who can live in the fish bowl, and people who can't."

One other worry about Wright began to surface in late 1987, and it went to his presumed strength: deal-making. The only deals Wright had done at NBC were the acquisition of the TV station in Miami and the NBC Radio sale. Welch was looking for "one big bang. My job in this area is to keep asking them: 'How are you going to deal with network erosion?' "

Bob Wright had a "big bang" deal in mind—buying all or part of the Turner Broadcasting System, including CNN. Ted Turner, whom Wright knew fairly well from his days with Cox Cable, was financially overextended, having spent $1.4 billion to acquire MGM/UA Entertainment. To meet the debt payments, the Atlanta buccaneer was forced to swallow his pride and sell, for $560 million, 37 percent of his company. The buyers included the nation's two largest cable-system owners—Time, Inc. and Tele-Communications, Inc. The new partners held seven of the fifteen seats on Turner's board, and they began to squeeze.

Each partner wanted something. Pay-cable viewership had leveled off, and Michael Fuchs, president of Time-owned Home Box Office, admitted, "I'm dying to get into live news." Time and CNN might pool their correspondents and save money. John Malone's TCI, with nearly a quarter of the nation's cable installations, wanted to keep Turner in friendly hands and thus guarantee the continued supply of inexpensive programming to his cable systems. If Time and TCI couldn't control CNN, they were determined not to let it belong to a broadcast competitor such as NBC. Control, of course, is what Turner himself wanted, and to succeed he had to keep his investors apart, and impotent. "Sometimes it's better to have three bosses than one boss," observed Fuchs. But Turner needed cash. If he sold more stock to Time or TCI, he risked losing control of his company.

In November 1987, Bob Wright and NBC entered the picture. If Turner could induce his old friend from Cox Cable to become a minority investor, he would get the cash he needed, he would keep control, and perhaps he would get NBC to program for his cable channels. Turner would be comfortable with NBC, more comfortable than he would be with the relative strangers from Cap Cities/ABC, who were also in hot pursuit. "I like Bob Wright," Turner said around this time. "It's a game, and I want to like my teammates." Seeing that there was no way to swallow all of Turner Broadcasting, at least not immediately, Wright chased what GE refers to as an "alliance," a partnership along with Time, TCI, and Turner.

NBC offered what cable wanted: programming strength. And Turner offered NBC an opportunity to "amortize News and Sports, and even Entertainment costs," said Thomas S. Rogers, the former Congressional aide who assisted Wright in these negotiations. "It would give us more shelf space. . . . We want to be like Procter & Gamble and have four to five brands, not just one."

Within NBC there were fears that the network would be competing against itself. But these concerns were not openly debated as Wright and Turner met throughout November and December. The differences between the parties were vast—Turner wanted Wright to pay twenty dollars a share ($400 million) for 20 percent of Turner Broadcasting, and Wright offered twelve dollars a share ($250 million); Wright wanted more say in Turner Broadcasting, and Turner wanted him to have less; Time didn't want NBC at all. By mid-January, the parties decided their interests could not be harmonized. Bob Wright and Jack Welch would not have their "big bang." Not yet, anyway.

With Turner off the table, there were no other cable deals in sight—another cable-programming network, even if one were available, would be too expensive. So Wright met with cable operators to explore joint ventures, met with colleagues from GE Credit to map plans for the financial arm of GE to become the banker and part owner of cable and broadcast properties, met with Hollywood studio heads looking for joint alliances and approval to lift the fin-syn rules, met with Tartikoff to explore buying a studio or making NBC Productions a studio in its own right, met with Time, Inc. to explore a merger between these two communications giants. Wright also looked at Europe, where state-run television was being turned over to private owners. To help him sort through NBC's European options, Wright retained McKinsey & Company to probe everything from joint ventures to selling select NBC programs to European broadcasters. In much of Europe television was not free, since the consumer paid a monthly fee, just as cable viewers did in the U.S. With two revenue sources—advertising and subscription fees—European TV revenues by 1993 were projected to climb to $19 billion, or two-thirds the revenues of the U.S. networks and local stations. More boldly than either ABC or CBS, Wright was pursuing a deal.

Outside NBC people praised Wright. Inside Wright still felt that he had to convince his team to accept his leadership. He was the CEO, yet he felt like a salesman. He had to sell News to cut costs. He had to convince Sports to lower license fees and to either bring cable in as a partner or lose network sports. He had to sell the affiliates, NABET, Hollywood, and the government, on how the old ways of doing things were passé. By the end of 1987, he couldn't get his own team—ten months after a task force had been formed—to agree on a visions and values statement. "They've had a great deal of difficulty coming up with a uniform opinion," Wright explained. "In many respects, NBC is a united Afghanistan—a series of fiefdoms with different views of life."

Executive row at 30 Rock was contributing to Wright's sense that NBC was fragmented and bureaucratic. His sixth-floor suite of offices and private dining room were flanked by the offices of the group executive vice presidents, whom Wright and Welch thought superfluous. Under Tinker, these senior executives were like a college of cardinals, meeting weekly. Under Wright, they seldom met at all. Instead of firing the executives, Wright froze them out.

"He didn't make you feel at ease," said executive vice president Bob Walsh, who had applauded the merger with GE. "In the old chairman's council we would have known a lot more about the Turner negotiations up front." Then Walsh added, "It may be no one wants to hear my opinions." The senior vice presidents had come to refer to themselves with a degree of fatalism as "the lump-sum group," who would take their generous RCA retirement packages when it was time. They talked often at the end of a day about this severance, about the glories of the Tinker years, about their many shared memories. "Since there's no interaction with the CEO," said Bud Rukeyser, "my guess is that the sixth floor will go away."

Following Irwin Segelstein, Bob Butler, and Gene McGuire, Bob Walsh announced in December that he would retire in a year, and in the meantime Al Jerome, president of the television stations division would report directly to Wright; Arthur Watson, president of NBC Sports, would now report to executive vice president Al Barber instead of Walsh. Wright hoped Ray Timothy would stay. Timothy helped hold the system together; he had standing among affiliates, advertisers, and Tartikoff's people on the Coast. Like Gene Jankowski at CBS, Ray Timothy was a respected ambassador.

Wright also wanted to keep Bud Rukeyser, who had something GE lacked: credibility with the TV press. Reporters listened to him;

Rukeyser could steer them from publishing damagingly false stories. In October Wright gave him a 10 percent raise. Still, Rukeyser wasn't sure he'd stay, even after Wright boosted his bonus in January. In contrast to Wright, Rukeyser believed the networks had a bright future. Bud Rukeyser loved NBC. Only during Fred Silverman's brief, temptestuous reign from 1978 to 1981 did he leave for a comparable job at *Newsweek*. But as soon as Silverman was fired, he was back, this time with Grant Tinker. People liked to drop by Rukeyser's office, to dip into his crystal NBC brandy glass filled with Red Hots and to gossip or discuss press strategy. Although business executives usually pretend to ignore what the press says, in fact it is usually a preoccupation. TV reporters, like the Nielsen ratings or earnings reports, are another way to keep score. And Rukeyser was NBC's link to the press.

Larry Grossman had no idea that Wright had engaged Ed Scanlon to commence a quiet search for a new NBC News president. By late 1987 Grossman saw Wright as a basically decent man who, beneath his intensity, hid a sense of humor. Grossman was ecstatic when Wright approved three separate requests for four prime-time hours in December—a Tom Brokaw one-on-one interview with Mikhail Gorbachev, a two-hour debate among the Republican and Democratic presidential contenders, and a sitdown with President Reagan and the network anchors.

Just as Grossman brightened, however, more trouble arose at a November 5, 1987, meeting with Wright and ten senior News executive producers. Wright requested the session, saying that he wanted to learn more about how News operated. He would meet with the people who produced *Nightly News, Today,* and the weekend news, just as he had done when he met with Tartikoff's staff. The initiative was welcomed, just as at CBS Larry Tisch's offer to visit news bureaus in Europe was. The more Bob Wright understood the complicated process of News gathering, the better the chances that he would sympathize with News. Perhaps he would even venture to praise a news report or program he had seen.

But the meeting in Grossman's office went poorly, and was a reminder that Wright did not share the same value system. Each producer tried to do what Wright later complained to Bud Rukeyser was a "show and tell." Wright interrupted, saying: *I want to get into issues. You, Marty Ryan. Are you happy with Maria Shriver? Or would you rather have Deborah Norville hosting* Sunday Today? Wright tried to be provocative, noting, as had Jack Welch, that he found Maria Shriver "shrill" and Boyd Matson like "white bread." Garrick Utley, he said, was "black coffee." Larry Grossman saw Wright's lips moving but heard Jack Welch. News producers were appalled. How could Wright speak of *team spirit* and then criticize some players publicly? Wright received no response to his criticism of Shriver or Matson. Undeterred, he wondered what they thought of Bob Jamieson or Chris Wallace? No one wanted to play that game either.

Wright thought they were defensive. Wright was looking to mix it up, to banter, to goad, to do what he had always done at GE. He came away more convinced than ever that News was insular. When he met with Tartikoff's team, Wright had been impressed by how "critical" they were of shows and talent. Not so in News. "I would love to see more of that. More self-criticism," said Wright. "They call themselves creative and suggest the West Coast is not. That's wrong. . . . Tartikoff is a creative head, Grossman's not. Brandon can be the producer and talk to people as a creative director and encourage those kinds of discussions much more easily than Larry can."

Grossman was appalled by Wright's ignorance. It was ridiculous, he felt, for Wright to expect "the same frank discussion he gets in Hollywood—'*The Cosby Show* script stank!' " *Today* producer Marty Ryan would never publicly say, "We're unhappy with Willard!" And the reason was that Marty Ryan, not some Hollywood studio, was responsible for Willard Scott. "It's like expecting parents to sit around and complain about their children," said Grossman. "You don't say, 'Maria is shrill' in a group where each guy feels you're talking about their family. The way you do it is one-on-one."

Part of the reason Wright felt alienated from Grossman and News, was that he didn't understand the journalistic value system. News people are by nature suspicious. It is their job. They don't applaud at presidential press conferences. They aren't supposed to advise the people they cover. They keep their distance. They worry that politicians and diplomats will try to mislead or seduce them. They want an arm's-length relationship with the business side, to be shielded from "friends" of the boss and advertisers. Among themselves, reporters talk in swaggering, smart-alecky shorthand. Among outsiders, they sound rehearsed. Observed Grossman, who as an outsider himself had come to understand the news culture: "Hollywood is fun. People are fast and funny and open and full of gossip. It's very seductive, for all of us. News, on the other hand, is full of restrictions and journalistic guidelines and separation of church and state. It is a real priesthood. It is very unkind to outsiders, as any priesthood is."

It might have been easier for Wright to understand this world if

NBC News made money, or generated ratings, or didn't provoke complaints from advertisers, members of Congress, or the White House. Bob Wright came off as a scold to News because he was one. He worried about leaks. He worried News wouldn't confront its losses, wouldn't look honestly at its own processes. He worried News wouldn't tell him the truth. And now people like Bud Rukeyser were telling him that even though he was the CEO, sometimes he should keep his mouth shut, and speak to News only through Larry Grossman.

"Are you saying I can't talk directly to producers?" Wright exclaimed to Rukeyser incredulously.

"Yes, it's inappropriate. News has to be insulated. Marty Ryan shouldn't have to go around each day wondering how Bob Wright feels."

The gap between Wright and News widened because of Wright's irritation with Grossman. The awkward relationship did not improve —not even after Grossman, at the annual Fairfield Budget review in December, vowed to Wright and Welch to shrink the 1989 News budget to $259 million and to cut its head count from 1,362 employees in 1986 to 1,126 by the end of 1988, and to 1,067 in 1989.

Wright was harsh on Grossman at his personnel evaluation in mid-December. Following GE's personnel policy, starting in December 1987 each top NBC executive would meet twice a year with Wright to review department plans and to be evaluated. There would be a meeting in the spring for what was called a Session C, at which they would sketch their division goals for the next three years. In December they would meet again for a Session C-2, at which Wright would gauge whether they had achieved their objectives. Here they would be judged as achievers, as managers, as leaders. Joining Wright at these sessions, beginning in December of 1987, was Ed Scanlon. Wright planned to let Grossman know he was disappointed. Grossman entered Wright's office with the same intent.

Grossman went on the offensive: "News has proportionately contributed more than any other division to the downsizing of NBC. Of the five hundred NABET positions cut, two hundred came from News. And we did it without evidencing the loss on air, without public complaint. Yet News has received little recognition for this achievement. The only time we hear from the sixth floor is when it comes to money. It's important that there be some psychic reinforcement for what we're doing!"

Wright looked puzzled and said he did not understand. "I think

I've shown lots of interest in News," he said. "I visited China. I've met with your producers and had a brown-bag lunch with people from News. Besides, everyone's a grown-up and doesn't need hand-holding." Wright told Grossman he was too reactive, not sufficiently entrepreneurial. He believed that network news was overproduced, and therefore at a disadvantage against low-cost competitors like CNN. He appreciated NBC News's efforts to produce quality pieces, but added, "We have a very different manufacturing process for News than our competitors." News had to be produced differently, which meant more cheaply. There was room for improvement elsewhere, Wright said, including News management.

Who is your backup? asked Wright, the same question he would ask each of the executives reporting to him. Grossman said his deputy, Tim Russert, would be his choice. Wright made it clear he thought well of Russert's abilities but said Russert, thirty-seven, needed more seasoning as a manager. Privately, Wright would pencil in the name of Al Jerome, president of the station group, as a potential successor to Grossman.

Like every executive, Grossman was graded between 1 and 5, with 1 indicating "significant improvement necessary" and 5 representing the "top 15 percent." 3 signified "solid performance," and a 4 "exceeds most employees." For his management skills Wright said he was grading Grossman a 2—"improvement is needed."

Wright was unhappy with Grossman yet uncertain he should make a change. He saw Grossman as "an outsider" within his own news division, but replacing Grossman with another outsider might be disruptive. He wanted more of a business manager, but wasn't sure News would swallow this. He respected Al Jerome as an executive, but worried that he lacked News experience. He wanted to fire Grossman, yet was afraid of bad press.

Not surprisingly, Grossman left his personal evaluation meeting depressed, trapped in a familiar dilemma. Wright expected him to cut costs and represent the company to News, and News expected him to champion news first and money second. By his measure, he had had a good year—*Nightly News* came in first in the ratings thirty of the fifty-two weeks; *Today* and *Sunrise* were solid number-ones; he had Wright's approval to talk to Ted Koppel about joining NBC to host a weekly prime-time program and had hopes of success; News had pulled through the five-month NABET strike and had streamlined; they had achieved a coup with the exclusive Gorbachev interview and had managed to round up each of the Republican and Democratic presidential challengers for the prime-time debate, even if the one-minute answer time allotted each candidate was less than the time allotted for ads.

Grossman felt unappreciated. His contract ran out at the end of 1987, and he didn't have a new one. His division had lost writers, researchers, and producers. At a time when the network claimed it was different from local news because it offered more foreign reports and context, NBC News didn't have a resident correspondent on some continents, including South America and black Africa. Though he had shrunk his budget and even removed Boyd Matson as host of *Sunday Today* at the end of the year, Grossman got little praise from Wright or Welch, or from his own organization. He was depressed.

It might have been easier if he had had a stronger bond with Brokaw, but Grossman had the same kind of awkward relationship with his anchorman that he had with Wright. Publicly the two men denied they were feuding, but more than just lifestyle or personal chemistry separated them. Grossman found Brokaw defensive, a prima donna, and sometimes a bully—the same criticism that had been lodged at one time or other against all three anchors. Brokaw, on the other hand, was not alone in finding Grossman indecisive and lacking in news judgment. "I'd like someone who could excite me and the people around here," said Brokaw. "We all need an editor."

One other matter regularly came between them: a coanchor. By late 1987 Larry Grossman was convinced that Brokaw alone was not the anchor of the future. In 1982, after hosting *Today* for five years, Brokaw had been selected by Tinker to replace John Chancellor as anchor, "to appeal to a younger audience," recalled former RCA chairman Thornton Bradshaw. Now, after a thirty-week surge as number one earlier in 1987, *NBC Nightly News* had slipped to number three. Grossman worried that this was no accident. He knew all the arguments about the importance of lead-ins and how news was at a disadvantage against game shows, for publicly he made these same arguments. But Grossman really did not believe that Peter Jennings had moved into second place because *The Oprah Winfrey Show* was ABC's lead-in to its local and then network newscast, or because NBC affiliates juggled Brokaw's time slots so that *Nightly News* was thrown up against popular game shows. Grossman sensed, and some executives at CBS and ABC privately agreed, that Tom Brokaw lacked authority. This was unfair, since Brokaw is a serious student of national and international affairs. But to some extent this impression was fed by Brokaw's past identification with the less substantial *Today* show, and his boyishly handsome looks. Once when Brokaw did a standup outdoors at a Geneva summit and snow transformed his dark hair to white, Grossman cried: "That's the image we want!" While many congratulated Brokaw on orchestrating the interview with Gorbachev, Grossman thought the anchor betrayed a lack of authority when he failed to interrupt the Soviet leader. "Tom's lack of a sense of history was obvious," Grossman would say later. "He came out hollow."

Brokaw bought none of this. His ratings dip, he was sure, had nothing to do with his boyish looks or a lack of authority. "How do you explain why a year ago we were twenty-two straight weeks as number one?" he said. He wasn't intimidated by Gorbachev, he said; no, he was a victim of a format that permitted the Soviet leader to filibuster, leaving Brokaw in the position of looking rude if he interrupted or meek if he did not. Brokaw had had a golden career, succeeding in every job he had ever held, from local anchor to chief White House correspondent to *Today* host. At NBC he was called "Duncan the Wonderhorse." But now he was trying to understand his falloff—and even asked Tartikoff if he could explain it. Tom Brokaw was confused: "I keep asking and asking and asking, and I don't get clear answers. I am befuddled by it."

Brokaw sensed, correctly, that Grossman was maneuvering to saddle him with a coanchor. He had won that showdown in December of 1986, when Grossman wanted to hire Diane Sawyer as coanchor. Now Sawyer had a window in her CBS contract that allowed her to leave for an anchor job at another network. Grossman wasn't trying to get rid of Brokaw; he respected his abilities as a journalist and interviewer. But he thought Sawyer would add another dimension to the newscast. Grossman said he had presented to Wright the idea of a dual anchor, with one on the road and the other in a studio, or one on air and the other off reporting a story. Grossman said Wright agreed, but that Brokaw still howled.

Wright suggested to Brokaw that he and Grossman seek a truce. At lunch during the holiday season, Grossman alluded to the war between Dan Rather and former CBS News president Ed Joyce in 1985, a conflict that undermined Joyce with his superiors and helped lead to his dismissal. "I hear we have a Dan Rather/Ed Joyce problem?" Grossman said.

"No, Larry. I'm going to tell you what I think. You ought to be here more and not out making speeches so much." Brokaw suggested that Grossman consult others in News and urged that he act more like a leader internally. Brokaw remembers they had a "civil conversation."

Grossman remembers one other thing about lunch: Brokaw again vetoed Diane Sawyer as coanchor.

By the end of 1987, neither Brokaw nor Grossman trusted each other. While Grossman stewed, Brokaw acted. He honestly believed Grossman was hurting News. He knew that Tom Ross, who served as Grossman's liaison to Wright and GE, had been told by Wright in the late fall to set up some meetings with respected print journalists, preferably in their forties, who also had some managerial experience. Wright never told Ross he planned to replace Grossman, but Ross suspected as much. Brokaw suspected it as well, for Ross shared this information with him. Ross felt he had, in his words, "worked hard to save Larry's job," but it was hopeless. "Grant Tinker brought in Larry because he knew he was a decent, stable, and intelligent guy. He was a respectable caretaker. But that's not what these guys want. Larry is caught in the middle. He's doing what Grant Tinker wanted, but not what the new guys want."

Ross shared Brokaw's belief that the news division needed fresh leadership. Over the coming months, Ross would suggest a platoon of journalists for Wright to consult—James Hoge, publisher of the *Daily News;* his brother Warren Hoge, assistant managing editor of *The New York Times;* Robert Kaiser, assistant managing editor of *The Washington Post;* Roger Ogden, vice president and general manager of KCNC, NBC's Denver station; Michael J. Davies, publisher of the Hartford *Courant.* Although these gentlemen were not told this was his intention, Wright was "comparison shopping," as Ed Scanlon referred to the process. Wright would have lunch or dinner with each on the pretext that he wanted to discuss, say, First Amendment issues, and he would size them up. Wright did not mention Grossman's job. He had no intention of replacing Larry Grossman until he—and Jack Welch—found someone they liked. Usually Tom Ross would sit in on these meals, including lunch with Kaiser at the Century Club and dinner with Warren Hoge at David K's restaurant.

A full-fledged conspiracy bloomed, involving Wright, Welch, Scanlon, Brokaw, Ross, and, after a while, Gordon Manning, another Grossman deputy. In effect, Brokaw and Ross were participating in selecting their own boss, which was odd. Odder still was that Ross, the man Grossman chose to reinforce his ties to Wright and Welch and whom he had personally assigned to gather intelligence, had become a double agent. Even odder was that Larry Grossman—the man who scheduled a get-acquainted dinner during the sixth game of the

World Series—didn't have a clue as to what was going on behind his back.

Despite his difficulties with Grossman and News and the executives on the sixth floor, Bob Wright had reason to be pleased at the end of his first full year on the job. Powered by Tartikoff's entertainment division, the NBC network and its stations generated record profits of $500 million in 1987. NBC had widened its prime-time lead over CBS and ABC. NBC was a major contributor to GE's own 17 percent earnings rise, in the best year the global company had had in some fifteen years. Since becoming president of NBC in September of 1986, Wright had reduced the number of NBC employees from 8,465 to about 7,000. He had gained some leverage over the unions. Not only had NBC saved $25 million in NABET costs, it had shown that the new order was determined to do things differently. While Wright hadn't made a cable or Hollywood deal, he was confident one would be coming. And as for his network competitors, neither CBS nor ABC seemed about to make any programming breakthroughs; the Fox network he felt lacked the platform enjoyed by the Big Three to promote its shows, and thus would not compete for mass audiences. Wright had replaced some key NBC executives with members of his own team, and had induced the City of New York to grant tax abatements in return for NBC's agreement to stay put and modernize its 30 Rockefeller Plaza studios and offices.

Although he was unaware that Lilly Tartikoff was urging her husband to leave NBC while he was the ratings winner and to devote more time to Calla, their young daughter, Bob Wright hoped to keep Tartikoff at the network for a few more years. In the fall of 1987, Wright and Welch had taken Tartikoff to lunch and given him a $200,000 bonus. Tartikoff provided arcane skills, plus something else: He was the perfect son. "He's got wonderful taste about things," rhapsodized Jack Welch. "He'll talk about what people could be doing without taking shots. He does it all. He's a classy guy. . . . He has his ego in total balance with his set of values. I mean, he's got a family. He loves sports." Welch described the GE officers' meeting in September, to which he invited Tartikoff. They played tennis together as partners in a round robin. "Maybe he's a hundred times a better player than I am, or maybe eighty times," said Welch. "He was better than most of the players there. Yet he's just got a nice manner. Everyone feels comfortable. Everyone in GE likes him. I mean, he just fits."

Welch and Wright also felt good that everyone at the network was now cost-conscious. One could tell how NBC had changed by the language. The GE lingo was now spoken, or understood, by just about everyone. No one scratched his head anymore when Al Barber said in a meeting: "That's a *no-brainer!*" (no problem) or "We'll give you *air cover*" (follow-through) or *"Sign up to the program"* (join the team).

But just as Grossman didn't sense the conspiracy to replace him, Wright didn't sense the depth of hostility within NBC to its new owners. Within a few months, Al Barber became a figure of scorn. People began to refer to him as "Boxcar Barber," calling him a gaseous know-it-all, a reaction that revealed something larger than a rejection of his personality. It represented as well the general malaise infecting NBC at the end of 1987. The number-one network had achieved great success, but too few employees were enjoying it. "It's a less happy place," said Natalie P. Hunter, vice president of Finance and Administration for NBC News, who joined the network in 1980. "It's hard to be happier than we were at NBC working for Grant Tinker and when we had just risen from the depths of number three. People have felt their pride was stolen." Like others, Hunter believed the less congenial atmosphere would "eventually" lead to NBC's demise.

People at NBC felt that Wright was too pessimistic about the future of the network business. They talked about GE's Crotonville training facility as if it were a Cambodian reeducation camp. They knew that NBC, which had so far been spared, was expected to start sending executives there in 1988. They would be assigned to teams of eight and sent north, where they would row twelve miles to Hurricane Island, there to endure a swimming competition, climb up and down a one-hundred-foot cliff by rope, swing from trees, squeeze through a spider's web of holes, and tiptoe across a plank high above the ground, all while their team was timed. It did not comfort those at NBC to know their GE compatriots viewed them as just a well-known brand name. During a Crotonville lunch with young executives from four different GE businesses, for example, Hani Ayoub of the lighting division applauded the merger with NBC because its "brand awareness" would "strengthen the GE name."

"The average consumer doesn't know GE owns NBC," replied Beth Davis, who worked for Construction Equipment.

"Then we have to do a better job," said Ayoub. "Millions of people are watching. There is no reason you can't modify the NBC logo."

There remained a fundamental philosophical divide at NBC, and not just between the parent company and the network. Wright stressed that NBC was in the communications business, including cable, while longtime NBC executives stressed the broadcasting business. Bud Rukeyser, whose job it was to sell NBC to the press and the public, was having a hard time selling it to himself. He was torn between love for his job and "genuine affection for Wright," yet he disdained the direction in which Wright and GE were steering his beloved network. "Part of me says stay and help him," said Rukeyser as 1987 drew to a close. But with $1 million awaiting him as a lump-sum retirement package, Rukeyser wanted out. He recalled the story of the starlet on the movie set where everyone is miserable. The starlet inches up to the assistant director and whispers, "Who do I have to fuck to get out of this movie?"

Those, he sighed, are "my feelings exactly. I've got to get out. The fact that they think I'm now a part of their team fills me with guilt."

Bob Wright had little patience for the angst within NBC. Even when he tried to reach out—as when he conducted his first teleconference for employees on January 12, 1988—communication went only one way. By contrast to the way Tinker used to do it, or to ABC, where Tom Murphy and Dan Burke fielded employee questions twice a year on closed circuit, Wright in his maiden appearance spoke to, not with, employees.

But in other ways, Wright was changing. Asked at a press conference what he had learned, Wright joked: "Well, I now type all my own letters." Wright now knew he was always on a public stage. Before he appeared at a press conference, he rehearsed potential questions and was coached by GE consultant Jack Hilton, author of *How to Meet the Press: A Survival Guide.* He had also begun to learn, as had Cap Cities, the limits of cost cutting. We've got to keep costs under control, he told an industry luncheon, "but not at the expense of the product." Only 20 percent of NBC's costs were personnel; the rest were earmarked for the Hollywood studios and for sports and news programming, and what was left over was for equipment and depreciation costs. This wasn't the boxcar or jet-engine business, where GE could predict 10 percent growth. If Brandon Tartikoff came up with a few surprise hits—a few *Golden Girls*—they could grow 40 percent! After seventeen months Wright was a bit more humble than when he arrived at NBC in September of 1986. He was acutely aware of the limits government imposed on the networks. And even where Wright had freedom—to buy another station or two, to become a cable programmer—the "deals" and "alliances" were too expensive or slow in coming.

* * *

Grant Tinker was now back on the West Coast and in the fourteen-acre, $50 million studio he had built for his production company in Culver City, which he expected would make him happy. But he felt guilty about the network he had left behind. He didn't agree with Wright's effort to chase after cable and other businesses, believing it would erode the network audience further. Grant Tinker thought the network was "a very good business," and he cited as proof not ABC or CBS's dwindling profits but the $500 million NBC earned.

Something else bothered Tinker, what was by now a familiar refrain: that Wright and Welch felt little sense of "public obligation." "It doesn't have to be spelled out. It's got to be there in spirit," Tinker said. A network had to be willing to lose money in News, to break into prime time for an important story, to insist on quality programs even if the ratings sometimes suffered, to forego a series that was in bad taste even if it would boost ratings. There was no romance. NBC was not just another product line, to be discarded if it didn't work out.

These thoughts congealed for Tinker at a wistful January 15, 1988, farewell dinner Phyllis and Bud Rukeyser hosted at their Central Park West apartment for the departed Bob Butler and Gene McGuire. Only the nine former members of Tinker's chairman's council and their wives were invited—Butler, McGuire, Irwin Segelstein, Bob Walsh, Ray Timothy, Cory Dunham, Larry Grossman, Tinker, and Rukeyser. "We spent the evening remembering the things we accomplished together," said Tinker. They talked, remembers Rukeyser, about "the present NBC as if something was lost." Despite Jack Welch's vow to retain Tinker's team, five of the nine had left or were about to. "There's a ten little Indians aspect to this thing," said Rukeyser. "One by one people are leaving. There's a feeling of inevitability. We all look back on that time with fondness and sadness. We knew at the time that it was as good as it gets."

19

WHAT'S THE FREQUENCY, LARRY?: CBS IN THE SECOND HALF OF 1987

Throughout his business career, Larry Tisch made money doing the unexpected. When other investors bought stocks, he bought bonds; when they sold, he waited. When others shed insurance companies or oil tankers, he acquired them. Now as Bob Wright stalked deals to diversify NBC, as his friend Tom Murphy presided over a publishing, cable, broadcasting, and Broadway powerhouse, and as such cunning companies as Rupert Murdoch's News Corporation, Michael Eisner's Disney, Steve Ross's Warner Communications, Japan's Sony, Germany's Bertelsmann, and France's Hachette, among others, jostled to become vertically integrated, Larry Tisch's CBS went in another direction. Tisch was shedding, not acquiring, companies. Since becoming CEO in September 1986, Tisch had sold CBS's book publishing operations for $500 million, its musical publishing unit for $125 million, its Latin American and Spanish publishing company, had closed the CBS Technology Center in Stamford, Connecticut, and withdrawn from its joint Trintex venture with IBM and Sears.

Then, in June 1987, while Wright was trying to acquire cable programming, Tisch sold CBS's final cable holding, its one-third interest in SportsChannel, which consisted of four regional sports networks it had acquired jointly with the Washington Post Company and cable pioneer Charles F. Dolan's Cablevision Inc. in 1984. Despite the common wisdom that said sports would increasingly migrate from the networks to cable, despite the proliferation of more than two dozen regional sports cable channels, despite evidence that these were natural homes for local teams, Tisch sold. He believed, incorrectly it turned out, that cable prices were at their peak—nearly two years later NBC paid more to become a partner with Dolan in SportsChannel. Tisch was also wrong in his belief that regional sports channels had peaked, for by 1990 they reached thirty million homes and their ad revenues had jumped by 50 percent each year since 1985.

Larry Tisch unloaded one other asset that summer; in July he sold for $650 million the twenty-one publications of the CBS magazines division, including *Woman's Day* with its nearly six million circulation. At the time the price seemed generous. Within a year, the same magazines would be sold by their new owners for $1 billion. A year later, however, as the magazine business faced ad losses and cost increases, it became clear that the new owners, Hachette, had grossly overpaid.

By the summer of 1987, his first anniversary as CEO, Tisch had narrowed the CBS communications empire to broadcasting—including the CBS network, four CBS-owned TV stations, eighteen AM and FM radio stations, a joint venture with Fox producing movies and CBS shows for video-cassette release—and the Records Group. As a businessman, Larry Tisch believed in "sticking to his knitting," which he defined as the broadcasting rather than the communications business.

Tisch liked things kept simple. He was devoted to family, Israel, and shareholder value. In business he always stripped things to their essence. He believed that stations and cable were overpriced, and would eventually drop. He believed that America would one day plunge into a recession, enabling those with ready cash to acquire properties at bargain prices. Because he always worried first about the downside, he avoided debt and disparaged the junk-bond financing pushed by Michael Milken of Drexel Burnham Lambert. When the recession came, he warned, many companies would not be able to meet their interest payments or to sell assets. With his divestitures, Larry Tisch now sat on a $1.5 billion pile of cash.

Although Tisch had shed debt and saved shareholders money, as he had promised to, he had not overcome the suspicions of directors who had reluctantly agreed to make him CEO only after receiving assurances that he would not dismember CBS. Nine months later, Tisch had done exactly that, and many CBS directors felt duped.

Once again, the board came to believe it had a responsibility to protect CBS from Larry Tisch. "Not only do they have a fiduciary responsibility, but they don't want to look like patsies," observed a CBS executive who welcomed an assertive board as a counterweight to Tisch. Wanting CBS to remain a communications company, the directors had united to block the sale of CBS Records. Three directors—James Wolfensohn, Harold Brown, and Walter Cronkite—voted against the sale of CBS Magazines. At the July board meeting, Wolfensohn and Brown in particular asked: *What do you plan to do with all this cash? What is your strategy down the road for CBS?*

To Larry Tisch, these were the questions nonbusinessmen like Brown would ask. Tisch didn't believe in strategic planning departments, task forces, memorandums. Nor did he believe in committees of the board and group think. Tisch was accustomed to steering his businesses alone, and believed his investment record justified ceding him a free hand. Larry Tisch was proud of what he and his brother had accomplished in the hotel business. Loews was among the first hoteliers to recruit entertainers and offer a smorgasbord of activities, which transformed hotels into resorts. Larry Tisch was proud of his vision in spotting the hidden value of insurance companies. Or oil tankers. Larry Tisch didn't fancy lectures on *vision* from his board or anyone else.

He was, however, going to get lectured. The board had too many reasons to be uneasy about the future. In April 1987, one of the CBS executives whose name Tisch had submitted to the board the previous December as a possible future CEO—Peter Lund—left his job as president of the television stations division to become president of Multimedia Entertainment, syndicator of such shows as *Donahue.* The opportunity, explained Lund, offered 50 percent more than he was earning at CBS, plus significant stock options. Even worse than Lund's departure, from the directors' point of view, were the circumstances surrounding it. They learned his salary had been only $210,000, a pittance by network standards. Why, if Tisch held Lund in such esteem, did he not pay him more? Why didn't he know that Lund was unhappy and had decided weeks before to depart? There seemed something cold, almost indifferent, about Tisch to the directors, as if Lund were just another figure flitting across his Quotron machine.

The Lund affair also provoked troubling questions about Gene Jankowski, Lund's boss. Lund was one of five people who reported directly to Jankowski, but in his ten years at CBS, Lund told friends, he never once had an intimate conversation with Jankowski. The gregarious Jankowski tended to be uncomfortable in private encounters. He avoided confrontations, a reason his regular staff meetings were usually so bland—"What's going on in your department?" he would ask in front of all the other department heads.

These were among the reasons Jankowski was not included on Tisch's short list of possible successors. Directors knew that Jankowski had his fingers on Tisch's pulse, not on the pulse of those below him.

It was News president Howard Stringer—not Jankowski—who told Tisch that Lund was thinking of leaving. Even the way Lund's successor was chosen revealed Jankowski's hesitant leadership. The suggestion to appoint Stringer's deputy, Eric Ober, a former general manager of WBBM in Chicago, came not from Jankowski, said Lund, but from Stringer, who talked to Tisch.

Why, directors and others wondered, didn't Tisch fire Jankowski? Jankowski's aides said Tisch knew he needed Jankowski's relationships with affiliates and advertisers, needed what colleagues called his Boy Scout image. Gene Jankowski drove in from Connecticut daily and rarely missed a 7:30 A.M. mass at St. Patrick's Cathedral. He conveyed decency, dignity, was a wonderful cheerleader. There was another reason, said Jay Kriegel, and this was that there were day-to-day decisions "that Larry doesn't want to make," particularly decisions about how to allocate an executive's time. Yet if Tisch wished to communicate directly with a vice president, Jankowski did not stand on ceremony. The bottom line for Tisch, said an intimate, is that "he runs the place and Gene does anything Tisch wants. Gene is loyal."

Loyal, yes. But also unrealistically optimistic. CBS had slipped into second place that summer in both prime-time and news ratings. Tisch was alarmed; yet the serene Jankowski said, "I happen to think we're in the best possible position of the three networks."

The CBS board worried that internally no one would stand up to Tisch. Neither Jankowski nor Tisch had a strong bedside manner, one because he shied from sticky situations, the other because he had no patience for them. Despite Tisch's vow to bring back the stock option plan he had suspended in the fall of 1986, after nine months the plan remained suspended. Would there be more layoffs? More cuts? More reorganization? Many in the news division, for example, were already complaining of the toll Tisch's cuts had taken. In September 1987, *Evening News* senior producer Andrew Heyward complained that employees in many bureaus "haven't had a day off since May." Some CBS executives, including Tony Malara, the head of Affiliate Relations who had been demoted by Tisch, contemplated early retirement. Records president Walter Yetnikoff and Tisch were now estranged, the more so after the straightlaced Tisch kept hearing that Yetnikoff drank and behaved weirdly.* The volatile Yetnikoff wailed openly that Tisch didn't consult him and was preoccupied with the wrong things, such as the price of a bagel at the Beverly Hills Hotel. Like Bob Wright,

* A few years later Yetnikoff would enter treatment for alcohol abuse.

Tisch was stingy with praise. "I don't have the foggiest idea what Larry thinks of me as a manager," sighed one executive.

Persistent rumors that Tisch planned to transform CBS into a family affair heightened tensions. His son Andrew visited CBS News's Tokyo bureau and its Los Angeles station, KCBS. Photocopied clips mentioning the visits were circulated internally like contraband, exciting rumors that Tisch was grooming his sons for high positions within the company. Many executives were shaken when in June Tisch hired as his special assistant Steven D. Warner, twenty-eight, whose father was a Rye neighbor and weekend tennis partner. Warner, who looked as if he'd just jumped out of bed, his shirttail protruding from his trousers and his hair uncombed, was given an office next door to Tisch's and the freedom to poke around. It didn't matter that Warner had worked at CBS News and Sports for four and a half years, or that he had an M.B.A. from Harvard. He was seen as family. As was Jay Kriegel, who had worked on and off with the Tisch brothers and Loews for more than a decade and was now spending more time at CBS. So influential was Kriegel becoming that people at CBS began to refer to him as "the Consiglieri." In fact, Tisch was determined to bring Kriegel to CBS and had offered him Lund's job before he gave it to Eric Ober. (After consulting an old mentor, David Burke of ABC, Kriegel turned it down.)

Even fans of Tisch were concerned about his impact on morale. "He has made effective business changes," said Phil Jones of KCTV in Kansas City, head of the CBS affiliate board. "But he's done it in such a way that he has lost a sense of family." Family is "important in his personal life, but he doesn't seem to recognize it in his business life." While many affiliates, including Jones, respected Tisch the businessman, they were uneasy that he wouldn't spend the money necessary to propel CBS upward. They worried that he would treat affiliate compensation as a cost rather than an investment, would fail to see that compensation was what bound stations to the network. "We're in an emotional entertainment business," said Phil Jones. "Larry's such a practical businessman. He doesn't want to pay attention to the emotional side."

Unlike Murphy and Burke, Larry Tisch seemed oblivious to the unhappiness at the network. Rarely did he venture from his corner office. He had no confidant, no extra set of eyes, no hands-on manager, as he did at Loews with brother Bob. There were no staff meetings. His managers were compartmentalized; they did not sit around and kick about ideas or dialogue. This was the way he managed at

Loews. Larry Tisch was a man alone. With single-minded intensity, he targeted the changes CBS should make.

Tisch was watching more television, but still didn't know the players. One night that fall, he went to dinner at Primavera, a favorite Manhattan restaurant, and spotted Barbra Streisand at a table with *Saturday Night Live* producer Lorne Michaels, among others. "Barbra!" Tisch exclaimed, coming over to their table. He held her hand and recalled how they were both at a dinner to raise funds for Israel. At one point Michaels politely introduced Tisch to the table: "This is [agent] Sue Mengers. This is my date, Miranda Guinness. This is Brandon Tartikoff."

Tisch immediately turned his back on Streisand, and proceeded to discuss the networks with Tartikoff. "He's the only man in America who would turn his back on Barbra Streisand!" declared one guest, who found him rude. What surprised Lorne Michaels, who did not think Tisch rude, "was that Tisch didn't know Brandon."

"I'm interested in prodding our people to do new things," Tisch said at that time. "But I don't think I have the ability to say 'This program should be done' or 'This program shouldn't be done.' I want to set certain standards. I don't want junk." He applied this antijunk pledge to the nine-month-old *Morning Program* hosted by Mariette Hartley and Rolland Smith. Despite all the enemies he had made by chopping CBS News, Tisch liked his news straight, unadorned with smiles, starlets, and happy talk. He preferred the days when Charles Kuralt and the news division were running *CBS Morning News.* He had agreed to allow *The Morning Program* to be produced independently of CBS News starting in January 1987, and now he was sorry. As were the affiliates, who were regularly receiving dismal 1 and 2 ratings for *The Morning Program* and complaining loudly. If they were to be trounced by *Today* and *Good Morning America,* Tisch felt, at least CBS should be proud of its product.

In the summer Tisch told News president Stringer he wanted the program returned to News's auspices. That is why Stringer proposed to hire Kathleen Sullivan away from ABC as cohost, which meant raiding Tom Murphy's stable. To get Sullivan, Stringer said they might have to pay her $1 million.

Do it! Tisch said.

"Larry's focus has changed," said Jay Kriegel. "The first year his focus and obsession were on finances and the economics of the company. Sometime in August his obsession switched to programming." The nudge was "what happened in the news division."

Stringer and Kriegel, who were both in their mid-forties and had equally quick tongues, became buddies. With Kriegel's quiet support and Tisch's public backing, Bud Grant had reluctantly placed News's *West 57th* on CBS's prime-time schedule. Now Stringer hatched other program ideas, which Tisch welcomed. Stringer had a concept for a weekly one-hour documentary—*48 Hours*—to offer a fly-on-the-wall view into the workings of a hospital, a campaign headquarters, and so on—all in a forty-eight-hour period. Stringer hoped to put *48 Hours* on the CBS midseason schedule in early 1988.

Unlike Bob Wright, Tisch identified with News and drew close to his News president in a cozy relationship that made other CBS divisions uneasy. At a time when CBS hovered near third place, Hollywood insisted it was a serious error to overload the twenty-two-hour prime-time schedule with one to two additional hours of low-rated news programs. "CBS is making all kinds of mistakes," said Jeffrey Sagansky, Tartikoff's former deputy who would one day join CBS. "I can't believe that CBS with all its troubles would put on another news hour. Sure it's cheaper. But it will lead to more affiliate preemptions."

Also in the summer of 1987, CBS's flagship station in New York, WCBS, wanted to bump the *CBS Evening News* down a half hour to 6:30 P.M. The ratings of the three evening newscasts had continued their steady decline, having together lost 13 percent of the audience since 1981. More serious, after five straight years as the ratings leader, Rather was now in third place. Stringer and executive producer Tom Bettag, forty-three, disagreed over how to recoup. Stringer wanted to return to longer pieces and a mix of stories; Bettag and Rather wanted to stay with a harder news approach, including what Stringer considered too many brief wire-service-type headline stories. Stringer believed, as did his predecessor, Van Gordon Sauter, that CBS News was often "elitist." When Fred Astaire died in June, ABC and NBC both reported the event. CBS did not. Stringer thought this was a mistake, that television is a "mass medium" and most viewers would want to know that the lengendary Astaire had died.

There was another conflict between Stringer and Rather/Bettag. Like Arledge and Grossman, Stringer believed the executive producer, not the anchor, should be the boss. Stringer would have been less concerned if Bettag ran the show. But Bettag seemed to play supplicant to Rather. "Dan is the most experienced, savviest person we have in this news division," he said. "He brings the qualifications that I don't bring, that Howard doesn't bring. Howard and I were pups when Dan was in full bloom."

Rumors circulated that summer, which were true, of Stringer's intention to replace Bettag, perhaps with Mark Harrington, who had been his deputy when Stringer was Rather's executive producer, or with Bettag's number two, Andrew Heyward. Bettag obviously believed the rumors, for in September he and his wife Claire had what they called their final "celebratory steak dinner." They wondered how they could keep the house and pay for their son Andy's college tuition.

All that summer the newsroom was tense. Rather was depressed, and it showed. Jonathan Alter, the *Newsweek* media critic, wrote, "so far this month, Rather has changed his on-air delivery from intense to studied mellow to somewhere in between." The stray piece of good news for the newscast was the planned shift to people meters in September: Initial tests revealed that when the new Nielsen measuring system took hold Rather might come in first instead of third. Of course, in a way this "good" news was as irrelevant as the "bad," for less than a single ratings point—a switch by several hundred thousand viewers—separated Rather, Brokaw, and Jennings.

And then came Dan Rather's very odd behavior in Miami. The news division was quarreling with Sports, whose games sometimes ran long, particularly on weekends. This robbed Rather of precious minutes or preempted entire newscasts, as happened during the basketball playoffs in the spring. Rather worried about the affiliates, since nearly half the CBS stations now aired his newscast earlier, and ran syndicated shows at 7 P.M. Rather was agitated that news was becoming secondary and that the affiliates had too much power over the network. He was convinced that the stations were too easily stampeded, as they had been when he was covering the civil rights revolution and many Southern station managers phoned to complain about his "trashy Northerners."

For an assortment of reasons—to cement relations with affiliates, to personalize news, to rivet attention on stories, to allow the anchors to escape from behind their desks—the three anchors were traveling more, doing their newscasts from the studios of affiliates. To cover Pope John Paul II's trip to Miami on Friday, September 11, Rather's broadcast was set to originate out of empty space on the eleventh floor of the Biscayne Boulevard building that housed CBS's Miami bureau. At about 6:10 P.M., or twenty minutes before the 6:30 newscast (the anchors do a second live feed at 7 P.M.), Rather learned that the women's semifinal match of the U.S. Open was deadlocked between Steffi Graf and Lori McNeil, the first black woman in tennis to reach the semifinals. Rather was concerned, since this was the very first week of the new people-meter rating system and *CBS Evening News* hoped to bounce back to first place. But now Rather was hearing that CBS Sports expected that the match might push back or even eliminate the newscast. Incensed that a mere tennis match might supplant news, Rather and Bettag called Stringer in New York.

This is unprecedented and unacceptable! Rather roared into the phone. *Why are we doing tennis? It kills us in the ratings.*

I agree, but there's a lot of interest. It's a close match, and for the first time ever there's a black woman competing to get into the finals, said Stringer.

If Sports is going to cut into the newscast, they may as well fill to the hour, Rather said, meaning that Sports should fill the time until 7:00 or 7:30 P.M. With the pope in Miami, Rather didn't want to do a truncated broadcast. *I will be in position at six-thirty and ready to do the news. But if you don't come to me at six-thirty, don't come to me until seven.*

Stringer said he would call Gene Jankowski and plead News's case. Rather hung up hoping the matter would be resolved to News's satisfaction and went to have his makeup applied. Meanwhile, Stringer reached Jankowski at home, and Jankowski agreed to a compromise: *If the match is tied at 5 all or if Steffi Graf wins in the next ten minutes, CBS Sports will go right to Rather. But if the match stays at 4 all, or if Lori McNeil wins, Sports will stay with the match.*

What happened next is murky. Stringer and his deputy, Mark Harrington, phoned Bettag at around 6:25 and described Jankowski's compromise. They told Bettag that the match would end soon. But Sports did not have a direct telephone hookup to CBS's makeshift Miami studio, and since WTVJ, the Miami CBS affiliate, ran its own local news between 6:00 and 6:30, Bettag had no direct confirmation of this.

Minutes before airtime, Rather reached for the phone. "I am not bluffing. Hear me straight," he barked, according to an eight-page, handwritten memo Tom Bettag wrote to himself the next day. "Come to me at 6:30, or don't come to me. I won't be there." Eager to placate Rather, Stringer issued no commands, and Rather moved to the anchor desk to have his microphone hooked up.

Bettag remained on the phone with Harrington, insisting that Rather was serious. *Make sure Sports stays on the air if the match spills past 6:30.*

When 6:30 came and the match was tied, Rather angrily left the set. Bettag, who was still on the phone with Harrington, hung up and hurried to catch up with the anchor. There was no private phone in the temporary studio for Rather to use, and Rather, who was smoking mad, wanted a heart-to-heart with Stringer. So he marched back across the long outdoor corridor to an office he had used earlier in the day. He wanted to tell Stringer that he wasn't interested in doing a ten-minute newscast. Let Sports stay on the air. He would rather start the second newscast from the top at 7 P.M. "My view is that a semifinal tennis match is not as important as the visit of the pope to this country," said Rather. He was not going to allow News to be trivialized. As Rather barreled along the outdoor corridor to his office, he told Bettag to stay behind and monitor the situation.

The CBS Miami affiliate was not carrying the semi-final, so Rather could not see with his own eyes that the match was about to end. But when Bettag learned that it was almost over, he raced from the studio along the outside corridor, and met Rather about sixty yards away. Rather was still agitated, but Bettag told him, "Hold your thought. Don't move. I've got to go back and find out what's going on." Bettag hustled back to the studio, while Rather waited alone in the corridor.

At 6:32 P.M., CBS Sports, thinking Rather was waiting at the anchor desk, went off the air.

The next six minutes were chaotic. The network went black. There was no "Please stand by," no announcer's voice warning viewers of technical difficulties, no four-minute tape that was ready to roll of Rather introducing the pope's visit. There was only black space.

Panicked, Bettag dashed back to Rather, never thinking of the four-minute taped opening of the newscast he could have put on the air. Feeling that he had given fair warning to Sports, Rather hesitated. If he went back on the air now, News and Dan Rather, not Sports, would be blamed. He wanted to think, but he had no time. Nor did he have a choice. He walked back to the set at a regular pace, so as not to be out of breath. And, wrote Bettag, "we decided to take one minute" extra so that Rather could "cool" off.

Meanwhile, Andrew Heyward, Bettag's deputy, was in the control room, where the director of the newscast had told New York not to switch to Miami because Rather was not in his chair. Why didn't Heyward just give the order to roll the tape they had of the pope's visit? Or tell correspondent Richard Roth, who was in the studio, to take Rather's seat while Heyward looked for him? Because, Heyward said, "The managing editor had said we're not going on if we don't go on at 6:30. And he and the executive producer had left." To overrule them, Heyward said, "would have been disloyal. It would have been creating a potentially irrevocable break with Dan and the organization."

This preoccupation with Rather's feelings may explain why none of the News people in the studio had run out to the corridor where Rather and Bettag were arguing and shouted for the anchor to hustle onto the set. When asked to explain, people in News went blank, or said they would speak only off the record. The consensus was that Rather was having a tantrum and Bettag was frantically trying to calm him down and get him on the air, an impression affirmed by Bettag's own eight-page memorandum. Many believe, as did executives in New York, that Rather was simply testing Sports to see who would blink first. Rather denies this: "We did not know we were in the black. As soon as I heard, I came back." Aware that Rather was in Miami with his producers, and aware that Stringer had alerted Bettag at about 6:25 P.M. that the match was about to end, CBS executives were unconvinced by this explanation. One Black Rock executive said, "Implicit in Dan's position was: 'I can decide whether I will go on the air.' "

In a way, Rather's behavior reflected a basic conflict within Rather between his desire to be a likeable host and his desire to be a tough newsman. "The difference between a reporter and an anchor is like the difference between a D.A. and a judge," observed Howard Stringer. "Dan is an outstanding, aggressive reporter. Walter Cronkite defined an anchor for all time as this judge—fair, reliable, the opposite of an aggressive, assertive D.A. Dan, deep down, really admired Ed Murrow. He thought Walter Cronkite was too much of a news reader. In Miami Dan was saying, 'How dare they give sports priority over news!' It was Dan being the D.A."

Tom Bettag believed that what happened in Miami reflected News's declining clout at the network. In the past a News president could have said, "We're going to take over the air from tennis," but Stringer could no longer do this. Bettag thought Rather got a bum rap. Kindly Walter Cronkite, he felt, was more arbitrary, less collaborative, but hid this with a silky personality. "Walter used to have sole control over the writers and producers," remembered Bettag, who was an associate producer on the Cronkite broadcast. "We used to have what we called 'magic time,' which was the amount of time Walter had on camera. Walter would be angry if the time that was left him was under a certain point. Walter's first question when he walked in was, 'What's my magic?' "

Inside the CBS family, the reaction to the six-minute gap was surprisingly muted. Back in New York on the night of the incident, Larry Tisch tuned to the 7 P.M. newscast, which Rather did live. Tisch thought Rather looked relaxed. He had no idea that starting at 6:32 there had been six minutes of blank airspace. When Tisch learned of the incident later, he faced a dilemma. If he suspended his star anchor, Rather would be "damaged goods," and there would be more stories about troubled CBS. If he fired Rather—which would be expensive, since his $3.5 million yearly contract did not run out until 1994—who would replace him? "Larry really believes when Dan is relaxed he's the best anchor," said Jay Kriegel. So Tisch took a call from Rather that weekend, and accepted his explanation. Stringer faced a similar dilemma. He had wanted to fire Tom Bettag that summer but hesitated. To replace him now would make Bettag the scapegoat at a time when Tisch was publicly forgiving Rather. Ironically, the incident saved Bettag's job.

Publicly Dan Rather seemed philosophical. He was pleased with Tisch's reaction. "Right from the beginning his was an understanding ear," he said. Rather saw the anchor as "a symbol," and felt the weight of that responsibility. "When you're a reporter you're not a symbol. You take responsibility for your own work, but you don't have to take responsibility for other people's work." An anchor did. An anchor also endured the "frustration" of knowing he was both a journalist and a celebrity. "No matter how good you are," he said, "at some point you get spread-eagled. On better days you smile and say, 'It goes with the territory.' "

On worse days in 1987, Rather thought a lot about giving up his $13,409-a-day salary.* But there was a part of Rather that craved danger. Born in 1931, he was raised in Houston, where his father worked as a pipeliner in the oilfields. After graduating from Sam Houston State College, Rather took a job as a radio disc jockey on KSAM. He saw himself as a risk-taker. When he got hungry at the radio station, he would often put on a long-playing record, hop into his 1937 Plymouth pickup truck, race to the Dairy Bar two miles away, where he ordered two hamburgers to go, and then rush back to the station before the record ended. Later, Rather braved Hurricane Carla for KHOU-TV in Houston, thrived while covering the civil rights movement in the South for CBS in the sixties, did not flinch

* Rather's daily income assumes a five-day work week—261 days—and excludes time off for vacations.

when he stood up to Richard Nixon as CBS's White House correspondent in the seventies.

In the previous year alone, Dan Rather had walked picket lines, faced down Larry Tisch on behalf of CBS News, survived being punched and kicked by mysterious muggers, and had become a favorite media target. And then Miami. There were those who thought Rather was muddled, vexed by his different roles, wanting to please by donning sweaters, yet wanting to draw the line with his "From Murrow to Mediocrity?" warning. One day a good ol' boy, the next a prosecutor. Rather thought he was misunderstood. One reason he could walk away from the anchor job, Rather said, is that "I know who I am and what I am. I could be happy being the AP man in McAllen, Texas. The reason is because I like news."

Some believed Rather might one day have to take that job in Texas. Those who tracked the standings of the newscasts at the three networks believed that Miami, on top of the other incidents involving Rather, would eventually hurt him. Viewers expect from their network anchor security, a feeling of calm, balance, control. Rather was coming off hot, not cool. And the network research revealed Rather was slipping. Before Miami, CBS's chief research analyst, appropriately named Poltrack, observed that Rather's numbers "have in the last year declined. . . . All our research shows it's ABC and Peter Jennings that are moving up." David Poltrack hastened to add that Rather's Q, or likeability, scores were still the highest of any anchor. His negatives, however, were higher than those registered for Jennings or Brokaw, and his audience was older. There was a core group of viewers who wouldn't watch Rather, and those who remained loyal were dying off. Rather's ratings would perk up with the new people meter, but in a medium which placed a premium on personality, his long-term prognosis was bleak.

In September 1987, around the time of the Miami incident, Larry Tisch was struggling with his board over a matter directors thought had long been settled, the sale of CBS Records. Before the September 9 board meeting, a CBS director bet another director "a quarter that even though it wasn't on the agenda Tisch would propose to sell the records division." He won the bet, as Tisch announced in executive session that the Sony Corporation had made an offer to buy CBS Records. "It could sell for as much as $2 billion," Tisch said.

The board had no choice but to meet and explore the matter, and a special session was called for the next day. On September 11—the same day the network went black for six minutes—*The Wall Street Journal* reported that CBS was pondering an offer from Sony, and CBS announced that it would "consider and respond to Sony's inquiry in due course." Tisch was ready to sell, but his board, including Paley, was not. Before the month was out, Tisch was forced, again, to tell Sony that CBS Records was not for sale.

Then the stock market intervened. On October 19 the market crashed. CBS's stock fell from $199 to $152 on October 20. Tisch raced over to Loews, where he spent the next two days in front of his Quotron, monitoring the market. Immediately Tisch spotted a silver lining: Perhaps the market plunge could rescue the sale. The swings of the market might remind the board that Records was an unsteady business, and that a recession was just around the corner. CBS needed to fortify itself with cash. Because the Japanese yen was overvalued, Tisch also knew Sony might be unaffected by the market crash. He had to be sure Sony would still pay $2 billion, but first he had to win over Bill Paley.

Bill, CBS's stock is down. The way to strengthen it is to sell Records. How can we reject a $2 billion offer? he said.

Paley, at eighty-six, was feeling old. He tired easily. He came to the office most mornings, but was home in the afternoon. He had suffered a hip injury that fall and was now in a wheelchair attended by a nurse, who regularly entered his office to administer medication. Paley's resistance weakened. Seated one morning that fall among his Picassos and Rouaults, the white-haired CBS founder looked postcard perfect in a navy blue suit, white shirt with CBS cuff links, polka-dot tie, and white breast-pocket handkerchief coming to a just-so point. Asked about the potential sale of CBS Records, he admitted to being torn between sentiment and shareholder value. "My mind has to be adjusted from time to time," he said. It was easier rejecting $1.2 billion. "Suddenly it's $2 billion. You've got to give it respect and attention."

Within days of the crash, Tisch telephoned Sony and this time promised to deliver Paley, and thus the board, if they still wanted to go forward. In November, with Paley and the board's approval, Tisch finally got rid of CBS Records and its pesky president, Walter Yetnikoff.

Tisch and Paley would be allied on another matter—firing Bud Grant. Before injuring his hip, Paley had decided to be more assertive in programming. He hadn't really immersed himself when he first returned to the network a year ago, he said. But now he would, as the tapes of pilots and new shows piled on his desk attested. CBS, which had been number one in prime time for two decades ending in 1976, and then reclaimed the lead in 1979 for another six years, was now a feeble second, and slipping. Paley believed he could still spot the broad appeal of a zany actress like Lucille Ball, could still guess the shows viewers would like. And he sensed an opportunity to fill a vacuum. While professing admiration for Tisch as "one of the brightest businessmen I've ever seen," Paley added, "He's not as well acquainted on the programming side of the operation."

Paley was now obsessed with firing Bud Grant, and by that fall Tisch was on his side. On a visit to L.A., Paley solicited suggestions from Grant Tinker and Robert Daly about a replacement. Heading both lists was Jeff Sagansky. Paley consulted with Tisch and Jankowski, for whom Sagansky had once worked in the CBS finance department, before he left to join Tartikoff at NBC. In late August, Jankowski met with Sagansky, who was now head of production at Tri-Star, and asked whether he might be interested in the job. Sagansky perked up. But then he thought of his friend Tartikoff, and how uncomfortable it would be to compete against him. More important, Tri-Star had recently merged with Columbia, and he had a large moral and financial stake in its success. No, the timing was all wrong, said Sagansky.

Tisch and Paley pressed forward. "Bud wasn't reaching out to the community, to the writers and producers," Tisch explained. People kept telling him Bud Grant was lazy, burned out after seven years as Entertainment president and fifteen years at the network. And though Tisch and Paley had signed off on the fall 1987–88 schedule, it was a disaster. By October—five weeks into the new season—ABC had snatched second place from CBS. All but two of CBS's nine new shows ranked in the bottom fifty of the top one hundred network series, and such highly touted new series as *Beauty and the Beast* and *Frank's Place* barely escaped these depths. By fall CBS had added a second movie night on Saturdays, and before the season ended there would be a third movie night—Tuesdays. Two months into the new season, CBS would ax half its new fall entries. By the end of October —long after rumors that he was about to be ousted swept Hollywood —Grant was terminated.

The decision to fire Bud Grant was made before CBS decided on his successor. Neither Tisch nor Paley felt his deputy, Kim LeMasters, thirty-eight, had the seasoning or the kind of relationships with writers and producers to move up; yet they wanted to keep LeMasters—and believed they could—as number two. In searching for a replacement, in September Paley consulted Dr. Robert M. Batscha, president of the Museum of Broadcasting, which Paley helped found and where he served as chairman. Batscha urged Paley to hire producer Steven Bochco, who would later make his precedent-setting deal to create ten series for ABC.

Paley was excited by the idea. He admired Bochco's *L.A. Law* and *Hill Street Blues.* They were the kind of programs Paley liked to associate with CBS.

Batscha, who kept in touch with Bochco, said he would make the call.

"You said to me once that you had always fantasized about running a network," Batscha said to Bochco on the phone. "Do you still?"

"Yes, why?"

"Would you be willing to come back to New York and talk to Bill Paley about running CBS?" said Batscha.

Bochco, who had been born in New York forty-three years earlier, flew to his hometown in mid-October to see Paley and Tisch, separately. Bochco wondered if he should ask CBS for a ticket or offer to pay himself. His lawyer advised: "You'll find out more about them by not asking."* Bochco was excited. "I liked the idea of the challenge," he said. He thought of the things he would change at a network—the restrictions imposed by the censors from Program Practices, the script notes from junior executives, the sameness of most series.

Bochco met Paley at the chairman's Fifth Avenue apartment on a Friday morning. For two hours the tall, thin, silver-haired Bochco, who moves around his Hollywood office in jeans and often pauses to take a few cuts with a baseball bat parked near his desk, stretched his long legs in a sitting room overlooking Central Park. He sat across from the white-haired patriarch, who began by telling the younger man that he was the best writer in television today.

Paley talked about how he built the network, about the nineteen straight golden years CBS reigned as number one with shows like *I Love Lucy.* At noon Paley rose, put his hand on Bochco's shoulder, and said, "I think you're going to run CBS and I think you should do it."

"In all candor, it's a tough sell," said Bochco. "There are compelling reasons not to. But I wouldn't be here unless I was interested."

* Bochco says he was never reimbursed.

"Could you come back at 2:00 and meet Mr. Tisch?" asked Paley.

Bochco returned, and the three men chatted amiably for fifteen minutes, but the job was never mentioned. Before he left, Tisch asked if Bochco and his actress wife, Barbara Bosson, who was featured in *Hill Street Blues,* could join him and Billie and their son Tom for dinner that night. Bochco agreed, and stayed behind to chat with Paley. If by some chance Bochco didn't take the top job, Paley said that he wanted to work out a development deal.

Two hours into dinner at an Upper East Side restaurant, Tisch finally raised the subject of Bud Grant's job. Bochco agreed that CBS had to do a better job of courting talent and quality. His model was Grant Tinker, who picked talent and then got out of the way. A crucial task was to discover new prodigies. But Bochco reminded Tisch: *It's expensive. There are writers on L.A. Law who make $8,000 per show—more than I made as executive producer of* Hill Street Blues. *Plus they are paid an extra bundle for each show they write. Some writers make $300,000 to $500,000 a year! Writers who also produce make a lot more.* Bochco said he wouldn't be interested in the job until June at the earliest, since he wouldn't want to be held responsible for shows now in development. But he would need a sense that the network was willing to pay money to compete.

No problem, said Tisch. *We will pay whatever it takes to attract talent. The head of CBS Entertainment will have wide latitude to make decisions.* Bochco never brought up salary, nor did Tisch.

"You're the guy for the job," Larry Tisch said as they were ready to stand up and leave. "I hope you'll consider this."

"I will consider it, and not keep you hanging," said Bochco.

"Please think hard about this," said Billie Tisch, a warm, relaxed person whom the Bochcos found enchanting. "We really want you."

As they went their separate ways that night, Tisch thought "we had a 50 percent chance" of getting him. Bochco thought the odds were better. "If I had to make up my mind right then and there, I'd have taken the job," he recalled just a few weeks later.

Bochco envisioned few obstacles at first. His wife was supportive. He gave no thought to the CBS bureaucracy. He had not talked to Gene Jankowski, and assumed, "I wouldn't have reported to him. I wasn't going to report to a guy I didn't know. I would have reported to Tisch."

Bochco flew back to Los Angeles the next morning and consulted with three people: his lawyer, Tinker, and Tartikoff. His lawyer opposed the move, explaining that he would be taking a cut in pay, no matter what CBS was willing to offer. Besides, it would represent a conflict between his network duties and his financial interests, since Bochco would have to sever his ties to two series—NBC's *L.A. Law* and ABC's *Hooperman.* And if either were sold in syndication, he would not receive a penny. The advice from Tinker was equally unsettling, and stayed with Bochco: "It will not be good for your tennis game or your marriage."

Tartikoff told Bochco he was in love with a job that didn't exist. Bochco had a romantic notion that he would be able to concentrate on prime-time series, recruiting talent, fussing with scripts. Wrong, Tartikoff said. Bochco would also have to work on daytime soap operas and quiz shows and Saturday morning children's programs. "Only 15 percent of your time is spent creating," Tartikoff told him. Another 15 percent would go toward what Tartikoff called "the Prince Phillip agenda for the network"—making speeches, taking meals and meetings with people as a courtesy. Another quarter of Bochco's time would be spent in meetings about new series or series in trouble. Not to forget the time devoted to promotion, scheduling, planning, and "people handling," including the care and feeding of a staff. Nor the affiliate conferences, the sessions with advertisers, the budget reviews, the management meetings back at Black Rock, and maybe a little maneuvering between Tisch and Paley.

By Wednesday, Bochco had made up his mind and called Tisch. He explained the reasons—particularly the financial reasons—why he could not accept. Tisch understood, and said he hoped they could work out a production deal. Bochco then made the same call to Paley, who reacted just as Tisch did. "Promise me you won't make a decision without talking to us?" said Paley. Bochco agreed, and put his lawyer to work negotiating a potential production deal with both CBS and Brandon Stoddard, who also wanted to pursue a long-term arrangement with Bochco.

Meanwhile, Kim LeMasters was upset. He had worked at CBS since 1976, except for one year when he worked for Disney. He had both the energy and the experience to run the entire department. He knew about Bochco. He knew Bud Grant was to be fired. He had heard rumors about other contenders. He would have to be pretty thick not to realize he was being passed over. LeMasters confided in Howard Stringer, whom he trusted, and the News president counseled him to campaign for the job. First, said Stringer, he should court Tisch's princes, Jay Kriegel and Steve Warner. The taciturn LeMasters had always brushed past Steve Warner, barely concealing his contempt.

Without realizing it, LeMasters had spawned a potent detractor, someone who cared about and watched television and whose opinions were welcomed by Tisch.

In October 1987, LeMasters launched a full-scale campaign for the job. First he phoned Warner and held a confessional—out gushed his hurt, his loyalty to CBS, his frustrations with the "lazy" Bud Grant, his plea for a friend and ally. The conversation went on so long—two hours—that for the first time since rejoining the network in June Warner closed the door to his narrow office so that his next-door neighbor, Larry Tisch, could not overhear his conversation.

Warner was seduced, and the next day he told Tisch, "Kim deserves a chance." The CEO agreed to consider him, but first he dispatched Jankowski to Los Angeles for some serious hand-holding.

Wanting his own eyes and ears on the scene, Tisch had Warner fly west too. Warner would stay three weeks, and LeMasters would become his new best friend. But Paley was telling Tisch he wanted LeMasters as well as Grant ousted, that he wanted to start fresh. Warner weighed in on Friday—the first time he had ever taken such a strong position—and said if both LeMasters and Grant left it would wreck the entertainment department and send a terrible signal of disloyalty and panic.

Though Tisch didn't want to lose LeMasters, he agreed with Paley: They had to explore other options. Tisch and Paley decided to pursue two Hollywood program suppliers recommended by Tinker—Robert Harris, president of the MCA Television Group, and Richard Berger, president of MGM/UA. One other candidate, NBC's Warren Littlefield, was sent a feeler by a Hollywood agent, who like other agents often passed along information that placed those they do business with in their debt. "The agent was asked to see if there was any interest on my part," said Littlefield, who said there wasn't. Paley and Tisch then interviewed Harris and Berger, and this time Jankowski was involved, lunching with Harris and having a drink with Berger. Tisch invited Harris, but not Berger, to dinner with him, Billie, and Tommy Tisch. The dinner went well, and Tisch said he wanted Harris for the job. But over the next week Harris couldn't persuade MCA to release him from his contract.

The boyishly handsome LeMasters first heard about Harris on Monday evening while driving home. His wife, Donna, reached him on the car phone. She was crying, and told her husband that *Entertainment Tonight* had just reported that Bob Harris was offered Bud Grant's job. "I'm so sorry," she said.

LeMasters jerked his four-wheel-drive red Chevrolet Blazer over to the side of the road and immediately phoned Jankowski with an ultimatum: *Either I get the top job, or I leave.* LeMasters heatedly announced that he would call Tisch and come east. The next morning Jankowski phoned and soothingly urged LeMasters to delay the trip; Tisch wanted a few more days. LeMasters accepted Jankowski's judgment, knowing that Jankowski was quietly pushing him for the top job.

Tisch was determined not to act impulsively. First he wanted to measure how Hollywood really felt about LeMasters. The feedback was mixed at best. Grant Tinker said LeMasters was "not a good listener," an essential quality if a programmer is to attract gifted people to write and produce shows for CBS. Tinker was worried that LeMasters, thirty-eight, lacked enough self-confidence to nurture talent. The basic knock on LeMasters was that he was rigid, not unlike his stepfather, former John Birch Society member and eight-term California congressman John H. Rousselot. But rigidity can also be a strength, the conviction to stick with what you believe, which is the argument LeMasters's proponents advanced. Disney's Michael Eisner, for whom LeMasters (as well as Tartikoff and Stoddard) once worked, extolled LeMasters's certitude.

Internal support for LeMasters came from Jankowski, Warner, the increasingly influential Jay Kriegel, whom LeMasters had also courted, and from Howard Stringer. The support from Stringer was crucial, since Tisch respected him as a programmer. Stringer, in fact, identified with LeMasters in a way only a fellow former number two could. Stringer assured Tisch that if LeMasters got the number-one job, they might see another Kim, a more assertive, self-confident man. "Number-two jobs don't tell you much about a person," said Stringer, who spoke from experience. "You get lost in the shadows. You've got to be loyal, and that is viewed as sycophancy. If you come up with good ideas, they're stolen or get lost in the void. Everything has to go through your boss. So you often feel indecisive and weak. When you deal with subordinates you want to say *yes* or *no.* But if you don't know what your boss thinks, you convey indecisiveness and weakness. Your self-worth deteriorates."

Kim LeMasters became president of CBS Entertainment on November 9. CBS seemed happy. So did NBC. "I have a regard for his competitiveness," observed rival Brandon Tartikoff wickedly. "But I can take him every day of the week. In the last year and a half I've been mostly competing with myself." Within the Hollywood colony, the knowledge that he was Tisch's third choice for the job—perhaps fourth or fifth if Sagansky or Littlefield had been interested—meant LeMasters was not dealing from strength. It didn't help that LeMasters in effect reported to five people: Tisch, Paley, Jankowski, Warner, and Kriegel. "I keep Larry and Gene and Jay and Steve Warner and Mr. Paley informed," explained LeMasters.

Tisch made one other major appointment before 1987 was over: On December 3 he announced that Jay Kriegel would join CBS as senior vice president. The press release said the bespectacled Kriegel, who has a mop of thick gray hair and is uncomfortable when separated from a phone, would "coordinate" external relations, run government affairs, including Washington lobbying efforts, and oversee some special projects, reporting directly to Tisch. Kriegel's job would be broader than his vague title, for he would become Tisch's alter ego. He had been associated with the Tisches for more than a decade and was like a fifth son. "To me," said Tommy Tisch, "Jay is the single greatest piece of managerial, intellectual, and political horsepower in one person." Kriegel would become the ultimate staff man—free to roam and question everything, responsible for little. Although he didn't know how to operate a VCR and didn't know the difference between *Dallas* and *Dynasty,* Kriegel could decode Tisch for other CBS executives, could help them shape arguments in ways Tisch might find persuasive. "Larry can be scary if you don't know him," explained Kriegel. "He's so quick, so unadorned, so free to say what he thinks. He doesn't guard his questions or ideas." Nor, Kriegel would add, did Tisch care much for how he communicated: "One of Larry's problems is that he talks in shorthand and doesn't explain himself well. He is the most self-confident man I've ever met."

Long before his December appointment, Kriegel was trying to perform the role of peacemaker, the kind of role this Harvard-educated lawyer failed to perform as Mayor John V. Lindsay's chief of staff, when his brainpower was undermined by his arrogance. Now he listened, and spent a lot of time over at CBS News, which was what he knew best. Kriegel grew close to Stringer and championed placing *West 57th* on the prime-time schedule. With Stringer's encouragement, he spent a long evening reassuring Rather of Tisch's noble intent. "I owe him a lot," Stringer said at the time. "The revival of the news division would not have happened without him."

By the end of the year, Kriegel spoke of "a new collegiality" at CBS, emphasizing the relatively young, aggressive members of the team—Stringer; LeMasters; Eric Ober, president of Television Stations; Neal

H. Pilson, president of Sports; and Tony Malara, whom Kriegel had persuaded Tisch to promote. Pointedly, Kriegel did not include Jankowski or himself. But the "new collegiality" did not extend to Bill Paley and the CBS board. Paley was never comfortable with Tisch's determination to sell parts of the company he had assembled. Nor was he thrilled with Tisch's programming intrusions, an area he considered his domain. He was lukewarm, at best, toward the LeMasters appointment and agitated when Bochco decided to sign a production deal with ABC rather than CBS. Bochco noticed the tension between Paley and Tisch when he was negotiating to produce shows for CBS. Paley would call him daily, he said, pushing him to sign a production deal. Tisch, chilled by stories of Bochco's cost overruns at *Hill Street Blues,* resisted. He knew that Bochco had tangled with MTM over "creative differences," which the studio said was his inability to manage costs and Bochco said was its tendency, with Tinker gone to NBC, to treat Bochco like an ant. Tisch communicated his anxiety internally, and the deal CBS offered Bochco carefully limited the network's downside risks. Bochco was offered a mere six-series commitment; CBS did not agree to swallow any deficits; there were penalties if a series failed to last thirteen weeks; and there was no signing bonus. "They were hedging their bets," said Bochco, who chose the ten-series offer and $5 million signing bonus from ABC. Paley phoned the next day.

"Hi, Mr. Paley. How are you, sir?" said Bochco.

"Not good," answered Paley. "I'm very unhappy with how our negotiations went."

"CBS wasn't competitive with ABC," said Bochco, who explained the relatively paltry proposal he had received from CBS.

"Well, it was very nice meeting you, and good luck!" Paley said before slamming the phone down.

Bochco did not take it personally. "I realized he was not angry with me," he said. "He was angry with Larry Tisch." Paley, he sensed, felt manipulated, as if he were being "humored" by Tisch. "With all of Paley's art on the walls and the fact that he is a lion, he can't get what he wants anymore. It was sad." said Bochco.

"Not at all!" Tisch snapped when asked if there was any tension between him and Paley. Embarrassed by a published report in *New York* magazine that spoke of these tensions, Tisch wrote a letter to the magazine complaining of the "total misrepresentation of my relations with Bill Paley," and adding: "Bill and I came in as a team, and we continue as a team in every sense of the word."

What was true was that publicly Tisch treated Paley with respect. And his relationship with Paley was a quantum leap better than Paley's had been with Tom Wyman and his immediate predecessors. But it was not "a team in every sense of the word." Sometimes Tisch could not hide his impatience toward the enfeebled older man. Paley had won back his company from Wyman, only to lose it to Tisch.

Tisch's relations with his board of directors did not improve with the November sale of CBS Records. If anything, the sale had "emboldened" the board to become more assertive. Directors congratulated themselves for resisting Tisch's efforts to sell Records in 1986. Had they not held firm, directors assured themselves, they would have sold the company for $1 billion, not $2 billion. When Tisch again made noises in December about making two nominations to the board—"Arthur Liman would be a great addition to the board; Bob Tisch would be a great addition to the board," he said—directors were implacably opposed and the matter died, for the time being.

The board's aggressiveness continued to rile Tisch, sometimes diverting his, and the board's, attention from the larger issue of lost network viewers, of the advances made by cable and independent stations and the VCR. Tisch's relations with some directors—Frank Thomas and Henry Schacht—had ripened. With others, the Cold War persisted. "It's hardly a representative board for a media company in the twentieth century—geographically, by race, by sex, by age," said a Tisch intimate of the eleven white males, one black, and one woman director. "What that board needs is more energy." Four directors were past seventy—Paley, Cronkite, Gilpatric, and Marietta Tree. Tisch expected all but Paley to retire. The continued absence of Bob Tisch rankled him. They had always been partners. Their offices at Loews were connected. Bob owned 12½ percent of CBS, just as Larry did. Still, the board resisted inviting him to join, which sometimes created tension between the brothers.

As 1987 was nearing its end, Larry Tisch sometimes felt unappreciated, and not just by his fellow directors. He got much worse press notices than either Tom Murphy or Bob Wright. The press said he had a credibility gap. They said he was in over his head in the entertainment business. "I never read anything about me," Tisch declared, before reciting from memory some of the unkind things that had been written. He was convinced journalistic standards had declined; now the media regularly printed gossip as news and did not check facts. The best retort to critics, he insisted, were the facts.

The facts, Tisch believed, demonstrated that he had accomplished much in his first sixteen months. Costs had been cut; through the sale of CBS Records and other assets as well as layoffs, he had slimmed the overall number of CBS employees from about 19,000 to 7,026; he had won new flexibility to hire part-time workers and saved what chief financial officer Fred Meyer estimated to be $20 million in CBS's new IBEW labor contract. CBS's profits were also up. This was all the more impressive, he thought, since 1987 ad revenues dipped 2 percent and network after-tax profits fell to about $30 million. Despite numerous hurdles, CBS profits rose in 1987 to $136 million after taxes, nearly double the $72.4 million earned in 1986. A large chunk of these earnings came from the $1.5 billion of cash that Tisch had put into treasury bills, commercial paper, bonds and other money-market instruments, and from record earnings at CBS's four owned stations. While other companies were rocked by the October stock market collapse, Tisch could boast that his prudent investments had sheltered CBS. "Financially, no one can ever refer again to CBS as a troubled company," he said. "At the end of the year, when the Records deal closes, we'll have over $3 billion in cash." And CBS's stock price, which began the year at $127, closed the year at $158, or almost $35 more per share than the average price Tisch had paid.

Tisch could point to nonfinancial accomplishments as well. "We've changed the culture," said Tisch. "We're less meeting-oriented and more action-oriented." Tisch made quick decisions. However, even with the changes he had wrought, Tisch, like his NBC and ABC counterparts, was not satisfied. He wanted to cut more. Around the first of the year he hired Ed Grebow as senior vice president, with responsibility to supervise Personnel, Facilities, Data Processing, and the 2,500 employees of Operations and Engineering. Tisch had come to know Grebow when he had been an investor in the Bowery Savings Bank, where Grebow had been executive vice president as well as a friend of Tom Tisch's. His chief mission, like Coopers & Lybrand's before, was to "reduce expenses," Grebow said. If anything, Grebow was more militant than his boss. "People here don't know anything other than the CBS way," said Grebow. "Larry has not changed the culture here. He's made some progress. But this is still a company that likes to spend money." Take the CBS Tampax machine. Grebow once boasted to a roomful of European technology experts that he had saved CBS four hundred dollars a month on Tampax. What happened, he explained to the startled executives, was that CBS had dispensers in its ladies' rooms that sold Tampax for five cents each when they cost CBS thirteen cents. The result, said Grebow, was that female employees were ripping off the company, using CBS as their local supermarket. Outraged, Grebow ordered the price jacked to twenty-five cents. What outraged CBS employees was that Grebow bragged about it.

Almost daily Grebow excited Tisch with the latest outrage he had uncovered. Like the time he reported that CBS paid for the home TV antennas of its executives, as if they wouldn't have TVs if not for their job! Or when Grebow found that CBS used seventy-four types of CBS envelopes in the stockroom, and ordered that it eliminate all but two, legal and regular size. These discoveries still drove Tisch crazy.

But as with the other new network owners, experience had rendered Tisch more moderate. Now, instead of automatically ordering layoffs when he detected waste, Tisch chose in December 1987 to rely on attrition to reduce the corporate staff by two hundred. By now he was acutely aware, he said, "of the ramifications of every word I say or act I do. I give an extra ten-second pause."

Tisch remained less sensitive to the human relationships within the company. The same people issues that bedeviled Bob Wright at NBC chased Tisch at CBS. Internal communications were bad, and morale was worse. While praising many of Tisch's changes, Fred Meyer, the Swiss-born chief financial officer, spoke for many fellow executives when he said that colleagues at CBS were now "a little bit in their foxholes. They are not sure the shelling has stopped. As a result, internal communications between people, initiative, creativity, brainstorming, and maybe even good comradeship are a little bit in hibernation right now."

Outside CBS this view was widely shared. Unlike Tom Murphy and Dan Burke, Tisch had not been raised in the TV business, and unlike Bob Wright, he did not have Brandon Tartikoff. Hollywood was distressed by more than Tisch's penny-pinching. One of Hollywood's major young executives said of Tisch's CBS: "They are not taken seriously. They have no attachment to or love of the product. There's nothing in Larry Tisch's life that suggests it. He's not a great collector of art. He's not looked at as an intellectual. Look at Steve Ross. He's a great collector of talent, at making a home for talent. It's not that he's creative. Steve Ross is one of the most extraordinary guys at making people feel great."

Why couldn't Tisch hire someone to do it for him? Because, answered this executive, "Does anyone want to work for him? Is he fun to work for? How generous would he be? I'm sure I'd be on his short list to be the head of the network. I can't think of why I'd want to work for him. . . . What you need in any creative environment is the talent and the absolute right to fail. If you don't have it, and believe it, you'll never succeed in a big way. The reason is that most creative things are, by definition, most risky." And Tisch had trained himself to minimize risks.

Tisch ignored such criticism, saying he was satisfied with what he had done. And within the next few years he would hire widely respected executives. In the meantime, he especially took pride in what he had accomplished with CBS News. "I think the morale of the news division is terrific," he said. "I got a call from Dan Rather this morning and he said how good morale was and how appreciative News was of new News programming." Tisch had returned the morning schedule to CBS News, and had nudged *West 57th* onto the prime-time schedule. After Stringer's division won awards for cinema-verité documentaries on a street corner *(48 Hours on Crack Street)* and in the Soviet Union *(Seven Days in May),* Tisch announced that a weekly *48 Hours,* anchored by Rather, would debut sometime in January 1988. In all, CBS News would claim three hours of prime time, three more hours than NBC and two more than ABC. And this did not include *Nightwatch* at 4 A.M., a two-hour interview program for insomniacs. After twenty years, *60 Minutes* was still among the top ten rated shows. Despite the Miami incident, Dan Rather's newscast had won the ratings contest for twenty straight weeks. News was even adding employees, with its budget swelling by 27 percent in 1988, to $348 million. "The place is sky high and starting to get a little cocky again," said a thrilled Howard Stringer.

Strategically, Tisch took pride in something else. He had imposed his personality on the company by simplifying CBS. He had always said: *Get the core business under control first. Once that's in order, expand.* At his CNA insurance company, Tom Tisch remembered, the herd would clamor: " 'Larry, why don't you put more business on the books? Why don't you go out and buy an insurance agency rather than rely on independent agents? Why don't you become a financial supermarket?' Larry always said, 'Let's focus on the main issues. Today, CNA is the strongest company in the insurance business in America." At CBS, Tisch resisted advice from those who beseeched him to vault into cable, the way ABC had and NBC was trying to do. "I don't understand it," Larry Tisch said. "Our business is the network. I don't want our people to take their eye off the ball. . . . In the long run, the potential profitability is not there in cable. I don't mean a well-run cable company won't make $20–$30 million a year. But when you compare that to the $300 million NBC makes at the network, you shouldn't jeopardize that." A much more fruitful diversion of energies, he felt, would be to get the federal regulations on the networks lifted so CBS could produce unlimited hours of its own programs and then sell reruns to local stations. Unlike Bob Wright, he did not think the world was on fire, and believed that time might be on the networks' side. And while he knew that his friend Tom Murphy and Cap Cities were cautious, they were in too many businesses for his taste. Tisch would stake his reputation on the networks.

There were those who didn't believe Tisch really meant what he said about cable, believed he was playing the game the way he did bridge, exploiting the cards he was dealt. Until the price of cable companies or stations fell, he wasn't going to buy; it was not a matter of principle with Tisch, but price. A close Tisch advisor confirmed, "He would love to have a cable outlet at the right price." In other words, Larry Tisch the trader was probably doing what he had always done: waiting to buy cheap.

Perhaps not. There was confusion because Tisch did not share his thoughts. If there was a strategy it was "in the head of Larry Tisch," said Donald D. Weir, Jr., then senior vice president in charge of CBS's international efforts, who felt Tisch was mistaken to shun cable. It simply was not Tisch's style to brainstorm. Unlike NBC or ABC, which conducted ongoing dialogues among executives, at CBS top executives could remember no specific discussions about whether to get into cable before Tisch decided they should not. Nor was strategy Tisch's strong suit. He played bridge, not chess, a game more reliant on cunning than strategy. Tisch had the patience to wait for an investment to pay off, but not the inclination to puzzle out seven moves ahead.

Because he didn't tell directors what he was thinking, or sometimes told them things they thought were untrue, the CBS directors began to wonder whether Tisch might be scheming to merge CBS into Loews, or sell it. Asked if there was "tension" between Tisch and the board, Roswell Gilpatric answered carefully, "I think there is a guarded attitude on the part of the outside directors concerning business strategy." By the end of 1987, the directors sensed they had voted for Tisch and gotten Ted Turner, minus the vision. "He has done an LBO liquidation of the company, just as any raider would do," complained one director who was seen by Tisch as an adversary. He had radically transformed CBS from a broad-based communications company to broadcasting. And he had done so at a time when the broadcasting business was declining. Yet because the outside directors owned but 7,567 shares among them, they were defensive, this director admitted. Which is why Paley became so important to them. "If he could get Paley to go along, we'd do it," explained a director. One director was so depressed that he was thinking of leaving, and said other directors wanted out as well.* Of one thing this director was certain: "I don't know what his plan is, but he has one."

The long-running dispute over the future direction of CBS erupted at the January 13, 1988, CBS board meeting, provoked by a report from Fred Meyer. With the sale of Records to Sony now complete, Meyer reported, CBS had more than $3 billion in cash. At Tisch's direction they had invested these funds in short-term money-market instruments or seven-year treasury notes.

Directors interrupted Meyer and began questioning Tisch: *Now that we have all this cash, what is your strategy for using it? CBS has only four stations. Do we plan to buy more? Do we plan to invest in cable? Overseas? A Hollywood studio?* In short, did Tisch know what he was doing?

Tisch rose from his end of the long table and said he would do something, in time. Relax, he seemed to be saying. Stations and cable were too expensive. Federal fin-syn regulations precluded a network from buying a studio. CBS already spent plenty on programming. CBS earned about $10 million overseas and was expanding its efforts, but overseas offered no panacea. Already, he warned, political resistance to American cultural hegemony was growing. And to buy anything overseas was expensive. Then, in what Ros Gilpatric referred to as "Larry just passing off ideas," Tisch suggested that CBS could act like a holding company, tapping its cash to invest in companies the way Loews did. "A company selling very cheaply is Aetna," Gilpatric recalls Tisch saying. "Larry is not a precise man," said another director, who remembered that Tisch had said, "I have no plans for the money. We could invest it in T-bills, at 9 percent interest. Or I might come back at a later date seeking authorization to invest in securities. We might want to invest in something else. For instance, I got word of a Sterling Drug fight and there is a possibility we could be a white knight there. Or at Federated Department Stores. I'm sure they would welcome us."

The directors were shaken. What did an insurance company, a pharmaceutical concern, or a retailer have to do with a broadcast com-

* None would leave, at least not until 1990, when Gilpatric, then in his eighties, decided to step down. Cronkite and Newton Minow would depart in early 1991.

pany? Directors said they were interested in growing their entertainment business, not plunging into unrelated fields, as CBS did, for instance, when it bought an ill-fated toy company and the Yankees.

Tisch declared: *The problem with stations and cable is that they cost more than they are worth. And government regulations prevent us from buying cable systems. Or producing programs. Or financing them in exchange for a residual interest. Or from syndicating programs. Or from making certain types of business arrangements with our affiliates.*

"Shouldn't we look at what we'd like to do without regard to restraint and then see if there is some action we can take to try and remove the restraints?" said Henry Schacht. Like others, Schacht didn't like the idea of CBS as a holding company. After ventilating this issue, the board agreed, according to the antiseptically written minutes, to "avoid investing" in "the long-term holding of investments" and in any acquisition unless it was first "agreed upon by the board. It was further agreed that the Board should regularly consider and discuss at subsequent meetings the future business strategy for CBS. . . ." Sometime soon, the board said it expected from Tisch a report on CBS's strategy.

The board was not reassured by Tisch's responses, in part because directors and Tisch started from different assumptions. Larry Tisch was profoundly pessimistic about the future of the economy and the stock market. He wanted to avoid debt and conserve cash. He was wary of those companies that accumulated debt to make acquisitions. "No one ever repealed the business cycle," Tisch observed. "I don't want to be the guy who drowns in an average of twelve inches of water. . . . Sometimes you don't have to have a growth strategy. Sometimes you need a preservation strategy." If that strategy led CBS to become a holding company, he said: "Philosophically, I have no problem with it. What is General Electric? There are very few pure companies left in America."

Despite a sluggish year for broadcasting, CBS profits would be up in 1988, he predicted. And 40 percent of its profits would be from interest. "What difference to shareholders does it make if the money is from interest? . . . My definition of building for the future is creating value for the shareholders of CBS."

Which gets to the third assumption Tisch rejected: Value was more important than the initial price. "The best security—say IBM—at the wrong price is a much more risky investment than a lousy company bought at the right price," said a close business associate of Tisch's.

"The price should determine the investment. Larry believes that." Asked why others were buying when he was not, Tisch declared: "I'm smarter than they are. Sure I can make a 6 percent return on my stations. I want 15 percent. Why should I pay because stations are in style?"

But Tisch's 9 percent return on treasury bills looked better the first year than it would in subsequent years. "If you take $100 million and put it into treasury bills and you made 9 percent versus, say, 7 percent on a station, that first year you would get $9 million from the treasury bills and $7 million from the station," said one investment banker, who did a quick computation. "But the second year the cash flow of the station grows. Plus you're building asset values. The station appreciates, the treasury bill does not. It's simplistic for Tisch to say stations are overpriced."

"The number-one question before the board is what is our strategy," said director Frank Thomas in early 1988. Members of the board, including Paley, wanted to plunge into the cable business. "I think we should" invest in cable, said Paley. "It's a coming thing. It's really our game, except that the distribution system is different."

While CBS directors were worried that Tisch lacked a strategy, the members of the affiliate board worried that he had one. Many station owners thought Tisch was utterly without sentiment, a dollars-and-cents man who didn't value the network/affiliate "partnership." When the affiliate board members gathered in Hawaii in mid-January, as they do every third year for a meeting with network brass, they intended to tell Tisch this was uppermost on their minds. If cable was seen as the wave of the future, they feared Tisch would ride that wave. What many affiliates and CBS directors shared was suspicion of Larry Tisch.

Tisch confounded the affiliates' suspicions. At this confab, he listened, seemed to be more relaxed on the tennis court, seemed to be paying more attention to their pal, Tony Malara. And what he said pleased them. During the course of the Tuesday morning round-table discussion in the Kula Room of the Westin Maui, an affiliate asked: *What are your intentions toward cable?*

"We know NBC is going down that path," Phil Jones remembers Tisch saying. "We don't think that's the way to go. We have no plans to pursue cable as an alternative business." Let NBC and ABC talk of hedging their bets on cable, he would not. To program for cable, he declared, was to build up a weak competitor. "You're comparing an elephant and a fish," Tisch recalls saying. "We're a giant." The "new"

Tisch left little doubt that in the debate then raging, he sided with traditional broadcasters.

But behind the new mask, the old Tisch lurked. Privately he confided to select associates that his objection to cable was based less on principle than on cost. For now, cable was too expensive, so why not assuage the CBS affiliates? Nevertheless, he admitted, "My mind is open on everything." If CBS's entertainment division got back on its feet and could withstand the diversion, if cable prices dropped, if the networks were deregulated and allowed to acquire cable systems, or if the affiliates made his life miserable, Larry Tisch the trader would do as he wished. Even after the euphoric Hawaii meeting, Phil Jones had few illusions about the "new" Tisch. "I believe him as of January 1988," Jones said. Perhaps, Jones feared, Larry Tisch really did agree with the nontraditional, expansionist strategy of the new owners of ABC and NBC, choosing only to take a different route to reach the same destination. Or perhaps Tisch didn't have the foggiest notion what he would do next.

20

THE PRODUCERS: PALTROW AND SPELLING

Bruce Paltrow wore his standard summer uniform—dungarees, polo shirt, and sneakers—as he sat behind a bare black metal desk in a dusty suite of five offices on West Fifty-seventh Street in Manhattan. His headquarters was bereft of any decoration, save for the production schedule for the pilot of *Tattinger's,* his new NBC series. As executive producer, Paltrow was a juggler. He commuted back and forth to California to keep an eye on *St. Elsewhere,* the successful series he had helped launch six years earlier on NBC. To film *Tattinger's,* he had to assemble a cast and hire a production staff of about eighty, including art and set decorators to design Nick Tattinger's restaurant, as well as carpenters, construction grips, a director of photography, and sound mixers. It was already September 1987, and there were scripts to be assigned and edited, locations to be scouted, cartons to unpack, bank accounts to open, money to be cajoled from NBC so Paltrow could begin shooting on October 26.

Tattinger's would take place in a restaurant, which, Paltrow and NBC believed, would give the series a "franchise," the way the hospital in *St. Elsewhere* gave Paltrow's talented team of writers—Tom Fontana, Mark and John Tinker, Robert DeLaurentis, Channing Gibson—an opportunity to write individual stories without losing focus. The series would open with Nick Tattinger's return from Europe, where he had gone to recover from a gunshot wound. He was coming home to attend his daughter's debutante ball. Once back in New York, Nick discovers that his former restaurant is going to seed and will be sold to a real estate developer, a thug who belongs to the right establishment clubs. The developer orders people to be roughed up or killed as casually as he bulldozes buildings, which is what he intends for the restaurant. So Nick decides to remain in New York and fight.

NBC hoped the series would attract the kind of hip, young urban audiences advertisers pay premiums to reach. "I love the script," said Perry Simon, who headed NBC's Drama Programs. The network expected *Tattinger's* to debut in the fall of 1988, which is why it gave Paltrow and his studio, MTM Enterprises, a thirteen-episode pledge, a commitment that was expected to cost NBC $12.5 million, including the $55,000 Paltrow would receive each week as executive producer.

Simon, accompanied by Warren Littlefield and NBC casting chief Joel Thurm, came east in mid-October 1987 to help Paltrow cast the remaining actors. They had already settled on Stephen Collins, who had starred recently on NBC in *The Two Mrs. Grenvilles,* as Nick Tattinger, and on Blythe Danner to play his ex-wife, Hilary. For the audition, the West Coast contingent joined Paltrow, three writers, and Collins in a room at NBC's 30 Rockefeller Plaza offices. Paltrow was determined to select an unconventional ensemble cast, much as they had done for *St. Elsewhere.* Among others, they chose stage actors Simon Jones and Roderick Cook, comic Jerry Stiller, and such accomplished veterans as Jack Gilford and Uta Hagen. NBC would defer to Paltrow on casting decisions.

The network was less pliable over the budget. The morning casting session over, Paltrow and Tartikoff's team repaired to the NBC cafeteria to debate money over tuna fish sandwiches.

"How much are we short to pay for Stiller?" asked Joel Thurm, who knew Jerry Stiller wanted $17,500 per episode to play a character budgeted for just $8,500.

But a few thousand more for Stiller wasn't the big obstacle. "I have huge budget problems," Paltrow said. The pilot alone was now expected to cost $2.8 million, and NBC had agreed to pay only $2 million as its license fee. Which meant that the studio that employed Paltrow, MTM, had to pick up the $800,000 difference. Each of the remaining episodes, said Paltrow, would cost an average of $1.2 million, but NBC had initially agreed to pay only $800,000 weekly. In other words, MTM would again have to make up the difference, gambling that the series would stay on NBC for at least four years. If it did, MTM could make a fortune by selling reruns in the syndication marketplace. However, by 1987 this was even more of a gamble since the market for reruns of one-hour shows had shriveled. "We're prepared to eat $300,000 an episode," said Paltrow the businessman. "We're not going to eat $400,000."

Expenses escalated—the set construction and decoration came in at

$500,000, and that didn't include the cost of Hilary's apartment; the rent for the Plaza Hotel ballroom to shoot the debutante party was $30,000 for a single day. Aware of the new network owners' preoccupation with costs, and of cost overruns on NBC's *Miami Vice* and ABC's *Moonlighting,* Paltrow said he was trying to be frugal; instead of paying $115,000, as he did to the director of his last pilot, he would direct the pilot himself for only $25,000. But Paltrow said he needed NBC to sweeten its license fee, and Warren Littlefield promised to talk with NBC's Business Affairs people and get back to Paltrow that afternoon.

The license-fee question would float, unresolved, for months. In the meantime, Paltrow went forward with plans to build three sound stages and offices on a West Twenty-third Street pier to house his production company. A television series involves more intensive work than a movie or a stage play. A movie is made over a period of months and there is time to reshoot scenes; a TV series episode takes about a week to shoot, and if Paltrow doesn't get it right on the day he rents the Plaza, there is no going back. "The theater is different pressure," said Collins, a personable, gum-chewing New York actor. "Once a play is running it's a three-hour day, or six hours for matinee day. Here, every day is a twelve-hour day. I've probably been offered twenty series since mine [*Tales of the Gold Monkey*] went off the air. I turned them down. It's like joining the marines. But this is Bruce Paltrow, New York, a good script. It will take nine, ten months a year. It's like falling in love."

Like many members of the *Tattinger's* entourage, Collins loved Paltrow; loved his calm, the way he heaped praise on everyone or, when dissatisfied with a performance, the way he would pull an actor aside and whisper to avoid embarrassing anyone. Like the Tom Hanks character in the movie *Big,* Paltrow was a kid hiding in an adult body. He still talked fast and retained his Long Island accent (dog came out as dawg), still giggled mischievously over a *St. Elsewhere* scene in which actor Ed Flanders dropped his pants and half-mooned the audience, still went away once a year to ski with his brother and six other pals he grew up with. "He's a nice guy," said Jim Finnerty, Sr., his production manager. "The business hasn't ruined him."

For the *Tattinger's* pilot, Paltrow shot the interior scenes starting on November 2, 1987, at a studio in Long Island City. Perry Simon flew in to lend moral support. While Simon watched, Paltrow directed a scene in Hilary Tattinger's peach-colored dining room, a scene in which she instructed her daughters Winifred and Nina on the proper table placement of the Baccarat crystal, the Christofle silver and the English bone china. "Two daughters and not one domestic skill between you," exclaimed Hilary Tattinger. "What do they teach you at Spence?"

After watching the first eleven takes of this scene, Simon was uneasy. He found the dining room scene "a little bitchy. There's a difference between tension and bitchiness." Between comedy and whining. Simon, adopting what he said was his "Kissinger mode," inched up to Paltrow before the twelfth take and diplomatically whispered something.

"This is a comedy of manners!" responded Paltrow, polite yet firm. To play it softer, he said, would "take the energy out of the scene."

Simon retreated to the background. "He didn't want to hear it," Simon said. "But he was a gentleman about it."

Simon knew that his task was complicated by the fact that Paltrow and Danner were married. He could not say what he really felt, which was that the talented Broadway actress was putting too much starch into the role of an upper-class woman, was playing too hot for the small screen. Mass audiences, he feared, would not relate to her and the kids, would not find them *likeable.* The concern Simon and NBC had was not that the premise of *Tattinger's* was faulty, nor that the series could somehow mix three genres—drama, action-adventure, and romantic comedy. NBC worried that Paltrow would create a stylish but not very commercial series. A network programmer like Simon always thought of reaching a mass audience. The Nielsen ratings or the demos had long been the scorecard, but especially now with the desperation for ratings intensified because of fading network audiences and bottom-line–oriented network owners. Simon worried that the Baccarat crystal scene, like the upper-class teenagers, like the stage actors and strong ensemble cast that was similar to *St. Elsewhere*'s but contained no stars, would narrow Paltrow's potential audience.

But while Perry Simon approved the checks for NBC, he was not the boss. "That's what makes Paltrow what he is," Simon said. "He has his own vision. Lots of producers, if I made that comment to them they would just run in and change the lines." Simon hoped the Baccarat scene would come off as light comedy. As he departed at 2 P.M., he called out, "Keep it up. It looks great."

After he was gone, Paltrow said there would be no changes, even though he respected Simon. "You've got to realize, the network is always looking for the greatest common denominator, reaching the greatest number. I'm looking for reality." He had been through something similar when he did *The White Shadow* for CBS. Although it was a series set in a ghetto, CBS kept telling him to put in more white faces. "I was constantly writing scenes that served no function at all." He vowed not to do that again. "When I was doing *St. Elsewhere* they kept saying to me, 'Why do people have to be sick? Can't they get better?' They always want to turn it into *Dr. Kildare.*"

Tartikoff remained sky high. "I'm sure it's going to be a good pilot," he said at the time. Despite what in retrospect would appear to be the obvious pitfalls in trying to use a restaurant as an incubator for a weekly series, the savvy Tartikoff still hoped that *Tattinger's* would be "the next *Hill Street.*"

A month later, when he screened the pilot, Paltrow was dissatisfied, and had it reedited. Still, the only crimp in Paltrow's pre-holiday cheer was money. There was yet no agreement between his studio and NBC on a license fee. MTM told Paltrow not to show NBC the pilot until the network upped the license fee to $900,000 per episode. It was a game of chicken between two macho powers, Paltrow thought. He had some experience with the game, since a similar battle was waged over *St. Elsewhere.* The difference between the license fee NBC paid and the actual cost of *St. Elsewhere* for the entire season was $3.5 million, a figure that would rise to $4.5 million next season, said Paltrow. MTM was saying it couldn't continue with *St. Elsewhere* unless NBC raised its fee, and NBC replied that the studio could recoup its losses in syndication.

After the holidays, Paltrow viewed the reedited pilot and pronounced it "very good. Now I'll show it to anybody." First he showed it to MTM, and then on January 22 he screened it for Tartikoff and his team. When the lights went up, he recalled, Tartikoff rose and said, "It's great." (Tartikoff recalls saying it was "good.") Then they went off to Paltrow's office where Tartikoff gave him "notes"—he said he worried that the daughters might come off "mean-spirited," that the series should not dwell too much on the restaurant and food but become a meeting place for stories. The restaurant was to be the prop, the way Rick's was in *Casablanca.* Perry Simon assured Paltrow, "the scenes with Blythe and the kids were great."

Privately Tartikoff fretted—as did Simon—that the scene with the kids and the debutante ball was a "little too chi-chi." But, added Tartikoff, "Stephen Collins was better than I thought he'd be. Usually, actors have to grow into the part, as Don Johnson did on *Miami Vice.*" If anything, he thought the "notes" Paltrow and his team offered at the meeting were "stronger than mine." The NBC programming chief was still bullish.

By February 1988, Bruce Paltrow was flying. NBC had agreed to raise the license fee to $900,000 and to pay much of the cost of reshooting parts of the pilot, which Paltrow would do in late March so he could deliver the finished product in time for NBC's May Decision Week. While he was disappointed that NBC decided in January not to renew *St. Elsewhere,* Paltrow nevertheless gave himself a treat—a chauffeured black Mercedes to ferry him from his Upper East Side brownstone to the offices on West Twenty-third Street. "It says 'Big Jewish Car' on the side," Paltrow cracked. "I've almost gotten over my guilt."

Tartikoff was now thinking about *Tattinger's* as a 10 P.M. show, perhaps on Wednesday or Tuesday, or maybe even Sunday, and made a six-minute promo to boost the series to affiliates, advertisers, and the media. While excited about Paltrow's series, by the winter of 1988 Tartikoff was worried about NBC's schedule for the next fall. This was a critical year, he knew. None of NBC's 1987–88 shows was a "hit," and perhaps only *A Year in the Life* deserved to be called a "quality" series. Several of NBC's established hits—*The Cosby Show, Cheers, Family Ties, Miami Vice*—were getting older, and Tartikoff knew that NBC's younger audiences wouldn't stick with a series as long as older viewers did. NBC already had three weak nights—Tuesday, Wednesday, and Friday. Without a few new hits, Tartikoff worried that NBC would slip from first place, just as CBS had.

Tartikoff and the NBC programmers also lugged a psychological weight. If the challenge in 1987 was to prove they could succeed without Tinker, the challenge in 1988 had more to do with pride. Critics no longer thought of thirty-eight-year-old Tartikoff as a boy wonder. Tom Shales of *The Washington Post,* whom he read daily, described the midseason debut of *The Highwayman,* an action-adventure series, as "possibly the worst Tartiplop ever," a series "for people who find Sylvester Stallone off-puttingly intellectual." Now ABC was being hailed as the "quality" network. In Hollywood it was assumed that NBC would falter.

Tartikoff knew there was some truth to the critics' claim that NBC was choked with obligations to established talent, which discouraged newcomers. NBC had made a deal with Stephen J. Cannell, TV's most prolific producer, who then had three series on NBC *(Hunter, J. J. Starbuck,* and *Sonny Spoon),* one on CBS *(Wiseguy),* and one on Fox *(21 Jump Street).* The deal, admitted Tartikoff's deputy, Warren

Littlefield, was this: If Cannell agreed to move *Hunter,* a top-twenty rated show, to Tuesdays, NBC would not yank his mediocre *J. J. Starbuck.* "It was tit for tat," said Littlefield. NBC had also in the past year given Bill Cosby's producers Thursday at 8:30 P.M. to produce what Tartikoff knew was a pedestrian spinoff, *A Different World.* Critics, and Hollywood, asked: Are Tartikoff & Company too locked into a few producers? Was NBC in trouble? The competitive Tartikoff was determined to prove the critics wrong.

Tartikoff also thought about the possibility of a Writers Guild strike in March. The Alliance of Motion Picture and Television Producers wanted the nine thousand members of the Guild to accept smaller residual payments for reruns in the domestic or foreign syndication market or on video cassette, even though these markets were exploding. A strike could disrupt the pilots being made in March or April, and thus NBC's ability to decide its fall schedule in May. The longer the strike, the greater the odds that the fall season would be delayed.

All of these reasons, plus fatigue, led Tartikoff to make a tentative decision to leave the network in a year, or in June of 1989. He was tired after eight years as Entertainment president. To prepare for the succession, he had already stepped back a bit, become more of "a coach," as Littlefield described him. But to leave comfortably, Tartikoff felt this was the year in which NBC had "to plant the right seeds." He thought NBC could remain number one for another four or five years if he could come up with four to five solid new shows. To plant these seeds, he made early series commitments, without even asking to see scripts first, with a roster of outstanding writer/producers and directors, including Bruce Paltrow; Susan Harris, Paul Witt, and Tony Thomas *(Golden Girls);* Ed Weinberger, an original producer of *The Cosby Show;* Charles Shyer and Nancy Meyers, who directed the popular Diane Keaton movie, *Baby Boom;* Lowell Ganz and Babaloo Mandel, who helped create such acclaimed comedies as the movie *Splash* and the ABC series *Happy Days;* Bill Blinn, who produced such family fare as *Our House* and *Aaron's Way;* and Aaron Spelling, who had produced more network hits than anyone.

Several series—such as *Tattinger's*—were meant to be NBC's principal contenders for Emmys, but the series that Tartikoff believed could be NBC's next 40-share show was Spelling's *Nightingales.* No matter the Moral Majority, the growls against rock music lyrics, the conservative Reagan Revolution. Tartikoff's reading of the national mood was that the time had come to loosen up, to flaunt some voluptuous, drop-dead looking women. Besides, Tartikoff said, "I always believe in betting on people who have something to prove."

Aaron Spelling was indeed obsessed. "We have not had a pleasant two years with ABC," said Spelling. "We'd love to have a quick hit on another network." This way Spelling could prove Stoddard and ABC wrong, prove that Stoddard in particular, and Hollywood and the critics in general, were elitist. There was, he believed, too much "meaningful" reality television. Viewers didn't want to think when they flicked on their sets.

Nightingales was an escape into sexual fantasy. That was the sole premise behind the one-sentence pitch Spelling had lobbed at Tartikoff. It was the core of the plot and character sketch for the two-hour movie pilot Spelling next sent over to NBC, and of his December 15, 1987, meeting at NBC with Tartikoff.

"I have a couple of ideas. Would you like to hear them?" is how Spelling remembers Tartikoff's opening gambit.

"Sure."

"Have two male nurses in it," advised Tartikoff. "It will be like the cock in the henhouse." It would add humor, too.

Spelling left the meeting pleased, the more so when he received a call from Tartikoff that night expressing continued enthusiasm for the project. Perry Simon was more dubious. "It was okay. It wasn't great," he said of the ideas sketched in the meeting. Simon was nervous that too many of the characters outlined were not "fresh," that too often the women defined themselves in relation to men. Yet Simon was quick to add, "I think it can be very commercial. I don't think we'll win any Emmys for this one. But if it's done right, it doesn't have to be an exploitive show. We can present contemporary working women." Somehow the usually incisive Simon and Tartikoff managed to convince themselves that the tackiness of the concept would not be apparent to viewers.

Tartikoff dug himself in deeper. In late January he called Spelling, told him he had read his new outline or "bible," as it's called, and without even reading the first script Tartikoff upped the ante. Now if the two-hour movie and series didn't make NBC's schedule, Tartikoff said he would substitute another thirteen-week series commitment. Spelling hadn't worked with another network since the early seventies, and he was swooning. "It's always easier to work with a partner than a boss," he said, no longer feeling like a relic. "Brandon doesn't think

Aaron is ten years behind the times," said a Spelling vice president, Ilene Chaiken.

Unlike *Tattinger's,* Spelling's *Nightingales* didn't have a script, a director, a cast, locations, sets, or wardrobes. Spelling had to assemble these elements by the end of March in order to shoot the two-hour movie in April and edit and deliver a tape to Tartikoff in early May. Casting, particularly for the roles of the student nurses, was crucial, and a casting session took place in Spelling's two-story brick bungalow on what was once the Samuel Goldwyn Studios in Hollywood.

The hopeful actresses and actors trooped into an office large enough to accommodate a small convention. When they entered, their eyes froze on Spelling's immense desk at the far end of the room, elevated as if it were a throne. They noticed the five seating areas, the Waterford crystal glasses arrayed above the bar, the walls covered in raw silk, the fox skins used as throws on the oversized L-shaped couch that seats perhaps twenty-five. The room was designed by Candy Spelling, who wanted everyone to be both comfortable and awed. "I was putting my husband on a pedestal," she explained. "I felt that if his office was very big but warm," Aaron and his guests would relax more. "That was part of it. The other was that if visitors had a long walk from the end of the office to his desk then he has the upper hand."

Thirty-two actors were invited to audition on the afternoon of March 16, 1988. Each would enter Spelling's office at ten-minute intervals to read dialogue from *Nightingales.* They would be questioned and inspected by Spelling, his partner and vice chairman, Doug Cramer, and seven other members of Spelling's team. Each time an actor walked in, Spelling, who wore a gray V-neck sweater over a pale blue shirt, would rise. As he did, the pipe would come out of his mouth, and in a whisper the rail-thin producer would offer a genuine, even effusive greeting. To each actor he tried to say something nice. To Traci Lin, a twenty-year-old with straight blond hair who asked if she could smoke and who wore a short white blouse that bared her midriff when she lifted her arms, he said, "Nice transitions, Traci."

No one said a word about the first three auditions, but when Traci Lin left the room, Spelling said, "Anybody want to talk?"

"After you," said Cramer.

"I love this girl Traci!" proclaimed Spelling, closing his eyes as he often does when he speaks. "Great transition. Everybody else was screaming. . . . We have to really like her. . . . I also liked her because she lit a cigarette." Spelling then stood up and, patting the back of his legs, noted, "She has a little"—baby fat.

The group was certain Kim Morgan Greene was too close to thirty to play a student nurse. "You've got to think of playing the role for five years," said Cramer, to general agreement. They were sure that Gail O'Grady—stunning in a tight black leather skirt, black sweater with the sleeves casually rolled up, no makeup, blonde hair combed straight back with feathered bangs, and prominent breasts—was a contender to play Julie in what they called the bathing suit scene, a scene requiring a knockout body. "I like the hairdo, which is *today,*" said Spelling. And, because she was obviously well endowed, Spelling added, "We don't have to see her in a bathing suit!" On the other hand, they weren't sure about Kristian Alfonso, who wore dark sunglasses, a camel-colored cowboy jacket over a long green billowy dress that reached down to the heels of her cowboy boots. "Anybody ever seen her in a short dress?" asked Spelling as soon as she was out of the room.

"I think she has a nice body," reassured talent coordinator Tony Shepherd, who had done his homework.

From among these actors, and several whom Spelling saw earlier, they planned to select three or four finalists for each part, then audition these for Tartikoff at NBC a week later. It was at this NBC session that they would debate which of the two finalists would play Julie, the tease who seduces the doctor in his swimming pool during the bathing suit scene. One faction wanted to go with the better actress, the other with the better body. To settle the matter, Tartikoff walked off with Spelling, and together they resolved the dispute. The body won.

The final cast, including Susan Walters, Chelsea Field, Britta Phillips, and Kristy Swanson, was announced by NBC on the first day of shooting, April 7. The locale of the series had been changed from Dallas to L.A. The press release described *Nightingales* as "eight student nurses living in a Los Angeles university residence. . . . The students, who have chosen nursing for a variety of personal reasons" —one is in the Federal Witness Protection Program, one is fleeing a history of drug abuse, one has a secret child, one is a peach-cheeked virgin from a Midwest farm—"arrive at Nightingale House with high hopes."

Around the time of the announcement, people at NBC were developing a belated case of the jitters. "The core of a commercial property is there," said Warren Littlefield. "I wish the writing were better." But a jury of one, Brandon Tartikoff, was sold. "Brandon considers it an important commitment," said Perry Simon, who found the scripts only "fair" but hoped "great casting" might "triumph over medium material." In any case, everyone at NBC was confident that they could fix any problems. It was worth fixing, thought Tartikoff, because a network needed both an *A-Team* and a *Hill Street Blues.* Spelling, he believed, was a perfect counterpoint to Paltrow. Tartikoff sought Emmys and mass appeal, unaware that with these two shows he would achieve neither.

With *Tattinger's,* Tartikoff and Paltrow failed to see that a restaurant would not provide the same "franchise" for a one-hour action-adventure drama as a hospital or a law firm, which deals with life and death matters, not peach melba and surly chefs. Unlike Rick's place in *Casablanca,* which vibrated with the dangers of Vichy France and World War II, there was no compelling larger drama taking place at Nick Tattinger's restaurant. The restaurant itself was only a clumsy prop for an action-adventure series. And the one-hour form was too long for a romantic comedy. How could someone as shrewd and experienced as Tartikoff miss what, in retrospect at least, seems obvious? The simple answer is that Tartikoff had confidence in the Paltrow group: "They do my favorite dramatic series on TV—*St. Elsewhere.* They know what's needed," he said. The more complicated answer comes in several parts. First, picking hit shows is like catching fish with one hand, owing as much to luck as to skill. Second, even the best programmers delude themselves, becoming so attached to people or ideas that they are blinded. Sometimes they are blinded by their own hubris. Tartikoff, with help from his capable team, had resurrected NBC. Together they had seized first place, demonstrated their ability to pick hits, to choose actors, fix scripts. They could fix *Tattinger's* and *Nightingales.*

Both Spelling and Paltrow were only dimly aware of each other's projects in the spring of 1988. Neither knew the other. And, of course, neither knew both of their projects would fail. Paltrow, who does not disparage people—"They got kids to feed, too," he likes to say—nevertheless referred to Spelling's project as "the sweaty nurses" show. But he didn't see it as a competitor, even though he knew that both his series and Spelling's were hour-long dramas and that NBC had, at most, openings for four new dramas. Bruce Paltrow felt he and his team were golden. Never for a moment did he think that *Tattinger's* would flop.

Spelling, on the other hand, no longer felt golden. He is a natural worrier—during May Decision Week he traditionally took to bed, ill with fright that ABC might reject a series. Spelling worried that *Nightingales* would be rejected. And despite the obvious differences between the two projects, Spelling worried that *Nightingales* and *Tattinger's* might collide. "Our two shows, I fear, are competing," he said, more presciently than he knew.

21

TABLOID TV

Brandon Tartikoff was merely joining a parade when he decided to do *Nightingales.* As competition for viewers had intensified, Rupert Murdoch's Twentieth Century Fox was among the first to transfer to television the sex and violence that sold copies of Murdoch's *National Star* and *New York Post.* Since its debut in the fall of 1987, Fox was a ratings winner with *A Current Affair,* which featured lurid accounts of true crimes and other sensational material. In addition to *A Current Affair,* Fox introduced *America's Most Wanted,* a popular series about actual fugitives, some of whom were apprehended as a result of the show. Tabloid TV, as it was called, was hot. Audiences flocked to syndicated talk shows hosted by Oprah Winfrey, Phil Donahue, and Geraldo Rivera, which tantalized viewers by offering interviews with witches, bigamists, bigots, male strippers, child molesters—what critics dubbed the Freaks of the Week.

Everywhere there was evidence—despite the Reagan Revolution's much ballyhooed return to "traditional values"—of relaxed sexual standards. Calvin Klein and other advertisers flaunted sex to sell jeans. Men no longer wore shirts on daytime soap operas, and beds became a favorite prop. The dimple displayed by the Cosmopolitan girl was no longer on her chin. And even family-oriented sitcoms featured dialogue that just a few years before would have been scrubbed clean. "Do you use any protection?" asked the teenage girl from under the sheets on NBC's *Valerie,* whose 8:30 P.M. time slot meant it was targeted at kids.

NBC News joined the parade when it presented a one-hour prime-time special, *Scared Sexless,* on December 30, 1987. Hosted by correspondent Connie Chung, *Scared Sexless* did something no network news documentary on defense or race relations or any other serious topic had done in a long time—it magnetized an audience. Nearly a third of the viewing public watched it, as the special achieved an astonishing 30 share and a 17.5 rating. On her quick tour of the subject, Chung peeked in on singles bars, on gay sex and AIDS, on unwanted pregnancies; she listened in on sex education classes and interviewed such "experts" on sex as actors Alan Alda and Goldie Hawn, as well as Los Angeles Raiders running back Marcus Allen.

To escape the "boring" tag viewers sometimes pin on serious news, NBC billed *Scared Sexless* as a "special," rather than as a "news documentary." Bob Wright, who had tried and failed to persuade News president Larry Grossman to use actors like Don Johnson to host news documentaries, was thrilled by the ratings *Scared Sexless* drew. For the first time in Larry Grossman's memory, Wright actually praised a News product, dispatching letters of congratulations to correspondent Chung and her producers.

Many within NBC News sensed a line had been crossed. Network news, like newspapers themselves, had always flirted with entertainment as opposed to news values. Network news flaunted graphics and music and too rarely permitted people to complete a sentence. They cluttered the morning news shows with celebrity interviews, and when the network did a cutaway at a ball game or a supermarket counter they tried to linger on a pretty face. Newspapers also offered screaming headlines and conflict and gossip. But at heart, a network newscast, like most newspapers, took its news obligations seriously. Traditionally, when a network did a one-hour documentary—be it on Nixon's first one hundred days or India—it took a weighty subject and explored it soberly, expecting a low rating. True, News did offer such ratings pleasers as a tour of the White House hosted by Jackie Kennedy. But these were not the rule. Because *Scared Sexless* was designed less to explore the subject of sex than to tease an audience, many journalists agreed with a ranking NBC News executive who found the Chung special "really embarrassing."

But *Scared Sexless* supplied the ratings now demanded from News. Larry Grossman had made a Faustian bargain, the same one his hero, Edward R. Murrow, had made when he hosted the celebrity-oriented *Person to Person* in order to help fund CBS News's hard-hitting *See It Now* documentaries; the same bargain network news made in 1989 when they used actors to re-create scenes. ABC News, which later apologized and vowed it would not happen again, used actors on *World News Tonight* when there were no pictures of alleged Soviet spy Felix Block. NBC and CBS, on the other hand, would regularly and unapologetically use actors to re-create scenes on such news magazine shows as *Yesterday, Today and Tomorrow* (NBC) and Connie Chung specials (CBS). Re-creations or docudramas were also not new to the networks—in the fifties the late John Houseman produced *Seven Lively Arts* for CBS, which often devoted its full hour to dramatizations of historical events and featured actors such as Jason Robards. But these were either done for the entertainment division and did not bear the stamp and credibility of News; or fell under the auspices of News, in which case the subjects were historical, the participants usually dead, and thus the docudrama was not a substitute for reporting, blurring the distinction between fact and fiction.

Within a week of the *Scared Sexless* telecast, Larry Grossman announced that NBC News would soon offer specials on such eye-popping subjects as *Women Behind Bars, American Men in the 80s,* and *Stress.* The specials, the NBC News press release emphasized, would "highlight the life-styles of various individuals." Sandwiched between were some sober documentaries on the homeless and on Islam, to be hosted by Tom Brokaw, but these were not to be the thrust of NBC News's documentaries. Over the next three years, the traditional barriers between news and entertainment would continue to collapse.

Preoccupied with profits, Wright and Welch invited Sid Feders, who produced *Scared Sexless,* to lunch. Only at the last minute did they think to invite Grossman, Feders's boss.

Behind *Scared Sexless,* behind tabloid TV and syndicated *Titanic* specials, crouched a dirty little secret: Viewers were bored. They craved excitement. Their attention span had shrunk. Increasingly, programmers assumed the only way to keep their attention was with surprise or shock. The sense spread throughout the industry that sock-em-in-the-nose novelty was the way to trap viewers. *Nightingales* would be novel because *Charlie's Angels* had been off the air for nearly a decade. Just as ABC's *Roseanne* or Fox's *The Simpsons* would offer even more oddball families than *The Honeymooners* or *All in the Family.* Just as sending the *Today* show, *Good Morning America,* or the three anchors on the road might electrify viewers with a sense of immediacy, of something different. Novel news specials would, it was hoped, liberate the news divisions from corporate pressure to reduce losses.

By jumping aboard the tabloid TV bandwagon, NBC News was sliding down the slope Neil Postman, in his book *The Disappearance of Childhood,* ascribed not to the malevolence of TV executives but to something more banal, something that had started long before Bob Wright, Larry Tisch, or Tom Murphy appeared on the scene. Television, Postman wrote, "requires a continuous supply of novel and interesting information to engage and hold" an audience. Television has a constant need for material. "The bias and therefore the business of television is to move information, not collect it." Unlike print, television "cannot dwell" on a subject. "There may, for example, be fifty books on the history of Argentina, five hundred on childhood, five thousand on the Civil War. If television has anything to do with these subjects, it will do it once, and then move on."

22

ABC, NBC, AND CBS TAKE DIFFERENT ROUTES, 1988

The new owners had streamlined and pared costs, but by early 1988, two years after they had taken over, the networks had not recaptured lost viewers. In the war with the small but mobile armies of the new video democracy, the networks were being outflanked. In 1988 alone, the three network share of the prime-time audience would drop to 68 percent—compared to 92 percent in 1976; the number of channels available to the average home increased in a single year from twenty-two to twenty-eight, four times as many as were available in 1976; cable television entered 2.4 percent more homes, now reaching 51.1 percent of Americans, compared to just 15 percent in 1976.

The new owners could not keep the combined profits of the three networks from shrinking. No matter Brandon Tartikoff's brilliance, or the weapons each network mustered—big-event sports programming, miniseries, Steven Bochco, Dolly Parton—the loss of network viewers would be irreversible. By 1991, the three-network share of viewers would fall to nearly 60 percent; six out of ten homes would be wired for cable, and a VCR would be in nearly three out of four homes. The day-to-day preoccupation with overnight ratings, with the internal battle between ABC, CBS, and NBC, often diverted attention from this more momentous external battle between the Big Three and the Little Twenty-Eight—or 150—channels.

The new owners were more mindful of the external threat than their predecessors had been, but the ground was shifting under their feet, and each would be humbled by this strange new world. Among the three, by early 1988 ABC was clearly the best managed and the most pleasant place to work, and thrived with eight mighty TV stations and potent cable and publishing investments. Gradually ABC was gaining in the ratings, though NBC continued to hold a sizeable lead. Despite record profits, many NBC employees were dispirited, feeling they were robbed of the right to enjoy hard-won victories. While each network news division had difficulty adjusting to the new order, only NBC would provide anything like the spectacle of News president Larry Grossman's murder—or was it suicide? Of the three networks, NBC was the most aggressive about changing the old culture, about seeking deals or alliances to yield fresh revenues. Like ABC, NBC envisioned itself as a worldwide communications colossus. CBS headed in a different direction, shedding its varied communications assets to concentrate on broadcasting. Nevertheless, for the first time ever, CBS dropped into third place in 1988. Its morale was low, its strategy unclear, its affiliates restive, its anchor volatile, its leadership uncertain.

As 1988 began, Tom Murphy saw too little evidence of programming progress at ABC. He had given his pal, Brandon Stoddard, everything he had asked for, from miniseries money to Dolly Parton. Yet ABC's prime-time ratings languished. Of the eight new weekly ABC programs Stoddard had introduced in the fall of 1987, none was a hit and only two—*thirtysomething* and *Hooperman*—seemed to have a shot at a second season. Cost overruns and turmoil beset *Dolly,* and continued to beset *Moonlighting*. Tom Murphy was frustrated, the more so because he had fallen under the spell of Mike Dann, who told him Brandon Stoddard was screwing up.

Mike Dann served as a kind of private tutor to the programming neophytes from Cap Cities. Murphy and Burke listened when the sixty-seven-year-old Dann talked because he had done it all in network television. Beginning in 1948, for ten years Dann had held a variety of jobs at NBC, including Entertainment head under General Sarnoff. In his next incarnation, Dann spent fifteen years at CBS, where he wound up running the entertainment division for William Paley. After leaving CBS in the early seventies, Dann set up shop as a television programming consultant, and his clients included ABC Video Enterprises. Already on the payroll and in the ABC building when Cap Cities arrived, and because he impressed Murphy with his reservoir of knowledge, Dann began tutoring Murphy in September 1987.

Dann was not shy. He immodestly considered Tartikoff as good a scheduler as he once was, and declared that Stoddard and his principal scheduler, Ted Harbert, were in over their heads against Tartikoff. By January 1, 1988, Dann was not alone in this opinion. "There is a malaise around the building," said one despondent executive. "We're a beleaguered ABC. Third place seems permanent." Stoddard had been given near total freedom for two years, and ABC was still mired in the cellar. No longer was it just Aaron Spelling complaining that Brandon Stoddard was an elitist snob. ABC president John Sias grumbled that Stoddard paid too little heed to daytime and late-night programming, which made no sense since "We make no money on prime time." Disney chairman Michael Eisner said he had warned Stoddard at least twenty times that he was unhappy with the promotion done for his 7 P.M. *Disney Sunday Movie.* So when ABC's option on the Disney show lapsed at the end of 1987—Stoddard told Tom Murphy he was unaware that it had—Eisner jumped to NBC.

A pattern was forming in the collective mind of Murphy & Burke about their once sainted programmer. For two years they were bemused when Stoddard boasted, "you're talking to a guy who has no sense of numbers whatsoever." Although they had never been happy with Stoddard's managerial skills, they had been convinced he had a magic programming touch. No longer. Stoddard and his team "are ignorant of the business consequences of what they do," complained Dan Burke. "At some point you've got to introduce a business element and budget."

What finally convinced Murphy and Burke that Stoddard needed help was Stoddard's decision to schedule a two-hour pilot of *China Beach* after the 1988 Super Bowl, perhaps the most desirable launching pad for any new show. This series about nurses in Vietnam was too earnest and had too much female appeal to follow the mostly male Super Bowl audience. What ABC needed after the Super Bowl, Mike Dann argued, was a half-hour comedy, not a drama that wouldn't start till about 10:30 P.M. and wouldn't end until after midnight, long after the mass audience had gone to bed. Plus, Murphy knew, a two-hour *China Beach* would inflame affiliates, since it would eradicate the late local news.

When Murphy learned that Sias knew nothing of Stoddard's decision, he exploded and told him to order Stoddard to replace *China Beach* with a new half-hour comedy, *The Wonder Years.* Stoddard, who reported to Sias only on paper, at first resisted. "Brandon was almost fired over *China Beach* because he didn't talk to anyone first and because he was obstinate," said one ABC executive. "At the same time, Dann was buzzing in Murphy's ear."

Tom Murphy had been in charge of ABC for two years, but this was the first time he had overruled Stoddard. At first he admitted he was "intimidated" by programming. For the first two years after the merger, Murphy spent about half the day at his Cap Cities brownstone on East Fifty-first Street. In January 1988, all that changed. From then on Murphy spent all his time at ABC's offices. Now he wished he had followed his own instincts and stayed with *Our World,* wished he had left *20/20* on Thursday night, wished he had rejected the miniseries *Amerika* and the extravagant *War and Remembrance.* After two years, said Murphy, "I declared myself a veteran. For better or worse, it's my football."

Grabbing the ball, Murphy consulted with Stoddard and together they made a series of midseason programming and scheduling changes. Some of the moves worked. By February, ABC's prime-time schedule had begun to perk up. *The Wonder Years* reached forty million viewers after *Super Bowl XXII* and was placed on ABC's schedule, where it thrived. Murphy was more assertive, but his relationship with Stoddard, whom he liked and found to be a man of character and wit, remained solid. Never once did Murphy disparage Stoddard to Dann or others, as, say, Bill Paley openly disparaged his executives, or as Larry Tisch, Bob Wright, and Jack Welch sometimes did.

ABC's ascent continued in February with the Winter Olympics in Calgary, Canada. These games not only propelled ABC into second place in the prime-time ratings, they also gave Cap Cities renewed appreciation for showmanship in general and for Roone Arledge in particular. Arledge, who invented modern Olympics coverage, produced these games along with director Roger Goodman from the control room in Calgary. Dan Burke was in attendance most nights, and Tom Murphy on several. They marveled as Arledge commanded camera positions, created heroes and suspense, juggled live events with tape, and transformed potential tedium into drama. "I was in awe of what they did," said Murphy. As Murphy and Burke learned that crafting a schedule was not a science, so they learned that producing and orchestrating what gets on the air could be an art. Throughout the organization a sense spread that Murphy and Burke were coming to think less about costs and more about the magic of television. "The Cap Cities people went up to Calgary and saw what a network does," said Mike Mallardi. "They came away with a real appreciation."

More good news arrived in March when Ted Koppel, who had been working without a contract for a while, agreed to remain at ABC. What was unusual about the new arrangement with Koppel was that the contract was with his production company. The newsman would continue to anchor *Nightline,* would produce at least four prime-time specials for ABC, and would even be free to sell up to three documentaries a year to competitors if ABC passed on them. What was remarkable, given Cap Cities' indifference to losing David Hartman and its refusal to make Peter Jennings managing editor, was that it now allowed Koppel to sell his own product, to select his own subjects. Koppel had become his own boss. Whatever the precedent-setting perils of this agreement, there was rejoicing that Koppel would remain at ABC.

There was also rejoicing over Peter Jennings. With a new executive producer, Paul Friedman, the anchor had relaxed. "We're having a good time. We get along well," said Jennings. He told of how he deferred to Friedman on the selection of a story and after it ran walked into Friedman's office and said, "The piece was tacky."

"You're wrong," Friedman responded simply.

Instead of triggering a war, Jennings laughed and left. "I trusted his judgment," said Jennings. The producer and the anchor now regularly reviewed the day's stories. "It has been such a pleasure working with the man," Friedman said a month after taking the job. What others saw in Jennings as capriciousness Friedman saw as the perfectionism of a man of "high standards." Roone Arledge and David Burke were ecstatic with the new, relaxed Jennings. "It's like night and day," said David Burke. "It manifests itself on the screen. He's more vibrant. More importantly, every conversation with Peter is not a confrontation. It's a conversation." Viewers obviously noticed something, for in February Jennings began occasionally to edge into first place in the weekly ratings race, a pattern that would solidify into a permanent lead beginning in 1989.

The entire network seemed exuberant. ABC Sales was, by March, bullish about the various series Stoddard had in development, particularly an oddball comedy about a mom who can't stand her kids starring comedienne Roseanne Barr. Sales was excited about selling Jennings and Koppel, about the prospects of ending the season in May in second place. Sales knew that the battle was as much psychological as real. "Our market is all emotional," admitted George Cain of Sales.

Intangibles, as Cain suggested and Tom Murphy was learning, mattered, because feelings often become facts. Using Cap Cities' traditional dollars-and-cents scorecard, ABC had a paper loss of $100 million on the Winter Olympics. But a P&L statement did not account for the ratings boost enjoyed by the eight owned ABC stations, which generated an extra $19 million. Nor did it count the promotional value of the Olympics, which allowed ABC to showcase new programs. Nor could it count goodwill. How to calculate the worth of transporting a total of 1,200 advertisers to Calgary, of treating each to free room, board, transit, and three hundred dollars' worth of custom-fitted cowboy boots and hats? If the Olympics nudged ABC into second place in the season's rating race, the sales department would gain a psychological edge over advertisers, which would translate into an economic advantage since ABC could then charge a premium for spots on the number-two network.

Therefore it mattered to ABC when, at the end of April, their network bested CBS and took second place in the prime-time contest. Logic suggested that too much should not be made of this number-two finish, since without a boost from the Winter Olympics, World Series, and Super Bowl, ABC's regular series programming would have finished third. But network psychology often had less to do with logic than feelings. People at ABC brushed aside the unpleasant information that during this 1987–88 season all three networks lost viewers. They brushed aside Ted Turner's March announcement that he and the major cable operators would in October 1988 inaugurate Turner Network Television (TNT), offering to cable channels sitcoms, made-for-TV movies, and miniseries, as well as film classics from the 3,300 movies in the MGM/UA library Turner had acquired in 1986. And the new network would be given to subscribers as part of their basic cable package rather than as a service—like HBO or Showtime—viewers had to pay extra for. No one at ABC Sales expected that Turner would steal their advertising dollars, certainly not right away. And, Sales assured themselves, they were safe because there were already more than sixty cable networks competing for openings on cable boxes that had space for only thirty-five or so channels.

In the spring of 1988, what ABC was able to sell advertisers, affiliates, the press, the Hollywood community—and itself—was that in the traditional three-network competition CBS, not ABC, was number three. Inevitably, the new network owners, like the old, sometimes looked away from the external threat, became caught up in the exhilarating daily ratings battle. "It's a business tailor-made for competitive human beings," observed Dan Burke. "Just think about it: You get a little fix every morning when the national overnights come in at 8:30. . . . On Saturday and Sunday there's a recording you can call in our research department to get the overnights. You can't go a Saturday and Sunday without a fix!"

In the three-network competition, ABC was gaining. Compared to

NBC and CBS, ABC had suffered the smallest audience declines during the 1987–88 season. Unlike CBS, its schedule was not dominated by aging shows—the average life of its series was two years, compared to just over six for CBS. And ABC was a strong number two in its demographics, with more youth and urban appeal than CBS had. With shows like *China Beach, The Wonder Years, Moonlighting,* and *thirtysomething,* ABC was doing distinctive television. And with its lineup of Tuesday, Wednesday, and Friday 8:00 comedies, ABC had the table setters to entice viewers on several nights. ABC now had more top thirty shows than CBS. And even with eroding audiences, the stakes remained huge. A series ranking in the top third of one hundred Nielsen-rated shows would, over the course of the two showings a network was licensed to run, earn from three to six times what the studio was paid in license fees. A series that landed in the middle third of the ratings about broke even. "The bottom one-third," said Dan Burke, "is where you lose your ass." Of the three networks, in 1988 CBS had the most shows in the bottom third.

The gloom that attached itself to ABC's schedule earlier in the winter had lifted by late spring. When the schedule began to click and the new one for the fall was set and greeted with enthusiasm by the advertising community, "all of a sudden people's frustrations with each other got better," said Dan Burke. By May Tom Murphy could appear before the annual meeting of Cap Cities/ABC shareholders and boast of the "progress" made on the prime-time programming front.

The enthusiasm was palpable at the annual ABC affiliates meeting in Los Angeles in June. Instead of grumbling, as they had in prior years, general managers relaxed, enjoyed mingling at dinner with Burt Reynolds, Julie Andrews, and Debbie Allen. Even at the business meeting on the last day of the confab, not one grenade was hurled at Sias, Murphy, or Burke. When ABC pushed a joint task force to study future issues, including reduced compensation, the stations went along. It was a lovefeast. Even the ever-guarded David Burke joined in, noting the way Murphy and Burke now managed to make people feel good. The change reminded David Burke of when he served as chief of staff to New York governor Hugh Carey: "The first two years he was in a panic—'What if I fail?' In year three and four he said, 'I'm not going to fail.' " Now in Cap Cities' third year as ABC's parent, David Burke, much later than most old hands, had the feeling that "the siege is broken."

With affiliates sold on the prime-time schedule, ABC's immediate task was to sell advertisers. In June, before the summer upfront sales effort, advertisers prepare their analyses and guesses concerning each network's prime-time schedule. The guesses are crucial, for they place a value on each show. It is these estimates that help the advertiser determine both a price for a series and which shows are likely to reach denture users or potato chip munchers. By estimating the share of audience reached, the agencies also establish the minimum audience guarantee the advertiser will demand from the network; if the series dips below the guarantee, the network must offer free ads, called "make goods." In the negotiations between buyer and seller, these estimates are closely guarded secrets, for if an advertiser values Aaron Spelling's *Heartbeat* at a higher share than ABC does, he overpays; if ABC guesses *Moonlighting* will do a 28 share and it does a 30 share, the network undercharges.

The McCann-Erickson analysis was fairly typical. Joel M. Segal, McCann's executive vice president, summoned his ad agency team to a conference room to estimate how each network series would fare. The stakes were significant, for the agency would expend $250 million of its clients' advertising dollars in the upfront market. "Let's start with Monday at 8:00," Segal announced to the two dozen or so media buyers and researchers, most of them in their twenties. Together they reviewed the shares and ratings for each night in the season just concluded, talked about the age of a series, its demographic track record, its lead-ins, the competition on the other networks. Whatever the facts, Segal and his team were judging a new series based on a single pilot. Some, like Segal, watched each pilot in the spring but little television the remainder of the year. After more than thirty years in advertising, Segal relied on hunches.

He assumed, on the basis of a hunch, that the average share points among the three networks would be 68 at the start of Monday evening. Which meant that 32 percent of the viewers were watching something else. When they discussed *Who's the Boss?* on Tuesday at 8 P.M., several of the buyers wanted to lower its estimated shares from 34 to 33 because they liked a new CBS entry, *TV 101*. "Why?" asked Segal, who noted that *Who's the Boss?* showed no Nielsen evidence of "tiring." Nor was it clear, he said, that the CBS series would appeal to the younger viewers watching *Who's the Boss?*.

In the end, Segal would concede that since Grant Tinker's studio was producing *TV 101* maybe they should boost its share and lower *Who's the Boss?* to a 32 share, which they did. Segal guessed, correctly it turned out, that viewers "are mad at *Moonlighting*" because of too few original episodes and that it would slip; he guessed, incorrectly, that a new series, *Roseanne,* would do less well (a 28 share) than another comedy, *Growing Pains.* Although this process qualifies as neither science nor art, it happens that the differences between McCann-Erickson's estimates and ABC's were marginal. Of the twenty-two prime-time hours, the only series Segal's group pegged to do better than what the network was willing to guarantee was Spelling's *Heartbeat* on Thursday at 10 P.M. Segal guessed it would attract 18 to 19 percent of viewers, and ABC guessed 17.

For ad executives like Joel Segal, the next step in June was to collect advertising budgets from his clients. For ABC Sales, the next step was to gauge how much advertisers might spend upfront, how much NBC and CBS might charge, and then to formalize ABC's final strategy. Much of what each would do in the coming weeks was what Jake Keever called "psychological warfare." ABC Sales promoted the network's second-place finish in the ratings race; advertisers countered that without sporting events, ABC would have been third. The ad agencies leaked word to the press that they expected to spend little, thus hoping to depress network prices; the network leaked word of growing demand, hoping to provoke a stampede. "The upfront market is the Information Age equivalent of a Middle Eastern souk," wrote Randall Rothenberg in *The New York Times.* "The networks demand impossible prices and the ad agencies complain to the networks about lackluster programming and audience fragmentation." In the end, decisions are made based on intangibles—*feelings.*

While feelings were always a factor, some facts complicated the advertising/network marketplace. The mix of advertising dollars spent on television had changed. In 1980, $81 billion was spent marketing products and services in the U.S., of which 40 percent, or $32 billion, was earmarked for advertising and the rest for sales promotion, which included direct mail, billboards, store posters, giveaways. Back then, of the money spent on advertising, just over $8 billion went for television, with 6 out of every 10 TV dollars going to the networks. Seven years later, the total dollars spent on marketing had doubled. While TV spending jumped to nearly $18 billion, the share of dollars going to the networks declined from $6 to $5 out of every $10 spent on TV. Cable, the Fox network, and other independent TV stations and syndicators, not to mention the affiliated stations, now siphoned the extra dollars.

Another factor adding to the uncertainty within ABC Sales was the new people meter rating system, introduced the previous September.

Both buyer and seller were still unsure of its accuracy, the more so since one of two rivals to Nielsen in the ratings measurement business —AGB Television Research—measured the same shows and got different results. One of the rating systems had to be wrong, though there was no way of knowing which. (Nor was anyone likely to find out. Since cost-conscious ABC and NBC were reluctant to pay for three ratings services, the upstart AGB went out of business in the summer of 1988, leaving the field to the dominant Nielsen service and to Arbitron.) More uncertainty was added by the Hollywood writers strike, now entering its fifth month, which threatened the start—and quality—of the fall season. Without original episodes the network would have to air repeats, which attract smaller audiences and lower prices.

On top of all this, the advertising business was reeling from its own shocks. The two years between 1987 and 1988 saw a rash of ad agency mergers. Would merged agencies spend less? Or would clients, dubious about the loyalty of worldwide agencies that sometimes represented two or more competitors, pour more dollars into direct marketing? Could this be the year, people at the three networks wondered, when advertisers finally revolt and refuse to pay more to reach a smaller audience?

Dan Burke was gloomy about network sales. "The tone of the market today is significantly worse than last year," Burke said in June. ABC, which had sold $985 million worth of advertising in the 1987 upfront market, expected to sell only about $800 million in the 1988 upfront.

But so far this was just a *feeling,* and could be overcome by other *feelings.* The upfront begins "almost like witchcraft," said Joel Segal in early July. "It's a feeling in the air." The "feeling" started to come over people on July 7. The upfront began, and was over, within days. It was the fastest upfront in memory. "It was almost a stampede," said ABC Sales's Robert Wallen. "I honestly don't know why."

Nor did people at ABC quite know why upfront sales exceeded expectations, though they offered a guess. With no end in sight to the Writers Guild of America's strike, they guessed that advertisers opted for the security of the guaranteed rating the network offered in the upfront but not in the year-round scatter market. Perhaps. In any case, while the networks vie to create a stampede, they don't always control the result. Instead of selling 75 to 78 percent of its inventory upfront, ABC decided to placate its customers and sold nearly 90 percent.

In all, the three networks took a total of $3.4 billion in upfront prime-time orders, with just over $1 billion going to ABC. Not only did 1988 turn out to be the largest dollar upfront ever, it was also one in which the networks were able to boost their prime-time cost per thousand between 5 and 10 percent, with CBS on the low end, NBC at the top, and ABC in the middle. The money collected by the networks rose more than anyone expected. Despite the continued erosion of network audiences, despite the rise of cable and other competitors, or the palpable buzz that perhaps the networks were dinosaurs, the three networks were in better shape in mid-1988 than they were when their ownership changed hands in 1986. ABC in particular seemed to have gathered new momentum in both Entertainment and News.

All of which suggested that in their negotiations with advertisers the networks came out better than they should have. Or as Irving A. Gross, who had been selling advertising at ABC for twenty years, said of his customers: "If they only held out until September, we'd panic. They have someplace else to go—Fox, cable, syndication. The networks have no place to go." The dread was that a day of reckoning lay ahead. Someday soon advertisers might discover that their *feelings* about the importance of displaying their products on the networks was out of sync with the *facts* of where viewers had gone.

By 1988, people at ABC seemed to be pulling in a single direction. But at NBC the cultural gap between new and old remained vast. Bob Wright had been on the job for nearly a year and a half and still seemed determined to bend NBC to his value system. Toward this end, he scheduled an all-day meeting of his president's council on February 5, 1988, to discuss NBC's future strategy. He circulated a memo from vice president Don Carswell asking each executive to imagine: *How would you run NBC in 1990 if we borrowed a substantial sum of money to take NBC private in a leveraged buyout?* Further, they were asked to imagine that in order to meet interest payments they had to slash $80 million in costs the first year and hold costs constant in year two. Carswell explained: "Wright is trying to make the point that if you own the business you run it differently than a business you don't own." Wright was still trying to get his team to think about the future as he envisioned it.

Wright's team thought more about the competition from ABC and CBS. As the date of the meeting approached, Grossman visited other executives to promote his own vision of the future. Working from a three-page, single-spaced memo he had drafted, the News president said NBC should "explore ownership in cable, global opportunities and aggressively engage in program production." But Grossman said this perfunctorily, for like his colleagues he believed broadcasting—the NBC network and its owned stations—was the *core business,* and not just because it delivered the bulk of NBC's profits. Unlike Wright or Welch, Grossman did not see cable or Fox or video cassettes as the competition. "I see virtually no prospect of achieving in our lifetime the earnings from cable, global initiatives or program and feature production that we are accustomed to getting from network broadcasting," Grossman's memo read. So he proposed what he called a "knock-out strategy," one that took advantage of NBC's total of $500 million in profits to "overpay," if necessary, to lock up every major sporting event, to chase "every major star and talent" in Hollywood in order to "force up the cost for the competition," to ally "with major broadcasters abroad," to build a "news delivery capacity that will outstrip ABC and CBS." Grossman's goal was to force ABC or CBS to get out of the network business. Larry Grossman had wanted Wright to spend more money on News in the fall of 1986; now he wanted him to spend more on the network itself.

When the council gathered in the fifty-third-floor former RCA boardroom on February 5, several senior executives expressed their belief in the core business and advanced the idea of a "knock-out strategy" before Wright cut them off. "I'm not sure what you mean by 'knock-out strategy,'" Wright snapped. "To talk about a 'knock-out strategy' implies that we're not doing things we should do. Everything Brandon has suggested we do we're doing." Wright said he objected to their constant chant about "the core business."

In turn, many NBC executives objected to Wright's constant talk of "new" business or "new" assumptions when the old business was prospering. Why did Wright keep referring to the networks as "a mature" business when NBC's profits outraced those of most companies within GE? Why did he object to identifying NBC's core business as the network? Before this meeting broke at 2 P.M., task forces were formed to prepare for a fuller discussion of "future" issues at NBC's April management retreat.

Wright was puzzled by all this—no other word would do—paranoia! *Am I not spending—and losing—money on News and Sports?* By his reckoning, too many executives at NBC were like those playwright John Osborne described as "people who look forward to the past." To Wright the core business was everything that appeared on a TV screen. It was immaterial whether the signal entered the home through a copper cable wire, or was bounced off a local station's antenna and transmitted over the air, or was relayed from satellites to rooftop dishes. To Wright, it all boiled down to one issue. He had a product to sell, and cable was another way to sell it. That was Wright's intellect speaking.

Perhaps Wright's emotions were engaged in a more complicated way. Maybe Wright talked less about the core business "because he knows less about the core business than we do," observed Don Carswell. "He talks about things outside that he knows a lot more about than we do." Or perhaps Wright talked more about *tomorrow* because he wanted to get away from Grant Tinker's *yesterday*. Many of Wright's colleagues believed he wanted to break from the past, separate himself from Tinker.

As he rode the elevator alone with Wright after the meeting, Communications chief Bud Rukeyser told his boss the session had ended badly. "The truth is we're all confused by your attitude toward the core business. We feel you're only interested in futures."

Wright demurred but finally said, "Since there's so much confusion, maybe I ought to call everyone together again and clarify this." To reassure executives, he scheduled another meeting in the boardroom that very afternoon at 4 P.M. Wright felt no sense of defeat in doing this. Progress was slower than he would have liked, but no one was any longer debating, as they had done a year before, whether NBC should do business with cable. Now the debate was over whether he believed in the future of broadcasting.

In a confidential report that reached Wright's desk around this time, Noel M. Tichy, who was on leave from the University of Michigan's Graduate School of Business and who joined GE in 1985 to head its management education operation at Crotonville, observed in a written report in December 1987 that NBC's culture was "in transition" but was nonetheless resistant to GE and its values. "For the most part, deep ambivalence reflects the feeling about change. The further down in the organization the less felt need for change." Employees didn't understand why a network that was doing so well should be asked to act as if it were troubled. They bridled at the "harshness" and "toughness" of GE, didn't understand why being number one or number two was such an important GE value, why "change" was *good* and "stability" *bad*. Wright needed to better articulate to the organization "why change is needed." He should get more NBC employees to visit GE's Crotonville training center to be exposed to GE values. And he should do a better job, Tichy wrote, of "communicating" his vision.

Communication became a buzzword around the corridors of NBC late that winter. Prompted by McKinsey's probe of the news division, Grossman had begun a series of meetings—dubbed "the Group of 24" —inviting a disparate group of twenty-four correspondents, field producers, writers, bureau chiefs, engineers, and cameramen from all over the world to meet and discuss their feelings. Starting on March 1, 1988, the second Group of 24 was invited to New York for three days of intense discussions about how News should be managed. Determined to improve internal communications, Bob Wright agreed to meet with them.

His chair in the sixty-fourth-floor conference room was circled by a horseshoe-shaped table. It was not meant to appear so, but it was as if the blue-suited Wright were the defendant and the Group of 24 the jury. For the next hour they questioned Wright, seeking reassurance. "What is your vision of the news division in 1995?" asked one NBC journalist.

"My sense is we'll have a more cooperative affiliate/network relationship," said Wright. "The interrelationships won't be as stiff as today. . . . I don't know whether our correspondents will be associated with local stations. But there will be more integration of local and network."

This upset people, for network news made sharp distinctions between its product and that of the local stations. Most of us "think of ourselves as a Mercedes" versus "the Chevrolets of local news," declared another member of the Group of 24.

NBC's surveys indicated that viewers can tell the difference between a local and a network newscast, said Wright matter-of-factly. Rather than seeking to mollify or to compliment—he seemed almost incapable of doing that, as if it would be a signal to relax—Wright said, "I think the distinction is one of experience." But, he was quick to add, the old distinctions were dissolving. No longer does the network alone cover breaking national or international stories. "That's where technology has not been our friend," said Wright. With satellites and network feeds, stations can go anywhere.

After a time, Larry Grossman rose and said he'd like to ask the question on the minds of many in this room and throughout NBC News: "Is GE running NBC or is NBC running NBC?"

Grossman had obviously hit Wright's hot button, for suddenly NBC's president became animated. Wright sputtered about how there were 914 million outstanding shares of GE on the market, many of them owned by pension funds. "GE has a fiduciary management responsibility. As long as I'm here, NBC has to be sensitive to what GE shareholders think. We have here at NBC the most autonomy any public company could grant. The perception you have is that NBC is GE, and to a certain extent it is. We're not the Ford Foundation. . . . But ultimately, the company has got to recognize we are part of General Electric."

The audience heard, correctly, that Wright's obsession was "shareholder responsibility." News had traditionally worshipped another totem—the "public trust." A member of the group asked Wright: "Can you give us GE's view of News? Is it a public trust?"

"Well, it isn't a public trust. I can't understand that concept," said Wright, explaining that GE employees also had a public trust—to produce safe consumer products, for instance.

"What is it about the public trust concept that gives you trouble?" the journalist persisted.

"It doesn't tell me anything," said Wright. "The news product and news programs are very important. But does 'public trust' tell me we must put on 2.6 hours a day of news? How many hours a day does 'public trust' mean?" What the journalists wanted to hear from Wright was: *I believe NBC News has a responsibility to report the news honestly and fearlessly, no matter the cost.* But they heard nothing of the sort.

Wright, weeks later, would refer to this session as a "tough" meeting, one in which he felt the journalists were willing to discuss only part of their "public trust"—"We have promised people we will provide them special, accurate, and thorough information." But the other part—an agreement "to do all this in the context of a business" —they resisted.

The meeting left Larry Grossman unsettled. "For a group whose whole being is the 'public trust,'" the meeting was "a real culture shock," he said. "I don't know what their standards are," said one producer of Wright and GE. "I don't know whether they want me to go after the best possible story and do the best editing, or whether they want me to do it okay and cheap." That was the *feeling* within NBC News.

At the time, News had more concrete reasons to fret. Everyone in the news division had witnessed NBC's disappointing 9 share for its coverage of the New Hampshire primary. And everyone saw that NBC, like CBS and ABC, had scaled back prime-time coverage of the Iowa presidential caucuses in February, as well as the twenty primaries and caucuses held on "Super Tuesday" in March. They saw that News had less freedom to interrupt prime-time programs for breaking events, that documentaries were an endangered species—unless they were saucy hours like *Scared Sexless.* No longer did the network assign a correspondent, producer, and camera crew to each presidential candidate that year; instead, they dispatched a lone producer. "My fear is that in the future I'm an unaffordable commodity," said Ken Bode, NBC's premier political reporter, who would quit the network after this campaign.

The broader fear within News was that the cost cutting wouldn't stop. "If this were the end of the cutbacks, we could live with it," observed Cheryl A. Gould, senior producer of *Nightly News.* "I welcome the challenge of having to think more creatively about how we conduct our business. My worry is that it's not going to stop here. I don't know where the process ends."

On the last of their three days in New York, Grossman sensed that he had to counter the despair among the Group of 24, and so he joined them in a private room at Bellini's restaurant for dinner. It was Boots and Larry Grossman's wedding anniversary, but these people had come from all over the country and from as far away as Rome, Frankfurt, London, and Grossman thought he should attend to tell them they were terrific.

This very decent man was in deeper trouble than he knew. Larry Grossman had no idea that two key members of his team—Brokaw and Ross—were discreetly searching to find his successor. Grossman didn't know that Brokaw was urging the GE chairman and Wright to stay Grossman's execution until the end of 1988 so as not to disrupt NBC News in the thick of a presidential contest.

All Grossman knew for sure was that NBC News was no longer golden. "What used to be a spoiled child has been reduced to a stepchild," Grossman said. "Everybody's going to have to learn how to live with GE. And GE's going to have to learn to live with NBC. I suppose I'm the litmus test. For two years I've had a difficult time."

Grossman had to think about a presentation he would make to Wright and Welch on the morning of March 4. He was to reveal how the news division would incorporate the McKinsey recommendations, curb costs, achieve a break-even budget by 1990. Grossman usually relied on deputies to present his budgets. This time he was determined to prove his own proficiency. This would be his first budget audience with the chairman of GE since their November 1986 summit. To be sure he was properly prepped, Grossman conducted dress rehearsals.

At 9 A.M. on March 4, Grossman and his staff were joined by Welch, Wright, finance chief Al Barber, Personnel head Ed Scanlon, and John Stewart of McKinsey. They fanned about the round table that dominated Grossman's gray-carpeted office. Welch peeled off his jacket, and everyone else followed suit. "Okay, let's get down to business," he said. The meeting would stretch over three hours, and Welch was stunned by a new Larry Grossman. Gone, said one participant, was "the aura of the intellectual," replaced by "an account executive." Working from a twenty-page budget packet distributed to everyone in the room, Grossman went through his budget plan in great detail. The News budget, he said, would dip from $257.8 million in 1987 to $245.9 million this year, and down to $237 million by 1990, when they would, he was happy to report, break even. News would have to do three things: boost revenues; make sharp cost reductions; and exclude from the accounting the $40 million the network charged to News as its share of corporate expenses. Since personnel costs represented three-quarters of the News budget, the staff would be hardest hit. Employment in News would drop from a high of 1,362 in 1986 to 1,000 in 1990. News would eliminate all twenty-four NABET desk assistants, shrink the pool of correspondents from 79 to 59, cut producers from 312 to 219, slice nearly a third of its 143-person foreign bureaus, and rely more on foreign news services like Visnews.

"This is very good," the usually impatient Welch would say more than once.

"We learned from McKinsey the importance of strong management," said Grossman. Of the 5,900 stories NBC News taped in 1987, he said, roughly half were planned stories with a long lead time. While almost all the breaking stories got on the air, only about two-thirds of these planned stories did, yet they consumed 75 percent of News personnel's time. In the future, said Grossman, they had to manage and track these better. They would rely more on NBC stations to cover domestic news.

Welch couldn't believe what he was hearing. Larry Grossman sounded like a convert! He even heard Grossman say the protective wall between News and other divisions should be lowered. News hoped, Grossman said, to coproduce with Entertainment and Sports a ninety-minute magazine show. And to those who said news programs should be held to a much lower Nielsen rating standard, Grossman dissented: "We would never tolerate a *West 57th* or *48 Hours.* We would never tolerate anything less than an 18 share!" Nor would

News shirk new business opportunities—in programming for cable, in selling programs overseas, in packaging news programs for the syndication market, in making and selling news video cassettes.

"This is a terrific job," Welch announced when Grossman had finished. "You've got a lot to be proud of. You're on your way."

As Welch rose to leave, Grossman interrupted. "One last thing, Jack," he said. "There's not a person in the place who believes GE cares about News. And since we bought into your priorities, it's important you buy into ours." He wanted some recognition of the good job NBC News had done in snaring the Gorbachev interview and the debate among the presidential contenders. He wanted Welch to make a statement extolling NBC News.

"I have no problem with that," Welch responded. "I'll be honest, I did until I saw this. . . . I know what you guys accomplished—the debate, Gorbachev. But without this"—he tapped the twenty-page document—"Gorbachev is hogwash!"

"Jack, when we started with McKinsey," interjected Grossman's deputy, Tim Russert, "most people in the news division thought this"—he, too, tapped the document—"was hogwash and thought what mattered were debates and Gorbachev and other journalistic pursuits. But now people accept the fact that to be fiscally responsible is part of the challenge of fulfilling their journalistic responsibility."

"Nice, nice," said Welch.

"That's a very important point," said John Stewart of McKinsey, who as usual said little. "What we have here, Jack, are two religions"—he put his hands together—"which have come together. They showed some respect for your religion. It's time you showed some respect for theirs."

"This is a terrific job," said Welch, rising again. Welch was so pleased that, privately, he told Wright he was in "less of a hurry" to decide on Grossman's fate, though he shared Wright's sense that Grossman was not a galvanizing leader.

At last Welch had seen solid evidence that GE was imposing its cost-conscious, think-about-tomorrow culture on NBC. Never for a moment did he think of NBC as anything but a part of GE, one unit among many, offering "corporate added value" everyone could share. Jack Welch would drive home this point just hours after his March 4 morning meeting with Grossman and News. He had set aside the entire day for NBC. This afternoon Bob Wright would show him NBC's renovation plans for 30 Rock, including new studios and GE's New York offices. The vice president of NBC's facilities, Henry

Kanegsberg, unrolled for Welch a design sketch of the interior of the building and mentioned that still emblazoned near the top of 30 Rock were the letters *RCA,* a landmark on the New York skyline. Wright was going to change the name of the building from RCA to NBC.

Stop, Welch said. Since the building did not already bear the name NBC, he announced that he wanted it known as the *GE* building. It was, he would explain later, "a gut call," a choice of whether "to merchandise" a $3 billion company (NBC) or a $40 billion company (GE). The billboard space was too valuable to deny GE.

NBC employees felt even more like cogs in the GE wheel. Another shudder went through the company when GE decided for "synergy" and "efficiency" reasons to merge NBC's government relations office in Washington with GE's. How, people at NBC wondered, could the same lobbyist for GE's nuclear power efforts also lobby for the network? Would the GE lobbyist now promise a senator tickets to the Letterman show? An audience with NBC News, whose credibility depended on being perceived as disinterested? But Wright and Welch insisted on a merged lobbying office to marshal all its political forces to win support for regulatory changes.

The unhappiness at NBC was reflected in a survey conducted in February and March among 7,000 employees. Of the 5,400 responses, an astonishing 60 percent offered unsolicited written comments. Three out of four respondents said NBC was a "worse" place to work since GE became the corporate parent; only 2 percent said it was a "better" place. No doubt, a degree of employee unhappiness was inevitable in an industry whose foundations were trembling. GE's arrival coincided with these industry-wide changes. It was predictable that network employees would blame GE for an insecurity they would have felt anyway. Nor were the networks alone. Deregulation had also shattered the tranquility of the airline and telecommunications businesses. All across America, automation and the steady shift from blue- to white-collar jobs produced insecurity, which is why workers were often willing to accept contracts that sacrificed pay hikes for job guarantees.

Even so, the NBC survey was a rebuke to Bob Wright and GE. In spite of its ratings success and record profits, the survey revealed that NBC was a melancholy place to work. And why not? After all, wasn't Jack Welch trying to make employees feel less secure? Wasn't insecurity a natural result of constant "downsizing," layoffs, and poor communications? This was hardly a revelation, since a year earlier, at the March 1987 management meeting in Florida, there were furious complaints about inadequate internal dialogue. And just this past December, Noel Tichy's report described the anxiety employees felt. What was surprising was how little had been done to reassure people.

In the wake of the employee survey, Bob Wright moved fast. In a candid six-page April letter to all employees, he wrote, "You've spoken out loud and clear about your most pressing concerns and, I assure you, you have been heard. Our commitment now is to work on improving communication within our company." Wright said he was asking each department head to meet with employees to discuss the results and to begin a series of "work-out" sessions to provide two-way communication.

Few NBC employees were more despondent than Bud Rukeyser. RCA may have been hopelessly bureaucratic, but network employees had felt that they worked for NBC, not RCA. Rukeyser could not bear the thought of selling "the merchandising leverage" GE would gain by renaming the RCA building. He believed in "the core business" and felt Wright and Welch did not. He believed a pleasant work environment and patient leadership translated into success and felt NBC was a less happy place.

Wright was genuinely sorry to accept Rukeyser's resignation and awarded him a generous severance. Rukeyser felt liberated. "I'll never again have to go to a meeting with twenty people and talk about downsizing," he said. Within weeks of leaving NBC, he rejoined Grant Tinker as senior vice president of Tinker's fledgling studio.

With Rukeyser's resignation, Wright worried "about the appearance of a mass departure of executives." He had taken care to "spread out" executive departures. But with Rukeyser joining Bob Walsh, who had announced his resignation in December, and with a new head of Personnel and a new chief financial officer, Wright felt he had lost some flexibility. Perhaps now was the wrong time to replace Grossman.

By Spring, the mood at NBC had not yet appreciably changed but the tone from the top had. Mindful of the depressing employee survey results, in his opening remarks to the 150 or so people attending the annual management meeting in Scottsdale, Arizona, in April 1988, Bob Wright showered praise on nearly every division, including News. He emphasized that GE was not interested in selling NBC, for the network was "the principal reason" GE had acquired RCA. Nor, he said, is there a "group of people in Fairfield, Connecticut, who are busy planning the future of NBC. That's what I do. That's what you do."

Between golf and tennis, for the better part of three days NBC managers continued the hypothetical LBO discussion they had begun in February. Their tone had changed as well. Instead of talk about the "core business" and "knock-out" strategies, at this meeting the reports from the seven group leaders suggested there was much more willingness to acknowledge that the networks were "a mature" and even "a declining business." Few any longer challenged NBC's move into cable or other growth businesses. Suddenly NBC executives were tossing out ideas to effect change—to eliminate NBC's annual affiliate convention or to pare affiliate compensation; to induce the stations to share rising sports license fees; to sell NBC-owned stations in declining markets. Within the seven groups, a few executives even asked: Should the network get out of non-money-making businesses like Sports and News?

Jack Welch attended the retreat and was thrilled. When Bob Wright introduced him at the final session, the chairman rhapsodized about the new and "exciting way" his managers were now confronting reality. "You really do have the toughest job in the world in trying to change. Because you are trying to change when today feels so good. And I can sympathize with the people who filled out those forms in the attitude survey. . . . They read every day you're number one, they feel all these things and they say, 'What the hell is this about?' So you people in this room have one enormous challenge."

But as pleased as Welch was with the progress NBC had made, he wanted it understood there was no perfect antidote for employee anxiety. This was the marines, and theirs was an endless struggle to stay fit, poised for battle. Everywhere he went within GE, Welch said, he was always asked: "When will this end?" Welch paused, fixing his blue eyes on the NBC management team. "And the awful answer is never. . . . In the world of the eighties and the nineties it won't end."

At the end of the meeting, NBC executives were flying. They had gotten the applause they had earned. They had heard from Welch and Wright a pledge to "the core business" they had not heard before. Larry Grossman had heard, for the first time publicly, "a ringing endorsement" for News.

Meanwhile, Grossman had to cope with another controversy, one arising from the Phoenix retreat itself. Grossman had instructed vice president Tom Ross to use NBC News's regular electronic newsletter to report the complimentary things Welch and Wright had said about News. "But don't make it a puff piece," he cautioned Ross over the phone from Las Vegas, where Grossman was speaking to the National

Association of Broadcasters. "Don't make it sound like nothing was done at the meeting except that News came in for lavish praise." Thus the newsletter contained this sentence: "The news division came under criticism by some members of the management team, with a few suggesting the best way to assure economic success is to eliminate the division entirely."

Within days, Peter Boyer reported in the *Times* that NBC News was still under pressure, and quoted that sentence from the newsletter. Boyer's story, said Grossman, was "true, but it wasn't accurate," for it missed the endorsement News had received. And though it was true that there had been a few stray suggestions that NBC might consider getting out of the money-losing news business, the idea wasn't even mentioned by any of the seven discussion leaders in their summaries.

Not surprisingly, Bob Wright and Jack Welch were irritated by the *Times* account, and they did not blame the reporter. Both men attributed this latest imbroglio to Grossman's News "macho." Once again they felt he was trying to prove to his troops that he would fight GE on their behalf. By their lights, Grossman was forgetting the lesson Jack Welch tried to impart back in November of 1986, when he jabbed a finger in Grossman's chest and bellowed, "You work for Bob Wright. You work for GE!"

Soon after this incident Wright speeded the search for Grossman's replacement. He had, by the end of April 1988, seen ten potential candidates, but one complaint or another was lodged against each. Some candidates were said to lack flair, others stature. Some would not leave their print careers for television. Complicating matters were implicit divisions between Wright and his secret allies in News. Brokaw and Ross were more interested in finding someone with strong news judgment; Wright was more interested in someone with a management or business background. An Editor versus a Publisher.

Wright was talking separately to Ed Scanlon, who quietly helped in the search, and to Brokaw, by whom he ran each name. Brokaw suggested ABC News executive vice president David Burke, but Wright did not want to recruit a News president from another network. Brokaw continued to look, and conferred with Ross and with News consultant Gordon Manning, who had been so instrumental in persuading the Soviet leadership to induce Gorbachev to sit with Brokaw in December. They reviewed the ten or so names already considered.

The next day Manning came back to Brokaw with a slip of paper. "Listen, this guy is better than those bozos," he said, handing Brokaw a single name—Michael G. Gartner.

"Bingo!" Brokaw exclaimed.

Unlike Grossman, Gartner had a long and distinguished journalistic career. He started at age fifteen at the *Des Moines Register*. Then he spent fourteen years at *The Wall Street Journal*, rising to Page One editor. In 1974, he was named executive editor of the *Des Moines Register*, which is where Gartner became even better known to journalistic vagabonds who pass through every four years during the Iowa presidential caucuses and are desperate for independent sources. On paper, Gartner looked perfect. He had been both a reporter/editor and a businessman. When Gannett acquired the Iowa paper in 1986, Gartner walked away with about $4 million on the deal, and used some of the proceeds to buy parts of two Iowa newspapers—the *Daily Tribune* in Ames, and a weekly in Algona. Soon thereafter, Gannett recruited him to run two of their Louisville, Kentucky, newspapers—the *Courier-Journal* and the *Times*—which he promptly merged, cutting the staffs by joining them. Gartner also had stature: His byline appeared every three weeks over a column in *The Wall Street Journal;* he was past president of the American Society of Newspaper Editors; and he was a member of the Pulitzer Prize board. Gartner also conveyed a sense of conviction: He was a well-known absolutist when it came to the First Amendment, believed that government should never—ever—interfere with the press. Finally, Gartner was thought to possess pizzazz: He wore bright bow ties and suspenders and was known for his acerbic wit. And he was young enough—forty-nine—to stay the course.

He was, Brokaw thought, perfect.

Brokaw passed the name on to Wright, who passed it on to Ed Scanlon, who conferred with public relations advisor Jack Hilton of Hilton/Sucherman Productions, whose clients included GE and NBC. Hilton and his partner, Stuart Sucherman, a former public television executive, advise and prep corporate leaders to handle media interviews, including NBC interviews. Sucherman knew Gartner.

"Bob Wright is interested in press and First Amendment issues," Sucherman said to Gartner when he telephoned. "The next time you're in New York would you have lunch with him?"

Gartner, Wright, and Sucherman lunched on May 26. They said nothing about the NBC News job. Instead, they talked about journalism and the First Amendment, about whether television should be treated differently under the Constitution than newspapers. Gartner said he didn't believe in the Fairness Doctrine or the equal time rules the federal government imposed on television but not on newspapers.

They infringed free speech. Gartner's absolutist position on the First Amendment dovetailed with Wright's push for deregulation, providing an intellectual—as opposed to a business—rationale for their elimination.

Wright said Gartner "was very unusual. He spent most of the time interrogating me as to what I thought network News was and where it was going. What kind of a future did it have? I was quite taken with his approach." Gartner's questions exhibited what Wright and GE prized: "a willingness to search" for answers, to question settled assumptions. When Wright steered the conversation around to Gartner's background, what he encountered was a fellow businessman. Gartner told how, when he joined the *Des Moines Register* in 1974, the newspaper had a "slipshod distribution system." It had never prepared for when the trains might stop delivering papers, as they did in 1958 when the railroad was phased out. The *Register* had to find different means to distribute the newspaper, and Gartner did. Like a GE man.

At the end of lunch, the men shook hands, agreeing to keep in touch. Gartner said later that he had no idea of Wright's true agenda. When Wright returned from lunch he summoned Ed Scanlon and asked for a thorough background check on Gartner. Within weeks, Scanlon had dined with Gartner in Washington. It was at this dinner, said Gartner, that he first sensed that NBC was interested in more than his First Amendment views. Wright then saw Gartner a second time, in Washington, and came away equally impressed, particularly by Gartner's "shockingly candid" account of how the Bingham family mismanaged the Louisville paper before Gartner was summoned by Gannett, and why Gartner's impatience to get things done made him so frustrated that he left Louisville after only eighteen months. Like Wright, Gartner seemed frustrated with an elitist journalistic culture.

Meanwhile, events within the news division were conspiring against Larry Grossman. The *Nightly News,* which then provided 60 percent of NBC News's revenues, had not won a ratings week throughout the first six months of 1988. By June, Grossman reported that News revenues had fallen $30 million under budget. Once again, he would have to cut the News budget, this time by 120 employees. By summer, he would have reduced the total News work force by 28 percent since the arrival of GE. Larry Grossman was a sensitive man, who loved his job. Yet he had reasons to hate it. People in News blamed him for not resisting the cuts. Wright continued to complain about his leadership and privately grumbled, "Larry's yessing me to death."

And Welch, much to Grossman's discomfort, wondered aloud at a Fairfield strategic planning session in early July why NBC didn't have a Morton Downey, Jr.-style loudmouth interviewer hyping its ratings.

By early summer, Grossman learned that Peter Boyer of the *Times* was checking out a story that Tom Ross was heading a search for a new NBC News president. Grossman didn't believe it. He invited Ross into his office and told him of the rumor. But instead of asking Ross directly whether it was true, Grossman rambled on about how the rumor was so preposterous it couldn't be true. He truly couldn't imagine such a conspiracy. He was a gentleman.

As Ross sat there, dreading a direct question from his boss—*Are you an assassin?*—Grossman went on about how his position had actually grown "stronger," about how pleased Welch and Wright were with his budget plan. Just then, Grossman's secretary stuck her head in the door to say that George Paul, the director of the *Today* show, was on the line. Grossman swirled to pick up the receiver behind his desk, and as he did Tom Ross slipped from the office, escaping the dreaded question.

The new owners of NBC and ABC were following distinct but calibrated strategies. While Jack Welch and Bob Wright set out to instill insecurity, to impose GE's culture on NBC, Tom Murphy and Dan Burke set out to make ABC employees feel secure by accommodating differences even as they altered the culture. Larry Tisch, by contrast, brought no management philosophy. Within CBS, Tisch was often perceived as a Scrooge-like figure, impatient with the idea of management retreats or conversations about teamwork. He was not interested in new business opportunities, like Wright, or passionate about broadcasting, like Murphy and Burke. To CBS employees, Tisch seemed passionate only about costs. While NBC in 1988 was a thriving network not enjoying its success, and ABC was becoming successful and enjoying it, during the first half of 1988 CBS was both unhappy and unsuccessful.

Only part of the unhappiness was the result of CBS's poor ratings. Although CBS had a new programming chief in Kim LeMasters, its prime-time schedule was in a tailspin. The average age of its best-rated series was just over seven years, compared with just over two years for ABC and just over three for NBC; and CBS's viewers were themselves getting older. Nearly half of them were fifty or older. Spirits might have soared if employees felt confident that LeMasters or Jankowski knew how to fix the schedule. LeMasters himself was brimming with confidence—ABC's *The Wonder Years,* which would become a hit, he called "boring." Encouraged by Tisch to be bold, this season LeMasters installed a block of four half-hour comedies on Tuesday night and vowed to keep them there until they built an audience. Weeks later the comedies were yanked from the schedule. Publicly, CBS executives feigned optimism; privately, said one senior executive in the winter of 1988, "They are batshit about falling into third place." While each rating point in prime time was worth about $100 million extra to the network, more than money was involved. "You're dealing with whose penis is bigger," said the executive.

CBS News added to the malaise on the night of January 25, 1988. It had arranged a live interview between Rather and Vice President Bush, the frontrunner for the Republican presidential nomination. The interview would be the first extensive on-camera confrontation with Bush to probe his role in the Reagan administration's Iran-contra affair. Did the vice president know of the planned arms-for-hostages swap? If Bush did know, why was he silent? How could he deny knowledge of the swap when an Israeli antiterrorist expert, Amiram Nir, said he briefed Bush not once but three times? Did Bush know the White House was circumventing the Congress to funnel monies to the contras?

Rather was in CBS's New York studio, and Bush was seen on a split screen from his Capitol Hill office. As the vice president's microphone was adjusted, he was alerted to watch the preceding piece, a five-minute investigative profile of the contradictory claims Bush had made concerning his role in the scandal. Bush, who at the time was worried about his "wimp" image, seemed to be smoking mad when the red light went on and Rather introduced him. The two men, both somewhat stiff TV performers on their best days, traded punches for an extraordinary nine minutes. Excluding commercials, the interview consumed 40 percent of the actual newscast. Rather hit Bush with tough questions—Were you "irrelevant" or "ineffective"? And Bush alternated between hurt innocence and belligerence. When Rather prefaced a question with, "I don't want to be argumentative, Mr. Vice President," Bush snapped back, "You do, Dan."

After taking a few more shots from Rather, Bush unloaded a planned haymaker: "It's not fair to judge my whole career by a rehash of Iran. How would you like it if I judged your career by those seven [six, actually] minutes when you walked off the set in New York [Miami, actually]?"

Rather seemed frozen for a moment, and then switched back to Iran-contra questions. When Rather kept pressing Bush to meet with reporters and Bush kept evading a direct response, producer Tom Bettag started yelling into Rather's earpiece to zipper the interview. Abruptly Rather injected the final word: "I gather the answer is no. Thank you very much for being with us, Mr. Vice President."

In many ways, the interview was a triumph for Rather, who dared ask impertinent questions of a man who had managed to avoid them. And polls taken after this encounter revealed that 79 percent of Americans believed Bush "knows more about the arms-for-hostages deal than he has told the public." But it didn't matter. Bush won the encounter. Calls of protest poured into CBS—from viewers, from affiliates, from Republican politicians—while Bush basked in his new macho image. People tended to ignore the substance of Rather's questions and Bush's evasions. CBS, like the rest of TV News, had come to live by images, by evocative "moments," not the linear logic of print. Viewers "hear" the pictures, not the words. And what they heard was Rather's "rudeness." With Walter Cronkite as the model, viewers had come to expect their anchors to perform as gracious hosts, polite, judicious, cool. Instead they saw the hot, prosecutorial side of Rather's personality. Rather was going against the grain of a medium which had grown up wanting to please, to have its actors or anchors be "likeable." "So much of what we do on television is to try to balance left and right," explained anchor Peter Jennings. "Therefore what we wind up with is the squishy middle. You don't see pointed documentaries. There are so many ifs, buts, and maybes that the audience loses the chance to have its mind spurred."

In the long run, said Tom Bettag, it "was as good an interview as you can do." In the long run, said a depressed member of the CBS hierarchy, Rather would be hurt by this encounter: "Miami told everyone he had a bad temper. Bush told them he was rude. These are bad negatives. I don't know how to reverse them." According to a *Los Angeles Times* poll taken after the confrontation with Bush, Rather's "unfavorable" standing among viewers was triple that of Brokaw or Jennings. Like others who only whispered it, ABC News vice president David Burke thought we were witness to the slow death of Dan Rather, anchorman. "His inventory of 'strange' events is too long," said Burke, who with Roone Arledge had almost succeeded in bringing Rather to ABC in 1981. "If I were his manager I'd be pessimistic because there's something wrong. And since I can't identify what it is, I can't fix it. I feel sad. I like him."

After the Bush confrontation, Rather's newscast fell into second place. This depressed people, but not as much as the sense within CBS News—a sense shared with NBC News—that the head of the network did not share their values. While Tisch said he "would never interfere with News," an incident took place on March 12 that received no public notice but undermined this assurance and reminded the handful of network people who had heard about it of Tom Wyman's August 1986 warning that if the interests of News clashed with the interests of Israel, Larry Tisch would choose Israel. The incident occured in an unusual setting—a birthday dinner hosted by Barbara Walters and her husband, Merv Adelson, for Federal Reserve Board chairman Alan Greenspan. Hamburgers and hot dogs catered by Glorious Food were served, along with hats and horns for fourteen guests. Billie and Larry Tisch came to Walters's New York apartment, as did Henry Kissinger, Oscar de la Renta and Annette Reed, Felix and Liz Rohatyn, Roone Arledge, Children's Television Workshop president Joan Ganz Cooney and her husband, financier and former secretary of commerce Pete Peterson, and Greenspan's steady date, NBC News Capitol Hill correspondent Andrea Mitchell; they were joined after dinner by real estate developer and *U.S. News & World Report* publisher Mortimer Zuckerman and his date, ABC producer Susan Mercandetti.

During dinner the talk got around to a topic then much in the news: Israel's treatment of the Arab community on the West Bank and its relations with the press. Since the *intifada* or Palestinian uprising in the disputed territories had begun in December of 1987, the beleaguered Israeli government was using force to quell it, which provoked a raging controversy. Kissinger had some weeks before said he would banish all cameras on the West Bank, arguing that TV cameras incited riots and unnecessarily tarnished Israel's reputation. Critics replied that the cameras were only recording, not precipitating, the riots. Kissinger, they claimed, was asking the democratic government of Israel to pattern itself after the racist government of South Africa, which in 1987 censored all broadcast pictures.

A long and at times heated discussion ensued. According to Arledge, Tisch argued "that television ought be banned from the occupied territories" because it provoked and sensationalized the uprising, transforming an Israeli police action into what appeared to be a denial of civil rights. Arledge countered that Tisch—like Lyndon Johnson, who scapegoated the media during the Vietnam War—was blaming the messenger rather than the policy. Tisch, joined by Walters and Zuckerman, denied taking this posture. "I never recommended keeping the press out," Tisch said. Yet eight other guests insist that he did.* Tisch later conceded: "It's a dilemma. If I were president of Israel I don't know what I'd do."

After dinner, guests pounced on Arledge for Peter Jennings's coverage of the Middle East. "There was a general feeling that Peter Jennings was more sympathetic to the Arab cause," recalls Walters, who remembers that her husband criticized Arledge for a Jennings newscast comparing the actions of Israel with those of South Africa. Over the years, Tisch had complained to Leonard Goldenson and others that he considered Jennings "anti-Israel," and had once confronted Jennings directly with this assertion. This night Tisch and others, with Zuckerman acknowledging that he was the most vociferous, lashed out at Jennings's and the media's Middle East coverage. "I've just come back from Israel," Zuckerman said, according to Arledge, "and I didn't see a single stone thrown. If anything, we've missed the story. Not a single Arab has been killed on TV. The media are unfair. Why doesn't ABC mention Palestinian atrocities?"

"We do!" responded Arledge.

"A reporter's pad is different from a camera because it doesn't invite" crowds and magnify demonstrations, said Tisch, who added that the press should tell viewers or readers when demonstrations were "staged" or when the press was invited in by the PLO.

The discussion was never impolite—these were social friends—but several guests came away deeply distressed by Tisch's behavior. What disturbed them was that the president of CBS seemed to say that the perceived interests of Israel took precedence over the interests of CBS News. Tisch's reflex, they felt, was to defend Israel, not his network; he was blaming Jennings and the press for reporting Israeli excesses, not Israel for committing them. For those like Arledge, who sometimes worried whether the new owners shared the same commitment to the public trust as the original owners, this was a particularly worrisome encounter.

The encounter remained private, and caused Tisch no public embarrassment. But Tisch's posture toward the Middle East would be felt by CBS News. Ranking News executives conceded they were always mindful of Tisch's passionate interest in the subject, the more so after an incident several months later. On October 23, 1988, *60 Minutes* aired a Mike Wallace piece on the American Israel Public Affairs Com-

* Five guests confirmed this to this author directly, and three told this to close friends.

mittee (AIPAC), the pro-Israel lobby. Wallace's report explored how AIPAC used the large sums of money it raised to punish political candidates portrayed as insufficiently pro-Israel. "The clout of AIPAC here on Capitol Hill is enormous," Wallace said, standing outside AIPAC's Washington headquarters. Though Wallace balanced AIPAC's critics with its defenders, the piece ignited fears that it would provoke the wild claim made by anti-Semites for centuries—*The Jews are too powerful!*

Several days after the piece ran, Tisch attended a cocktail party at River House, the elegant apartment building on Manhattan's East Side, hosted by *Wall Street Journal* publisher Warren H. Phillips in honor of Joan Konner, who had just been named dean of the Columbia School of Journalism. "Hi, boss," said a smiling Don Hewitt as he approached Tisch.

"Don't you 'Hi, boss' me," said Tisch to the executive producer of *60 Minutes.* "I can barely see straight I'm so angry with you." And with that, Tisch turned his back on Hewitt. Mike Wallace recalls that when he ran into Tisch at the same party, Tisch ignored him, as he would on subsequent occasions, until the Wallaces and the Tisches made peace at a dinner some months later. To friends—and to at least one CBS correspondent and his producer, who are based overseas—Tisch referred to Wallace as a "self-hating Jew." Tisch acknowledges, "There may have been parts of the program I didn't think were well done." But he denied berating Hewitt; "I kidded him about the program," he said. And he denied calling Wallace a "self-hating Jew." Few who were aware of these incidents believed Tisch.

The real fear at CBS News was not that Tisch would directly order something censored. The fear was that Tisch's attitude could lead to self-censorship, the same concern those at NBC News had when they heard of Jack Welch's phone call to Larry Grossman about a GE story. Mike Wallace said he did not share this concern. "After the AIPAC piece on *60 Minutes,* Harry [Reasoner] did a piece on a lawyer in Israel who defends Palestinians," said the veteran correspondent. And in December 1990, Wallace came right back with another piece—on the killing of about twenty rock-throwing Palestinians by Israelis—that also inflamed many of Tisch's friends. The AIPAC incident, and CBS News's unwillingness to back off, Wallace said of Tisch, "taught him a fact of life: Larry Tisch should not, and will not, meddle with news coverage on CBS because of his personal leanings, understandings, tendencies." Whether the next generation at CBS News—who might not enjoy either the same clout or courage as Wallace and Hewitt, or Hewitt's ten-year contract—would be able to resist was less certain.

An old mob expression—"The fish stinks from the head"—sums up another major source of unhappiness at CBS. Larry Tisch's personality, it was said, hampered the network. Even such staunch Tisch allies as CBS vice president Ed Grebow worried about his communication skills. "Larry is brilliant," said Grebow. "But Larry doesn't communicate his vision well. Part of being a manager is getting your managers to agree on a shared vision. We haven't done that." Chief financial officer Fred Meyer, who left CBS in March of 1988,* echoed a larger point, one shared by CBS directors. Whatever success Tisch had at cost cutting, said Meyer, was mitigated by two factors. The first was that the networks were not "a healthy business anymore. . . . I believe it is quite likely that from now on only one network will be profitable and the other two will be only marginally profitable. There's a limited amount you can cut out of costs. The game is to regain the number-one slot." Which brought Meyer to point two: "Part of my thinking was: Is Larry the kind of guy to fly by the seat of the pants and sign up some big producers to make us jump to number one again? When he says, 'We will not hold back,' I take him at face value. But he's so much associated with cost control that whether he says it or not the LeMasters and Jankowskis still act as if he is looking over their shoulders. Tisch . . . just may not be the kind of person to run this business." Nor, lamented Meyer, did Tisch have a strategy for the future.

Surely CBS lacked a strategy to avoid tumbling into third place. In its thirty-six years CBS had never finished last, and Tisch did not want it to happen on his watch. Nevertheless, it did. The prime-time season officially ended on April 17, and the results were wretched for CBS. Nielsen showed that CBS had lost 15 percent of its audience, compared to NBC, which lost 10 percent, and ABC, which lost 3 percent. CBS, which had finished first in twenty-six of network television's thirty-five seasons, had to return to advertisers about $65 million worth of free make-good spots.

By the spring of 1988, CBS employees, already fearful of layoffs, were made doubly insecure by rumors in the entertainment press that *Larry Tisch may sell CBS.* The rumors were so intense that Tisch addressed a three-page memorandum to all employees denying that he

* Both Meyer and Tisch say Meyer left voluntarily.

planned to sell. Tisch said he and Loews were "long-term" investors, who believed "in quality businesses—and by that standard, there could be no better investment in America than CBS." The rumors were followed by two books on CBS, neither favorable. One was by the *Times*'s influential television writer, Peter Boyer, and the provocative title was a conclusion, *Who Killed CBS?* The other—*Prime Times, Bad Times,* was a readable kiss-and-tell book written by former News president Ed Joyce. "These books have had a terribly corrosive effect," complained Jay Kriegel. While not denying their impact, Dan Rather had an interesting way of dealing with them: He didn't read them. When *Vanity Fair* excerpted part of Boyer's book that winter, producer Tom Bettag suggested Rather read the article after the Friday broadcast, not before. Rather packed it in his briefcase for the weekend. He was prepared to open it in Connecticut when his wife, Jean, asked if he wanted to walk in the woods.

"Screw it," Rather said, "I'd rather walk in the woods."

He returned, glanced at the cover of the magazine, and did not pick it up for the remainder of that day, or the next. He arrived at work Monday, and colleagues asked what he thought of the excerpt. "By that time I felt pretty good," recalls Rather. "I liked the feeling of being able to say, truthfully, 'I didn't read it.'" Nor had he read Joyce's book.

Jankowski, on the other hand, dealt with the books the way he always did with bad news. They had no impact on morale at CBS, he said, which was now "higher than it was in March of 1987" because employees were more secure. "We don't feel we're a third-place network."

The words did not erase CBS's third-place finish, nor Larry Tisch's Hollywood woes. "We have a communications problem in Hollywood," Jay Kriegel admitted at the time. Much of Hollywood thought Tisch neither watched nor cared about what appeared on the small screen. Tom Murphy put people at ease with his reassuring phone calls and relaxed air, and Bob Wright left Hollywood to Brandon Tartikoff, but Larry Tisch unnerved people.

Coaxed by Kriegel and Steve Warner, Tisch sought to improve his Hollywood persona by holding a series of relaxed, get-acquainted sessions with writer/producers. In early May he met with Aaron Spelling, who in addition to *Nightingales* had just done a pilot for CBS and looked forward to meeting Tisch, the more so since he was still upset about a CBS encounter the day before. Spelling had screened his one-hour action-adventure pilot, *The Pretenders,* for LeMasters, who brusquely walked in just as the lights dimmed, said "Hello, hello," pointedly sat alone in the front row, and when the lights went up offered only a few perfunctory compliments before rushing back to his office. Spelling hoped that out of the Tisch meeting might come some encouragement for his series.

The meeting was scheduled for May 4 at 3:30 P.M. For the occasion, Spelling took unusual pains with his wardrobe, wearing business as opposed to Hollywood attire—white shirt, black and white polka-dot tie, and a light gray sports jacket with dark slacks. Entering the lobby of CBS's Entertainment complex on Beverly Boulevard in Hollywood, Spelling signed in and was directed to an elevator. No one waited to greet him upstairs, so the producer sat in the third-floor reception area for five minutes until a secretary appeared to say, "We're running a little late." A few moments later she reappeared to lead Spelling to LeMasters's corner office, explaining that he was off screening pilots. Waiting inside were Tisch and Warner.

"You're a legend in your own lifetime," said Tisch, warmly extending his hand.

"I've heard so much about you," responded Spelling in a voice just above a whisper. Instead of suggesting that they sit on a comfortable corner couch, Tisch remained true to his no-frills style and beckoned Spelling to sit on an aluminum swivel chair at the small table LeMasters used as a desk. Spelling was neither offered coffee or a cold drink, nor invited to peel off his jacket. Tisch asked Warner not to leave but to join them.

"I know you're famous for your house," said Tisch, trying to make a joke but actually raising a sensitive subject.

Spelling closed his eyes, understandably defensive about the ridicule he had received for buying six acres of land and Bing Crosby's old house in Holmby Hills, demolishing it, and erecting in its place a sixty-five-thousand-square-foot castle. "I'll tell you," Spelling finally responded, "you start off in a small town in Texas like I did . . ."

"How do you shut off that thing?" Tisch interrupted, distracted by the live television set. Steve Warner reached over and pressed the remote-control device at Tisch's fingertips.

". . . The house is twice as big as I wanted," Spelling continued, explaining that his two children will love the space, the indoor bowling alley, the three kitchens.

The two men wandered onto the subject of flying, and Tisch was surprised to learn of Spelling's well-known aversion to airplanes. "Do you ever come to New York?" he asked.

"Four years ago," said Spelling. "By train."

"When was the last time you flew?"

At the end of World War II. Spelling told Tisch that his mother had heard incorrectly that his plane had crashed, and when he arrived home the family was already in mourning. Seeing Aaron alive, his mother fainted. When she awoke, Spelling promised her he would never again fly.

"That's a two-hour movie!" joked Tisch.

"That's the reason for buying the house," said Spelling.

"If you don't travel you've got to have a big house," said Tisch, who told of escaping Manhattan on weekends to his home in Rye.

"Everything I've read, good or bad, didn't tell me of your character," said Spelling, offering a compliment.

"Some of the things you read about yourself I say, 'Is that me?'" said Tisch.

The tempo of the conversation picked up. For the next ten minutes they swapped stories about how they had each suffered at the hands of journalists. Tisch spoke about the recent books on CBS, about how he was made out to be a heartless cost cutter, about unsubstantiated rumors that he planned to sell CBS. Spelling went on about the terrible insults gossip columnists heaped on his wife and their new home, about TV critics and "the Bel-Air elite" who "don't hang out at supermarkets" and know how common folk feel.

Tisch said that he and Billie would love to have dinner some night with the Spellings.

"I'd love it," said the producer. "You're not disliked in this town."

"Oh, I didn't think that," said Tisch. "I've been associated, in a way, for forty years with this business."

"It's important that the head of the network be out here a lot," said Spelling.

"I'm determined to be," answered Tisch, who reassured Spelling, "I really enjoy what I'm doing. I love going to the office. I think people should work until they're ninety-five, if they can."

Spelling concurred, telling how his dad died a year after he retired, and how Leonard Goldenson hadn't been sick a day—until he retired.

"We've made leisure a goal," said Tisch, who at sixty-four was the same age as his guest. Tisch told how pleased he was when he saw an entire family at work in a Chinese laundry or a Korean vegetable market. "This isn't so terrible. They're working. They're together. We all make such a fetish making sure people don't work past nine to five.

I spent the first ten years of my life working seven days a week. It's not so terrible."

Forty minutes after the meeting began, Tisch rose to thank Spelling for coming. Either because he didn't want to usurp LeMasters's role or because he was unaware of Spelling's pilot, he said nothing about it. Nor did he mention *The Love Boat, Fantasy Island, Dynasty, Charlie's Angels,* or any of the more than 2,500 hours of shows Spelling had produced. They would keep in touch.

Two weeks later, when Tisch, Paley, Jankowski, and other New York executives flew west to decide on the fall 1988 schedule, Spelling's pilot was dropped. Tisch screened a total of thirty-six pilots during May's Decision Week and, as typically happens, network participants emerged after a week all pumped up, their judgment clouded by the exhausting ordeal they had just endured. Weeks later, no one was any longer certain that CBS had found the shows to propel it out of third place.

Morale sank. While Black Rock did not conduct an employee survey, as NBC did, or hold retreats for middle managers, as ABC did, Ed Grebow didn't need a questionnaire to know how employees felt. "Morale is bad," he said. "The rumors around this place are horrible." The unhappiness became so intense that Grebow hired an industrial psychologist. "I don't plan to tell Larry," said Grebow. "He'd go crazy. Larry doesn't think morale is a key problem. He thinks morale has never been good at CBS."

People outside the network also doubted that CBS's eight new series would help, an assessment that would prove correct. Critics noted that while most TV watchers were women, CBS's schedule was dominated by male-oriented programming about mobsters (*Wiseguy*), soldiers in Vietnam (*Tour of Duty*), and private detectives (*Jake and the Fatman*), plus two news magazine shows. Advertisers joined the generally negative chorus.

The 206 affiliated stations were openly rebellious about the schedule and much else. Affiliate Relations vice president Scott Michaels told his staff: "We need some tangible, visible [proof] that we're moving ahead." Privately Michaels would say, "The affiliates . . . are not going to buy the words till they see some action. They want to see something other than a memo saying 'CBS is not for sale' or 'We want to be number one.' We have a credibility problem here that has to be fixed."

CBS needed some good news, and Larry Tisch would buy it. On the morning of May 25, Michaels took a call from Sports president

Neal Pilson. Michaels's face immediately liquefied into a smile. "We did? We got 'em!" he exclaimed. "Sensational! I love ya!" Michaels slammed the phone down and called his staff: "The '92 Olympics are going to be on our schedule!" Within seconds, whoops filled the corridors.

Larry Tisch, who in 1987 had let cable get a piece of the NFL schedule and had passed on Steven Bochco and buying a bustling Miami station for $270 million, announced that he had agreed to pay $243 million to telecast the 1992 winter games from Albertville, France. It was an extraordinary sum, not just because of Tisch's penny-pinching reputation, but because it was $43 million above the minimum set by the International Olympic Committee. His friend Tom Murphy's network had dropped out of the bidding, saying there was no way to make money even at the minimum price. More astonishing, CBS paid approximately $68 million more than NBC bid. Even Pilson predicted only "modest profits" from the games.

Like the other new owners, Tisch now believed that the bottom line was not all that mattered in the network business. After nearly six months of damaging headlines, he knew the Olympics might pacify the affiliates and get the press off his back. "The Olympics," said Jay Kriegel, who every six months or so would trumpet a "new" Tisch, "will be a symbolic turning point for Larry Tisch and CBS. It's been a terrible period here from January through May. . . . This starts the movement up. The place needs a lift. People need to see a future, and this is a future. This is a signal that Larry is prepared to invest in what gets on the screen."

Prodded by Kriegel, the "new" Tisch would send one other signal he hoped would encourage affiliates on the eve of their annual meeting in Los Angeles. On May 31, 1988, he elevated Scott Michaels's boss, Tony Malara, from vice president to president of the affiliate relations division, and announced he would now report directly to Gene Jankowski.

CBS's affiliate relations department thought it had something to sell when it met in Los Angeles for the annual convention with its 206 stations. An affiliate convention celebrates the new schedule with a lavish spread of food and drink, with loud music and garish sports jackets and a caravan of Hollywood stars. It is meant to be a gathering of true believers, and there are, Martha Sherrill of *The Washington Post* once observed, "more slogans than in a new socialist country." For three full days five hundred or so adults are bombarded with preachments, platitudes, chants, bromides, ear-splitting music, and snappy MTV-like images flitting across screens.

"CBS. Television you can feel," was the slogan that accosted delegates when they arrived on Saturday, June 11, for a welcoming reception around the reflecting pools of the Century Plaza Hotel. The opening meeting was scheduled for 9 A.M. Sunday, and only the affiliate representatives were invited. Network officials and the press were specifically excluded. This private session would be followed later in the morning by a meeting with the network, also off-limits to the press.*

"Third place is on everybody's mind," said Ben Tucker as he sipped coffee moments before the morning session was to begin. Tucker wore a bushy mustache and a deep tan, which along with a small case of jitters gave him a friendly aura. Tucker, thirty-eight, was executive vice president of Retlaw Broadcasting, which owns four stations in western states, and the new chairman of the CBS Affiliate Advisory Board. "Business is soft all over," he said. "When you're third and business is not good, you've got trouble."

More trouble than Tucker imagined, for at this session the complaints from CBS's affiliates were harsh. The affiliate board sat between two enormous ficus trees at a pink-linen-draped table. They were on an elevated platform in the Century Room, facing about five hundred casually dressed station representatives sitting on pink, felt-covered folding chairs. Tucker and members of his board quickly recapped what had been discussed at the meeting the previous night with Tisch and CBS executives. Expecting routine questions, Tucker welcomed colleagues to step up to microphones.

One delegate complained about Jankowski's leadership. Another about Tisch's. Within moments a long line of affiliates snaked behind the microphone stands, eager to vent their anger. Twenty years ago, these stations might have been awed by the big boys from the network. Or by the Tiffany aura. Or by Paley's charm. But now station managers were besieged by new competitors and financial pressure from group owners. And CBS's numbers were not good.

There were questions about Rather, and whether he, not Stringer, was really running News. Another board member groused that he'd never seen Jankowski sweat, but "I think under his clothing there was

* The affiliate board allowed this author into the meeting on condition that I not identify speakers from the floor.

probably some dampness. He certainly doesn't give us" any sense of comfort because he's so damn impassively confident.

"I think we've been hearing lip service for three, four years," an affiliate shouted from the floor. "We have to ask the tough questions. If we ran our stations and our groups the way they run their network we'd be in serious trouble."

"Do you as a board need a strongly worded resolution from this affiliate body?" asked an affiliate from the floor.

"No," responded Ben Tucker, who was eager to head off a storm.

"The good news on Tisch's dealings with us is that I believe he is committed to act," said former affiliate board chairman Phil Jones. "The bad news is that, as you know from the marketplace, throwing money at the problem is not the answer. He needs a plan. And we're not hearing it."

Another affiliate stepped to the microphone and preceded his question with a complaint: *We have five-year plans, why doesn't CBS?* My question, he continued, is simply this: "Are they prepared to put a broadcaster at the head of the network" who can make us win again?

Applause rippled through the ballroom.

Another impatient affiliate complained: "The suggestion we can go through Tony and Gene to get to Tisch is wrong. While Tisch disarms us, he intimidates them. If we are to get Tisch's attention, it has to come from the affiliate body."

Another affiliate asked: "Let's just not be nice. . . . Do we need a formal resolution?"

Again, a roar of applause.

We don't need a formal resolution, said Ben Tucker, who was torn between loyalty to the affiliates and the network. "The board recognizes that CBS is as intensely convinced of these problems as we are." Probably a majority of the affiliates did not believe that, but after a short break they would have an opportunity to hear from the network because Tisch & Company were about to enter.

At 10:30 A.M. the network brass—Gene Jankowski, Tony Malara, Kim LeMasters, Tom Leahy, Howard Stringer, Neal Pilson, and David Poltrack, led by Tisch in a beige gabardine suit—filed in, taking seats at the table facing the affiliate body. "It's really important to convey the concerns of our meeting," said Ben Tucker, leaning forward at the table and looking directly at Tisch. The best way to do this, he said, would be to turn to the audience and let network officials hear from their partners.

We had hoped to open with some comments from Gene Jankowski, and then respond to questions, interjected Tony Malara.

"I don't want to get away from questions, but Tony is absolutely right," said Jankowski. Resplendent in a pink button-down shirt and tie with a navy blazer, his hair neatly combed, Jankowski read from scripted notes. "This country is going through a tough period" economically, he began, and there is much "confusion in the media world." Some say the networks are dinosaurs. Cable and technology threaten. "But it's important to point out that over the last year and a half this company" has confronted its problems and responded with good programs, with an improved distribution system, and by investing more money in sports and pilots. We made Tony Malara president to "elevate" the importance of this body. We enhanced our promotion effort by moving Tom Leahy to supervise it. Admittedly, in promotion and marketing "we have done a lousy job," conceded Jankowski. But all that will change, he assured them. The "partnership" is what counts: "Without you, we're nothing. . . . It's important that we're frank with each other."

Larry Tisch stared inscrutably at the affiliates, his head resting on his fist. When Jankowski finished, the affiliates remained silent. Finally Tony Malara broke the quiet by announcing that CBS would unveil its new promos Tuesday morning.

Duane Harm, president of KWTV in Oklahoma City, stepped to the microphone, determined to provoke the "frank" dialogue Jankowski said he invited.* "We all want the network to succeed," said Harm in a voice that commanded attention. "But we would be remiss if we didn't give you the spirit of the morning meeting. . . . We are concerned the network doesn't have a plan, and you are reacting to crisis. We also question whether Tisch should not consider, if the network doesn't turn around, stepping up to a higher position and letting the network be run by a broadcaster."

Tisch's expression remained impenetrable. Except for the tapping of his pencil on the pink tablecloth, he didn't move. But his face turned bright red.

Jankowski defended Tisch, praising the financial integrity and rigorous management Tisch had restored to CBS. "Larry gave us the muscle I haven't seen since Paley and Stanton were running the place."

Tisch cut him off: "I think the network is being run by broadcast-

* Although this author was the only journalist present, in published accounts Harm would be identified and would confirm his comments at this meeting.

ers. I am not a broadcaster. But I do take full responsibility for what happens at CBS. We have gone through a disastrous period. I will spare no resources—anything it takes to get back to number one, we will spend. But just keep in mind that the people running the network are professionals. I think we're on the right track. This is a very difficult period. . . . Money is no object. I spent the first year getting our house in order. We have the highest earnings in history. But that's meaningless unless we're number one."

The affiliates, for all their anger, nevertheless wanted to be polite and perhaps felt they had humbled Tisch enough. They erupted with applause.

Do we know why viewers are fleeing the Rather newscast? one speaker asked. *Is it because of the Bush interview? The six-minute gap?*

We have lots of research, Stringer answered. ABC and NBC had been forced to cut as much, but they have escaped without the headlines. "No News division could have gone through this year" without harm, said Stringer. "We've done for loyalty what the Boston Strangler did for door-to-door salesmen!" Everyone laughed, including Tisch.

Stringer then became serious, explaining that the network news business was changing before their eyes. All three network newscasts have lost audience, he said, as viewers no longer waited until 6:30 or 7 P.M. to learn what happened that day. It was also true, he acknowledged: Research indicates that "the audience is polarized by our anchor." Many viewers did not like Rather. But there was nothing new to this, said Stringer. Rather's vulnerabilities were offset by his great strength, which "is authority." Research, Stringer importuned, "is only a tool." Research does not tell who does the best journalistic job. What News needs now is a period of quiet. Stringer noted that NBC didn't even have a prime-time magazine show while CBS had three; and *48 Hours* came in second to *Cosby* in the ratings on Thursday, ahead of ABC. "You ought to be proud of that show," he admonished. "We're in suicide alley. Give us some credit for committing suicide bravely!"

Laughter and applause filled the room, for Stringer was a popular figure among affiliates. Unlike some in News, he was not scornful of the stations. He came to their conferences, attended their football games, and conversed with their spouses. Unlike Jankowski, he did not insist that bad news was good news. And he fought back.

"Don't be so impatient!" admonished Stringer. *West 57th* and *48 Hours* were shows their competitors would be proud to air. *It took* 60

Minutes *eight years to become a hit.* Cheers *was ranked eighty-eighth in the ratings after its first year on NBC. Give us time.*

Again, applause.

But the long line at the microphones remained, and the questions continued. *We don't let our anchors go to the general manager,* said one local News director, referring to Rather's ability to go above Stringer's head to Jankowski or Tisch.

Stringer rose to Rather's defense: *You should pause before you abandon an anchor who's been in first place six of the last seven years. Many of you have told me how annoyed you were by the disloyalty of Ed Joyce for writing a book about his network. What about your loyalty?*

Larry Tisch was no longer looking straight ahead; his eyes were on Stringer, enraptured, as if he were noticing something for the first time. "I get your message," concluded Stringer. "I'm not deaf. . . . But let's not all step on the hands hanging onto the cliffs here!"

"These meetings would be no fun without Howard!" exclaimed an affiliate from the floor, prompting Stringer to answer: "By the way, in case you haven't noticed, I'm not alone up here!"

Ben Tucker turned to Kim LeMasters and asked if CBS was doing anything different in program development.

No, answered LeMasters, who then fielded a barrage of questions about programming. With his smoothly confident broadcaster's voice, LeMasters spoke with certitude about how CBS had finally awakened to the fact that it had lost its comedy franchise and younger viewers to ABC and NBC, and how, once again, CBS was innovating.

To the affiliates, LeMasters was overselling, again. One irate affiliate asked: "What formal mechanism do you have to take full advantage of several hundred experienced broadcasters here in providing to you the feedback as to those shows you're planning to put on?"

LeMasters hesitated before saying there was no "formal mechanism" and that, to his knowledge, neither ABC nor NBC had one either. LeMasters seemed annoyed by the question. "The danger in seeking too much feedback is that a committee that starts out to make a horse ends up with a camel," he said.

The affiliate representative was standing, shaking with anger. "I wonder if any of my colleagues here feel they would like to have a formal method of providing some feedback to the network about how they feel about the new shows?" he asked.

Like a thunderclap, the applause in the hall said *yes.*

"I don't hear you, Kim, talking about 'together,' " said the affiliate rep. "I hear 'camels.' I've seen a lot of camels in the last year!"

"How do we get there?" LeMasters asked.

"The word is: Listen," said the affiliate sharply.

"I'm really here to listen," said LeMasters politely.

Despite the reassuring steps Tisch had taken as their "partner"—deciding not to cut affiliate compensation, refusing to seek a deal with cable, restoring *The Morning Program* to News, buying the 1992 Winter Olympics—there were no expressions of gratitude or support from the affiliates. Not, that is, until a rural Southern affiliate stepped to the microphone and declared: "I like the Tisch philosophy. I look over at NBC and I see Bob Wright, and his loyalty is not to NBC. It's to GE. I look at Tom Murphy. He has ESPN. He, in essence, is competing with ABC's affiliates. I look at Mr. Tisch and I see he got rid of nonbroadcast things. He's not competing against us the way ABC is and NBC are going to be. . . . If we weren't associated with CBS, we wouldn't have the CBS identity. So I'd like to thank Tisch for his devotion to broadcasting."

Only tepid applause greeted this statement, for the affiliates were clearly not in a celebratory mood. They wanted the network to take risks many local stations dared not take. They wanted the network to be run by broadcasters even though many stations were not. No matter. The affiliates had listened to too many promises, too much "good news" from Gene Jankowski. When they looked up they saw Larry Tisch, looking bored, doodling, not laughing when others did, seemingly not paying attention—except when Stringer spoke. They saw Jankowski, who seemed more concerned with Tisch's feelings than theirs. The affiliates needed to scream, and Jankowski was the true target of their fury. They blamed him not just for the poor ratings or promotion campaign, but for not leveling with them. Stringer listened to their bleats, agreed with some, challenged them on others. Yet when they criticized Jankowski it was like driving a fist into Jell-o. There was no resistance, nothing solid.

From the floor one affiliate shouted: *Gene keeps saying he wants our feedback. He acts as if he's never heard what we're saying before. I tell the affiliate relations department what I think all the time. Doesn't he talk to Scott Michaels? Doesn't he talk to Tony Malara? Or don't they tell Gene what we say?*

To this outburst, Jankowski responded solicitously, "Call us when you've got" a problem. It was already 12:45 P.M. They had gone an hour and fifteen minutes longer than planned. The program had called for a press conference at 11:30 and a luncheon at 12:30. And there was no end in sight. Reporters and lunch waited outside, but few affiliates left their seats, except to approach the microphone. The meeting would not conclude until 1:50 P.M.

At an afternoon press conference after the closed session with affiliates, a scribe asked Tisch how he responded to reports that the affiliates were furious and complained that he lacked a strategic plan. "I didn't hear that at our meeting," Tisch declared, untruthfully. Privately, Tisch flicked aside the criticism because he truly did not comprehend why anyone would be mad at him. He was earning 9 percent on the cash he had invested for CBS. Forget the ratings. With his cost reductions and streamlined management, he believed he had saved the network. He expected CBS to earn $60 to $100 million from the network in 1988, $40 million from radio, $160 million from its four TV stations, and $275 million from its cash investments. He deserved applause, he thought. Larry Tisch simply didn't think he was their target. "I think they lost confidence in Jankowski," he explained a week after the conference.

When Jankowski heard that some thought he was the reason for much of the affiliates' ire, he was puzzled. "Why would they be angry with me?"

No question, falling into third place heightened the frustrations of affiliates. But something extraordinary had erupted in that ballroom. People seemed to want more than a change in the ratings; they wanted a change of management. The affiliate body had heard Gene Jankowski predict a winning CBS season for 1987–88, and they were now third. They had heard him predict that the network share of audience would grow, and it didn't. Something Rather said about his friend Jankowski sums up why the affiliates were exhausted by him. "If Gene Jankowski were in Hitler's bunker when the Russian troops were approaching," Rather had said admiringly, "and Hitler asked, 'What's that noise?' Jankowski would have said, 'Don't worry, my Führer. It's our spring offensive!' "

"Howard, you're going to be the next president of the Broadcast Center," Eric Ober whispered to his friend as he and Stringer waited for an elevator moments after the closed affiliate session ended. Ober, who ran CBS's owned stations division, sat in a front row at the meeting and saw how Tisch brightened when Stringer spoke. Of Stringer, Ober said, "He took tough questions on News and didn't take any shit. And at the same time he didn't insult them." The way LeMasters had.

A process of elimination led Ober to Stringer, as it did, simultaneously, Jay Kriegel. Though Kriegel was new to broadcasting, he was experienced as both a staff man and a political head counter. It was clear that Jankowski was no longer protecting Tisch from the affiliates. When Kriegel's mind raced over the possible internal candidates to replace Jankowski, who else was there but Stringer? Sports president Neal Pilson was a good executive, but he lacked the bedside manner a vulnerable network especially required. Tom Leahy? Like Jankowski, he was too much a part of the old culture. With Peter Lund gone, there was no one else.

In the wake of the affiliate conference, another wave of rumors struck CBS. Many concerned Jankowski. People were on edge—so on edge that Kriegel telephoned Peter Boyer at 12:30 A.M. one night in June to berate him about one of his stories. (Kriegel consulted people about barring Boyer from entering any CBS building. The idea was not implemented.)

Jankowski, however, seemed serene. On a hot, sticky day late in June, Jankowski's brow was dry, not a hair out of place. Looking model-perfect in his gray suit, a bright red paisley foulard spilling from his breast pocket, the personable CBS Broadcast Group president spoke in a relaxed way of his achievements. He had, he said, "created an environment where people are proud to work," a "creative environment freer of distractions and insecurity." Despite painful cutbacks, Jankowski was confident that he had managed "to foster an atmosphere of teamwork." "Never once," he said, had he talked to Tisch about leaving. Why should he? His contract ran until 1990. The optimism that once served CBS so well had by June 1988 become a form of self-deception. "I do feel very comfortable that our position this fall will be better," Jankowski announced. "Our shows are better than the competition."

23

TARTIKOFF: "IT'S EASIER WHEN YOU DON'T KNOW YOU'RE GUESSING"

By the end of the 1987–88 prime-time season, programmers at CBS and ABC had reason to feel that they had tried to halt an NBC tank with their bare hands. In May, NBC achieved its third straight prime-time season triumph with an average 16 percent rating, compared to ABC's 13.7 and CBS's 13.6. NBC won on Monday, Thursday, and Saturday nights, and finished second on the other four nights. As he was about to decide his fall 1988–89 schedule, Brandon Tartikoff and his team were confident—too confident—about the series they would throw against the competition.

Take NBC's preoccupation with *Nightingales,* for example. Tartikoff & Company had invested more than NBC's money in Spelling's soap opera. It had become a fixation at NBC's Burbank offices, where Tartikoff expected it to be a huge hit. In April, when the dailies of *Nightingales* were sent over to NBC to give the network an early look at the daily shooting, staffers avidly congregated for a peek. "It's like a porn fest, guys coming in to watch the dailies," laughed Warren Littlefield. One day, as they were transfixed by a locker-room scene—the student nurses romping about in G-strings, lace panties, and bras, with the camera shifting to slow motion as it froze on a nurse pulling a nylon stocking up a shapely leg, gliding languidly from the ankle to the calf to the thigh to the hip, pausing for a split second on the crotch—Littlefield turned to Perry Simon and said, "I think we went too far!"

No one in the room disagreed. In fact, there was already a murmur in Hollywood that without Tinker, Tartikoff would misbehave. This year all three networks had relaxed their broadcast standards restrictions. They now winked at steamy commercials such as Revlon's for Intimate perfume, in which viewers were shown a half-naked woman enjoying what appears to be an orgasm as a male hand gently rubs an ice cube on her body. The broadcast standards departments, which sometimes sanitized language or ethnic stereotypes—and were accused of homogenizing network television—would in the summer of 1988 be drastically slashed as a cost-cutting measure at the three networks; NBC alone would reduce its staff by two thirds, to seventeen. Bob Wright defended these moves by insisting that since NBC was now one of twenty-three networks it was "no longer in a position to impose arbitrary standards." By 1989 the relaxation of these standards would help unleash an advertiser and viewer revolt—with Aaron Spelling's *Nightingales* often cited as a prime example of the new vulgarity—and Wright would be compelled to restaff Broadcast Standards.

But in April 1988 Spelling was encouraged by NBC's reaction to the dailies and by Tartikoff's supportive phone calls. "This is not *Hill Street Blues.* It won't break any new molds," Spelling said. "It won't win any awards. . . . We will say some things about young women. But it's not a documentary about nursing." The series aimed to entertain, Spelling said; to provoke envy and empathy among females, lust among males.

Spelling sounded as if he knew what he was talking about. In retrospect, it is clear he did not. When the two-hour *Nightingales* pilot was completed on May 1, the producer sat in his vast office the next day, his hands jammed into the pockets of blue velour Ellesse sweat pants, and said, "I think it's one of the best things we've ever done. It's the only time in a long time I loved every daily. My main fear right now is cutting it." His edited version ran twenty minutes long, and he had just two days to cut before screening it for Tartikoff. Of all the projects he was working on—two pilots for ABC, a pilot for CBS, the tenth year of *Dynasty,* the continuation of *Heartbeat* on ABC, a remake of *Charlie's Angels* for Fox, several made-for-TV movies—the project Spelling said he cared most about was *Nightingales.* "This is one I conceived," he said. This one yelled: *40 share!* This series would prove to Stoddard and other Hollywood snobs that Aaron Spelling had not lost his touch.

After screening the pilot for his own people, which Spelling said was "fantastic," he invited the director, Mimi Leder, his partner, Douglas Cramer, and a dozen others back to his office for a discussion. Unfailingly generous with praise, kisses, and hugs, Spelling said he wanted to share a few concerns with his staff. "I thought we had too many shots of the girls in G-strings and their bottoms in the locker room," he told them.

The staff disagreed. The locker-room scene was accompanied by music, it had a *Miami Vice feel,* they said. Director Mimi Leder insisted she opposed exploitative scenes and didn't think this one was. Nor did she think the network would object, especially since NBC had passed along to her a tape of a Diet Pepsi commercial with young women, nipples erect, in lingerie and T-shirts. That's the feel, the sensuality, NBC told her they hoped to capture in *Nightingales.*

"It seemed to me a little long," said Spelling. "How long was it?"

"One hundred and twelve seconds," said a production assistant.

"I would beg you to take twelve seconds out of it," said Spelling.

Easy to do, said the production assistant.

"I just feel like we're selling sex," said Spelling, inhaling deeply on his pipe. "It's up there in neon lights."

Spelling was nervous about a second scene, one in which Becky, the golden-haired, sweetly innocent nineteen-year-old student nurse who left the convent and her Midwest farm, is kissed for the first time. The camera closes in on a tongue as it plunges into her mouth, then withdraws and glides down her swanlike neck, and up, then dives into her ear. "I hate the tongue sticking in at fifty miles per hour," said Spelling, sighing deeply and wrinkling his nose. "And I hate the tongue licking her neck!"

"It was their third date!" exclaimed Doug Cramer.

"I'll give you the tongue in the mouth, but not the tongue on the neck!" said Spelling.

"My main fear is that we have everything to lose and nothing to gain," Spelling continued. "If it doesn't work that's all they'll pick on." And as a storyteller, he worried that the scene was "out of character." In real life he felt "a nice kid" like Becky "would freak out." Spelling was trying to sell a series. He didn't want the kissing to be seized upon as a way to dismiss *Nightingales.* For years Spelling had been attacked for exploiting women. He could sniff it coming again. Already, NBC's Broadcast Standards department had sent him a note based on the dailies, questioning the locker-room scene. They wanted the nurses to wear slips. Spelling had persuaded Perry Simon to overrule them, but he didn't want to push the kissing scene. He didn't want NBC to worry about what his enemies—the TV critics—would write. "Licking her neck won't sell this series. But it can kill it!" sighed Spelling.

"Aaron is a prude," said Doug Cramer, smiling. "But so is a large part of America."

In the end, the series would die. But in May 1988 no one in this room—or at NBC—sensed that *Nightingales* was neither good storytelling nor really sexy. Many of these people had enjoyed great success, and yet they dug themselves deeper and deeper into a hole from which there was no exit. Before the staff meeting broke, Spelling made a decision to kill the tongue scene outright. A moment later he had second thoughts. As the staff filed from his office, Spelling asked them back. Perhaps, he said, they should save the scene on a reel and tell the network about it? "If they want the tongue, we can put it back in."

On the day he was scheduled to screen *Nightingales* for NBC, Spelling had a headache. He told the film editor that morning, "I don't want to show the tongue. Even if they say they want it in, it still has my name on it. . . . I don't need another article!" He had once been ridiculed for posing Farrah Fawcett in a wet T-shirt, though he claims she made the decision on her own, enticed by a $1 million advertising fee. At 5:30 P.M. on May 4, Brandon Tartikoff arrived at Spelling's bungalow screening room, accompanied by members of his staff and joined by Spelling's team.

Tartikoff slipped into a seat beside Spelling, who as the lights dimmed nervously announced that the pilot was still more than three minutes too long and, "We have two scenes that are iffy, and we'd like your opinions."

When the lights went up, Tartikoff rose and said, "Nice job," gently, ambiguously. Unlike LeMasters, who quickly excused himself after viewing Spelling's pilot at CBS that spring, Tartikoff asked if they could go to Spelling's office to talk about it.

Nearly two dozen people bunched together around the oversized L-shaped couch—except CAA agent Bill Haber, who purposefully sat to one side on a straight chair, out of the line of conversation. "It has a sense of style," said Tartikoff. His biggest problem was whether "we are trying to recreate *Charlie's Angels* ten years later." On the other hand, Tartikoff thought "it really has a contemporary feel." Carefully, Tartikoff and Perry Simon went through what they liked and didn't like. Tartikoff didn't like the 120 or so seconds in the locker room. "I think the locker-room scene crosses the line," he said.

Spelling said nothing.

"I'm not saying lose the locker room. I'm saying PG it," said Tartikoff, who added, "The kissing scene with Becky seemed like an eternity!"

"I think the actual kissing can be cut by a third," announced Spelling.

"I like that scene," said director Leder.

"I want it to be beautiful," said Spelling. "I don't want it to be dirty."

Leder polled the women in the room, and was surprised that they agreed with Spelling and Tartikoff.

"How about the kissing on the ear in the scene?" asked Doug Cramer.

Spelling interceded, insisting that he didn't like it. Period. Then he said, "We're not going to tell what we took out!"

"We took out the tongue!" said Leder.

"No, we took out a tongue going up and down a neck!" said Spelling.

For an hour the "note session" went on. When Tartikoff rose to leave, Spelling thanked him profusely and pledged to get the finished pilot over to NBC by May 11.

With the NBC team gone, Spelling told his director, "Mimi, those were the best notes we ever had in our lives!"

"I think they were very excited about it," said Leder.

"You could hear a pin drop in the screening room," said Spelling.

"We have a hit. Let's not fool with it," said Cramer.

But two days later, when they heard nothing further from the network—no one assured them that *Nightingales* would make the schedule, no one said that it was fantastic!—Spelling's team was not so certain it had a hit. "Aaron would feel better if he got more enthusiasm from Brandon," said Ilene Chaiken, Spelling's creative affairs vice president. "My feeling is that Brandon is not a game player. He would have said 'It was terrific!' if he thought it was terrific." After a pause, she added, "I think?"

NBC did not think the pilot was "terrific," particularly compared to other NBC dramas like *Tattinger's, Midnight Caller,* and *Dream Street* that arrived around the same time. *Nightingales,* said a disappointed Warren Littlefield, was "recycled television." It didn't "feel fresh," didn't have a distinctive style or look, as *Miami Vice* did. And it made no pretense to grappling with ideas, as *L.A. Law* did. But Tartikoff honestly believed the public was ready for sexual escape, and he trusted Spelling's storytelling skills. Tartikoff was scurrying to find a huge hit that might restore network audiences and keep NBC in first place. *Nightingales*'s fate, Tartikoff suspected, would be determined by the research, not taste. But it would not be easy. He worried that critics would savage it. And how, he plaintively asked three days after screening it, could he justify bumping a serious one-hour drama series like *A Year in the Life* for a piece of fluff like *Nightingales*? How could he give it a place on NBC's schedule over programs from producers he had obligations to?

Tartikoff had a lot on his mind as May's Decision Week neared. He had made thirteen-week series commitments to four comedies and two dramas, and to reject any of these now would be expensive because he would be paying millions for shows he would not air. Perhaps he would have to say no to the four pilots made by NBC Productions. It was in NBC's interest to produce its own shows but not to appear to play favorites. There was also the continuing writers strike to contend with, a strike that had interrupted pilot production and threatened to disrupt the start of the fall season. Tartikoff had to think about how his competitors might arrange their schedules and about how to maneuver his own lead-ins—a series with strong male appeal like *In the Heat of the Night,* about a southern sheriff played by Carroll O'Connor, should not precede a series with female appeal like *Nightingales.*

The entire year was a prelude to Decision Week. All of the series ideas, the internal meetings to refine show concepts and to match them with talent, all the courting, all the negotiating, all the scripts and dailies and pilots—all led to this single week in May when Tartikoff and his team in Burbank, joined by a delegation of New York executives, would no longer have time to cast a new lead, to reedit a script, to get it right a third or fourth time. Decision Week was the finish line.

To Lilly Tartikoff her husband's mood around Decision Week was an annual squall. Fifty weeks or so a year, she said, he rarely complained when burdened with dozens of scripts, rarely talked about escaping. But Decision Week, she said, produced his "annual depression: He hates the town. He hates everybody. He wants to move to Colorado. He's nervous. He knows he's going to be graded." And after eight years of doing this, Tartikoff knew how easy it was to fail.

Tartikoff knew that ABC, like NBC in 1984–85, was the new media darling. And, this year, Tartikoff had begun to think about his own future. He had entrusted more responsibility to his deputy, Warren Littlefield, and to Perry Simon and Michele Brusten, the heads respectively of Drama and Comedy. They had all been together for nearly a decade. This year he would try to do something that he was not very good at: share credit. For the first time he was wondering whether, a year shy of his fortieth birthday, he wasn't burning out. Maybe it was time to move on? This year, he said, was "probably" his last.

But by Monday, May 9, retirement was not on Tartikoff's mind. "I'm always excited, and nervous," said Warren Littlefield, describing his own feelings that morning. "This is the big game. It's like taping up in the locker room."

From New York Wright led a delegation of fourteen executives. Joined by Tartikoff and twenty-five or so members of his Burbank team, for the better part of the next seven days they spent most daylight hours in the huge third-floor conference room above Tartikoff's office watching pilots on one of three TV sets, waiting for Tartikoff to unlock the wall-mounted wooden cabinet containing the magnetized scheduling board with cards for each possible fall series.

"Welcome to Burbank," said Warren Littlefield on Monday afternoon, the first day of Decision Week. "The message loud and clear is demographics." The red-bearded Littlefield, one of the few executives in a coat and tie, explained to the New York visitors that they had made a special effort to attract more young viewers, the kind advertisers wanted. Littlefield dispensed cards so that each executive could rate the twenty-eight pilots from 1 (weakest) to 5 (strongest). A smiling Tartikoff passed out T-shirts showing a horse with an X through its head. This year, he said, there would be "no horses," a reference to the president of NBC's owned stations group, who once said: "If there are any horses in any of these pilots, I'm out of here!" The affiliates wanted urban shows that young women shoppers could identify with. Tartikoff praised his team for doing "great work," and said that "the main concern is coming up with a schedule which we can sell. The second concern is to maintain" NBC's reputation for quality. And third, no matter what critics may say, "we're still in the business of entertaining and getting as many people as possible into the tent."

The lights dimmed and the first pilot appeared on the screens. It was *Something Is Out There,* an action-adventure series about a cop and a beautiful visitor from another solar system.

When the lights went back on, Bob Blackmore, executive vice president for Sales, said, "The demos are there! It's got *urban.*"

"If you don't have good ratings, good demos don't matter," said Research chief William Rubens, underlining a running conflict between Sales and Research. "*Slap Maxwell* on ABC had a 12 rating. It probably had good demos. . . . It's a mistake for us to think of unmass appeal."

This mini-debate was but one of many that Tartikoff would adjudicate this week—between Sales, which cared about ratings but was preoccupied with urban-oriented demos, and Research, which cared about demos but first thought of ratings; between Al Jerome representing NBC's seven owned large city stations, eager for 10:00 shows that played well to urban audiences and provided strong lead-ins to the late news, and many suburban and rural affiliates that prefer the older appeal of shows like *Matlock* or *In the Heat of the Night;* between existing and new series, old and new relationships; between research reports suggesting a series would be weak, and a gut feel it would be strong. Then there were the conflicts within Tartikoff's entertainment division—between Business Affairs, which thought first of costs and contracts, and therefore tended to favor cheaper shows with more pliable stars, and programmers, who thought first of what appeared on the screen; between the Comedy and Drama Development teams, each pushing for time, rooting for its own shows; among entertainment division executives, each wanting to advance careers.

Bob Wright was aware of these conflicts, but with Tartikoff in charge he relaxed, donning a sports shirt and summer slacks and zipping from his downtown L.A. hotel to NBC's Burbank offices in a rented white Mustang convertible. "It's a good thing Brandon has a sense of balance. . . . He's not a moralist," Wright said on day one, meaning that Tartikoff was willing to offer a mix of programming, from highbrow to lowbrow. "It's why my job is a lot easier."

On day two, Perry Simon introduced *Tattinger's,* mentioning that it came from the people who created *St. Elsewhere* and that it was "female oriented." The audience responded modestly—*Tattinger's* rated a 3.19 out of a possible 5 on their scorecards; ten pilots would rate higher, seventeen lower. But the *Tattinger's* score alarmed no one. Paltrow and his team were proven winners, which is why Tartikoff had given them a thirteen-week commitment. And Pier Mapes, the executive to whom Sales reported, was confident NBC could sell each thirty-second spot on it for $150,000 to $200,000, versus the $110,000 the network averaged for a prime-time spot (or the $275,000 per thirty-second spot on *L.A. Law).* Mapes would induce advertisers to pay a premium for *Tattinger's* because the series was set in New York City, because it had "glitz" and Gershwinesque music and Armani clothes—ingredients viewers would "identify with," he said. Though a restaurant was not an ideal setting for an action series, Tartikoff was confident that *Tattinger's* had writers good enough to make the series better than the pilot. And he was confident that, together, they could fix any problems.

About another pilot they would screen on this second day—*Dream Street*—Tartikoff was more ambivalent. The idea for the series, Perry Simon explained, came from a *Rolling Stone* magazine cover story on Bruce Springsteen. Why not, NBC said, do a "sexy, passionate series about young, sexy people living and working in New Jersey," a blue-collar series, set in a place like Hoboken, that would feel like *American Graffiti.* NBC recruited Ed Zwick and Marshall Herskovitz, who had created ABC's *thirtysomething.* Pier Mapes and his Sales people reacted enthusiastically to the urban demographic appeal of the series; the programmers reacted more circumspectly, anxious about the brooding characters with thick accents, the dark look of the show (much of it was shot at night) and the absence of likeable characters—a girlfriend had an illegitimate child, her current boyfriend was in the refrigeration business, and another main character was a low-level mobster. Tartikoff sat in the front row, rarely revealing his feelings, but noted that the lead actress had pimples. "Maybe we can get Clearasil to sponsor it," he said.

"It's too urban," said senior vice president Lee Currlin, a man in his mid-fifties who once programmed for CBS and who now headed Program Planning out of New York. Currlin was the one person in this room Tartikoff would treat as an equal. "There's nobody to like" so far, said Currlin. The execution is "terrific, but it's too dark and grainy for me." The Sales people liked it, he would say later, because "It's young. Urban. Good demos . . . All the things that will make it fail!"

Bob Wright thought *Dream Street* "was terrific." It would be his favorite among all the pilots screened that week. But NBC's CEO attended the screenings as a member of the audience rather than as a decision maker. He entrusted power to Tartikoff, and had other business to conduct over the four days he was out here—negotiations with Bryant Gumbel's West Coast agent over a proposed $2 million contract, discussions with studio chiefs over their common stance toward the writers strike, and secret talks about deals. This year Wright was much more enthusiastic than he had been last. At the end of day two, after he had viewed nine pilots, Wright said, "This year there is a high level of excitement. The production level is incredible. Brandon ought to be thrilled this year."

For Tartikoff the thrills were outweighed by new sources of torment. When day two ended, Tartikoff retreated to his office and was already concerned that he had two quality dramas—*Tattinger's* and *Dream Street*—competing for what he thought might be the same 10 P.M. time slot on Wednesday. He had some counterprogramming ideas, particularly on Tuesday nights, where he hoped to throw *Matlock* and *In the Heat of the Night,* both dramas with older male stars, against the youthful appeal of ABC's *Who's the Boss?* and *Moonlighting.*

If he made these moves, however, Tartikoff knew he would agitate Sales, and perhaps blur NBC's youthful image. Tartikoff also wanted to sneak *Nightingales* onto the schedule and even shifted the screening date so that Wright could see it on Thursday before he left town. He was under no illusions, however. He expected that Aaron Spelling's pilot would neither screen well among NBC executives, nor score well when NBC Research tested it with viewers.

Something else troubled Tartikoff: He didn't like the way his deputy was behaving. Tartikoff could not fail to notice the shirt and tie Littlefield had worn on the first two days and how he sat beside Wright at most screenings as if he were the host, introducing Perry Simon or Michele Brusten, who in turn introduced the pilots. Littlefield had different roots from Tartikoff's, and perhaps this was a source of friction. He was a working-class kid from Montclair, New Jersey, who had attended Hobart College, a small school in upstate New York. Instead of remaining aloof from the antiwar movement, as Tartikoff did at Yale, Littlefield was arrested while protesting Nixon's secret bombing of Cambodia. He had bounced from job to job until Tartikoff hired him in late 1979 to work in Comedy Development. Ever since, in his relationship with Tartikoff, Littlefield played the long-suffering mate, sometimes enduring verbal or mental abuse, sometimes seething quietly that he was treated like a kid though he was only several years Tartikoff's junior. At other times, Littlefield enjoyed the success he had helped engineer.

Brandon Tartikoff is a man of awesome talents with a beguiling personality, but a glaring shortcoming was his tendency to hog the credit. He competed with everyone, whether in scheduling against ABC and CBS, or against Littlefield, or on the softball diamond, where he vies for the batting title as if it were a Nielsen championship; so as not to miss a Saturday softball game, Tartikoff has been known to drag his wife and daughter from a New York hotel to catch a 5:30 A.M. flight to L.A. The tension with Littlefield flared a few days before, when the staff celebrated Littlefield's birthday with cheesecake and candles. One colleague remembered that Tartikoff did not join in singing happy birthday. Nor did he take a piece of cake. At the end of day two of Decision Week, Tartikoff groused, "Warren, it is clear, is auditioning for the job. If he goes over the line, I'll have to pull him back."

On day three, Research made a presentation to the assembled executives. NBC Research tested pilots in three ways. During or just before Decision Week, Research showed the pilots to small focus groups, or sneak-previewed them on four cable channels around the country, or invited four hundred viewers to a movie theater in Hollywood. When people watched at home over a cable channel, Research polled them by telephone; those who came to the theater or to a focus group registered their opinions by turning a dial signifying what they liked or did not, producing a kind of electrocardiogram of a pilot. It was just such a reading, for instance, that guided producer Michael Mann when he reshot the pilot for *Miami Vice* and altered some of the characters. Tartikoff waited for the research, but he knew that research was not the last word. "The more familiar the pilot, the better it does," he said. A then unfamiliar actor—Don Johnson, who had failed in six other pilots—tested poorly on the initial *Miami Vice.* Nor did *Hill Street Blues* test well, except in more sophisticated cable homes. Viewers were confused because instead of the traditional single story line there was a series of interlocking stories. Breakthrough shows—like *Hill Street Blues* or *All in the Family*—tend not to test well because they are unfamiliar. Shows with more familiar formats—like the saccharine *Highway to Heaven*—tested strong but did not become a hit.

During the fall and winter NBC tested episodes and actors in series already on the air, thus helping Tartikoff decide whether to renew a series, expand a character, or replace a lead. In the past year, for example, Research had heavily tested Kirstie Alley, the new female lead of *Cheers,* who replaced Shelley Long. Research also tested shows on CBS and ABC to help Tartikoff decide how to counterprogram against them.

The tendency of those who work in Research is to dress up what they do as a science, something Research chief Bill Rubens did this Wednesday morning. Between 1982 and 1986, he reported, 80 percent of the pilots Research rated "strong" were successful; 83 percent of those rated "weak" were flops. What was hard to predict, he admitted, were those series testing in the middle range—those whose prospects were considered "moderate." The problem, of course, is that most pilots fall in this middle category; since half succeed, picking a winner from this batch is a guessing game. At CBS *The Mary Tyler Moore Show* had tested "weak". While *I Love Lucy* had tested "strong," at first the researchers and programmers turned down Desi Arnaz to play Lucille Ball's husband, since they said viewers would not accept a Cuban bandleader as her mate. Testing, as Tartikoff was fully aware, could be misleading, for it measured first impressions, which change, as does the quality of a series. Unlike *The Cosby Show,* few series become instant hits; they take time to build an audience, which requires a programmer with patience rather than a researcher's printout.

Harder numbers were provided Wednesday afternoon, when Gerald Jaffe of Research offered an overview of the season just ended. The three-network share of audience had declined 7 percent, he said. NBC's audience fell by 14 percent on Thursday nights and 20 percent on Fridays. On three nights the three networks dipped below a 70 percent share of audience, and on Saturday they fell to 65 percent. Everyone in the NBC screening room was reminded that their enemies were not just ABC or CBS but cable channels and Fox and independent stations and the VCR and pay-per-view and even extra leisure time, which had liberated Americans from their homes.

As a result the networks were desperate for hits. This is why Tartikoff pushed so hard for *Nightingales,* which he screened the next morning, on day four. It was to be Bob Wright's last day in Burbank, and as the group settled into their seats, Perry Simon announced: "We're going to try to wake you all up with Aaron Spelling this morning. . . . Sex in the morning!" This produced a few chuckles, and Simon went on to describe how Tartikoff and Spelling had started with a one-line premise: "Student nurses in Dallas in the summer and the air conditioning doesn't work." But Simon described it differently. This is a series, he grinned, about "a group of young women struggling with their identity and aspirations. . . ."

The audience was still giggling as the room went dark and a set of drop-dead legs filled the screen, high heels loudly clicking on a marble floor. They were about to preview the tried and true Spelling formula, accompanied by with-it music and fashions.

The good-natured laughter soon turned to snickers when David, the handsome twenty-three-year-old California Lothario, kisses Becky, the innocent blonde from a Midwest farm, who announced that she had once been in a convent. A moment later, after Becky blushingly says she is a virgin, David responds, "Becky, I'll never make you do anything you don't want to do."

"Sure!" exclaimed several members of the audience in unison.

Betty Hudson was laughing—out of control, hysterically—as were others. Perry Simon squirmed in his seat and whispered, "The cat's out of the bag!"

Executives laughed throughout the entire second half of this two-hour pilot. They laughed when Dr. Roger Taylor plunged his tongue into the mouth of the student nurse in the bathing suit scene. They laughed right through David and Becky's third date when he nibbled on her ear, and as his tongue glided up and down her neck.

When the credits rolled on the screen and the lights returned, the audience hissed. "I thought it was offensive," exclaimed Leslie Lurie, head of Creative Affairs at NBC Productions. Lurie spoke not just for the women in attendance, but for the men as well. *Nightingales* received nearly the lowest grade of the twenty-eight pilots they would watch—averaging a 1.58 out of a possible 5.

Except for Tartikoff, almost no one in the room wanted to pay attention to Research chief Rubens's reminder that all but five NBC executives had stalked out of the *Highway to Heaven* screening. Yet it tested well, so well that it made NBC's schedule. Like Tartikoff, Rubens thought the real test for *Nightingales* was how it would do in both the cable test and in the Hollywood theater on Thursday night.

Bob Wright, like Tartikoff and Rubens, was not giving up on the series. The Spelling show, he said before heading back to New York tonight, "is a good idea for us." It was the kind of series NBC's schedule lacked. It offered women the kind of stories once featured in romance magazines. Wright believed that *Nightingales* would test well and that Tartikoff could resist the criticism of fellow executives or critics. Brandon, he would say, is "the toughest executive at NBC. He gets right to the point. He will cut you off or move on if you have nothing to contribute." To Wright, whether to air *Nightingales* was simply a business decision.

By Thursday evening everyone was eager for Tartikoff to unlock the magnetic scheduling board at the other end of the conference room. "Brandon should be getting itchy by now," said Lee Currlin, his quiet, older confidant from New York.

Throughout the week Tartikoff and Currlin whispered to each other, but during the screenings Tartikoff would say to Currlin, "Don't tell me what you think yet." Nevertheless, by the fourth day of Decision Week Currlin was certain that Tartikoff had already decided on NBC's schedule and was only awaiting the research results. Unlike Grant Tinker—who often disparaged research and once told Tartikoff to ignore the poor research report on *ALF* and remember instead that the comedy made him and everyone else who screened it laugh—Lee Currlin believed in research. "If the research comes out very poorly for a show we thought was terrific, it would be tough to schedule it," he said. Conversely, if the research said viewers liked Spelling's *Nightingales,* Tartikoff was prepared to overrule everyone in this room who hated it.

Spelling was on Tartikoff's mind, and at 6:00 Thursday evening he phoned the producer but missed him. Having to run off to an early dinner with Wright before the NBC president caught his plane, Tartikoff entrusted the call to Simon. Tartikoff's way was to treat "talent" well; he understood the insecurity of people whose work and livelihood awaited the judgment of others. "It's like college interviewing," observed the chairman of International Creative Management, Jeff Berg. Or like opening night. After a day's screenings, Tartikoff & Company always took care to make the calls and relay how the pilot played. At 7:40 P.M., Spelling called Simon back.

"You and I talked about this long before the screening. The room we showed *Nightingales* to is not our target audience," said Simon to the producer, tiptoeing between reassurance and candor. "At one or two points the audience responded as if it were camp. Then it became a mob psychology. Then there was more laughter. The biggest part I picked up on was the revelation that she was a nun. In the room today that was a critical moment. Research will play a role here. I hope there will be some things from Research that allow us to say to the room, 'Look, they like Chelsea. They like Bridget.' "

Spelling reminded Simon that his hit series, *Charlie's Angels,* did not score well with research, registering a "weak" 5.7 when tested in 1976 at the ASI Theater. *How did the women in the audience respond?* he asked.

"The women in the room were the most vocal," answered Simon. "My guess is that they feel that's how they have to present themselves," he said soothingly. Simon added: "There's going to be a lot more discussion." He then announced that he had to rush off to the ASI theater, where Research had invited a test audience of four hundred to sample Spelling's pilot.

Though the ASI was a Hollywood movie theater on Sunset Boulevard, the invited audience was right out of *Back to the Future.* More than a few women fixed their hair in buns; some men wore powder-blue polyester outfits. Attached to each seat was a knob, which viewers were instructed to turn one way or the other when they liked or disliked something. Connected to the knobs were wires that traveled to a third-floor, glass-walled office overlooking the auditorium, where they were attached to a computer that compressed the four hundred responses into a single black line that rose or fell between the boundaries of 0 (the lowest score) and 10 (the highest score). 8 or above was considered "high"; a "moderate" was between 6.5 and 8; anything below a 6.5 was "weak." Also considered "weak" was a needle that did not rise steadily as the show unfolded. Three other machines deciphered the demographic responses, including the differing reactions of women and men.

Perry Simon and Ted Frank from NBC Research were joined in the control room by several Spelling representatives, led by Ilene Chaiken. All eyes remained glued to the wavy lines. For the first forty-five minutes the needle hovered between a dismal 5 and 6. It climbed slightly above 6 when a skimpily clad Samantha gyrated in a nightclub dance routine. But as the dance ran on, the needle fell below 6 again.

"They're getting bored," whispered a worried Simon. Usually in a dramatic series the needle score builds slowly. This time, the needle wasn't cooperating. After the first hour, Simon said, "They're just not into it. There's no build."

The first snickers came, as they did in the NBC screening room, when Becky mentioned she had been in the convent, followed by loud laughter when David vowed not to "make you do anything you don't want to do." With the laughter the needle fell. The problem with the pilot, an NBC programmer would say later, was that people like prurience but they don't like to feel they're watching pornography. "You've got to disguise the larceny," he said. This *Nightingales* failed to do. The mystery was how smart people could have been so dumb as to miss this.

Spelling's people recovered their spirits when the shapely Julie appeared in the bathing suit scene and the needle instantly jumped above 7. But then it plunged again. It kept dropping when David's tongue licked Becky's long neck.

The show averaged a "weak" 6.1 score. As Ilene Chaiken walked to her car, she admitted, "We're a bit devastated by the results." She knew *Nightingales* was Spelling's pet project. However, she also knew the decision was sealed. "We have very little hope *Nightingales* will be on the schedule," Chaiken said as she slipped behind the wheel of her car and drove off into the night.

Tartikoff had yet to go to the scheduling board by the end of day five, yet the new season's schedule was taking shape in his mind. He knew that he probably couldn't put *Nightingales* on the schedule, even though he desperately wanted to. Like Spelling himself, Tartikoff seemed driven to prove something. When people told him *Nightingales* was so bad it was almost camp, Tartikoff bristled: *Batman* and Vanna White were also camp! When people warned him that the audience would laugh at it, Tartikoff remembered how NBC executives laughed at other shows—like *The A-Team*—that became hits. A network had to offer a range of choices, he believed. Grant Tinker believed that too. But where Tinker might have steered Tartikoff away from an embarrassment like *Nightingales,* Bob Wright and Jack Welch loved tough guys, welcomed Tartikoff's poke-em-in-the-eye attitude.

By Saturday morning—day six—Tartikoff finally wandered upstairs to the conference room and unlocked the scheduling board which contained all the likely series to be shown by NBC, ABC and CBS, but not Fox. By mid-1988, Fox still provided its 118 affiliates with only two full nights of broadcasting—Saturday and Sunday—and this year would lose $80 million. But this would be the last year Tartikoff would build his schedule without considering Fox's plans. By 1989 Fox would be on the magnetic board, and by the fall of 1990 its hit, *The Simpsons,* went head-to-head with the mighty Cosby. As he stared at the board in May 1988, Tartikoff knew that NBC would be first to announce its schedule and therefore he had to guess what ABC and CBS shows he would be programming against. Assuming that ABC kept *thirtysomething* on Tuesdays at 10, he wanted to move his *Midnight Caller* card into the same time slot because the ABC show "is very female" and *Midnight Caller* was a male-oriented series. He liked the idea of a show with urban appeal like *Tattinger's* at 10 P.M. on Wednesday, against CBS's *The Equalizer* and ABC's *Dynasty,* which appealed to older viewers. He toyed with several cards to lead off Wednesdays at 8, including *Unsolved Mysteries,* an inexpensively produced imitation of Fox's successful *America's Most Wanted* that had attracted respectable ratings for NBC when it aired as specials. "The only way to get *Year in the Life* on the schedule is Monday at 10:00," said Tartikoff, who a year earlier had hailed the series as "one not seen on the air since *Family* at ABC." Studying the schedule board as he pondered this move, Tartikoff knew that placing *A Year in the Life* on Monday at 10 P.M. would mean scrapping a movie night and coming up with another hour of fresh programming at 9 P.M. to compensate for the two-hour movie. He didn't feel he could do that.

Before Tartikoff could go on, Ted Frank entered the conference room, arms bulging with folders containing the latest test results. As the jeans-clad executives ate club sandwiches, Frank coolly reviewed the findings. Tartikoff asked Frank to review the results of *Nightingales* with some precision. Frank said it was their lowest rated drama. The character the audience related to best was Samantha, he said, and the least was Becky. While Samantha got a relatively good 25 Q (likeability) score, the series itself received a Q score of 8 among men and only 10 among women.

Almost instantly Tartikoff returned to the board and placed *Nightingales* off to the side, on a magnetized panel known as "Death Valley." After a few minutes, Tartikoff excused himself to go to his office for a meeting, and the group dispersed.

Forty-five minutes later they reconvened, and Tartikoff returned to the board. This time, *A Year in the Life* was on his mind. "Part of me wants to pick it up," he said. The other part worried that the Emmy-winning series lacked a cast of recognizable stars and that its creators were too infatuated with the characters they had introduced to allow them to grow. There were other issues, including: Should he give some special consideration to two drama series, *Oakmont Stories* and *Sonny Spoon,* since they were produced by NBC Productions? That night nothing would be resolved.

Sunday—day seven—would be Decision Day. With the exception of Bill Rubens and his Research contingent, plus Lee Currlin, most of the New York executives had returned home. Tartikoff, in jeans, spent a good part of the morning with Research, talking about the test results for the pilots, talking about "the audience flow" from, say, a reality-based series like *Unsolved Mysteries* to a comedy, talking about the vulnerabilities of ABC or CBS shows. It was obvious that Tartikoff knew more about ABC and CBS's likely fall schedule than he was supposed to.

Why was Tartikoff so conversant with the plans of his competitors? One reason is that Hollywood agents are sometimes double agents. During Decision Week, they prowl the halls or pick up the phone and trade news in exchange for information about their clients. Agents know more than anyone else about what all the networks are doing. In Hollywood agents have four sources of clout—their clients, their treasure-trove of information, their power as an informal employment placement service, and their longevity. Network programmers come and go, but agents like Bill Haber of CAA or Alan Berger, his television counterpart at ICM, are fixtures. "The more the changeover of buyers," said Haber, "the more insecure and thus the more dependent they become on the seller."

At 1 P.M. Tartikoff wandered upstairs and headed for the board once more. Poor research results meant that he couldn't use *Oakmont Stories* to lead off Wednesday night, and he pushed its card off to the side. He made it clear that no one could tamper with *Empty Nest.* He had a commitment to its producer, Susan Harris, to place it at 9:30 P.M. Saturday, behind her hit show, *Golden Girls.* He didn't tell the group, but Tartikoff also had obligations to Gary David Goldberg to try to keep his new series, *Day by Day,* behind Goldberg's *Family Ties* on Sundays; he had commitments as well to Johnny Carson for *Amen,* to Bill Cosby for *A Different World,* and to Michael Eisner to run the Disney series on Friday rather than Sunday night. As good as he was at nurturing talent, Tartikoff didn't then appreciate fully the message he was unintentionally sending to some members of the Hollywood community: NBC had become a closed shop.

Others sat around the conference table eating roast chicken, but a tense Tartikoff ate only strawberries. And stared at the board. He took a break to meet with the producers of *A Year in the Life,* at which he asked them to review where, if the series were renewed, they planned to take their characters in the coming season. Tartikoff was not reassured by their answers, which prompted him to consign this series to Death Valley when he returned to the board at 2:30 P.M. Near the end of the day, Tartikoff made decisions he would reverse the next day, including a decision to place *The Incredible World of Disney* on Friday at 8:00.

Monday morning—day eight—Tartikoff arrived at the board and started pulling off cards. He focused intently on the *Nightingales* card, which was still in Death Valley. The only spot that would have made sense for the student nurses was 10:00 on Wednesday, he said. But that time slot had belonged to *A Year in the Life,* and to bump a "quality" series for Spelling's would have enraged the critics. "I would have done it," he said, if research suggested Spelling's series was a 35 share! But now *A Year in the Life* was also in Death Valley, replaced by *Tattinger's.* Tartikoff was nervous that the pilot was "a little chi-chi" for network TV. A network programmer has an unwritten list of things that don't play with mass audiences—like psychiatric therapy sessions, spoofs which viewers might not know how to interpret, downbeat shows, and thick ethnic accents. All were no-no's, like Cuban bandleaders playing a lead—before Desi Arnaz came along. Despite slight misgivings, Tartikoff was convinced *Tattinger's* would improve because "there is no better writing group working in television than those guys." One last time, he reached up to retrieve *A Year in the Life,* moving it to 10 P.M. on Tuesday and *Midnight Caller* to Friday at 9:00. This thought lasted about a minute.

Pondering the board, Tartikoff said he was uncomfortable with *Dream Street;* it was too dark, and so he kept it off the final schedule even though it was Bob Wright's favorite pilot. It's a measure of the freedom Wright granted Tartikoff that none of the executives in Burbank, including Tartikoff, even knew *Dream Street* was Wright's personal favorite. Network television is that rare business where the CEO often stands off to the side while underlings decide the product line.

Before he closed the scheduling board at 9:20 A.M. to head for the airport and New York, Tartikoff glanced one final time at the year ahead. He had tentatively decided on six and one-half hours of new series for the fall, only one of which—*Sonny Spoon*—came from NBC Productions.* Tartikoff was unhappy that only one new series from the 1987–88 season—*A Different World*—would return. But this year, unlike last, he felt he had some winners: New comedies like *Dear John* and *Empty Nest* might one day replace *Cheers* and *The Cosby Show;* dramas like *Tattinger's* or *Midnight Caller* might replace *Miami Vice.*

Tartikoff had one final chore before heading for New York, and that was to deliver the bad news to Aaron Spelling.

Tartikoff would tell Spelling he didn't make NBC's fall schedule, but he eased the rejection by telling him the network planned to air *Nightingales* as a two-hour Monday movie in early summer, preceded by one and one-half times the usual amount of promos and advertising. "If it gets a huge rating," Tartikoff said, "it would prove both of us right." At that point NBC would order a full thirteen weeks of one-hour shows and Spelling could be ready to go on the NBC schedule as a midseason replacement.

Spelling was depressed. "I've never been in this situation before," said the producer whose series were always welcomed as surefire hits. He was convinced that, aside from *Dynasty,* which had been on the air nine years and had plunged from number one in 1984–85 to thirty-ninth this season, he might be off the air entirely at ABC and CBS. He was angry at both ABC and CBS. Yet despite the rejection of *Nightingales,* Spelling said of NBC: "They've been as helpful, as generous and kind as can be. I still think it's a good show, and could be a hit."

Tartikoff was also depressed, for different reasons. The three networks together spent nearly $500 million on developing new series, ordering up ninety or so pilots even though they knew there were maybe only a couple of dozen outstanding writer/producers or stars

* Though the three networks collectively were allowed to own and produce nine hours of prime-time entertainment programs this year and fifteen the next few years, they would produce but two hours this fall—*Sonny Spoon* and ABC's *Moonlighting.*

that could carry a series, and maybe a dozen television directors. The pilot process, Tartikoff knew, was irrational. Yet he had just done it, again, for the ninth year. On the other hand, by the time he left for the airport, Tartikoff was beginning to pump himself up to sell the schedule to advertisers, affiliates, and the press. Then, as he entered the first-class cabin, he bumped into Bill Haber, and the two men fell deep into conversation.

Haber went to New York every year at this time to be close to the action on behalf of his clients. By 1988, he had known Tartikoff for thirteen years, Stoddard for nineteen, and LeMasters for seventeen. Not only known them, and their deputies, but recommended them for jobs, done them favors, negotiated with them, listened to their problems. Tartikoff spent time on the plane with Haber because he, like Alan Berger, who headed the TV department at ICM, was a power. Haber's partner, Michael Ovitz, who runs CAA, used to indulge in a game with friends, asking them to name the ten most powerful figures in Hollywood. At the time, Ovitz would nominate himself, tentatively. By 1990, after he had helped engineer the sale of Columbia to Sony and MCA to Matsushita, Ovitz no longer had to play this parlor game since he was commonly hailed as Hollywood's new king.

A stewardess interrupted Tartikoff and Haber and asked, "Are you Brandon Tartikoff?"

"Yes."

"Do me a favor? Renew *A Year in the Life,*" she said.

The stewardess could hardly have depressed Tartikoff more. He was so vexed over cancelling this series, and by rumors that ABC was about to pick it up, that he had even mentioned it to Jack Welch. *Don't worry. The show's a turkey!* Welch reassured him.

Tartikoff did not believe it was a *turkey,* though he was disappointed in its growth. What he did believe was that the media would clobber NBC. Staring out the window of the DC10 as it climbed through the clouds, he fretted that cancelling the series "sends a signal out there that NBC is different. Not that NBC is not doing quality things. But they'll say, 'Once upon a time you renewed *St. Elsewhere.*' Once upon a time NBC bet on quality."

Tartikoff's prediction proved correct. FAT CAT NBC TOO GREEDY read a New York *Daily News* headline. NBC's reputation as the "quality" network was further tarnished when later that spring it was revealed that Tartikoff had contracted for a two-hour Geraldo Rivera prime-time special—*Devil Worship: Exposing Satan's Underground*—from 8 to

10 P.M. on October 25. News of the Rivera special appeared in newspapers on the same day Tartikoff was unveiling *Nightingales* as a two-hour movie. Cleverly scheduled against a June 27 baseball game, and heralded by waves of promotion—"Six beautiful women. Six shocking secrets!"—Spelling's movie turned out to be the most watched show on any network that week, capturing a 34 share and 18 million viewers.

Spelling was euphoric when the ratings arrived the next day; more so when Tartikoff called to say, "I'm picking you up," meaning he expected Spelling to have the series ready to step in as a midseason replacement.

Within days, Aaron Spelling's cold phone became hot. Brandon Stoddard now cooed into the receiver. CBS, which had snubbed his pilot, invited him to lunch. Once again, he was King Aaron.

But his reign was brief. While Spelling readied his series in the fall of 1988, Bruce Paltrow's *Tattinger's* premiered to weak reviews and an audience that fell by 3.3 million viewers from its first to its fourth episode. *Newsday's* TV critic, Marvin Kitman, asked: How could the creators of *St. Elsewhere* and "seven of TV's greatest creators/writers/producers . . . have cooked up such a mess of a show?" By December, after its audience had shrunk from a 25 to a lowly 13 share, Tartikoff pulled the plug on Paltrow's series and announced that it would be replaced on Wednesdays at 10:00 by *Nightingales.*

Nightingales premiered on February 22, 1989, and attracted 22 percent of the available audience, a reasonably good result. But the ratings quickly dropped. Nurses associations protested that the series didn't show what nurses actually did but displayed them as sex objects. Parents complained that *Nightingales* was pornography. Advertisers panicked and said that the controversy was hurting their "friendly" products. In March 1989, Pier Mapes warned Tartikoff at lunch: "We can't sell it. People don't want to be associated with that show." Tartikoff had to cancel *Nightingales,* leaving Aaron Spelling, by mid-1989, without a series on any network, including Fox, for the first time in twenty-five years.

Nightingales and *Tattinger's* had failed. So had *Dream Street* when Tartikoff placed it on NBC's midseason schedule. All of which, and more, led Tartikoff to muse: "It gets harder. I think I know too much now. At first, I did things and learned from mistakes. It was easier to do then because you didn't know you were guessing."

One nonguess at the end of the 1988–89 season was that NBC was left with a schedule very vulnerable to attack.

24

ABC, NBC, AND CBS, SUMMER 1988 THROUGH 1989

Throughout the summer and fall of 1988, before his show flopped, Aaron Spelling was possessed. He would make *Nightingales* a hit, prove to the Hollywood colony that he had not lost his touch. Spelling was getting ready to do the series as a winter replacement, recruiting new writers, dropping actors, adding contemporary music and young directors. Among those consulted was his good friend Suzanne Pleshette, the actress who once starred in *The Bob Newhart Show.* Spelling wanted an actress to play house mother to the eight student nurses, and thought Pleshette would be perfect. At fifty-one, she was still attractive and shapely. And her husky voice would convey authority.

I'd love to be a Nightingale! said Pleshette.

Great, said Spelling, thinking she had agreed to be the house mother.

No, said Pleshette. She wanted to be one of the student nurses!

Pleshette eventually accepted the role of house mother. But like her, in the summer and fall of 1988 the three networks deluded themselves. NBC was certain that the 1988 Summer Olympics would provide a big ratings boost, and assumed that no matter how coarse the stunt—putting on *Nightingales,* or made-for-TV movies such as *Sex Tapes* and *Swimsuit,* or the Geraldo Rivera special on satanism—NBC would not tarnish its crown. NBC News believed a new president would relieve corporate pressures on News. ABC believed that it could close the gap between its second-place finish and NBC's, believed it had a surefire hit in *War and Remembrance,* the most expensive miniseries in history. CBS believed it could escape third place, overtaking ABC with its own "quality" schedule, its own determination to patiently wait for its series to build an audience. Each network believed that management changes would improve its competitive standing. Each had great hopes that it could halt the erosion of network audiences. Each failed.

Against an expanding field of competitors, the three networks continued their decline. For the sixth straight year, the networks' share of the viewing audience would slip, from 72 in 1987 to 67.2 percent by April 1989. In those households with cable, the network audience plunged to 56 percent. Two of every three lost viewers were claimed by cable, which had hooked up 55 percent of all homes by the start of 1989. The Fox network and other independent stations took one out of every five viewers. Sixty-four percent of all TV homes had a VCR. Network advertising had grown a miserly 2.5 percent over the past three years, while advertising on cable and in barter syndication surged 22 percent. The three networks finished in the same order in 1988–89 as they had the previous season—NBC, ABC, and CBS. But in the race against the future, the networks were losing.

Late in August 1988, a summit meeting was held in Tom Murphy's office on the thirty-ninth floor of the ABC building. The meeting was John Sias's idea, for Sias was frustrated. He was responsible for the network but he lacked the authority to run it. To make matters worse, Mike Dann floated free of any management constraint, fluttering near Tom Murphy's ear, sending Murphy memos about how to produce *Mission Impossible* in Australia at a bargain price of $700,000 an episode. The normally ebullient Sias had become subdued, depressed.

Brandon Stoddard had similar concerns. Like Sias, he bridled at Mike Dann's private pipeline to Tom Murphy and was frustrated by his own duplicative lines of communication to Murphy, Sias, and Burke. But he was less unhappy than Sias since Murphy still gave him the kind of programming freedom Kim LeMasters of CBS could only envy. And ABC had won twenty-one Emmy Awards that summer, more than either NBC or CBS, including Emmys for the outstanding drama series *(thirtysomething)* and the best comedy series *(The Wonder Years)*.

The August summit meeting to address tangled internal communications included Murphy, Dan Burke, and Sias. They spent the morning dissecting the issue. In the afternoon they invited Stoddard to ventilate his views.

As a consequence of the summit, Mike Dann lost his exclusive access to Murphy; in fact, he would lose his ABC office and was relocated to Cap Cities' Fifty-first Street headquarters, where he was told to confine himself to helping out with Cap Cities' cable operations. Sias was given more managerial oversight of Stoddard's entertainment division, and would now chair ABC's budget reviews on his own. "John no longer has to talk to both of us," said Burke.

The less obvious outcome of the August summit was that Brandon Stoddard lost still more power. With Murphy ceding authority, Sias would become more of a boss to Stoddard. "The honeymoon with Brandon is over," said Sias a few weeks later.

But at the start of the 1988–89 season, it appeared that the "honeymoon" was still on. *Roseanne* became the first new superhit on any network in several seasons. Two other new shows—*The Wonder Years* and *China Beach*—averaged an impressive 25 share. But there were failures, too. *War and Remembrance,* which ran for almost thirty hours and cost $110 million, was a dud, trailing NBC during the week in November when the first eighteen hours were shown. ABC's schedule was still weak on three nights. Only one of Stoddard's new hour-long dramas would last the season. *Moonlighting* slipped precipitously in the ratings, and was finally cancelled in February. Stoddard's initial mid-season replacements did less well than CBS's; in fact, powered by its hit miniseries, *Lonesome Dove,* by February 1989 CBS threatened to pass ABC and claim second place.

Murphy and Burke were not happy. "We have more troubled half-hour and hour shows than successes," said Burke. Cap Cities had given Stoddard the authority he demanded, had gone along with him on miniseries and *Dolly* and agreed to be patient with *Moonlighting.* ABC's Emmys and press clippings were small comfort to the businessmen running Cap Cities. They wanted to see costs under control. "Brandon always felt it was our responsibility to prevent him from spending us into bankruptcy," said Tom Murphy, "and that was very difficult for us." Decentralization worked only if Cap Cities believed that the entertainment division was well managed. With Stoddard, they lacked that assurance. By the winter of 1989, they no longer believed their Brandon was as good as NBC's Brandon.

In March of 1989, Tom Murphy flew to L.A. and fired his pal Stoddard. "Brandon didn't love the job," explained Murphy. He "didn't love the action. There hasn't been a Saturday or a Sunday when I didn't get the ratings. Brandon would go home on the weekends and not get the ratings till Monday morning!" Stoddard loved producing, and was almost relieved to accept an expanded job as head of ABC Productions. In Stoddard's place, Murphy immediately installed Sias's thirty-seven-year-old deputy, Robert Iger. With Stu

Bloomberg staying on as Iger's principal programmer, Murphy was convinced he had a team in place that could build on Stoddard's successes. "Iger keeps score the way we keep score," said Murphy. For those who kept score of internal ABC battles, this was a win for John Sias.

By the end of the 1988–89 season, ABC would lengthen its ratings lead over third-place CBS. And in the 1989–90 season, ABC began to gain on NBC, narrowing the ratings gap and actually passing NBC as the number-one network among select demographic groups, such as young men. Murphy would come to praise Stoddard as the architect of ABC's resurgence, crediting him for such series as Bochco's *Doogie Howser, M.D.*

Management changes improved ABC's lines of communication, but a more aggressive John Sias could not boost the network's dismal 1988 profits. While Cap Cities/ABC's overall operating income rose to $816 million in 1988, and its stock price went to $362, from $344 at the close of 1987, the ABC network lost $4 million. By contrast, ABC's eight owned stations earned more than $400 million. In the four years since Cap Cities had announced its merger with ABC, Tom Murphy ruefully said, network profits totalled just $115 million on revenues of $10 billion.

By June 1988, CBS was in considerably worse shape than ABC. Immediately after the disastrous June affiliate meeting, Kriegel knew Tisch was ready to remove Jankowski as president of the Broadcast Group. Kriegel had a candidate for the job, but first his boss had to overcome a personal hurdle. Larry Tisch could be ruthless in ordering his executives to terminate underlings, but he trembled at the thought of doing the dirty deed himself. Always there was Bob Tisch or another executive to do it. "Contrary to what everyone thinks, I'm too soft," said Tisch, explaining why Jankowski survived as long as he did.

The first moves were made by Kriegel, who with Tisch's knowledge began meeting in June with his friend Howard Stringer to feel him out about becoming president of the Broadcast Group. Stringer had not yet signed his new contract and felt spent. He had picked up the leavings of two controversial News presidents, endured painful budget cuts, expansive egos, and a news division split into factions. He was tired of holding Dan Rather's hand, tired of the politics within News, tired of conducting meetings and reading about them in the press the next day. CBS News, he would later tell a press conference, "believed in the primal scream theory of public relations!"

Stringer also knew there were serious questions to be confronted about the future of nightly newscasts. Every year the three newscasts lost 3 to 4 percent of their audience. Game shows regularly trounced News in the ratings race. Would network news have to imitate Fox's lurid *A Current Affair,* or Morton Downey, Jr., or Geraldo Rivera, in order to attract viewers? Would News have to submit to endless rounds of budget cuts? How could you justify sending three hundred News employees at a cost of $10 million to cover a political convention, as CBS did this summer, when viewers were tuning out? Would each network have to slash its seventy to ninety highly paid correspondents, replacing them with competent but lower-paid reporter/producers who expected less airtime and fed many of their stories to a dozen or so star correspondents? Would network news lose its coveted half hour each evening? Would it instead become a packager, selling pieces to stations like an Associated Press wire service? Would CNN prevail over the networks in a crisis—as in 1991 during the war with Iraq—because CNN had twenty-four hours of airtime and two sources of revenue to sustain a worldwide news-gathering operation?

Stringer felt it was time to move on. He worked well with Tisch and Kriegel. He was experienced at functioning collaboratively. While Stringer had little experience in Hollywood, unlike most executives who ran a network he actually knew his way around an edit room and had produced more than six hundred broadcasts, not counting his three years as executive producer of the *Evening News.*

Larry Tisch first broached the topic to Stringer over dinner at Parioli Romanissimo on June 28. While Tisch did not technically offer Stringer the job since he had yet to talk to Jankowski or his board, signals were exchanged. They left dinner knowing an offer had been rendered and accepted. To replace Stringer at CBS News, the two men talked about ABC's David Burke, whom neither knew, except by reputation and the importunings of Jay Kriegel.

Kriegel had known Burke since 1965, and Burke was his candidate. They had met when Burke was a legislative aide to Senator Ted Kennedy and had retained a Harvard Law professor to craft a defense of the proposed Voting Rights Act. The professor brought along his prized third-year law student, Jay Kriegel, and Burke was impressed. Although they barely saw each other over the next twenty-odd years, on the few occasions Kriegel had to make a tough career choice, he consulted Burke. Kriegel invited Burke to lunch in late June. At the end of the meal, Kriegel said, "Would you like to be president of CBS News?"

"I don't know," said Burke, genuinely flabbergasted. Kriegel had expressed nothing but praise for Howard Stringer, and now Burke couldn't understand why CBS would want to replace him. No, no, Kriegel explained. They were thinking of replacing Jankowski and elevating Stringer. Before he would talk to Tisch or Stringer, Burke would have another meal with Kriegel.

Like Stringer, Burke had been a number two and was ready to move up. In many ways, he really managed ABC News. People came to him for answers they couldn't get from the less accessible Arledge. He was a popular figure at ABC News, where he had never been entirely comfortable with Cap Cities, particularly with John Sias. David Burke kept his distance, believing his primary mission was to educate, not to advance shareholder values.

At fifty-two, David Burke wanted to be president of CBS News. For the moment he forgot the misgivings he had voiced about Larry Tisch and his values in 1986: "With me it always comes down to the last day in the hospital room when you've got to make an account of yourself. Larry Tisch may be in that hospital room and be very pleased with the stock market price of his company. But those are not my values." Burke also squelched doubts he harbored about whether Dan Rather could survive as an anchor after a series of "strange events," including Rather's belligerent encounter with George Bush.

The next hurdle for Burke was a July 5 dinner with Stringer. It was an exploratory meeting, and no offer was made or accepted. Stringer left believing Burke was, in his words, "a grown-up," a man with a keen sense of probity. Two nights later Burke dined with Tisch in a private suite at Loews's Regency Hotel. Before going to dinner the ever-correct Burke informed Roone Arledge. "I hope it happens for you," Arledge told his friend. "But for us I hope it doesn't happen." At dinner Tisch was careful not to offer the job formally, wanting first to get his board's assent. But the job was his, as Burke told Arledge the next day.

While the Stringer/Burke maneuvers progressed, Gene Jankowski seemed as oblivious to them as Larry Grossman had been to NBC's search for his own successor. As late as June 29, Jankowski asserted that he had no intention of leaving. In early July, Jankowski got wind of the plot, visited Tisch, and told him he would like to go off and run his own company. Tisch was spared having to fire Jankowski.

The eight days between July 5 and July 13, 1988, when the appointments of Stringer and Burke were announced, were tense. Burke worried that if Tom Murphy learned of his new job he might call his friend Tisch and urge him to rescind the offer. Arledge was distressed about losing Burke, yet even though Burke told him on Friday, July 8, that he planned to leave, Arledge chose not to alert his superiors until after the weekend. "The way he handled the whole thing was as decent and generous as anything I've ever experienced in my professional life," said Burke.

Tisch and Stringer worried about press leaks, since the circle of those who knew widened to include at least a dozen people. The secret held for an entire week. Larry Tisch had one final worry as the announcement approached: the reaction of Tom Murphy. He decided, as a courtesy, to call Murphy just before the July 13 announcement.

If Murphy had persuaded Tisch to pull back, or for some other reason David Burke's appointment was aborted, Tisch said he had a backup in mind. Someone who had been a working reporter as well as an editor and publisher—someone whose name kept surfacing every time Tisch asked his publishing friends to name a journalist who was also a businessman. "If David Burke fell through," said Tisch, "I planned to talk to Michael Gartner."

But Burke did not fall through, and Murphy did not resist. In his best "okay pal" style, Murphy put Tisch at ease. *Congratulations. You picked a good man.* Privately, Murphy was upset. He had been disturbed when CBS hired Kathleen Sullivan away from ABC in September 1987, but not as much as he was now. The unspoken gentleman's compact was over. "Tom said to me," recalls Arledge, " 'Past statements are no longer operative.' " Arledge, who was not permitted to chase Diane Sawyer in 1986, could now do so.

The decision would come back to haunt CBS. With a wink from his boss, Arledge began courting Sawyer, taking her to quiet lunches, telling her CBS and *60 Minutes* were underutilizing her talents, that she was getting lost among the five correspondents on that show. He said he wanted her to join ABC and cohost a new prime-time magazine show. When Arledge woos talent he is as ardent as someone in love. Because Arledge is usually so remote, the target is all the more impressed.

Sawyer wasn't given that special feeling at CBS. Oh, sure, she got it from Tisch and Paley, who treated her like a queen. But she barely knew her new boss, David Burke. And he offended her by proposing that CBS could give her more visibility if she became chief White House correspondent. Recently and happily married to director Mike Nichols, Sawyer was not about to move to Washington, which to her would be a step down. Yes, she wanted more camera time; but she also wanted stature and a vehicle to showcase her talents. Perhaps she would have felt better if Broadcast president Howard Stringer was her champion. Yet Sawyer drew no comfort from her former News boss, who treated her warily, mindful of how she flaunted her social ties to Tisch and Paley.

Early in 1989, Sawyer succumbed to Arledge's advances, shocking the communications world by leaving CBS. She would cohost ABC's *Prime Time Live* and would become a backup anchor to both Jennings and Koppel. She would be paid $1.7 million, and over the course of a five-year contract her pay would rise. After years of being hailed as the trailblazer for network news, the network with the strongest bench of correspondents, suddenly CBS was yesterday. Tomorrow belonged to ABC News and its stars. Arledge would cleverly underline this message with ABC's own Mount Rushmore advertising campaign, one featuring head shots of Jennings, Koppel, Barbara Walters, David Brinkley, Sam Donaldson, Hugh Downs, and Sawyer. The ad, and the talk of ABC's bench strength, including such outstanding reporters as Jeff Greenfield, James Wooten, Brit Hume, and the lucid commentary of George Will, made Larry Tisch somewhat defensive. "Diane Sawyer is a star in the media of New York City," he said then. "She's not a star around the country. . . . I think they have two stars at ABC—Barbara Walters and Ted Koppel. A star is someone who can get on a show and make it work."

In Sawyer's case, Tisch proved correct. She would not send her magazine show soaring in the ratings. But he wrongly left out Jennings, and perhaps Brinkley. By the fall of 1988, executive producer Paul Friedman had quietly introduced some of the new format changes he had proposed in early 1987. Relaxed with a new producer and format, by 1989 Jennings had steered *World News Tonight* into first place; by 1991 he would open an extraordinary two-ratings-point lead over number-two NBC, while Rather's newscast continued its slow but steady descent.

ABC strove to make a larger point, one Tisch seemed to miss. Once again, the new owners of ABC were deliberately sending a different signal than either CBS or NBC. They were telling the world they believed in News; to prove it they would spend to become the best. They would pause to celebrate success and rhapsodize about what News put on the air. No signal of their commitment was clearer than Murphy and Burke's public pledge that Arledge would have two years to make *Prime Time Live* work. For two years he and Sawyer and her cohost, Sam Donaldson, could ignore the tyranny of the ratings. The internal message was just as important, and it was, simply: *We love news.* Arledge himself was given a new contract, a five-year deal in which his salary would start at just under $3 million—a nearly $1 million pay boost—and he would receive additional stock. After a difficult several years of adjustment, Roone Arledge was, in effect, appointed "emperor for life."

The success that ABC would achieve was, CBS believed, within its own grasp when Stringer became president of the Broadcast Group in August 1988. Stringer set out to end the "defensiveness" at CBS, to get people to confront "bad news," to make CBS a more relaxed work environment. "The place is hungry for an aggressive message," Stringer said then. "All victims get tired of feeling like victims. . . . The key is to take away fear." With Jankowski gone, Tisch stepped back. "I want to give Howard more room," he said. During his first month, Stringer inspired a series of management changes in the entertainment division, including hiring producer Barbara Corday as a deputy to Kim LeMasters.

LeMasters could feel the pressure from his original benefactor. For while Stringer had been impressed with LeMasters's decisiveness, he quickly detected traces of an authoritarian personality. So he nudged LeMasters to accept a strong deputy, to reach out to Hollywood talent. Privately Stringer guessed LeMasters had ten months to prove how good he was.

Ten months was too long for Bill Paley, who hadn't wanted to give LeMasters the job in the first place. The CBS chairman wanted LeMasters fired. Paley was not alone in his rage. In the all-important November sweeps period, which helps determine the advertising prices stations can charge, for the first time in the history of television the independent stations trounced a network—CBS—in the ratings. CBS series were performing below the audience guarantees promised advertisers. While CBS had said it would patiently stay with "quality" shows, by December it had cancelled four of its eight new series, including two by Tinker; by February, after moving it three times, CBS would cancel a third Tinker series, *TV 101,* which they had billed as an emblem for the new CBS. The network was in turmoil. Paley moaned that LeMasters should be fired. Tisch groused at how expensive entertainment programs were, and said there should be more news and sports in prime time. Advertisers and the affiliates were restive.

And Stringer was feeling like a trapped mouse. "We could make money with cheap programming, but we'd lose affiliate clearances," he said. "So the networks are trapped by a marriage which is now a bit of a death dance. We are trapped by ratings, which means we always have to go for a mass audience. We are trapped by a high-cost apparatus, which is part of a mature industry. We are trapped by Fox, which if it takes away a 10 share from us on Saturday or Sunday, that is the difference between profit and loss for us. The only way out of the trap is good programming." Hits. And even when CBS had hits—as they did with *Murder, She Wrote* and *Dallas*—the network ran into another trap. For the studios did not have to renew when their four-year contracts with the networks expired. That winter, for instance, Universal, which owned *Murder, She Wrote,* and Lorimar, which owned *Dallas* and *Falcon Crest,* threatened to move these series to another network unless CBS hiked its weekly license fee. Resist, and CBS risked losing these hits; comply, and risk network profits. CBS surrendered, augmenting *Murder, She Wrote*'s weekly license fee by 60 percent, to $1.8 million. Worse, its license fees to Lorimar escalated to the point that, by 1990–91, when *Dallas*'s ratings dropped, the network lost $30 million on the series.

Desperate to boost sagging morale, to prevent more affiliate preemptions, and to hush the drone from critics, in December 1988 Larry Tisch did what he had done in May: bought CBS some good news. For $1.06 billion, CBS acquired the rights to televise four years of major league baseball, including the All Star game, all postseason games, and twelve games during the season. CBS's winning bid topped by $400 million the bids of both ABC and NBC. Tisch actually agreed to pay 25 percent more for four years than NBC and ABC paid to split the previous six-year package; and that package, one top ABC executive said, would leave the two networks with a loss of $250 million. There was "no way anyone could have seduced us into the baseball deal Larry made," observed Dan Burke. Baseball was the second of what would become, over the next few years, a $3.6 billion CBS spending spree to lock up major sports franchises. These ventures stunned broadcasters, for they were made by a man who declined to sweeten his bid for NFL games and who refused to buy WTVJ in Miami, instead buying a small independent station, WCIX, because it cost much less.

"Maybe I'm living in a fool's paradise . . . but I'm really pleased with what's happening at CBS," Larry Tisch said as 1988 came to an end. With sports he had some guaranteed ratings winners and a platform from which to promote CBS series. With the interest on its $3 billion in cash, CBS would have record profits, even though network profits were off for the third straight year and limped in at about $40 million. The CBS board had finally relented and invited brother Bob to join, and relations between Tisch and the directors had thawed. CBS stock, which cost the Tisches about $125 per share and closed 1987 at $158, ended 1988 at $171. With Stringer, the network was a more informal place, which suited Tisch. He saw evidence that CBS Entertainment was turning around. "Stringer is making all the right moves in California" and doing a good job of bolstering Kim LeMasters and his team, said Tisch, who was equally enthusiastic about David Burke, the new president of CBS News.

From his first day, August 1, 1988, David Burke was determined to change CBS News. Burke felt News needed an outsider to run it, someone who could impose discipline. There were too many factions, he thought, and too many people at CBS News fought their battles in the press. He wanted the news division to concentrate on covering news, not making it.

No sooner was he in the building than Burke summoned Rather and the executive producers and key staff members to a conference room. His jacket off, the round-shouldered Burke stood before nearly two dozen people in his starched white shirt, and told them: "I come out of a Massachusetts political background and there are two things I know well: politics and bullshit. And I hate both! We come to work every day in an occupation that may be the most enjoyable. We don't work for Metropolitan Life. We all have obligations and a public trust. One thing that I have observed and that will have to stop is that we don't come to work every day to talk to the press. We come to work to do our profession. I don't enjoy self-aggrandizement at the expense of this institution and profession."

No more leaks!

In coming months, Burke would italicize his message by boasting how he never returned the phone calls of newspaper reporters. He kept his office door shut, rarely walked the halls to schmooze, the way Stringer had. He fired Stringer's two deputies and established his authority over Dan Rather.

Burke went out of his way to be sensitive to Rather's concerns, particularly his problems during the 1988 presidential contest. The Bush campaign tried to repay Rather and CBS for its take-no-prisoners interview on the Iran-contra scandal by denying interviews to CBS. At one point Rather dispatched his producer, Tom Bettag, to Washington to smooth differences with Bush's campaign chairman, Lee Atwater. Bettag was kept waiting, and then Atwater saw him for only a moment, before brushing him off on an aide. "It was a clear back of the hand," said Rather, who came to view the press as "spineless" during the campaign, a characterization Burke did not disagree with.

But Burke would not coddle Rather, as he felt his predecessors had. He ordered Rather to be less accessible to reporters fishing for stories about CBS. He took away Rather's de facto veto over the assignment of correspondents. He would, before the end of the year, terminate Rather's great friend, David Buksbaum, vice president in charge of Special Events, an experienced producer who was known within CBS as "the vice president for Rather," a man who always looked out for Rather's interest. "I want people to respond to me," explained Burke, who felt Buksbaum had too much power. Rather wasn't happy, but he got the message that Burke was the boss. So did others. Tisch applauded Burke's toughness. He was pleased that CBS News made $50 million after expenses of $330 million in 1989.

Tisch would be less pleased with what he came to see as Burke's imperiousness. He mostly blamed Burke for letting Sawyer slip away. He blamed Burke's stubborn remoteness for some of the bad press CBS News received, including the time Burke refused to publicly denounce stories that CBS and Rather had aired footage from Afghanistan they knew was doctored. Burke believed the reports were so ludicrous they were beneath comment; Tisch believed Burke's silence needlessly incriminated CBS News. And Tisch had come to feel that Burke was judging him, as indeed he was. What Tisch was hearing from people within News only confirmed this. As they got to know him, News employees often came to admire Burke. He was a man of standards, of compassion. But too few got to know him. Often, they referred to Burke as "the headmaster." "I am the outsider, like a bottle of bleach poured over them," said Burke, explaining his mission. With few strong allies within News, Burke had no way to counter Tisch's growing disenchantment. Six months into his new job, Burke acknowledged that he had been remote because he was "trying to send a message." He said he would change. Yet he did not.

David Burke succeeded in establishing his authority. But many people felt that he focused on the wrong need—better management—when perhaps he needed to replace his disputatious anchorman, since the nightly newscast continued to lose viewers. ABC president John Sias said he hoped Rather stayed "there a long time." ABC worried that Burke would snatch his friend Ted Koppel away and bounce Rather, an idea Burke had in mind as a possibility, but not until Koppel's contract expired in 1990.

David Burke's moral rectitude would leave him isolated. He was wary of Tisch because he thought a news division had to keep the business types at a distance. Soon after starting work at CBS, Burke was asked if he was as worried about Tisch as he had been about Cap Cities. "Oh, yes," he said. "But I don't know enough yet. He hasn't picked up the phone." Burke hadn't picked up the phone either. He would also keep his distance from Stringer, wanting to establish his own record, feeling that Stringer was preoccupied with getting Entertainment back on its feet, and fearful that Stringer didn't have the fortitude to resist Tisch or Kriegel. But in the process Burke lost a potential ally and shield. Most puzzling of all, Burke drew away from the man who maneuvered his appointment and who he thought was really running CBS, Jay Kriegel. He came to see that Kriegel had a constituency of one: Larry Tisch. But as the months passed, Burke came to hold Tisch in contempt. He became increasingly alarmed that Tisch had the mindset of a Wall Street trader, changing his opinions in an instant, quickly losing interest and wanting to move on to the next trade. What Tisch didn't lose interest in were costs and budgets. This preoccupation drove Burke nuts, as did Tisch's crude opinions. Burke told friends how he wanted to fire *60 Minutes* commentator Andy Rooney early in 1990 for alleged racist statements and Tisch purportedly shrugged. Kriegel might be dependent on Tisch, but Burke was determined not to be.

Burke would not bend, so eventually he would break. In August 1990, two years after he took the job, David Burke was fired.

Back in July of 1988, Bob Wright had two pressing management issues on his mind: getting rid of Larry Grossman as NBC News president and retaining Brandon Tartikoff. Two meetings with Michael Gartner convinced Wright that he had found the man he wanted for Grossman's job. Gartner was both a publisher and an editor. He was, above all, an outsider, someone with enough detachment to devise a strategy for News, which was uppermost on Wright's mind. Bob Wright wanted someone to puzzle out what to do about NBC's nightly newscast. The three network newscasts reached only 60 percent of viewers, a loss of two and one-half million viewers in just three years. Since the nightly newscast provided nearly two thirds of NBC News's revenues, unless the erosion ceased, Wright wasn't sure network news had a future. Convinced that Gartner was a soul mate, Wright was eager to make a change.

Gartner was summoned to Atlanta during the 1988 Democratic National Convention in mid-July, and met with Wright and Personnel chief Ed Scanlon all morning in Wright's hotel suite. "I spent the first two hours arguing that it would be a mistake for these guys to hire me," recalls Gartner, a slim man whose trademarks are bow ties, half glasses that slide down his long, thin nose or dangle from a black cord around his neck, and a bluntness that impresses some as candid, others as prickly. Gartner lost the argument, and by the end of the morning had signaled his eagerness for the job. While Wright and Scanlon boarded the GE jet Wednesday afternoon to get Jack Welch's benediction, they asked Gartner to stay behind to meet privately with Brokaw on Thursday. A lunch in New York with Chairman Welch would be scheduled for the following Wednesday.

Meanwhile, the rumor that he was about to be fired stalked Grossman in Atlanta, so he phoned Wright and they arranged to meet Friday afternoon at 30 Rock.

"You've done a terrific job," Wright told Grossman. "But it's time to bring someone else in. I don't have anyone yet." Wright assured him his severance would be generous, and they agreed that Grossman could make the announcement the following Thursday, after they returned from a president's council meeting in Los Angeles on Tuesday.

Grossman was feeling almost relaxed by Monday afternoon when he boarded the GE jet bound for Los Angeles, and Wright beckoned him to a nearby seat. His exit would be dignified. With a full salary, provisions for an office and secretary for a year, plus bonus, plus GE stock and a sweetened lump-sum retirement benefit, he would have financial security. "To me it was very sad, but a great relief," said Grossman.

Within twenty-four hours the story that he was fired leaked. Anonymous quotes disparaged his leadership of NBC News. All that was missing was the name of his successor. Grossman felt awful.

Welch felt the leak stripped him of his prerogatives as chairman. One of his primary tasks was to judge candidates for major jobs, and now he was being rushed. What if he didn't like Gartner? Jack Welch didn't like to be crowded.

Welch's misgivings would dissolve over a plate of pasta at a midtown Manhattan restaurant. Instantly he liked Gartner. He was reassured that Gartner did not view the GE culture as alien. At one point during lunch Welch brought up the controversy aroused by the decision to rename 30 Rock. Welch leaned over and asked: "What do you think of changing the name of the building to GE?"

"I'm glad you're trying it and hope the fight lasts eight years," said Gartner, explaining that he considered it "a trivial issue. Let them get worked up about something like that rather than what I consider a plan to bring order and progress to the news division."

The next day Michael Gartner was named president of NBC News, its sixth president in twelve years.

In what even detractors considered a classy exit, Larry Grossman met with reporters, showered NBC News with praise, stayed to debrief Gartner, and disappeared. The major culprit, he thought, was Tom Brokaw. "My sense is that it was inevitable and that Tom spurred it on," said Grossman a few weeks later, looking relaxed in blue jeans and sneakers in his small, plant-filled Greenwich Village apartment. Though he exaggerated the anchorman's role, Grossman was not alone in blaming Brokaw. Critic Tom Shales wrote that the execution of Grossman proved "Brokaw's power at NBC may be even greater than anchor Dan Rather's at CBS."

The simple truth is that Brokaw did play a powerful role, first in conveying dissatisfaction with Grossman, then in reviewing possible candidates, then in passing on Gordon Manning's suggestion of Michael Gartner. It is also true that Brokaw, like all network stars, can be temperamental. "You can't go through life being paid millions," observed an NBC official, "and having nearly the same recognition as a president but with a higher approval rating, being able to get tickets for anything, to get anyone on the phone, to walk into a room and everyone feels they know you, to never have to be introduced, to never have to stand in line—what do you think it does to you? Given all this, Brokaw handles it pretty well."

There is a competing truth, one less palatable to Larry Grossman. Despite his sense of public obligation, his decency and popularity with the TV press or NBC affiliates, Grossman lacked a broad internal constituency. As chief of correspondents—the job Grossman gave him—Brokaw spoke for more than himself. He knew that Grossman's NBC News colleagues generally liked him as a man but did not respect him as their leader. Or, as Brokaw accurately put it, "I was really representing, in addition to my own feelings here, a consensus point of view."

While the Grossman/Gartner machinations were going on in July, Bob Wright and Jack Welch despaired of keeping Brandon Tartikoff.

They expected him to flee the network early in 1989 to run a studio or become a producer and make millions. After nearly ten years at the helm of NBC Entertainment, he would want to try something new. Tartikoff had said as much to them. When Wright attended a Sun Valley retreat in July sponsored by the investment banking firm of Allen & Company, however, he picked up an amazing piece of information. Several studio heads and entertainment company CEOs told him they had tried to hire Tartikoff, only to come away convinced he wouldn't leave NBC. Brandon, they said, too much enjoyed being a powerful buyer, creating shows, refining and scheduling and promoting and packaging them.

Wright wasn't sure they were correct, but he returned excited, and visited Jack Welch at his Connecticut home the next weekend. "Jack, I have a hunch," Wright said. "Brandon likes GE. He likes the atmosphere. These people told me, 'Don't be so sure Brandon wants to move on.' " Wright wanted to structure a package to keep Tartikoff at NBC.

Welch, too, was excited. Together he and Wright explored how to pay Tartikoff more money, particularly if his salary came directly from GE. What if they enlarged his NBC responsibilities to chair a Program Development Group to oversee NBC Sports, the owned stations, cable, and even some News programming? What if they boosted NBC Productions' development budget by 50 percent, to $150 million? What if they awarded new contracts to retain key members of Tartikoff's team? The ideas became proposals, and in late July Welch took them to the Compensation Committee of his board. "I told the board there was a chance," recalls Welch. The board concurred, and Welch phoned to invite the Tartikoffs to Nantucket in August.

For three days Brandon and Lilly Tartikoff, Welch and his steady date, attorney Jane Beasley (now his second wife), Bob and Suzanne Wright, and one of Welch's closest friends, attorney Anthony LoFrisco and his wife, Eleanor, played golf, ate, laughed, drank, and talked. Welch and Wright talked privately with Tartikoff about breaking down walls between divisions at NBC. A way to do that, they said, and make better use of Tartikoff's brilliant showmanship, was to enlarge his role. He should critique, if not supervise, everything NBC put on the air. They talked about how they saw him as Wright's backup—"Brandon has that option," said Wright. They talked about the challenge of staying number one. And they talked about money, offering Tartikoff a contract ending July 1, 1992, and paying him about $5 million annually, not including bonus incentives pegged to

NBC's Nielsen ratings, plus additional GE stock. Staggered, Tartikoff stalled for a few weeks.

Tartikoff rethought his future. From a financial standpoint, the GE offer was as munificent as those from the studios. At a studio it would be two years before his first picture appeared in movie theaters. And the people he would work for were not, he thought, "as smart as Welch and Wright." He wasn't ready to become an independent producer, prowling the halls of the three networks to peddle pet projects. The more Tartikoff thought about the challenge of proving he could stay number one, of trying to defy the historical cycle of boom and bust, the more excited he became. He was feeling almost euphoric. He believed he had a strong fall schedule. He had confounded the critics by winning a July ratings week with *Nightingales.* He believed, correctly, that he was smarter than his competitors. He was now rich. By enlarging his programming responsibilities, Wright and Welch offered new frontiers to conquer. There were reasons for Brandon Tartikoff to believe he was Superman, reasons to remain at NBC.

When Michael Gartner first appeared on the third floor that summer, he wowed the people in News. He was thought to bring strengths Grossman lacked. He was an experienced editor and businessman; he was decisive; he quickly mastered the News budget. And he seemed politically astute—he immediately established a regular Friday 7:05 A.M. breakfast in the NBC cafeteria with Personnel chief Ed Scanlon, who had the ear of both Wright and Welch. But it soon became apparent that Gartner's political skills were aimed more at his NBC peers and superiors, for he was less adroit with underlings or with NBC's various constituents. At his maiden meeting with TV critics in August 1988, Gartner was asked whether he would have supported an NBC PAC, and instead of enunciating why it would be wrong for News to risk losing the appearance of impartiality, Gartner chose to dodge and dismiss it as "a hypothetical question" since the issue had not arisen "during my tenure."

Unlike Grossman, Gartner saw himself as "the middle part of the hourglass, filtering material that's running each way" from Wright and from News. He did not see himself as News's champion. What zeal he displayed was as a member of the GE team, as when he took care to review drafts of his speeches with Ed Scanlon. Gartner wasn't defensive about GE, like Grossman. GE, he said, had become "a whipping boy" for NBC employees who did not want to face the future. Of *Nightly News* he said—as Wright had to the NBC affiliate board in

November 1987—"Maybe it is a dinosaur." Gartner even said he had "no preconceived notions" about whether *Nightly News* should be a separate half hour each night or just sold as story packages to stations. People at NBC News came to think that Gartner instinctively sided with Wright, as an incident that occurred in September suggested.

George Bush and Michael Dukakis were to engage in the first of two presidential debates on Sunday, September 25, from 8:00 to 9:30 P.M. This was a night on which NBC expected a ratings surge since it owned the Olympics. Air the commercial-free debate live and NBC would lose an estimated $8 million in advertising. Not air it and the network would be criticized for abandoning its public trust. At a meeting of his president's council in early September, Bob Wright asked: Should NBC carry the presidential debate live? Traditionally, the Entertainment and Finance people fought such preemptions, while News advanced them. This time, members of the president's council were in for a surprise.

The most hawkish voice against carrying the debate live was News president Gartner, who declared: *NBC has long been committed to the Olympics. Since these dates were known by both political parties, there is no reason NBC should alter its schedule. Especially since ABC, CBS, and CNN will carry the debate live. We're offering something different—the Olympics. I'm not of the view that this presidential debate is the most significant thing in our democracy. I've been to too many debates that don't make news. Their argument is that if NBC doesn't run the debate it will drain forty million viewers. My response is, 'That's what freedom is all about!' Other networks, including cable and Fox, are not abandoning their regular programs.* As a First Amendment absolutist, Gartner said he didn't believe the government had any business telling NBC News what to do, or even making suggestions. "If the issue was news versus entertainment, I would do it," he remembers saying. "But this is news versus news. The Olympics are news." He would tape the debate and run it later that night.

With Gartner on his side, Wright had a chorus. On September 11, NBC announced that it would stick with the Olympics and as a public service would air the debate later that night.

The next day, pressure began to build on NBC. Wright received calls from the chairmen of the Democratic and Republican National Committees, as well as from Congressman Edward Markey, chairman of a house committee with regulatory power over the broadcast industry. Wright spoke only to Markey, asking Gartner to return the other calls. Counsel Cory Dunham reported a riot of congressional anger.

By the end of the day, Bob Wright's resolve weakened. But Gartner was implacable. "No way we're going to change!" he told Communications chief Betty Hudson late that day. Not without reason, he was outraged that the head of a News organization should be pressured by politicians.

By the next morning, Gartner's staff began to wear him down. They said that there were no major Olympic finals scheduled for Sunday evening. The political protests, they argued, were not on behalf of a candidate or a narrow cause, but were meant to advance democratic participation. If there was any chance NBC might retreat later, better to make a quick decision now. This way NBC could cut its public relations losses early. "They said," recalls Gartner, " 'It's the thing to do for appearances' sake, and for the sake of News.' "

Reluctantly Gartner yielded. He phoned Wright, who at this point was relieved to back off. On September 13 NBC announced that it would cover the debate live. When Wright's statement was read aloud, cheers erupted in the third-floor NBC newsroom.

The cheers were short-lived. By November, revenues fell below budget. NBC News, which was budgeted to lose $54 million in 1988, would by year end lose $70 million. To cut the 1989 budget to $245 million, Gartner ordered $55 million in savings.

By January 1989, after Gartner's first five months, many in News would have hailed the return of Larry Grossman. While Grossman's niceness sometimes conveyed weakness, Gartner came off as unduly combative. *Today* show host Bryant Gumbel was so offended by his brusque manner that he stopped talking to his new boss; Gartner snapped that Gumbel was a spoiled brat. Journalists within NBC News were offended when, without explanation, Gartner summarily transferred correspondent Ken Bode from politics to Congress, removed Chris Wallace as moderator of *Meet the Press,* and hardballed correspondent Connie Chung in negotiations over a new contract. NBC News was generally thought to have the weakest bench of the three networks, and to demote three of its best-known correspondents seemed to make little sense. When all three chose to leave and Gartner ho-hummed as if this were a nonevent, the shock reverberated throughout NBC News. The anger was muted but not dispelled when Gartner managed to lure CNN anchor Mary Alice Williams to NBC. Of NBC News, Gartner said, "It's a pretty vicious place. Larry Grossman and I agree on that." What was unusual, he said, was that "I wasn't just getting stabbed in the back. I was getting stabbed in the front."

Although he had a distinguished journalistic career, people convinced themselves that Gartner didn't care about NBC News. They grumbled that he returned home to Iowa on weekends, where his family remained. They groaned about the column he wrote every third week for *The Wall Street Journal*'s editorial page, at the bottom of which he chose to identify himself thus: "Mr. Gartner is editor and co-owner of the *Daily Tribune* in Ames, Iowa, and president of NBC News in New York."

By the spring of 1989, Gartner was distressed as well, but for different reasons. "I haven't even gotten into issues of journalism here," he said. "It's been all budgets and personnel and getting comfortable with people." And meeting with affiliates, and TV critics, and general managers from the owned stations. Feeling surrounded by assassins and spoiled children, Gartner declared, "I decided that I had to manage like a dictator." At his first annual NBC affiliate convention this spring, when station managers complained about this or that, as they customarily did, instead of deflecting the criticism or cracking a joke, Gartner barked at one affiliate representative, "As I said to you when I wrote . . ." Sometimes when others spoke, he looked up at the ceiling. He appeared arrogant. "The affiliates think I'm a jerk," said Gartner afterward. "I'm blunt. I'm not adept at small talk."

Enter Tartikoff. True to his promise, Bob Wright came to rely on Tartikoff for more than the entertainment schedule. When he was disappointed in NBC's handling of the 1988 Seoul Olympics, for which he had paid $300 million, he consulted Tartikoff. The games, hosted by Bryant Gumbel, attracted a 30 share, up only three points from the audiences NBC had achieved the previous year. Wright and Welch thought NBC had overpaid by $100 million. And they were upset at the staid way the network packaged the contests. "They are running a semi-news operation rather than a heroic sports event," complained Welch. "It's as if the shuttle went up and they were talking about Franco-American relations." Tartikoff confirmed that NBC's effort lacked showmanship, and recommended that Wright clean house, replacing Arthur Watson as head of NBC Sports. To replace Watson, Tartikoff suggested his buddy, Dick Ebersol, who had been Roone Arledge's deputy at ABC Sports before becoming a network programmer and an independent producer. Ebersol, he said, would want broader jurisdiction, perhaps over the *Today* show, where his old friend Bryant Gumbel presided. Dick Ebersol's appointment was announced by Wright in April 1989.

What wasn't announced at the time was that Wright had agreed to cede to Ebersol dominion over *Today.* Although it was still in first place in the morning, Wright knew that Gartner thought the main problem with *Today* was that "they spend money like drunken sailors." Wright was aware, as well, that Gumbel would not talk to Gartner, that tempers were frayed by a leaked Gumbel memo ridiculing members of the *Today* family. Ever so slowly, younger female viewers were leaving *Today.* But when Wright broached the subject of Ebersol to Gartner, the News president was at first pliable, and then resisted. Gartner had consulted Brokaw, among others, who argued that *Today* should report to News—unlike *Good Morning America,* which did not. The serious journalist in Brokaw and Gartner agreed: To take *Today* away from News would be another surrender to entertainment values.

Wright was furious. He felt that Gartner, like Grossman, was braying for the priesthood. But he felt powerless to force the issue since it would look terrible if he fired another News president. Wright smoldered. Gartner's obstinancy fused in his mind with other incidents. He was disappointed that Gartner had gotten into so many quarrels, was by his own admission "a television naif," and had been unable to focus on larger issues, including how to jump-start Brokaw's newscast, which was stuck in third place and had actually lost 13 percent of its viewers in 1988. "I think he's impatient having to deal with so many constituents in reaching his objectives," said Wright. "And he's not a guy long on patience." Asked in the spring of 1989 if he were pleased with Gartner, Wright implied that he was not: "I feel very sorry for him. I have a lot of empathy. I would like it if he had a more positive reception. He's a very honest person. He's not devious. I think he is being diverted. I wish that weren't the case."

By late spring, Jack Welch was openly disenchanted with Gartner. He said Gartner was getting sidetracked by "arguments about the mechanics of news gathering" rather than acting like a producer and overhauling what appeared on the screen. Instead of a publisher, now Welch and Wright wanted a producer. Gartner, said the GE chairman, was wasting his political capital on "details about news gathering." Nor was he, by Welch or Wright's lights, attacking the basic self-satisfaction within News. They watched the press cover the presidential campaign like firefighters, racing from horse race story to poll story to "photo opportunities," rarely adjudicating the truth of the charges heaved by each candidate, and allowing a mere 9.8 seconds for each interview or soundbite. What Welch and Wright did not know, though it would have enraged them if they had, was that despite the criticism there were no postmortems at the networks immediately after the campaign. At NBC there were only "corridor postmortems," said Brokaw. At CBS there were a few casual conversations at haphazard dinners. At ABC, Peter Jennings wrote a memo to Arledge suggesting a formal postmortem, but Arledge responded that a discussion on Ted Koppel's *Nightline* would suffice.

To outsiders like Welch and Wright, such behavior reeked of complacency and conceit. It would have infuriated them to learn that despite constant complaints from correspondents about getting too little airtime, network news producers actually had trouble getting correspondents to do pieces longer than the usual two-minute report. Over at ABC, for example, executive producer Paul Friedman was having difficulty inaugurating a longer segment called *American Agenda*. He had assumed that a dozen correspondents would jump at the chance to have a regular beat, a subject they could master in depth, and the luxury of spending days and even weeks on a single five- to seven-minute story. Wrong. Friedman found he couldn't recruit enough top-flight correspondents because few wanted to forego the satisfaction of a nightly fix of airtime. "The system has become so corrupt that your success as a correspondent is too often measured by how often you get on the air," lamented Friedman. Wright and Welch had expected Michael Gartner to alter such attitudes.

But Gartner hadn't advanced the GE cultural revolution as they had expected him to. Nor did he bring anything to the table as a producer. NBC News looked the same. Less than a year after they had gotten rid of Grossman, Wright and Welch were ready to fire Gartner. Early in the summer of 1989, Wright confided this to Tartikoff, who had his own frustrations with the way Gartner was handling a joint effort with Entertainment to devise a news magazine show. Wright said he was ready to make a change—if Tartikoff knew of an outsider who could fix what appeared on the screen. Having worked with a public relations/advertising executive (Grossman) and a journalist/businessman (Gartner), Wright was ready to try a producer. If there was a model for what Wright wanted, it was Roone Arledge.

Don Ohlmeyer, said Tartikoff.

Bingo. Ohlmeyer had been a brilliant executive producer of NBC Sports, and now headed his own successful production company. What a team—Tartikoff, Ebersol, and Ohlmeyer. The three men were friends. And Ohlmeyer occasionally played golf with Jack Welch; it was Ohlmeyer who warned Welch in 1986 that Tartikoff was about to leave NBC. Great idea, said Wright. Welch was equally enthusiastic, and Wright offered Ohlmeyer the job. But Ohlmeyer declined, and Gartner stayed at NBC.

Gartner and Ebersol became close—Ebersol was "a genius," Gartner said. That summer Gartner made Ebersol a senior vice president of News with responsibility for the *Today* show. Although Gartner in June had said the principal problem with *Today* was its management, now he and Ebersol decided its true plight was the slow but steady flight of younger viewers from *Today.* They discussed with Wright the idea of replacing veteran John Palmer with Deborah Norville as a news reader and putting her on the set alongside Gumbel and cohost Jane Pauley. Norville might appeal to the younger viewers they were losing. Each of these men—like Grossman and Russert before them—was smitten with Norville. They thought she did a good job reading the early morning news on NBC's *Sunrise.* Young professionals who found thirty-nine-year-old Pauley a bit frumpy would identify with Norville's natty clothes and brisk manner. Men would look at her and swoon. Welch was even consulted on the move and chimed his support. They would put Norville on the set beside Pauley and Gumbel, hoist her pay to $1 million, and watch the demos rise. It was the GE way: *Make tough decisions. If it ain't broke, fix it!*

Instead, they broke it. Norville was put on the set and Pauley, with reason, felt she was about to be replaced. Headlines tortured NBC. Pauley resigned from the show, becoming an instant heroine. *Today's* ratings collapsed, leaving the show in second place.* Gartner, like Ebersol, was chastened. He had, he said at the end of his first full year, learned some lessons. "I've been this way all my life and no one ever said, 'Hey, he has a chip on his shoulder.' " To make himself more congenial, Gartner went to "charm school," to be coached before public appearances by consultant Jack Hilton and his partner Stuart Sucherman. Gartner learned a second lesson. The true problem, he said, was the superficiality of the TV press. "Nobody ever looks at content," Gartner observed. "Everybody looks at salaries or nonessential things. No one looks at the content of news or the economics. They look at meaningless shit: Were we first or was another network first by thirty seconds in saying that Jim Wright resigned this afternoon? The question should be: On nightly news, who did the

* Responding to *Today's* ratings slide, in the spring of 1991 Norville announced that she wanted to spend more time with her infant son and would leave NBC. When Katie Couric, a warmer personality and a more skilled interviewer, replaced Norville, *Today's* ratings began to climb.

best job explaining the story to the American public?" If critics merely wanted more warmth and the TV press was preoccupied with the wrong thing—the horse race—it followed that Gartner's tribulations might be fixed with a dash of public relations. In this, he was as mistaken as Suzanne Pleshette had been regarding *Nightingales.*

On the surface, despite Gartner's or *Today*'s woes, NBC in 1988 and 1989 had few problems. Still number one in the ratings, the network had retained TV's reigning genius, Brandon Tartikoff. When the 1988–89 season ended in April 1989, Tartikoff would lead NBC to its fourth straight ratings triumph, winning a record forty-seven consecutive weeks and topping second-place ABC by 24 percent. This season, once again, Tartikoff burnished his reputation as a scheduling whiz. To attack ABC's conclusion of *War and Remembrance,* for instance, he not only posted the farewell episode of the long-running *Family Ties* against it but extended the series an extra ten minutes to 9:10 P.M., following it with a popular movie, *Ferris Beuller's Day Off.* These maneuvers allowed NBC to snatch the Sunday ratings lead from ABC. NBC's profits were also robust, with after-tax network earnings of $280 million in 1988. Jack Welch then said he expected to see NBC "widening the gap" over CBS and ABC and generating, over the next three years, a total of $1.2 billion in cash for its parent company. NBC's profits looked even better compared to the losses at ABC and the slim profits at CBS.

But the broadcast industry's problems were real, and brought to mind the story of the three network executives stalked by a lion while on safari in Africa. Suddenly, one executive kneeled, loosened his knapsack, and laced on his running shoes.

"Why are you doing that?" asked the two other network executives. "We can outrun him!"

"I'm not worried about outrunning the lion," said the kneeling executive. "I'm worried about outrunning you!"

Once again, 1988 was a winner-take-all year for the three network competitors, with one winner and two losers. Smaller audiences translated into fewer network advertising dollars. The Big Three, which in 1984 luxuriated in profits of $800 million, had by 1988 seen their combined profits dwindle to less than half that. Although 1989 turned out to be a more robust advertising year than anticipated, and profits at NBC, ABC, and CBS rose, perhaps it was an aberration. With increased competition and the continued flight of viewers from the networks, Jack Welch would, in time, be proven wrong. NBC would not supply GE with the expected cash. By the end of the 1989–90 season, NBC's ratings and demos would start to fall, as would NBC's profits.

Although it would not become apparent for a year or two, the bottom was falling out for NBC. The 1988–89 season marked the third straight year in which Tartikoff & Company had failed to introduce a new hit.* By May 1989, even though NBC's victory margin had grown, its own ratings actually declined by 2 percent. Even the mighty Cosby's ratings dipped. While several of NBC's new series—*Midnight Caller, Unsolved Mysteries, Dear John, Empty Nest*—would flower beyond this year, none shot up the charts, the way ABC's *Roseanne,* a series Tartikoff had turned down, would. Nor were NBC's successes, modest as they were, the hour-long dramas that had given NBC its reputation for quality. Tartikoff's leading candidate to retain NBC's aura—Bruce Paltrow's *Tattinger's*—had bombed. And its replacement—Aaron Spelling's *Nightingales*—was an embarrassment.

Tartikoff fell into a funk before the 1988–89 season ended. He had been savaged in the press for his Geraldo Rivera special on satanism, and by nurses groups for *Nightingales.* His network, which like the others rejected ads for condoms, would not hesitate to promote shows featuring sex and violence. NBC began the 1988–89 season convinced, in Warren Littlefield's words, that "sex sells," that it was pushing "the boundaries," and ended the season pushing prurience. So depressed was Tartikoff that he refused to attend the August 1989 Emmy Awards ceremony. Picking at a cold breakfast, he said, "I feel like Orel Hershiser setting a record and then hearing someone complain, 'He's scuffing the ball!' "

A year later, at the end of the 1989–90 season in April 1990, Tartikoff's NBC was no longer setting records. True, the network had racked up its fifth straight prime-time ratings victory. But its audience dropped by 9 percent over the previous year, its key demos by 13 percent. For the fourth straight season, NBC did not produce a new hit, while ABC did in midseason with *America's Funniest Home Videos. Cosby* was knocked from its number-one perch by ABC's *Roseanne.* The broadcast community was seized by speculation that ABC might actually overtake NBC in the new season, beginning in the fall of 1990.

* I am not counting *A Different World* as a genuine hit because even Tartikoff conceded that this mediocre series initially owed its strength to its 8:30 P.M. Thursday time slot, between *Cosby* and *Cheers.*

While ABC gained compared to NBC and CBS, which lost viewers, the actual size of ABC's evening audience remained flat. Even though 1989 was a generally better profit year for the networks, their combined profit margin was only 10.2 percent (a low of 1 percent for CBS, a high of 17 percent for NBC); by contrast, the profit margins for cable systems averaged 42 percent, and for affiliated stations 38 percent.

NBC's cycle of ratings leadership appeared near its end, but so did the ability of the Big Three to galvanize mass audiences. None of the twenty-three new series introduced by the three networks in the fall of 1989, nor of the twenty-two introduced in the fall of 1990, became a hit. Network programmers came to defend series that ranked in the bottom third of the ratings—like ABC's *Twin Peaks*—if they had good demos. Or they defended shows that cost relatively little to produce—like *America's Funniest Home Videos,* reality shows like CBS's *Top Cops,* or sometimes even news specials. This opened the network door to talented movie directors like David Lynch and John Sayles, who once shunned television as a giant glob factory, and to more news in prime time. But it also opened the door to more schlock and to more network narrowcasting. Slowly but perceptibly, the networks switched from a focus on mass appeal to a focus on demos and costs. By imitating their cable and other competitors in search of the right audience fragments, the networks further loosened their grip on the mass audience.

Brandon Tartikoff thought the game was over. There was no longer any way, he felt, to combat the fragmented audience. The viewer, not the programmer, was now boss as the three-network share of the prime-time audience dropped to 64 percent at the end of 1989; in summer, when the networks save money by running repeats, their combined share had fallen to nearly half the available audience, which is what the networks by 1991 were averaging on midseason Saturday nights. The expansion of cable did not abate. Nor did the pressure from the Fox network, which by 1989 had three nights of programming, a genuine hit in *The Simpsons,* and had turned a profit, earning $33 million. So Tartikoff chose, in 1990, to step up to chairman of the entertainment division, letting Warren Littlefield try his hand as president. Wright and Welch wanted Tartikoff to stay, and he said he would for a while. But unless GE acquired a studio for him to run, Tartikoff planned to leave in 1991 and finish an autobiography about his network experiences. The title of the planned book conveyed his impish humor but also an emerging conviction that the networks were destined to decline further. The book would be called *The Last Great Ride.*

Sadly, on New Year's Day, 1991, Tartikoff and his daughter Calla, eight, were driving to a bowling alley in Lake Tahoe, Nevada, where the Tartikoffs have a vacation home. Blinded by the late afternoon sun, Tartikoff did not see an approaching car as he made a left turn. He was seriously injured, with a fractured pelvis, broken ribs, and assorted lacerations. After a lengthy hospital stay, he recovered physically. Calla Tartikoff suffered a severe head injury; her recovery would come, but more slowly.

By the end of the eighties, optimists like Gene Jankowski were gone. No one any longer proclaimed that the networks could recover lost viewers or halt further erosion. No longer could the networks blame faulty people meters or the absence of hits. By 1990, even the hits no longer attracted the same mass audiences they once did. Instead of a 50 share, a 30 share now won the week.

To improve profits and cope with lost viewers, the three networks had limited options. One option was cost cutting, but the new owners had already slashed network jobs by approximately 30 percent, to about six thousand employees. Cutting costs was not a growth strategy, as the new owners learned. To keep costs down, they ran more repeats and invested in fewer specials, and the flight of viewers accelerated. They knew that picking hit shows was a way to grow, but hit series were a rarity. Worse, they seemed almost an accident. No one at either CBS or ABC, for instance, saw the promise of *The Cosby Show* when they turned it down; Tartikoff had missed the potential of *Roseanne.* After they screened the pilot in 1990, people at ABC from Tom Murphy down thought Steven Bochco had delivered a huge hit with *Cop Rock,* a police music-drama with songs by Randy Newman; it bombed. Buying stations was another option for growth, but stations were expensive and both ABC and NBC were near the ceiling the government allowed. Pressures intensified on the networks to find fresh sources of revenues.

A common target remained government regulations. The networks continued to work toward an agreement with the Hollywood studios to lift the financial interest and syndication restrictions. The networks' case was strengthened by the 1989 merger of Warner Communications and Time, Inc., and by Sony's subsequent purchase of Columbia Pictures and Matsushita's of Universal. By 1991, five of the Big Eight Hollywood studios were owned by foreign giants. How could the government treat the networks as a monopoly when its suppliers were so powerful? Why tie the hands of American networks and not those of studios owned by foreign nationals? When negotiations between the networks and the studios broke off in 1990, each camp tried to convince the FCC to rule in its favor when the old rules would lapse in 1991. At least one other potential source of revenue was linked to a Washington decision—the reregulation of the cable industry. But this, too, was some time away.

The new network owners themselves had real differences concerning future strategies. NBC had been the most aggressive of the three in seeking deals. Unlike Tisch, Wright believed that cable was a potential partner, not a competitor. When his efforts to link up with Ted Turner failed in late 1987, Wright unsuccessfully pursued other cable alliances. He decided that it would be cheaper, and enhance his leverage, if NBC inaugurated its own cable-programming service. In the summer of 1988, Wright announced CNBC, a twenty-four-hour-a-day consumer-oriented business news programming service that would debut in April of 1989. It was an expensive start-up (about $50 million), with modest immediate results—CNBC reached only a third of the 33 million subscribers of its nearest competitor, the Financial News Network (FNN).

Bob Wright was convinced he needed other outlets, so he turned to Cablevision, which owned regional sports and news channels and was run by Charles F. Dolan, a cable pioneer. Wright had helped finance Cablevision when he ran GE Capital—Dolan "was in hock to us," said Jack Welch. In December 1988, NBC announced a joint venture with Dolan's Cablevision. For $137.5 million in cash, NBC became a 50 percent owner of Cablevision's seven regional sports channels, in News 12, their all-news channel on Long Island, and in two other small cable services, Bravo and Rainbow Network Communications; in return, Cablevision would own 50 percent of CNBC. Together, they would create SportsChannel America, skimming the excess sports programming from NBC and the regional sports channels and funneling these to a new cable service. NBC's partnership with Cablevision led Wright—despite his October lament that NBC had lost $100 million on the 1988 Summer Olympics—to bid for the 1992 Summer Olympics in Barcelona. NBC's $401 million winning bid was the first joint network/cable partnership, and the first to offer a pay-per-view component, since a special package of the games would be made available to viewers willing to pay an extra fee of $95 to $175.

NBC, unlike ABC, was not content with an incremental, grind-out-a-yard-at-a-time approach to the future. Bob Wright was looking to heave some touchdowns. Wright would, in 1989 and 1990, connect in quick order with Westinghouse Broadcasting, which agreed to distribute to its cable customers programs made by NBC Productions. He, the Tribune Company of Chicago, and ten cable operators completed a deal to invest in the NuCable Resources Corporation, which provides and markets digital video systems, including classified advertising on television. He hooked up with Reuters and the BBC when NBC acquired 38 percent ownership of Visnews, the world's largest television news agency. With overseas television in turmoil—just 15 percent of Europe was then wired for cable, entrepreneurial money was chasing after private broadcast channels everywhere, and the demand for programming was rising faster than the supply—Wright completed investment deals with a television network in Australia, linked up with Yorkshire Television to form Tango Productions, which would produce and distribute programs to Europe, and had NBC News enter into a joint news-gathering agreement with the Nippon Television network of Japan to share overseas stories.

A company, like a country or a street corner, develops its own distinctive culture. The GE culture was shaped by a belief in technology. Not surprisingly, Bob Wright scrambled to link NBC to potentially profitable future technologies. Wright also made a financial arrangement with Interactive Network, which invited viewers to participate in game shows or to choose the camera angle and replays during sports contests. He joined with the David Sarnoff Research Center and Thompson Consumer Electronics, the largest TV-receiver manufacturer in the U.S., to race Japan and Europe to develop high-definition television that was compatible with American TV sets. He made a third gamble when, in early 1990, NBC allied with Rupert Murdoch, Hughes Communications, and Cablevision in creating a partnership that would, they hoped, produce by 1993 a direct broadcast satellite service. Such a service would allow programmers to reach consumers directly through individual satellite dishes placed on roofs or in backyards, thus bypassing traditional distributors, whether local TV stations or the cable box.

In consultation with Wright, by early 1989 GE Capital had directed $3 billion of its $43 billion in assets into loans or investments for twenty-one cable, broadcast, or communications deals, including a $200 million investment in Viacom and large positions in five cable companies. And in early 1991, Wright bid and eventually won the right to buy CNBC's chief rival, FNN, and merge the two. In less than three years, Bob Wright had run the football equivalent of the two-minute drill, driving NBC downfield with one deal after another. By 1991, both Wright and Welch knew that in the global game they were playing, they had flung some potential touchdown passes. But it would be years before they learned if any were caught.

CBS under Larry Tisch had adopted a conservative defensive game plan. The deals he made were designed to save money—he signed a joint agreement to share news bureaus and news footage with the Tokyo Broadcasting System in 1990. But buying cable properties or launching his own was so expensive, said Tisch, that the economics were cockeyed. "That strategy is not going to work, for NBC or anyone. Suppose when they are all finished that it makes $20 million a year. So what? By then they will have $500 million invested in it." No, Tisch's strategy was always to wait. After selling off assets, he would invest CBS's $3 billion cash hoard not in overpriced cable or station properties but in treasury bills, waiting for the recession, allowing CBS to acquire properties cheap. Though muted, differences between Tisch and his board persisted into 1990, with Tisch unwilling to invest in the broadcast or cable business, and the board anxious to see an offensive strategy.

Tisch believed he was more patient than Wright, and more confident in the network business. Four months before he fired Kim LeMasters in November 1989 and replaced him with Tri-Star president Jeffrey Sagansky, Tisch said he was optimistic that in a year—starting with the prime-time season beginning in September 1990—CBS would enjoy a renaissance. "I think 1989 will be our bottom year, and starting in 1990 we'll be looking at a real reversal at the network." Under Sagansky and Stringer, CBS's prime-time schedule did begin to rebound, as Tisch predicted.

But with Tisch it was sometimes hard to tell when he spoke from the heart. Despite his anti-cable stance to affiliates, for instance, by the end of that year CBS made a joint bid with John Malone's TCI for the 1992 Summer Olympics, and sought a cable partner on all subsequent sports bids. More quietly, Malone said that he had held discussions with CBS about testing the appeal of some network series on cable. If Tisch's flirtation with cable wasn't confusing enough, he baffled broadcasters and even some members of his board by spending liberally to lock up sports events and movies before they could appear on cable, investing a stupefying $3.6 billion on sports, including the rights to major league baseball games and the 1992 Winter Olympics, and another $50 million for ten Universal movies, including *Field of Dreams.*

Tisch, who had been ridiculed as cheap, was now derided as profligate. Naturally, he didn't like it. His record as an investor was not to be sneezed at. It seemed so unfair to be the target of those who claimed he was too cautious, and of those who said his sports strategy was not cautious enough; of those who asserted that he lacked a strategy, and those who said he had the wrong strategy. One set of critics had to be wrong—unless they were both right! Unless, that is, Tisch proved too cautious in the station and cable properties he refused to buy, and too incautious in what he would pay for sports and other "good" news. A common critique among CBS directors throughout 1989 and well into 1990 was that CBS under Tisch at best had a strategy that waited for an event—a recession—over which Larry Tisch had no control. Of course, when a recession finally struck in 1990, Tisch's decision to squirrel cash into safe treasury bills seemed vindicated. The cautious strategy made sense—if, that is, he was now prepared to buy broadcast and cable properties at bargain prices.

Apparently he was not. In December 1990, on the same day that he imposed a CBS wage freeze, Tisch announced that CBS would spend $2 billion to buy back up to 44 percent of its stock, including stock owned by Tisch's own Loews Corporation and founder William Paley, who had passed away that fall, unhappy, feeling cut off from his once robust child. For Tisch and Loews, the difference between his own purchase price and the stock buyback price meant a tidy profit of about $180 million. But for CBS, said a depressed CBS policy maker, "It means we have no big future in the media world. We can't buy anything." What it meant to this executive and others was that Tisch had a hidden offensive plan after all—to sell CBS.

Perhaps. The vulnerability of this argument is its assumption that Tisch would sell CBS simply to make money when his motive in acquiring it had more to do with vanity. By 1991 the questions were: Had Tisch tired of his new vocation and was he now ready to discard it—for a profit? And who would buy it?

Of the three companies, Cap Cities/ABC had the most balanced portfolio of holdings. It had ESPN and other money-making cable investments. Each of ABC's eight owned stations was number one in its urban market. It was a powerhouse in publishing and the theater. It had invested in a variety of new technologies, including interactive television and an electronic billboard to deliver promotional messages in supermarkets. It would make several overseas deals, including 40 percent ownership of WTN, a worldwide news service, an agreement to exchange entertainment, news, and sports with the Japan Broadcasting Corporation or NHK, as well as stakes in Tele Munchen, a German media conglomerate, and ABC/Kane Productions, which was set up to sell nonfiction programming to foreign and domestic markets. Warren Buffett had staked an initial claim to 6.3 percent of Coca-Cola's stock, which he said was a passive investment; skeptics were left to note the nice fit between the world's best-known product and a communications company with worldwide aspirations.

ABC, unlike NBC, was not playing for quick touchdowns. Cap Cities was also a creature of its own culture. It was a company that grew by relying on cautious acquisitions and careful cost cutting. Success taught Cap Cities that rewards came to the slow and sure. So they adopted an incremental growth strategy, one more cautious than NBC's but bolder than CBS's. They were steady and predictable; they would not take big risks on sports, as CBS would. Nor would they jump to acquire Time, Inc., which Tom Murphy said would have made "a perfect partner." Murphy and Time chairman Dick Munro, who were fellow IBM board members, negotiated from November 1988 to January 1989. They had gotten so far as to agree to call the merged company Time/ABC. But they couldn't get the FCC to waive the rules allowing a network to be a cable operator, and Time was the second largest. The ever careful Murphy also decided that the price was too steep, and not just the financial price. The two men, who were past sixty, were also apart on a successor, with Murphy insisting on Dan Burke, and Munro on his number two, Nick Nicholas. Though it would have been a blockbuster deal, as Warner's merger with Time became, Murphy walked away from it. ABC just didn't take big flyers, mindful of the downside. Yet it did take some chances, as with ESPN, Bochco, and Diane Sawyer.

It was this impression of *balance* that both shaped the new culture at ABC and created a sense among broadcasters and others that ABC was the network to watch. Even Jack Welch said it. "It appears to me from where I sit that ABC is steadily rebuilding and making progress in a tough environment," he said late in 1988. There were varied ways to measure this progress. A 1989 *Broadcasting* magazine poll of securities analysts found Wall Street touting Cap Cities/ABC as a great stock to buy, and its stock price at the close of 1989 rose to $564 a share, while its overall after-tax profits reached $485.7 million and

ABC network profits climbed to $165 million. In prime time, the youthful reach of ABC's shows would help narrow NBC's demographic lead. In the morning, in the wake of the Jane Pauley fiasco, *Good Morning America* shot past the *Today* show. In the evening newscast race, Peter Jennings and ABC News came to be seen as the best of the three news organizations, as Jennings's and ABC's handling of the 1991 war with Iraq seemed to certify. In sports, while CBS suffered heavy losses and NBC lost its baseball franchise, ABC Sports turned a modest profit.

Perhaps, it was said, intangibles helped explain ABC's resurgence. Morale was far better at ABC than at either NBC or CBS, and one reason was the sense of security executives imparted throughout the organization. In a business convulsed by change, ABC's communal executive dining room took away a feeling of *us* and *them,* as did Dan Burke's effort, once ABC's offices were combined in a campus-like setting on West Sixty-sixth Street, to try to breakfast and lunch three or four times a week in the employee cafeteria. Murphy and Burke were professional managers who set out to make their minions feel comfortable. Rarely did they snarl at employees, as Wright and Tisch sometimes did. They took time to chat with workers. Probably no decision had as much impact on overall ABC morale as Murphy and Burke's effort to do all the layoffs just once. They did, and nearly 2,000 employees felt the pain. But by late 1987 the layoffs ceased for four long years. Over time, ABC employees came to trust that they need not fret daily about losing their jobs. Layoffs were a last, not a first, resort. At NBC or CBS, every time business dipped or costs escalated, the terror of layoffs returned. Because ABC employees felt more secure, perhaps they were more willing to take risks, to talk back to their bosses, to devote more time to their work with fewer distractions.

People came to credit ABC's relative success—as they did NBC's under Grant Tinker—to understanding, patient, and generous leadership from people who understood broadcasting. Even when Tom Murphy reached sixty-five and stepped down as CEO in June 1990, no one was alarmed, because his successor was a worthy fellow broadcaster, Dan Burke, and because their relationship was so symbiotic that no one expected Murphy to walk off into the sunset. Nor would anyone have expected to hear Larry Tisch or Bob Wright passionately say what Tom Murphy did at an emotional thank-you dinner in his honor at the Waldorf Astoria Hotel: "I always thought it was something special to be a broadcaster. The part of the network most dear to my heart is the news division. Edward R. Murrow was one of my heroes. . . . The greatest personal satisfaction I have gotten out of being associated with ABC is when the slide goes up and you see the ABC logo and it says under it, 'More Americans get their news from ABC News.' "

Tom Murphy was saying something special, something that Peter Jennings and Tom Brokaw and Dan Rather and other journalists who come to work each day at the networks craved to hear. Sure they wanted to see evidence that management would invest money in correspondents or bureaus. But they also wanted to know that their boss understood their work was a calling, not just a job.

They wanted to hear something else, something that Murphy would also say, as if by reflex. Before the applause subsided, Murphy hushed the crowd, modestly took the credit everyone had bestowed upon him, and cast it out onto the ballroom floor, inviting one of his executives to stand and bask in the spotlight alone. When the light reached Roone Arledge, Murphy announced: This is "the genius behind the great ABC News operation."

Murphy was saying, simply: *We love you.*

And the love was sometimes reciprocated. During the evening, after toastmaster Peter Jennings paid a brief but poignant tribute—"Tom, we are proud to work for you"—sportscaster Jim McKay rose to lift his glass. "Frankly, when Cap Cities took over some five years ago," said McKay, looking at Murphy, "all we knew about them was that they were supposed to be 'lean and mean' and run a taut ship. Didn't sound like us, did it, Roone? Well, we found they were lean but really weren't mean at all. . . . We found this was a business organization that used words like integrity and honor and responsibility, and meant them."

In a period of turmoil in television, ABC was simply a better place to work. This was not because it had invented some new management technique like GE's "work-out sessions" or just because ABC was rising in the ratings. No, it was because in addition to keeping its eyes on the bottom line, Cap Cities/ABC was more sensitive to its employees. Sure, Murphy and Burke thought the network world was on fire. But they took the time to mingle and laugh, to give pats on the back, to share credit. In the middle of an earthquake, they radiated a sense of security.

25

THREE BLIND MICE, 1990-91 AND BEYOND

Since 1985, when this story began, the networks have been staggered by an earthquake that struck as if in slow motion, cracking their foundations. By the end of the 1990–91 season, the damage was unmistakable. In a single season, they had lost 5 percent of their viewers, as the three-network share of audience fell to 62 percent. Since 1976, the three networks had lost one out of three viewers.

The big gainer, again, was cable. By 1991, cable had extended its reach another couple of percent, to nearly 60 percent of all homes. Compared to the previous year, the change was incremental. Compared to 1976, when 15 percent of homes had cable, the change registered a 10 on the Richter scale. Cable now topped independent stations as a viewing choice, attracting 23.5 percent of the nightly TV audience; another 14.8 percent tuned to the three-hundred-plus independent stations. The Fox network, which now supplied programming to half these independent stations on five out of seven nights, was another gainer; by the end of the 1990–91 season, Fox attracted 11 percent of viewers (a 6.4 percent rating), though by the end of the season it had lost some momentum. The VCR was now in nearly three out of four American homes. The average viewer enjoyed thirty-three channel options, and stores sold TV sets capable of receiving nearly two hundred channels from cable or a satellite dish.

Not only were viewers fleeing, but once again, no network produced a certifiable hit in the 1990–91 season, although each tried oddball shows, hoping to catch the public's fancy. Brandon Tartikoff had said that NBC and the other networks were experimenting more, shedding familiar formulas. With *Twin Peaks* and *The Simpsons* as models, they cooked up a stew of singing cops, cartoon sitcoms, and so on. "Tried and true equals dead and buried," declared Tartikoff. The experiments flopped. That someone as smart as Tartikoff could no longer divine a hit only deepened the depression at the networks.

Perhaps because viewers had so many choices, they were latching onto the familiar. A better motto for the season would have been: "Tried and true equals alive and well." The most watched show on television was NBC's nine-year-old *Cheers.* The top ten was dominated by familiar hits such as *60 Minutes* and *The Cosby Show.* The advances CBS made this year were, in part, powered by clever scheduling of nostalgic specials—the best of *The Ed Sullivan Show, The Mary Tyler Moore Show,* and *All in the Family.*

The earthquake's toll was clearer by the end of the season. After winning five straight prime-time contests, NBC's ratings collapsed, falling 13 percent, from a 14.6 average to 12.7 in 1991. CBS, with a surprising 12.3 rating, not only won the February ratings sweeps for the first time since 1985 but was in contention to finish number one. NBC limped in third some weeks, and when he returned from the hospital in mid-February, Tartikoff jumped back into his programming sandbox with a vengeance. By the close of the season in mid-April, NBC barely squeaked to a sixth straight first-place finish, just two-tenths of a rating point ahead of second-place ABC's 12.5 rating. Although it finished third for the fourth straight year, with a 12.3 rating, CBS was the only network to not only gain viewers but also to attract new younger ones. Despite Tisch's management style and sometimes gruff manner, CBS, under Broadcast president Howard Stringer and Entertainment chief Jeff Sagansky, was poised to make a run at first place in the 1991–92 season.

Nevertheless, the "good" news wasn't so good for any of the three networks. Though ABC edged NBC as the network with the best demographic profile, its performance trailed expectations. ABC actually lost 3 percent of its viewers over the same period the year before. CBS's audience gains were a modest 2 percent. In touting these gains, or proclaiming that CBS might come in first in 1991–92, CBS executives sometimes sounded like cancer patients boasting that they had had a terrific night's sleep. And it should be remembered that CBS's ratings gains were offset by mammoth Sports losses, prompting Larry Tisch to urge major league baseball to renegotiate its contract with CBS. Although NBC was number one, it had been abandoned by nearly one fourth of its viewers since the 1987–88 season. Equally unsettling, NBC faced the future without Brandon Tartikoff, who announced in May 1991 that he would head Paramount Studios.

On top of this, a recession began to pound the networks in 1990, and profits sank. At the end of the year, having been belted by huge baseball losses, the CBS network would lose about $30 million. While the ABC network earned about $225 million in 1990, by the fourth quarter its profits had begun to tumble. At NBC, Bob Wright did not meet his $465 million profit goal for 1990, as after-tax earnings fell to $340 million, half of which came from the network. Privately, Larry Tisch confessed early in 1991 that he feared CBS's network losses could climb above $200 million in 1991, and perhaps as high as $300 million. Dan Burke, who had succeeded Tom Murphy as CEO, said it was "easily possible" that the ABC network would lose money in 1991. And early in the year, Wright alerted Jack Welch that NBC would miss its overall $340 million target for 1991 by perhaps $120 million, and that the network might lose money.

Falling revenues and rising costs invoked new economies at the networks. In December 1990, Tisch ordered yet another round of cuts, this one totaling $70 million; he also brought in McKinsey & Company to help him streamline and take a closer look at how to spend money more intelligently. By February, long before McKinsey's report was ready, a gloomy Tisch was impatiently pressing for $200 million in cost savings, including $100 million immediately. Period. End of discussion. To CBS employees, Tisch was like a Scud missile—they never knew where or when he would strike. Dan Burke, like Tisch, said ABC would seek to alter functions and better analyze its spending; he, too, foresaw nothing but trouble ahead for the networks. Unlike Tisch or Wright, he said he would struggle to avoid layoffs, though he wouldn't make an ironclad pledge. (For the first time in four years, ABC ordered layoffs in July 1991.) Unlike Tisch, he would follow a deliberate, nonconfrontational process and not just issue sudden commands. Wright early in 1991 asked each NBC division to devise a cost-saving restructuring plan, including massive layoffs.

Surprisingly, Jack Welch seemed less alarmed than Wright, Tisch, or Burke. In shirtsleeves, and leaning forward, never back, in a leather swivel chair in the conference room next to his office in the newly named GE Building at 30 Rock, one floor above Bob Wright's renovated suite, Welch insisted the network falloff was aberrational—"a one-year thing." He would not insist on brutal measures to meet profit goals. "To ask NBC to grow its profits in this environment is ludicrous," he said. Fingering a chart of the various GE businesses, he said he would offset NBC's declining earnings with higher profits from Aircraft Engines, Power Systems, and Medical Systems. GE was a diversified company, as to a lesser extent was Cap Cities. "Tisch has a different problem," said Welch. "He has no other source of income. I'm at the table with three kings, three queens, two jacks. . . . I've got more options. That's the strength of GE. I'm going to have a very nice first quarter. NBC's going to have a terrible first quarter." Still, Welch applauded Wright's efforts to downsize, to remind his troops that this was the marines; the struggle never ceased.

What explains the sudden collapse of network revenues? The causes are many: The recession obviously gutted advertising budgets; as network audiences shrank, advertisers sought other outlets; the decision of the networks to try and make up for lost revenues by running from 4 (ABC) to 8 percent (NBC and CBS) more ads altered the psychology of the marketplace, shifting leverage to advertisers who had no reason to panic since they now knew network time wasn't scarce. The war with Iraq took a toll as well. In its first days, the war cost each network up to $6 million a day in lost advertising; NBC calculated that the Gulf War cost it $50 million between August 2, 1990, when Iraq invaded Kuwait, and February 1991, when a ceasefire was achieved.

In a less quantifiable way, the war in the Gulf may have cost even more. Instantly, the public glimpsed the cataclysmic changes in the television industry. Viewers realized that CNN, not the three networks, was the channel of convenience for live, up-to-the-minute news. With relatively few overseas bureaus—by mid-1991 each network had shrunk to between four and nine bureaus, not including a handful of offices scattered elsewhere—the networks no longer qualified as a worldwide news service, if they ever did. Even though the war boosted interest in news, by early 1991 the three network newscasts together attracted only 54 percent of those watching television, a loss of nearly one out of three viewers in less than a decade. All at once, everyone seemed to be talking about whether network news had a future—indeed, whether the networks had a future.

Rewind to 1986.

It's clear, in retrospect, that in many ways the new owners succeeded in changing the old culture. They tamed the unions, forced News and other divisions to spend less, convinced everyone that the good times had stopped. Doing business with cable was no longer heresy. Nor was the idea of producing and selling programs to a network rival, as ABC announced it was prepared to do. Nor was the idea that the four News networks should pool their efforts on Election Day exit polls, saving about $10 million each in the process. The new owners had forced their organizations to recognize new competitors. How could they not? It was now commonplace for the media to identify Fox and CNN as "networks"; programs that had once been "free"—movies, the Olympics, boxing matches, football games, perhaps one day the Super Bowl or World Series—viewers now paid to watch. Already the nearly $18 billion the cable industry collected in revenues dwarfed the $9 billion gathered by the three networks.

Quietly, the new owners had curbed affiliate compensation. In constant dollars, by 1990 the roughly $500 million the three networks together paid their affiliates had declined. Impatient with reducing compensation one station at a time, in late 1990 Larry Tisch announced that CBS would slash compensation across the board by 20 percent, or by about $30 million. Over breakfast in 1991, Tisch exploded: "In five years there won't be any compensation!" Maybe in five years, guessed Dan Burke, "the stations will pay compensation to the networks. Maybe the networks will be a cooperative and the affiliated stations will have to buy a stake in it."

Some of the changes advanced by the new owners were worrisome. At NBC, for example, both Welch and Wright emphasized the importance of a "boundaryless" company, one without walls among News, Entertainment, Sales, and other divisions. Inhibitions would dissolve, it was said, and ideas would gush like oil. At NBC's annual management retreat in 1990, many of the 160 executives questioned why Sales or Entertainment couldn't have more input into news specials, or why News tended to keep its distance from the rest of the company, as if it were somehow special. Sounding as if he were singing for his supper, Don Browne, the new executive News director and deputy to Michael Gartner, proclaimed that henceforth News would be "lean and mean" and "at the cutting edge." He and Gartner welcomed ideas from Sales and Marketing and Entertainment for a Jane Pauley magazine show, Browne assured fellow executives. Although "barriers in the news division" were "coming down," by God, more work remained to be done!

The working assumption at this conference was that all barriers were bureaucratic. Overlooked was the fact that some barriers were meant to protect, say, News from entertainment values or from advertiser pressure, or to protect consumers or children from hidden advertising. The panic for profits had provoked Bob Wright to suggest that maybe Don Johnson of *Miami Vice* could host some news documentaries, and Jack Welch to propose that publishers pay to induce the *Today* show to interview their authors. Although the weakening of the walls that traditionally stood between News and the rest of the company began before the new owners arrived, that process was now surely accelerated. Increasingly the networks pressured their local stations to promote network entertainment shows and stars on its newscasts, thus tarnishing the independence a newscast needs to retain the trust of viewers—the "big shill factor," Verne Gay of *Newsday* called it. News re-creations knocked down the walls, as did most docudramas, including ABC's version of Bob Woodward and Carl Bernstein's *The Final Days,* complete with invented dialogue. The new owners speeded the trend to hold news to the same ratings standard as entertainment shows. If a news documentary or special couldn't approximate the desired Nielsen numbers, it usually got the hook. Slowly but perceptibly, the center of gravity—the value system—shifted within much of network news. Which probably helps explain why NBC's newest magazine entry—*Exposé*—in April 1991 aired a sensationalist eleven-minute report on Senator Charles S. Robb's alleged extracurricular escapades, why *NBC Nightly News* closed a newscast earlier that month with an exclusive interview with a man who claimed he had been Merv Griffin's lover, or why CBS News dabbled in re-creations of news events. Each lowered the wall between network news and such tabloid-TV fare as *A Current Affair.*

Network Sales scaled some walls of its own by conniving with advertisers to camouflage commercials. Increasingly the networks, like the movie studios, accommodated advertisers by letting products be plugged within a program or film. For example, Coca-Cola induced CBS and Grant Tinker to let an actor on Tinker's *TV 101* ostentatiously gulp from a can of Coke. As profit pressures mount and mass markets splinter into hundreds of distinct market segments, advertisers will holler to knock down more walls. "A network is not in the program business. It's not in the news business or the sports business. It's in the business of selling advertising," said Roy J. Bostock, president of the world's ninth-largest ad agency, D'Arcy Masius Benton & Bowles. To sell more advertising, he said the networks had to be more willing to hide ads within shows. Or to name sporting events after products. Or to allow advertisers a say in programming or to own entire shows, as they often do in daytime soap operas and as they once did in prime time. Or to enter joint ventures with the network. Perhaps the networks and local stations can let popular weathermen talk about, say, Anacin, in the middle of a weather report.

Of course, this blurring is not unique to the networks. Entrepreneur Chris Whittles's Channel One provides "free" televised news to public schools, giving advertisers access to a captive student audience. Plugs for Pepsi-Cola are tucked within "Magic Johnson's Fast Break" video game for kids, and ads for Federal Express or Philip Morris are sandwiched between the covers of some books. Infomercials on television and advertorials in magazines are dressed to look like journalism, yet are paid advertisements. We have "The Virginia Slims Tennis Tournament," and even the annual dinner of P.E.N., the eminent international writers' organization, is billed as the P.E.N. MontBlanc dinner.

The new owners, led by Bob Wright, helped awaken the networks to the encroaching earthquake. In this, they were right. But in their quest to tap fresh revenue, they rushed to eliminate barriers that actually protected their investment. In their haste to impose a new order, to defend shareholder rights, sometimes they failed to see the unintended damage to their investment and to their public trust.

In other ways, the new owners had changed and become more like the old ones. Larry Tisch and Tom Murphy set out to curb Hollywood costs under their control, slashing the budgets for their self-produced series and made-for-TV movies. But within a few years, they were copying NBC's 1986 decision to produce more of its own shows. "We should have done it sooner," admitted ABC's Murphy. "We didn't because we went through a learning process. There were too many other things on the table." The new owners began by focusing on costs and ended thinking more about revenues. No one any longer had to sell them on the magnetic power of hit shows, or the importance of spending time in Hollywood.

In countless ways, the new owners had changed. They were zigging and zagging more, no longer assuming that a straight line was the quickest route to reach such goals as paring station compensation. Employee morale was no longer gruffly dismissed as an excuse to avoid cutbacks. In an extraordinary attempt to generate good feeling, at NBC's 1990 management retreat a more relaxed and likable Bob Wright mobilized his executives to spend an entire day doing a good deed. At 7 A.M.,with Motown music as a backdrop, Wright led a contingent of 160 overalled executives on a sometimes Chaplinesque contest to erect a playground for the Barnyard Community Center, to repair its asphalt, plant nine hundred shrubs and trees, and to fix and paint this after-school program center in the Coconut Grove section of Miami. For NBC executives it was a memorable, shared experience.

The new owners were determined to reduce sports rights fees and star salaries, yet both rose. They might want to change it, but the habit among the three networks was like the rule of thumb in the arms race: If one superpower acquired a weapon, the other wanted it. So they became bigger spenders, as Larry Tisch did when he paid $3.6 billion to broadcast sports or $50 million to acquire ten movies from Universal. Despite their caution in spending money, Murphy and Burke would approve multiyear contracts for Steven Bochco, James L. Brooks, and other Hollywood talent, as well as for Diane Sawyer.

Sometimes the new owners felt compelled to make decisions they knew might be counterproductive. For instance, in 1990 NBC agreed to pay the producers of *The Cosby Show* a nearly $3 million weekly license fee, or about $75 million annually; this expenditure cut in half NBC's $100 million profit from its entire Thursday night schedule. Even so, Wright was relieved that he had refused to pay Cosby's producers the $100 million they had demanded, or to pledge to keep one of their other series—*Grand*—on the air for at least two years. Nevertheless, NBC paid dearly to keep Cosby. In 1991, NBC would face the same problem when *The Cosby Show* and four other popular shows were up for renewal. One of these was the comedy hit *Cheers,* which ranked number one in the 1990–91 season. As he contemplated the $120 million license-fee demand from Paramount, which produced *Cheers,* Jack Welch was angry. Yet he didn't dismiss Paramount out of hand, as he might have just a few years before. Welch did not want to lose *Cheers.* NBC was already paying the producers $35 million a season. To retain *Cheers,* he said that winter, NBC would be willing to pay $50 million, and might, if a gun were at its head, pay slightly more. But not much more. Welch was certain Dan Burke of ABC would refrain from a bidding war, as he had refrained from bidding on sports franchises. Burke had already signaled this to Wright when their paths crossed at an industry breakfast; Burke had refused to allow his Entertainment people to even meet with and receive a proposal from Paramount. It says a lot about Welch's new flexibility, and about Larry Tisch's new reputation for extravagance, that Welch's main concern, with ABC neutralized, was whether CBS would outbid NBC. After a tense few weeks, NBC retained *Cheers,* paying about $70 million for the privilege.

Why were the new owners, three shrewd, cautious investors, sometimes so extravagant? One reason is that they had learned the value of investing in hits. Since they didn't control their producers, they had to pay what the Hollywood market demanded. Their affiliates also demanded attractive products, particularly sports. And in the network business, like any other, you keep customers happy.

Another reason is that their peer pressure group changed. "When the new owners come in, no matter who they are, they come into an established system," observed CAA agent Bill Haber. "When David Puttnam came in and tried to change the motion picture business, he failed." What happened to the new network owners, said Haber, is what happens to isolated cells in the human body: "The amoebic reaction breaks down their cells, not the other way around. Think of it as a giant corpuscle. The outside body absorbs the new cell." But this is not the complete answer.

Still another factor was how human "logic"—ego, vanity, anger, pride, even panic—sometimes triumphed over business logic. The networks were a strange new world for these conventional businessmen. Good news wasn't just measured in stock prices and profits. They became so eager to hush critics, to calm affiliates, to send a reassuring message to Hollywood and Washington, that they occasionally overspent. Sometimes it was simply the desire for victory that proved irresistible. "In no other business do you get a report card every day from overnight ratings," said a ranking ABC executive. "Over a period of time your competitive ego gets determined to fight hard for these things." To win.

The desire to win is more pronounced in a business that imposes unusual constraints on the power of the chief executive. The new owners thought they would be hailed for cost cutting, yet were vilified instead. Surely it was no fun for Larry Tisch to come home to his Fifth Avenue apartment and see Local One stagehands handing out leaflets telling neighbors, "Next time you see Larry Tisch in the elevator or the lobby, tell him you are outraged with his efforts to destroy the lives of his employees." Nor was it much fun for Tisch to admit, as he did early in 1991, that "we overpaid" for sports. Nor was it fun for these businessmen to spot what they believed to be waste, and yet do nothing for fear that cuts would ignite a public furor. Larry Tisch, who believed when he first acquired stock in CBS that it was "just like every other business," would eventually conclude that he had been "much too glib." The mysteries of programming, the difficulties of dealing with two-hundred-plus affiliates, of appeasing government regulators and fulfilling a public trust while under a public microscope, said Tisch, "set network television apart and complicated the normal logic of business planning and budgeting." Even Jack Welch, who believed that networks were different from other businesses only in the attention the media lavished on them, acknowledged that daily press coverage—including a story that very day that NBC had curbed its distribution of photocopied press clippings!—had an effect on an organization and its leaders, sending spirits up or down, producing energy or lethargy.

Fast forward to the future.

The network owners know that they will encounter increasingly negative publicity, more audience erosion, more cost cutting, as they struggle to shrink their organizations. In the future, sports will probably continue to migrate to cable and pay channels, since these can better afford to subsidize the salaries of Roger Clemens and Dwight Gooden. Maybe some or all of the networks will program fewer hours each day. To save money, maybe game shows or even syndicated programs will be stripped into prime-time hours. It is no longer unthinkable that one of the Big Three might abandon the network business altogether.

Unless network news consolidates more of its functions with other networks or local stations or overseas news services, as each is vying to do, it is likely to see its influence ebb. It is possible that one or more networks will abandon news, merge its overseas operations, or eliminate a nightly newscast and instead sell news packages to stations. Increasingly, news is viewed as an important but expensive luxury. The three networks together spent about $1 billion on news in 1991, compared to about $200 million by CNN. News "isn't the strategic center of what happens here," declared Jack Welch in early 1991. While Welch praised Michael Gartner, Tom Brokaw, and NBC News for their work, he nevertheless noted, pointedly, "Fox doesn't have news." Because news was now available on local stations, CNN, PBS, and elsewhere, in the view of Welch and no doubt others, "News is not the core of the asset." This was his financial calculus.

Journalists have a different calculus, which is why the clash between shareholder responsibility and the public trust will not subside. As he sat one night in a Miami bar reflecting on NBC's 1990 management retreat and how executives who attended seemed to have "bought into" the GE lingo and value system, Gerry Solomon was morose. He had been at NBC News for seventeen years, and he was now the executive producer of *Sunday Today* and *Meet the Press,* but when his contract expired in 1991 he said he might want out. Here's why: "The argument we hear all the time is that 'quality' counts. But the definition of 'quality' has changed at the networks. They are not talking about the quality of the reporter"—they would just as soon send a green local reporter to cover unrest in Nicaragua as they would the experienced Garrick Utley. "They are talking about the 'quality' of the payoff to the network." He meant that Welch and Wright were talking about costs. Yet journalists talked about "ephemeral things" like "credibility" and "calling" and the "quality" of the product. "GE doesn't know these things because they can't be quantified," he said.

If news, or sports, or other network functions become expendable, will the three networks themselves die?

Probably not. Certainly there are powerful forces with a stake in strong networks, starting with advertisers. Ten years ago, said Roy Bostock, 60 percent of a company's marketing budget was earmarked for advertising and only 40 percent went into promotion. Today, he said, only 40 percent went to advertising. "That's a major part of the problem that the networks have." It's also a problem for the advertising business, "because how goes the television business is how goes the advertising business." With advertising growth stalled, agencies often saw their fate linked to the networks. Hollywood studio chiefs, as Disney chairman Michael Eisner and Warner chairman Bob Daly acknowledged, also had an interest in vibrant networks. The networks were their biggest single customer; no one else could match the license fees paid by the networks, or their mass audiences; no one else could create an audience for shows that can be sold to syndication, which is where the studios make big money.

The public also has a stake in the networks. Whatever its failings, a mass medium creates a sense of community. Americans grow up believing diversity is good and bigness is bad, which is often true. But it is also true that the public has an investment in a common communications system, in the larger public purpose a network can perform when it brings a disparate population together to share an experience. Often this potential is unrealized. But it was fulfilled when the networks became the nation's common church after John F. Kennedy and Martin Luther King, Jr., were assassinated; when nearly three quarters of all viewers tuned to the miniseries *Roots;* and when the new owners sacrificed ad revenues to offer live coverage during the first week of the 1991 war with Iraq. Ev Dennis, executive director of the Gannett Center for Media Studies at Columbia University, observed: "We have shared values that are enhanced by three networks. For the same reason we don't favor five hundred languages in the country. It does create a national consensus of values and of what we think is important. We could be like Italy, where the newspapers are weak," TV is dispersed, and there is no national consensus. The stability of the American government and society, he said, owed something to the networks.

It is also true, however, that the variety of choices now available to the TV viewer enhances the diversity of the culture. For nearly two decades the federal government has sought to deregulate television in order to encourage a greater range of choices; yet at the same time, government has long proclaimed the public's right to free television. The two goals sometimes war. As is often true in a democracy, individual freedom may not mean equal access. Freedom of choice may belong only to those who can afford to pay for the opportunity. If there were no networks, how many citizens could afford—or have access to—cable or pay TV? How could fifty cable and pay-TV channels, none with more than 2 percent of the audience, subsidize quality programs at prices all consumers could afford? Will the public tolerate limiting major events to cable when only 60–70 percent of the nation actually has cable? Will they pay fifteen to twenty dollars for a football game, as they now do to watch a championship fight on pay-per-view? While he has a personal interest in building this case, Larry Tisch correctly identifies the public-policy question looming down the road: "The issue is the future of free television. Will citizens have to pay fifty dollars to see the Super Bowl? Or ten dollars to see a made-for-TV movie? That question will be there. And when the crisis comes, it will be too late." Ten years from now, he predicted, Congress may wake up and call for an investigation of who killed free TV.

Because powerful interests—the public, the government, advertisers, local stations, and the studios—have a stake in network television, it is entirely possible that government will one day pass legislation to protect "free" TV. It might one day suspend the fin-syn rules, encouraging the studios and the networks to merge, thus enhancing the economic viability of the networks. Perhaps the U.S. government will one day do what a Canadian government task force recommended in May 1991. The Canadian government, they urged, should impose a three-year moratorium on new broadcast and cable licenses in order to preserve economically struggling broadcast networks and stations.

What is certain about the future is this: The networks can never recapture their monopoly. No matter what advertisers or the studios or the government say, having tasted the power to choose, viewers will continue to insist on programming for themselves, just as they increasingly opt for the convenience of shopping at home through catalogues. It may be unclear how the networks will tap other sources of revenue, or with whom they will ally themselves. It may be unclear what technologies will emerge—high-definition TV, direct broadcast satellites, fiber optics, digitalized signals, among countless others. What is clear is that the programmer will be king.

A decade ago, Michael Eisner, then a top Paramount executive, told of a visit he made to the Consumer Electronics Show in Las Vegas. There he wandered among the exhibits for videocassettes and video discs, giant screens and miniature television sets, hundred-channel cable systems and backyard dishes, car phones and home computers. "Everywhere the call of technology. The music of progress was in the wind," he remembered. Eisner panicked when he realized that his studio, Paramount, was not even on the main exhibition floor. "Somehow, we had missed not only the show, but the boat." Were the studios not part of the brave new world of tomorrow? Then as Eisner walked past the exhibits of the latest technologies he noticed that each was playing movies starring Warren Beatty, John Travolta, or some other American star. None promoted "Fukkatsu No Hi from Japan."

The future, Eisner realized, belonged to "the product," the entertainment shows and movies produced mostly by Hollywood. Everything else—the VCR, the cable wire, the local stations, the satellite dish, even the networks—was merely a way of distributing his product.

What seems certain is that if the networks are to survive and perhaps thrive, they must be permitted to produce and own and sell more of the product. The networks need to find a way out of their trap, which is that they rely on a single source of revenue and are but three channels in a 150-channel universe. Standing alone, the networks may die. With additional revenue sources or partners, the good times may return.

Each new network owner approaches the future in his own fashion. Tisch backs into it, one careful step at a time. He comes to the office alone most mornings, as he has done from day one, taking an express elevator programmed to stop only on the thirty-fifth floor. He places his briefcase on a plain wooden desk largely clear of piles of papers, glances at his phone message slips, and walks through a vestibule to his private dining room, where he sits at a small polished wood table, surrounded by the valuable art that Bill Paley collected. On most days, Tisch sees only those who visit his corner suite. Larry Tisch now wears Hermès ties, finer wool suits, and enjoys the respectability of his membership on the boards of the Metropolitan Museum and the New York

Public Library. But he still follows the hour-to-hour bounces of the market, still talks to his four sons and brother Bob perhaps more than to any CBS executive, and leaves early most days to play bridge.

As he sipped coffee and breakfasted on a croissant in the seclusion of his CBS dining room in early 1991, Tisch held to some simple convictions. Costs, not revenues, he still believed, were the key to CBS's future. He dismissed the notion that a relaxation of the fin-syn rules would mean riches for the networks. He still did not believe the networks were a growth business, but he was certain that "if it were run properly, the CBS network could earn $200 million a year." Tisch was not just referring to more cost cutting, though he did believe he could squeeze another $200 million out of CBS's costs. "Do you keep *Dallas* on the air? That's a $30 million decision," he said, noting that CBS paid $30 million more to Lorimar for the series than it received in advertising revenues. "How does the network split the time between half-hour and hour shows?" Does it abandon sports? How many hours of news should it program? "This is not just a question of cost cutting," said Tisch. "It's a question of making the right decisions." Tisch sounded, much as he did in 1986, like a man fiercely determined to defend shareholders by cutting costs. Once again, he was convinced that because he had right on his side the fallout would be slight.

Larry Tisch in the winter of 1991 also sounded like a seller. As he neared his sixty-eighth birthday, Tisch admitted that none of the Tisch offspring was, or planned to be, involved in CBS. And after he was gone, Tisch said there was a "big question" whether Loews would remain CBS's major shareholder. Though he now says, "I have no *intention* of selling," this is not what he once proclaimed: *CBS is not for sale at any price.* Tisch insisted he wasn't sure a network and a studio made a good fit. Was Tisch the trader being coy? With only two major studios apparently shopping to buy a network—Eisner's Disney and Paramount—it was possible that Tisch was waiting for the perfect price, but by then the trade might have passed him by.

Dan Burke also ate breakfast as he talked about the immediate future in early 1991. At sixty-one, he had been rewarded with the CEO prize in 1990 when Tom Murphy honored his word and stepped aside. Like Murphy, he was informal, a natural pol. He wore button-down shirts and chewed nicotine gum rapidly, as if he were exercising his jaw. If Tisch kept his distance, Burke took the opposite tack. Striving to escape the confines of ABC's chain of command, he now took fewer meals in the vice presidents' dining room. Instead he breakfasted and lunched three or four times a week in ABC's employee cafeteria, carrying his own tray through the line and each time sitting down alongside a group of network employees. Hunched over corned beef hash in the cafeteria one February 1991 morning, waving to assorted engineers and secretaries, Burke spoke of the future. Like Tisch, he wanted to make "structural changes," including greater efforts to reduce compensation, or to slim news costs by inducing ABC's affiliates to provide the network with domestic news or to consolidate overseas bureaus. Like Tisch, his short-term prognosis for the networks was bleak. The networks would, he said, continue to "diminish." There would be networks in five years, he guessed, but: "I don't know whether there will be four. One may be out of sports. Or news. Or may program less than twenty-two hours a week of prime time."

But if Tisch's CBS was playing defense, waiting for a turnover, Dan Burke's Cap Cities/ABC was prepared to go for a first down, to be a bit more aggressive. With $1.3 billion in cash on hand, and the ability to borrow a lot more, with Cap Cities' stock trading at around $440 per share—up about $200 from when it acquired ABC—by the winter of 1991 Dan Burke said he could "hear the elephants moving in the jungle." Clearly, he was cautiously on the prowl for a deal. Burke still believed in creating a vertically integrated communications giant. To this end, he said, "anything is possible"—a merger with a studio, a partnership, the sale of the network. Maybe.

Jack Welch and Bob Wright, more than either Tisch or even Burke, saw the future as more of an opportunity than a problem. From his fifty-third-floor window in the GE Building at 30 Rock, Welch could see the Statue of Liberty. No buildings impeded his view of Central Park or Wall Street, or of the falling afternoon sun. Welch seemed surprisingly mellow for a man who acknowledged, as he did this winter day in 1991, that NBC's cable investments and other alliances had made "no marks on the wall," and who was aware that NBC's profits were in a nosedive. Nevertheless, Welch said he wasn't concerned. He had led GE to become a global superpower, now the second most valued company in the world, and about to pass IBM as number one. He still rooted for, and had his heart broken by, the Boston Red Sox, still occasionally stuttered, still paced his office in shirtsleeves. The new quarters might be dressed in elegant light wood and painted earth colors, but Jack Welch's booming voice could still be heard from behind solid wood doors. Welch remained an electric, sometimes terrifying, presence. Whether one worked for GE Jet Engines, Plastics, Appliances—or NBC—the sense was that Jack, as he's called, was everywhere.

Welch's success at GE had confirmed his faith in alliances, as well as his willingness to gamble. Because he believed a network was a critical link in the vertical integration of the communications business, he also believed that networks would endure. "I don't know how it will shape up, but a network is a wonderful asset," he said. A network was crucial to any future entertainment superpower. To him it was a given that a network and a studio were a natural fit. Such an alliance might be set in motion by the FCC when it relaxed the fin-syn rules, as he expected it would in April 1991.

"I am open to an asset play with NBC," said Welch, who was willing to buy a studio, or sell NBC, though preferably only part of it. He wanted to make an alliance. "You have to end up looking like Fox," he said. He wanted to own a studio, and a network, and stations, and cable, and a publishing arm, and newspapers, and magazines, and the direct broadcast satellites to deliver programs to the home. "I like Fox's position. But someone can be a bigger Fox." He would like to add theme parks, he said, which sounded as if Welch was thinking of a merger with Disney.

Such a merger was made less likely by the FCC ruling in April 1991. The FCC did relax the rules somewhat, permitting the networks to produce up to 40 percent of their prime-time programs, to seek studio partners to engage in some domestic syndication, and to compete in the $2 billion and fast-growing foreign syndication marketplace. But except for Fox, which was exempt from the rules as long as it agreed to stay under fifteen hours of programming, the ruling continued the ban on network participation in the lucrative first-run syndication business. And the fine print on how the networks would be allowed to compete in the syndication marketplace, moaned network executives, was another legal straitjacket. Bitterly "disappointed" in the ruling, Tom Murphy said, "What we received was a myriad of new hoops and hurdles that can only complicate our business dealings." In the short run, the rule changes offered no financial relief to the networks, since it usually takes at least four years on the air before reruns of a network show can be sold, which means that even if the networks could produce a series of hits in the 1991–92 season, they wouldn't enter the rerun market until 1996, at the earliest. In the long run, if this new set of strictures is not altered by the courts or the FCC, Welch's idea of a network-studio alliance is dubious, though this did not halt the rumors when Brandon Tartikoff bid farewell to NBC to become head of Paramount Pictures. To marry a network, a studio like Paramount would have to divorce itself from the first-run syndication business and agree not to produce shows for other networks. Network executives guessed they would not make such an uneconomic choice. And a studio would have to overlook the relatively poor economics of the broadcasting business. By mid-1991, Wall Street analysts were guessing that if Welch sold NBC he would fetch less than its book value, and that Tisch might have done better putting his money in a savings account than in CBS. Once again, there seemed to be no way out for the networks, as Jack Welch and his fellow network owners were reminded that the government policed their fate.

When Welch looked forward he was, in a sense, looking back, thinking of the networks as a nineteenth-century European nation-state. The communications business is made up of five sovereign powers—the networks, cable, the independent and affiliated stations, the Hollywood studios, and the telephone companies. Each wants to dominate. The outcome of the struggle between them is uncertain. And it is made more uncertain because of the deterrent power of the one true superpower—Washington. The federal government has the power to liberate the networks to compete or to merge with the Hollywood studios, to reregulate cable, to define a high-definition standard all broadcasters must use, to free the phone companies to enter the programming business or the cable companies to enter the telephone business, to impose restrictions on mergers or new licenses or on American programs sold overseas. What was certain was that GE and Cap Cities, each in its own way, wanted to vie with Sony, Matsushita, Murdoch, Time Warner, Bertelsmann, and others to become a global communications superpower. It appeared unclear whether Larry Tisch had a long-term strategy, unless it was to sell CBS.

No one can know which of these sovereign powers will join forces to shape the vertically integrated communications colossus of the future, if indeed this is the future. No one yet knows what government will do. Or what programs viewers will select. Will the networks and Hollywood merge, as Welch thinks? Will the telephone companies become the distribution arm for Hollywood or network programmers? Will cable replace the networks as Hollywood's distributor? Will the networks become a cooperative, with affiliates cementing a partnership through common ownership? Will technology and direct broadcast satellites make all distributors, from stations to networks to cable companies, obsolete? Will "free" TV become extinct? Will Congress tolerate a World Series or Super Bowl available only to pay-cable subscribers?

Neither Jack Welch nor Larry Tisch nor Dan Burke knows where this process will end. Will Welch overreach, as GE seemed to do when it bought the investment house of Kidder, Peabody and struggled to mesh two distinct cultures? Will Burke be too cautious? Will Tisch wait for a moment that will never come?

In 1991, as this book ends, the earthquake continues. This is a story without an end. It may be too soon to know who will survive. But it is not too soon to conclude that without fresh sources of revenue the once-mighty network lions seem as vulnerable, and sometimes as bewildered, as three blind mice.

AFTERWORD TO THE VINTAGE EDITION

For six years I was a visitor to a distant celestial body, the planet Television. This Martian knew few of the natives or local customs, and yet I was graciously welcomed by tribal leaders from the three networks.

Six years later I left, awed by the peculiar wonders I encountered on this voyage.

I learned that television is that rare business in which the CEO rarely consumes his company's primary product—entertainment programming.

I learned that even if they lose money—as CBS did in 1991 (and may in 1992)—the networks still preen when they win the prime-time ratings race, like three vain toughs battling for bragging rights to a street corner.

I learned network officials can sound like cancer patients, who, after a rare peaceful night of sleep, delude themselves into believing their long nightmare is over. So when the prime-time season ended in April 1992 and for the first time in 15 years the networks enjoyed a modest gain—1 percent—in viewers, the same network executives who privately believe more channel choices will ultimately steal viewers nevertheless publicly proclaimed that the cancer of eroding audiences had been arrested.

I learned television is a business in which vertically integrated Hollywood studios nonetheless pretend that frail networks are monopolies.

I learned that station managers love to complain about the "bean counters" running the networks—but that they too often behave more like accountants than broadcasters.

I learned it's a business in which advertisers will pay more even as network audiences shrink, in which advertisers insist on knowing the demographic audience profile for each show—but seem not to want to know whether viewers are zapping their commercials.

It's a business in which people feign lack of interest in what the press reports—yet can recite every word written about them.

It's a business covered by armchair reporters in distant cities, by those who too often fly in formation and whose primary sources are often in the News division, which knows next to nothing about business.

I learned it's a business citizens eagerly denounce as all-powerful, while those who run the networks often feel powerless. The CEOs would like to eliminate cash compensation to their affiliates and pare another thousand employees from their payroll, but they fear an avalanche of protests if they did so. To outward appearances, the owners of the networks are business lions. Yet they sometimes feel like trapped mice.

I learned that television (and technology in general) is mightier than any army or barbed-wire border because it obliterates national boundaries, reaching nearly everyone and making possible "the global village" Marshall McLuhan prophesized.

A TV network, I also learned, is a renter, not a landlord. Because the networks own neither the manufacturing process (the programs) nor the means of distribution (the stations), a congenial work atmosphere matters. When you think about it, that's what's implied in the phrase *He's a broadcaster*. A broadcaster understands that TV is a touchy-feely business, that he or she—usually he—cannot bark commands but instead must persuade people to cooperate. A broadcaster often makes gut decisions based on feelings, not facts. If a broadcaster is chary with compliments or pats on the back, morale sags. If broadcasters just rely on quantifiable market research to determine whether to air a new show, they forget the many hits—*Charlie's Angels, Hill Street Blues*—that tested poorly. If Steven Bochco or Jim Brooks feels he will receive more freedom, he will make his home at ABC, as each has.

The entertainment business is not the Marines. Success, as Grant Tinker demonstrated at NBC, often comes to those who create a sense of security and a shared vision. One reason ABC is a happier place to work—and the only network to earn a profit in 1991 even though it finished third in the nightly ratings race—is that top management made a concerted effort to provide a sense of security, to make people feel good. Larry Tisch and Bob Wright meant to say: *You can't relax.* Instead employees heard: *You can't enjoy.*

Feelings matter, which is why I come away from my visit to the planet Television acutely aware of the collision between business and human logic. If they were merely slaves to business logic, the men who acquired control of the three networks in 1986 might not have done so. Strict business logic might compel the CEOs to eliminate the nearly $400 million the three networks now spend on affiliate compensation. If he listened just to business logic, Larry Tisch would not have invested $3.6 billion to lock up sports rights for CBS. Nor would the three owners spend as much time as they do worrying about the three-network overnight Nielsen ratings when the real competition comes from forty channels, not three. On this planet—as in Washington, D.C.—things like pride, vanity, character, macho competitiveness, even panic—the stuff of human logic—often triumph over dollars-and-cents logic.

"No man," Robert Louis Stevenson wrote, "lives in the external truth among salts and acids, but in the warm, phant-as-mag-or-ic chamber of his brain, with painted windows and storied wall."

Still, the new network owners arrived in 1986 armed with some powerful business logic. They concluded, correctly, that the once mighty networks—like the Big Three auto companies—had grown fat and smug. They were right to cut costs, right to fret about their responsibility to shareholders, right to spread a sense of alarm about new competitors who in the past decade have snatched away one-third of network viewers.

But they were wrong to arrive—as many newly minted CEOs do—and announce that everything that happened yesterday was wasteful. They worshipped so intently at the shrine of shareholder responsibility that they seemed cavalier to those whose religion was the public trust. While it's true that a network is, from a strict dollars-and-cents standpoint, merely a billboard for advertisers, such cold logic ignores the romance of the television business. The journalists who work in News believe they have a civic duty, a responsibility to distill the truth, to educate. Most folks who inhabit this peculiar planet—be they in Entertainment or News or the stations or sales—go to their office each day believing they work for the public good.

Which brings to mind something that F. Scott Fitzgerald once said. An intelligent person, he wrote, is someone who can keep two or more competing truths in mind and still function. What was odd about the clash of new and old values at the networks was how otherwise intelligent folks could not always keep the two competing truths—of responsibility to shareholders and to the public—in mind at the same time.

Since my return from the planet Television, I have done my share of radio call-in shows. Everyone asks about the natives and their customs. And everyone seems to believe the networks are too powerful, too liberal, too prurient.

Yet I return from my voyage unimpressed by network power. Despite their business talents, the three new network owners have been powerless to halt the erosion of their audience. They'd like to cut more, but dare not. They'd like to produce more of their own shows and syndicate these, to own more stations and even a few cable boxes, but government won't allow it. NBC did not want to pay $70 million in 1991 to renew *Cheers,* but it did. ABC does not want to pay such steep license fees for *Monday Night Football.* Yet it does.

Like three blind mice, the owners are trapped. Not because they are stupid but because they confront a series of Hobson's choices. They can refuse to lose money by not paying the NFL what it wants to broadcast games—but then the games will migrate to cable. They can reduce costs by relying on local stations to cover domestic news—but then they weaken the authority and perhaps the credibility of network news. They can decline to pay the license fees demanded by the Hollywood studios—and risk losing such hits as *Murder, She Wrote* or *Cheers;* but if they pay the price demanded, they remove the profits from hits. In the short run, they can stop programming certain parts of the day to save money; but in the long run they risk losing more money by strengthening syndicators and by lessening the reliance of stations on their network. They can get into the cable business—but how can they get into cable without weakening their main business, which is broadcasting?

The future of the planet Television cannot be mapped with any certitude. Powerful institutions—the Hollywood studios, cable, the networks, stations, and telephone companies—vie for dominance. In their daily battles, there will be victories, defeats, mergers, and alliances as giants compete to become global communication superpowers. Government will have a profound say in who succeeds or fails, because government regulations both hinder and help each rival. No one can know what government will do—not even those in government pretend to know—so it's impossible to precisely chart the future.

But some things are clear. Government should offer some regulatory relief to the networks, as I expect it will. Those who produce programs will always have a seat at the table.

And many of the networks' adversaries should do another think. Even though they don't always acknowledge it, those who frequently grouse about the networks—the stations, the studios, advertisers—have a stake in the networks. Crippled networks will not help the stations, who receive free programming from them. Nor will it help the studios or advertisers. For only the networks regularly reach a mass audience—and thus pay the steep license fees the studios demand, or connect with the eyeballs advertisers crave.

Nor will the demise of the networks necessarily serve the interests of viewers, who have a stake in free TV. What happens if, within this decade, the networks are out of the sports business and viewers discover they can only watch the World Series or the Super Bowl on pay per view? And then only if they have—or can afford—cable.

What happens if network news, which is where most Americans still get their news, becomes less reliable?

What happens if the networks abandon expensive miniseries or one-hour dramas?

In a democracy in which there is already too little sense of community, what happens if citizens lose a common source of information and shared values? What happens when 400 languages replace three?

What happens when the means of communications slip into fewer corporate hands even as viewers gain more channel choices? It is a certainty that the quest to become vertically integrated Goliaths will lead communications giants to seek mergers and alliances. But will the future offer citizens greater political liberty yet fewer independent information outlets?

Many things surprised me on my visit to the planet Television. But what truly stunned me was how little these momentous issues are discussed, how otherwise intelligent people don't always glimpse what seems so obvious to this Martian.

Which suggests a final thought: Perhaps there are more than three blind mice?

—Ken Auletta
June 1992

CAST OF CHARACTERS

THE NETWORKS

ABC: In March 1985, it was announced that Capital Cities Communications had acquired ABC. After waiting for government approval of the sale, Cap Cities officially took command on January 3, 1986. Some of the players:

ROONE ARLEDGE: When he was made president of ABC News in 1977, critics sneered that Arledge was a sports producer who would bring entertainment values to News. He put ABC on the map, running both the sports and news divisions until Cap Cities took over and stripped him of Sports. At first dispirited, Arledge took a couple of years to bounce back. To his employees, he was often as visible as Howard Hughes. But by 1988 the new owners hailed him as a genius and soon awarded him an emperor-for-life contract.

STEVEN BOCHCO: The creator of *Hill Street Blues* and *L.A. Law* was offered the presidency of CBS Entertainment in 1987. When he said no, ABC offered him a ten-series commitment to produce shows for them. He accepted.

WARREN BUFFETT: "The 800-pound gorilla." Probably America's most successful postwar investor. To help them finance the merger with ABC, Buffett bought 20 percent of the stock, and then ceded his voting rights to Tom Murphy, CEO of Cap Cities, and his COO, Dan Burke.

DAN BURKE: Cap Cities' number two since 1972. Because of his rigorous standards and withering stare, he was sometimes known as "the Cardinal." While Chairman Murphy focused on strategy, Burke ran the business from day to day. In 1990, Murphy stepped down as CEO and handed the baton to his pal Burke.

DAVID BURKE: Arledge's deputy was the Last Angry Man at ABC, determined to protect News's public trust obligations from the depradations of the businessmen running the network. After ten years as Arledge's number two, he got a chance to run his own show when CBS made him News president in 1988.

RON DOERFLER: Cap Cities' longtime chief financial officer.

PAUL FRIEDMAN: Became executive producer of Peter Jennings's *World News Tonight* in 1988, relaxing both the anchorman and the newsroom.

LEONARD GOLDENSON: "The Patriarch." In his seventy-ninth year and uneasy with his designated successor, the founder of ABC sold the network to Cap Cities.

ROBERT IGER: Went from ABC Sports to Business Affairs, and then became deputy to network president John Sias. In 1989, when he was thirty-eight, he was appointed to run ABC's entertainment division.

PETER JENNINGS: He failed as anchor of the evening news when he was twenty-six, because viewers perceived him as callow. By the time he was fifty, he was the very model of an authoritative anchor.

JAKE KEEVER: The head of ABC Sales doesn't look like a typical salesman, with his fifty-inch waistline.

BILL LORD: As executive producer of *World News* until late 1987, his relationship with Jennings was tempestuous.

MICHAEL MALLARDI: Was chief financial officer at ABC. After the merger, he became president of the owned station group and Video Enterprises.

PATRICIA MATSON: Was communications chief under both the old and the new ABC.

TOM MURPHY: As chairman and CEO for more than twenty years, he built Cap Cities into a colossus. With a ready "Hi ya, pal" and a perfect row of white teeth, he was a natural pol. But no one underestimated his toughness.

FRED PIERCE: Like the son Leonard Goldenson never had. But he resented Goldenson's decision to sell ABC, and after the merger he stiffly resisted the new order. Rather than accept a lesser position running just the network, he quit as ABC president in January 1986.

JOHN SIAS: Ran Cap Cities Publishing until he was asked to step in as network president in January 1986. Longtime colleagues appreciated this former paratrooper's zany sense of humor; others thought he had a screw loose.

BRANDON STODDARD: "The Prince." The president of ABC Entertainment was treated like royalty when Cap Cities took over, because Murphy, Burke, and Sias felt insecure about their own programming judgment. By 1989, they were spending more time in Hollywood, and felt that their Brandon was no Tartikoff, so they replaced Stoddard with Iger.

STEVE WEISWASSER: Was a partner in Cap Cities' D.C. law firm. He became full-time counsel to ABC/Cap Cities in January 1986, and in late 1990 became number two to network president Sias, inviting speculation that he might one day run the network or all of Cap Cities.

CBS: Larry Tisch began buying CBS stock in July 1985. By September 1986, his company, Loews, owned 25 percent and he was made president of CBS.

TOM BETTAG: Dan Rather's executive producer was so fierce a defender of the anchorman and traditional news that some called him the chief of the Red Guards. He was replaced in early 1991. Soon thereafter he became executive producer of ABC's *Nightline*.

HAROLD BROWN: Former secretary of defense in the Carter administration and a member of the CBS board. Offended Tisch because CBS's largest shareholder could not abide being lectured by someone he considered brilliant but a dunce when it came to business.

DAVID BURKE: "The Headmaster." Left ABC and replaced Howard Stringer as president of CBS News in July 1988. But the wariness he had felt toward the new owners of ABC grew into contempt for the owner of CBS. Burke became isolated, and was fired in 1990.

PETER DEROW: The president of CBS Publishing. Little more than one month after pledging to retain all division presidents, Tisch terminated Derow. He was the first person Tisch had ever fired face to face.

DAVID FUCHS: Inside CBS, this longtime aide to Broadcast president Gene Jankowski was popular. He was less successful as chief of communications, since he did not believe a company had an obligation to communicate to the press.

ROSWELL GILPATRIC: Was the longest-serving member of the CBS board, the person who told William Paley what he didn't always want to hear. Although he had once been Tisch's lawyer, he became a Tisch adversary on the board.

BUD GRANT: The longtime president of CBS Entertainment. By 1985–86, when CBS fell from first place, he was widely perceived to be burned out. He was fired in the fall of 1987.

DON HEWITT: Producer of *60 Minutes,* the biggest money-maker in TV history, and a power within CBS.

GENE JANKOWSKI: He was known as "the Salesman," and not just because he grew up in CBS Sales. Ever the optimist, Jankowski managed to survive as president of the Broadcast group through Tisch's first two years as CEO.

PHIL JONES: General manager of KCTV in Kansas City and chairman of the CBS Affiliate Advisory Board from 1986 to 1988.

JAY KRIEGEL: "The Consiglieri." This former chief of staff to New York mayor John V. Lindsay had been associated with the Tisch brothers for a decade when he was brought in to help douse the fire ignited by Tisch's March 1987 News budget cuts. He joined CBS as senior vice president in the fall of 1987.

KIM LEMASTERS: Although he was Bud Grant's deputy, he was the fifth choice to succeed Grant as president of CBS Entertainment in 1987. Having assumed the post by default, he was not reassured when he had, in effect, to report to five people. He got the job at thirty-eight and lost it by the time he was forty.

RICHARD LEIBNER: Dan Rather and Diane Sawyer's agent. Had the delicate task of satisfying the desire of one client (Sawyer) to become an anchor without alienating his main client (Rather). The perfect solution was to move Sawyer from CBS.

ARTHUR LIMAN: William Paley's lawyer and Larry Tisch's friend. Throughout the struggle to oust Tom Wyman as president, Liman was the link between Paley and Tisch. Once they became allied, Wyman's days were numbered.

PETER LUND: Ran the Stations division at CBS and was on Tisch's short list to one day become CEO, but left in 1987 for a more lucrative opportunity. He returned to CBS in 1990.

TONY MALARA: Supervised affiliate relations. At first, the loquaciousness of this former station general manager and local Republican party chairman offended Tisch. But Tisch came to feel he needed to pour syrup on restive affiliates, and the popular Malara made a comeback.

ERIC OBER: Succeeded Peter Lund as head of the owned stations group in 1987, and became president of CBS News in 1990.

WILLIAM PALEY: The founder of CBS was genuinely thrilled on that September 1986 day when he was restored as chairman of CBS. But his power was not restored. For the first time, Paley had to contend with someone who owned more CBS stock than he did, and he was not happy. He died in 1990.

DAN RATHER: Succeeded Walter Cronkite as anchorman in 1981 and had a run of five straight years as number one. But as he became enmeshed in a series of strange incidents, his "likability" among viewers fell, as did his ratings.

JEFF SAGANSKY: Left as Brandon Tartikoff's deputy at NBC in 1985 to take a top position at Tri-Star Pictures. He might have been Tartikoff's first choice to succeed him, but that vacancy seemed a long way off. After first spurning a CBS feeler to replace Bud Grant in 1987, he accepted the job as CBS Entertainment president in late 1989.

VAN GORDON SAUTER: When he was terminated as News president on September 11, 1986, a producer ran through the newsroom shouting, "The wicked witch is dead!" His departure neither ended the clash between those advocating "hard" vs. "soft" news nor restored the good times to CBS News.

DIANE SAWYER: After her friends Paley and Tisch interceded to keep Sawyer at CBS and *60 Minutes* in 1986, she joined ABC in early 1989 for the opportunity she sought at CBS, a coanchor position.

FRANK STANTON: For nearly three decades as president, Stanton, as much as Paley, was responsible for establishing CBS as the Tiffany network. Paley, in an action he came to regret, let Stanton retire at sixty-five. But Stanton retained his respect and was one of the few people Paley turned to for advice. Cut adrift from the place they loved, Paley and Stanton lunched together regularly.

HOWARD STRINGER: After being educated at Oxford, he joined CBS News as a researcher, rising during a period of twenty years to head the documentary unit, to produce Rather's newscast, and to become deputy to two News presidents. He replaced Sauter as News president in the fall of 1986, and Jankowski as Broadcast group president in the summer of 1988.

FRANK THOMAS: The president of the Ford Foundation has served on the CBS board since 1970, and was a pivotal figure in the board's affairs.

BOB TISCH: All through their successful business career the two brothers had been partners—until CBS. Although Bob owned an equal percentage of CBS stock, directors resisted inviting him to join the board until 1989. His sometimes brusque brother missed Bob's bedside manner at CBS.

LARRY TISCH: "The Missile." After a legendary career as an investor and after basing his business decisions on dollars-and-cents logic, Tisch began investing in CBS in the summer of 1985 for reasons having to do partly with vanity. He moved straight ahead, and replaced Tom Wyman as CEO on September 10, 1986. Critics said his management of CBS demonstrated that he had spent too many years alone by his Quotron machine and didn't know how to relate to people; supporters said he was a financial genius.

STEVE WARNER: A longtime family friend of the Tisches', he worked at CBS before Tisch arrived. He served as Tisch's aide until early 1989, when he moved to the West Coast as a CBS Entertainment executive.

JAMES WOLFENSOHN: The CBS director and former tennis partner who first introduced Tisch to CBS and Wyman. Before long this investment banker and chairman of Carnegie Hall regretted the move, fretting that Tisch was acquiring CBS without paying a premium for the privilege.

TOM WYMAN: CEO and chairman of CBS for nearly six years. After a yearlong struggle, he was booted out in September 1986.

WALTER YETNIKOFF: The president of CBS Records was thrilled when Tisch arrived. The feeling did not last, and the two men came to detest each other, one reason the records division was sold to Sony in 1988.

NBC: GE announced that it would acquire RCA, the parent company of NBC, in December 1985. The merger was officially blessed in the summer of 1986.

JOHN AGOGLIA: The head of Business Affairs for NBC Entertainment. He ran the business side of NBC's Hollywood efforts, while the programmers decided what to put on the air.

AL BARBER: "Boxcar Barber." A former colleague of Bob Wright's who ran the boxcar division at GE, he joined NBC in the fall of 1987 with the hope that he would become chief operating officer. Instead he was eased out in 1990, and became COO of NBC's cable arm.

THORTON BRADSHAW: RCA chairman from 1981 to 1986. Decided that RCA's electronics and defense businesses could not compete with world giants and that his chosen successor lacked the heft to lead the company. He steered the sale of RCA, which had been NBC's parent for fifty years.

TOM BROKAW: Anchor of the *Nightly News* since 1982, and known around NBC as "Duncan the Wonderhorse" because he had succeeded at everything he had ever tried—except to boost *Nightly* to number one.

ROBERT BUTLER: Was chief financial officer until he was fired in August 1987.

DICK EBERSOL: Former *Saturday Night Live* producer who became NBC Sports president in the spring of 1989, and that summer became a senior producer in News as well.

ROBERT FREDERICK: In 1981, when employed by GE, he lost out to Jack Welch in a competition to head the company. Joined RCA as number two, and became CEO in 1984. Nevertheless, he again lost the prize when Bradshaw, despite the opposition of Frederick, engineered the sale of RCA.

MICHAEL GARTNER: This former *Wall Street Journal* editor and businessman was appointed president of NBC News in July 1988 because it was thought he combined the qualities of a publisher and an editor. Within a year, News employees pined for his less prickly predecessor.

LARRY GROSSMAN: This former advertising and public relations executive left the presidency of PBS when an old friend, Grant Tinker, asked him to become NBC News president in 1984. He spent two glorious years under Tinker and two miserable ones under GE.

J. B. HOLSTON: The first GE employee assigned to work at NBC, he managed NBC's efforts to find new business opportunities overseas.

AL JEROME: President of the NBC division that supervises the seven stations owned by the network.

WARREN LITTLEFIELD: After serving for years as deputy to Entertainment president Brandon Tartikoff, he longed for his own spotlight. Littlefield became president of NBC Entertainment in 1990 when Tartikoff became chairman, the expectation being that Tartikoff would soon leave. When Tartikoff did leave in the spring of 1991, Littlefield got his chance.

BRUCE PALTROW: The talented executive producer of *St. Elsewhere* and a much-ballyhooed 1988 NBC series that failed: *Tattinger's.*

TOM ROGERS: Former congressional aide responsible for telecommunications policy who joined NBC in January 1987 to work on future strategies. Believing that the networks were "yesterday's" business, he was put in charge of finding "tomorrow's" businesses. Supervised all of NBC's cable efforts.

BUD RUKEYSER: Was NBC's chief of communications for nearly twenty-five years, and left on his own in the spring of 1988 when he could no longer bring himself to extoll the joys of "downsizing" (layoffs).

TIM RUSSERT: Served as News deputy to Larry Grossman, and moved on to become NBC News's Washington bureau chief and a regular panelist on *Meet the Press.*

ED SCANLON: Was RCA personnel chief and the official who worked most closely with GE to integrate the two companies. Because GE president Jack Welch thought of him as a superb "fingertip," he was appointed in late 1987 to run personnel at NBC. Distrusted by some longtime network officials, he nevertheless wielded enormous power.

PERRY SIMON: Held a series of important jobs with NBC Entertainment, including head of both drama and comedy development. In 1990, he was made number two to Littlefield.

AARON SPELLING: Probably the most prolific producer in TV history, and certainly one of the richest, responsible for such escapist series as *Charlie's Angels* and *Fantasy Island.* After his exclusive arrangement with ABC lapsed in 1988, he pitched a single sentence idea to NBC—"Student nurses in Dallas in the summer and the air conditioning doesn't work"—which became the 1988 series *Nightingales.* It flopped.

BRANDON TARTIKOFF: No one has ever run a network entertainment division longer, and few have done it as well. His bosses usually thought of him as a son; his underlings spent half the time holding him in awe and the other half resenting how he hogged the spotlight. He left the network in May 1991 to hear Paramount Pictures.

RAY TIMOTHY: Was executive vice president of NBC. A popular ambassador to the affiliates and advertisers, this representative of "the old culture" decided he was not entirely comfortable with "the new culture" and left NBC in 1989.

GRANT TINKER: Starting in 1982, this former producer engineered the resurgence of NBC. He succeeded in no small measure not because he mastered budgets or cost cutting but because he concentrated on what appeared on the screen—and because he imparted a sense of security to those who worked at NBC, making it a pleasant place to work.

ROBERT WALSH: Along with Timothy, Butler, and Rukeyser, this executive vice president had operating departments report to him and served as a kind of senior counselor to the NBC chairman. He announced his retirement at the end of 1987.

JACK WELCH: GE chairman since 1981, who would achieve his goal of passing IBM as the world's most valued corporation in 1991. An electric presence throughout GE, Welch believes employees are spurred when they are insecure.

ROBERT WRIGHT: Spent most of a brilliant business career at GE. In August 1986, at age forty-three, was selected by Welch to run NBC. Unlike Grant Tinker, he spoke more of responsibility to shareholders than to the public trust, and concentrated more on deal making. Because he was often out of the office, executives sometimes referred to him as "the Bumble Bee."

ADDITIONAL CHARACTERS

BOB DALY: The head of Warner Brothers. Spearheaded the Hollywood studio negotiators in their ongoing battle with the networks. William Paley tried desperately to lure him back to run CBS.

MARTIN DAVIS: The man who let Diller and Eisner get away from Paramount long dreamed of owning a network. When the company he headed, Paramount Communications (formerly Gulf + Western), sat on a mountain of cash in 1991, Davis let it be known he was still interested in owning a network. Hired Brandon Tartikoff in May 1991 to head Paramount Studios.

BARRY DILLER: After success as an ABC programmer in the seventies and as head of Paramount Studios earlier in the eighties, he was put in charge of Twentieth Century Fox and its efforts to pioneer a fourth network.

MICHAEL EISNER: After being passed over for the Paramount job that belonged to Diller, this former ABC programmer was lured to the chairmanship of the sleepy Walt Disney Studios. Within a few years, Disney was a Hollywood powerhouse and a potential rival bidder to own a network.

JOSEPH FLOM: The well-known mergers and acquisitions lawyer advised Leonard Goldenson in his negotiations with Cap Cities and, starting in 1985, helped craft CBS's defenses against predators.

MARTIN LIPTON: The father of the "poison pill" and other corporate defenses against raiders, Lipton was involved in the takeover at each network, advising Cap Cities, RCA, and Larry Tisch.

JOHN MALONE: He is the CEO of the Denver-based Tele-Communications, Inc. While other companies are better known, TCI owns nearly one quarter of the cable boxes in America and much of the programming on them. While many communication companies strive to become vertically integrated monopolies, Malone has already accomplished this.

RUPERT MURDOCH: With ownership of Fox and seven stations, with publications all over the world and direct broadcast satellite services, Murdoch early on laid out a vision of a worldwide communications colossus. Will rising debt payments choke that vision?

FELIX ROHATYN: The investment banker who acted as matchmaker in the sale of RCA to GE.

STEVE ROSS: The chairman of Warners Communications vies with Murdoch, Eisner, Cap Cities, and GE, among others, to become a worldwide communications company. Like Murdoch, his dream could be frustrated by debt obligations, particulary stemming from his 1989 merger with Time, Inc.

TED TURNER: Once dismissed as a loon for starting a superstation in 1976 and for proposing a 24-hour cable news network, the Atlanta buccaneer was subsequently hailed as a visionary. Ironically, had he succeeded in acquiring CBS in 1985, he might be dismissed today as a buffoon.

NOTES

INTRODUCTION

PAGE 3: Estimates of the number of lost network viewers cannot be precise. Nielsen can measure that the average primetime rating for the three networks was 56.3 in March 1976, and plunged to 37.8 in March 1991. But while the ratings fell, the American population and the number of TV sets rose. The estimate of up to 10 million lost network viewers is a conservative one.

PAGE 3: The 1991 three-network zero-profit estimate comes from Larry Tisch interview, Feb. 12, 1991, and March 13, 1991 (he projected that CBS would lose from $200 to $300 million); from Dan Burke interview, Feb. 13, 1991 (Burke said ABC might lose money); and from Jack Welch interview, Feb. 14, 1991 (Welch said that NBC profits were already $120 million below its $340 million projection).

PAGE 4: National poll of news viewers by Birch Scarborough Research, cited in Kevin Goldman, "Weak War Coverage Isn't the Only Problem at *CBS Evening News*," *The Wall Street Journal*, Feb. 7, 1991.

PAGE 4: Cable revenues from Paul Kagan Associates.

PAGE 6: Joseph A. Schumpeter, "Capitalism, Socialism and Democracy," Harper & Row, 1942.

PAGE 6: Janet Malcolm, "The Journalist and the Murderer," *The New Yorker*, March 13 and 20, 1989.

CHAPTER 1

PAGE 9: Bob Wright interview, April 7, 1989, and Tom Brokaw interview, March 10, 1989.

PAGE 11: Larry Grossman interview, Nov. 30, 1989.

PAGE 11: Tom Brokaw interview, March 10, 1989.

PAGE 12: Jack Welch interview, May 24, 1989.

PAGE 12: Bob Wright interview, April 7, 1989.

PAGE 12: Peter J. Boyer, *New York Times*, Oct. 21, 1986.

PAGE 13: Robert Wright interview, April 7, 1989.

PAGE 13: Alberta Grossman interview, Dec. 11, 1989.

PAGE 14: Dinner menu supplied by Alberta Grossman, Dec. 11, 1989, interview.

PAGE 14: Larry Grossman interview, March 2, 1989.

PAGE 14: Tom Brokaw interview, March 10, 1989.

PAGE 14: Bob Wright interview, April 7, 1989.

PAGE 15: Larry Grossman speech, "The Murrow Legacy," Washington State University, April 12, 1990.

PAGE 16: Jack Welch interview, May 24, 1989.

PAGE 16: Jack Welch interview, July 1, 1987.

PAGE 17: Jack Welch interview, April 15, 1988.

PAGE 17: Jack Welch interview, Oct. 4, 1988.

PAGE 17: "Cable TV Facts," Cable Television Advertising Bureau, 1986.

PAGE 18: A. C. Nielsen Media Research reports.

PAGE 18: NBC "News Division Review," Dec. 11, 1987.

PAGE 19: Tom Brokaw interview, April 7, 1989.

PAGE 19: Bob Wright interview, Nov. 11, 1986.

PAGE 19: Larry Grossman speech, "The Murrow Legacy," Washington State University, April 12, 1990.

PAGE 19: Marshall McLuhan, *Understand-*

ing Media: The Extensions of Man (New York: McGraw-Hill, 1964).

PAGE 19: Garrick Utley report from Belize on *NBC Nightly News,* Aug. 19, 1985.

PAGE 19: Jack Welch interview, May 24, 1989.

PAGE 20: Larry Grossman interview, Jan. 17, 1987.

PAGE 21: Bob Wright interview, April 7, 1989.

PAGE 21: Tom Brokaw interview, April 7, 1989.

PAGE 21: Jack Welch interview, May 24, 1989.

PAGE 22: Larry Grossman interviews, Nov. 30, 1989 and May 2, 1990.

PAGE 23: Account of Welch/Grossman meeting from Larry Grossman interview, Nov. 30, 1989; Jack Welch interview, May 24, 1989; and Bob Wright interview, April 7, 1989.

PAGE 23: Larry Grossman interview, April 6, 1987.

CHAPTER 2

PAGE 24: HBO FCC petition recounted in J. Fred MacDonald, *One Nation Under Television* (New York: Pantheon Books, 1990), p. 244.

PAGE 25: William Paley interview, Nov. 12, 1987.

PAGE 25: Brandon Tartikoff interview, May 16, 1988.

PAGE 25: David J. Londoner, "The Changing Economics of Entertainment," report by Wertheim & Co., April 1978.

PAGE 25: Memo from Jim MacGregor to James Abernathy, ABC's response to "The Changing Economics of Entertainment," April 12, 1978.

PAGE 26: Jake Keever interview, Feb. 9, 1987.

PAGE 26: For another illustration of the networks' giddy optimism, see the 1982 CBS Annual Report to Shareholders, including the claim from its report, "The Road to 1990," which projected: "It is our belief that the networks and their affiliated television stations will continue to grow despite an increasingly competitive marketplace."

PAGE 27: Account of Michael Mallardi speech based on interviews with Mallardi on June 25, 1987 and April 6, 1988.

PAGE 29: Leonard H. Goldenson, *Beating the Odds* (New York: Charles Scribner's Sons, 1991).

PAGE 29: Fred Pierce interview, Oct. 7, 1987.

PAGE 30: Kenneth Bilby, *David Sarnoff and the Rise of the Communications Industry* (New York: Harper & Row, 1986).

PAGE 31: Erik Barnouw, *Tube of Plenty: The Evolution of American Television* (Oxford, England: Oxford University Press, 1975).

PAGE 32: For a description of how the public interest assumptions changed under Reagan, see Victor E. Ferrall, Jr., *The Impact of Television Deregulation on Private and Public Interests, Journal of Communication,* Vol. 39, No. 1., Winter 1989.

PAGE 33: Fowler quote from *Business Week,* Aug. 5, 1985.

PAGE 33: Fowler quote from *New York Times,* Jan. 19, 1987.

PAGE 33: Bud Rukeyser interview, Dec. 9, 1988.

PAGE 33: John Malone interview, April 11, 1989.

PAGE 34: Roone Arledge interview, Sept. 30, 1987.

PAGE 35: Tom Murphy interview, April 7, 1989.

PAGE 35: Fred Pierce interview, Oct. 14, 1987.

PAGE 35: Capital Cities/ABC's Annual Report, 1985.

PAGE 36: Tom Murphy interview, April 7, 1989.

PAGE 36: James Burke interview, Feb. 1, 1989.

PAGE 36: Capital Cities/ABC Annual Report, 1985.

PAGE 36: Tom Murphy interview, April 7, 1989.

PAGE 37: Tom Murphy interview, July 16, 1987, and Tom Murphy speech to ABC affiliates, June 4, 1986.

PAGE 37: Goldenson, *Beating the Odds.*

PAGE 38: Leonard Goldenson interview, March 4, 1987.

PAGE 38: Tom Murphy interview, July 16, 1987, and *Business Week* account, April 1, 1985; and Goldenson, *Beating the Odds.*

PAGE 38: Fred Pierce interview, Oct. 14, 1987.

PAGE 39: Dialogue from Tom Murphy interview, July 16, 1987.

PAGE 39: Capital Cities/ABC Annual Report, 1985.

PAGE 39: Warren Buffett interview, May 21, 1987.

PAGE 40: Berkshire Hathaway, Inc. Annual Report, 1985.

PAGE 40: Warren E. Buffett letter to shareholders, Berkshire Hathaway, Inc. Annual Report, 1980.

PAGE 40: Warren Buffett interview, May 21, 1987.

PAGE 40: Warren Buffett speech to Cap Cities/ABC first management retreat, Jan. 16, 1986.

PAGE 40: Warren Buffett interview, May 21, 1987; and Buffett as quoted in Goldenson, *Beating the Odds.*

PAGE 41: Tom Murphy interview, July 16, 1987.

PAGE 41: Tom Murphy interview, April 7, 1989.

PAGE 41: James Burke interview, Feb. 1, 1989.

PAGE 41: Warren Buffett interview, May 21, 1987, and Buffett interview in Goldenson, *Beating the Odds.*

PAGE 41: Dan Burke interview, May 28, 1987.

PAGE 42: Dialogue based on interviews on above dates with Buffett, Daniel Burke, Murphy, and Ronald Doerfler.

PAGE 42: Telephone call with Murphy recounted by Warren Buffett in Goldenson, *Beating the Odds.*

PAGE 42: Dan Burke interview, May 28, 1987.

PAGE 42: Cap Cities/ABC notice of annual meeting of shareholders, May 19, 1988.

PAGE 43: Berkshire Hathaway, Inc. Annual Report, 1985.

PAGE 43: Martin Lipton interview, June 10, 1987.

PAGE 44: Dan Burke interview, May 28, 1987.

PAGE 45: Martin Lipton interview, June 10, 1987.

PAGE 45: Dan Burke interview, Jan. 19, 1988.

PAGE 45: John Carmody, "The TV Column," *USA Today,* March 21, 1985.

PAGE 46: Barbara Walters interview, April 11, 1989.

PAGE 46: Fred Pierce interview, Oct. 14, 1987.

PAGE 46: Jake Keever interview, May 27, 1987.

PAGE 46: Dan Burke interview, May 28, 1987.

PAGE 47: David Burke interview, June 4, 1987.

PAGE 47: Fred Pierce interview, Oct. 14, 1987.

PAGE 47: Barbara Walters interview, April 11, 1989.

CHAPTER 3

PAGE 49: Susan F. Rasky, "Wyman Faced Doubts from the Start," *New York Times,* Sept. 11, 1986.

PAGE 50: Network's owned stations profit margins from Eric Ober interview, March 4, 1988.

PAGE 50: Tom Wyman interview, Feb. 1, 1988.

PAGE 50: Larry Tisch interview, Nov. 21, 1985.

PAGE 50: Dan Tisch interview, Dec. 3, 1985.

PAGE 51: Larry Tisch interview, Dec. 10, 1985.

PAGE 52: James Wolfensohn interview, Dec. 20, 1985.

PAGE 53: Tom Wyman interview, Dec. 19, 1985.

PAGE 53: Roswell Gilpatric interview, Dec. 16, 1985.

PAGE 54: Bob Tisch interview, Nov. 18, 1985.

PAGE 54: Larry Tisch interview, March 14, 1986.

PAGE 54: Jack Welch interview, July 1, 1987.

PAGE 54: Bob Wright interviews, May 27, 1987, and April 7, 1989.

PAGE 54: Al Neuharth, *Confessions of an S.O.B.* (Garden City, N.Y.: Doubleday & Company, 1989).

PAGE 55: Tom Wyman interview, Dec. 19, 1985.

PAGE 55: James Wolfensohn interview, Dec. 20, 1985.

PAGE 55: James Wolfensohn interview, Dec. 20, 1985.

PAGE 55: Tom Wyman interview, Dec. 19, 1985.

PAGE 55: Henry Kravis interview, Oct. 13, 1987.

PAGE 56: Tom Wyman interview, Feb. 1, 1988.

PAGE 56: Peter Derow interview, Nov, 6, 1986.

PAGE 56: James Wolfensohn interview, Oct. 28, 1987.

PAGE 56: Larry Tisch interview, Nov. 21, 1985.

PAGE 56: William Paley interview, Jan. 14, 1986.

PAGE 57: Jimmy Tisch interview, Dec. 2, 1985.

PAGE 57: Larry Tisch interview, Nov. 29, 1985.

PAGE 57: William Paley interview, Jan. 14, 1986.

PAGE 58: Martin Lipton interview, Nov. 7, 1985.

PAGE 58: Tom Tisch interview, Dec. 2, 1985.

PAGE 58: Larry Tisch interview, Nov. 21, 1985.

PAGE 59: Larry Tisch interview, Feb. 10, 1986.

PAGE 59: Larry Tisch interview, Nov. 11, 1985.

PAGE 60: Larry Tisch interview, Nov. 11, 1985.

PAGE 60: Billie Tisch interview, Dec. 3, 1985.

PAGE 61: Billie Tisch interview, Dec. 3, 1985.

PAGE 61: Larry Tisch interview, Jan. 4, 1986.

PAGE 62: Larry Tisch interview, Feb. 10, 1986.

PAGE 63: Leonard Goldenson, *Beating the Odds* (New York: Charles Scribner's Sons, 1991).

PAGE 63: Frank Stanton interview, Feb. 5, 1988.

PAGE 63: Mortimer Zuckerman interview, Nov. 11, 1985.

PAGE 63: Larry Tisch interview, Feb. 10, 1986.

PAGE 64: Franklin A. Thomas interview, Dec. 4, 1985.

PAGE 64: Tom Wyman interview, Feb. 1, 1988.

PAGE 64: Tom Wyman interview, Dec. 19, 1985.

PAGE 64: Larry Tisch interview, April 10, 1986.

PAGE 65: *New York Times,* Nov. 14, 1985.

PAGE 65: *New York Times,* Nov. 14, 1985, and Feb. 12, 1986.

PAGE 66: William Paley interview, Jan. 14, 1986.

PAGE 67: Larry Tisch interview, April 10, 1986.

PAGE 67: Roswell Gilpatric interview, Sept. 16, 1986.

PAGE 67: CBS 10-K filing with the SEC for the year ending Dec. 31, 1987.

PAGE 68: Walter Yetnikoff interview, April 13, 1988.

PAGE 68: Billie Tisch interview, Dec. 3, 1985.

PAGE 69: Larry Tisch interview, Nov. 11, 1985.

PAGE 69: Larry Tisch interview in *Channels* magazine, Feb. 1987.

PAGE 70: CBS Annual Report, 1985.

PAGE 70: Gene Jankowski speech to the International Radio & Television Society Newsmaker luncheon, Jan. 15, 1986.

PAGE 70: Dan Tisch interview, Dec. 3, 1985.

PAGE 70: Roswell Gilpatric interview, Dec. 16, 1985.

PAGE 71: James Wolfensohn interview, Dec. 20, 1985.

CHAPTER 4

PAGE 72: Felix Rohatyn interview, Oct. 1, 1986.

PAGE 73: Julius Barnathan interview, July 16, 1990.

PAGE 73: Casmir Skrzpcak interview, March 29, 1988.

PAGE 74: Peter J. Boyer, "A Triumphant NBC Faces an Uncertain Future," *New York Times,* April 12, 1986.

PAGE 74: Thornton Bradshaw interview, Oct. 6, 1986.

PAGE 75: Thornton Bradshaw interview, Sept. 30, 1987.

PAGE 75: Thornton Bradshaw interview, Oct. 6, 1986.

PAGE 75: Grant Tinker interview, May 22, 1987.

PAGE 76: The growth of TV sets from J. Fred MacDonald, *One Nation Under Television,* (New York: Pantheon Books, 1990), p. 61.

PAGE 77: Thornton Bradshaw interview, Oct. 6, 1986.

PAGE 77: Thornton Bradshaw interviews, Sept. 30, 1987, and Oct. 6, 1986.

PAGE 78: Michael Eisner interview, May 9, 1988.

PAGE 78: Thornton Bradshaw interview, Sept. 30, 1987.

PAGE 78: Michael Eisner interview, May 9, 1988.

PAGE 79: Jack Welch address to the Economic Club of Chicago, Feb. 20, 1986, and GE "Report to Share Owners," April 22, 1987, and April 23, 1986.

PAGE 79: Jack Welch interview, April 15, 1988.

PAGE 79: Jack Welch "Report to Share Owners," April 23, 1986.

PAGE 80: Account of first Welch, Bradshaw meeting from: Jack Welch interview,

July 1, 1987; Felix Rohatyn interview, Oct. 1, 1986; Thornton Bradshaw interview, Sept. 30, 1987.

PAGE 80: Jack Welch interviews, July 1, 1987, and Dec. 16, 1987.

PAGE 80: Thornton Bradshaw interview, Sept. 30, 1987.

PAGE 80: Bob Wright interview, April 7, 1989.

PAGE 81: Bob Wright interview, April 7, 1989.

PAGE 81: Thornton Bradshaw interview, Sept. 30, 1987.

PAGE 81: Grant Tinker interview, May 19, 1987.

PAGE 82: Jack Welch interview, July 1, 1987.

PAGE 82: Jack Welch interviews, July 1, 1987, Dec. 16, 1987, and initial offering price confirmed by Welch's press office on Aug. 27, 1990.

PAGE 82: Thornton Bradshaw interview, Sept. 30, 1987.

PAGE 82: L. J. Davis, "Did RCA Have to Be Sold?" *New York Times Magazine,* Sept. 20, 1987.

PAGE 83: Thornton Bradshaw interview, Sept. 30, 1987.

PAGE 83: Jack Welch dictated "Chronology of RCA/GE Discussions," Dec. 1986.

PAGE 83: Tom Brokaw interview, April 20, 1987.

PAGE 84: Account of Bradshaw's announcement from Irwin Segelstein interview, April 15, 1987; Robert Butler interview, Aug. 12, 1987.

PAGE 84: GE press release, Dec. 12, 1985.

PAGE 84: Martin Davis interview, Nov. 4, 1987.

PAGE 85: Brandon Tartikoff interview, April 30, 1987.

PAGE 85: Bob Walsh interview, Dec. 15, 1987.

PAGE 85: Chairman's message, GE Annual Report, 1985.

PAGE 85: James Traub, *Channels,* Sept. 1986.

PAGE 85: Alan Riding, *New York Times,* Jan. 12, 1987.

PAGE 86: Television Factbook, No. 57. (Washington, D.C.: Warren Publishing, Inc., 1989); Morton Research report for Lynch, Jones & Ryan, Jan. 31, 1990; and Rance Crain, "Mega-Merger: Deal Making Over Product Making," a presentation to the Gannett Center for Media Studies, Jan. 17, 1990.

PAGE 86: Ben H. Bagdikian, *The Nation,* June 12, 1989.

PAGE 87: Jack Welch interview, July 6, 1987.

PAGE 87: Welch aphorism from *Fortune,* Jan. 5, 1986.

PAGE 87: Jack Welch, Hatfield Fellow Lecture, Cornell University, April 16, 1984.

PAGE 87: GE *Monogram,* Vol. 65, no. 1 (Winter 1987).

PAGE 87: James P. Baughman interview, Nov. 17, 1987.

PAGE 88: Larry Grossman interviews, April 25, 1988, and May 22, 1990.

PAGE 88: Bud Rukeyser interview, May 24, 1990.

PAGE 88: Bob Walsh interview, Dec. 15, 1987.

PAGE 88: NBC press release on *Misfits of Science,* Fall 1985.

PAGE 89: Tony Schwartz profile of Tartikoff, *New York,* Sept. 30, 1985.

PAGE 89: Steve Oney, "That Championship Season," *California,* Feb. 1984.

PAGE 89: Brandon Tartikoff interview, Jan. 14, 1987.

PAGE 89: Steven Bochco interview, Aug. 20, 1987.

PAGE 90: Grant Tinker interview, May 20, 1987.

PAGE 90: Jack Welch interview, July 1, 1987.

PAGE 90: Grant Tinker interview, March 2, 1989.

PAGE 91: Brandon Tartikoff interview, Oct. 25, 1988.

PAGE 91: "20 Questions: Brandon Tartikoff," *Playboy,* June 1982.

PAGE 92: The concept of Tartikoff as "the good son" comes from Lynn Hirschberg, "The Man Who Turns on America," *Rolling Stone,* Oct. 22, 1987.

PAGE 92: Jeffrey Katzenberg interview, April 18, 1988.

PAGE 92: Jeff Sagansky interview, Nov. 25, 1987.

PAGE 93: Dick Ebersol interview, Nov. 19, 1987.

PAGE 93: Jack Welch interview, Nov. 25, 1987.

PAGE 94: Figures on profitability of prime time from Al Barber interview, Feb. 26, 1988.

PAGE 94: Figures on top seventy-five network shows from Dan Burke interview, June 3, 1988.

PAGE 94: Jack Welch interview, Dec. 16, 1987.

PAGE 94: Grant Tinker interview, Nov. 25, 1987.

PAGE 94: Lynn Hirschberg, "The Man Who Turns on America," *Rolling Stone,* Oct. 22, 1987.

PAGE 95: Brandon Tartikoff interview, Jan. 14, 1987.

PAGE 95: Brandon Tartikoff interview, Oct. 25, 1988.

PAGE 95: Brandon Tartikoff interviews, Jan. 14, 1987 and April 30, 1987.

PAGE 95: Jack Welch interview, Dec. 16, 1987.

PAGE 96: Brandon Tartikoff interview, Feb. 11, 1988.

PAGE 96: Jack Welch interview, Dec. 16, 1987.

PAGE 97: Jack Welch interview, Oct. 4, 1988.

PAGE 97: Brandon Tartikoff interview, April 30, 1987.

PAGE 97: Lilly Tartikoff interview, May 13, 1988.

PAGE 98: Account of breakfast from Thornton Bradshaw interview, Sept. 30, 1987 and Jack Welch interview, Dec. 16, 1987, and confirmed by Tinker intimates.

PAGE 98: Ray Timothy interview, Dec. 2, 1986.

PAGE 99: Jack Welch interview, Dec. 16, 1987.

PAGE 99: The lack of social intimacy between Welch and Wright from Suzanne Wright interview, Jan. 7, 1988.

PAGE 100: Jack Welch interview, July 1, 1987.

PAGE 100: Thornton Bradshaw interview, Sept. 30, 1987.

PAGE 100: Larry Grossman interview, June 18, 1987.

PAGE 100: Bob Walsh interview, Dec. 15, 1987.

PAGE 101: Bob Butler interview, Aug. 2, 1987.

PAGE 101: Jack Welch interview, July 1, 1987.

PAGE 101: Jack Welch interview, July 1, 1987.

PAGE 101: Jack Welch interview, Oct. 4, 1988.

PAGE 101: Bob Wright interview, April 7, 1989.

PAGE 102: Jack Welch interview, Oct. 4, 1988.

PAGE 102: Suzanne Wright interview, Jan. 7, 1988.

PAGE 102: Grant Tinker interview, May 19, 1987.

PAGE 102: Bob Wright interview, May 27, 1987.

PAGE 102: Bob Wright interview, Nov. 26, 1986.

PAGE 103: J. B. Holston III interview, April 14, 1987.

PAGE 105: Peter J. Boyer, *New York Times,* Aug. 27, 1986; NBC videotape of Aug. 26, 1986, press conference; and GE press release, Aug. 26, 1986.

PAGE 105: Bob Wright interview, May 27, 1987.

PAGE 105: Bud Rukeyser interview, Dec. 8, 1986.

PAGE 105: Bud Rukeyser interview, Dec. 8, 1986.

PAGE 105: Bob Wright interview, Nov. 26, 1986.

PAGE 106: Bob Walsh interview, Dec. 15, 1987.

PAGE 106: Grant Tinker interview, March 2, 1989.

CHAPTER 5

PAGE 107: David Burke interview, Feb. 3, 1989.

PAGE 108: Stephen Weiswasser interview, July 23, 1987.

PAGE 109: David Burke interview, Feb. 3, 1989.

PAGE 109: Dan Burke interview, Dec. 20, 1988.

PAGE 109: Dan Burke interview, May 28, 1987.

PAGE 109: Fred Pierce interview, Oct. 14, 1987.

PAGE 109: Tony Thomopoulus interview in Leonard Goldenson, *Beating the Odds* (New York: Charles Scribner's Sons, 1991).

PAGE 110: Brandon Stoddard interview, Feb. 4, 1988.

PAGE 111: Tom Murphy and Dan Burke interview, Nov. 26, 1986; also, Murphy vowed to avoid programming decisions at ABC from day one, and said as much *The MacNeil/Lehrer Newshour,* transcript, March 20, 1985.

PAGE 111: Tom Murphy interview, Oct. 14, 1986.

PAGE 112: Goldenson, *Beating The Odds.* (New York, Charles Scribner's Sons, 1991).

PAGE 112: Tom Murphy interview, April 7, 1989.

PAGE 112: Tom Murphy interview, Nov. 26, 1986.

PAGE 112: Tom Murphy interviews, April 7,

1989, and during the Oct. 19, 1988, press tour.

PAGE 113: Marc Cohen interview, May 31, 1988.

PAGE 113: Cap Cities/ABC Annual Report, 1985.

PAGE 114: Ron Doerfler interviews, Oct. 6, 1987, and June 4, 1990.

PAGE 114: Dan Burke interview, May 28, 1987.

PAGE 114: Fred Pierce interview, Oct. 14, 1987.

PAGE 114: Pierce hiring a psychic was first reported by Huntington Williams, *Beyond Control: ABC and the Fate of the Networks* (New York: Atheneum, 1989).

PAGE 114: Dan Burke interview, Nov. 14, 1989.

PAGE 115: Dan Burke interview, May 28, 1987.

PAGE 115: John Sias interview, June 6, 1987.

PAGE 115: Account of the Pierce meeting from Dan Burke interview, Oct. 30, 1987; Fred Pierce interview, Oct. 14, 1987.

PAGE 115: Roone Arledge interview, Sept. 30, 1987.

PAGE 115: John Sias interview, June 6, 1987.

PAGE 116: Tom Murphy interview, July 16, 1987.

PAGE 116: Ron Doerfler interview, July 23, 1987.

PAGE 116: John Sias interview, Dec. 16, 1986.

PAGE 117: Facts on waste from: Phil Beuth interview, Jan. 5, 1988; Stephen Weiswasser interview, Sept. 28, 1987; and Tom Murphy press conference, Oct. 24, 1986.

PAGE 117: Roone Arledge interview, Sept. 30, 1987.

PAGE 118: Fred Pierce interview, Oct. 14, 1987.

PAGE 118: Dan Burke interview, May 28, 1987.

PAGE 118: Richard Connelly interview, Nov. 11, 1987.

PAGE 119: Patricia Matson interview, Oct. 7, 1986.

PAGE 119: Peter W. Barnes, *Wall Street Journal*, Jan. 10, 1986.

PAGE 119: Sias anecdote from Joel M. Segal interview, April 8, 1988.

PAGE 119: John Sias interview, June 6, 1987.

PAGE 120: Dan Burke interview, Oct. 30, 1987.

PAGE 121: Roone Arledge interview, May 16, 1989.

PAGE 121: Dan Burke interview, Dec. 20, 1988.

PAGE 121: Roone Arledge interview, Sept. 30, 1987.

PAGE 122: Roone Arledge interview, May 26, 1988.

PAGE 123: Ron Doerfler interview, July 23, 1987.

PAGE 123: John Sias interview, Nov. 11, 1987.

PAGE 123: Tom Murphy interview, Oct. 22, 1987.

PAGE 123: Phil Beuth interview, Dec. 7, 1987.

PAGE 124: Phil Beuth interview, Jan. 1, 1988.

PAGE 124: Dan Burke interview, May 28, 1987.

PAGE 124: Fred Pierce interview, Oct. 14, 1987.

PAGE 125: Richard Wald interview, Oct. 2, 1987.

PAGE 126: Dan Burke interview, May 28, 1987.

PAGE 126: Dan Burke interview, May 28, 1987.

PAGE 126: Patricia Matson interview, April 14, 1987.

PAGE 126: David Burke interview, March 11, 1987.

PAGE 127: Tom Murphy interview, Nov. 26, 1986.

PAGE 127: David Burke interviews, Nov. 14, 1989 and Feb. 3, 1989.

PAGE 127: David Burke interview, March 11, 1987.

PAGE 127: David Burke interview, June 16, 1987.

PAGE 128: Audio tape made by ABC of Warren Buffett's remarks to ABC's Jan. 1986 management retreat.

PAGE 128: Brandon Stoddard interview, Feb. 4, 1988.

PAGE 128: Dan Burke interview, Oct. 30, 1987.

PAGE 128: Peter Jennings interview, Oct. 4, 1986.

PAGE 129: Roone Arledge interview, May 16, 1989.

PAGE 129: Dan Burke interview, May 28, 1987.

PAGE 129: John Sias interview, Dec. 16, 1986.

PAGE 130: Marc Cohen interview, May 31, 1988.

PAGE 130: Robert S. Wallen interview, July 29, 1987.

PAGE 130: Mark Mandala interview, July 8, 1987.

PAGE 130: John Sias interview, June 6, 1987.

PAGE 130: Dan Burke interview, May 28, 1987.

PAGE 131: Peter J. Boyer, "The Spendthrift Turns Miser at ABC," *New York Times,* April 2, 1986.

PAGE 131: John Sias interview, Dec. 16, 1986.

PAGE 132: Josh Mankiewicz interview, Nov. 20, 1989.

PAGE 132: Roone Arledge memo to news division heads, May 2, 1986.

PAGE 132: John Sias interview, Dec. 16, 1986.

PAGE 132: Peter J. Boyer, "Can a Strictly Non-TV Type Pull ABC from Doldrums?" *New York Times,* March 12, 1986.

PAGE 133: David Burke interview, June 4, 1987.

PAGE 133: Richard Connelly interview, Nov. 11, 1987.

PAGE 133: John Sias interview, June 6, 1987.

PAGE 134: John Sias interview, Nov. 11, 1987.

PAGE 135: Text of Tom Murphy speech to ABC affiliates, June 4, 1986.

CHAPTER 6

PAGE 136: Larry Tisch interview, March 4, 1986.

PAGE 136: Tom Wyman interview, Dec. 19, 1985.

PAGE 137: CBS chronology sent by George Vradenburg III to Kenneth E. Wyker, Securites and Exchange Commission, Nov. 6, 1986.

PAGE 137: CBS form 10-K filing with the SEC for the fiscal year ending Dec. 31, 1987.

PAGE 137: Larry Tisch interview, March 10, 1988.

PAGE 137: Larry Tisch interview, Feb. 5, 1986.

PAGE 138: Jay Kriegel interview, Nov. 12, 1985.

PAGE 138: Tom Wyman interview, Feb. 1, 1988.

PAGE 138: Wyman 1980 dinner conversation from James H. Rosenfield interview, Jan. 20, 1988.

PAGE 138: Larry Tisch interview, March 14, 1986.

PAGE 139: Larry Tisch interview, Nov. 21, 1986.

PAGE 139: Larry Tisch interview, Feb. 5, 1986.

PAGE 140: Frank Thomas interview, Dec. 4, 1985.

PAGE 140: Andrea Stone, "Tisches Have Eyes for CBS," *USA Today,* March 24, 1986.

PAGE 141: Bob Tisch interview, April 2, 1986.

PAGE 141: Tom Wyman interview, Dec. 19, 1985.

PAGE 141: Larry Tisch interview, Dec. 10, 1985.

PAGE 141: Fred Meyer interview, Oct. 9, 1987.

PAGE 142: Larry Tisch interview, Dec. 10, 1985.

PAGE 142: Tom Wyman interview, Dec. 19, 1985.

PAGE 142: William Paley interview, Jan. 14, 1986.

PAGE 143: Robert Daly interview, Nov. 24, 1987.

PAGE 143: For a fuller account of Paley and CBS's preoccupation with appearances see Sally Bedell Smith, *In All His Glory: William S. Paley, The Legendary Tycoon and His Brilliant Circle,* (New York: Simon and Schuster, 1990).

PAGE 143: Wyman complained about the Daly rumors to George Vradenburg, interview, Nov. 4, 1988.

PAGE 143: *New York Post,* April 15, 1986.

PAGE 143: *Washington Post,* May 20, 1986.

PAGE 143: Text of Tom Wyman budget presentation to CBS board, Sept. 10, 1986.

PAGE 144: Tom Wyman interview, Feb. 1, 1988.

PAGE 144: For a superb account of Paley's early years at CBS and how he created a sense of "the Tiffany network," see Smith, *In All His Glory: William S. Paley, The Legendary Tycoon and His Brilliant Circle.*

PAGE 144: Fred Meyer interview, Oct. 9, 1987.

PAGE 145: Ken Auletta, "Gambling on CBS," *New York Times Magazine, Part 2: The Business World,* June 8, 1986.

PAGE 145: Tom Wyman interview, Feb. 1, 1988.

PAGE 145: Larry Tisch interview, March 10, 1988.

PAGE 145: Tom Wyman interview, Feb. 1, 1988.

PAGE 146: Fred Meyer interview, Nov. 5, 1986.
PAGE 146: Roswell Gilpatric interview, Feb. 8, 1988.
PAGE 146: William Paley interview, Feb. 10, 1987.
PAGE 146: CBS annual proxy statement, 1986.
PAGE 147: Tom Wyman interview, Feb. 1, 1988.
PAGE 147: Larry Tisch interview, Sept. 2, 1986.
PAGE 147: Larry Tisch interview, March 1, 1988.
PAGE 148: Tom Wyman interview, Feb. 1, 1988.
PAGE 148: Michel Bergerac interview, Oct. 28, 1986.
PAGE 149: Frank Thomas interview, Feb. 23, 1988.
PAGE 149: Larry Tisch letter to Tom Wyman, June 12, 1986.
PAGE 149: Marietta Tree interview, Jan. 20, 1987.
PAGE 150: Tom Wyman interview, Feb. 1, 1988.
PAGE 150: Larry Tisch interview, March 10, 1988.
PAGE 150: Roswell Gilpatric interview, Sept. 16, 1986.
PAGE 150: Larry Tisch interview, March 10, 1988.
PAGE 151: Martin Lipton interviews, June 10, 1987, and Sept. 18, 1986.
PAGE 152: Roswell Gilpatric memorandum to file, June 18, 1986; the dialogue at this meeting was confirmed by Larry Tisch.
PAGE 152: James Wolfensohn interview, Nov. 5, 1986.
PAGE 152: Martin Lipton interview, June 10, 1987.
PAGE 152: Roswell Gilpatric notes on session with Larry Tisch, June 18, 1986.
PAGE 153: Michel Bergerac interview, Oct. 28, 1986.
PAGE 153: Frank Thomas interview, Feb. 23, 1988.
PAGE 153: Larry Tisch interview, March 10, 1988.
PAGE 154: Peter Derow interview, Nov. 6, 1986.
PAGE 155: Michel Bergerac interview, Oct. 28, 1986.
PAGE 155: Michel Bergerac interview, Oct. 28, 1986.
PAGE 156: Tom Wyman memo to CBS board of directors plus enclosures, July 18, 1986.
PAGE 156: Fred Meyer interview, Dec. 17, 1986.
PAGE 156: Tom Wyman interview, Feb. 1, 1988.
PAGE 156: Fred Meyer interview, Nov. 5, 1986.
PAGE 157: Larry Tisch interview, March 10, 1988.
PAGE 157: George Vradenburg III interview, June 1, 1987.
PAGE 157: Tom Wyman memo to CBS directors, plus enclosures, July 29, 1986.
PAGE 157: Roswell Gilpatric interview, Sept. 16, 1986.
PAGE 157: Kay Gardella, "The Net Effect Is Negative," New York *Daily News,* Aug. 25, 1986.
PAGE 157: George Maksian, "No Mountain Climbing For Brokaw," New York *Daily News,* Aug. 6, 1986.
PAGE 158: Van Gordon Sauter interview, Sept. 9, 1986.
PAGE 159: *Channels,* Oct. 1986.
PAGE 159: Van Gordon Sauter interview, Sept. 9, 1986.
PAGE 159: Mike Wallace interview, March 17, 1989.
PAGE 160: Martin Lipton interview, June 10, 1987.
PAGE 160: Larry Tisch interview, March 10, 1988.
PAGE 160: William Paley interview, Nov. 12, 1987.
PAGE 160: Tom Wyman interview, Feb. 1, 1988.
PAGE 160: James Wolfensohn interview, Feb. 17, 1988.
PAGE 160: George Vradenburg III correspondence and enclosures to the SEC, Nov. 6, 1986.
PAGE 161: Gene Jankowski interview, Feb. 19, 1987.
PAGE 161: David Fuchs interview, Sept. 22, 1986.
PAGE 162: Fred Meyer interview, Dec. 17, 1986.
PAGE 162: Peter Derow interview. Nov. 6, 1986.
PAGE 162: Mike Wallace interview, March 17, 1989.
PAGE 162: Grant Tinker interview, May 19, 1987.
PAGE 163: Frank Thomas interview, Feb. 23, 1988.
PAGE 163: James Wolfensohn interview, Nov. 5, 1986.
PAGE 163: Tom Wyman interview, Feb. 1, 1988.

PAGE 163: Tom Wyman interview, Feb. 1, 1988.

PAGE 163: Larry Tisch interview, March 1, 1988.

PAGE 163: Peter J. Boyer, "CBS News Chief Responds to Critics," *New York Times,* Aug. 25, 1986.

PAGE 164: Van Gordon Sauter interview, March 16, 1988.

PAGE 164: Tom Wyman interview, Feb. 1, 1988.

PAGE 164: Tom Bettag interview, Sept. 29, 1987.

PAGE 164: Jonathan Alter and Bill Powell, "Civil War at CBS," *Newsweek,* Sept. 8, 1986.

PAGE 164: Larry Tisch interview, March 10, 1988.

PAGE 164: Tom Wyman interview, June 5, 1990.

PAGE 164: Marietta Tree interview, Jan. 20, 1987.

PAGE 165: Frank Thomas interview, Feb. 23, 1988.

PAGE 165: Michel Bergerac interview, Sept. 15, 1987.

PAGE 166: George Vradenburg III interview, Feb. 2, 1988.

PAGE 167: Francis T. Vincent, Jr., interview, Feb. 6, 1987.

PAGE 167: Francis T. Vincent, Jr., interview, Feb. 6, 1987.

PAGE 167: Tom Wyman interview, Feb. 1, 1988.

PAGE 168: Herbert Allen, Jr., interview, Oct. 6, 1986.

PAGE 168: CBS filing with the SEC, Nov. 6, 1986.

PAGE 168: Tom Wyman interview, Feb. 1, 1988.

PAGE 168: Francis T. Vincent, Jr., interview, Feb. 6, 1987.

PAGE 169: Frank Stanton interview, Feb. 5, 1988.

PAGE 169: Larry Tisch interviews, March 1, 1988, and March 10, 1988.

PAGE 169: Frank Stanton interview, Dec. 21, 1987.

PAGE 169: Larry Tisch interview, March 10, 1988.

PAGE 169: Larry Tisch interview, Sept. 2, 1986.

PAGE 170: Peter Jennings interview, Feb. 18, 1988.

PAGE 170: Alter and Powell, "Civil War at CBS."

PAGE 170: Alter and Powell, "Civil War at CBS."

PAGE 171: Don Hewitt interview, Oct. 31, 1986.

PAGE 171: Mike Wallace interview, March 17, 1989.

PAGE 171: Tom Wyman interview, Feb. 1, 1988.

PAGE 171: Arthur Liman interview, Nov. 26, 1987.

PAGE 171: Fred Meyer interview, March 7, 1988.

PAGE 172: Marietta Tree interview, Jan. 20, 1987.

PAGE 172: James Wolfensohn interview, Nov. 5, 1986.

PAGE 172: CBS chronology and attachments filed with the SEC on Nov. 6, 1986.

PAGE 172: Larry Tisch interview, March 10, 1988.

PAGE 173: Paley's remarks from Arthur Liman interview, Nov. 26, 1986.

PAGE 173: Marietta Tree interview, Jan. 20, 1987.

PAGE 174: Marietta Tree interview, Jan. 20, 1987.

PAGE 174: Frank Thomas interview, Feb. 23, 1988.

PAGE 174: Michel Bergerac interview, Oct. 28, 1986.

PAGE 174: William Paley interview, Feb. 10, 1987.

PAGE 174: Van Gordon Sauter interview, Sept. 9, 1986.

PAGE 174: Jankowski's optimistic assessment of Wyman's fate from Sept. 9 statement to Broadcast executives, Gene Lothery interview, June 11, 1988.

PAGE 175: Tom Wyman interview, Feb. 1, 1988.

PAGE 175: Fred Meyer interview, Dec. 17, 1986.

PAGE 175: Fred Meyer interview, Oct. 9, 1987.

PAGE 176: Patrick Callahan interview, Aug. 26, 1988.

PAGE 176: Copy of Peter Derow notes, Sept. 10, 1986.

PAGE 176: Fred Meyer interview, Dec. 17, 1986.

PAGE 176: Michel Bergerac interview, Oct. 28, 1986.

PAGE 176: James Wolfensohn interview, Feb. 17, 1988.

PAGE 176: Tom Wyman interview, Feb. 1, 1988.

PAGE 177: Roswell Gilpatric interview, Sept. 16, 1986.

PAGE 177: CBS board minutes, Sept. 10, 1986.

PAGE 177: Tom Wyman interview, Feb. 1, 1988.

PAGE 177: Larry Tisch interview, March 10, 1988.

PAGE 178: James Wolfensohn interview, Feb. 17, 1988.

PAGE 178: Roswell Gilpatric interview, April 20, 1987.

PAGE 178: Michel Bergerac interview, Oct. 28, 1986.

PAGE 178: See, for example, *New York Times, Wall Street Journal,* and *Washington Post* stories of Sept. 12, 1986.

PAGE 179: Francis T. Vincent, Jr., interview, Feb. 6, 1987.

PAGE 179: Peter J. Boyer, "Ex-CBS Chairman Tells of Takeover," *New York Times,* Jan. 21, 1988.

PAGE 179: Van Gordon Sauter interview, March 16, 1988.

PAGE 179: James Wolfensohn interview, Feb. 17, 1988.

PAGE 180: The board dialogue paraphrased from CBS board minutes, Sept. 10, 1986 and from eyewitness accounts.

PAGE 180: Larry Tisch interview, March 10, 1988.

PAGE 180: Roswell Gilpatric interview, Sept. 16, 1986.

PAGE 181: Marietta Tree interviews, Jan. 20, 1987, and April 15, 1987.

PAGE 181: Michel Bergerac interview, Oct. 28, 1986.

PAGE 182: Michel Bergerac interview, Oct. 28, 1986.

PAGE 182: James Wolfensohn interview, Oct. 28, 1987.

PAGE 182: Larry Tisch interview, March 10, 1988.

PAGE 182: Marietta Tree interview, April 15, 1987.

PAGE 182: Michel Bergerac interview, Sept. 15, 1987.

PAGE 183: Gene Jankowski interview, July 15, 1987.

PAGE 183: Larry Tisch interview, March 10, 1988.

PAGE 183: CBS press release, Sept. 10, 1986.

PAGE 183: CBS board minutes, Sept. 10, 1986.

PAGE 184: Van Gordon Sauter interview, March 16, 1988.

PAGE 184: Gene Jankowski interview, July 28, 1988.

PAGE 184: Dan Rather interview, April 22, 1988.

PAGE 184: CBS press release, Sept. 10, 1986.

PAGE 185: Kati Marton interview, Sept. 11, 1986.

PAGE 185: Molly Parnis interview, June 5, 1990.

PAGE 185: Peter J. Boyer, "At CBS News, a Feeling of Relief," *New York Times,*, Sept. 11, 1986.

PAGE 185: Monica Collins, "Old Partners, New Marriage: Paley, CBS," *USA Today,* Sept. 11, 1986.

PAGE 185: The Cincinnatus analogy was first used, to my knowledge, by Sally Bedell Smith, "Paley's Latest Feat: His Return," *New York Times,* Sept. 11, 1986.

CHAPTER 7

PAGE 187: Phil Beuth interview, Jan. 5, 1988.

PAGE 187: Tom Murphy interview, April 7, 1989.

PAGE 187: Ron Doerfler interview, Oct. 6, 1987.

PAGE 188: Stephen Weiswasser interview, Sept. 28, 1987.

PAGE 188: ABC's 1986 News profit from John Sias interview, Dec. 16, 1986.

PAGE 189: Account of News budget review from Richard C. Wald interview, Oct. 2, 1987.

PAGE 189: John Sias interview, Nov. 11, 1987.

PAGE 189: News reductions from Ronald Doerfler interview, Oct. 6, 1987.

PAGE 189: William Grimes interview, Jan. 5, 1988.

PAGE 189: Tom Murphy press conference, Oct. 14, 1986.

PAGE 189: Explanation of ABC defensiveness from Herbert A. Granath interview, Feb. 24, 1988.

PAGE 190: Dick Wald interview, Oct. 22, 1986.

PAGE 190: Dan Burke interview, May 28, 1987.

PAGE 190: James Burke interview, Feb. 1, 1989.

PAGE 190: Dan Burke interview, Nov. 14, 1989.

PAGE 191: James Burke interview, Feb. 1, 1989.

PAGE 191: Stephen Weiswasser interviews, Sept. 28, 1987, and June 5, 1990.

PAGE 192: Dan Burke interview, Jan. 19, 1988.

PAGE 192: Dan Burke interview, June 3, 1988.
PAGE 193: Dan Burke interview, June 3, 1988.
PAGE 193: Dan Burke interview, Oct. 30, 1987.
PAGE 193: Dan Burke interview, May 28, 1987.
PAGE 193: Christopher Isham interview, Aug. 12, 1986.
PAGE 193: Ted Koppel interview, July 20, 1988.
PAGE 193: Dick Wald interview, 22, 1986.
PAGE 194: Christopher Isham interview, Aug. 12, 1986.
PAGE 194: Leonard Goldenson interview, March 4, 1987.
PAGE 194: David Burke interview, March 11, 1987.
PAGE 195: Roone Arledge interview, Jan. 15, 1987.
PAGE 195: Roone Arledge interveiw, Jan. 15, 1987.
PAGE 195: Roone Arledge interview, Jan. 15, 1987.
PAGE 196: Cable facts from "Cable TV Facts 1988," a publication of the Cable Television Advertising Bureau, 1988.
PAGE 196: Richard McDonald interview, Nov. 17, 1986.
PAGE 196: Rupert Murdoch, Chief Executive's Review, The News Corporation Ltd. Annual Report, 1986.
PAGE 197: John Sias interview, March 17, 1987.
PAGE 198: Val Pinchbeck interview, Dec. 10, 1986.
PAGE 198: Michael Fuchs interview, Sept. 24, 1986.
PAGE 200: Aljean Harmetz, "Now Playing: The New Hollywood," *New York Times,* Jan. 10, 1988; and "Network Television in Transition," a report prepared by the CBS Broadcast Group, Aug. 1987.
PAGE 201: Bob Butler interview, Dec. 8, 1986.
PAGE 201: Letter from Michael P. Mallardi, president of the ABC Broadcasting Group, to Robert A. Daly, chairman and chief executive officer of Warner Brothers Inc., Oct. 30, 1986; and John Lippman, *Variety,* Oct. 31, 1986.
PAGE 202: Robert Daly interview, Nov. 24, 1987.
PAGE 202: Francis T. Vincent, Jr., interview, Feb. 6, 1987.
PAGE 202: Mark Mandala interview, Dec. 15, 1986.
PAGE 203: John Sias interview, March 17, 1987, and Peter J. Boyer, "ABC News to Adjust Pay Overseas," *New York Times,* Nov. 18, 1986.
PAGE 203: Reported in Huntington Williams, *Beyond Control: ABC and the Fate of the Networks* (New York: Atheneum, 1989).
PAGE 203: Fred Pierce interview, Oct. 14, 1987.
PAGE 204: David Burke interview, March 11, 1987.
PAGE 204: Peter J. Boyer, "Move of 'World News' Hints at a Power Shift," *New York Times,* Nov. 13, 1986.
PAGE 204: Brian Donlon, "Time Ticks as Networks Fight to Save 7 P.M. News," *USA Today,* Nov. 18, 1986.
PAGE 204: Erik Barnouw, *Tube of Plenty* (Oxford, England: Oxford University Press, 1982), p. 187.
PAGE 205: Dan Burke interview, May 28, 1987.
PAGE 205: Michael Mallardi interview, June 25, 1987.
PAGE 205: Peter Jennings interview, Dec. 4, 1986.
PAGE 205: John Sias interview, June 6, 1987.
PAGE 206: Stuart Hirsch interview, Nov. 17, 1986.
PAGE 206: Peter Jennings interview, Dec. 4, 1986.
PAGE 207: John Sias interview, June 6, 1987.
PAGE 207: Larry Grossman interview, Jan. 17, 1987, and John Sias interview, July 11, 1990.
PAGE 207: Billie Tisch interview, at CBS affiliate convention, May 19, 1987.
PAGE 207: Gene Jankowski interview, July 15, 1987.
PAGE 208: Figures on ABC preemptions in the seventies from Les Brown, *Television: The Business Behind the Box* (New York: Harcourt Brace Jovanovich, 1971).
PAGE 208: Tom Murphy interview, April 7, 1989.
PAGE 208: Tom Murphy interview, July 16, 1987.
PAGE 208: Ray Timothy, NBC executive presentation to employees, Jan. 12, 1988.
PAGE 208: Bob Wright interview, Oct. 29, 1987.
PAGE 209: Stephen Weiswasser interview, Sept. 28, 1987.

PAGE 209: Pier Mapes interview, May 14, 1988.

PAGE 209: John Sias interview, March 17, 1987.

PAGE 209: Tom Murphy interview, April 7, 1989.

PAGE 210: Ron Doerfler interview, Aug. 23, 1987.

PAGE 210: Dick Wald interview, Oct. 2, 1987.

PAGE 210: Bob Murphy interview, May 6, 1987.

PAGE 211: David Adams essay, "The Best of Intentions, The Worst of Results: A Small Saga," unpublished, 1980.

PAGE 211: Mark Mandala interview, Dec. 15, 1986.

CHAPTER 8

PAGE 213: Melissa Ludlum interview, Nov. 6, 1986.

PAGE 213: Bob Wright interview, May 27, 1987.

PAGE 213: NBC Corporate Planning Chart, "1987 Estimated Operating Income of Major National TV Programming Services," Dec. 1986.

PAGE 214: Grant Tinker interview, May 19, 1987.

PAGE 214: Description of NBC's strategic approach under Tinker from Ellen Agress interview, June 24, 1987.

PAGE 214: Suzanne Wright interview, Jan. 7, 1988.

PAGE 214: Bob Wright interview, May 27, 1987.

PAGE 215: Bob Wright press conference, Oct. 22, 1986.

PAGE 215: Mark Frankel, "The Sweet Buy and Buy," *Channels,* Sept. 1986.

PAGE 215: Description of Wright's proposal to have Don Johnson host news documentaries from Larry Grossman interview, Jan. 17, 1987.

PAGE 215: Tom Brokaw interview, Oct. 21, 1986.

PAGE 216: Bob Wright interview, Nov. 26, 1986.

PAGE 216: Tom Brokaw interview, Oct. 13, 1987.

PAGE 216: Larry Grossman interview, Oct. 15, 1986.

PAGE 217: NBC budget numbers from transcript of Robert Butler presentation to NBC management meeting, March 23, 1987.

PAGE 217: Bob Wright interview, Nov. 26, 1986.

PAGE 217: Bob Wright interview, Oct. 22, 1986.

PAGE 218: Bud Rukeyser interview, Dec. 9, 1988.

PAGE 218: Jack Welch interview, July 1, 1987.

PAGE 218: Bob Wright interview, May 27, 1986.

PAGE 218: Peter J. Boyer, "Key NBC Officials Resist 5% Budget-Cut Request, *New York Times,* Oct. 21, 1986.

PAGE 219: Tom Brokaw interview, Oct. 21, 1986.

PAGE 219: Steve Friedman interview, Dec. 17, 1986.

PAGE 219: Tom Brokaw interview, Oct. 21, 1986.

PAGE 219: Bud Rukeyser, memorandum to Bob Wright, Oct. 14, 1986.

PAGE 220: Bob Wright interview, May 27, 1987.

PAGE 220: Bob Wright memo to Senior NBC Officers, Oct. 24, 1986.

PAGE 220: Bob Butler interview, Aug. 12, 1987.

PAGE 221: Bud Rukeyser interview, Dec. 8, 1986.

PAGE 221: Figures on NBC profits from Bob Butler budget presentation, March 23, 1987.

PAGE 221: Perry Simon interview, April 29, 1987.

PAGE 221: Warren Littlefield interview, Nov. 23, 1987.

PAGE 222: Jack Welch interview, July 1, 1987.

PAGE 222: Brandon Tartikoff interview, April 30, 1987.

PAGE 222: John Agoglia interview, April 30, 1987.

PAGE 222: Michele Brusten interview, May 1, 1987.

PAGE 222: Bob Wright letter to NBC executives, Nov. 14, 1986.

PAGE 223: Bob Wright interview, Nov. 26, 1986.

PAGE 223: Jack Welch interview, July 5, 1987.

PAGE 223: Bob Wright interview, Nov. 26, 1986.

PAGE 223: Bob Wright memo from Marilyn Harris et al, "The Dynamo," *Business Week,* June 30, 1986.

PAGE 224: Bob Wright memorandum to Corey Dunham, Nov. 6, 1986.

PAGE 224: Brandon Tartikoff news conference, Jan. 6, 1987.

PAGE 224: Peter J. Boyer, "NBC Head Proposes Staff Political Contributions," *New York Times,* Dec. 10, 1986.

PAGE 224: Bud Rukeyser interview, Dec. 18, 1986.

PAGE 224: Bob Wright interview, Oct. 29, 1987.

PAGE 224: Jack Welch interview, Jan. 13, 1987.

PAGE 224: Jack Welch interview, Jan. 13, 1987.

PAGE 225: J. B. Holston III interview, April 14, 1987.

PAGE 225: Larry Grossman interview, June 18, 1987.

PAGE 225: Larry Grossman interview, May 5, 1987.

PAGE 226: NBC Summary of the Meeting of the NBC Affiliate Board, November 10–13, 1986.

PAGE 226: J. B. Holston III, interview, April 14, 1987.

PAGE 227: Description of Welch/Grossman encounter from, among others: Larry Grossman interview, Jan. 17, 1987; Bob Butler interview, April 8, 1987; Jack Welch interview, Jan. 13, 1987.

PAGE 227: Jack Welch interview, Jan. 13, 1987.

PAGE 227: Bob Wright interview, April 7, 1989.

PAGE 227: Bob Wright interview, Nov. 26, 1986.

PAGE 227: Bob Wright interview, Nov. 26, 1986.

PAGE 227: Jack Welch interview, Oct. 4, 1988.

PAGE 228: Bob Wright interview, May 27, 1987.

PAGE 228: Larry Grossman interview, Jan. 17, 1987.

PAGE 228: Larry Grossman interview, Jan. 17, 1987.

PAGE 228: Jack Welch interview, July 1, 1987.

PAGE 228: Bob Wright interview, March 17, 1987.

PAGE 229: Larry Grossman interview, April 1, 1987.

PAGE 229: Larry Grossman interview, Jan. 17, 1987.

PAGE 229: Jack Welch interview, July 1, 1987.

PAGE 229: Larry Grossman interview, April 6, 1987.

PAGE 229: Edwin Diamond, "Mr. Wright?" *New York,* Jan. 19, 1987.

PAGE 229: Peter J. Boyer, "NBC Cancels Magazine Show '1986,'" *New York Tmes,* Dec. 10, 1986.

PAGE 229: Bob Wright interview, March 17, 1987.

PAGE 229: Grant Tinker interview, Nov. 25, 1987.

PAGE 230: John Stewart interview, March 13, 1987.

PAGE 230: Tom Ross interview, Aug. 10, 1988.

PAGE 230: Tom Ross interview, April 1, 1987.

PAGE 231: Larry Grossman press conference transcript, Oct. 22, 1986.

PAGE 232: Larry Grossman interview, Aug. 10, 1988.

PAGE 232: NBC Research study of the three network newscasts, 1984.

PAGE 233: Richard Leibner interview, March 3, 1987.

PAGE 233: Bob Wright interview, Oct. 29, 1987.

PAGE 234: Larry Grossman interview, Aug. 10, 1988.

PAGE 234: Tom Brokaw interview, May 30, 1990.

PAGE 234: Tom Brokaw interview, Jan. 6, 1987.

PAGE 234: Larry Grossman interview, Jan. 17, 1987.

PAGE 235: Tom Brokaw interview, May 22, 1988.

PAGE 235: Larry Grossman interview, Aug. 10, 1988.

PAGE 235: Timothy J. Russert interview, Feb. 27, 1987.

PAGE 235: Larry Grossman interview, Jan. 17, 1987.

PAGE 235: Bob Wright interview, May 27, 1987.

PAGE 235: Bud Rukeyser interview, Jan. 14, 1987.

PAGE 235: Suzanne Wright interview, Jan. 7, 1988.

PAGE 236: Al Barber interview, Nov. 4, 1987.

PAGE 236: John J. Gabarro, *The Dynamics of Taking Charge* (Cambridge, Mass.: Harvard Business School Press, 1987), p. 8.

PAGE 236: Al Barber interview, Nov. 10, 1987.

PAGE 236: Bob Wright interview, Nov. 26, 1986.

PAGE 236: Bob Wright interview, May 15, 1987.

PAGE 236: Bob Wright press conference, Oct. 22, 1986.

PAGE 237: Bob Wright interview, Oct. 22, 1986.
PAGE 237: Bud Rukeyser interview, Jan. 14, 1987.
PAGE 238: Franklin J. Havlicek interview, Feb. 17, 1987.
PAGE 238: Suzanne Wright interview, Jan. 7, 1988.
PAGE 238: Bob Wright lunch interview with TV press, Oct. 22, 1986.
PAGE 238: Donald Carswell interview, June 15, 1987.
PAGE 239: Figures from Bob Butler presentation to NBC management meeting, March 23, 1987.
PAGE 239: NBC Corporate Planning Chart, "1987 Estimated Operating Income of Major National TV Programming Services," Dec. 1986.
PAGE 239: Brandon Tartikoff interview, Jan. 14, 1987.
PAGE 240: Edward L. Scanlon interview, Dec. 1, 1987.
PAGE 240: Grant Tinker interview, May 19, 1987.
PAGE 240: Jack Welch interview, Jan. 13, 1987.

CHAPTER 9

PAGE 241: Mark N. Vamos et al, in "The Bad Days at Black Rock Aren't Over Yet," *Business Week,* Sept. 29, 1986, reported on Tisch's attitude toward the Wells Fargo guards.
PAGE 241: Patrick Callahan interview, Aug. 26, 1988.
PAGE 241: Fred Meyer interview, May 6, 1987.
PAGE 242: *New York Times* charts on CBS debt, Sept. 12, 1986.
PAGE 242: Larry Tisch interview, *Broadcasting,* Oct. 27, 1986.
PAGE 242: Margaret A. Elliot and Nancy J. Perry, "CBS Braces for the Tisch Touch," *Fortune,* Oct. 13, 1986.
PAGE 242: Quoted by Bill Powell and Jonathan Alter, "The Showdown at CBS," *Newsweek,* Sept. 22, 1986.
PAGE 242: CBS proxy statement, 1986.
PAGE 242: Gene Jankowski interview, Feb. 23, 1988.
PAGE 243: Larry Tisch interview, July 29, 1987.
PAGE 243: Van Gordon Sauter interview, March 16, 1988.
PAGE 243: Richard Cohen interview, Nov. 18, 1987.
PAGE 244: Van Gorden Sauter interview, March 16, 1988.
PAGE 244: Larry Tisch interview, July 29, 1987.
PAGE 244: CBS memorandum from Laurence Tisch, Sept. 11, 1986.
PAGE 245: Larry Tisch interview, July 29, 1987.
PAGE 245: Interview with Larry Tisch, *Broadcasting,* Oct. 27, 1987.
PAGE 245: David Fuchs interview, Sept. 22, 1986.
PAGE 245: Francis T. Vincent, Jr., interview, Feb. 6, 1987.
PAGE 245: Geraldine Fabrikant, "Tisch Rules At Selling CBS Parts." *New York Times,* Sept. 15, 1986.
PAGE 246: Robert Pittman interview, Jan. 22, 1988.
PAGE 246: Larry Tisch interview, Dec. 20, 1988.
PAGE 246: Robert Pittman interview, Jan. 22, 1988.
PAGE 247: William S. Paley letter to the FCC and accompanying legal memorandum, Oct. 1, 1986.
PAGE 247: Kevin Goldman, "Cronkite, Stanton Join Search for CBS Chiefs," *Newsday,* Sept. 16, 1986.
PAGE 247: Larry Tisch letter to *Newsweek,* Oct. 6, 1986.
PAGE 248: Larry Tisch interview, March 10, 1988.
PAGE 248: Frank Stanton interview, Feb. 5, 1988.
PAGE 248: John Carmody, "The TV Column," *Washington Post,* Sept. 16, 1986.
PAGE 249: Account of what Tisch said during dinner from Andrew Heyward interview, March 10, 1987, among others.
PAGE 249: Larry Tisch interview, July 29, 1987.
PAGE 249: Larry Tisch memo to the Organization, Oct. 1, 1986.
PAGE 249: Tisch's instructions to Flanagan recounted in Fred Meyer interview, May 6, 1987.
PAGE 249: Thomas C. Flanagan interview, Nov. 9, 1987.
PAGE 250: Details of CBS cost reductions from Larry Tisch interview, July 29, 1987; "A Cut Above the Ordinary," *Time,* Dec. 22, 1986; and Peter J. Boyer, "Trauma Time on Network TV," *New York Times,* Nov. 2, 1986.
PAGE 250: Larry Tisch interview, *AFTRA,* Summer 1987.
PAGE 250: Flanagan's attitude toward mi-

nority advancement program from Fred Meyer interview, Oct. 9, 1987.

PAGE 251: Walter Yetnikoff interview, April 6, 1988.

PAGE 252: Peter Derow memo to the file, Oct. 16, 1986.

PAGE 252: Larry Tisch interview, July 29, 1987.

PAGE 253: Larry Tisch interview, Nov. 13, 1986.

PAGE 253: Grant Tinker interview, Nov. 25, 1987.

PAGE 253: Peter W. Barnes, *Wall Street Journal,* Oct. 3, 1986.

PAGE 254: Burton R. Benjamin interview, Feb. 24, 1987.

PAGE 254: David Burke interview, Nov. 18, 1987.

PAGE 254: Don Hewitt interview, July 28, 1988.

PAGE 254: Roone Arledge interview, July 17, 1988.

PAGE 255: Walter Cronkite eulogy to Burton R. Benjamin held at the Society for Ethical Culture, Sept. 30, 1988.

PAGE 255: Burton R. Benjamin interview, Feb. 24, 1987.

PAGE 256: Howard Stringer interview, Oct. 9, 1986, and confirmed, June 1, 1990.

PAGE 256: Burton R. Benjamin interview, Feb. 24, 1987.

PAGE 256: Howard Stringer interview, Oct. 30, 1986.

PAGE 256: Larry Tisch interview, Nov. 13, 1986.

PAGE 257: Larry Tisch interview, Dec. 20, 1988.

PAGE 257: Larry Tisch interview, Nov. 30, 1987.

PAGE 257: "Larry Tisch and the New Realism at CBS," *Broadcasting,* Oct. 27, 1986.

PAGE 257: Larry Tisch interview, July 29, 1987.

PAGE 258: For an account of the discussions concerning the sale of CBS Records see Peter J. Boyer, "What a Romance: Sony and CBS Records!" *New York Times Magazine,* Sept. 18, 1988.

PAGE 258: Walter Yetnikoff interview, April 13, 1988.

PAGE 259: Peter Boyer, "What a Romance!"

PAGE 259: Larry Tisch interview, June 22, 1988.

PAGE 259: William Paley interviews, Nov. 12, 1987, and Feb. 10, 1987.

PAGE 259: Walter Yetnikoff interview, April 13, 1988.

PAGE 259: Michel Bergerac interview, Sept. 15, 1987.

PAGE 260: Frank Stanton interview, Feb. 5, 1988.

PAGE 260: Larry Tisch interview, July 29, 1987.

PAGE 261: Larry Tisch interview, July 29, 1987.

PAGE 261: Tisch's exploration of a proxy fight to remove CBS directors comes from three Tisch intimates.

PAGE 261: Michel Bergerac interview, Sept. 15, 1987.

PAGE 264: Account of dialogue between Larry Tisch and Tony Malara based on interviews with most of the attendees.

PAGE 264: CBS proxy statement, 1986.

PAGE 264: Larry Tisch interviews, July 29, 1987, and Nov. 30, 1987.

PAGE 264: Larry Tisch interview, July 29, 1987.

PAGE 265: CBS press release announcing reorganization, Dec. 15, 1986.

PAGE 265: Tony Malara interview, Dec. 18, 1986.

PAGE 266: Bagel story from Walter Yetnikoff interview, April 6, 1988.

PAGE 268: Jim Jensen letters to Larry Tisch, Dec. 30, 1986, and Jan. 14, 1987.

PAGE 268: Larry Tisch interview, May 5, 1988.

PAGE 268: Wyman/Backe anecdote about Jankowski from one of the participants.

PAGE 268: Gene Jankowski question to author, Feb. 24, 1988.

PAGE 269: Tony Malara interview, June 1, 1987.

PAGE 269: Gene Jankowski interview, July 15, 1987.

PAGE 269: Eric Ober interview, Sept. 23, 1988.

PAGE 269: Larry Tisch interview, July 29, 1987.

PAGE 269: Larry Tisch interview, Dec. 22, 1986.

PAGE 270: James Wolfensohn interview, Feb. 17, 1988.

PAGE 271: Larry Tisch interview, Dec. 22, 1986.

PAGE 271: Richard Leibner interview, Nov. 4, 1986.

PAGE 271: Howard Stringer interview, Dec. 20, 1986.

PAGE 272: Analysis that viewers seek authority from a network anchor from Eric Marder Associates survey research report, July 1987.

PAGE 272: Eric Ober interview, Sept. 15, 1987.

PAGE 272: Anecdote about Sawyer call to Stringer from Eric Ober interview, Oct. 6, 1987, and confirmed by one other source.

PAGE 272: Richard Leibner interview, March 3, 1987.

PAGE 273: Mark Harrington interview, March 13, 1987.

PAGE 273: Howard Stringer interview, May 11, 1987.

PAGE 273: Burton R. Benjamin interview, Feb. 24, 1987.

PAGE 273: Larry Tisch interview, April 10, 1987.

PAGE 275: Fred Meyer interview, May 6, 1987.

PAGE 275: CNN figures from Ed Turner interview, Aug. 12, 1987, and from N. R. Kleinfield, "Making News on the Cheap Pay Off," *New York Times,* April 19, 1987.

PAGE 275: CNN overseas sales from *Broadcasting,* Dec. 8, 1986, and Jan. 26, 1987.

PAGE 275: Tom Bettag interview, March 10, 1987.

PAGE 275: Dan Rather interview, April 22, 1988.

PAGE 275: Howard Stringer interview, Oct. 7, 1987.

PAGE 275: Larry Tisch interview, March 10, 1987.

PAGE 276: Dan Rather interview, April 22, 1988.

PAGE 276: Dan Rather interview, Oct. 23, 1986.

PAGE 276: Dan Rather interview, March 10, 1987.

PAGE 276: Dan Rather interview, April 22, 1988.

PAGE 277: Larry Tisch interview, April 10, 1987.

PAGE 277: Tom Bettag interview, March 10, 1987.

PAGE 277: Gene Jankowski interview, July 15, 1987.

PAGE 277: Michel Bergerac interview, Sept. 15, 1987.

PAGE 278: Roswell Gilpatric interview, March 16, 1987.

PAGE 278: Larry Tisch interview, Jan. 27, 1987.

PAGE 278: CBS Broadcast Group projected revenues and profits for 1986 and 1987, prepared in Dec. 1986.

PAGE 279: Rich MacDonald research report on CBS, the First Boston Corp., Dec. 15, 1986.

PAGE 279: Larry Tisch at annual shareholders meeting in New York, May 13, 1987.

PAGE 279: What a network spends on all programming taken from speech by Daniel B. Burke to Cap Cities/ABC shareholders, May 19, 1988.

PAGE 279: Scott Ticer and Mark Ivey, "OK, Larry and Bill, Take Your Places. It's Showtime," *Business Week,* Jan. 26, 1987.

PAGE 279: Frank Stanton interview, Feb. 23, 1987.

CHAPTER 10

PAGE 280: John Sias interview. June 6, 1987.

PAGE 280: John Sias interview, Nov. 11, 1987.

PAGE 280: Transcript, Brandon Tartikoff press conference, Jan. 6, 1987.

PAGE 281: Figures on network costs from Daniel B. Burke speech to the annual meeting of Cap Cities/ABC shareholders, May 19, 1988.

PAGE 281: Network losses from NFL games from Peter Lund interview, Sept. 30, 1986.

PAGE 281: Dan Burke interview, Jan. 19, 1988.

PAGE 282: Ted Turner, "Inside Cable" panel at the New York Cable Television Advertising Bureau Convention, March 31, 1987.

PAGE 283: Lester Wunderman interview, April 4, 1988.

PAGE 283: John Sias interview, Dec. 16, 1986.

PAGE 283: Brandon Stoddard interview, Feb. 4, 1988.

PAGE 283: Tom Murphy interview, Oct. 14, 1986.

PAGE 283: Barry Diller interview. Nov. 26, 1987.

PAGE 284: Merv Adelson interview, March 17, 1987.

PAGE 284: Lorne Michaels interview, Oct. 23, 1987.

PAGE 284: Sammy Davis, Jr., anecdote from Leonard H. Goldenson, *Beating the Odds,* (New York: Charles Scribner's Sons, 1991).

PAGE 284: Les Brown, *Television: The Business Behind The Box,* New York: Harcourt Brace Jovanovich, 1974.

PAGE 284: Robert MacNeil, *The People Machine: The Influence of Television on Amer-*

ican Politics (New York: Harper & Row, 1968).

PAGE 284: Newton N. Minow speech quoted in Erik Barnouw, *Tube of Plenty* (Oxford, England: Oxford University Press, 1975).

PAGE 285: Richard Salant appearance before panel, "Ethics And Broadcasting: Profits Versus Social Responsibility," sponsored by the Center for Communication, Inc., Feb. 18, 1987.

PAGE 285: Figures on the news documentary from Burton R. Benjamin, "The Documentary: An Endangered Species," a speech to the Annenberg School of Communication, University of Pennsylvania, Feb. 12, 1987.

PAGE 286: Roone Arledge interview, Jan. 15, 1987.

PAGE 286: John Sias interview, March 17, 1987.

PAGE 286: John Sias interview, June 6, 1987.

PAGE 286: David Burke interview, June 4, 1987.

PAGE 287: Paul Friedman interview, Feb. 11, 1987.

PAGE 287: Roone Arledge interview, Sept. 30, 1987.

PAGE 288: Peter Jennings interview, Jan. 12, 1987.

PAGE 288: Peter Jennings interview, April 4, 1987.

PAGE 288: Lynn Darling, "Country Boy Makes Pretty Good," *Esquire,* March 1986.

PAGE 288: Frank Reynolds anecdote from a family friend.

PAGE 289: For an account of Jennings's early years see Robert Goldberg and Gerald Jay Goldberg, *Anchors: Brokaw, Jennings, Rather and the Evening News,* (New York: Birch Lane Press, 1990).

PAGE 289: Bill Lord interview, April 3, 1987.

PAGE 290: David Burke interview, March 11, 1987.

PAGE 290: Tom Brokaw interview, Oct. 21, 1986.

PAGE 290: Tom Bettag interview, Feb. 18, 1987.

PAGE 290: Barry Dunsmore toast to Peter Jennings, Aug. 6, 1988.

PAGE 290: Peter Jennings interview, April 1, 1987.

PAGE 291: Av Westin memo, "Days of Penury, Days of Affluence," Feb. 12, 1987.

PAGE 291: Bud Rukeyser interview, April 1, 1987.

PAGE 291: Description of how News eased pain of layoffs from Richard Wald interview, Oct. 2, 1987.

PAGE 292: John Sias interview, March 17, 1987.

PAGE 292: David Burke interview, June 4, 1987.

PAGE 292: John Sias interview, March 17, 1987.

PAGE 292: John Sias interview. June 6, 1987.

PAGE 294: Roone Arledge interview, Sept. 30, 1987.

PAGE 294: David Burke interview, June 4, 1987.

PAGE 294: Jake Keever interview, June 29, 1988.

PAGE 294: Brandon Stoddard interview, Feb. 4, 1988.

PAGE 296: Tom Murphy interview, July 16, 1987.

PAGE 296: Tom Murphy interview, July 16, 1987.

PAGE 297: John Sias interview, June 6, 1987.

PAGE 297: Brandon Stoddard interview, Feb. 4, 1988.

PAGE 299: The account of this encounter with News has been pieced together from the following: David Burke interview, June 4, 1987; Tom Murphy interview, July 16, 1987; Roone Arledge interview, July 17, 1988; Dick Wald interview, Oct. 2, 1987; John Sias interview, June 6, 1987; Brandon Stoddard interview, Feb. 4, 1988; and Dan Burke interview, May 28, 1987.

PAGE 299: Dan Burke interview, Nov. 14, 1989.

PAGE 299: Patricia Matson interview, July 8, 1987.

PAGE 300: John Sias interview, June 6, 1987.

PAGE 300: Dick Wald interview, July 20, 1988.

PAGE 300: Roone P. Arledge memorandum to "All Hands, All Bureaus Including New York," May 18, 1987.

PAGE 300: Jake Keever interview, May 27, 1987.

PAGE 301: Brandon Stoddard interview, Feb. 4, 1988.

PAGE 301: Dan Burke interview, Dec. 20, 1988.

PAGE 301: John Sias interview, Sept. 28, 1988.

PAGE 301: Tom Murphy interview, July 16, 1987.

PAGE 302: Mark Mandala interview, Dec. 15, 1986.

PAGE 302: Estimated revenues from extra rating points based on Robert Butler presentation to NBC management meeting, March 23, 1987.

PAGE 302: Daytime dollars estimated by Robert Butler, presentation to NBC management meeting, March 23, 1987.

PAGE 303: A. C. Nielsen Media Research, "The 1987 Nielsen Report on Television."

PAGE 303: American viewing habits taken from: ABC Sales, "Network Television as Easy as ABC," 1987, and William Rubens speech to the American Film Institute Producers' Caucus for Women in Television, March 17, 1987.

PAGE 303: Cost per thousand figures from Mark Mandala interview, Dec. 15, 1986.

PAGE 304: Information on number of spots and average price from Robert S. Wallen interview, July 29, 1987.

PAGE 304: Jake Keever interview, July 22, 1987.

PAGE 305: Jake Keever interview, April 14, 1987.

PAGE 305: Audience composition numbers from Ray Warren interview, April 22, 1987.

PAGE 306: ABC Sales meeting, April 22, 1987.

PAGE 306: Ray Warren interview, April 22, 1987.

PAGE 307: ABC Prime Time, Schedule Rationale/Audience Estimates, Fall 1987, a brochure put out by ABC Sales in June of 1987.

PAGE 307: Tom Murphy interview, May 28, 1987.

PAGE 308: Marvin S. Mord speech, "The Transition to People Meter!" given to the National Association of Broadcasters, March 30, 1987.

PAGE 308: Jake Keever interview, April 22, 1987.

PAGE 309: Estimate on number of ad messages from Alison Leigh Cowan, "Ad Clutter: Even in Restrooms Now," *New York Times,* Feb. 18, 1988.

PAGE 309: Sarah Stiansen, "Non-Verbal Messages in Ads Gain New Importance," *Adweek*'s Marketing Week, Jan. 4, 1988.

PAGE 309: The shift in advertising spending from speech by Thomas F. Leahy, president CBS marketing division, to the Rochester Advertising Council 39th Annual Dinner, June 23, 1988.

PAGE 310: Unpublished internal ABC Sales document, "1987–88 Primetime Mini-Game Plan," June 17, 1987.

PAGE 310: Memorandum from Robert Blackmore and Donald Carswell to Robert Wright sketching NBC's upfront strategy, June 24, 1987.

PAGE 310: Speech by Madelyn Nagel to a woman's organization in which she quoted Chin, 1987.

PAGE 311: Elaine Chin interview, June 30, 1987.

PAGE 312: Irwin Gotlieb interview, March 13, 1989.

PAGE 313: Pete Tyrrell interview, June 16, 1987.

PAGE 313: Pete Tyrrell interview, Aug. 13, 1987.

PAGE 314: Pete Tyrrell interview, June 16, 1987.

PAGE 314: Jake Keever interview, June 30, 1987.

PAGE 314: Jake Keever interviews, June 27 and June 30, 1987.

PAGE 315: Jake Keever interview, July 8, 1987.

PAGE 316: Jake Keever and Dan Burke interview, July 8, 1987.

PAGE 316: Ray Warren interview, July 8, 1987.

PAGE 316: Jake Keever interview, July 14, 1987.

PAGE 316: Ray Warren interview, July 20, 1987.

PAGE 317: Upfront sales figures from George Cain interview, July 12, 1988.

PAGE 317: Breakout of ABC total advertising revenues from Robert S. Wallen interview, July 27, 1988.

PAGE 317: Average unit price increases from John Sias interview with Security Analysts, Hotel International, Oct. 26, 1987.

PAGE 317: Robert Blackmore interview, Aug. 21, 1987.

PAGE 318: Ray Warren interview, July 20, 1987.

PAGE 318: Pete Tyrrell interview, Aug. 13, 1987.

PAGE 318: Robert Blackmore and Donald Carswell memo to Robert Wright, NBC, June 24, 1987.

PAGE 318: A. C. Nielsen Media Research, "The 1987 Nielsen Report on Televison."

PAGE 319: Dan Burke interview, Oct. 30, 1987.

PAGE 319: Peter Jennings interview, Oct. 20, 1987.
PAGE 319: Peter Jennings interview, Oct. 20, 1987.
PAGE 319: Peter Jennings interview, April 1, 1987.
PAGE 320: Dan Rather interview, March 3, 1988.
PAGE 320: Peter Jennings interview, April 1, 1987.
PAGE 320: Peter Jennings interview, Oct. 20, 1987.
PAGE 320: Dan Burke interview, Oct. 30, 1987.
PAGE 321: "New Season: Race for 2d Place," *Variety,* Sept. 30, 1987.
PAGE 321: David Burke interview, Feb. 17, 1988.
PAGE 321: Roone Arledge interview, May 26, 1988.
PAGE 321: Dan Burke interview, June 3, 1988.
PAGE 321: Dan Burke interview, Dec. 20, 1988.
PAGE 321: Interview with Tom Murphy on the public trust from *AFTRA,* 50th Anniversary issue, July 1987; and Tom Murphy interview, July 16, 1987.

CHAPTER 11

PAGE 323: Jack Welch interview, Jan. 13, 1987.
PAGE 324: Martin Pompadur interview, Nov. 18, 1987.
PAGE 324: Larry Tisch interview, Jan. 27, 1987.
PAGE 324: Peter Lund interview, March 6, 1987.
PAGE 324: Bob Walsh interview, Dec. 15, 1987.
PAGE 324: J. B. Holston III interview, April 14, 1987.
PAGE 325: Bob Wright interview, April 7, 1989.
PAGE 325: Thomas S. Rogers interview, Jan. 15, 1988.
PAGE 325: Bob Wright interview, Oct. 29, 1987.
PAGE 325: Bob Wright remarks to NBC management meeting in Boca Raton, Fla., March 23, 1987.
PAGE 326: Jack Welch address to GE's annual meeting of shareholders, Montgomery, Ala., April 22, 1987.
PAGE 326: Jack Welch interview, July 1, 1987.
PAGE 327: Transcript and tape of Jack Welch speech to NBC management meeting, March 22, 1987.
PAGE 327: Warren Littlefield interview, April 29, 1987.
PAGE 327: Grant Tinker interview, May 18, 1987.
PAGE 327: Sparky Anderson's managerial technique described in Murray Chass, "Tigers are Hearing the Right Words." *New York Times,* Aug. 17, 1988.
PAGE 327: Robert Daly interview, Nov. 24, 1987.
PAGE 328: Steve Ross interview, Feb. 3, 1988.
PAGE 328: Steve Ross interview, Feb. 3, 1988.
PAGE 328: Bob Wright interview, Sept. 29, 1988.
PAGE 328: Jack Welch interview, Dec. 13, 1989.
PAGE 328: Jack Welch interview, May 24, 1989.
PAGE 329: Transcript of Robert Wright presentation to annual NBC management committee meeting, March 23, 1987.
PAGE 329: Transcript of Robert Wright closing remarks to the Annual NBC management meeting, March 24, 1987.
PAGE 329: Robert Butler presentation to NBC management meeting, March 23, 1987.
PAGE 329: Tom Ross interview, April 1, 1987, and Tom Ross confidential memo to Larry Grossman, April 13, 1987.
PAGE 329: Bob Wright interview, May 15, 1987.
PAGE 330: Jack Welch interview, July 1, 1987.

CHAPTER 12

PAGE 331: Larry Tisch breakfast with author, March 10, 1987.
PAGE 332: Dan Rather, "From Murrow to Mediocrity?" *New York Times* op-ed page, March 10, 1987.
PAGE 332: Tom Shales, "Darkening Skies at CBS News," *Washington Post,* March 10, 1987.
PAGE 333: A. M. Sperber, *Murrow: His Life and Times* (New York: Freundlich Books, 1986).
PAGE 334: Larry Tisch telephone conversation with Howard Stringer witnessed by author, March 10, 1987.
PAGE 334: CBS News budget cuts from Fred Meyer interview, March 7, 1988.

PAGE 335: Tom Brokaw interview, April 20, 1987, and Tom Brokaw, *Washington Post* op-ed page, April 19, 1987.

PAGE 335: Richard Cohen interview, Nov. 18, 1987.

PAGE 336: Dan Rather interview, March 3, 1968.

PAGE 336: Dan Rather interview, Feb. 18, 1987.

PAGE 336: Dan Rather interview, March 10, 1987.

PAGE 337: Richard Cohen interview, Nov. 18, 1987.

PAGE 337: Dan Rather interview, March 10, 1987.

PAGE 337: Andrew Heyward interview, March 10, 1987.

PAGE 338: Eric Ober interview, March 17, 1987.

PAGE 338: Peter J. Boyer, "Sadness Turns to Anger Over CBS Dismissals," *New York Times,* March 9, 1987.

PAGE 339: Larry Tisch interview, March 10, 1987.

PAGE 339: Larry A. Tisch memorandum to the CBS news division, March 9, 1987.

CHAPTER 13

PAGE 340: John Stewart interview, March 13, 1987.

PAGE 341: Bud Rukeyser interview, May 11, 1987.

PAGE 341: James P. Baughman interview, Nov. 17, 1987.

PAGE 341: John Stewart interview, March 2, 1987.

PAGE 341: Larry Grossman interview, April 6, 1987.

PAGE 341: Larry Grossman interview, April 1, 1987.

PAGE 341: Larry Grossman interview, May 5, 1987.

PAGE 342: Larry Grossman memo to Robert Wright, April 2, 1987.

PAGE 342: Larry Grossman interview, April 6, 1987.

PAGE 342: Larry Grossman interview, May 5, 1987.

PAGE 345: Bob Wright interview, May 15, 1987.

PAGE 345: Three-volume McKinsey & Co. report to NBC News, June 1987.

PAGE 346: Larry Grossman memorandum to "All Network News Bureaus and Staff," June 9, 1987.

PAGE 346: Larry Grossman interview, July 29, 1987.

PAGE 346: Tom Brokaw interview, Oct. 13, 1987.

PAGE 347: Garrick Utley interview, June 24, 1987.

PAGE 347: Tom Brokaw interview, Oct. 13, 1987.

PAGE 347: Jack Welch interview, July 1, 1987.

PAGE 347: Larry Tisch interview, July 29, 1987.

PAGE 347: Larry Grossman interview, May 5, 1987.

CHAPTER 14

PAGE 349: Robert Daly interview, Nov. 24, 1987.

PAGE 350: Jay Kriegel interview, Dec. 15, 1987.

PAGE 350: Keynote speech by Francis T. Vincent, Jr., to the National Association of Television Program Executives, New Orleans, Jan. 22, 1987.

CHAPTER 15

PAGE 352: Bud Rukeyser interview, Sept. 25, 1987.

PAGE 352: Jack Welch interview, April 15, 1988.

PAGE 352: Brandon Tartikoff interview, April 29, 1987.

PAGE 352: Bob Wright interview, Sept. 29, 1988.

PAGE 354: Brandon Tartikoff interview, April 30, 1987.

PAGE 355: Steven Bochco interview, Aug. 20, 1987.

PAGE 355: Brandon Tartikoff press conference, May 13, 1987.

PAGE 355: Brandon Tartikoff interview, April 30, 1987.

PAGE 355: Brandon Stoddard interview, Feb. 4, 1988.

PAGE 355: Michael Dann interview, June 29, 1988.

PAGE 356: Brandon Tartikoff press conference, July 25, 1987.

PAGE 356: Brandon Tartikoff presentation to advertisers for NBC 1987–88 program season, Waldorf Astoria Hotel, May 13, 1987.

PAGE 356: Les Brown, *Television: The Business Behind the Box* (New York: Harcourt Brace Jovanovich, 1971).

PAGE 357: Bob Wright interview, May 15, 1987.

PAGE 357: Brandon Tartikoff interview, Feb. 11, 1988.

PAGE 357: Brandon Tartikoff interview, Aug. 20, 1987.

PAGE 357: Brandon Tartikoff interview, April 27, 1987.

PAGE 357: Jeff Sagansky interview, Nov. 25, 1987.

PAGE 357: Brandon Tartikoff interview, Aug. 20, 1987.

PAGE 358: Brandon Tartikoff interview, Jan. 14, 1987.

PAGE 358: I borrow from David Ansen of *Newsweek,* who artfully described David Lynch's ABC series, *Twin Peaks,* as a show in which the "mannerisms threaten to overwhelm the matter." *Newsweek,* June 4, 1990.

PAGE 359: Jeff Sagansky interview, Nov. 25, 1987.

PAGE 359: Facts on the failure rate of shows from following sources: Gene Jankowski interview, Nov. 13, 1986; interview with Earle H. "Kim" LeMasters III, quoted in Kevin Goldman story in *Wall Street Journal,* March 21, 1990; and a one-hour film, *Making Television: Inside CBS.*

PAGE 359: Letter from Maurie Goodman, vice president of NBC's Broadcast Standards, to Gary David Goldberg, Aug. 12, 1987.

PAGE 359: Steven Bochco interview, Aug. 20, 1987.

PAGE 359: Brandon Tartikoff interview, Aug. 20, 1987.

PAGE 360: Brandon Tartikoff interview, Nov. 23, 1987.

PAGE 361: Brandon Tartikoff interview, Feb. 11, 1988.

PAGE 361: Grant Tinker interview, Nov. 25, 1987.

PAGE 361: Bruce Paltrow interview, Sept. 29, 1987.

PAGE 361: Perry Simon interview, Sept. 28, 1987.

PAGE 361: Bruce Paltrow interview, Oct. 26, 1987.

PAGE 362: Aaron Spelling interviews, Feb. 11, 1988, and May 3, 1988.

PAGE 363: Candy Spelling interview, May 3, 1988.

PAGE 363: Aaron Spelling interview, May 3, 1988.

PAGE 363: Aaron Spelling interview, Feb. 11, 1988.

PAGE 364: Brandon Tartikoff interview, Feb. 11, 1988.

PAGE 364: Brandon Tartikoff interview, Nov. 23, 1987.

PAGE 365: Spelling's first visit to NBC described in Lynn Hirschberg, "The Man Who Turns on America," *Rolling Stone,* Oct. 22, 1987.

PAGE 365: Aaron Spelling interview, Feb. 11, 1988.

PAGE 365: Warren Littlefield recalled Tartikoff's remarks and staff reaction to *Nightingales* in interview, Nov. 23, 1987.

CHAPTER 16

PAGE 367: Warren Littlefield interview, Nov. 23, 1987.

PAGE 367: CBS Affiliate Relations staff meeting, Nov. 3, 1987.

PAGE 367: Harry Waters and Betsy Carter "Affiliates' Lib," *Newsweek,* June 7, 1976.

PAGE 367: I. Martin Pompadur interview, Nov. 13, 1987.

PAGE 368: CBS 1986 preemption data from David Olmstead interview, Jan. 2, 1988.

PAGE 368: CBS affiliate clearance figures from Tony Malara presentation to CBS affiliate convention, May 20, 1987.

PAGE 368: Scott Michaels interview, March 17, 1987.

PAGE 368: Viacom profit margins from Frank Biondi interview, Feb. 2, 1988.

PAGE 369: Jeffrey B. McIntyre interview, July 8, 1987.

PAGE 369: Fred Friendly interview, Feb. 24, 1987.

PAGE 369: Phil Jones interview, Sept. 22, 1987.

PAGE 370: The value of network adjacencies to KCTV's late-night schedule from Patrick W. North interview, Sept. 23, 1987.

PAGE 370: Phil Jones interview, Sept. 22, 1987.

PAGE 371: Patrick W. North interview, Sept. 23, 1987.

PAGE 371: The cost and value of KCTV's late-night schedule from Phil Jones interview, Sept. 23, 1987.

PAGE 371: CBS presentation to its affiliates regarding Billy Graham specials, March 1988 regional affiliate meeting.

PAGE 371: Economics of Billy Graham specials and local news from Patrick W. North interview, Sept. 22, 1987.

PAGE 371: KCTV revenues and costs from Phil Jones interview, Sept. 23, 1987.

PAGE 372: Patrick W. North interview, Sept. 22, 1987.

PAGE 372: Information about KCTV clearances for CBS from Jeffrey B. McIntyre interview, Feb. 16, 1988.

PAGE 372: David Adams interview, Dec. 12, 1986.

PAGE 372: Phil Jones interview, Sept. 23, 1987.

CHAPTER 17

PAGE 375: Barry Diller interview, Nov. 26, 1987.

PAGE 377: Laurence Hyams presentation to ABC Sales staff meeting, Nov. 10, 1987.

PAGE 377: Aaron Spelling interview, Feb. 11, 1988.

PAGE 377: A. C. Nielsen Media Research reports for the 1976–77 and 1986–87 television seasons.

PAGE 377: Brandon Tartikoff speech to the Association of National Advertisers, Oct. 19, 1987.

PAGE 377: ABC Sales staff meeting, Nov. 10, 1987.

PAGE 378: Jake Keever interview, Jan. 12, 1988.

PAGE 378: ABC make goods losses in fall of 1987 from George Cain interview, Jan. 6, 1988.

PAGE 378: AM and FM Radio Chart printed in *Newsweek,* Dec. 19, 1988, from Radar Data, Statistical Research, Inc.

PAGE 378: Dan Burke interview, Nov. 12, 1987.

PAGE 378: John Sias interview, Sept. 28, 1988.

PAGE 378: Tom Murphy interview, Nov. 12, 1987.

PAGE 379: Text of Brandon Tartikoff press conference, Oct. 26, 1987.

PAGE 379: Tom Murphy interview, Oct. 22, 1987.

PAGE 379: ABC press release announcing Steven Bochco contract, Nov. 10, 1987.

PAGE 379: Steven Bochco interview, Nov. 26, 1987.

PAGE 379: Bruce Paltrow interview, Dec. 15, 1987.

PAGE 380: Larry Tisch interview, Nov. 30, 1987.

PAGE 380: Brandon Tartikoff interview, Nov. 23, 1987.

PAGE 381: John Sias interview, Sept. 28, 1988.

PAGE 381: Dan Burke interview, Jan. 19, 1988.

PAGE 381: David Burke interview, Feb. 17, 1988.

PAGE 381: Dan Burke interview, June 3, 1988.

PAGE 381: David Burke interview, Nov. 18, 1987.

PAGE 382: Paul Friedman interview, Feb. 11, 1987.

PAGE 382: Peter Jennings interview, Oct. 20, 1987.

PAGE 382: Peter Jennings interview, Oct. 20, 1987.

PAGE 383: Peter Jennings interview, Dec. 30, 1987.

PAGE 383: Paul Friedman interview, Feb. 18, 1988.

PAGE 383: Roone Arledge interview, May 26, 1988.

PAGE 384: David Burke on Center for Communications panel on the future of news, sponsored by the Gannett Center, March 1, 1988.

PAGE 384: David Burke interview, Nov. 18, 1987.

PAGE 384: David Burke interview, July 6, 1988.

PAGE 385: Dan Burke interview, Jan. 19, 1988.

PAGE 385: Mimi Gurbst interview, March 31, 1988.

PAGE 385: Dan Burke interview, Jan. 19, 1988.

PAGE 385: Peter Lund interview, Dec. 16, 1987.

PAGE 386: Michael Fuchs interview, Dec. 13, 1987.

PAGE 386: John Sias interview, Sept. 28, 1988.

PAGE 386: Dan Burke interview, Dec. 20, 1988.

PAGE 386: Cap Cities/ABC Annual Report, 1987.

PAGE 386: ABC's 1987 profits from Tom Murphy interview, April 7, 1989.

PAGE 387: Michael W. Miller and Mathew Winkler, "A Former Trader Aims to Hook Wall Street on—and to—His Data," *Wall Street Journal,* Sept. 22, 1988; and L. J. Davis, "Television's Real-Life Cable Baron," *New York Times Magazine,* Dec. 2, 1990.

PAGE 387: Jack Welch interview, April 15, 1988.

PAGE 387: ABC Video Enterprises, Inc., Annual Report, Feb. 1988 and Capital Cities/ABC Annual Report, 1987.

PAGE 387: Herb Granath interview, Jan. 19, 1988.

PAGE 387: Dan Burke interview, Oct. 30, 1987.

PAGE 388: Herb Granath interview, Feb. 24, 1988.

PAGE 388: Young & Rubicam *Press Notes,* Feb. 1, 1988.

PAGE 388: Martin Davis interviews, Nov. 4, 1987 and April 30, 1990.

PAGE 388: Robert Daly interview, Nov. 24, 1987.

PAGE 389: Warren Buffett interview, March 8, 1988.

PAGE 389: Tom Murphy interview, April 6, 1988.

PAGE 389: Michael Eisner interview, May 9, 1988.

CHAPTER 18

PAGE 391: Bob Wright interview, Feb. 23, 1990.

PAGE 392: RCA employment reductions based on interview with Edward L. Scanlon, RCA's senior vice president for Personnel, Dec. 1, 1987.

PAGE 392: Tom Brokaw interview, Oct. 13, 1987.

PAGE 392: Larry Grossman interview, July 29, 1987.

PAGE 392: Larry Grossman interview, Jan. 22, 1989.

PAGE 392: Text of Larry Grossman news conference, July 26, 1987.

PAGE 393: Roy Rowan, "ABC Covers Itself," *Fortune,* Nov. 17, 1980; and A. M. Sperber, *Murrow: His Life and His Times* (New York: Freundlich Books, 1986), p. 347.

PAGE 393: Jack Welch interview, Dec. 13, 1989.

PAGE 394: Robert Wright speech to the Cable Television Administration & Marketing Society in San Francisco, Aug. 17, 1987.

PAGE 394: Material on NBC revenues from Al Barber interview, April 25, 1988, and transcript of Robert Butler budget presentation to the March 23, 1987, NBC management meeting.

PAGE 394: Jack Welch interview, July 1, 1987.

PAGE 394: Bob Butler interviews, Sept. 21, 1987, and Aug. 12, 1987.

PAGE 395: Grant Tinker interview, March 2, 1989.

PAGE 395: Bob Wright interview, Oct. 29, 1987.

PAGE 395: Al Barber interview, Nov. 4, 1987.

PAGE 395: Al Barber interview, Nov. 4, 1987.

PAGE 395: Al Barber interview, Nov. 10, 1987.

PAGE 396: Ed Scanlon interviews, Dec. 1, 1987, and Jan. 27, 1988.

PAGE 396: Grant Tinker interview, March 2, 1989.

PAGE 396: Ed Scanlon interview, Aug. 11, 1988.

PAGE 396: Bob Wright letter to *New York Times,* Sept. 26, 1987.

PAGE 396: Bob Wright interview, Oct. 29, 1987.

PAGE 397: Jack Welch interview, Dec. 16, 1987.

PAGE 397: Bob Wright reviews his Phoenix speech and charts in a Feb. 3, 1988, interview.

PAGE 397: Jack Welch interview, Dec. 16, 1987.

PAGE 397: Bob Walsh interview, Dec. 15, 1987.

PAGE 398: Bob Walsh interview, Dec. 15, 1987.

PAGE 398: Jack Welch interview, Dec. 16, 1987.

PAGE 398: Larry Grossman interview, Oct. 19, 1987.

PAGE 398: Bud Rukeyser interview, Oct. 19, 1987.

PAGE 398: Jack Welch interview, Dec. 16, 1987.

PAGE 399: Ed Scanlon interview, Dec. 1, 1987.

PAGE 399: Jack Welch interview, July 1, 1987.

PAGE 399: Noel M. Tichy, "Transformational Leadership," a 1985 monologue and lecture distributed at GE's Crotonsville training center.

PAGE 400: James P. Baughman interview, Nov. 17, 1987.

PAGE 400: Jack Welch interview, Dec. 16, 1987.

PAGE 400: Michael Fuchs interview, Dec. 13, 1987.

PAGE 400: Ted Turner interview, April 7, 1988.

PAGE 401: Bob Wright on a panel discussion, "Strategic Outlook of the Communications Industries," sponsored by the Center for Communications, April 25, 1988.

PAGE 401: Tom Rogers interview, Jan. 15, 1988.

PAGE 401: Bob Wright interview, Oct. 29, 1987.

PAGE 402: Bob Wright interview, Feb. 3, 1988.

PAGE 402: Bob Walsh interview, Dec. 15, 1987.

PAGE 402: Bud Rukeyser interview, Sept. 25, 1987.

PAGE 402: Bud Rukeyser interview, Oct. 28, 1987.

PAGE 403: Bud Rukeyser interview, Oct. 27, 1987.

PAGE 403: Bud Rukeyser interview, Nov. 6, 1987.

PAGE 404: Bob Wright interview, March 31, 1988.

PAGE 404: Larry Grossman interview, Dec. 3, 1987.

PAGE 405: Bud Rukeyser interview, Dec. 1, 1987.

PAGE 405: Larry Grossman "News Division Review," NBC News document, Dec. 11, 1987.

PAGE 406: Larry Grossman interview, Feb. 26, 1988.

PAGE 406: Bob Wright interview, Feb. 3, 1988.

PAGE 406: Bob Wright interview, March 31, 1988.

PAGE 406: Larry Grossman interview, Dec. 3, 1987.

PAGE 407: Larry Grossman interview, April 25, 1988.

PAGE 407: Tom Brokaw interview, March 1, 1988.

PAGE 407: Thornton Bradshaw interview, Oct. 6, 1986.

PAGE 408: Larry Grossman interviews, Aug. 10, 1988, and Nov. 30, 1989.

PAGE 408: Tom Brokaw interview, May 22, 1988.

PAGE 408: Larry Grossman interview, Dec. 8, 1988.

PAGE 408: Tom Brokaw interview, Nov. 30, 1988.

PAGE 409: Larry Grossman interview, Dec. 8, 1988.

PAGE 409: Tom Ross interview, Aug. 10, 1988.

PAGE 409: Tom Ross interview, Aug. 10, 1988.

PAGE 409: Ed Scanlon interview, Jan. 27, 1989.

PAGE 409: Tom Ross interview, Aug. 10, 1988.

PAGE 410: Jack Welch statement on 1987 earnings contained in GE booklet, "Globalization: Perspective from the Operating Managers Meeting," Jan. 5–6, 1988.

PAGE 410: Ed Scanlon interview, Jan. 27, 1988.

PAGE 410: Lilly Tartikoff interview, March 17, 1988.

PAGE 410: Jack Welch interview, Dec. 16, 1987.

PAGE 411: Al Barber interview, Nov. 4, 1987.

PAGE 411: Al Barber interview, Nov. 10, 1987.

PAGE 411: Al Barber interview, Nov. 10, 1987.

PAGE 411: Natalie P. Hunter interview, Jan. 6, 1988.

PAGE 411: Eugene S. Andrews interview about Crotonsville, Nov. 17, 1987.

PAGE 411: Luncheon interview between author and GE employees at Crotonsville, Nov. 17, 1987.

PAGE 412: Bud Rukeyser interview, Dec. 22, 1987.

PAGE 412: Bob Wright press conference, July 27, 1987.

PAGE 412: Jack Hilton, *How to Meet the Press: A Survival Guide,* (New York: Dodd, Mead & Co., 1987).

PAGE 412: Bob Wright speech to IRTS luncheon, Waldorf Astoria, Oct. 28, 1987.

PAGE 412: NBC costs from Bob Butler interview, Dec. 8, 1986.

PAGE 412: Robert C. Wright press conference, Jan. 5, 1988, Century Plaza Hotel, Los Angeles.

PAGE 413: Grant Tinker interview, March 15, 1988.

PAGE 413: Bud Rukeyser interview, Jan. 24, 1988.

CHAPTER 19

PAGE 414: CBS press release, Nov. 26, 1984.

PAGE 415: Dennis Kneale, "Regional Sports Cable Networks Score Big Gains," *Wall Street Journal,* Sept. 24, 1990.

PAGE 416: Peter Lund interview, Dec. 16, 1987.

PAGE 416: Peter Lund interview, March 16, 1987.

PAGE 417: Peter Lund interview, Dec. 16, 1987.

PAGE 417: Jay Kriegel interview, Dec. 15, 1987.

PAGE 417: Gene Jankowski interview, July 15, 1987.

PAGE 417: Andrew Heyward interview, Sept. 29, 1987.

PAGE 418: David Burke interview, Sept. 9, 1988.

PAGE 418: Phil Jones interview, Sept. 22, 1987.

PAGE 418: Phil Jones interview, May 19, 1987.

PAGE 419: Lorne Michaels interviews, Jan. 21, 1988, and May 31, 1990; incident confirmed by one other participant.

PAGE 419: Larry Tisch interview, Nov. 30, 1987.

PAGE 419: Larry Tisch interview, July 29, 1987.

PAGE 419: Howard Stringer interview, Oct. 7, 1987.

PAGE 419: Tom Murphy interview, April 7, 1989.

PAGE 419: Jay Kriegel interview, Dec. 15, 1987.

PAGE 420: Larry A. Tisch memo to employees in which he hailed CBS News as "the most distinguishing feature of the television network," Oct. 16, 1987.

PAGE 420: Jeff Sagansky interview, Nov. 25, 1987.

PAGE 420: Howard Stringer interview, June 30, 1987.

PAGE 421: Tom Bettag interview, Sept. 29, 1987.

PAGE 421: Jonathan Alter, "Dan Rather's Struggle," *Newsweek,* Aug. 24, 1987.

PAGE 422: Tom Bettag memo to the file, Sept. 12, 1987, and interview, Oct. 31, 1990.

PAGE 423: Dan Rather interview, Feb. 18, 1987.

PAGE 423: Peter J. Boyer, "CBS Explains 'Evening News' Incident," *New York Times,* Sept. 14, 1987.

PAGE 423: Tom Bettag interview, Sept. 29, 1987; Dan Rather interview, June 4, 1990.

PAGE 423: Tom Bettag interview, Sept. 29, 1987.

PAGE 424: Andrew Heyward interview, Sept. 29, 1987.

PAGE 424: Dan Rather interview, April 22, 1986.

PAGE 424: Howard Stringer interview, Dec. 2, 1989.

PAGE 424: Tom Bettag interview, Sept. 29, 1987.

PAGE 424: Tom Bettag interview, Feb. 23, 1988.

PAGE 425: Larry Tisch interview, Nov. 30, 1987.

PAGE 425: Jay Kriegel interview, Sept. 28, 1987.

PAGE 425: Dan Rather interview, April 22, 1988.

PAGE 425: Dan Rather interview, March 3, 1988.

PAGE 426: Dan Rather, *The Camera Never Blinks: Adventures of a TV Journalist,* (New York: William Morrow & Co., 1977).

PAGE 426: Dan Rather interview, March 3, 1988.

PAGE 426: David Poltrack interview, Aug. 12, 1987.

PAGE 427: Peter W. Barnes, "CBS Directors Expected to Meet to Decide on Selling All or Part of Record Division," *Wall Street Journal,* Sept. 11, 1987.

PAGE 427: CBS statement, Sept. 11, 1987.

PAGE 427: William Paley interview, Nov. 12, 1987.

PAGE 427: For a superb account of the sale see Peter J. Boyer, "What a Romance! Sony and CBS Records," *New York Times Magazine,* Sept. 18, 1988.

PAGE 428: William Paley interview, Nov. 12, 1987.

PAGE 428: Grant Tinker interview, Nov. 25, 1987, and Robert Daly interview, Nov. 24, 1987.

PAGE 428: Jeff Sagansky interview, Nov. 25, 1987.

PAGE 428: Larry Tisch interview, Nov. 30, 1987.

PAGE 429: For a good synopsis of Bochco's work see Harry F. Waters, "Lust for Law," *Newsweek,* Nov. 16, 1987.

PAGE 429: Robert Batscha interview, Jan. 20, 1988.

PAGE 430: William Paley interview, Nov. 12, 1987; Steven Bochco interview, Nov. 26, 1987; and Larry Tisch interview, Nov. 30, 1987.

PAGE 430: Steven Bochco interview, Nov. 26, 1987.

PAGE 431: Grant Tinker interview, Nov. 25, 1987.

PAGE 431: Brandon Tartikoff interviews, Oct. 28, 1987, and Nov. 23, 1987.

PAGE 432: Howard Stringer interviews, Jan. 8, 1988, and Feb. 29, 1988; Steve Warner interview, Dec. 8, 1987.

PAGE 432: Warren Littlefield interview, Nov. 23, 1987.

PAGE 432: Robert Harris interview, Nov. 24, 1987; Larry Tisch interview, Nov. 30, 1987.

PAGE 433: Kim LeMasters interview, March 15, 1988.

PAGE 433: Grant Tinker interview, March 15, 1988.

PAGE 433: Michael Eisner interview, May 9, 1988.

PAGE 433: Howard Stringer interviews, Dec. 4, 1987, and Jan. 8, 1988.

PAGE 433: Brandon Tartikoff interview, Nov. 23, 1987.

PAGE 434: Kim LeMasters interview, March 15, 1988.

PAGE 434: CBS press release announcing appointment of Jay L. Kriegel, Dec. 3, 1987.

PAGE 434: Tom Tisch interview, Feb. 2, 1988.

PAGE 434: Jay Kriegel interview, Dec. 15, 1987.

PAGE 434: Howard Stringer interview, July 22, 1988.

PAGE 434: Jay Kriegel interview, Feb. 17, 1988.

PAGE 435: Steven Bochco interview, Nov. 26, 1987.

PAGE 435: Larry Tisch interview, Nov. 30, 1987.

PAGE 435: Larry Tisch letter to *New York,* Dec. 7, 1987.

PAGE 436: Larry Tisch interview, Nov. 30, 1987.

PAGE 437: CBS proxy statement, April 7, 1988.

PAGE 437: Larry Tisch interview, Nov. 30, 1987.

PAGE 437: Cost savings taken from CBS Form 10-K filing with the SEC, Dec. 31, 1987, and from Fred Meyer interview, March 7, 1988.

PAGE 437: CBS 1987 Annual Report, and CBS Form 10-K filing with the SEC, Dec. 31, 1987.

PAGE 437: Larry Tisch interview, Nov. 30, 1987.

PAGE 437: Larry Tisch interview, March 1, 1988.

PAGE 437: CBS's conversion from optimism to skepticism was conveyed in "Network Television in Transition," a report from the CBS Broadcast Group, Aug. 1987.

PAGE 437: Ed Grebow interview, March 29, 1988.

PAGE 438: Larry Tisch interview, Nov. 30, 1987.

PAGE 438: Fred Meyer interview, Oct. 9, 1987.

PAGE 438: Fred Meyer interview, March 7, 1988.

PAGE 439: David Lieberman, *Newsweek,* Feb. 22, 1988.

PAGE 439: Howard Stringer interview, Dec. 4, 1987.

PAGE 439: Tom Tisch interview, Feb. 2, 1988.

PAGE 439: Larry Tisch interview, May 5, 1988.

PAGE 440: Larry Tisch speech before the Administrative Conference of the United States, Washington, D.C., Nov. 4, 1987.

PAGE 440: Donald D. Weir, Jr., interview, April 13, 1988.

PAGE 440: Roswell Gilpatric interview, Feb. 8, 1988.

PAGE 442: CBS board meeting minutes, Jan. 13, 1988.

PAGE 442: Larry Tisch interview, Aug. 10, 1988.

PAGE 442: Larry Tisch interview, March 1, 1988.

PAGE 443: Larry Tisch interview, Aug. 10, 1988.

PAGE 443: Frank Thomas interview, Feb. 23, 1988.

PAGE 443: Phil Jones interview, Feb. 12, 1988.

PAGE 444: Larry Tisch interview, March 1, 1988.

PAGE 444: Larry Tisch interview, March 1, 1988.

PAGE 444: Phil Jones interview, Feb. 12, 1988.

CHAPTER 20

PAGE 446: Perry Simon interview, Sept. 17, 1987.

PAGE 446: Cost figures for *Tattinger's* from Jim Finnerty, Sr., interview, Nov. 9, 1987.

PAGE 447: Stephen Collins interview, Oct. 26, 1987.

PAGE 449: Jim Finnerty, Sr., interview, Nov. 9, 1987.

PAGE 449: Bruce Paltrow and Perry Simon interviews, Nov. 2, 1987.

PAGE 449: Brandon Tartikoff interview, Nov. 23, 1987.

PAGE 449: Bruce Paltrow interviews, Dec. 15 and 22, 1987.

PAGE 449: Bruce Paltrow interview, Dec. 1, 1987.

PAGE 449: Bruce Paltrow interview, Jan. 11, 1988.

PAGE 449: Bruce Paltrow interview, Jan. 29, 1988.

PAGE 450: Brandon Tartikoff interview, Feb. 11, 1988.

PAGE 450: Bruce Paltrow interview, Jan. 22, 1988, and Feb. 9, 1988.

PAGE 450: Tom Shales, "Dead End," *Washington Post,* March 4, 1988.

PAGE 451: Warren Littlefield interview, Feb. 10, 1988.

PAGE 451: Warren Littlefield interview, May 6, 1988.

PAGE 452: Brandon Tartikoff interview, Feb. 11, 1988.

PAGE 452: Aaron Spelling interview, March 17, 1988.

PAGE 452: Aaron Spelling interview, Feb. 11, 1988.

PAGE 452: Perry Simon interview, Jan. 4, 1988.

PAGE 452: Perry Simon interview, Feb. 10, 1988.

PAGE 452: Aaron Spelling interview, Feb. 11, 1988.

PAGE 453: Ilene Chaiken interview, May 5, 1988.

PAGE 453: Candy Spelling interview, May 3, 1988.

PAGE 454: Casting session in Aaron Spelling's office, March 16, 1988.

PAGE 454: Account of final NBC casting session from Ilene Chaiken interview, April 4, 1988.

PAGE 454: NBC press release announcing *Nightingales,* April 7, 1988.

PAGE 454: Warren Littlefield interview, March 17, 1988.

PAGE 455: Perry Simon interview, March 15, 1988.

PAGE 455: Brandon Tartikoff interview, Feb. 11, 1988.

PAGE 455: Bruce Paltrow interview, May 5, 1988.

PAGE 456: Aaron Spelling interview, May 3, 1988.

CHAPTER 21

PAGE 457: NBC's *Valerie,* April 27, 1987.

PAGE 458: Larry Grossman interview, Feb. 26, 1988.

PAGE 459: Information about early docudramas on CBS from Shad Northshield interview, Oct. 7, 1986.

PAGE 459: NBC News press release, Jan. 6, 1988.

PAGE 459: Dennis Kneale, "TV Is Going Tabloid As Shows Seek Sleaze and Find Profits, Too," *Wall Street Journal,* May 18, 1988.

PAGE 460: Neil Postman, *The Disappearance of Childhood* (New York: Laurel Books, 1982).

CHAPTER 22

PAGE 461: A. C. Nielsen Media Research, "The 1989 Nielsen Report on Television"; and "Cable TV Facts 1988," Cable Television Advertising Bureau, Spring 1988.

PAGE 462: Mike Dann interview, June 29, 1988.

PAGE 462: Mike Dann interview, June 29, 1988.

PAGE 463: John Sias interview, Nov. 11, 1987.

PAGE 463: Michael Eisner interview, May 9, 1988.

PAGE 463: Brandon Stoddard's miscalculation on the Disney deal was confirmed by his ally, Marc Cohen, who said, "Brandon was wrong on the option date." Marc Cohen interview, May 31, 1988.

PAGE 463: Brandon Stoddard press conference transcript, Jan. 9, 1988.

PAGE 463: Dan Burke interview, June 3, 1988.

PAGE 463: John Sias interview, Sept. 28, 1988.

PAGE 464: Tom Murphy interview, April 6, 1988.

PAGE 464: ABC press release, Feb. 2, 1988.

PAGE 464: Mike Dann interview, June 29, 1988.

PAGE 464: Tom Murphy interview, April 6, 1988.

PAGE 464: Mike Mallardi interview, April 6, 1988.

PAGE 465: Ted Koppel's contract terms from David Burke interview, July 6, 1988, and Ted Koppel interview, July 20, 1988.

PAGE 465: Peter Jennings interview, Feb. 18, 1988.

PAGE 465: Paul Friedman interview, Feb. 18, 1988.

PAGE 465: David Burke interview, Feb. 17, 1988.

PAGE 465: George Cain interview, June 22, 1988.

PAGE 465: ABC Olympics financial results from Tom Murphy interview, April 6, 1988.

PAGE 466: Details on what ABC Sales spent in Calgary from Robert S. Wallen interview, March 11, 1988.

PAGE 466: John Helyar and Laura Landro, "Turner Plan for Cable Network Draws Large Measure of Skepticism," *Wall Street Journal,* March 30, 1988.

PAGE 466: Dan Burke interview, June 3, 1988.

PAGE 467: Dan Burke interview, Dec. 20, 1988.

PAGE 467: Text of Thomas Murphy remarks to the Cap Cities/ABC annual shareholders meeting in Chicago, May 19, 1988.

PAGE 467: "ABC-TV to Affiliates: Use Us or Lose Us," *Broadcasting,* June 13, 1988.

PAGE 467: David Burke interview, July 6, 1988.

PAGE 468: Joel Segal meeting at McCann-Erickson attended by author, June 6, 1988.

PAGE 469: ABC Research report, "Primetime Schedule Rationale, 1988–89 Season," June 1988.

PAGE 469: Jake Keever interview, April 19, 1988.

PAGE 469: Randall Rothenberg, "Big Sales of Network Times Prove a Disturbing Point," *New York Times,* July 29, 1988.

PAGE 469: Marketing and advertising figures from speech by Thomas F. Leahy, president CBS marketing division, to the Rochester Advertising Council, June 23, 1988.

PAGE 470: Dan Burke interview, June 3, 1988.

PAGE 470: ABC's 1987 upfront sales figures from George Cain interview, July 12, 1988.

PAGE 470: Joel Segal interview, July 11, 1988.

PAGE 470: Robert S. Wallen interview, July 27, 1988.

PAGE 470: Estimate on what ABC hoped to sell in 1988 upfront from Robert S. Wallen interview, July 27, 1988.

PAGE 471: Irving A. Gross interview, July 27, 1988.

PAGE 471: Draft of "NBC Values Statement," Feb. 4, 1988.

PAGE 471: President's council meeting attended by author, Feb. 4, 1988.

PAGE 471: Donald Carswell interview, April 13, 1988.

PAGE 472: Larry Grossman memo, Jan. 25, 1988.

PAGE 473: Account of president's council meeting from Bud Rukeyser interview, Feb. 5, 1988.

PAGE 473: Don Carswell interview, April 13, 1988.

PAGE 473: Bud Rukeyser interview, Feb. 5, 1988.

PAGE 474: Noel M. Tichy, "NBC Shared Values Focused Group Interviews," Dec. 7, 1987.

PAGE 475: Meeting of Bob Wright and the Group of 24 attended by author, March 1, 1988.

PAGE 475: Bob Wright interview, March 31, 1988.

PAGE 475: Larry Grossman interview, March 1, 1988.

PAGE 476: For a superb and full account of how network news is better, and sometimes worse, than in the "golden days" of television see David Shaw, "TV News: Demise Is Exaggerated," *Los Angeles Times,* Dec. 28, 1986.

PAGE 476: Ken Bode interview, July 7, 1988.

PAGE 476: Cheryl A. Gould interview, Feb. 16, 1988.

PAGE 476: Larry Grossman interview, April 25, 1988.

PAGE 478: Larry Grossman interview to review his presentation, March 9, 1988, and NBC News budget presentation, March 4, 1988.

PAGE 478: Larry Grossman interview, March 9, 1988.

PAGE 478: Tim Russert interview, March 11, 1988.

PAGE 479: Bob Wright interview, March 31, 1988.

PAGE 479: Jack Welch interview, April 15, 1988.

PAGE 479: Words like "synergy" are common to Welch's speech. For example: Jack Welch presentation to Wall Street analysts, Dec. 12, 1988.

PAGE 479: Description of Welch's decision to rename 30 Rockefeller Plaza from Jack Welch interview, April 15, 1988; and Bud Rukeyser interview, March 4, 1988.

PAGE 479: NBC Employee Survey Results, a fourteen-page compilation of the survey results, April 1988.

PAGE 480: Bob Wright letter to employees, April 1988.

PAGE 480: Bud Rukeyser interview, April 15, 1988.

PAGE 480: Bud Rukeyser interview, March 10, 1988.

PAGE 480: Bob Wright interview, March 31, 1988, and memo to all employees concerning Rukeyser's resignation, March 29, 1988.

PAGE 480: Bud Rukeyser interview, April 15, 1988.

PAGE 481: Bob Wright interview, March 31, 1988.

PAGE 481: Transcript of NBC management meeting in Scottsdale, Arizona, April 4–7, 1988; and Donald Carswell case study for the April 1988 management meeting.

PAGE 481: Bob Wright interview, March 31, 1988.

PAGE 481: Transcript of NBC management meeting in Scottsdale, Arizona, April 4–7, 1988.

PAGE 482: Larry Grossman interview, April 25, 1988.

PAGE 482: Peter J. Boyer, "NBC News Still Has Money Worries," *New York Times,* April 12, 1988.

PAGE 483: Tom Brokaw interviews, Aug. 1, 1988, and Nov. 30, 1988.

PAGE 483: Michael Gartner interview, Sept. 13, 1988; text of Michael Gartner press conference, Aug. 6, 1988.

PAGE 484: Bob Wright interview, Sept. 29, 1988.

PAGE 484: Michael Gartner interview, Sept. 13, 1988.

PAGE 484: Michael Gartner interview, Sept. 13, 1988.

PAGE 484: Bob Wright interview, Sept. 29, 1988.

PAGE 484: Larry Grossman interview, July 6, 1988.

PAGE 484: Bob Wright interview, Sept. 29, 1988.

PAGE 485: Larry Grossman interview, July 6, 1988.

PAGE 485: Tom Ross interview, Aug. 10, 1988.

PAGE 486: Kim LeMasters at CBS regional affiliate meeting, Feb. 5–10, 1988, CBS tape.

PAGE 486: Larry Tisch interview, Feb. 24, 1988.

PAGE 487: *CBS Evening News,* Jan. 25, 1988.

PAGE 487: Poll results from *Time,* Feb. 8, 1988.

PAGE 487: Peter Jennings interview, Oct. 20, 1987.

PAGE 487: For a compelling account of how the networks often play it safe see Mark Hertsgaard, *On Bended Knee: The Press and the Reagan Presidency,* (New York: Farrar Straus Giroux, 1988), p. 258.

PAGE 487: Vivid examples of how Ronald Reagan's presidency was judged by pictures, not words or deeds, is provided by Martin Shram, *The Great American Video Game: Presidential Politics in the Television Age* (New York: William Morrow & Co., 1987), pp. 23–26.

PAGE 487: Tom Bettag interview, Nov. 18, 1988.

PAGE 487: *Los Angeles Times* poll quoted in John Carmody, *Washington Post,* Jan. 29, 1988.

PAGE 487: David Burke interview, Feb. 17, 1988.

PAGE 489: The account of this dinner is pieced together from interviews with two thirds of the guests, including: Barbara Walters interview, April 11, 1989; Larry Tisch interview, June 22, 1988; Roone Arledge interviews, May 16, 1989, and May 26, 1988; Mortimer Zuckerman interview, Sept. 4, 1988.

PAGE 489: Soon after I interviewed Mortimer Zuckerman about this dinner he telephoned his friend Larry Tisch to warn I was "out to get him" and Tisch should not talk to me. For several months, Tisch refused to see me. At first Zuckerman denied making this call, but after Tisch accidentally blurted —"Mort Zuckerman warned me not to talk to you!"—Zuckerman conceded he had made the call.

PAGE 490: Confrontation between Tisch and Hewitt confirmed by, among others, David Burke, in an interview on Feb. 3, 1989.

PAGE 490: Mike Wallace interview, March 17, 1989.

PAGE 490: Larry Tisch interviews, Dec. 20, 1988, and Aug. 10, 1989.

PAGE 490: Mike Wallace interview, March 17, 1989.

PAGE 491: Ed Grebow interviews, March 8, 1988, and March 29, 1988.

PAGE 491: Fred Meyer interview, March 7, 1988.

PAGE 491: A. C. Nielsen Media Research, "1989 Nielsen Report on Television."

PAGE 492: Larry Tisch memorandum to all CBS employees, March 31, 1988.

PAGE 492: Jay Kriegel interview, June 12, 1988.

PAGE 492: Peter J. Boyer, *Who Killed CBS? The Undoing of America's Number One News Network,* (New York: Random House, 1988); Ed Joyce, *Prime Times, Bad Times: A Personal Drama of Network Television* (New York: Doubleday & Co., 1988).

PAGE 492: Dan Rather interview, March 3, 1988.

PAGE 492: Gene Jankowski interview, June 29, 1988.

PAGE 492: Jay Kriegel interview, April 22, 1988.

PAGE 493: Screening at CBS attended by author, May 4, 1988.

PAGE 493: Aaron Spelling interview, May 4, 1988.

PAGE 495: Meeting between Larry Tisch and Aaron Spelling attended by author, May 5, 1988.

PAGE 495: Ed Grebow interview, March 29, 1988.

PAGE 495: CBS Affiliate Relations staff meeting, May 24, 1988; and Scott Michaels interview, May 24, 1988.

PAGE 496: Scott Michaels interview, May 25, 1988.

PAGE 496: Larry Tisch memorandum to all CBS employees, May 25, 1988, and Dennis Kneale, "CBS Defends Price in Bid to Broadcast '92 Olympics," *Wall Street Journal,* May 26, 1988.

PAGE 496: Jay Kriegel interview, May 24, 1988.

PAGE 496: Martha Sherrill, "NBC's Pride of Peacocks," *Washington Post,* June 6, 1990.

PAGE 497: Ben Tucker interview, June 12, 1988.

PAGE 498: Private meeting of CBS affiliates attended by author, June 12, 1988.

PAGE 502: Closed session of the June 12, 1988, meeting between CBS network officials and their affiliates attended by author.

PAGE 503: Larry Tisch press conference, June 12, 1988.

PAGE 503: Larry Tisch interviews, June 12 and 22, 1988, and July 27, 1988.

PAGE 503: Gene Jankowski interviews, June 13 and June 29, 1988.

PAGE 503: Dan Rather interview, April 22, 1988.

PAGE 503: Eric Ober interviews, July 14, 1988, and Sept. 23, 1988.

PAGE 504: Jay Kriegel interviews, June 12, 1988, and Dec. 28, 1988.

PAGE 504: Gene Jankowski interview, June 29, 1988.

CHAPTER 23

PAGE 505: Warren Littlefield interview, April 25, 1988.

PAGE 506: Size of NBC Broadcast Standards staff reduction from Betty Hudson interview, Aug. 17, 1988.

PAGE 506: Bob Wright appearance on panel sponsored by the Association of National Advertisers, Feb. 7, 1989.

PAGE 505: *CBS Evening News,* Dec. 28, 1987.

PAGE 506: Aaron Spelling interview, April 11, 1988.

PAGE 506: Aaron Spelling interview, May 2, 1988.

PAGE 507: Aaron Spelling interview, screening, and staff meeting on *Nightingales,* May 2, 1988.

PAGE 508: Aaron Spelling interview, May 3, 1988.

PAGE 508: Aaron Spelling interview, May 4, 1988.

PAGE 508: Bill Haber interview, May 6, 1988.

PAGE 509: Screening of *Nightingales* and notes session in Aaron Spelling's office, May 4, 1988.

PAGE 509: Ilene Chaiken interview, May 6, 1988.

PAGE 509: Warren Littlefield interview, May 6, 1988.

PAGE 510: Brandon Tartikoff interview, May 7, 1988.

PAGE 510: Lilly Tartikoff interview, May 13, 1988.

PAGE 510: Brandon Tartikoff interview, May 9, 1988.

PAGE 510: Brandon Tartikoff interview, May 10, 1988.

PAGE 511: Warren Littlefield interview, May 9, 1988.

PAGE 512: For the first time, a network permitted reporters to be present during Decision Week. I was joined from May 9–16, 1988, by Richard Turner, then of *TV Guide,* who wrote an excellent two-part article, "Watch the Master Strategist Plot to Stay No. 1," *TV Guide,* Oct. 8 and 15, 1988.

PAGE 512: Bob Wright interview, May 9, 1988.

PAGE 512: NBC memo compiling the reaction of executives to pilots, May 1988.

PAGE 512: Pier Mapes interview, May 10, 1988.

PAGE 513: Brandon Tartikoff interview, May 10, 1988.

PAGE 513: Lee Currlin interview, May 10, 1988.

PAGE 513: Bob Wright interview, May 10, 1988.

PAGE 514: Brandon Tartikoff interview, May 10, 1988.

PAGE 515: Analysis of how NBC Research functions and past tests results from

Ted Frank and William Rubens interviews, May 13, 1988.

PAGE 517: Leslie Lurie interview, May 12, 1988.

PAGE 517: William Rubens interview, May 12, 1988.

PAGE 517: Bob Wright interview, May 12, 1988.

PAGE 517: Bob Wright interview, Dec. 8, 1987.

PAGE 517: Lee Currlin interview, May 12, 1988.

PAGE 518: Jeff Berg interview, May 14, 1988.

PAGE 518: Author present as Perry Simon spoke with Aaron Spelling, May 12, 1988.

PAGE 519: ASI Theater screening of *Nightingales* attended by author, May 12, 1988.

PAGE 520: Brandon Tartikoff interview, May 14, 1988.

PAGE 520: Dennis Kneale and Johnny L. Roberts, "Fox Broadcasting to Post Bigger Losses Than Expected," *Wall Street Journal,* June 20, 1988.

PAGE 521: Brandon Tartikoff presentation to advertisers of NBC's 1987–88 prime-time schedule, May 13, 1987.

PAGE 521: Brandon Tartikoff press conference, May 18, 1988.

PAGE 521: Bill Haber interview, May 6, 1988.

PAGE 522: NBC's commitments to producers confirmed by Michele Brusten interview, May 15, 1988.

PAGE 523: Brandon Tartikoff interview, May 16, 1988.

PAGE 523: Aaron Spelling interview, May 16, 1988.

PAGE 524: Bill Haber interview, May 6, 1988.

PAGE 524: Alan Berger interview, Nov. 24, 1987.

PAGE 524: Greg Dawson, "Fat Cat NBC Too Greedy," New York *Daily News,* June 8, 1988.

PAGE 525: Aaron Spelling interview, Dec. 29, 1988.

PAGE 525: Marvin Kitman, "Make the Restaurant Public," *Newsday,* Jan. 10, 1989.

PAGE 525: Pier Mapes lunch recounted by Brandon Tartikoff in interview, Sept. 26, 1989.

PAGE 525: Brandon Tartikoff interview, May 16, 1988.

CHAPTER 24

PAGE 526: While Spelling chivalrously denied that his friend Suzanne Pleshette asked to be a Nightingale, I trusted the veracity of the anecdote because it came from a then-senior Spelling executive, Ilene Chaiken, who said Spelling told her of the incident, and because it was told to me at the time it happened, and with humor rather than malice. Ilene Chaiken interview, Sept. 29, 1988.

PAGE 527: A. C. Nielsen Media Research, "1989 Nielsen Report on Television."

PAGE 527: Figures on growth of cable networks and cable advertising from Bob Wright teleconference with NBC employees, Nov. 22, 1988.

PAGE 527: Description of summit meeting from: John Sias interviews, Sept. 28, 1988, and July 11, 1990; Tom Murphy interview, April 7, 1989; and Dan Burke interviews, Nov. 14 and Dec. 20, 1989.

PAGE 528: John Sias interview, Sept. 28, 1988.

PAGE 528: Dan Burke interview, Dec. 20, 1988.

PAGE 528: Tom Murphy interview, April 7, 1989.

PAGE 529: Tom Murphy interview, April 7, 1989.

PAGE 529: ABC's ratings from internal ABC Sales report, Nov. 1988.

PAGE 529: ABC profits from Tom Murphy interview, April 7, 1989.

PAGE 529: Larry Tisch interview, Aug. 10, 1988.

PAGE 529: Larry Tisch interview, July 27, 1988.

PAGE 530: Howard Stringer press conference, Aug. 4, 1988.

PAGE 530: Howard Stringer interview, Feb. 29, 1988.

PAGE 530: David Burke interview, Sept. 9, 1988.

PAGE 531: David Burke interview, Feb. 3, 1989.

PAGE 531: David Burke interview, Oct. 18, 1988.

PAGE 531: Howard Stringer interview, Aug. 22, 1988.

PAGE 531: David Burke interview, Sept. 9, 1988.

PAGE 531: Gene Jankowski interview, June 29, 1988.

PAGE 531: Gene Jankowski interview, June 29, 1988.

PAGE 532: Roone Arledge interview, May 16, 1989.

PAGE 532: David Burke interview, Feb. 3, 1989.

PAGE 532: Larry Tisch interview, Aug. 10, 1989.

PAGE 532: David Burke interview, Sept. 9, 1988.

PAGE 532: Roone Arledge interview, July 17, 1988.

PAGE 533: For an account of Sawyer's negotiations with Arledge and its impact, see Edward Klein, "Winning Diane: How ABC's Roone Arledge Snatched Her Away from CBS," *New York,* March 13, 1989.

PAGE 533: Larry Tisch interview, July 28, 1988.

PAGE 534: Roone Arledge interview, May 22, 1990.

PAGE 534: Howard Stringer interview, Aug. 11, 1988.

PAGE 534: Larry Tisch interview, Dec. 20, 1988.

PAGE 534: Howard Stringer interview, Aug. 11, 1988.

PAGE 534: Jay Kriegel interview, Sept. 13, 1988.

PAGE 535: Howard Stringer interview, Dec. 30, 1988.

PAGE 535: Figures on negotiations with Universal and Lorimar from Howard Stringer interview, Dec. 17, 1990, Jay Kriegel interview, March 10, 1989, and Larry Tisch interview, Feb. 12, 1991.

PAGE 535: Larry Tisch interview, Dec. 20, 1988.

PAGE 535: Dan Burke interview, Feb. 13, 1991.

PAGE 536: Larry Tisch interview, Dec. 20, 1988.

PAGE 536: David Burke interview, Sept. 9, 1988.

PAGE 536: David Burke interview, Sept. 9, 1988.

PAGE 536: David Burke recalls his comments to CBS executives in Sept. 9, 1988 interview, and Tom Bettag interview, Nov. 18, 1988.

PAGE 536: David Burke interview, Sept. 9, 1988.

PAGE 537: One example of Bush's hostility to Rather and CBS News: In the final week of the presidential campaign Bush granted interviews to Peter Jennings and Tom Brokaw, but declined to be interviewed by Rather, according to Rather interview, Jan. 13, 1989.

PAGE 537: Dan Rather interview, Jan. 13, 1989.

PAGE 537: David Burke interview, Feb. 3, 1989.

PAGE 537: CBS News 1989 profits from top CBS executive.

PAGE 537: David Burke interview, Nov. 14, 1989.

PAGE 537: John Sias interview, Sept. 28, 1988.

PAGE 538: David Burke interview, Sept. 9, 1988.

PAGE 538: Bob Wright interview, April 7, 1989.

PAGE 538: News ratings numbers for the 1984–85 versus the 1987–88 season from A. C. Nielsen.

PAGE 539: Michael Gartner interview, Sept. 13, 1988.

PAGE 539: Larry Grossman interview, Aug. 10, 1988.

PAGE 540: Jack Welch interview, Oct. 4, 1988.

PAGE 540: Michael Gartner interview, Sept. 13, 1988.

PAGE 540: Larry Grossman interview, Aug. 10, 1988.

PAGE 540: Tom Shales, "The Brokaw Connection," *Washington Post,* July 28, 1988.

PAGE 540: Larry Grossman interview, Aug. 10, 1988.

PAGE 540: Tom Brokaw interview, Aug. 1, 1988.

PAGE 541: Bob Wright interview, Sept. 29, 1988.

PAGE 541: Jack Welch interview, Oct. 4, 1988.

PAGE 542: Terms of Brandon Tartikoff's 1988 contract confirmed by an executive intimate with its terms.

PAGE 542: Brandon Tartikoff interview, Oct. 25, 1988.

PAGE 542: Michael Gartner press conference transcript, Aug. 6, 1988.

PAGE 542: Michael Gartner interview, Sept. 13, 1988.

PAGE 542: Account that Michael Gartner reviews his speech with other executives from Ed Scanlon interview, Jan. 27, 1989.

PAGE 543: Michael Gartner reviews his speech to the president's council in Sept. 13, 1988 interview.

PAGE 544: Betty Hudson interview, Sept. 20, 1988.

PAGE 544: Michael Gartner interview, Sept. 14, 1988.

PAGE 544: Description of cheering NBC

newsroom from John Carmody TV column, *Washington Post,* Sept. 14, 1988.

PAGE 544: NBC News budget figures from Michael Gartner interview on NBC News budget, Dec. 14, 1988.

PAGE 544: For a description of Gartner's brusqueness see Jennet Conant, "Michael Gartner: What's Behind the Bow Tie?" *Manhattan inc.,* March 1989.

PAGE 544: Michael Gartner interview, Dec. 14, 1988.

PAGE 545: Michael Gartner interview, June 9, 1989.

PAGE 545: Michael Gartner interview, June 9, 1989.

PAGE 545: Estimate that NBC overpaid by $100 million for the 1988 Olympics from Bob Wright interview, Sept. 29, 1988.

PAGE 545: Jack Welch interview, Oct. 4, 1988.

PAGE 545: Brandon Tartikoff interview, Sept. 26, 1989.

PAGE 546: Bob Wright concedes Gartner at first resisted Ebersol's appointment to oversee *Today* in interview, Feb. 23, 1990.

PAGE 546: Michael Gartner interview, June 9, 1989.

PAGE 546: Bob Wright interview, Sept. 29, 1988.

PAGE 546: NBC News loses 13 percent of viewers from Bill Carter, *Baltimore Sun,* Jan. 10, 1989.

PAGE 546: Bob Wright interview, April 7, 1989.

PAGE 546: Jack Welch interview, May 24, 1989.

PAGE 546: The average campaign soundbite actually dropped from 42 seconds in the 1968 presidential contest to 9.8 seconds in 1988, according to Harvard fellow Kiku Adatto, "The Incredible Shrinking Soundbite," *The New Republic,* May 28, 1990.

PAGE 547: The absence of postmortems at ABC from Paul Friedman interview, Nov. 28, 1988, and Peter Jennings interview, Nov. 28, 1988; at CBS, from executive producer Tom Bettag interview, Nov. 18, 1988; and at NBC from Tom Brokaw interview, Nov. 30, 1988.

PAGE 547: Paul Friedman interview, Nov. 28, 1988.

PAGE 548: Both Welch and Wright concede Ohlmeyer was offered a position involving NBC News in the summer of 1989. It has been confirmed that the job was to become News President.

PAGE 548: Michael Gartner interview, June 9, 1989.

PAGE 548: Jack Welch acknowledged to NBC managers that he bore some responsibility for the Deborah Norville decision.

PAGE 549: Michael Gartner interview, June 9, 1989.

PAGE 549: Jack Welch interview, May 24, 1989.

PAGE 549: Network profits from Bob Wright presentation to NBC management retreat attended by author, Feb. 27, 1990; from Tom Murphy interview, April 7, 1989; and from CBS executive who requested anonymity.

PAGE 549: I first heard a variation of this joke from Wall Street analyst Chris Dixon, who spoke at an NBC management retreat in 1990.

PAGE 549: Estimate of $800 million three-network profit in 1984 from Larry Tisch interview, Dec. 20, 1988.

PAGE 550: Results of the 1989–90 season from Kevin Goldman, "NBC Remains No. 1 for Prime Time During Latest Season; CBS Is Third," *Wall Street Journal,* April 17, 1990.

PAGE 550: Brandon Tartikoff interview, Sept. 26, 1989.

PAGE 550: Network results in 1990 from Bill Carter, "Little Improvement in Sight As Networks End Bad Year," *New York Times,* Dec. 24, 1990.

PAGE 551: 1989 profit margins at the networks, cable, and stations from Bob Wright presentation to NBC management retreat attended by author, Feb. 26, 1990.

PAGE 551: Fox 1989 performance from Richard Zoglin, "The Fox Trots Faster," *Time,* Aug. 27, 1990.

PAGE 552: Cost cutting at NBC from Bob Wright memo to author, May 29, 1990, and from documents provided by both CBS and ABC.

PAGE 553: Bob Wright interview, Sept. 29, 1988.

PAGE 553: Jack Welch interview, Dec. 12, 1988.

PAGE 554: GE Capital investments provided by: Jack Welch interview, May 24, 1989; Welch presentation to financial analysts, Dec. 12, 1988; C. H. Biederman of the GE Capital Corp. in a Feb. 21, 1989, correspondence; and GE spokeswoman Joyce Hergenhan interview, July 10, 1989.

PAGE 555: Larry Tisch interview, Aug. 10, 1989.

PAGE 555: Larry Tisch speech before the International Radio and Television Society, Oct. 19, 1988.

PAGE 555: John Malone interview, April 11, 1989.

PAGE 557: Tom Murphy interview, April 7, 1989.

PAGE 557: Jack Welch interview, Oct. 4, 1988.

PAGE 558: "Picking Bulls and Bears of 1989," *Broadcasting*, Dec. 26, 1988.

PAGE 558: ABC 1989 profits from Cap Cities/ABC report, "1989–90 Television Season," distributed in early 1990.

PAGE 559: IRTS dinner honoring Tom Murphy, March 31, 1990.

CHAPTER 25

PAGE 560: Results of the Sept. 17, 1990, to Feb. 10, 1991, season from A. C. Nielsen Media Research.

PAGE 560: Tartikoff quoted in Bill Carter, "TV Networks Gamble to Win in the Prime-Time Stakes for Fall," *New York Times*, May 31, 1990.

PAGE 561: Numbers on the results of the TV season from Sept. 13, 1990, to Feb. 10, 1991, plus cable penetration and VCR ownership in 1990 provided by A. C. Nielsen Media Research.

PAGE 562: CBS losses from Larry Tisch interview, Feb. 12, 1991.

PAGE 562: ABC profits from Dan Burke interview, Feb. 13, 1991.

PAGE 562: NBC original 1990 profit projection from Bob Wright presentation to NBC management retreat attended by author, Feb. 26, 1990. Actual and projected NBC profits for 1990 and 1991 from Jack Welch interview, Feb. 14, 1991.

PAGE 562: Estimate of added advertising inventory at the networks from Dan Burke interview, Feb. 13, 1991.

PAGE 562: Larry Tisch interview, Feb. 12, 1991.

PAGE 562: Dan Burke interview, Feb. 13, 1991.

PAGE 563: Jack Welch interview, Feb. 14, 1991.

PAGE 563: Extra cost to NBC News of Gulf War from NBC News press release, Feb. 11, 1991.

PAGE 563: Cable revenue estimate for 1990 from Paul Kagan Associates.

PAGE 564: Larry Tisch interview, Feb. 12, 1991.

PAGE 564: Dan Burke interview, Feb. 13, 1991.

PAGE 564: NBC 1990 management retreat attended by author, Feb. 25–28, 1990, plus NBC transcript.

PAGE 565: Verne Gay, "This Is News?" *Newsday*, May 23, 1990.

PAGE 565: Roy Bostock interview, Jan. 6, 1989, and Dec. 17, 1988.

PAGE 566: Tom Murphy interview, April 7, 1989.

PAGE 566: Bob Wright interview, April 7, 1989.

PAGE 567: Jack Welch interview, Feb. 14, 1991.

PAGE 567: Dan Burke interview concerning *Cheers*, Feb. 13, 1991.

PAGE 568: Bill Haber interview, May 6, 1988.

PAGE 568: Leaflet handed out in front of Tisch's home by Local 1 of the IATSE in the spring of 1990.

PAGE 568: Larry Tisch interview, Feb. 12, 1991.

PAGE 568: Larry Tisch speech to the International Radio and Television Society, Oct. 19, 1988.

PAGE 569: Jack Welch interview, Feb. 14, 1991.

PAGE 570: Gerry Solomon interview, Feb. 27, 1990.

PAGE 570: Roy Bostock interview, Jan. 6, 1989.

PAGE 570: Ev Dennis interview, Feb. 8, 1989.

PAGE 571: Larry Tisch interview, Feb. 12, 1991.

PAGE 571: Jill Vardy and Richard Silkos, "Shake-up Urged for Broadcasters," *The Financial Post of Canada*, May 10, 1991.

PAGE 572: Text of Michael D. Eisner speech to the TV Academy Forum Lunch, Jan. 27, 1981.

PAGE 573: Larry Tisch interview, Feb. 12, 1991.

PAGE 574: Dan Burke interview, Feb. 13, 1991.

PAGE 575: Jack Welch interview, Feb. 14, 1991.

PAGE 575: "Murphy Calls Fin-Syn Ruling 'Trojan Horse,'" *Broadcasting*, April 22, 1991.

BIBLIOGRAPHY

Adelman, William. *Pilsen and the West Side: A Tour Guide.* Chicago: Illinois Labor History Society, 1983.

Aldrich, Nelson W., Jr. *Old Money: The Mythology of America's Upper Class.* New York: Alfred A. Knopf, 1988.

Allen, Frederick Lewis. *Only Yesterday: An Informal History of the 1920's.* New York: Perennial Library, Harper & Row, 1964.

Arlen, Michael J. *The Camera Age: Essays on Television.* New York: Farrar, Straus & Giroux, 1981.

———. *The Living Room War.* New York: Viking, 1969.

Barnouw, Erik. *A History of Broadcasting in the United States.* Vol. I, *A Tower of Babel: To 1933.* New York and London: Oxford University Press, 1966.

———. *A History of Broadcasting in the United States.* Vol. II, *The Golden Web.* New York and London: Oxford University Press, 1968.

———. *A History of Broadcasting in the United States.* Vol. III, *The Image Empire From 1953.* New York and London: Oxford University Press, 1970.

———. *Tube of Plenty.* New York: Oxford University Press, 1975.

Bagdikian, Ben. *The Media Monopoly.* Boston: Beacon, 1983.

Bedell, Sally. *Up the Tube: Prime Time TV and the Silverman Years.* New York: Viking, 1981.

Bessen, Stanley M.; Kattermaker, Thomas G.; Metzger, A. Richard, Jr.; and Woodbury, John R. *Misregulating Television: Network Dominance and the FCC.* Chicago: University of Chicago Press, 1984.

Bilby, Kenneth. *The General: David Sarnoff and the Rise of the Communications Industry.* New York: Harper & Row, 1986.

Birmingham, Stephen. *"Our Crowd": The Great Jewish Families of New York.* New York: Berkley Books, 1984.

Blair, Gwenda. *Almost Golden: Jessica Savitch and the Selling of Television News.* New York: Simon and Schuster, 1988.

Blum, Richard A., and Lindheim, Richard D. *Primetimes: Network Television Programming.* Boston: Focal Press, 1987.

Boyer, Peter J. *Who Killed CBS?: The Undoing of America's Number One News Network.* New York: Random House, 1988.

Brooks, Tim, and Marsh, Earle. *The Complete Directory to Prime Time Network TV Shows 1946–Present.* New York: Ballantine Books, 1988.

Brown, Les. *Television: The Business Behind the Box.* New York: Harcourt Brace Jovanovich, 1974.

Burrows, William E. *On Reporting the News.* New York: Simon and Schuster, 1985.

Campbell, Robert. *The Golden Years of Broadcasting: A Celebration of the First 50 Years of Radio and TV on NBC.* New York: Charles Scribner's Sons, 1976.

Christiansen, Mark, and Staith, Cameron. *The Sweeps: Behind the Scenes in Network TV.* New York: William Morrow and Company, Inc., 1984.

Clarke, Gerald. *Capote: A Biography.* New York: Simon and Schuster, 1988.

Clurman, Richard M. *Beyond Malice: The Media's Years of Reckoning.* New Brunswick, New Jersey: Transaction Books, 1988.

Cowan, Geoffrey. *See No Evil: The Backstage Battle over Sex and Violence on Television.* New York: Simon and Schuster, 1979.

Donaldson, Sam. *Hold On, Mr. President!* New York: Random House, 1987.

Downie, Leonard, Jr. *The New Muckrakers.* Washington, D.C.: The New Republic Book Company, Inc., 1976.

Dunne, John Gregory. *The Studio.* New York: Simon and Schuster, 1969.

Dygert, James H. *The Investigative Journalist: Folk Heroes of a New Era.* Englewood Cliffs, New Jersey: Prentice Hall, Inc., 1976.

Ellerbee, Linda. *"And So It Goes": Adventures in Television.* New York: G. P. Putnam's Sons, 1986.

Epstein, Edward Jay. *News from Nowhere: Television and the News.* New York: Random House, 1973.

Foley, John; Lebdell, Robert C.; and Trownson, Robert, eds. *The Southern California Conference on the Media and the Law.* Los Angeles: Times Mirror Press, 1977.

Friendly, Fred W. *Due to Circumstances Beyond Our Control . . .* New York: Vintage Books, 1968.

———. *The Good Guys, the Bad Guys and the First Amendment: Free Speech vs. Fairness in Broadcasting.* New York: Vintage Books, 1977.

———. *Minnesota Rag.* New York: Random House, 1981.

Gabler, Neal, *An Empire of Their Own: How the Jews Invented Hollywood.* New York: Crown Publishers, Inc., 1988.

Gannett Foundation Report, *Emerging Voices: East European Media in Transition.* New York: Gannett Center for Media Studies, October 1990.

Gans, Herbert. *Deciding What's News.* New York: Pantheon, 1979.

Gates, Gary Paul. *Air Time: The Inside Story of CBS News.* New York: Harper & Row, 1978.

Gilder, George. *Life After Television: The Coming Transformation of Media and American Life.* Knoxville, Tennessee: Whittle Direct Books, 1990.

Gitlin, Todd. *Inside Prime Time.* New York: Pantheon Books, 1985.

Goldberg, Robert, and Goldberg, Gerald Jay. *Anchors: Brokaw, Jennings, Rather and the Evening News.* New York: Carol Publishing Group, 1990.

Goldenson, Leonard H., and Wolf, Marvin J. *Beating the Odds: The Untold Story Behind the Rise of ABC.* New York: Charles Scribner's Sons, 1991.

Goldstein, Tom, ed. *Killing the Messenger: 100 Years of Media Criticism.* New York: Columbia University Press, 1989.

Goldstein, Tom. *The News at Any Cost: How Journalists Compromise Their Ethics to Shape the News.* New York: Simon and Schuster, 1985.

Hanhardt, John. *Video Culture: A Critical Investigation.* Rochester, New York: Rochester Studies Workshop Press, 1986.

Halberstam, David. *The Powers That Be.* New York: Alfred A. Knopf, 1979.

Harris, David. *The League: The Rise and Decline of the NFL.* New York: Bantam Books, 1986.

Henderson, Amy. *On the Air: Pioneers of American Broadcasting.* Washington, D.C.: Smithsonian Institution Press, 1988.

Hertsgaard, Mark. *On Bended Knee: The Press and the Reagan Presidency.* New York: Farrar, Strauss & Giroux, 1988.

Hess, Dick, and Muller, Marion. *Dorfsman and CBS.* New York: American Showcase, Inc., 1987.

Hill, Doug, and Weingrad, Jeff. *Saturday Night: A Backstage History of "Saturday Night Live."* New York: Beech Tree Books, 1986.

Howe, Irving. *World of Our Fathers: The Journey of the East European Jews to America and the Life They Found and Made.* New York: Touchstone, 1983.

Issacson, Walter, and Thomas, Evan. *The Wise Men: Six Friends and the World They Made.* New York: Simon and Schuster, 1986.

Joyce, Ed. *Prime Times, Bad Times: A Personal Drama of Network Television.* Garden City, New York: Doubleday, 1981.

Katz, Jon. *Sign Off.* New York: Bantam Books, 1991.

Kluger, Richard. *The Paper: The Life and Death of the New York Herald Tribune.* New York: Alfred A. Knopf, 1986.

Lardner, James. *Fast Forward: Hollywood, the Japanese and the Onslaught of the VCR.* New York: W. W. Norton & Company, 1987.

Leonard, Bill. *In the Storm of the Eye: A Lifetime at CBS.* New York: G. P. Putnam's Sons, 1987.

Levinson, Richard, and Link, William. *Off Camera: Conversations with the Makers of Prime Time Television.* New York: New American Library, 1986.

MacDonald, J. Fred. *One Nation Under Television.* New York: Pantheon Books, 1990.

MacNeil, Robert. *The People Machine.* New York: Harper & Row, 1968.

———. *The Right Place at the Right Time.* Boston: Little, Brown, 1982.

Mankiewicz, Frank, and Swerdlow, Joel. *Remote Control: Television and the Manipulation of American Life.* New York: Times Books, 1978.

Matusow, Barbara. *The Evening Stars: The Making of the Network News Anchor.* Boston: Houghton Mifflin Company, 1983.

Mayer, Martin. *About Television.* New York: Harper & Row, 1972.

McLuhan, Marshall. *Understanding Media; The Extensions of Man.* New Jersey: New American Library, 1964.

Metz, Robert. *CBS: Reflections in a Bloodshot Eye.* New York: Signet, New American Library, 1976.

Miller, Mark Crispin. *Boxed In: The Culture of TV.* Evanston, Illinois: Northwestern University Press, 1989.

Miller, Merle, and Rhodes, Evan. *Only You Dick Daring! or How to Write One Television Script and Make $50,000,000.* New York: Sloane and Associates, 1964.

Neuharth, Al. *Confessions of an S.O.B.* Garden City, New York: Doubleday, 1989.

O'Connell, Mary. *Connections: Reflections on Sixty Years of Broadcasting.* New York: National Broadcasting Company, Inc., 1986.

Ornstein, Robert. *Multimind: A New Way of Looking at Human Behavior.* New York: Doubleday, 1986.

Paley, William. *As It Happened: A Memoir.* Garden City, New York: Doubleday, 1979.

Paper, Lewis J. *Empire: Willaim S. Paley and the Making of CBS.* New York: St. Martin's Press, 1987.

Persico, Joseph E. *Edward R. Murrow: An American Original.* New York: McGraw-Hill, 1988.

Pollak, Richard, ed. *Stop the Presses, I Want to Get Off!* New York: Random House, 1975.

Postman, Neil. *The Disappearance of Childhood.* New York: Dell Publishing Company, Inc., 1982.

Powell, Jody. *The Other Side of the Story.* New York: William Morrow and Company, Inc., 1984.

Powers, Ron. *The Beast, the Eunuch and the Glass-Eyed Child: Television in the 80's.* New York: Harcourt Brace Jovanovich, 1990.

———. *The Newscasters.* New York: St. Martin's Press, 1978.

Rather, Dan, and Gates, Gary Paul. *The Palace Guard.* New York: Harper & Row, 1974.

Rather, Dan, with Herskowitz, Mickey. *The Camera Never Blinks.* New York: Ballantine, 1977.

Said, Edward W. *Covering Islam: How the Media and the Experts Determine How We See the Rest of the World.* New York: Pantheon Books, 1981.

Schram, Martin. *The Great American Video Game: Presidential Politics in the Television Age.* New York: William Morrow and Company, Inc., 1987.

Schwartz, Tony. *Media: The Second God.* New York: Random House, 1981.

Servan-Schreiber, Jean-Louise. *The Power to Inform.* New York: McGraw-Hill, 1974.

Shirer, William L. *20th Century Journey: A Memoir of a Life and the Times.* Vol. II, *The Nightmare Years: 1930–1940.* New York: Bantam Books, 1985.

Simons, Howard, and Califano, Joseph A., Jr. *The Media and Business.* New York: Vintage Books, 1979.

Simons, Howard, and Califano, Joseph A., Jr. *The Media and the Law.* New York: Praeger Publishers, 1976.

Smith, Sally Bedell. *In All His Glory: The Life of William S. Paley—The Legendary Tycoon and His Brilliant Circle.* New York: Simon and Schuster, 1990.

Sperber, A. M. *Murrow: His Life and Times.* New York: Freundlich Books, 1986.

Swanberg, W. A. *Citizen Hearst: A Biography of William Randolph Hearst.* New York: Charles Scribner's Sons, 1961.

Trotta, Liz. *Fighting for Air: In the Trenches with Television News.* New York: Simon and Schuster, 1991.

Williams, Huntington. *Beyond Control: ABC and the Fate of the Networks.* New York: MacMillian Publishing Company, 1989.

INDEX